James Robert Miller Jr.

# THE MINISTERS MANUAL FOR 1958

---

THE VOLUME FOR THIS YEAR, BEING A STUDY AND PULPIT GUIDE, AND HANDBOOK OF SUGGESTION AND INSPIRATION FOR PASTORS, EVANGELISTS, MISSIONARIES, BIBLE READERS AND ALL OTHERS REGULARLY CALLED UPON FOR CHRISTIAN ADDRESS FROM PULPIT OR PLATFORM

*THIRTY-THIRD ANNUAL VOLUME*

# *The* MINISTERS MANUAL

*(Doran's)*

## *A Study and Pulpit Guide for the Calendar Year 1958*

THIRTY-THIRD ANNUAL ISSUE
OF THIS "MINISTERS WORKING TOOL"

*Compiled and Edited by*
REV. M. K. W. HEICHER, PH.D.
*and*
REV. G. B. F. HALLOCK, M.A., D.D.

HARPER & BROTHERS PUBLISHERS
NEW YORK

G-G



*Library of Congress catalog card number: 25-21658*

# *Foreword*

This is the thirty-third annual issue of *The Ministers Manual.* For one-third of a century it has helped to relieve the tremendous pressure of responsibility on ministers and laymen and its wide geographical circulation in such countries as Brazil, Burma, and Norway indicates its value.

For those who do not have access to public libraries and other inspiring aids it is "a mine of information and inspiraton." Within this one volume there is a book of sermon outlines and condensations, a book of prayers, and a book of children's sermons.

Section VII, Outlined Sermons for Sunday Mornings and Evenings of the Church Year, with Aids to Public Worship, follows in general the Christian Year. The Lenten Season, the Communion Service, and the Missionary Message are in Sections IV, V, and VI. The Questions of Religion and Life in Section II represent real needs arising from real perplexities. The list should suggest many sermon themes.

As in the previous issues, it is the purpose of this *Manual* to "communicate the Christian gospel"; to strike the universal and essential notes; and to emphasize the importance of each part of the Christian service of worship.

Except for a few pages in Section I, Calendars and Other Convenient Clergy Helps, the volume is entirely new and retains the section headings of the earlier issues. For convenience the Christian Endeavor Topics have been grouped in Section I.

M. K. W. H.

*Pilgrim Place*
*Claremont, California*

# CONDENSED TABLE OF CONTENTS

*(A Complete Alphabetical Subject Index Immediately Follows)*

# CONTENTS ACCORDING TO SUBJECT

## General Alphabetical Index

# SCRIPTURAL INDEX

Complete with the exception of references to which there is practically no comment or material.

## OLD TESTAMENT



## NEW TESTAMENT

# SECTION I. *Calendars and Other Convenient Clergy Helps*

## 1. *Civil Year Calendars for 1958 and 1959*

# 1958

**JANUARY**

| S | M | T | W | T | F | S |
|---|---|---|---|---|---|---|
| — | — | — | 1 | 2 | 3 | 4 |
| 5 | 6 | 7 | 8 | 9 | 10 | 11 |
| 12 | 13 | 14 | 15 | 16 | 17 | 18 |
| 19 | 20 | 21 | 22 | 23 | 24 | 25 |
| 26 | 27 | 28 | 29 | 30 | 31 | — |

**FEBRUARY**

| S | M | T | W | T | F | S |
|---|---|---|---|---|---|---|
| — | — | — | — | — | — | 1 |
| 2 | 3 | 4 | 5 | 6 | 7 | 8 |
| 9 | 10 | 11 | 12 | 13 | 14 | 15 |
| 16 | 17 | 18 | 19 | 20 | 21 | 22 |
| 23 | 24 | 25 | 26 | 27 | 28 | — |
| — | — | — | — | — | — | — |

**MARCH**

| S | M | T | W | T | F | S |
|---|---|---|---|---|---|---|
| — | — | — | — | — | — | 1 |
| 2 | 3 | 4 | 5 | 6 | 7 | 8 |
| 9 | 10 | 11 | 12 | 13 | 14 | 15 |
| 16 | 17 | 18 | 19 | 20 | 21 | 22 |
| 23 | 24 | 25 | 26 | 27 | 28 | 29 |
| 30 | 31 | — | — | — | — | — |

**APRIL**

| S | M | T | W | T | F | S |
|---|---|---|---|---|---|---|
| — | — | 1 | 2 | 3 | 4 | 5 |
| 6 | 7 | 8 | 9 | 10 | 11 | 12 |
| 13 | 14 | 15 | 16 | 17 | 18 | 19 |
| 20 | 21 | 22 | 23 | 24 | 25 | 26 |
| 27 | 28 | 29 | 30 | — | — | — |

**MAY**

| S | M | T | W | T | F | S |
|---|---|---|---|---|---|---|
| — | — | — | — | 1 | 2 | 3 |
| 4 | 5 | 6 | 7 | 8 | 9 | 10 |
| 11 | 12 | 13 | 14 | 15 | 16 | 17 |
| 18 | 19 | 20 | 21 | 22 | 23 | 24 |
| 25 | 26 | 27 | 28 | 29 | 30 | 31 |
| — | — | — | — | — | — | — |

**JUNE**

| S | M | T | W | T | F | S |
|---|---|---|---|---|---|---|
| 1 | 2 | 3 | 4 | 5 | 6 | 7 |
| 8 | 9 | 10 | 11 | 12 | 13 | 14 |
| 15 | 16 | 17 | 18 | 19 | 20 | 21 |
| 22 | 23 | 24 | 25 | 26 | 27 | 28 |
| 29 | 30 | — | — | — | — | — |
| — | — | — | — | — | — | — |

**JULY**

| S | M | T | W | T | F | S |
|---|---|---|---|---|---|---|
| — | — | 1 | 2 | 3 | 4 | 5 |
| 6 | 7 | 8 | 9 | 10 | 11 | 12 |
| 13 | 14 | 15 | 16 | 17 | 18 | 19 |
| 20 | 21 | 22 | 23 | 24 | 25 | 26 |
| 27 | 28 | 29 | 30 | 31 | — | — |

**AUGUST**

| S | M | T | W | T | F | S |
|---|---|---|---|---|---|---|
| — | — | — | — | — | 1 | 2 |
| 3 | 4 | 5 | 6 | 7 | 8 | 9 |
| 10 | 11 | 12 | 13 | 14 | 15 | 16 |
| 17 | 18 | 19 | 20 | 21 | 22 | 23 |
| 24 | 25 | 26 | 27 | 28 | 29 | 30 |
| 31 | — | — | — | — | — | — |

**SEPTEMBER**

| S | M | T | W | T | F | S |
|---|---|---|---|---|---|---|
| — | 1 | 2 | 3 | 4 | 5 | 6 |
| 7 | 8 | 9 | 10 | 11 | 12 | 13 |
| 14 | 15 | 16 | 17 | 18 | 19 | 20 |
| 21 | 22 | 23 | 24 | 25 | 26 | 27 |
| 28 | 29 | 30 | — | — | — | — |
| — | — | — | — | — | — | — |

**OCTOBER**

| S | M | T | W | T | F | S |
|---|---|---|---|---|---|---|
| — | — | — | 1 | 2 | 3 | 4 |
| 5 | 6 | 7 | 8 | 9 | 10 | 11 |
| 12 | 13 | 14 | 15 | 16 | 17 | 18 |
| 19 | 20 | 21 | 22 | 23 | 24 | 25 |
| 26 | 27 | 28 | 29 | 30 | 31 | — |

**NOVEMBER**

| S | M | T | W | T | F | S |
|---|---|---|---|---|---|---|
| — | — | — | — | — | — | 1 |
| 2 | 3 | 4 | 5 | 6 | 7 | 8 |
| 9 | 10 | 11 | 12 | 13 | 14 | 15 |
| 16 | 17 | 18 | 19 | 20 | 21 | 22 |
| 23 | 24 | 25 | 26 | 27 | 28 | 29 |
| 30 | — | — | — | — | — | — |

**DECEMBER**

| S | M | T | W | T | F | S |
|---|---|---|---|---|---|---|
| — | 1 | 2 | 3 | 4 | 5 | 6 |
| 7 | 8 | 9 | 10 | 11 | 12 | 13 |
| 14 | 15 | 16 | 17 | 18 | 19 | 20 |
| 21 | 22 | 23 | 24 | 25 | 26 | 27 |
| 28 | 29 | 30 | 31 | — | — | — |
| — | — | — | — | — | — | — |

# 1959

**JANUARY**

| S | M | T | W | T | F | S |
|---|---|---|---|---|---|---|
| | | | | 1 | 2 | 3 |
| 4 | 5 | 6 | 7 | 8 | 9 | 10 |
| 11 | 12 | 13 | 14 | 15 | 16 | 17 |
| 18 | 19 | 20 | 21 | 22 | 23 | 24 |
| 25 | 26 | 27 | 28 | 29 | 30 | 31 |
| — | — | — | — | — | — | — |

**FEBRUARY**

| S | M | T | W | T | F | S |
|---|---|---|---|---|---|---|
| 1 | 2 | 3 | 4 | 5 | 6 | 7 |
| 8 | 9 | 10 | 11 | 12 | 13 | 14 |
| 15 | 16 | 17 | 18 | 19 | 20 | 21 |
| 22 | 23 | 24 | 25 | 26 | 27 | 28 |
| — | — | — | — | — | — | — |
| — | — | — | — | — | — | — |

**MARCH**

| S | M | T | W | T | F | S |
|---|---|---|---|---|---|---|
| 1 | 2 | 3 | 4 | 5 | 6 | 7 |
| 8 | 9 | 10 | 11 | 12 | 13 | 14 |
| 15 | 16 | 17 | 18 | 19 | 20 | 21 |
| 22 | 23 | 24 | 25 | 26 | 27 | 28 |
| 29 | 30 | 31 | — | — | — | — |
| — | — | — | — | — | — | — |

**APRIL**

| S | M | T | W | T | F | S |
|---|---|---|---|---|---|---|
| — | — | — | 1 | 2 | 3 | 4 |
| 5 | 6 | 7 | 8 | 9 | 10 | 11 |
| 12 | 13 | 14 | 15 | 16 | 17 | 18 |
| 19 | 20 | 21 | 22 | 23 | 24 | 25 |
| 26 | 27 | 28 | 29 | 30 | — | — |
| — | — | — | — | — | — | — |

**MAY**

| S | M | T | W | T | F | S |
|---|---|---|---|---|---|---|
| — | — | — | — | — | 1 | 2 |
| 3 | 4 | 5 | 6 | 7 | 8 | 9 |
| 10 | 11 | 12 | 13 | 14 | 15 | 16 |
| 17 | 18 | 19 | 20 | 21 | 22 | 23 |
| 24 | 25 | 26 | 27 | 28 | 29 | 30 |
| 31 | — | — | — | — | — | — |

**JUNE**

| S | M | T | W | T | F | S |
|---|---|---|---|---|---|---|
| — | 1 | 2 | 3 | 4 | 5 | 6 |
| 7 | 8 | 9 | 10 | 11 | 12 | 13 |
| 14 | 15 | 16 | 17 | 18 | 19 | 20 |
| 21 | 22 | 23 | 24 | 25 | 26 | 27 |
| 28 | 29 | 30 | — | — | — | — |
| — | — | — | — | — | — | — |

**JULY**

| S | M | T | W | T | F | S |
|---|---|---|---|---|---|---|
| — | — | — | 1 | 2 | 3 | 4 |
| 5 | 6 | 7 | 8 | 9 | 10 | 11 |
| 12 | 13 | 14 | 15 | 16 | 17 | 18 |
| 19 | 20 | 21 | 22 | 23 | 24 | 25 |
| 26 | 27 | 28 | 29 | 30 | 31 | — |
| — | — | — | — | — | — | — |

**AUGUST**

| S | M | T | W | T | F | S |
|---|---|---|---|---|---|---|
| — | — | — | — | — | — | 1 |
| 2 | 3 | 4 | 5 | 6 | 7 | 8 |
| 9 | 10 | 11 | 12 | 13 | 14 | 15 |
| 16 | 17 | 18 | 19 | 20 | 21 | 22 |
| 23 | 24 | 25 | 26 | 27 | 28 | 29 |
| 30 | 31 | — | — | — | — | — |

**SEPTEMBER**

| S | M | T | W | T | F | S |
|---|---|---|---|---|---|---|
| — | — | 1 | 2 | 3 | 4 | 5 |
| 6 | 7 | 8 | 9 | 10 | 11 | 12 |
| 13 | 14 | 15 | 16 | 17 | 18 | 19 |
| 20 | 21 | 22 | 23 | 24 | 25 | 26 |
| 27 | 28 | 29 | 30 | — | — | — |
| — | — | — | — | — | — | — |

**OCTOBER**

| S | M | T | W | T | F | S |
|---|---|---|---|---|---|---|
| — | — | — | — | 1 | 2 | 3 |
| 4 | 5 | 6 | 7 | 8 | 9 | 10 |
| 11 | 12 | 13 | 14 | 15 | 16 | 17 |
| 18 | 19 | 20 | 21 | 22 | 23 | 24 |
| 25 | 26 | 27 | 28 | 29 | 30 | 31 |
| — | — | — | — | — | — | — |

**NOVEMBER**

| S | M | T | W | T | F | S |
|---|---|---|---|---|---|---|
| 1 | 2 | 3 | 4 | 5 | 6 | 7 |
| 8 | 9 | 10 | 11 | 12 | 13 | 14 |
| 15 | 16 | 17 | 18 | 19 | 20 | 21 |
| 22 | 23 | 24 | 25 | 26 | 27 | 28 |
| 29 | 30 | — | — | — | — | — |
| — | — | — | — | — | — | — |

**DECEMBER**

| S | M | T | W | T | F | S |
|---|---|---|---|---|---|---|
| — | — | 1 | 2 | 3 | 4 | 5 |
| 6 | 7 | 8 | 9 | 10 | 11 | 12 |
| 13 | 14 | 15 | 16 | 17 | 18 | 19 |
| 20 | 21 | 22 | 23 | 24 | 25 | 26 |
| 27 | 28 | 29 | 30 | 31 | — | — |
| — | — | — | — | — | — | — |

## 2. *Ecclesiastical Year Calendar for 1958 (Including the Movable and Immovable Feasts)*

### JANUARY

**1—We.** Circumcision.
**5—Su.** 2nd Sunday after Christmas.
**6—Mo.** The Epiphany.
**12—Su.** 1st Sunday after The Epiphany.
**19—Su.** 2nd Sunday after The Epiphany.
**25—Sa.** Conversion of St. Paul.
**26—Su.** 3rd Sunday after The Epiphany.
**31—Fr.**

### FEBRUARY

**1—Sa.**
**2—Su.** Septuagesima Sunday.
**3—Mo.** The Purification.
**9—Su.** Sexagesima Sunday.
**16—Su.** Quinquagesima Sunday.
**19—We.** Ash Wednesday.
**23—Su.** First Sunday in Lent.
**24—Mo.** St. Matthias.
**26—We.** Ember Day.
**28—Fr.** Ember Day.

### MARCH

**1—Sa.** Ember Day.
**2—Su.** 2nd Sunday in Lent.
**9—Su.** 3rd Sunday in Lent.
**16—Su.** 4th Sunday in Lent.
**23—Su.** **5th Sunday in Lent.**
**25—Tu.** The Annunciation.
**30—Su.** Palm Sunday.
**31—Mo.** **Monday before Easter.**

### APRIL

**1—Tu.** Tuesday before Easter.
**2—We.** Wednesday before Easter.
**3—Th.** Maundy Thursday.
**4—Fr.** **Good Friday.**
**5—Sa.** Easter Even.
**6—Su.** **Easter Day.**
**7—Mo.** Easter Monday.
**8—Tu.** Easter Tuesday.
**13—Su.** First Sunday after Easter.
**20—Su.** Second Sunday after Easter.
**25—Fr.** St. Mark's Day.
**27—Su.** 3rd Sunday after Easter.
**30—We.**

### MAY

**1—Th.** St. Philip and St. James.
**4—Su.** 4th Sunday after Easter.
**11—Su.** 5th Sunday (Rogation) after Easter.
**12—Mo.** Rogation Monday.
**13—Tu.** Rogation Tuesday.
**14—We.** Rogation Wednesday.
**15—Th.** Ascension Day.
**18—Su.** Sunday after Ascension Day.
**25—Su.** Whitsunday (Pentecost).
**28—We.** Ember Day.
**30—Fr.** Ember Day.
**31—Sa.** Ember Day.

### JUNE

**1—Su.** Trinity Sunday.
**8—Su.** 1st Sunday after Trinity.

11—We. St. Barnabas.
15—Su. 2nd Sunday after Trinity.
22—Su. 3rd Sunday after Trinity.
24—Tu. Nativity of St. John the Baptist.
29—Su. 4th Sunday after Trinity.
30—Mo. St. Peter.

JULY

1—Tu.
4—Fr. Independence Day.
6—Su. 5th Sunday after Trinity.
13—Su. 6th Sunday after Trinity.
20—Su. 7th Sunday after Trinity.
25—Fr. St. James.
27—Su. 8th Sunday after Trinity.
31—Th.

AUGUST

1—Fr.
3—Su. 9th Sunday after Trinity.
6—We. Transfiguration.
10—Su. 10th Sunday after Trinity.
17—Su. 11th Sunday after Trinity.
24—Su. 12th Sunday after Trinity.
25—Mo. St. Bartholomew.
31—Su. 13th Sunday after Trinity.

SEPTEMBER

1—Mo.
7—Su. 14th Sunday after Trinity.
14—Su. 15th Sunday after Trinity.
17—We. Ember Day.
19—Fr. Ember Day.
20—Sa. Ember Day.
21—Su. 16th Sunday after Trinity.
22—Mo. St. Matthew.
28—Su. 17th Sunday after Trinity.
29—Mo. St. Michael and All Angels.
30—Tu.

OCTOBER

1—We.
5—Su. 18th Sunday after Trinity.
12—Su. 19th Sunday after Trinity.
18—Sa. St. Luke.
19—Su. 20th Sunday after Trinity.
26—Su. 21st Sunday after Trinity.
28—Tu. St. Simon and St. Jude.
31—Fr.

NOVEMBER

1—Sa. All Saints.
2—Su. 22nd Sunday after Trinity.
9—Su. 23rd Sunday after Trinity.
16—Su. 24th Sunday after Trinity.
23—Su. Sunday next before Advent.
30—Su. Advent Sunday (St. Andrew).

DECEMBER

1—Mo.
7—Su. 2nd Sunday in Advent.
14—Su. 3rd Sunday in Advent.
17—We. Ember Day.
19—Fr. Ember Day.
20—Sa. Ember Day.
21—Su. 4th Sunday in Advent.
22—Mo. St. Thomas.
25—Th. Christmas Day.
26—Fr. St. Stephen.
27—Sa. St. John the Evangelist.
28—Su. 1st Sunday after Christmas.
29—Mo. Holy Innocents.
31—We.

## 3. *Prominent Church Year Dates for Three Years*

Ash Wednesday, 1958, Feb. 19. 1959, Feb. 11. 1960, Mar. 2.

Palm Sunday, 1958, Mar. 30. 1959, Mar. 22. 1960, Apr. 10.

Good Friday, 1958, Apr. 4. 1959, Mar. 27. 1960, Apr. 15.

Easter, 1958, Apr. 6. 1959, Mar. 29. 1960, Apr. 17.

Trinity Sunday, 1958, June 1. 1959, May 24. 1960, June 12.

Ascension Sunday, 1958, May 15. 1959, May 7. 1960, May 26.

Whitsunday, 1958, May 25. 1959, May 17. 1960, June 5.

First Sunday in Advent, 1958, Nov. 30. 1959, Nov. 29. 1960, Nov. 27.

## 4. *A Table of Easter Sundays for the Years 1940-2000.*

1940, Mar. 24.
1941, Apr. 13.
1942, Apr. 6.
1943, Apr. 25.
1944, Apr. 9.
1945, Apr. 1.
1946, Apr. 21.
1947, Apr. 6.
1948, Mar. 28.
1949, Apr. 17.
1950, Apr. 9.
1951, Mar. 25.
1952, Apr. 13.
1953, Apr. 5.
1954, Apr. 18.
1955, Apr. 10.
1956, Apr. 1.
1957, Apr. 21.
1958, Apr. 6.
1959, Mar. 29.
1960, Apr. 17.
1961, Apr. 2.
1962, Apr. 22.
1963, Apr. 14.
1964, Mar. 29.
1965, Apr. 18.
1966, Apr. 10.
1967, Mar. 26.
1968, Apr. 14.
1969, Apr. 6.
1970, Mar. 29.
1971, Apr. 11.
1972, Apr. 2.
1973, Apr. 22.
1974, Apr. 14.
1975, Mar. 30.
1976, Apr. 18.
1977, Apr. 10.
1978, Mar. 26.
1979, Apr. 15.
1980, Apr. 6.
1981, Apr. 19.
1982, Apr. 11.
1983, Apr. 3.
1984, Apr. 22.
1985, Apr. 7.

1986, Mar. 30.
1987, Apr. 19.
1988, Apr. 3.
1989, Mar. 26.
1990, Apr. 15.
1991, Mar. 31.
1992, Apr. 19.
1993, Apr. 11.
1994, Apr. 3.
1995, Apr. 16.
1996, Apr. 7.
1997, Mar. 30.
1998, Apr. 12.
1999, Apr. 4.
2000, Apr. 23.

## 5. *List of Wedding Anniversaries with Distinctive Gifts*

Pastors find it convenient to have the full list, which follows. The most important are the "Silver" after 25 years, the "Golden" after 50 years, and the "Diamond" after 60, 70, or 75 years.

1st, Paper.
2nd, Cotton.
3rd, Leather.
4th, Fruit.
5th, Wooden.
6th, Candy.
7th, Wool.
8th, Pottery.
9th, Willow
10th, Tin.
11th, Steel.
12th, Silk.
13th, Lace.
14th, Ivory.
15th, Crystal.
20th, China.
25th, Silver.
30th, Pearl.
35th, Coral.
40th, Ruby.
45th, Sapphire.
50th, Golden.
75th, Diamond.

## 6. ANNIVERSARIES OF CULTURAL AND RELIGIOUS INTEREST IN 1958

1,700 years. Death of Cyprian, 258. The first African bishop to obtain the martyr's crown.

650 years. John Duns Scotus died in 1308. He was the greatest British medieval philosopher.

400 years. Elizabeth I of England ascended the throne in 1558.

350 years. Thomas Fuller, English divine and historian, was born in 1608. "Fuller was incomparably the most sensible, the least prejudiced, great man of an age that boasted a galaxy of great men."

350 years. Dec. 9, 1608, was the birth date of John Milton, England's great Puritan poet. He was also a champion of the freedom of the press. (See Section VIII, Evening Sermon for Dec. 7, in this *Manual.*)

300 years. Henry Purcell was born in 1658. He was an English composer of church and dramatic music of first rank; organist at Westminster Abbey, where he was buried.

300 years. Oliver Cromwell died Sept. 3, 1658. Great English Protestant, born Apr. 25, 1599. "He ranks among the giants. . . . And so the clodhopper became the king! It was *the text* that did it. His text: *'I can do all things through Christ that strengtheneth me.'*" F. W. Boreham, *A Bunch of Everlastings.*

250 years. William Pitt, constructive British statesman and orator, was known as "Pitt, the Elder." He was called also "The Great Commoner." As Prime Minister he built up the British Empire. He was born Nov. 15, 1708.

250 years. Charles Wesley, English Methodist hymn writer, was born Dec. 28, 1708 (?). Some say, 1707.

200 years. Jonathan Edwards died Mar. 22, 1758.

200 years. James Monroe was born Apr. 28, 1758. He was the fifth President of the United States, 1817-1825. He formulated the *Monroe Doctrine.*

200 years. Horatio, Lord Nelson was born Sept. 29, 1758. English admiral, hero of the Battle of Trafalgar.

200 years. Noah Webster, American lexicographer and scholar, was born Oct. 16, 1758. Best known for his dictionary.

200 years. On Nov. 5, 1758, Hans Egede, pioneer missionary to Greenland, died. His is one of the most heroic stories in missionary annals. "Estimated on the scale of motives and qualities, this apostle was a hero and his mission a triumph." (See Section VI in this *Manual.*)

150 years. Rev. Ray Palmer wrote the hymn, "My Faith Looks Up to Thee," at the age of 22. He was born in 1808.

150 years. Horatius Bonar, hymn writer, was born in 1808. Over one hundred of his hymns are still in use. "The best of them ran with the classics."

150 years. Salmon P. Chase, American jurist and statesman, was born Jan. 13, 1808. He was Secretary of the Treasury under Lincoln and Chief Justice of the Supreme Court from 1864 to 1873.

150 years. Jefferson Davis, President of the Confederate States of America, was born June 3, 1808. He died Dec. 6, 1889.

150 years. Samuel F. Smith, author of "My Country, 'Tis of Thee" and "The Morning Light is Breaking," was born Oct. 21, 1808.

150 years. Thomas Cook, English travel agent, was born Nov. 22, 1808.

150 years. Henry F. Chorley was born Dec. 15, 1808. His hymn, "God the Omnipotent! King, Who Ordainest," is a free rendering of the famous Russian national hymn.

150 years. Andrew Johnson, seventeenth President of the United States, was born Dec. 29, 1808.

100 years. In 1858 Dr. John G. Paton was sent out to begin his missionary service on the island of Tanna in the South Seas.

100 years. In 1858 Townsend Harris negotiated a new and more liberal treaty between the United States and Japan. This opened the long closed door to missionaries as well as to merchants.

100 years. On March 4, 1858, Matthew Calbraith Perry, commodore in the United States Navy, died. He negotiated the first treaty with Japan.

100 years. March 12, 1858, birth of Adolph S. Ochs, American journalist, publisher of the *New York Times,* 1896-1935. Died Apr. 18, 1935.

100 years. George Washington Goethals was born June 29, 1858. He was the builder of the Panama Canal and designer of the World War I merchant fleet. "Few men have served their nation better."

100 years. Maltbie D. Babcock, an American Presbyterian minister of peculiar gifts and powers, was born Aug. 3, 1858. Author of the well-known hymn, "This Is My Father's World."

100 years. Ando Hiroshige, Japanese landscape painter and color-print artist, died Sept. 6, 1858.

100 years. Michael I. Pupin was born Oct. 4, 1858. Died Mar. 12, 1935. Eminent American electrical scientist, inventor, and teacher, born in Serbia. Autobiography, *From Immigrant to Inventor.*

100 years. Theodore Roosevelt, the twenty-sixth President of the United States, 1901-1909, was born Oct. 27, 1858. Died Jan. 6, 1919. Soldier, man of letters, statesman, reformer, naturalist, sportsman.

100 years. On Nov. 9, 1858, the New York Symphony Orchestra gave its first concert under Leopold Damrosch.

100 years. Robert Owen, English idealistic reformer, died Nov. 17, 1858.

100 years. Selma Lagerlöff, Swedish novelist and first woman member of the Swedish Academy, was born Nov. 20, 1858.

100 years. Giacomo Puccini, Italian operatic composer, was born Dec. 23, 1858. Operas: *La Boheme, La Tosca,* and *Madame Butterfly.*

50 years. The first Boy Scout troop was organized in England in 1908.

50 years. Grover Cleveland, twenty-second (1885-1889) and twenty-fourth (1893-1897) President of the United States, died June 24, 1908.

50 years. Joel Chandler Harris, creator of Uncle Remus, was born Dec. 10, 1848, and died July 3, 1908. He was a Southern journalist and author.

50 years. William Mason, pianist, composer, and one of America's greatest teachers of music, died July 14. 1908.

50 years. July 24, 1908. A bloodless revolution in Turkey, by which that most absolute and tyrannical monarchy in the world gave place to a constitutional government.

50 years. Daniel Coit Gilman, first president of Johns Hopkins University and one of the founders of its school of medicine, died Oct. 13, 1908. Born July 6, 1831.

50 years. Edward A. MacDowell died Dec. 18, 1908. American composer. First professor of music at Columbia University.

## 7. FUNERAL MEDITATIONS

Since the Funeral Meditations that follow are given for their suggestive value, they are printed as they were actually used.

The occasion should tell us when it is wise to use any form of sermon or meditation when conducting a funeral service. The great Scripture passages which are generally read have power to comfort, strengthen, and bring peace. No other words can take their place. But sometimes a few well-chosen personal remarks are necessary.

A. The funeral of one who had been a house servant in many homes of the community. The Scripture Readings included Luke 2:1-20, because it was the Christmas season.

The reading of the Christmas story is not inappropriate at this service for a number of reasons, and I would like to point them out.

I. Think of the value and dignity which was given to human life when the eternal God came down in Christ and took the form of our humanity, being born as a little Babe. After that we can call no human being common. "Never again can I belittle man, if the eternal Son became a man. Never again can I despise humanity if he was found in the likeness of humanity."

Sometimes we ministers are called by a mortuary to take a funeral service for a total stranger. I have sometimes felt that to be a great privilege—with no personal ties as I have today—because the human ties are very strong; the stranger shares with me a common humanity. For him Christ came; for me he came. Christ shared with us our humanity. That stranger carries dignity and worth, no matter who he may be. He is my brother in Christ—and I should find it high privilege to say a prayer at his passing.

There is a certain dignity, such as Alice carried, that comes upon us because Christ came unto us.

II. Then there shines from the manger at Bethlehem light upon human toil. The good news was told to shepherds, to working men who were toiling in the fields. They were workers, living sacrificing and strenuous lives for their flocks.

Human service was made holy because servants were permitted to bow down at his cradle. We remember, too, that the Babe became a carpenter, working with his hands. Later he said, "I am among you as one that serveth." Alice could have said that.

III. Then we should consider this, that the Coming of the Son is related to our Going as Sons. We are children of God.

His coming is related to her going, and to mine when that day arrives.

He came as Saviour so that we might be saved. He came down to the darkness of earth, so that we might walk in the light and ascend into the light of heaven.

So let us go out into the Christmas season with joy in our hearts because we have known Alice and because we greet again and take into our hearts the One who was Alice's Saviour.—H.

B. The funeral of a Christian mother. She left three children between 10 and 15 years of age.

There was once a small boy whose mother died when he was four years old. This boy grew through childhood and youth to manhood, and after the busy years of maturity he became an old man.

There was never a time that he didn't miss his mother; but in a certain way he always possessed her more wonderfully than if she had lived.

How did he possess her? In four ways; First, she personified his ideals. You see, loveliness of character was no longer an abstract thing—loveliness of character was his mother. He learned to know what love is, because love was his mother. He learned to know what faith is, because faith was his mother. And so with all the Christian virtues and graces.

Then, secondly, she carried his burdens. Though she could not be seen, his mother was always taking the load off his shoulders and from his heart. She bore the heartaches of his childhood, the perplexities of his youth, and the burdens of his later years.

Then, thirdly, she gave him courage. Sometimes life goes to pieces, or the bottom drops out of things. One cannot always be sure of the seen person by one's side. But this boy learned early that he could depend upon his mother. She gave him courage.

And then, fourthly, she always went before him. He would have to do his best because his mother was always out beyond him in his best. She was the courier that always went ahead into the promised land.

And so this mother became the heroine of the boy, the man, the old man. And she never failed him.—H.

C. The funeral of a man. His son needed a more courageous spirit.

The last passage I have read (Josh. 1) is an unusual one to use on an occasion like this. On the other hand it is often read at the beginning of a new year.

It tells of the death of Moses and places a great responsibility upon his successor Joshua. Three times the word of God is spoken to Joshua in this form, "Be strong and of good courage."

Through the death of our brother there is shift of responsibility. Hear then the word of God as spoken to Joshua. Let this word come to our own ears and hearts, "Be strong and of good courage."

Surely it is better to be strong than to be weak. It is better to face up to life bravely than to fall back into bitterness or discouragement. Surely it is better to show courage than to show cowardice.

There are great opportunities and compensations to be had in facing up to great responsibilities.

Note what the Lord said to Joshua, "Be strong and of good courage, I will be with you." Unseen, but very real, God walks beside the man who faces life with strength and courage. God reinforces the courageous person. When strength ebbs and weakness comes then God adds his strength. When courage falters God is alongside to help.

The second time that the Lord spoke to Joshua he told him to be careful to do according to the Book of the Law; it was to be meditated upon and followed. It is so to this day; we have a Book in our hands, which when read and meditated upon gives faith and courage to a man and directs him along the pathway of life.

The third time that the Lord spoke to Joshua he repeated his first promise, "Be strong and of good courage; be not frightened, neither be dismayed; for the Lord your God is with you wherever you go."—H.

## 8. SENIOR-YOUNG PEOPLE'S SOCIETY CHRISTIAN ENDEAVOR TOPICS FOR 1958

Selected and Arranged by the Topics Committee of the International Society of Christian Endeavor.



These topics are arranged to be used either singly or in the series or units as indicated.

### LOOK IN THE MIRROR! (three topics)

Jan. 5. 1. Who Do You Think You Are? Ps. 144:3, 4; Ps. 19; I Cor. 15.

Jan. 12. 2. Where Do You Think You're Going? Luke 14:25-33.

Jan. 19. 3. Who Do You Think Will Help You? Ps. 46:1; Ps. 60:11; Heb. 4:16.

### CHRISTIAN ENDEAVOR WEEK—YOUTH WEEK (two topics)

Jan. 26. 1. Lord, Help Our Unbelief. (Denominational Sunday—Beginning Christian Endeavor Week.) Mark 9:24.

Feb. 2. 2. For Christ and the Church. (Christian Endeavor Sunday.) Rom. 12:1.

### THINKING GOD'S THOUGHTS (three topics)

Feb. 9. 1. God Plans the World. Gen. 1:1, 2, 26, 27, 31; Ps. 8:1, 3-9.

Feb. 16. 2. God Sees Man's Failure. Gen. 3:8-13; Gen. 4:8-10; Deut. 9:18.

Feb. 23. 3. God Plans Man's Redemption. Gen. 3:15; Gal. 3:13; Col. 2:13, 14.

### HABITS THAT STRENGTHEN (four topics)

Mar. 2. 1. Let's Go to Church. Ps. 122; Ps. 84:1-4, 10-12; Heb. 10:25a.

Mar. 9. 2. Bible Reading—a Stabilizing Influence. Matt. 4:1-11; Ps. 119:1-11.

Mar. 16. 3. Prayer—a Joyous Power. Rom. 8:26; I John 5:1-15.

Mar. 23. 4. Giving that Lifts Me. II Cor. 9:1-7; I Cor. 16:2.

Mar. 30. Take Up Thy Cross (Palm Sunday.) Mar 11:1-10; Luke 9:23.

Apr. 6. I Know the Living Christ. (Easter.) John 4:39-42; II Cor. 13:1-4.

### DEVELOPING CHRISTIAN QUALITIES (three topics)

Apr. 13 1. The Halo of Humbleness. Phil. 2:1-11.

Apr. 20. 2. Trifling with the Truth. Acts 5:1-11.

Apr. 27. 3. A. Life-Long Loyalty. II Tim. 4:1-8.

May 4. A Christ-Centered Vocation. (Vocations Sunday.) Mark 8:34-38.

May 11. My Dream Home. (Christian Family Sunday.) Luke 10:38-42.

May 18. Christ, the Church, and Race Matt. 28:18-20.

May 25. "When the Day of Pentecost Had Come." Acts 2:1-14, 36-47.

### LET'S GO TO EUROPE (five topics)

June 1. 1. Paul Called to Europe. Acts 16:6-10.

June 8. 2. Paul Meets a Business Woman. Acts 16:13-15, 40.

June 15. 3. Paul Discovers Bible Students. Acts 17:10-14.

June 22. 4. Paul's Experiences in Athens. Acts 17:16-34.

June 29. 5. Paul in a Seacoast Town. Acts 18:1-11.

July 6. Christians Have the Most Fun. Col. 3:1-17.

ONENESS IN CHRIST (three topics)

July 13. 1. Christ Prays for Oneness. John 17; Eph. 4:3-6.

July 20. 2. A Realistic Look at Our Prejudices. Luke 6:27, 28; Luke 10:25-37.

July 27. 3. The Power of Christian Oneness. John 1:6-13; Matt. 12:26-30.

HABITS THAT HINDER (four topics)

Aug. 3. 1. Everybody Does It. II Cor. 6:14-18; I Pet. 2:9; Rom. 12:2.

Aug. 10. 2. Confidentially—Have You Heard? Zech. 8:16, 17; Rom. 13:7-10.

Aug. 17. 3. I Can Quit Any Time. Luke 16:13-15; Matt. 15:18; I John 3:7, 8.

Aug. 24. 4. I'll Do It Tomorrow. James 4:13-17; Prov. 6:6-11.

Aug. 31. Learning Never Ends. Prov. 2:1-7; Prov. 3:13-23; I Cor. 3:18, 19.

Sept. 7. Dating Etiquette. II Cor. 5:8-15.

Sept. 14. Evangelism through Recreation. I Cor. 3:5-17.

EVALUATION OF SUCCESS (two topics)

Sept. 21. 1. True Measure of Success. Eph. 4:11-16.

Sept. 28. 2. The Successful Youth Program. Luke 12:22-32.

Oct. 5. Let a Man Examine Himself. (World-Wide Communion Sunday.) I Cor. 11:23-29.

Oct. 12. The Near East. Acts 1:8.

Oct. 19. World-Wide Ideas. (United Nations Sunday.) Acts 17:26 (KJV); Mic. 4:3-5; Mic. 6:8.

Oct. 26. Love—a More Excellent Way. John 3:16; I John 4:7-21.

LIGHT FROM ANCIENT CHURCHES (five topics)

Nov. 2. 1. The Church that Misplaced Love. Rev. 2:1-7.

Nov. 9. 2. The Church that Suffered. Rev. 2:8-11.

Nov. 16. 3. The Church that Needed Repentance. Rev. 2:12-17.

Nov. 23. 4. The Church that Lived in Name Only. Rev. 3:1-6.

Nov. 30. 5. The Church the Spirit Couldn't Endure. Rev. 3:14-22.

PRECIOUS POSSESSIONS (four topics)

Dec. 7. 1. I Have an Altar. Deut. 6:4-9; Exod. 27:1-8; Matt. 14:22, 23.

Dec. 14. 2. I Have a Book. (Universal Bible Sunday.) Ps. 119:9-16; John 20:30, 31; II Tim. 3:14-17.

Dec. 21. 3. I Have a Saviour. (Christmas Sunday.) Isa. 9:6, 7; Luke 2:7-17.

Dec. 28. 4. I Have a New Year. Eph. 6:10-20; Ezek. 36:25-28.

# *SECTION II. Questions of Religion and Life*

The following questions were asked by persons of various age groups. In looking them over any minister may find many which are suggestive for sermonic treatment.

## QUESTIONS

1. Why doesn't God do something about war and injustice?
2. Is it wrong to be a doubting Thomas?
3. What is the principle of faith?
4. If the apostles were to preach and cast out demons, did they believe in witchcraft?
5. Are prayers answered?
6. If there is a God and he is good, why does he permit the innocent to suffer for the deeds of the evil?
7. Why does God allow people to suffer?
8. How can one best determine the will of Christ in regard to what vocation he should follow?
9. Do you think the old-fashioned gospel is too outdated to meet the needs of modern young people?
10. What part does God play in personal growth?
11. Has America reached the apex of its power?
12. What is the general opinion about young people smoking?
13. What seems a miracle can eventually be explained as we understand newly discovered laws. Do you believe in miracles?
14. In what way does intercessory prayer help when the person has not asked for your prayer?
15. How do you explain evil in the world?
16. Once you get a young person interested in coming to your Youth Group, how can you keep him interested in coming?
17. How can a minister fulfill the people's need of spiritual leadership if his role must be that of administrator, first of all, before that of pastor?
18. Is there any way to explain the many contradictions that can be found in the Bible?
19. With the many technological advances in modern warfare is it within the power of man to destroy himself?
20. If Christianity is really a monotheistic religion, how can we justify the worship of Jesus?
21. Is man's power and destiny controlled and limited by an infinite God?
22. Who is God?
23. What is there in the social teachings of Jesus that could restore world order and provide for economic justice?
24. In Matthew 12:48 why did Jesus ask, "Who is my mother, and who are my brothers?"

25. Is the Christian church on the whole trying to help juvenile delinquents or is it leaving the problem to non-Christian groups?

26. Conflict: Observation tells us that preaching integration too aggressively will stir up a hostile antagonism which will set the process back; empathy with Negroes tells us they deserve justice now. What should we do?

27. What is a Christian attitude toward the homosexual?

28. Problem: To reconcile realistic mistrust of communism's program with a feeling for human brotherhood with the friendly Russian common people.

29. What is sin?

30. What does the resurrection mean?

31. Is discontentment a sin? If so, how can I overcome it?

32. Should the church receive money from men who make their money wrongly, such as saloonkeepers, gamblers, etc.?

33. Should I give up something for Lent?

34. Can we always tell what our duty is?

35. How can politicians and business people follow the Sermon on the Mount?

36. Can a man be a Christian and not go to church?

37. Where are the dead?

38. How can I be true to my Christian calling when I am surrounded with so much that is unchristian?

39. In view of Christ's injunction "Judge not . . ." what justification can there be for such stands as excluding the Unitarians from Christian organizations or excluding other people from Christian churches because of personal differences?

40. Is there any place for superstition in religion?

41. How does one know he is "saved"? Is it a sudden awakening or can it be gradual?

42. Should a Christian tithe his "gross income" or his "take-home" pay?

43. Would helping a worthy Catholic family be included in tithing?

44. How can I teach my children respect for God? They sometimes act silly during prayers.

45. What is meant by "on the right hand of God"?

46. What are the psychological implications of teen-age "crazes"?

47. Do TV and radio commercials on alcohol and tobacco have an adverse effect on teenagers?

48. Is there a sane approach to TV from a family viewpoint? If so, what is it?

49. What is meant by "the overruling providence of God"?

50. How can the ecumenical movement be kept from overemphasizing church organization, for example by regarding merger of denominations as the all-important goal?

51. What is meant by "the quick and the dead"?

52. Is the widespread criticism of Dr. Peale's writings fair? Should not the church bring a gospel of trust and confidence and so of peace to those who are going through deep waters of anxiety and perplexity?

53. Has the swing away from the old "liberal theology" gone too far? Were there not beliefs in that conception which need to be conserved?

54. How can a large modern church avoid the danger of letting the machinery of manifold church organizations swallow up the energies of the church staff and so hinder the main work of the church?

55. How can I be popular and be a teetotaler?

56. What is meant by "the communion of saints"?

57. What is meant by "the resurrection of the body"?

58. Do Protestants pray for the dead?

59. Is it more difficult to be a Christian today than 100 years ago?

60. What do the words "Church Militant" mean?

61. What is meant by faith healing?

62. Are there times when a "white lie" is justified?

63. How can the Church make its influence felt in our national life?

64. How can criticism be constructive?

65. Should a Christian refuse the use of liquor as a medicine?

66. When Christ enjoined his followers to be perfect, as God is perfect, was he suggesting a possible human achievement?

67. Should a Christian practice forgiveness even when he does not actually feel it in his heart?

68. Does the Protestant church have any doctrine which parallels the Roman Catholic confessional?

69. Are "You" and "Your" proper pronouns to use when addressing God?

70. Does the Bible mention conscience?

71. How can the Lord's Prayer become meaningful to those who are, perhaps, too familiar with its words?

72. What is meant by the phrase "Lord God of Hosts"?

73. What does the Bible teach concerning interracial marriage?

74. Is resistance to evil strengthened by exposing oneself deliberately to evil temptations?

75. Did Jesus ever express himself in a humorous manner?

76. Is the United States of America a Christian nation in a legal sense?

77. Is the phrase "Kingdom of God" appropriate for use by persons who live in a republican form of government?

78. Can a Christian ever consider himself to be a "self-made" man?

79. What is the unpardonable sin?

80. What is the difference in meaning between the cross and the crucifix?

81. Can we accept the Ascension story literally?

82. How can good be brought out of evil?

83. Did the Puritans make any lasting contributions to American religious life?

84. Should spontaneous prayers be given in formal church worship?

85. In what ways can a person prepare his soul and spirit for church worship?

86. How can I clear my mind of unworthy thoughts during prayer?

87. What does the Bible teach about Hell?

88. Is it helpful to kneel during private prayer? Why?

89. How can an individual Christian do something to bridge racial tensions?

90. What is meant by vicarious suffering?

91. Should personal devotions come in the morning or the evening?

92. Is conversion necessary for all Christians?

93. Should a Christian obey a law against his convictions?

94. How can a man be released from a sense of guilt?

95. What is the Christian concept of man?

96. Do all world religions express a faith in God?

97. Should Christians feel obligated to work for church unity?

98. Do only Christians believe in the immortality of the soul?

99. Can immortality be proven or is it accepted on faith?

100. What does the word "Selah" mean?

# *SECTION III. Vital Themes for Vital Preaching. Church Year and Other Sermons in Outline*

## THOUGHT-KINDLERS

The most consecrated and studious ministers are most alert to hints and helps and suggested material for their sermons. To them nothing is more thought-awakening and stimulating than just topics and texts strikingly united. Each clergyman is also well aware of how often time is lost for lack of good sermon leads and in trying to conjure up usable ideas out of thin air. Anything which saves him from this time-consuming endeavor is so much to the good. The briefest hint may prove a great help, the very starting-point needed. Here are fifty thought-kindlers arranged roughly according to the Sundays of the Christian Year.

### 1. Topic: Assurance

TEXT: "Thou hast beset me behind and before, and laid thine hand upon me." Ps. 139:5.

I. He throws his hallowing grace over our yesterdays.

II. He enfolds us in our present journey.

III. He lights up tomorrow with eternal Hope.—J. H. Jowett.

Christian assurance should mean, not "I know that I am going to Heaven," but "I know that the love of God is to be trusted in life and in death, everywhere and always." "Though he slay me, yet will I trust in him." If it is of this kind, then assurance is not presumption, nor is it a scarcely attainable goal in the future, but a present fact. It is grounded in the words of the Lord and in his abiding promise.—Edgar P. Dickie.

### 2. Topic: "When They Had Prayed"

SCRIPTURE: Acts 4:23-38. TEXT: "And when they had prayed, the place was shaken where they were assembled together; and they were all filled with the Holy Ghost, and they spake the word of God with boldness." Acts 4:31.

They faced the world's intimidation with prayer.

I. Things conspicuously absent: 1. No reliance in any human agency. 2. No solicitude for personal safety.

II. On the other hand: 1. Recognition of God's creatorship and sovereignty over the world. 2. A turning to God's word for a message fitting their case. 3. They ask God to: (a) "Behold *their* threatening"; (b) Give *them* boldness and courage, not "Don't let them hurt us!"; (c) Enable them to speak thy word, "Ye shall be witnesses unto me"; (d) Accompany their word with his divine works.

III. What happened: 1. The place where they assembled was shaken. 2. All were filled with the Holy Ghost—God laid hold of each witnessing person. 3. They spoke the word of God with boldness. 4. The multitude of disciples were of one heart and soul. 5. The apostles "with great power" gave witness.—Joseph A. Vance.

**3. Topic: "And Noah Was Drunk"**

TEXT: "And Noah . . . was drunken." Gen. 9:20, 21.

Claude C. Douglas gives this as the strangest text he ever used. "What a picture! The old world was destroyed, and a new world was to be built, and the chief architect was drunk!" He should have had a great sense of responsibility. There are parallel situations in modern times. The world requires a new order. What about our architects, political, social, religious?

**4. Topic: The Wonder of Man**

TEXT: "Thou hast made him a little lower than the angels, and hast crowned him with glory and honour." Ps. 8:5.

I. He can search the heavens.

II. He can dominate the earth.

III. He can love his brother.

IV. He can worship God.—H.

**5. Topic: Unusual Opportunities**

I. The Opportunity in Detainment. "After these things Jesus walked in Galilee. . . ." John 7:1. Lingering in Galilee.

II. The Opportunity in Necessity. "And he must needs go through Samaria. . . ." John 4:4.

III. The Opportunity in Repetition. "So Jesus came again into Cana of Galilee. . . ." John 4:46.—H.

**6. Topic: He Is Our Brother**

TEXT: ". . . for he is our brother. . . ." Gen. 37:27.

INTRODUCTION: The Story of Philemon and Onesimus

I. Jesus crossed boundaries to be a brother to the Samaritan woman, the Roman centurion, the hated tax-gatherer, the Sidonian mother.

II. Brotherhood is Christianity according to Christ.

III. Opportunities for showing brotherhood.

ILLUSTRATION: John Drinkwater's great play put Lincoln in the place every man must occupy when he gave us his conversation with the old Negro preacher, Frederick Douglass. "But I am black, and you are white," said Douglass as he was bidden to take a chair. "No, no," said Lincoln, "we are just two old en talking together." Just two old men, each with a burden on his soul, facing the common challenge of Jesus. This is Christianity according to Christ.—Adapted from Frederick Stamm.

**7. The Magnetism of Jesus**

TEXT: "And I, if I be lifted up from the earth, will draw all men unto me. This he said, signifying what death he should die." John 12:32, 33.

I. Its nature. The mightiest of spiritual forces, this attractive power of Jesus, is the power of a person. "And *I,* if I be lifted up," says Christ. This power of a person is the greatest power the world knows. Whatever makes more real and vivid personality, the more powerfully attracts us. Now Christ is a real person. And this personal Christ is the cause and summation of Christianity as the sun is of the day. And the difference between Christ and all other religious teachers is that instead of pointing to his teachings, he points to himself as the substance and illustration of his teachings. And a more remarkable difference is that Christ does not, like other men, fall below his teachings. He is the One Excellent, and attracts with this power of an utterly pure personality.

II. The sphere of this attractiveness. It is universal. "Will draw all men." Christ is not for any time or race or section of the world, but for all times, climes, races.

III. The method of this attractiveness. There are two New Testament words for drawing—one signifying dragging; the other persuading. It is the last word which is used to set forth the attractive power of Christ. One may feel it. Who has not? But one may resist it.

**8. Topic: What Is the Christian Life?**

I. It is a spiritual life by the Holy Spirit, I Cor. 2:12-15.

II. It is a new life from God, II Cor. :17.

III. It is a hidden life in Christ, Col. .3.

IV. It is a holy life of obedience, .omans 6:19, 22.

V. It is a progressive life of perse-erance, II Pet. 1:5-8.

VI. It is a fruitful life of abiding, ohn 15:4-8.

VII. It is an eternal life, a free gift, John 5:11-13.—C. Edwards.

**. Topic: Why Join the Church?**

TEXT: "And they continued stedfastly n the apostles' doctrine and fellowship, nd in breaking of bread, and in prayers. . . And the Lord added to the church laily such as should be saved." Acts :42, 47.

INTRODUCTION: What is meant by "the :hurch"? We mean just now "the whole ompany of those who have accepted esus Christ as their personal Saviour, by vhatever name they may be called, and ave thereby become members of the Kingdom of Heaven, and are associated ogether for Christian worship, fellow-.hip and service." Why join the Church?

I. Because there is a Church to join. It was Christ's will to establish the Church.

II. Because Christianity cannot do without the Church. All that goes to nake up our religious life has been given us directly or indirectly through the Church.

III. Because of the reasons for which it was founded: 1. For fellowship. Chris-tianity knows nothing of a solitary religion. 2. For worship. This is an essential part of religion. 3. For service. —H. Mudie Draper.

**10. Topic: A Study in Private Devotions**

TEXT: Isa. 6:1-8.

I. An experience of awe in the pres-ence of God. Vv. 1-4.

II. A sense of sin, and confession of that sin. Vv. 5.

III. An experience of forgiveness. Vv. 6 and 7.

IV. A vision of duty and an experience of complete dedication to the service of God. V. 8.

**11. Topic: He Might Have . . .**

TEXT: "He stedfastly set his face to go to Jerusalem." Luke 9:51.

I. He might have remained in Galilee.

II. He might have delayed by the bluffs of Jericho.

III. He might have lingered in Beth-any.

IV. He might have gone through an open door.

**12. Topic: Rooted and Grounded in Love (Lent)**

TEXT: "That ye being rooted and grounded in love." Eph. 3:17.

The figure is doubled. It is taken from a tree and a building. For the stability and growth of a tree, root is necessary. To the stability of a building, founda-tion is necessary. This was part of Paul's prayer for his beloved Ephesian Chris-tians, that they might be rooted and grounded in love, that their religion might have deep roots and a firm foun-dation.

I. The grace he besought for them. To be "rooted and grounded in love." 1. Love toward God implies admiration for his person and character. 2. It in-cludes gratitude for his benefits and blessings. 3. It includes delight in his communion.

II. The importance of this grace. Rooting is for sustenance and founda-tion; grounded is for support. 1. The love of God is the essence of religion. 2. The love of God is the germ of holi-ness. 3. The love of God is the source of happiness.

III. Some characteristics of this grace. 1. It should be sincere and not senti-mental. 2. It should be permanent and not temporary. In this Lenten season seek to become "rooted and grounded in love."—G. H.

**13. Topic: The Uniqueness of Jesus**

I. Unique Oneness with God.

II. Unique Moral Authority over Men.

III. Unique Ministry of Salvation.

IV. Unique Mastery over the Powers of Evil.—J. S. W.

**14. Topic: Jesus was Right (Easter)**

TEXT: "If I say the truth, why do ye not believe me?" John 8:46.

It would help tremendously today if all Christians could find in Easter the same assurance and conviction that Christ's resurrection brought to the first disciples.

For them it was not primarily the assurance of a continuing life beyond the grave; they believed that already. What the Resurrection proved to them was that Jesus had been right—all that he had told them about God and prayer and spiritual values was true!

Three days before, it seemed that he had been wrong; and when his body was laid away in the tomb, all their high hopes had been buried with him. But now everything was changed.

I. Jesus was right: this is God's world, and he never forsakes his children.

II. Jesus was right: love and righteousness are the laws of life and nothing can ultimately triumph over them.

III. Jesus was right: first things first—"seek ye first the kingdom of heaven."

Thus, for those first disciples the Resurrection was God's endorsement of all that Jesus taught and was. As St. Peter stated later: "There is no other name under heaven given among men by which we must be saved."

We Christians must convince the world of that fact today. No one else has the responsibility.—John F. Scott.

**15. Topic: Signposts to Immortality (Easter)**

TEXTS: "Death is swallowed up in victury." I Cor. 15:54. "That mortality might be swallowed up of life." II Cor. 5:4.

There are many people who regard the Christian faith in immortality as irrelevant. They are not interested. This regard is often conjoined with real nobility of character.

The mind of man cannot rest satisfied there. 1. A man wants to know. 2. Life's transience becomes a desperately real fact, especially when death raids your deepest affection when it touches another whom you love. 3. Belief in the hereafter is no abstract article of faith. It matters personally and vitally and overwhelmingly. 4. Is it true? Is it man's invention or God's reality?

I. The first signpost to immortality is *the* fact of the reality of the unseen.

II. The second signpost is the rationality of the universe.

III. The third signpost is the character of God. It is vitally important to get this clear. Have you realized that what is at stake in all discussion about life beyond is nothing less than the character of God himself?

IV. A further decisive signpost is the Christian experience of regeneration. All down the Christian centuries countless men and women, entering into fellowship with Christ, have found eternal life *as a present possession.*

V. Finally, there is the signpost of the Resurrection of Christ himself.—James S. Stewart (*The Strong Name*).

**16. Topic: Present-tense Christianity**

Again and again the future tenses of the Old Testament become present tenses in the New. Something *has come* to pass and now *is.*

I. "We *have* peace with God through our Lord Jesus Christ. Rom. 5:1.

II. "I *am persuaded.*" Rom. 8:38.

III. "We *know* that we *have passed* from death to life." I John 3:14.

IV. "Hereby *know* we that we *dwell* in him, and he in us, because he hath given us of his Spirit." I John 4:13.

V. "I *am* crucified with Christ; nevertheless *I am alive;* and yet not I, but Christ *is alive in me.*" Gal. 2:20.—Suggested by J. S. Whale.

**17. Topic: Sin in Blossom**

TEXT: "The rod hath blossomed, pride hath budded. . . ." Ezek. 7:10.

I. Sin in blossom—beauty may be associated with evil. Yes, other evils than pride seem to have the blossoms that make the world exclaim—"Beautiful!" "Splendid!" "Great!"

II. Success is no test of moral right or wrong. Pride blossoms. So does envy. So does selfishness. Lowliness often seems sterile. So does love. So does prayer.

The Babylonians besieged Jerusalem and had success. Success is no test of moral right or wrong.

III. The forces of retribution are ever at work. Just as the circulation of sap through all the vessels of the tree, the influences of light and air, all the forces working out the mystery of growth are gradually and silently (though probably not silently if our ears were keener) preparing the hour of bud and blossom. All evil actions are ever setting toward retributive results. Professor John C. Bennett has given us a great word, "the self-defeating character of evil." Retribution results gradually, and sometimes silently, but ever surely, are tending to the crises that are days of judgment.—G. H.

### 18. Topic: A New Beatitude

A new beatitude is given by Leland Foster Wood, "Blessed are the homemakers: for they are the builders of mankind." Happy are true homemakers—but how may such happiness be assured? Four ways are suggested by Mr. Wood:

I. Happy is the home where the home is first. Many times the sons of great men are mediocer, because their fathers were so busy being great that they had no time to share the fundamentals of life with their sons.

II. Happy is the home where there is love and laughter.

III. Happy is the home where children are taught a Christian response to life.

IV. Happy is the home where God is in the parents.

### 19. Topic: Winsome Womanhood (Mother's Day)

TEXT: "Entreat me not to leave thee . . . thy people shall be my people, and thy God my God." Ruth 1:16.

Text generally used in treating "The Choice of Ruth." But reading between the lines we find suggested the religion of Naomi.

I. Its strength. Could bear transplanting to a foreign land. It is one thing to be religious at home surrounded by helpful influences. Another when in a strange land, different customs, etc. In Moab she did not do as the Moabites did. Did not compromise. Kept firm and true to her convictions.

II. Its beauty. "On the pillars, lily-work." A personality that could evoke such passionate devotion as Ruth expresses in the text must have been attractive. If the effect (Ruth's conversion) was great and beautiful, the cause (Naomi's personality) must have been equally so.

III. Its results. Conversion of Ruth. Led to Ruth's becoming the ancestress of the Messiah. Broke down barriers of 1. Domestic relationship. Mother-in-law! Such have generally poor reputations. 2. National prejudice. Much harder to impress foreigners than those of our own people. Yet her faith was so strong and beautiful that she won the devotion of a daughter-in-law from another race to herself, her people, and her God.—G. H.

### 20. Topic: Furrows

TEXT: "Thou settlest the furrows thereof (of the earth)." Ps. 65:10. See vv. 9-13.

INTRODUCTION: Walking through the fields.

I. There is no harvest without the plowshare. These brown lines are upsetting enough; they tear up old root growths, disturb things as they are for the sake of things as they ought to be.

II. The test of any time is what furrows it plows—and how it seeds them.

III. God has many ways of plowing his furrows. 1. Crusted habits need to be broken up. 2. Useless growths of mind and spirit turned under. 3. New powers of response released. 4. His plowshares are change, challenge, new occasions; sometimes even sorrow and disaster.

IV. Furrows and Seed are the price of the harvest.—Gaius Glenn Atkins.

### 21. Topic: The Source (Pentecost)

TEXT: Acts 2:1-21.

I. God is the flame at which we light our goodness.

II. God is the fire in which we burn our strife.

III. God is the key by which we find our powers.

IV. God is the door through which we enter Life.

(The four sentences are taken from a poem by William H. Hudnut, Jr.

**22. Topic: The Measure of a Church**

TEXT: "And there was given me a reed like unto a rod: and the angel stood, saying, Rise, and measure the temple of God, and the altar, and them that worship therein." Rev. 11:1.

Just as a person needs to check up on himself from time to time, just as a business needs to audit its own records regularly, so there comes a time when a church ought to stand back and look at itself.

A comprehensive and convenient outline for the task is suggested by one of the visions which came to John: "Then I was given a measuring rod like a staff, and I was told: 'Rise and measure the temple of God and the altar and those who worship there'" (R.S.V.). Let's think a little about the measure of a church.

I. The first thing John was told to do was to "measure the temple of God." It suggests that the first thing to do in measuring a church is to assess its building. Is it adequate?

II. The second thing John was told to do was to "measure the altar." It suggests that another crucial element in evaluating a church is its ministry—the ones who officiate at the altar. Look at the ministry of our church.

My prejudice in this disqualifies me from the task of evaluation, I simply ask the privilege of telling what we are trying to do. If there is a single phrase which describes our philosophy and our goal it is this: "a ministry to people."

1. We are trying to minister to people through pastoral care. 2. Through evangelism. 3. Through worship. In practice one can draw no sharp line between pastoral care, evangelism, and worship. Each interacts with the others.

III. The third thing John was told to do was to "measure those who worship there." The final question in measuring any church is, are the people adequate? 1. Are they adequate in resources? 2. Are they adequate in courage? 3. The only real question is: are we adequate in consecration?—Raymond E. Balcomb.

**23. Topic: The Supreme Test (Commencement)**

TEXT: "So they came and stood before the king." Dan. 2:2.

We must validate our claims to wisdom or goodness or strength or courage.

I. You must validate your claims before the king (in a democracy the people).

II. You must validate your claims before superior men.

III. You must validate your claims before yourself.

IV. You must validate your claims before God.—Suggested by Charles E. Park.

**24. Topic: Honorary Degrees (Commencement Season)**

TEXT: "And thou shalt put some of thine honor upon him." Num. 27:20.

Inasmuch as it is the custom of colleges and universities to grant honorary degrees, why not confer some honors upon plain people who will be overlooked by the classical schools, but who are eminently deserving of all the honor we can pay to them?

I. Let's give an honorary degree to the individual who refuses to be victimized by life, who although rich has not lost the common touch, who although on public relief keeps his soul clean and takes the first respectable job he can get, who although midway in life without achieving the dreams of his youth still keeps pressing on, who in spite of the death of loved ones maintains his faith in the goodness of God. They deserve the "Doctor of Victorious Living."

II. Let us pay tribute to the person who in his own community is known for his gentleness, who on the golf links and the highway gives the other fellow the right of way, who in his social business and church relationships is always friendly, generous, and charitable. To such let us give the degree of "Doctor of Goodwill."

III. In the name of Christ let us honor the person who suddenly finds himself face to face with life's grim realities only to discover within himself a person he did not dream existed. Through the years he has exhibited a character that entitles him to the degree of "Doctor of Courage."

IV. Let us give the degree of "Doctor of Steadfast Devotion" to those who live in obedience to the fifth commandment, sacrificing every personal desire, dream, and pleasure, in order to care for aged, sick, or dependent parents with unfailing patience.

V. Then there are young men who, because of their forthrightness and character, have earned the degree of "Doctor of Royal Manhood."

VI. And there are older men who have kept the fires of youth burning within their souls who ought to have the degree of "Doctor of Youthful Maturity."

VII. To a certain young woman who is most admired of her own crowd because of her womanly graces and conduct—achieved by her willingness to be different for conscience' sake—let us give the degree "Doctor of Splendid Womanhood."

But whether we award these degrees formally or not, we do accord these children of God an honor that no college can give.—W. Ralph Ward, Jr.

### 25. Topic: A Great Little Man

TEXT: "Verily I say unto you, Among them that are born of women there hath not risen a greater than John the Baptist: notwithstanding he that is least in the kingdom of heaven is greater than he."—Matt. 11:11.

I. John was little because he had no light in himself—but he was great because all his light was a reflection of Jesus.

II. John was little because all his work was preparatory—but great because it was completed by Jesus.

III. John was little because his knowledge was all imperfect. but great because he told about Jesus.

IV. John was little because of his failure, but he was great because he was God's success.—H.

### 26. Topic: The Appreciation of Liberty (Independence Day)

TEXT: ". . . the glorious liberty of the children of God."—Rom. 8:21.

For the appreciation of liberty ask and answer the following questions:

I. What is the true value of liberty?

II. What is the real meaning of liberty?

III. What are the aesthetic values of liberty?

IV. How can we show our gratitude for liberty?

V. Liberty may be depreciated; how can we add something to, that is appreciate (in contrast to depreciate), liberty?—H.

### 27. Topic: Two Kinds of Knowledge

TEXT: "I have heard of thee by the hearing of the ear: but now mine eyes seeth thee."—Job 42:5.

There are two kinds of knowledge, the knowledge of hearsay and the knowledge of the heart. The one is secondhand; the other is immediate.

I. We know *about* God: 1. From the heavens, nature. 2. From conscience. 3. From the Bible.

II. We know God: 1. Being likeminded with him. To understand truth. a man must be truthful. To understand purity, a man must be pure. . . . Religious knowledge is possible only to those who make the venture. John 7:17. 2. Communion with him.

QUOTATION: To most even good people, God is a belief. To the saints he is an embrace. They have felt the wind of his locks, his heart has beaten against their side. They do not believe in him, for they know him.—Francis Thompson. Adapted from Edgar P. Dickie.

### 28. Topic: The Spirit of the Christian Life

TEXT: "For God has not given us the spirit of fear; but of power, and of love, and of a sound mind."—II Tim. 1:7.

I. The text gives us a striking picture of the contrast between pagan religions and that of Christ. All pagan religions are characterized by slavish fear. The people fear their idols. They fear their priests. They fear the devil. They often worship him lest he should hurt them. The spirit of the Christian life is absence of fear.

II. God has given us the spirit of power. The word is more particularly courage. The spirit of the Christian is the very opposite of the cowardly spirit. There is liberty. There is power. There is efficiency.

III. God has given us the spirit of love. There is attraction. The love of Christ and of God is an endowment of the Spirit of God. Love brings both fearlessness and power and is a joyful experience.

IV. God has given another of the finest gifts, that of a sound mind. The gifts bestowed upon the Christian are intended to make him a well-rounded character. 1. This is seen in his right appraisement of the world. 2. It is seen in his mastery of self. 3. It is seen in his desire and power to know more of God and of his word and works—W. D.

### 29. Topic: Religion as a River

TEXT: "As rivers of water in a dry place."—Isa. 32:2.

This chapter is prophetic of a bright age that awaits the world. A river is a fit emblem of great benefits for God's people. For a river is of utmost value to the land through which it flows. As a metaphor this suggests or sets forth the benefits and benedictions that come to us through Christ. Some of the suggestions:

I. Vitality. Water is life. Religion is life. It quickens develops, brings fruition.

II. Motion. A river is not like a torpid pool or stagnant lake. It is active, essentially and permanently active. So is real godliness in the soul. It is a perpetual flow. It keeps all the powers of the soul in action.

III. Outflow. A river is an outflow. It has a fountainhead somewhere. So of religion in the soul. It is an emanation. There is a divine fountain from which it issues, a primal font, the love of God.

IV. Progress. 1. Progress as enlargement in its volume. 2. Progress toward its destination.—G. H.

### 30. Topic: Reverence

TEXT: "Hallowed be thy name."—Luke 11:2. See Isa. 29:13-14.

INTRODUCTORY: It is not reverent to treat God as a kindly grandfather. Reverence is the "creaturely attitude" toward God—the daily, hourly, glad remembrance that he is God above all else, that we spring from his creative love, that we depend utterly upon him for life of body, mind, and spirit, and that without him we are no longer men but animals. It is consciously, deliberately, and always to reverse the ordinary human order, and to set God at the center and ourselves at the circumference.

I. Reverence for Life. Reverence for God is reverence for the life which God creates. It is attempting to understand his amazing working, to think his thoughts after him, to try to bring life into tune with his will, into accord with his purpose of good. Easy to lose our sense of wonder.

II. Reverence for Man. For his name's sake. 1. Reverence yourself. "Know ye not that ye are the temple of God?" Reverence God in God's purpose for you. Each life counts in God's wondrous scheme of things. 2. Reverence our fellow men for what they are to God.

III. Reverence for the Redeemer. Truth perceived by Isaiah. Hallow God for his mercy in redemption. We Christions truly reverence God when we hold in constant and thankful remembrance all that he has done for us in Christ.—R. H. Sabin.

### 31. Topic: Firm-footed Progress

TEXT: "The law of his God is in his heart; none of his steps shall slide." Ps. 37:31.

I. Every life comes to stretches of road where the surface is very treacherous and where, unless we are well shod, we are in grave peril of an ugly fall. 1. There are slippery places on the Hill Difficulty. 2. In the Valley of Humiliation. 3. In the Valley of the Shadow. 4. On the Enchanted Ground. 5. In Vanity Fair.

II. It is the character of the heart that determines the character of our steps. 1. A weak heart. 2. A wobbly heart. 3. A strong heart.

III. If we are to march with safety over treacherous ground the law of God must be in the heart. When the Scriptures use the word "heart" its contents embrace all the executive powers of the mind, and the affections, and the will. When the law of God is in the heart it means that that holy law is operating in all these realms like the law of gravity in the material world, and it holds everything in one mighty and invisible leash. —John H. Jowett.

**32. Topic: Tarrying at Seir**

TEXT: "Ye have compassed this mountain long enough: turn you northward." —Deut. 2:3.

The human characteristic of staying in one place rather than to press on to new fields of achievement.

I. Some of us never get away from our past successes.

II. Some of us tarry by the mountains of our past failures.

III. Turn northward from the mountains of the past and face the future and its opportunities—Adapted from Lewis H. Chrisman.

**33. Topic: Summer Harvest for the Soul (Summer Season)**

TEXT: "He that gathereth in summer is a wise son."—Prov. 10:5.

During the growing days of summer our thought often turns to the coming harvests in field and orchard. May we not also think during this same season of harvests for the spiritual life, as well as of these temporal blessings?

Emerson's rare intuition has given us the couplet:

One harvest from the fields, homeward brought the oxen strong,
Another crop, thine acres yield, which I gathered in a song.

I. Harvest of nature in portrayals of God—in beauty, order, and providential care. Summertime intimacy with nature should be more revealing. Seeing God in field and forest is a fine art. It takes a Wallace Nutting or a Turner to catch these deeper meanings, to which we must add the faith vision of the Psalmist (Ps. 19).

II. Harvests of friendship, which reveal rare virtues. Travel and social intercourse are more varied when doors are open and porches are inviting.

III. Finer citizenship will be developed as we travel and converse. "America the Beautiful" sings not only of spacious skies but of patriot dreams, and of heroes whose sacrifices are brought to attention after visiting historic shrines.

IV. Summer worship will be equally fruitful although some make the excuse that indoor worship is not necessary at this season. Such worship sends us out better able to appreciate "God's outdoors." Esau was an outdoor man; but he missed the deeper meanings and lost his birthright. Contrast Van Dyke's "God of the Open Air."—C. R. S.

**34. Topic: Mountaintop and Valley**

TEXT: "Jesus taketh with him Peter, and James, and John, and leadeth them up into a high mountain apart by themselves; and he was transfigured before them."—Mark 9:2.

Those who go beneath the surface find that the transfiguration is one of the sublimest incidents in the life of Jesus. Three great facts are imbedded in the story.

I. The transfiguration was a vindication. 1. It was heaven certifying the genuineness of Christ's claim. 2. It was a vindication to Christ of the reality of his mission. 3. It was also a vindication to his disciples. They needed certitude. They got it on the mountaintop. 4. It is likewise a vindication for you and me, passing on to us, over the faith of these apostles, a faith that was tested out in the fiercest conflict.

II. The transfiguration was a revelation of immortality. 1. It was a revelation that demonstrated the reality of the spiritual world. 2. It was a revelation of the character of the resurrected body, of something that cannot be portrayed in words.

III. The transfiguration was a preparation. While it transpired on the mountaintop, a very different scene was enacting itself in the valley. 1. They are coming down from the mountaintop. It was not a place to stay. It was just a place to be equipped. 2. Watch the Christ at the foot of the mountain. He is not less radiant and sublime than he was on the summit. He is not afraid. He has no doubts. Heaven has just commissioned him afresh. 3. God gives us a great hour on the summit with him that we may give him a great day of service in the valley with our fellow men.—James I. Vance.

### 35. Topic: Your Heart in Your Work

TEXT: "He did it with all his heart, and prospered."—II Chron. 31:21.

These words express Hezekiah's thoroughness in the service of his God. We note:

I. The work to which the word "it" refers. 1. Work in God's great realm. 2. The king had his work. He did not shrink, shirk, or try in any way to get rid of it. It was his joy and he did not delegate it.

II. The king's prosperity—its conditions. 1. Concentration of energy—"he did it with all his heart"—a mark of sincerity, earnestness, and singleness of purpose. "He was a whole man to one thing at a time." 2. Enthusiasm. Hezekiah threw himself heartily into his work. (a) The spirit that moves things—mountains recede before its march. (b) The spirit that finds things—"Ye shall seek me and ye shall find me when ye shall search for me with all your heart." Results that are distinctive characteristics of success follow the wholehearted endeavors of earnest souls. —C. A. T.

### 36. Topic: What a Layman Can Do

I. Have faith in God, in man, in yourself—faith in the ultimate victory of right over wrong. Have faith in our leaders and in God's ability to use them for his purposes.

II. Be an island of calm confidence in a world of turmoil—not blind wishful thinking, but belief in the power for right of a God who cares.

III. Be friendly to everyone you meet. Throw a pebble of kindness into the pool of human relations to help overcome hatred.

IV. Pray repeatedly, realizing that you are using an overwhelming power for good. Use spot prayers more and more frequently during the day to try beneficially to condition destructive situations as they are reported.

V. Practice the exclusion of doubt and fear from the mind. Keep a record of constructive thoughts put into words during the day, and of destructive thoughts not uttered. Be sure the balance at evening is on the positive side.

VI. Develop the consciousness that there is a constructive answer—no matter how depressing events may seem.

VII. Look upon yourself as a child of God, made in his image—then love your neighbor as yourself.—Layman's Movement.

### 37. Topic: Are You Missing Something?

TEXT: "Bring ye all the tithes into the storehouse . . . and prove me now herewith, saith the Lord of hosts, if I will not open you the windows of heaven, and pour you out a blessing, that there shall not be room enough to receive it."—Mal. 3:10.

I. When you tithe, you achieve a richer life: 1. a sense of values, 2. a sense of direction, 3. a purpose for living, 4. a sense of being at one with God.

II. When you tithe, you reach out beyond your own church to serve 24 hours a day in hundreds of places to advance Christ's work. 1. You preach the Gospel. 2. You provide Christian education. 3. You bring healing in Christ's name. 4. You serve human need.

III. When you tithe, you give Christ to the World, and receive God's blessing.

Will you decide now to open the windows of heaven?

### 38. Topic: The Stubs in Your Checkbook

TEXT: "Let the thief no longer steal, but rather let him labor, doing honest work with his hands, so that he may be able to give to those in need."—Eph. 4:28 (R.S.V.).

Look at the stubs in your checkbook.

I. Deposits. 1. A record of your honesty. 2. A record of your industry. 3. A record of your economy.

II. Payments. 1. A record of your honesty. You pay your bills. 2. A record of your charity. 3. A record of your loyalty to the Kingdom of God.

The stubs in your checkbook are a kind of autobiography.—H.

### 39. Topic: Creative Worship

TEXT: "And the glory of the Lord shone round about them."—Luke 2:9.

I. Worship is the process of piercing the veil of flesh, with its appetites and passions, and revealing the glory and effulgence of spiritual life. When successfully accomplished, it brings the experience described by St. Luke, "And the glory . . ." Luke 2:9.

II. Worship is the process of becoming more like God.

III. Worship is the most important activity of man.

IV. No activity of man is so richly rewarding.

### 40. Topic: Shields of Brass

TEXT: I Kings 14:26, 27.

When Rehoboam did no longer have the gold shield in the temple he substituted brass . . .

I. When the Church no longer has power she substitutes program . . .

II. When the Church no longer has fullness she substitutes form . . .

III. When she no longer has reality she substitutes ritual . . .

IV. When she no longer has persecution she will have complacency.

### 41. Topic: The Imperatives of Protestantism (Reformation Sunday)

SCRIPTURE: Rom. 1:1-17.

INTRODUCTORY: 1. The divisions in the Church: Greek *vs.* Roman Catholic; Protestantism *vs.* Roman Catholicism. 2. It is not an imperative to increase the tensions between Protestantism and Catholicism. Protestantism is not a negative way. It is a restatement of the truth. It is positive.

I. It is an imperative to emphasize the central part that the Bible plays in our Christian faith. The Bible is the great channel of our convictions.

II. It is an imperative to emphasize the fact that Protestantism is a faith of free men.

III. It is an imperative to recover the doctrine of the priesthood of believers and live by it.

IV. It is an imperative that we should remember our unity in Christ.

We must give a Protestant witness—positive, vital, clear, growing.—Adapted from Harold J. Jones.

### 42. Topic: A Citizen of Zion

TEXT: "Lord, who shall abide in thy tabernacle? Who shall dwell in thy holy hill?" Ps. 15:1.

A real question. Not one of idle curiosity or of despair. Who is the man who could fellowship with God? One whose fourfold life is right.

I. Personal life right. 1. An upright walk. 2. A righteous work. 3. A truthful word.

II. Social life right. 1. Speak no evil of others. 2. Do no evil to others. 3. Believe no evil of others.

III. Public life right. 1. Overthrow evil persons, principles, practices. 2. Support honest men, methods, measures. 3. Maintain pledges.

IV. Business life right. 1. Receive no overlegitimate income. 2. Receive no illegitimate income.

Such character God requires, Christ illustrates, and the Holy Spirit develops.

### 43. Topic: Seven Pillars of Stewardship

TEXT: "Moreover it is required in stewards, that a man be found faithful." I Cor. 4:2.

A Christian Steward:

I. Reads the Bible daily together with the "literature of power."

II. Worships weekly with his fellow Christians.

III. Gives a certain number of hours

of Christian service each week for which he receives no pay.

IV. Glorifies God in times of recreation and in times of work.

V. Invests his money in enterprises useful to mankind.

VI. Sets aside a definite proportion of his income for the work of the Kingdom of God.

VII. Tells others of Christ and the joy he has known in serving him.—Douglas Horton.

### 44. Topic: Three Things to Count

TEXT: "So teach us to number our days, that we may apply our hearts unto wisdom." Ps. 90:12.

Numbering things is one of the healthful exercises of the spiritual life. Unless we count, memory is apt to be very tricky and to snare us into strange forgetfulness.

I. We need to number our days.

II. We must count our blessings.

III. We might well count our benevolences.—John H. Jowett.

### 45. Topic: A Parable of the Human Soul (Christmas)

TEXT: "There was no room for them in the inn."—Luke 2:7.

INTRODUCTORY: The story. Is this a parable of the human soul? Why was there no room for them in the inn? Might these be the reasons?

I. Because the inn was fully occupied—preoccupation.

II. Because they were not expecting him—nonpreparation.

III. Because the innkeeper was lacking in loving-kindness—no human sympathy.

IV. Because the innkeeper did not recognize the importance of his coming—no recognition.—H.

### 46. Topic: Portrait of God

TEXT: "We beheld his glory, the glory as of the only begotten of the Father, full of grace and truth." John 1:14.

For generations men had tried to imagine what God is like. Then God sent them his likeness in the person of his Son.

I. Jesus showed men that God is understanding and loving.

II. Jesus showed men the creative power of God.

III. Jesus helped men to see the truth and righteousness of God.

IV. Jesus revealed the mercy of God.

V. Eternally he shows men the glory of God. It shines in his resurrection, in the growth of his Church, in his triumph in human lives.—Harriet M. Lucas.

### 47. Topic: Christ in the Center of Advent (Advent)

TEXT: "For unto you is born this day in the city of David a Saviour, which is Christ the Lord." Luke 2:11.

I. The Christ of Expectation. Looking beyond mere tinsel and decorations, Christmas trees and presents, reverent hearts seek the Christ of Expectation. They rejoice in the hope of his coming.

II. The Christ of Incarnation. He comes in human flesh, born of Mary. He lies in a manger. Dr. F. W. Boreham said of Jesus' birth: "He was born a tiny babe at Bethlehem; he was as *human* as that! Yet angels filled the air with heavenly song—he was as *divine* as that!"

III. The Christ of Realization. He came in fulfillment of every hope and expectancy. All that the prophets had said of him was realized in his birth, for Jesus was God in flesh. Christ is blessed reality. Children call him Friend. The sinful call him Saviour. Philosophers call him Reality. Christians call him Lord.—Edward J. Rees.

### 48. Topic: The World's Best News (Christmas)

TEXT: "I bring you good tidings." Luke 2:10.

The four-lettered word, "News," plural in form but singular in number, points to the four corners of the compass—North, East, West, South—and the good news announced by the angel was to all people, wherever dispersed around the globe. The "tidings" heralded by the angel, telling of the birth of a Saviour, was good news indeed.

I. It was good because it brought light to a darkened world.

II. It was good because it brought healing to a sin-sick world.

III. It was good news because it brought peace to a world of turmoil and confusion.

IV. It was good news because it brought salvation.—Samuel J. Patterson.

**49. Topic: Again the Miracle (Christmas)**

I. The Miracle of the Star—it kindles our faith.

II. The Miracle of the Song—it stirs our joy.

III. The Miracle of the Babe—it gives us peace.—H.

**50. Topic: "At the Long Journey's End"**

TEXT: John 21:18-22.

These men, Peter and John, at the time of this incident were young men. They were just beginning in a way their life's career. But here the veil was lifted just a little and they were made to realize that some day they should be getting old. "But when thou shalt be old," said Jesus to Peter. "If I will that he tarry," was said concerning John. The words "Follow me" carry our minds back to the beginning of Jesus' relationships with these disciples, his words to Philip which were meant for all.

I. Here are words for life's beginning ventures—"Follow me!"

II. Here are words for life's enduring years—"Follow me!"

III. Here are words for life's long journey's end—just kept following me! —H.

# *SECTION IV. Outlines and Themes for Lenten Services. Ash Wednesday to Easter*

## FOR DEEPENING THE SPIRITUAL LIFE

**Series Title: What Jesus Did for His Friends**

SERIES TEXT: "I have called you friends." John 15:15.

Here are suggestions for a series of Lenten prayer meetings or sermons. They can easily be fitted into the needs of the group or congregation to whom they are given.

**1. What Jesus Did for Andrew**

BACKGROUND SCRIPTURE: John 1:35-42; John 6:1-14; John 12:20-22.

I. Jesus invited Andrew to visit him in his abiding place. What happened there was kept hidden in the hearts of Jesus and Andrew, but the Master must have penetrated into and touched the very soul of his new disciple. During the months that followed Andrew never wavered in his allegiance to Jesus, not until that awful day of crucifixion when the little group, for the most part, were thrown into panic and despair.

We of this century cannot abide *with* Christ in his abode, but we can abide *in* Christ, which is a far more intimate experience, and the secret of fruit-bearing lives, John 15:1-16.

Many homes have opened their doors to him and know the secret of his presence.

II. Jesus stirred Andrew to become a missionary. In that secret conversion he gave Andrew something to tell and a passion for the telling. The next day Andrew brought his brother to Jesus. Then Andrew, with what marvelous success, began his missionary activity. How many Christians have never borne effective witness, have never brought a single individual to Christ!

III. With the passing months and years Andrew became a winsome and attractive personality. This was the Lord's doing. His fisherman brother became the great Apostle Peter. Such greatness in the sight of men and the Church was not for Andrew. But who knows what estimates are put upon the lives of men in the Kingdom of God?

Overshadowed by his brother Simon, Andrew's heart never showed envy. Given a low place he shared the humility of his Master. Then, too, Andrew was a loving man, for it is "love than envieth not."

Jesus did much for his disciple and servant and friend Andrew, and it seems to me that the Master must have taken great satisfaction in him.—H.

**2. What Jesus Did for Matthew**

BACKGROUND SCRIPTURE: Matt. 9:9; Matt. 10:3; Mark 2:14-17; Mark 3:18; Luke 5:27-32; Luke 6:15; Acts 1:13.

I. Jesus called Matthew out of a low and despised occupation. It was Matthew himself, not Mark or Luke or John, who inscribes in his book his own name with a word of dishonor and shame beside it, the word "publican." Matthew, a Jew, living on the profits of collecting taxes from his fellow Jews for their Roman overlords, was not an honored person, to say the least. He had knowledge of Jewish tradition and must have known how despicable he was in the sight of his neighbors. Perhaps he despised himself. Many a man does! It is high service to deliver a man from his own self-despising. Such deliverance Jesus gave to Matthew. Matthew did not forget it; there the word stands in his own script—"publican." We recall John Newton, whom Christ delivered from his occupation of slave-dealer. John Newton sometimes forgot!

II. Jesus called Matthew into training for unique service. There is something for each man to do in the Kingdom. Each man has his own place. Each man is to have his own call, and make life an answer to a word previously spoken by the Master himself.

As A. B. Bruce points out in *The Training of the Twelve,* the most important part of their training, Matthew's training, consisted in the simple fact of being for years *with such a one as Jesus.*

III. Jesus called Matthew to record for all future generations the events of his life, the discourses and mighty works, which constitute the First Gospel. There is no record of this assignment; there is no proof that the final Gospel of Matthew was written by this apostle. On the other hand it seems that Matthew had much to do with collecting the material of the Gospel, especially the sayings of Jesus. These include The Sermon on the Mount, which itself includes The Beatitudes and The Lord's Prayer,—the precious fifth, sixth, and seventh chapters of the Gospel. What would we do without them?

But we are thinking not of the Gospel itself, but of the marvelous lovingkindness of Christ in choosing a publican to have a major part in spreading the Good News of Christ throughout the world and to all generations.—H.

### 3. What Jesus Did for Zacchaeus

Background Scripture: Luke 19:1-10.

Having reviewed what Jesus did for Matthew, the publican, it is natural for our minds to leap to another publican, or tax collector, and note what Jesus did for Zacchaeus.

I. Jesus gave him friendship. He honored his home with his presence. A publican had few or no friends; he was a disliked, or even hated, ciitzen. Probably his most intense need was for friendship. When the writer was a pastor in the so-called slum section of a great city his days were filled with interviews with persons requesting help, money, clothing, food, work, advice, etc.—scarcely ever was he asked for that which was needed most, friendship. Many other things were wanted; the thing needed was friendship.

"No man is useless while he has a friend."

What a thrill of joy, of hope, came over the publican when Jesus said, "Zacchaeus, make haste and come down; for today I am going to be your guest."

II. Jesus restored his self-respect. And this is no trivial matter. "By his distinguished presence" he changed the man. He restored him from a life of selfishness and graft to one of charity and honesty. That was something that could never happen without Christ's help. Zacchaeus could never help himself; his neighbors could only scorn him; had Jesus not passed by the soul of the man had continued to shrivel.

III. Zacchaeus was a lost man, but Jesus found him. Jesus said that "to seek and to save that which was lost" was his business. That was God's business, and Jesus was working at it. "My Father worketh hitherto, and I work." John 5:17.

No man need be hopeless, no man need despair on account of his condition—there is One whose purpose is to find the lost. It is a great experience to be found.

We must despair of no man's life, whatever it may show of abjectness, of despair, of lostness. It is Jesus' purpose to seek out and to save that which is lost.—H.

**4. What Jesus Did for Mary Magdalene**

BACKGROUND SCRIPTURE: Luke 8:1-3; Matt. 27:55, 56; Mark 15:40; John 19:25; Matt. 28:1-10; Mark 16:1-11; Luke 24:1-12; John 20:1-18.

Did any other ever receive more of the Master's grace than Mary of Magdala? Did any other ever show more ardent love in appreciation of what he had done?

I. First of all, he restored her sanity. The physician Luke, imbued with the ideas of his times, said that she was delivered from seven devils. She had been hopelessly insane—a battered body, a twisted mind, a ravaged heart, a torn soul, a broken spirit, a split personality, black bile—melancholia. Who can withstand seven devils tearing one's life to pieces?

When? Where? Under what circumstances did Jesus heal her? It seems to me that I can imagine how he healed her. He spoke just one word. With that word she was made whole. With that word the pieces of her personality came together again into wholeness. It was just her name that he uttered, "Mary!"—that was the word. "Mary!" —and then she was Mary. She was herself!

II. She became a loving soul—a woman of pure and ardent love. If her house had been empty the devils would have returned, but they could not enter again. She was filled with an ecstasy of love. It could not be otherwise—suppose that you had been cured of such insanity, suppose that you had had seven devils driven out by Jesus. Her devotion is easy to explain.

III. She was the first witness of his resurrection. Was ever higher honor given than this, to be the first to greet the Living, Resurrected Lord? What joy to be the messenger of good news, of the best news that any man ever heard! Again he used her name—"Jesus saith unto her, Mary."

IV. ". . . I ascend unto my Father and your Father; and to my God and your God." He brought her into the same relationship with the Father as was his own. Eternal life was hers; she was an Eternal Child of God.—H.

**5. What Jesus Did for Thomas**

BACKGROUND SCRIPTURE: John 11:16; John 20:24-29.

I. Jesus gave him courage. On a certain day in October, 1918, the Germans shelled the road from Fleville to St. Juvin in France. The Austrian "whiz-bangs" forced me into the ditch to escape the flying shrapnel. In the midst of it all a corporal came whistling down the road, and when he saw me in the ditch he exclaimed, "I prayed all night last night!" There was no doubt that his praying had given him courage. By the example of his courage I leaped from the ditch and joined him. By the contagion of his courage I made my way to Fleville walking by his side.

There was no doubt that it was dangerous for Jesus to go to Jerusalem when he received the news of Lazarus' death. The disciples needed courage to go with him. Jesus, as he went straight forward, by his example gave Thomas the needed courage. "Let us also go, that we may die with him," were the words of Thomas. We feel sure that he thus sparked the courage of all the others.

II. Jesus gave him certainty. Luther wrote, "What is more miserable than uncertainty?" I suppose that he meant, "Who is more miserable than an uncertain man?" Thomas revealed his misery by his absence from the Upper Room on the first Easter evening.

But who has greater ecstasy than a man who from such uncertainty is delivered unto certainty? The Lord showed him his hands and side. Thomas cried out, "My Lord and my

God!" I should like to have felt the rapture of that cry.—H.

### 6. What Jesus Did for Peter

BACKGROUND SCRIPTURE: John 1:40-42; Luke 22:31-34; John 18:10, 11, 15-18, 25-27; Luke 22:54-62; Acts 4:13; Mark 1:16-18; John 21:1-17.

I. He gave him a new *Name.* "Jesus put Peter under the power of a great expectation," says Frank W. Boreham. He was placed under the stimulus of what he was to become, by carrying the new name. Luke 22:31-34 is an instance of the same procedure on the part of Jesus—aware that Peter would deny him, nevertheless Jesus said, "when thou art converted [turned again], strengthen thy brethren." This expectation, he would turn again, would support Peter in an hour of great need.

II. He gave him a new *Nature.* Though Peter denied him, "the Lord has not done with Peter. He is still in the making! Someday he will justify his surname, 'The Rock!' Someday we shall find it written: 'When they saw the boldness of Peter they marveled'! Once a maid could make him tremble. Now he can stand in high places 'steadfast and immovable'!"—John H. Jowett. The shifting sand nature became solid Rock.

III. He gave him a new *Vocation.* The fisherman became a shepherd. The climax of that transformation is given in the last chapter of John's Gospel.—H.

### 7. What Jesus Did for John

BACKGROUND SCRIPTURE: The Gospel of John, especially the Prologue and the last chapter. The First Epistle of John.

I. John claimed for himself the distinction of being "that disciple whom Jesus loved."

"John responded to Jesus as no other disciple seems to have done. He was what Christ made him. He discerned what Jesus was always trying to teach his disciples—that love is the essence of religion. . . . In his first Epistle, which is a kind of guidebook to his Gospel, John brings out the office of love with remarkable clearness. So fully did he enter into the mind of Jesus in this respect, and in other particulars of his teaching, that the reader of his Gospel is often puzzled to know whether John is recording the words of Jesus, or speaking in his own language."—George P. Eckman.

II. Jesus gave to John a deep revelation of God. "This then is the message which we have heard from him, and declare unto you, that God is light, . . ." "God is love; and he that dwelleth in love dwelleth in God, and God in him." "There are three that bear record in heaven, the Father, the Word, and the Holy Ghost: and these three are one."

"The Prologue of John's Gospel contains three dominant ideas, which ideas are found throughout the entire Gospel: (a) The Son of God in his eternal being as creator of the universe, and the life and light of men. (b) The revelation of the Son of God to men, and their manner of receiving him. (c) The perfect disclosure of God the Father through the incarnation of the Son, as attested by personal experience." —G. P. E.

III. Jesus gave John long life in which to bear witness to his relationship with Jesus and the revelation of God which was his. It is generally agreed to by scholars that John attained a great age. Jerome says that he died about the year 100. If, as has been supposed, he was from 20 to 25 years old when called by Jesus, he was from 90 to 95 about the year 100.—H.

## LENTEN SERIES

### 1. Series Title: The Perfect Man

SERIES TEXTS: "Thou shalt be perfect with the Lord thy God." Deut. 18:13. "Let us go on unto perfection." Heb. 6:1.

I. Perfection of the Heart. II Chron. 16:9.

II. Perfection of Faith. I Thess. 3:10.

III. Perfection of Love. I John 4:17, 18.

IV. Perfection of Spirit. Matt. 5:48.

V. Perfection of Will. Col. 4:12.

VI. Perfection of Unity. John 17:23.

VII. Perfection of Word. James 3:2.

VIII. Perfection of Patience. James 1:4.

IX. Perfection of Steadfastness. I Pet. 5:10.—Peter Wiseman.

**2. Series Title: The Fruits of the Spirit**

SERIES TEXT: Gal. 5:22-23.

I. Love. I John 4:7.

II. Joy. John 15:11.

III. Peace. John 14:27.

IV. Longsuffering, patience (R.S.V.). Col. 1:11.

V. Gentleness, kindness (R.S.V.). Eph. 4:32.

VI. Goodness, generosity (Phillips). II Cor. 9:8.

VII. Faith, faithfulness (R.S.V.), fidelity (Phillips). I Cor. 15:58.

VIII. Meekness, gentleness (R.S.V.), adaptability (Phillips). James 3:17.

IX. Temperance, self-control (R.S.V.). I John 2:14b.—H.

## MAUNDY THURSDAY SERVICE

Maundy Thursday is the name given to Thursday of Holy Week. *Maundy* is a corruption of the Latin *Mandatum.* It refers to the Roman service of the washing of the feet, during which the choir sings the following words of John 13:34, *Mandatum novum do vobis,* etc.

It is most fitting to hold a Communion Service on Thursday evening of Holy Week and an appropriate text is John 13:34, 35: "A new commandment I give unto you, That ye love one another; as I have loved you, that ye also love one another. By this shall all men know that ye are my disciples, that ye also love one another."

The significance of these words of Jesus is deepened when we consider the occasion on which they were spoken, that of the Last Supper, before Jesus went to the garden of Gethsemane. They were spoken in the closest intimacy of the chosen twelve, though Judas had departed. Note, too, that the phrase "that ye love one another" is thrice repeated. He meant that it should not be forgotten, that this New Commandment should be obeyed.

I. There love should be mutual love. This is the true foundation of the unity of the Church. This is the foundation of the Universal Church, for love is of Christ, and God is love.

Each local church holds together, grows, does its service for Christ, on the basis of the mutual love of its members.

II. The love of Christ's followers is to be a Christlike love. The disciples were to love one another, "as I have loved you." Who of us would dare to think that we had come to any great degree of Christlikeness in our mutual love? Some have had a measure of attainment. Some have even laid down their lives for their brethren, as did Christ. But the "amazing love" of Christ is beyond our grasp, and yet we must ever seek to attain it. He who began a good work in us will perfect it unto the day of Christ.

III. The love of Christ's disciples is to reveal the nature of God. "A New Commandment I give unto you," said Jesus. The Ten Commandments, the Two Great Commandments, this New Commandment—what are these, if not revelations of God himself? When Christ was upon the Cross, he was revealing the very heart of God, the nature of God. His loving was God loving. Our loving is God loving. Love God; love your neighbor; love one another in the fellowship of the Church: our obedience is God's revelation of himself. Paul Tillich, writing of Elsa Brandström, who initiated a great work for the orphans of German and Russian prisoners of war, says, "She made God transparent in every moment."

IV. The love of God's people is to be a witnessing love. "By this shall all men know that ye are my disciples."

Our mutual love is witnessing, proclaiming love. It is convincing love; "all men know." Note the scope of its influence—*all* men shall know.

In the early Church the pagan world looked at the disciples of Jesus and said, "Behold, how these Christians love one another!" Jesus Christ conquers the minds of men and wins the hearts of men by love, the love of God, the love revealed from the Cross, the love manifested in the relationships of his followers. I wonder if anyone says today, "Behold, how those Christians love one another!"

Paul Tillich writes: "It is a rare gift to meet a human being in whom love—and this means God—is so overwhelmingly manifest. It undercuts theological arrogance as well as pious isolation. It is more than justice and it is greater than faith and hope. It is the presence of God himself. For God is love. And in every moment of genuine love we are dwelling in God and God in us."—H.

## SPECIAL GOOD FRIDAY SERVICE

### Theme: The Meaning of the Cross

A writer in the *Interpreter's Bible* says that any attempt on the preacher's part to define the Cross is like "trying to wrap a package with a piece of paper that is too small."

But though we can only imperfectly unfold the meaning of the Cross, we must unfold such meaning as we find and believe.

What then are some of the meanings Christians find in the Cross?

I. The first meaning of the Cross is that God takes sin seriously. Sometimes people ask, "Why can't God just forgive sin and let it go at that?" There are several reasons, as we see it, why God can't forgive sin without a Cross.

For one thing, God is holy love. We sentimentalize God and make him love. But God is holy love and such love cannot compromise the moral law which our disobedience has broken. And somehow the moral law must be honored and fulfilled. There must be what Paul called "a demonstration of His righteousness." This righteousness the Cross illumines. This is what the Cross is: God taking the consequences of law and judgment upon and into himself.

For another thing, to forgive without a Cross makes our sinning not very serious. But sin is serious and it involved God, in his redemptive aspect, in a Cross. Christians have always seen in the Cross the awfulness of sin and its terrible cost to God. The Cross reminds us that forgiveness and reconciliation with God has nothing in common with moral laxity or the extermination of evil.

II. A second meaning of the Cross is its power to shake our lives to their roots and move us to repentance. On the Cross we see a God not angry at us for our sin and disobdience but sorry for us and taking unto himself its consequences: "God was in Christ reconciling the world [us] unto himself." "With his stripes we are healed."

The great James Denny once asked Frank Cairns what he thought happened at Calvary. He replied: "If I had a son and he went wrong, dreadfully wrong, I couldn't give him up. But to redeem him a heart would need to break—my heart; and perhaps his as well. And at the Cross it comes home to me that I have broken my Father's heart; and yet that he can't give me up. And I can't bear it, grow sick of myself, and long to be quite different —and there and then begin to be it."

The moment we are willing to call ourselves sinners and see Goodness suffering for us, our despair turns to hope and joy. The goodness of the Cross, in what it reveals about God as Saviour, melts our heart of stone: "God be merciful to me, a sinner." If God is like this we say I cannot be his enemy.

Such love melts our resistance and wins us to his fellowship. If God is like the One Christ revealed, he is my God, and I must everlastingly belong to him. I must love him with all my heart and soul and mind. In that moment judgment becomes mercy. In that moment, the Most High and the Most Holy becomes the All-Loving too.

III. A third meaning of the Cross is that good can come of our evil. The Cross is a strange paradox; on one side it is evil; evil men doing to death the world's best Man; on the other side it is the divine love laying down his love as atonement for the very sin displayed in the Crucifixion. Out of the evil of the Cross has nevertheless come the redemption we sing about.

IV. A fourth and final meaning of the Cross is as a sign of perfect obedience. With far deeper truth than the Psalmist could say, Jesus could say: "I delight to do thy will, O God." In the Garden, he said: "Not my will, but thine be done."

He didnt want to die, "If it be possible that this cup pass." He wasn't playing a part. This was no sham drama. God's incarnation in a man meant real limitation, real growth, real discovery of the Father's will by the path of obedience, a real death. Here was perfect obedience.

Being a Christian now is something more than a comfortable affair of going to church and trying to be mildly decent. That's all that Christianity means to the big majority in our churches. We see the churches as a cult to make us happy, with peace of mind and all that sort of thing. But until we learn that discipleship is a costly affair, calling us to perfect obedience to God's will, and in all the areas of life—business, politics, race relations, the home, the school, our leisure time—we will not be "the salt of the earth" nor "the light of the world." But this is what, as followers of Christ, we are meant to be.—H. Richard Rasmusson.

## GOOD FRIDAY TEXTS AND THEMES

The Suffering Servant of God: Isa. 53.

The Determination that Determines Everything: "I determined not to know any thing among you, save Jesus Christ, and him crucified." I Cor. 2:2.—John H. Jowett.

Behold the Man: John 19:5. Behold, . . . there was in him (1) a new order of life and fellowship; (2) a new way of goodness; (3) pardon for the sinning; (4) hope for the forgotten; (5) reconciliation for the estranged; (6) blessing for the unborn . . . the Son of God and the Saviour of the world.—Gaius Glenn Atkins.

The offense of the Cross: Gal. 5:11. Why is the Cross an offense?

I. First, because it condemns the world. The Cross is a mirror in which we see ourselves as we are. What kind of a man am I? I look at the Cross, and hang my head in shame. It tells me plainly what role I play in the drama of life—whether I am another Herod, or an Annas, or a Judas, or another member of that milling, hungry mob, hoping to see the end of him. When I look at the Cross, I smite myself on the breast, and say, "Lord, be merciful unto me, a sinner."

An African convert once used this striking sentence, "The Cross of Christ condemns me to be a saint."

II. Second, because it is the power of God unto salvation. The Cross is more than a symbol, it is a sermon. It is Christ's appeal to every man to get right with God. A wayside crucifix, or the cross on an altar, is God's question, "Have you made your peace with me this day?" But it is more than a question; it is the offer of reconciliation, the power of God unto salvation for all who accept it. "God was in Christ reconciling the world unto himself."

III. Third, because it demands sacrifice and righteousness. The Cross is more than an object to adore. It is God's imperative, it is God's demand.—William R. Seaman.

Why Did Jesus Die?

TEXT: "That he might bring us to God." I Pet. 3:18.

Why did Jesus die? Why did he put his head in the lion's mouth by going up to Jerusalem? Why did he give himself into the hands of wicked men? Why did he offer himself upon the Cross? The simple answer is: to bring God to us, and to bring us to God.

I. The Cross brings God to us. At Calvary we have the complete unveiling of the heart of God. Here the very heart of God is laid bare for us to see that he is Holy Love. One of those who stood by the Cross summarized it when later he wrote, "God is love." The dying thief saw this. Here was love so deep and compassionate that it could listen to the plea of a criminal. The Roman centurion suddenly realized this and exclaimed, "Truly this was the Son of God."

II. The Cross brings us to God. In the Cross God comes to meet us wherever we are. He sees us, loveless and blind, defiled and lost, and takes on his heart the burden of our guilt. The Cross carries us home to God. It is our key to the Kingdom, to the Father's house, and to his love.

The Cross reveals to what length divine love will go to redeem sinful man. In his humility Christ becomes one with us. Our lovelessness, our iniquities, our self-will, are laid on him. "He hath borne our griefs, and carried our sorrows."

## QUOTABLE LENTEN POETRY

Think not thou canst sigh a sigh
And thy Maker is not by;
Think not thou canst weep a tear
And thy Maker is not near.
—William Blake.

THERE'S IMMEASURABLY MORE

We can only see a little of the ocean,
Just a few miles distant from the rocky shore;
But out there—far beyond our eyes' horizon,
There's more, immeasurably more.

We can only see a little of God's loving—
A few rich treasures from his mighty store;
But out there—far beyond our eyes' horizon,
There's more—immeasurably more.
—Anonymous.

THE WAY, THE TRUTH, AND THE LIFE

O thou great Friend to all the sons of men,
Who once appear'dst in humblest guise below,
Sin to rebuke, to break the captive's chain,
To call Thy brethren forth from want and woe!—
Thee would I sing. Thy truth is still the light
Which guides the nations groping on their way,
Stumbling and falling in disastrous night,
Yet hoping ever for the perfect day.

Yes, Thou art still the life; Thou art the way
The holiest know—light, life, and way of heaven;
And they who dearest hope and deepest pray
Toil by the truth, life, way that Thou hast given;
And in Thy name aspiring mortals trust
To uplift their bleeding brothers rescued from the dust.
—Theodore Parker.

## OUTLINES AND THEMES FOR LENTEN EVANGELISM

**1. Topic: The Way: He Calls, He Leads, He Sends.**

TEXT: Matt. 11:28; Mark 8:34; Matt. 28:19, 20.

I. When Jesus says "Come" it is a personal invitation and calls for decision and an answer. Who is your most welcome and easily entertained house guest? Is it not the person who adjusts herself or himself to fit the tempo and spirit of your household? The degree of adjustment determines the harmony.

In like manner when we accept the invitation of Jesus, we must make adjustments—sometimes gigantic adjustments—from our former ways of living. His invitation, and our acceptance of it, means obedience to his commandments to love the Lord with our whole selves and our neighbor as ourselves. To have harmony in this new relationship we must repent of our old ways.

Christ has promised us rest (complete adjustment) by taking his yoke. Oh, the strength we possess when we are yoked with the resurrected Christ!

II. When Jesus says "Follow me" our answer must be obedience or disloyalty.

Christ's requirements for following him are rugged! Who in his normal mind really likes to deny himself? Who wants a cross on his back? Who wants to love Christ enough to risk failure by this world's standards?

A sure sign of immaturity is the sacrifice of long-range values for immediate desires. Esau sold his birthright for a mess of pottage. A certain young ruler chose earthly riches rather than treasure in heaven.

In Christ's service we have to lose our lives to save them. We have to believe that whatever we ask of God in Christ's name, he will give it if it brings glory to him. To follow Christ demands continued self-discipline which makes our words witness with actual living, so that others may see and want to follow him.

III. When Jesus says "Go" it is a personal directive to go in his name to point the way. Will you go? What exciting adventure awaits you! An old philosopher, when asked what was the most exciting and happiest day in his life, replied, "It was the day a child walked down the road singing after I had told her the way to go."

If we are to direct others to Christ we must know him who is the Way. Our love for him will be shown by our radiant living (Christian style), which will demonstrate that we know the meaning of Christian stewardship.—Mrs. J. Russell Salsbury.

### 2. Topic: Darkness, Dawn, and Daylight

TEXT: "And he cometh to Bethsaida; and they bring a blind man unto him, . . . " Mark 8:22-26.

The coming of the Lord Jesus to any place or people always means blessing. And when we hear of the spiritually blind receiving sight, the lame walking, and the deaf hearing we know that Jesus is visiting the place. The Great Physician was now at Bethsaida.

I. The darkness. "They bring a blind man unto him."

II. The dawn. "I see men as trees walking."

III. The daylight. "He was restored, and saw every man clearly."

The blind man with his body dark, the world dark, the path dark, the future dark. All dark. A type of the sinner. His soul dark with sin. Path dark with uncertainty. The future dark with fear. Jesus touches such with his power, lets in his light, and sends them away rejoicing.—C. E.

### 3. Topic: A New Creature

TEXT: "If any man be in Christ, he is a new creature." II Cor. 5:17.

I. His judgments are new. His judgments of himself, of God, of the purpose of life, and of happiness are formed truthfully.

II. His purposes are new. His new purpose is to serve God. Every other purpose is subservient to this.

III. His desires are new. "Whom have I in heaven but thee?"

IV. His conversation is new. "He spake of things above."

V. His actions are new. He walks in Christ.—G. H.

**4. Topic: Under New Management**

A member of Alcoholics Anonymous said to a psychiatrist, "I have been changed."

The psychiatrist responded, "A person can't be changed."

"Then," said the former alcoholic, "I am under new management."

**5. Topic: The New Birth**

TEXT: "Jesus answered and said unto him, Verily, verily, I say unto thee, Except one be born anew, he cannot see the kingdom of God." John 3:3 (A.R.V.).

INTRODUCTION: The character of Nicodemus; a timid man, for he "came by night"; a sincere man, for he "came." To the sincere seeker truth will always be revealed.

I. The need of a new birth. John 3:1-3. Contrary to the evident expectation of Nicodemus, one cannot enter the Kingdom of God by natural birth, by increased knowledge, or by moral resolve; nor can the Kingdom of God be brought upon earth by evolution, by education, or by force.

II. The nature of the new birth. John 3:4-8. One can enter the Kingdom of God only by virtue of a spiritual renewal wrought by the Spirit of God, whose operation is mysterious, but is manifested in a new life.

III. The method of the new birth. John 3:9-15. This spiritual change involves, on the part of man, faith in a divine (v. 13) and crucified Saviour (vv. 14-15) who alone can give "eternal life."

CONCLUSION: Accept Christ and by open confession escape the poignant grief of Nicodemus who as a "secret disciple" came with his gifts of love when it was too late to be numbered among the disciples. Too late to be recorded in the pages of sacred history as an outstanding fearless witness for his Lord.—Charles R. Erdman.

**6. Topic: Daily Assurance**

I. Without guilt—forgiven.
II. Without fear—unafraid.
III. Without weakness—strong.
IV. Without restlessness—peaceful.

**7. Topic: Paul's Dramatic Metaphors**

I. The new life was passing from darkness to light. I Thess. 5:5.

II. The new life was passing from slavery to sonship. Gal. 4:7.

III. The new life was passing from captivity to liberty. Gal. 5:1.

IV. The new life was passing from death to life. Rom. 8:21.

## EVANGELISTIC TEXTS AND THEMES

To Me to Live Is—What? "For to me to live is Christ." Phil. 1:21.

Consecration: "Who then is willing to consecrate his service this day unto the Lord?" I Chron. 29:5. I. It is a personal consecration. "Who?" II. It is a voluntary consecration. "Who is willing?" III. It is an active consecration. "His service." IV. It is a reasonable consecration. "To the Lord." V. It is a prompt consecration. "This day."—T. K.

Get Thee Out: Gen. 12:1. I. "Get thee out." 1. Put your body in motion. 2. Lift your mind to a higher idea; to a larger devotion. 3. Exercise your will. 4. Put forward your intention. II. Live for tomorrow. III. Look for a city.—Suggested by Frederick Stamm.

The Incredible Love: "Consider the incredible love that the Father has shown us in allowing us to be called 'children of God'—and that is not just what we are called, but what we *are*. Our heredity on the Godward side is no mere figure of speech—which explains why the world will no more recognize us than it recognized Christ." I John 3:1, 2 (Phillips).

A Relevant Gospel: I. Relevant to everything that defiled man. II. Relevant to everything that paralyzed his will. III. Relevant to everything that destroyed his peace.—B. C. Plowright.

Who (or What) Is Your God? To ask *whether* a man believes in "God" is . . . to misunderstand the issue. The proper question, as the biblical writers never forget, is rather: What (or *who*) is his god? As Martin Luther succinctly puts it, "Whatever, then, thy heart clings to and relies upon that is properly thy god."—E. La B. Cherbonnier.

Put a Purpose into Life: "I have not hid thy righteousness within my heart: I have declared thy faithfulness and thy salvation: I have not concealed thy loving-kindness and thy truth from the great congregation." Ps. 40:10.

The Wasted Years: "I will restore to you the years that the locust hath eaten." Joel 2:25.

# *SECTION V. The Conduct of the Holy Communion*

Most Christian ministers have books of forms and procedures provided by their denominations to be used in the conduct of the Holy Communion. However, as Daniel Jenkins points out, "It is false to the spirit in which God desires that his people should serve him to make excessively precise rules about how the Lord's Supper should proceed. . . . It must be emphasized again that the fundamental structure of the service is more important than uniformity of practice in regard to details."

The "fundamental structure" includes prayer and meditation, the distribution of the bread and wine, the singing of hymns, the offering of thanksgiving; framed generally in a morning or evening service of worship. It should become the vehicle of the Real Presence of Christ, of the participants' awareness of His presence, and a means of grace.

The following suggestions, prayers, and communion meditations are offered as assistance to the minister in the preparation of the fundamental structure of the Communion Service.

## PREPARATION

It is most unfortunate that the custom of holding a "preparatory service" before Communion has lapsed in many churches. At least. the people might be urged to attend the midweek service next preceding the Communion Sabbath. This service could then have special reference to the service of the following Sunday.

In the preparatory services the origin, history, and significance of the Lord's Supper could be repeatedly explained. Those participating in the service as deacons or elders. or other officers of the church, would feel the importance of their responsibilities and thus develop the personal reverence and decorum which the Communion Service demands.

The participation of the people in the sacramental service would be more thoughtful, with deepened devotion, with greater consecration, followed by a greater awareness of Christ's Presence. The persistent calling attention to the preparatory service would bring an increasing attendance. The results would be felt throughout the whole life of the church.

A few themes for preparatory services follow.

### 1. "Let a Man Examine Himself"

TEXT: I Cor. 11:28.

"Let a man examine himself." The church asks us to do it every time we receive Holy Communion. Look at yourself, stripped and defenseless, and see yourself as you are, a sinner desperately in need of Christ. It is that need which makes confession easy and indispensable. It is that need which opens our hearts to Christ's entrance.

What about our prayers? If we do not pray as David prayed, seven times a day, do we pray at least thrice, as Daniel prayed? If not as Solomon, at length, do we at least pray briefly as the publican? If not like Christ, the whole night, at least for an hour? Here is Christ's promise "Ask, and ye shall receive." Do we pray for our world's redemption, for our congregation's spiritual growth, for our neighbor's forgiveness, for the coming of the kingdom?

What about our love? Do we love like Paul—yearningly for many souls? Do we love like Jeremiah—with tears for our country's repentance? Do we love like Christ—sacrificially, at Gethsemane, at Calvary? What of our love for God? Let us examine ourselves on these points before coming to the Sacrament.—William R. Seaman.

### 2. Approach

I. We approach the Eucharist, Thanksgiving; I will count my blessings and be thankful.

II. We approach the Communion; I will live in fellowship with God and my fellow men, and be joyful.

III. We approach the Lord's Supper; I shall be hungry for spiritual food and drink, and be vital.

IV. We approach the Sacrament, I will review and renew my vows unto the Lord, and be loyal.—H.

### 3. The Table of Christ

I. The Table of Christ is a place of devotion and desire.

II. A place of vision. Where Christ is seen and felt and known.

III. A place of forgiveness. Where Christ forgives us and we forgive one another.

IV. A place of power. Where the heart is braced and the spirit quickened.

V. A place of peace. "Where the heart's dull ache and acutest pain are soothed and stilled." Where comfort is found; where confidence is renewed; where a fuller trust is given.

VI. A place of hope. Where hope is kindled and life found sweet.

VII. A place of thanksgiving and joy.

We have a marvelous place of rendezvous next Sunday.

## PRAYERS FOR THE DAY

### 1. Root Out of Our Hearts All Pride

O Lord Jesus Christ, who didst humble thyself to become man, and to be born into the world for our salvation, teach us the grace of humility. Root out of our hearts all pride and haughtiness, and so fashion us after thy holy image in this world that in the world to come we may walk in thy likeness. To this end we humbly pray thee to bless all the ministries of thy grace. May there be unto us a savour of life unto life, quickening and enriching all the powers of our souls. Graciously remove the sin that daily alienates us from thy fellowship and which so constantly destroys our peace. Help us to destroy every form of idolatry that lingers in our hearts; the love of money, the longing for applause, the craving for ease, the quest of pleasure. Impart unto us the grace of devotion, that so we may worship thee with unwavering homage and in perfect loyalty and obedience. Wilt thou draw us into an intimacy of communion such as we have never had before. Leave us not in the far country where in our trespasses we may have wandered and become lost. Make us a way home and bring us into the realm of holiness and peace. Let this day be to all our souls one of the days of the Son of Man upon earth. Amen.—John H. Jowett.

### 2. We Remember Thy Loving-kindness

We remember before thee, O God, thy loving-kindness. Thy love ever issues in kindness; thy kindness ever reveals thy love. Thy mercy is ever over us and thy constant love follows us all the days of our life. On the sunlit day we lift up our heads and rejoice in thee; on the dark day we know that all things work together for good to them who are the called according to thy purpose.

We rejoice in thy loving-kindness become incarnate in our Lord Jesus Christ. He does us only good. He gives us wholeness, forgiveness, peace, eternal life. He lays down his life for us that we may be cleansed of all iniquity. By his stripes we are healed. This is loving-kindness like the great mountains: this is love "broader than the measure of man's mind."

Would, O God, that our gratitude were in the same measure as thy goodness. Enable us to show our thanks by the manner of our daily lives, by ourselves acquiring a heart of love and a will to do kindly deeds. In Jesus' name. Amen.—H.

### 3. In Whose Patient Love Our Lives Are Set

Almighty God, in whose patient love our lives are set, as we present ourselves to thee and think of thy redeeming grace, make thyself known to us in the breaking of bread.

We thank thee for Christ, the mediator and sacrifice for our sins and the sins of the world; for the perpetual memorial of the Sacrifice of the Cross whereby we are made partakers of this redemption.

In this holy hour, with contrite hearts, we confess our inconstancy of faith, our inconsistency in conduct, and our harboring hate and cruel devisiveness. Create within us clean hearts and renew within us a right spirit.

Unite all who are guests at thy table to live in thy will, labor in thy strength, love in thy name, and so promote the peace of thy Kingdom. May we give ourselves more completely to him, take up our cross uncomplainingly, and confess our Saviour before men in all tribulation with uplifted heads. Help us to recover unity by practicing fellowship. Hasten the day when there shall be one fold under one Shepherd.

We ask this in the name that is above every other name, even Jesus Christ our Lord, Amen.—From a church bulletin.

## MEDITATIONS AND OUTLINES

### 1. Theme: The Richness of the Sacrament

How rich and beautiful this Sacrament is! I. It is a service of worship and thanksgiving. A Eucharist in which we praise God for all his mercies, and above all, for his love in redemption.

II. It is a "means of grace" by which the living Christ unites us to himself and strengthens us for the battle of life.

III. It is a service of self-dedication in which we, pleading Christ's death for us, offer ourselves, soul and body, to his service.

IV. It is a service of fellowship. We have to grow into the meaning of the service. We can make it mean much or little. Those who find most help in it are those who are keeping closest to Jesus Christ in daily life.

### 2. Theme: The Bread of Life

TEXT: "I am the bread of life." John 6:35.

I. Jesus Christ claims to be the bread of life. His life will feed my life. His Spirit will feed my spirit, nourishing it, sustaining it, possessing it with the marvelous energies of his own communicated strength.

II. If Jesus Christ is my bread, it is his gracious purpose to feed me by imparting to me the force of his own life. I know that we are here on the borderland of impenetrable mysteries, but what I know is this, and of this I may be confident, that the mighty Christ has promised to be my bread, and that he will feed my life with his own life. It is one life feeding another life.

III. Everything in Jesus feeds everything in us. We are strengthened by the grace which is in the Lord Jesus. Everything in him is for everything in us. "We are made complete in him." All our hungers have their satisfactions in his bread. If the promise does not mean this, what can it mean? Take all the coronal capacities of your soul. Review them. There is hope, and there is veneration, and there is conscientiousness, and there is benevolence, and there is joy, and there are many others. The Lord Jesus Christ is the bread for all of them! He will feed your hope with his own visions. He will feed your consciousness with his own holiness. He will feed your benevolence with his own goodness. He will feed your joy with his own pleasure. "My joy shall be in you"; the joy of the Lord shall be your strength." Yes, the fullness of the Lord Jesus is the complement of all our emptiness. He is the food for all our cravings. His Spirit is the resource for our spirit. "I am the bread of life."—J.

**3. Theme: To Be Found at the Lord's Table**

TEXT: "So by all the stimulus of Christ, by every incentive of love, by all your participation in the Spirit, by all your affectionate tenderness, . . ." Phil. 2:1 (Moffatt).

I. The Stimulus of Christ.
II. The Incentive of Love.
III. The Fellowship of the Spirit.
IV. Affectionate Tenderness.

**4. Theme: The Bread of Joy**

TEXT: This do in remembrance of me." Luke 22:19.

I. The Passover. The Passover bread was "bread of affliction," a remembrance of Egypt. The Passover cup was the covenant made with Moses.

II. The New Feast. The bread of the Lord's Supper is bread of joy. It is bread unto life eternal. It is the Bread of Life, which if a man eat, he shall not die.

The new cup is a new covenant, being poured out for them. Here indeed is wine which maketh glad the heart of man!

Who am I that I should come to the banquet house to kneel at the Feast? I am not worthy to gather up the crumbs that fall from the Master's table. Yet it is for me that he instituted the Feast, and bids me "Come." Who is worthy to come, and who is truly prepared? He who believes these words, "Given, and shed for you, for the remission of sins."

"Lord, I believe, help thou mine unbelief."—Adapted from William R. Seaman.

**5. Theme: As We Gather at the Table**

I. We thank God for the Past. 1. Sacrifice. Luke 22:19; Matt. 26:28. 2. Salvation. I John 2:2.

II. We take heart for the present. 1. Sustenance. John 6:53. 2. Service. This sustenance is for service. I Cor. 11:26.

III. We rejoice in the future. 1. Sovereignty. Phil. 2:9-11. 2. Supremacy. Rev. 11:15.

**6. Theme: The Holy Supper**

TEXT: "This do in remembrance of me." Luke 22:19.

I. Let us think first of the Lord's Supper as a memorial. It supersedes the Passover of which it is said, "This day shall be unto you as a memorial." When Christ instituted the Supper he said, "This do in remembrance of me." It is a commemorative ordinance, in which we remember Jesus, who he was, what he did, how he suffered, and realize afresh the benefits of his redemption.

II. Let us think also of the Lord's Supper as a means of grace. We know of no more powerful way by which grace can get into men's souls—the souls of all Christian believers.

III. And let us think of it, thirdly, as a powerful witness for Christian truth. Think of the testimony of the frequent and world-wide observance of the ordinance. Think also of its preaching value, "For as often as ye eat this bread and drink this cup, ye do show forth the Lord's death till he come." It shows forth, proclaims, preaches, and in a most powerful way.—G. H.

**7. Theme: The Upper Room**

TEXT: "And he will show you a large upper room furnished: there make ready." Luke 22:12.

May *our* Upper Room be indeed prepared for Jesus. Indeed this Upper Room can be a place of many precious experiences and blessings. I would like to mention several of these.

I. First, it is a place of *penitence*.

II. This Upper Room becomes a place of *prayer*.

III. And the confidence that we have that Jesus answers our prayers leads to the third thought that the Upper Room is a place also of *pardon*.

IV. And so the Upper Room is a place of *peace*.

V. The Upper Room is a place of *Power*.

VI. We can make the Upper Room a place of *purpose*.

VII. This Upper Room of the Lord's Supper is also the place of *praise*, of thanksgiving.—H. G. C. H.

## SOME SUGGESTED LORD'S SUPPER TEXTS AND THEMES

A Great Bequest: "Peace I leave with you, my peace I give unto you: not as the world giveth, give I unto you. Let not your heart be troubled, neither let it be afraid." John 14:27.

Those Decisive Words: "And when he had given thanks, he brake it, and said, Take, eat, this is my body, which is broken for you: this do in remembrance of me." I Cor. 11:24.

The Inexhaustible Christ: "And they did eat, and were all filled." Luke 9:17.

Consecration: "And this they did, . . . but first gave their own selves to the Lord." II Cor. 8:5.

Experience, Not Theory: "O taste and see that the Lord is good: blessed is the man that trusteth in him. Ps. 34:8.

My Portion and My Cup: "The Lord is the portion of mine inheritance and of my cup." Ps. 16:5.

Minds Stirred to Remembrance: "I stir up your pure minds by way of remembrance." II Pet. 3:1.

## OFFERTORY SENTENCES AND PRAYERS

1. "Ye know the grace of our Lord Jesus Christ, that though he was rich, yet for your sakes he became poor, that ye through his poverty might be rich." II Cor. 8:9.

PRAYER: O Christ, who through thine obedience unto death, even the death of the Cross, hast redeemed us from sin and hast made us heirs of eternal life, wilt thou receive and bless what we now offer in worship unto thee. Accept it as an expression of the devotion of our hearts. We consecrate ourselves without reserve, withholding naught from thee, our Saviour and our Lord. Amen.—H. A. D.

2. Sentence: John 3:16.

PRAYER: Our Father who art in heaven, we praise thee for the gift of thine only-begotten Son, our Lord and Saviour, Jesus Christ. We thank thee also for the sacrament wherein we are reminded of the body broken and the blood shed for our salvation. Thanks be to God for his unspeakable gift! Receive now our offerings, O Lord, presented with love as a vital part of our worship. Amen.

3. "But whoso hath the world's goods, and beholdeth his brother in need, and shutteth up his compassion from him, how doth the love of God abide in him?"

PRAYER: Help us, O God, to be our brother's brother, aware of his need, compassionate and kind. Bless these offerings unto the welfare of our needy brethren in the world. In Jesus' name. Amen.—H.

4. "Every man according as he purposeth in his heart, so let him give; not grudgingly, or of necessity: for God loveth a cheerful giver."

PRAYER: Teach us, O God, in this act of worship by offerings, the joy of giving. As thou hast freely given us all things, even sparing not thine own Son, so would we make our gifts with free spirits and open hands. Through Jesus Christ our Lord. Amen.

## PRAYERS AT THE TABLE

### 1. May Our Lives Be Sanctified

Most holy and most gracious God, our Father, we come into thy presence to partake of the Holy Sacrament. We thank thee that our Lord, on the night in which he was betrayed, took common bread and common wine and sanctified them unto this uncommon use. By his blessing may these elements be made holy.

By that same blessing may our lives be sanctified. Deliver our minds from any profane thought, our hearts from any spirit of unforgiveness and our wills from any unworthy motive. Renew a right spirit within us.

Having received thy grace in this Sacrament, may be become channels of thy grace in the world about us, to the glory of thy name, and unto the proclamation of the Gospel of Christ. Amen.—H.

**2. All Things Are Ready, Lord**

All things are ready, Lord. The deed is done the word is spoken, "It is finished."

All things are ready, Lord. The house is furnished. The table is spread. The people are gathered. Their hearts are expectant.

We await thy blessing. By thy favor transform this house into an Upper Room. Transform the broken bread into the token of thy broken body, and the wine into the token of thy shed blood. Cause us to hunger and thirst after righteousness.

Nourish us, O Lord, our bodies that they may be whole, our minds that they may be clear, our souls that they may be vital, and our hearts that they may be loving. Then quicken us to love thee with all our heart and soul and mind and strength, to love our neighbor as ourselves, to love our brethren even as thou hast loved us. In Jesus' name. Amen.—H.

**3. As We Take . . . from His Hands**

Holy Father, we pray that we may have communion with thy beloved Son in the spirit of his holy living and dying. May we take to our duties as he took to his; bear our mortal burdens and the cross of our sacrifice, even as he bore his. May sin be to us what it was to him; and may our pain and sorrow only draw us deeper into his fellowship. As we take this perishable bread and wine from his hands, may we receive at the same time the spiritual food by which our souls are nourished. Thus may the bread which we break be to us the communion of the body of Christ, and the cup which we bless the communion of the blood of Christ. Amen.—John Hunter.

**4. The Bread of Life for a Hungry World**

O thou who has broken the Bread of Life for a hungry world, and satisfied its thirst with the Water of Life: grant to us, as we remember thee, all that makes life worth while. . . . We bless thee for this table around which the whole world may sit down and feel the Brotherhood, as from thy hand it receives the token of thy oneness with the human race. Take out of our hearts at this time and place the narrow and bitter feeling of superiority and pride. Make us humble in the presence of him who knelt to wash the feet of common men. Make us to feel the majesty of that divine act of service. . . . And from this table may we all arise to go out into the world of action to follow thee, cheered by the eternal presence, and fed by the abundant Life. Amen.—Adapted from Charles M. Sheldon.

## CLOSING PRAYERS

**1. We Give Thee Praise and Thanks**

Our heavenly Father, we give the praise and thanks that upon us the unworthy thou hast conferred so rich a benefit as to bring us into the communion of thy son Jesus Christ. Now also grant us grace, that we may never be unmindful of these things; but bearing them about, engraven on our hearts, may advance and grow as thy people in that faith which is effectual unto every good work; through Jesus Christ our Lord. Amen.—From a Communion folder.

**2. Send Us Out to Work**

We thank thee, O Lord, for the high privileges of this Sacrament with its new visions, new life, new fellowship with Christ. Send us out, if thou wilt, and through us send out many another to work for the extension of thy Kingdom throughout the world. Open our hearts that we may see Christ with hands outstretched to bless. Do with us what thou wilt, and as thou wilt. So shall the earth be filled with the knowledge of thyself as the waters cover the sea. And to thee be the glory and praise, now forevermore. Amen.—Author unknown.

**3. May We Surrender All Our Powers**

We thank thee, our Father, that thou hast gathered us about the table of our Lord. We have felt his gracious Presence. He hath fed us with the Bread of Life. He hath given our thirsty souls to drink. Now may we surrender all our powers to be held captive by thy will. In the strength of the blessings we have received, help us to minister to others. May we find the springs of joy in the ways of service. Deepen and broaden our compassions so that we may feel the urgent call of another's needs. Make us very sensitive to those who have no cry and who suffer and wait in silence. Give us holy mastery in the discernment of human sorrow, and make our feet swift and obedient in the ministry of relief.—Adapted from John H. Jowett.

## SOME CHOICE COMMUNION ILLUSTRATIONS

**1. Forgiveness**

"Against thee, thee only have I sinned." When we sin against others, we sin against God's creation and finally against him. So great is our transgression that only God can forgive us. Dr. Buttrick puts it in a parable: Into a great art gallery a fool walked and destroyed with his umbrella the most beautiful painting there. Who could forgive him? The artist could not. The owner of the picture could not. Something had been done that violated what had been known and loved in the world of beauty. Only Beauty herself can bow down over him and forgive this fool. Likewise, God himself must at great cost forgive us our far-reaching sin. This he did on a cross.—M. C. A.

**2. Love Never Fails**

When the venerable Professor Nitsch had reached his eightieth year, he said to a friend: "I can no longer see. I can no longer hear. I am not able to work, but I can still love. Love never faileth."

**3. A Sacred Feast**

"This do in remembrance of me." I think of a village in Bechuanaland, in a district not far from the place where Dr. and Mrs. Livingstone occupied the only permanent home they knew together in Africa. This village had no school or church, for there were very few Christians in that place. Service was held under a tree in the village open space and a large crowd had gathered, a crowd which was very reverent in demeanor. It was the intention to dispense the sacred Feast to the six or seven church members after the general service. I thought it would be fitting to hold that service just under the tree in that village open space. It is not often that Africans take upon themselves to advise a missionary against the course he proposes to take, but it was pointed out to me that a hut had been prepared in which to hold the Lord's Supper and it was added, "In any case this is too sacred a feast for heathen eyes to see!" And so I found it was the custom that only church members and catechumens are ever present at a Communion service.—P. M. Shepherd.

**4. Can We Turn the World Around?**

An engraver's error accounted for a strange mistake when the first proofs of a collection envelope for World-wide Communion Sunday came from the printer. North America on the cros-crowned globe was in its accustomed place, but with the Pacific coastline where the Atlantic seaboard ought to be, and South America was slanting off in the wrong direction.

There is a parable here for Christions, because they are inevitably and incurably world changers, turning the world around. That is something to think about as we gather at the world-around Communion table.

Christians can change the climate of that world, even though they cannot do much about its geography. When nations are tensed up with bitterness and hatred, Christians can cool tempers and ease tensions. When loyalties get twisted, Christians can straighten them out. When selfishness brings astigmatism of the soul and spiritual occlusion, and men forget that every man is a brother-man under God's fatherhood, Christians show the way to answer the posed question, "Who is my brother?"

Our thoughts, our prayers, our gifts on World-wide Communion Sunday are a mighty lever to turn the world around. —*Christian Advocate.*

**5. A Holy Feast**

One thinks of the universality of this Feast not only in regard to places but in other respects. There is also the universal acknowledgment of the holiness of this Feast. I have stated that the Africans not long emerged from heathendom judged the Lord's Supper too sacred for heathen eyes to see. In line with their thought in that respect was that they refrained from partaking of the Feast if they had been guilty of some more or less grave fault. Sitting at the Table I have noted one or another decline the bread and wine and seeing their refusal my heart became heavy. I knew that was the first public confession of fault. It is right that we preserve the thought of the holiness of the Feast and uphold the Apostle's injunction, "Let a man examine himself."—P. M. Shepherd.

**6. Great Experience**

When asked, during his exile, what the greatest experience of his life had been, Napoleon answered, "My first Communion."—C. L. W.

**7. Universal Unity**

There is universal unity in this Feast. We hear much these days about the racial Color Bar. How degrading that Color Bar can be some of us by close contact well know. With God there is no Color Bar at his Table. "There is neither Jew nor Greek, there is neither bond nor free, there is neither male nor female: for ye are all one in Christ Jesus." There is unity at this Feast as there is nowhere else. On arrival in an overseas mission field a missionary does not find it easy to adjust. The foreign country is so different; the ways of the people are so different; the habits and outlook, the background and environment—all are of strange pattern. Yet it never seems strange sitting with those of a different race at the Lord's Table.—P. M. S.

**8. A Moving Experience**

I think of the most moving of all missionary experience. Three or four huts had been chosen by the elders of the church at various parts of Molepolole village. On the Saturday those huts had been cleaned and garnished, and when I arrived on the Sabbath afternoon the old, infirm, and blind members no longer able to come the distance to the Central Church were gathered there. A table, covered with a white cloth, had been placed in the center of each of those huts. How grateful those old and crippled people were to know that they were still remembered as part of the Body of Christ, and that their missionary and African minister had asked them to gather, saying, "Let us keep the Feast." How they clasped the hand of fellowship and expressed their gratitude.—P. M. S.

**9. The Real Presence**

If a man goes out from his Communion to love and serve men better he has received the Real Presence. If he feels every thrill and tremor of devotion, but goes out as selfish as before, he has not received it. It was offered, but he did not receive it.—William Temple.

**10. The Cross**

In Chicago there is a unique Methodist church at the top story of a skyscraper. It is roofed with a Gothic spire which is crowned by a lofty cross, one of the highest points in the city. People come and go, doing their shopping, paying very little heed to that cross. But one day a man looking up at the cross became wildly excited. A crowd quickly gathered round, all looking at the cross. All traffic was stopped; the police rushed up to find out what was the matter. Someone shouted out: "It is the cross." "What's the matter with it?" And the reply came: "There is a man on it."—W. P. H.

**11. What Are They Going to Do Now?**

It was World-wide Communion Sunday. Members and friends of the First Methodist Church were celebrating their covenant with Christ.

Two more Tables were to be served and then every celebrant in the well-filled church would have partaken of the sacred emblems of the Lord's Supper.

The meaningful service, the music of the cherished old hymns, the oft-repeated words of Jesus as the sacraments were passed to grateful, penitent, kneeling ones brought full and warm response from all who worshiped there.

United as we were in the common act of worship and devotion we had opened wide the doors to let His Presence in, therefore many did not notice the presence of another.

A small one had escaped the upper nursery and had entered through the door in front and to the left of all the worshipers. The ushers who observed his coming said he stood for seconds—looking first at those who sat in the pews with spirits bowed and then his gaze was fixed upon his father as he passed the Cup to those who knelt before the rail.

"This Cup is the new covenant in my blood . . ." It was his father's pause that made me lift my head. I saw him then. His bright blond hair was lighted by a slanting ray of sun that pierced the upper windows on a sun-filled morning such as this. It caught him as a spotlight would were he performing in a drama or a pageant. Indeed so much a part of sacred drama did he seem that even I, his mother, didn't sense distraction. His father's pause was momentary . . . "which is shed for you," he continued. "Drink this in remembrance that Christ died for you, and be thankful."

The Table was dismissed. Our small son sought and found me. He neither sat not spoke; just leaned against the pew and watched. Another Table filled and emptied. A hymn was sung and then the benediction heard.

And then he spoke. It was between the amen of his father and the peal of the organ postlude—that sacred silent breath of time. He spoke, not loudly, but in the silence of that well-filled church it sounded loud and clear—"What *now,* mummy, what are *they* going to do *now*?"—Mazelle Wildes, Thomas, *Christian Advocate.*

# *SECTION VI. The Missionary Message*

It is increasingly important that ministers keep their congregations aware of the wide-sweeping changes going on in the field of Missions. There is even a change of name in progress, from *Foreign* Missions to *World* Missions. New inventions bring closer contacts between bases and stations and new methods are being used. With the larger co-operation between the denominations in the ecumenical movement, and the rise of strong younger churches able to share in the evangelization of contiguous or even distant areas, surely a new day has dawned. "Yet the divine arm of historic foreign missions is at the heart of *ecumenical missions* as it unites the world-wide Church in commitment, extends Christian frontiers and communicates Christ-centered power."

There is in the world a resurgence and revival of the non-Christian religions. Communism is a "demonic force" in many troubled areas. There are heavy restrictions and pressures, and in some cases persecution, determined to weaken Christian churches in many lands. Amid all this the Cross of Christ stands as the one Hope of the world.

## OUTLINES FOR MISSIONARY SERMONS AND ADDRESSES

### 1. Topic: What Is Our Work?

What is our work? It is defined explicitly in the famous Great Commission of our Lord to his disciples. "Go ye therefore and teach all nations . . . and, lo, I am with you alway, even unto the end of the world." Matt. 28:10, 20.

To make disciples is to carry the gospel of the worth and dignity of every soul as a child of God. It is to know that truth, and be persuaded of it, and live it, and share it until God's will is done on earth —God's will, which is fullness of life in the widest possible fellowship. And the dimension of the task in space is *all the world,* and the dimension of the task in time is *unto the end of the world.* That is what we are to be doing, today and tomorrow and the day after.

I. The Test of Extension. It is clear that if the work of the first disciples was to continue at all, the gospel must of necessity meet and survive two immediate tests. The first was the test of *extension.* Could it spread from person to person? And when it met the barriers between Jew and Greek, barbarian, Scythian, bond and free, could it break those barriers down? When it encountered a new language, and was translated, would anyone listen to it? When it was declared in the councils of rulers, would any head be bowed? When it found its way down a darkened alley and entered the door of a poor man's home, would any heart, heavy with its burden, be lifted up?

How absurd it would be to talk of preaching the gospel in all the world, if it meant nothing to the man across the street. How impossible to dream of a gospel for all nations, if it could not reach beyond the limits of a local Galilean cult. And yet how marvelously it did meet and survive that test of extension, so that even in the early days of Pentecost there were Parthians and Medes and Elamites and the people of Mesopotamia and Cappadocia and Phrygia and Egypt and Crete and Arabia, and Jews and Romans assembled together and united together in prayer and devotion. It could cross the old barriers of race and nation and class and creed. It might become a gospel for the whole world.

II. The Test of Duration. And the second test was the test of *duration.* Could this message not only break through the barriers that divided men, but could it transmit itself from father to son, from one generation to another? Could it survive the inevitable changes in outlook and purpose of young people coming of age? Could it endure the wear and tear of experience through the passing years? Could it endure the searching tests of scientific analysis and ethical judgment? And how wonderfully the gospel met and survived the test of duration as the faith of the fathers became the faith of their children, as new and deeper meanings in the gospel were found to interpret the unpredictable experiences of men.

So the work of the Church has gone on across the barriers of mountains and seas, and down through the long corridors of time, until today there is an unbroken fellowship of Christians in every nation encircling the world, and an unbroken company of pilgrims and followers marching together through the years.—Harold E. Nicely.

**2. Theme: The Fundamental Facts**

The fundamental facts of the case are these: I. That Christ laid mission work upon his followers and the matter therefore is not open to discussion. "Why call ye me, Lord, Lord, and do not the things which I say?"

II. By its very nature the Christian religion is a universal religion.

III. The turmoil in the world today reinforces the claims of Christ and Christianity.—**J. Hutchison Cockburn.**

**3. Theme: A Question and a Three-dimensional Answer**

Introductory: The Question. What is God's expectation of us as a church in the terms of our mission to the nation?

The answer is three dimensional, and is found in what has come to be known as the Great Commission: "Go ye into all the world, and preach the gospel to every creature." Mark 16:15.

I. The first dimension, marked in the opening words "Go ye," is *dedication.*

II. The second dimension is *direction*—God's emissaries are sent "into all the world." God's straight line of life and love, like all lines, goes someplace.

III. The third dimension is *doctrine.* "And preach the gospel," Christ commanded. 1. Preaching the gospel means preaching God's love. 2. Preaching the Gospel means preaching God's judgment. 3. Preaching the gospel means preaching God's control of history.

America is not only a mission field, but a potent missionary force.—Raymond I. Lindquist.

**4. Theme: Success That Seemed to Be Failure**

Text: "I said, I have laboured in vain, I have spent my strength for naught, and in vain: yet surely my judgment is with the Lord, and my work with my God." Isa. 49:4.

Hans Egede used this text for his farewell sermon at Godhaab, Greenland, sometime in August, 1736. He was about to return to Copenhagen, Denmark, after fifteen years of faithful labor for the conversion of the natives of Greenland without seeming success. As he stood to deliver his sermon he might have been a pathetic picture, but his judgment has been with God, and as Wilma M. Stubbs reminds us, "He has revealed the grandeur of seeming defeat."

Hans and Gertrude Egede, missionaries in the frozen North, must not be forgotten. Their story should be told this year, because the year marks the 200th anniversary of Hans' death on November 5, 1758.

I. Consider first his disappointments, his seeming failures and defeats.

1. It was in his heart to carry to the Norse settlements in Greenland the message of the old-time faith. Perhaps the descendants of Eric and Lief the Lucky had forgotten. Hans and Gertrude went out to bring back to the Christ the descendants of the brave Norsemen. When they arrived in Greenland they found no trace of Norse blood. There were only the fallen stones of buildings.

2. For fifteen years Pastor Egede and his wife grappled with the language of these small, dark-haired, olive-skinned Greenlanders, and sought to give them the Gospel. They had little apparent success. Though many of the Greenlanders gave assent to his teachings and desired baptism, he refused to perform the sacred rites because he discovered no fruits of their faith in their lives. He did not consider himself far wrong when later he learned that these apparently devout Greenlanders among their own people made mock of his preaching and praying.

3. Other difficulties and disappointments. A pestilence broke out at Godhaab carrying away two or three thousand natives. The colonists of the Danish settlement which was attempted were often in despair and burdened the missionaries grievously. When the pestilence had passed Mrs. Egede succumbed to the long burden of anxiety and privation and died on December 21, 1735.

II. Consider the fruits of the mission.

1. It was no small thing to stem the awful tide of pestilence. "The home of the missionaries was given over to the sick and dying. Without fear they moved among the natives in their villages, and won their love, if not their interest in higher thngs. One man voiced his conviction when he said, 'You have done for us what our own people would not do.' "

2. Hans and Gertrude Egede discovered Greenland to the world, and a way opened for Danish and Moravian missionaries to conquests which they had seen only afar off.

3. "These missionaries gave to Christian missions an example of splendid worth." "Estimated on the scale of motives and qualities, this apostle was a hero and his mission was a triumph."

4. The work for the people of the North was carried on by Paul, the oldest son of Hans and Gertrude. He prepared a grammar of the Greenland tongue, also a translation of a large part of the Bible and of numerous prayers and liturgies. He devoted himself unwearingly to the welfare of the Greenland mission until his death." (See *How Europe Was Won for Christianity* by M. Wilma Stubbs, Fleming H. Revell Company.)—H.

**5. Theme: An Open Door of Faith**

TEXT: "He had opened the door of faith unto the Gentiles." Acts 14:27.

The seal of the Missions Board set up by the King of Denmark, after the Tranquebar Mission had been established in 1714 by the pioneer missionaries, had this inscription: "To the Gentiles a door of faith is opened." This seal also showed a sailing boat.

No better motto could have been found for the mission. The work which began with the landing of the first two "royal Danish missionaries," the Germans, Bartholomaeus Ziegenbalg and Heinrich Pluetschau, at Tranquebar on July 7, 1706, was to become the parent mission of all Protestant missions in India, in a sense of all Protestant mission enterprises in the world.

This text can be used to introduce any sermon which sketches the history of missions in any land. In 1958 and 1959 attention will be directed to the opening of Protestant Christian work in Japan. The text can be applied to the work of the first century of Protestant Christianity in that land.—H.

**6. Theme: Our Missionary Message**

I. It is not a comparison of your religion and our religion.

II. It is not an argument to convert you to English or American Christianity.

III. It is to show you something we have seen and tell you something we have heard; that in the midst of the old creation there is a New Creation, and that this New Creation is manifest in

Jesus who is called the Christ.—Suggested by Paul Tillich, *The New Being*.

**7. Theme: Missions in the Book of Romans**

I. The missionary message. Rom. 1:14-16.
II. The missionary passion. Rom. 9:1-3.
III. The missionary argument. Rom. 10:11-16.
IV. The missionary ambition. Rom. 15:18-21.

## PRAYERS FOR MISSIONS AND FOR MISSIONARY OCCASIONS

**1. Call to Worship**

"O worship the Lord in the beauty of holiness: fear before him, all the earth."

"From the rising of the sun unto the going down of the same the Lord's name is to be praised."

This is the Day of Prayer. Did you hear the children of God singing in India, while yet it was dark with you? And are you aware of the multitudes singing to the north and to the south? And when you go to rest at night, will you sleep without a thought for those who will be singing and praising God over the shoulder of the world, where the sun is in the morning? Shall men be praising God around the earth all day long, and we be content to measure his worship by the hour, by the place, by the tribe?—United Church Women.

**2. A Prayer of Invocation**

Narrow not the influence of this service, O Lord, unto this hour and the space within these walls. May it be felt throughout eternity. Extend it unto the uttermost parts of the earth. That this may come to pass we invoke the presence of thy Holy Spirit.

And grant, O Lord, thy Spirit's presence wherever the Gospel is preached today, wherever men may worship, wherever men bear Christian witness, that thy Kingdom may come in the hearts of all men everywhere.—H.

**3. Prayer for Men of Faith and Courage**

Our heavenly Father, thy call is upon us, for thou hast summoned us into the highest service which the universe offers to mankind. We see on every side the work that is to be done, and we know that only those who have seen the vision of God's purpose can accomplish it. We join our hearts in the prayer for men of faith and courage to take up the tasks of leadership in this age which is upon us. And as we join in the call, we know that by the right kind of human service we can help to bring the Kingdom in this earth. Make us, therefore, we beseech thee, true citizens that we may be worthy of a place in the City of God. Through Jesus Christ our Lord. Amen. —L. S. Brown.

**4. Prayer for Missions throughout the World**

Thou who didst send forth thy disciples ino all the earth to teach men, wilt thou so incline the hearts of men to thy word and so move their stubborn wills toward thy purpose that we may see men's lives and characters changed and made Christlike.

Where organized opposition has set itself against the preaching of thy truth, and now seeks to abolish the liberty which thou didst bring to earth, may thine overmastering Spirit of righteousness and love enter in and work a miracle of grace, undermining every fortress of hate and cruelty.

Where, in lands of liberty, men and women are heedless of thy word as it is sung and preached and prayed and lived before them in the beautiful lives of their friends and neighbors, may the tender influences of thy Holy Spirit so move upon these indifferent hearts that thy truth may no longer be resisted. May the precious seed of thy truth find root in open minds and hearts, to thy praise and glory. Amen.—W. C. Covert.

**5. "Clear Our Vision, Lord"**

In this hour of worship clear our vision, Lord. Open our eyes that we may see. May our eyes run here and there throughout the whole earth to look into the faces of men and women and children—white faces and yellow faces, black faces and brown—some revealing well-being of body but ill-being of soul, and some of them showing hunger, and some showing sickness and weariness of life; some are despairing faces. Out of these faces may one face appear—that noble face, that gracious face, that loving face, revealing thee, O God—and from his lips may we hear him say, "Inasmuch as ye have done it unto one of the least of these, ye have done it unto me." Amen. —H.

**6. Prayer for the Church throughout the World**

O Lord of heaven and earth, who hast promised to reveal thy glory by Jesus Christ among all the nations; remember, we beseech thee, thy holy Church throughout all the world. Unite all who profess and call themselves Christians in the bond of a living faith as the body of Christ, and so replenish them and us with the grace of thy Holy Spirit that we may bring forth abundantly the fruits of peace and good works, and may turn many to righteousness through the preaching of the Gospel. And grant that, having persevered in the way of godliness to the end, we may with prophets, apostles, martyrs, confessors, and saints of all ages come into full communion with thee, and with one another, in thine eternal and glorious Kingdom; through our Lord and Saviour Jesus Christ.—From the Liturgy of the Reformed Church in America. Used in the opening service of the Amsterdam Assembly of the World Council of Churches.

**7. A Sioux Indian Prayer**

Great Spirit, you have been always, and before you nothing has been. There is no one to pray to but you. The star nations all over the heavens are yours, and yours are the grasses of the earth. You are older than all need, older than all pain and prayer.

Great Spirit, all over the world the faces of the living ones are alike. With tenderness have they come up out of the ground. Look upon your children, with children in their arms, that they may face the winds and walk the good road to the day of quiet. Great Spirit, fill us with the light. Give us the strength to understand and the eyes to see. Teach us to walk the soft earth as relatives to all that live. Help us, for without you we are nothing. Amen.—Pamphlet of United Church Women.

## SUGGESTED TEXTS AND THEMES

I. For Missionary Sermons.

Walls That Must Go: Josh. 6:1-16. "The walls of our modern world are spiritual but real. Like the ancient walls they must come down. They may protect for a time, but eventually they cost man his freedom."

Tear down the walls! God made of one
  All men who live upon the earth;
He is our Father, we his sons,
  Whatever be our human birth.

The Glad Prophecy: "From the rising of the sun even unto the going down of the same my name shall be great among the Gentiles . . ." Mal. 1:11.

The Dangerous Task Ahead: "The Church seeks not security . . . but to change the world. It is by nature a missionary movement, a revolutionary movement, a disturbing movement, a dissatisfied movement . . . filled with both righteous indignation and expectation . . . conscious ever of the tension between God's Holy Will and our unholy wills and corrupt communities."—Andrew T. Roy, Hong Kong.

The Missionary Message: "Say among the heathen that the Lord reigneth: the world also shall be established that it shall not be moved: he shall judge the people righteously." Ps. 96:10.

The Bread You Cast on Waters: "Cast thy bread upon the waters: for thou shalt find it after many days." Eccles. 11:1. A sermon on the success of the missionary enterprise, on one field, or throughout the world.

Down to Earth: "Missionary life is not up in the clouds; it is right down on the earth dealing with difficult situations."—Eugene A. Nida. Present some of the difficult situations.

"Lord, Who Is My Brother?" Hymn: "O brother man fold to thy heart thy brother."

Our Universal Obligation: "I feel myself under a sort of universal obligation, I owe something to all men, from cultured Greek to ignorant savage." Rom. 1:14 (Phillips).

II. For Missionary Preaching.

Missionaries on the field know the values of parallelism and contrast with the indigenous religions as they present the Christian Gospel. Local proverbs and well-known quotations give acceptable points of contact with the minds of their hearers. Here are a few suggested examples.

1. The Truth Shall Make You Free: "Ye shall know the truth, and the truth shall make you free."—Jesus (John 8:32).

"Teach ye the truth, lovely in its origin, lovely in its progress, lovely in its consummation."—Gautama Buddha.

2. The Road to Delhi and the Road to Jericho: "I met a hundred men on the road to Delhi and they were all my brothers."—Indian Proverb. Parable of the Road to Jericho: Luke 10:30-37.

3. The Great-mindedness of God: "When Allah gives he does not ask 'whose son art thou?' "—Turkish Proverb. "God sendeth rain on the just and the unjust."—Matt. 5:45.

4. The Inside of the Cup: "Woe unto you, scribes and Pharisees, hypocrites! for ye make clean the outside of the cup and of the platter, but within they are full of extortion and excess." Matt. 23:25.

"Though a man wash off his bodily filth, he will yet fail to please the deity if he restrain not his evil desires."—Shinto-Shoden-Kuju.

5. And a Saviour: Judaism gives a Law; Islam gives a Prophet; Buddhism offers a path; Hinduism offers enlightenment; but Christianity gives all these, and then offers a Saviour. No other religion has a Saviour from sin.—Brenton T. Badley.

6. The Supremacy of Love: I Cor. 13. "Bitter things become sweet through love; copper things become golden through love. Dregs become clear and bright through love; pains become salutary through love; through love a dead person is made living; through love a king is made a slave."—Islam. Sufism—Masnavi.

7. The First-class Person: "That first-class person who has removed from himself all sinfulness, who is free from haughtiness, free from impurity, self-restrained, who is an accomplished master of knowledge, who has fulfilled the duties of holiness: such may justly call himself a first-class person."—Buddhism, Mahavagga.

"Whosoever will be chief among you, let him be your servant. The son of man came not to be ministered unto, but to minister, and to give his life a ransom for many." Matt. 20:27, 28.

8. The Final Report: "God shall judge the secrets of men." Rom. 2:16. "The final report has to be presented."—Tao-Teh-Ching.

## CHOICE ILLUSTRATIONS ON MISSIONARY THEMES

### 1. The Real Ambassadors

Recently a Turk told a young American couple bound for the Near East: "The real ambassadors America sends are not the State Department men. They see and influence only our government officials. You missionaries are the real ambassadors. You work with the common folk and have the most lasting influence on our country. You are human and you treat us the same way."

### 2. Our Father

Among the Bakongo tribe in the Belgian Congo there are two words for father, *se* and *tata*. The early missionaries, in translating the New Testament, used *se* in speaking of God as our Father, not perceiving the distinction between the use of the two words. But *se* is not used when your father is present and you are speaking directly to him. So by using *se* the missionaries inadvertently were emphasizing what the natives believed; that God, who created the world, is not near; that you do not speak directly to him.

Later, as the missionaries taught them that in prayer we were to think of God being near, that we were actually in his presence, and could speak to him as we would to our earthly father, it was perceived that they should use the word *tata* and not *se.*—Peter A. MacDiarmid.

### 3. Impression of America

An Oriental visitor was leaving the United States at the end of his year's visit. To a question of his outstanding impression of America, he replied, "I am impressed by the size of your garbage cans."—Floyd Shacklock.

### 4. Increase in Stature

He was well past middle life, quite bent, with a face as seamed as a dried pod. Everyone looked surprised when he walked into the meeting all cleaned up. His shirt was white, if unironed, and it was topped by an unaccustomed bow tie.

He stood by the door awkwardly for a moment. Then he sidled up to one of his migrant camp neighbors.

"I haven't worn a tie for fifteen years," he said, fingering it self-consciously. "But I'm on the committee now."

"Me, too," said his neighbor. "This is the first time I ever felt higher than the beans."—Geraldine Sartain.

### 5. Waiting Along the Roadside

Mama Lufungula became a Christian and was so enthusiastic that the missionary gave her a New Testament, even though she could not read. He wrote of her: "Now she often sits by the roadside waiting for someone to come along who can read the Bible to her."

"Recently a student on his way home for the Christmas holidays came along that road. When Mama Lufungula saw the young man with a pencil clipped in his shirt and a book in his hand, she stopped him and said, 'Won't you please read from the Book for me? . . . The student read . . . 'For God so loved the world that he gave his only begotten Son. . . .'

"Mama Lufungula . . . is poor; she cannot read or write; she sits along the roadside waiting for someone to come along who can read to her from her Book."—*The Methodist Woman.*

### 6. Evangelism in a South Indian Town

In the previous week handbills advertising the service had been distrbiuted in the town. On Saturday evening volunteers visited streets in the town distributing handbills with a personal invitation to each house. Early on Sunday morning St. Mary's School children went out with banners in procession singing. To all the people who came out to see what the singing was about they gave an invitation. Similarly the Bible women and the Hospital had been calling people.

So on Sunday morning St. Mary's Church was full with four or five hundred Hindus and the rest Christians. There were some Moslems. There were educated and uneducated, rich merchants and coolies; vendors of tobacco and clay pots who left their wares in the vestry. There were women in silk saris with jewels and municipal sweepers brought in as they swept the street outside the church.

There was a most reverent atmosphere. The very best of our Telugu Christian music, including some lovely lyrics, was sung. By inviting the Hindus to Church in this way we aim at showing them what Christian worship is, as well as giving them an expostion of the Christian faith.

A convert from Hnduism gave a very well thought out presentation of the Christian message. At the end of the school children sang the beautiful Telugu lyric which is based on "Come unto me all ye that labour and are heavy laden." —*The South India Churchman.*

### 7. Toward Global Thinking

A serious roadblock to understanding the new global relations of the United States is misconception of simple geographical relationships. . . . The world is round any way you look at it. . . . The librarian of a New Hampshire public library, responding to a questionnaire regarding the use of globes, replied, "If people in general do not begin to think in terms of the world as a whole, they are probably doomed."

The roundness of the earth is very real in human relations. A globe is not merely an ornament nor a backdrop for photographs. . . . We cannot really comprehend many of our own national problems except in their true relationships to the whole. . . .

He who would solve world problems must understand them;

He who would understand world problems must visualize them; and

He who would visualize world problems should study them on the spherical surface of a globe.

It is not only the United States but also most of the other nations of the world that are experiencing global relations for the first time in their history. . . . It sometimes seems that vast new human energies would be released if we were to nourish faith in the integrity of the universe and its Creator, in the sound principles enunciated by our forefathers in each of our cultured worlds, and in the ability and desire of many of our fellow men of all lands to rise above the inane excesses of nationalism that sometimes seem to threaten to engulf us all. . . . When children begin early to see and think in world terms, realistically related to the roundness of the earth, the solution of world problems will become tractable.—From a Department of State Bulletin.

**8. The Motive of Service**

A celebrated movie star visited a leper colony and commented to the nurse, "How wonderful of you to serve these distressed people! Why, I wouldn't do it for a million dollars!"

"Neither would I," replied the nurse with gentle earnestness.

**9. Witness of a Navaho**

A Navaho Indian stepped forward and announced his decision to become a Christian, at a Navaho camp meeting. Here in his own words is the story of how Christianity gradually won over his life.

"I come to Protestant services all winter, but each time I left a big heavy bag of my sins over on the hilltop and came to church. I tried to be good while singing, praying, and even hearing the Word of God. Everything seemed to be all right while I was attending the church meeting, but the minute I got back to the top of that hill I picked up my heavy load of sins and started carrying them around again. I'd start doing evil things all over after hearing the Word of God. In spite of this I kept going to church, and I guess all the time my heavy load was getting smaller. Each time I left my load on top of the hill it seemed that way. Well, today I brought my load all the way in and have laid it before Jesus. I want Jesus to take it so I will not carry it back and forth anymore. It's much easier to carry the Bible."

**10. Demonstrating Christian Love**

Often we fail to appreciate the wonderful privilege we have in Christian fellowship. We tend to take it for granted. In Iran, an aristocratic Muslim became a Christian convert, even though it meant social ostracism from his family. He said that he really understood what Jesus meant when he said that if we lose our fathers and mothers by becoming disciples, he will repay the loss a hundredfold. For him this meant the members of the church whose love enfolded him in a fellowship more precious than he had known even with his own family. I wish every Christian congregation demonstrated such love.—Floyd Shacklock.

**11. Fulfilling the Divine Purpose**

Why do we find it hard to believe that it was the Great Spirit who summoned the fathers of the Indians to come thousands of years ago from Asia; that it was the same God who called the fathers of the whites to come hundreds of years ago from Europe, to meet in this last continental home for humanity? It was the God-implanted hope for a better life which brought to this continent people of every race, and it is not the nature of God to mock those who move at his behest. He has placed us in relation to one another here in America to bless us. We can defeat his purpose by refusing to care about one another, by indifference or self-seeking, by setting the superstitions of racism above the sure knowledge of brotherhood under one Father. We can begin to fulfill the divine purpose only by caring about those it is easy to forget but whose fate is bound up with our own, by using our hearts to hope, our minds to think, and our hands to work out our common destiny.—Harold E. Fey.

### 12. Bush Clinic

Dr. Evelyn A. Adams, physician and surgeon in charge of Nikol Mvolan Hospital in the sleeping sickness area of French Cameroun, makes monthly clinic trips to villages, where hundreds of patients have gathered to wait for her.

Dr. Adams has to use methods not generally used elsewhere. Her operating room is situated so that relatives, friends, and the curious can see with their own eyes that the doctor is *really* removing a tumor, and that it wasn't an evil spirit, after all, that was causing the swelling in the body. The tumors are taken from the operating room, exclaimed over by the bystanders, and buried in the forest by a relative, after the crowd has made remarks in praise of the wonderful doctor who can do such a marvelous thing. —*Monday Morning.*

### 13. We Did Not Know . . . Until You Came

A missionary was walking along a dusty road in India. As he approached a village, some villagers came near and fell to their knees. They were Harijans (outcastes, whom Gandhi called children of God) with whom the missionary and his colleagues had been working. The missionary made them rise, and said: "I am no god. Such reverence goes only to God." One of the villagers replied: "We did not know there was a God until you came."

### 14. A New Pattern

The church of Indonesia asked for the services of Mr. Itty (by name) of the church of India.

Mr. Itty, a Syrian Orthodox, was asked to serve in the Indonesian church, a church of Presbyterian theological background.

The Dutch Reformed Church of Holland paid his plane fare.

The YMCA deposited money, when he returned from Indonesia, for expenses when he first arrived in India.

The church in Indonesia paid his salary during the time he was on Indonesian soil.—Dorothy McConnell.

### 15. Insight from Japan

To a person who can read Chinese characters, there was (and probably still is) one aspect of the railway timetables in Japan which is puzzling and intriguing. Wherever one looked at the train schedules, one found them headed: "Going up" or "Going down." There was no reference to points of the compass, so far as one could see. Sometimes "Going up" indicated a southbound train and at other times an eastbound train. Finally, a friend explained that all over Japan trains that were going, even indirectly and often arbitrarily, toward Tokyo, where the Emperor was, were "Going up"; and those going away from Tokyo were "Going down." There was one central point of reference.

Is not this the secret of the practice of the presence of God? Even in activities that seem not to have the faintest relation to our Christian vocation, may there not be paths toward or away from God? . . . Whatever we are doing, are we "Going up"?—Wynn C. Fairfield.

### 16. Confused

A Chinese man who said he accepted Christ was asked to join the Christian church. "Which one?" he asked. "There are over a hundred kinds of Protestants here." He joined none of them.

# *SECTION VII. Outlined Sermons for Sunday Mornings and Evenings of the Entire Church Year. With Recognition Also of Special Days and Occasions and Thematic Aids to Public Worship*

## SUNDAY: JANUARY FIFTH

### MORNING SERVICE

**Theme: How to Live Triumphantly (New Year)**

Suggested Scripture Reading: Ps. 46.

Selected Hymns: "O God, our help in ages past."—Isaac Watts. "How firm a foundation."—Rippon's Selection. "Dear Lord and Father of Mankind."—J. G. Whittier. "He leadeth me, oh, blessed tho't."—Joseph H. Gilmore. "I need thee every hour."—Annie S. Hawks.

Call to Worship: "It is good for me to draw near to God; I have put my trust in the Lord God. My flesh and my heart faileth; but God is the strength of my heart, and my portion for ever." Ps. 73:28, 26.

Invocation: Almighty God, our eternal Father, with whom a thousand years are as one day, and one day as a thousand years, we the children of a brief time draw near to thee as we stand at the threshold of another year. Teach us so to number our days that we shall apply our hearts unto wisdom. Help us to realize the infinite significance of life's opportunities and choices. Give us calm minds and courageous hearts and contented spirits as we go forward to face the unknown experiences of the New Year. May we have in our lives a great renewal; so that old duties shall become fresh, old affections ardent, old aspirations filled with power, and old faith abundantly satisfying. And above all, teach us to walk this year in trustful fellowship with thee, our God. We ask in the name of Jesus. Amen.—G. H.

**Theme: How to Live Triumphantly (New Year)**

Text: "The Lord of hosts is with us. . . . Be still and know that I am God." Ps. 36:7, 11.

When Winston Churchill visited France during the dark days before the fall of the French Republic, he held a conference with the generals of the French Army. In characteristic Churchillian manner he dispensed with superficialities and put to the French generals the vital question: "Where are your reserves?" They answered, "We have no reserves."

And that of course was one of the major reasons for the tragic collapse of France: she had no reserves.

Anyone who is to meet these trying times without crumbling before the battering assaults of confusion and frustration, of tragedy and trouble which characterize so much of our present world, had better face realistically the fact that this truth about reserves applies to the individual life of the spirit quite as much as it does to the military situation of nations.

No one can live triumphantly in the present world without constantly being confronted by various kinds of crises. "Have you any fresh strength you can throw in at this critical moment? Have you any inward resources you can bring to the front in this dark hour? Where are your reserves?"

If the empire of strong character and purposeful living is not to collapse there must be adequate increments of extra spiritual power upon which one can draw to see him through when the enemies of the spirit launch their invasion.

I. Be Aware of God's Presence. One of the most effective ways of developing and maintaining such desperately needed reserves of the spirit is to nurture a sense of God's presence. The world's great personal victories are always won through reliance upon that unseen guidance and help which comes with the facing of life in a conscious fellowship with God. Here is St. Paul, for example, winning the most astonishing inner victories against the most formidable external odds! He did it, he said, by the power he received from his alliance with God. "If God be for us, who can be against us?" That is, if we have God on our side because we have first placed ourselves on his side, we are supported by the sort of spiritual reinforcements which can repulse any assault of evil.

From the time of Jesus down to the present those who face life with a consciousness of God's presence have inwardly found that they can count on inner reserves from which to draw strength in any time of critical need. One may call this experience by whatever name he may please: mysticism, illusion, wishful thinking. But no reasonable man can pretend that such experience is trivial to the person engaged in life's battle. When a sense of being reinforced by something greater than oneself can make an individual adequate to cope with existence, it hardly is a trivial matter.

II. Cultivate Inward Serenity. If one, going a step further, is to have the quality and quantity of spiritual reserve which can be depended upon to see him through in the hour of emergency, to provide that life does not collapse and become futile and meaningless, he must bring up the added spiritual resources which come from a well-cultivated sense of moral and intellectual serenity.

There are many ways by which to secure such needed poise and serenity. Some people are able to do this by occasionally going alone into the woods or among the hills or beside the sea. Others, for whom such withdrawal is impossible, learn to accomplish it by selecting a few minutes out of each day when the household is quiet and they can retire in solitude and sit quietly in meditative prayer.

Some individuals make provision for a few extra minutes, three or four times a week, to enter some empty sanctuary and sit in silent meditation as they draw upon the spiritual sources of strength and peace.

And more than one person has been kept out of the fields of futility and upon the road of meaningful living by relying on the divine promises as contained in the Bible. How steadying, for example, such words as these which come from the prophet Isaiah: "Thou wilt keep him in perfect peace whose mind is stayed on thee."

How each one may best go about the building of serene reserves against the incessant tumult of his existence, who can tell? There is one thing, however, that all of us should know: If we are to gain the stamina to stand up to life's crises, and to make the most of every opportunity, we must learn how to live without letting useless things, insignificant events and irrelevant associations so press upon us that we forfeit our sense of mission and wander vaguely in search of the lost way.

III. Trust Your Destiny to God. Religious faith assures us and reassures us, again and again, that the God whom we worship is able to deliver to the utmost those who put their trust in him; that his power is inexhaustible; that his love and mercy are omnipotent; that his will is sovereign; and that he holds our lives in the hollow of his hand. He created the dependable laws that govern the surrounding universe. There is nothing of which we need to be afraid, if we face the facts with him. In every emergency there is help for us from God. To him we may safely trust the future, and in this confidence we may call upon his reserves as a guarantee of victory.

To face the daily round with stamina and courage, and to make the spirit's citadel impregnable, demand of us that we keep our spiritual reserves at fullest strength, by nurturing a sense of God's presence, by cultivating an attitude of serenity in a chaotic world, and by learning to trust one's destiny to God. Where then are your reserves? Do you sustain your inner life at highest living and potential?—Adapted from Robert Clyde Yarbrough.

PRAYER: O thou who art from everlasting to everlasting, without beginning or end of days; replenish us with heavenly grace at the beginning of this year, that we may be enabled to accept all its duties, to perform all its labors, to welcome all its mercies, to meet all its trials, and to advance through all it holds in store for us with cheerful courage and a constant mind. O Lord, suffer us not to be separated from thee, either by joy or sorrow, or any sin or weakness of our own; but have compassion upon us, and forgive us, and keep us in the strong confidence of thine eternal love in Jesus Christ; that as thou hast called us to eternal life through him, so we may pass the residue of our years in the power of eternity; and to thy name shall be all the praise. Amen.

OFFERTORY SENTENCE: "Now that ye have consecrated yourselves unto the Lord, draw near and bring thank offerings into the courts of the Lord's house."

OFFERTORY PRAYER: Help us, O Lord, by thy Spirit in our hearts, to render during the coming year a faithful stewardship of our time and talents and wealth. Each morning open our eyes to some opportunity that thou hast placed in our way. In His name we now dedicate our offerings. Amen.—H.

SEED THOUGHTS: The 46th Psalm. Samuel Terrien points out that three aspects of the activity of God are in turn contemplated: I. God is the lord of creation. II. God is the lord of history. III. God is the lord of eternal peace.

God's omnipotent will shall prevail. Thus with utter serenity and calm the psalmist bade the people stand up and sing, "God is our refuge and strength."

Our Refuge and Strength. I. We need the *refuge* of God. Our finest strategy is sometimes "to rest in the Lord and wait." We can slay some of our enemies by leaving them alone. II. We need the *strength* of God. The defensive is changed to the offensive. We meet our enemy on the open field.

And so our God is our resource in the double warfare of active and passive crusade.—John H. Jowett.

### Choice Illustrations on the Theme

REINFORCED. Consider this statement from a letter recently received from a young man who went to college and found out for himself that the first year away from home requires some difficult adjustments: "It does a great deal," he writes, "for a person's morale to know that his church is behind him . . . Self discipline is facilitated by the knowledge that you are reinforced by something greater than yourself."—R. C. Y.

THE MARGIN OF OPERATION. Some people find themselves in precisely the same difficulty at the spiritual level as was the business firm financially when it called in an efficiency expert to diagnose its problems and received the verdict: "The trouble with you is, your margin of operation is too thin."—R. C. Y.

"GOOD NEW YEAR." So our friends in Scotland used to say it to us. They make more of New Year's Day than of Christmas. "Good" instead of "happy" they say. The Scot is often as careful in laying out his words as he is reputed to be in laying out his wealth. "A Good New Year" roots in a view of life. Popular etymology has connected the word "good" with the word "God." "God's New Year" is what our ancestors said to each other: "a new year with God in it!" That is our wish for one another.

"Happy" is a sister to "happen." Keep God in your new year, and there will be no monotony in it. God will cause good things to happen for you—new friends, a new vision of Christ, new work for him, and lasting riches. Professor Drummond used to say, "Others will be wishing you 'A Good New Year'; I will be wishing you 'A Good Eternity.'"—G. A. Frantz.

## Quotable New Year Poetry

### O God, Lead On!

Our God, lead on!
No matter what the path,
Or rough or smooth, we go
In Thy strength, by Thy grace,
To our appointed task.
Through shine or shadow, Lord,
Help us to follow Thee.
Make strife and hatred cease,
Make peace and truth prevail.
Into a brighter day
O God, lead on!

—N. B. Chester.

### The Gift of Tomorrow

If we could have a second chance
To live the days once more,
And rectify mistakes we've made
To even up the score . . .
If we could have a second choice
To use the knowledge gained,
Perhaps we might become at last
As fine as God ordained.
But though we can't retrace our steps,
However stands the score,
Tomorrow brings another chance
For us to try once more.

—Hilda Butler Farr.

### A Happy New Year

"A happy new year" it will be—if it's new:
New visions of all that is noble and true,
New powers for service, new knowledge of God,
New zeal for the ways that the heroes have trod,
New comforts, new courage, new graces, new joys,
New peace where the evil assails or annoys,
New friendships, new helpers, new faith and new love,
New treasures on earth, and new treasures above,
New wisdom, new glory, new health and new cheer,
Nothing old, all things new, in the happy new year!

—Amos R. Wells.

### Thoughts of the New Year

Let us walk softly, friend;
For strange paths lie before us, all untrod;
The new year, spotless from the hand of God
Is thine and mine, O friend!

Let us walk straightly, friend;
Forget the crooked paths behind us now.
Press on with steadier purpose on our brow
To better deeds, O friend!

Let us walk gladly, friend;
Perchance some greater good than we have known
Is waiting for us, or some fair hope flown
Shall yet return, O friend!

Let us walk kindly, friend,
We cannot tell how long this life shall last,
How soon these precious years be over past;
Let love walk with us, friend.

Let us walk quickly, friend;
Work with our might while lasts our little stay,

And help some halting comrade on the
way;
And may God guide us, friend!
—Author Unknown.

## EVENING SERVICE

**Theme: The Open Road**

TEXT: "And an highway shall be there, and a way, and it shall be called The way of holiness; . . . the wayfaring men, though fools, shall not err therein." Isa. 35:8.

"There shall be an highway, and a way, and it shall be called the Way of Holiness, and wayfaring men, though fools, shall not err therein." Thank God for that, he has not forgotten the plain man.

Despite all the conflict of doctrine and the din of voices, your duty, brother-wayfarer, is clear enough. Turn your face and your heart Christward, commit yourself and your way to him, and go straight ahead, doing your duty and fearing nothing. You are only a plain man, striving to live a religious life, very conscious of your failures and your need of higher help. Well, "there's a star to guide the humble," as the hymn says, "Trust in God and do the right."

I. There's a way of holiness for you, a broad macadamized road where you can walk and not mistake it, although—and this is Although number one—although you are not a scholar or a theologian. Now I do not wish even to seem to say anything derogatory here. Let us never forget what we owe to all patient, honest scholarship. But I am speaking of essential religion, and that can be proclaimed at a street corner to every passer-by and can be grasped and accepted by those who can neither read nor write. The Gospel of Jesus Christ is so adapted to the heart of man that an untutored savage can get hold of it.

Many a cultured believer who went to the War made the discovery that all that really counted in his creed when he was up against the elementary facts of life and death could be put in the simplest language, and ticked off on the fingers of one hand—that God is our Father, that Jesus brings us to him, that prayer is a real thing, that guidance comes when you want to do what is right, and that death is not the end. If you know that Christ is real, and that he is your friend, your feet are on the plain man's road, and you need not err nor fear.

II. Yes, my brother, there is a way of holiness for you, plain and clear, despite all the clamor of these days, although—and this is the second Although—you are a busy man immersed in affairs. You have your daily darg [work] to do that you and yours may live? Right! That's what God wants you to do. If sainthood requires seclusion and quiet and lots of time to meditate, you haven't any chance, you think. But it does not. The mark of sainthood is character, and only character. The saintliest man is the man who, whatever his calling, is like Jesus Christ, and he was once a carpenter in Nazareth. Why is it that one does not think of a carpenter or an engineer or a miner as a possible saint? I don't know. It's merely a stupid convention that hinders us, anyhow.

Plain man, this is your road and mine—once for all, claim your sonship in Christ Jesus, and then set yourself to live, everywhere and always, as God's son.

III. Ay, although—and this is the last Although—you feel that there is much wrong with the Church that should be your guide and the mediator of Christ's spirit to you. It cannot be denied that there are things amiss in the Church today. Where it should lead it is often silent, or it swings an enormous hammer to flatten out some poor little mouse of an abuse, while big cruel evils, like strong lions, stalk through the land unchallenged and unfought.

In spite of all that, stick you to the Church, plain man, for it is you and such as you who can help to mend it. Its shortcomings, however, will not excuse yours. Not even a dumb Church can alter your need of a Saviour or black the plain straight road to him. It matters not what others do or say, your duty is clear—to do justly, to love mercy, and to walk humbly with your God. That is the creed for a plain man, enough and more than enough for us all, if we try to live it. It's a long, long road, winding uphill all the way, but at least it is a clear road, and wayfaring men, though fools, shall not err therein.—Archibald Alexander.

**Suggested New Year Texts and Themes**

An Almighty Saviour: "Mighty to save." Isa. 63:1.

The Definite Aim: "This one thing I do." Phil. 3:13.

The Ships That Never Sailed: "Jehoshaphat made ships of Tharshish to go to Ophir for gold: but they went not; for the ships were broken at Eziongeber." I Kings 22:48.

The Path Unknown: ". . . I will lead them in paths that they have not known: . . ." Isa. 42:16.

Persistence in Well-doing: "And let us not be weary in well doing: for in due season we shall reap, if we faint not." Gal. 6:9.

Faith for Such a Year: "This is the victory that overcometh the world, even our faith." I John 5:4.

## MIDWEEK FELLOWSHIP MEETING TOPIC

(Church Night or Suggested Sermon Subject)

**Theme: "I'm Glad I'm Alive"**

TEXT: "Who knoweth whether thou art come to the kingdom for such a time as this?" Esther 4:14.

I. I'm glad I'm alive because, even in these times of mundane disaster, life can be made worth living. Even a catastrophe of evil can be met most nobly, bravely, and even happily, and life, therefore, be worth living.

II. I'm glad I'm alive because I'm an active member of the generation which is going to determine the destiny of the human race.

1. Inwrought in the whole concept of democracy is the idea that history is a matter not of a few outstanding men but of great aggregates of men. Events are determined not by a few heroes or leaders but by the mass of humankind. In that mass each one of us has his place and part. Some of us have a higher place than others, and play a larger part; but each one of us has some share in fashioning what later comes to be known as history. Speak a word, wave an arm, light a candle—and the universe is never the same again. 2. It is interesting to analyze the nature of personal influence to see how humbly it may begin and how grandly it may grow. 3. "They also serve who only stand and wait."

III. I'm glad I'm alive because I can bear witness unto the truth.

1. Example of Jesus. I think of Jesus in his times! It must have seemed to him as though there was nothing that he could do, and life therefore had no meaning. He was nothing but a poor carpenter of Nazareth, become now a preacher who was listened to by a few persons as humble as himself. What did he amount to? What could he do? But when he was arrested, and brought before the Roman governor, and asked to justify himself, he answered proudly, "To this end was I born, and for this cause came I into the world, that I should bear witness unto the truth."

2. That's something that we can do. What a time is this in which "to bear witness unto the truth"! Though there were nothing else for me to say, I should be glad to be alive today if only "to this end" and "for this cause."

In one place or another, in one way or another, we must all "serve" at this terrific moment of human history. We all have our work to do, our witness to bear, our post to hold. Whether we will or no, we are a part of this great drama of the ages. For this reason if for no other, we should be glad to be alive in this mighty age, "all of which we see and part of which we are."—Adapted from John Haynes Holmes.

## BULLETIN BOARD SLOGANS FOR THE MONTH

Never quit growing.

God gives you ideals; work toward them.

There is no right way to do a wrong thing.

"As a man thinketh in his heart, so is he."

Look backward with patience; look forward with vision.

As long as good men do nothing evil will triumph.

Keep your fears to yourself but share your courage with others.

"The human mind should be like a good hotel—open the year round."

"The only place where you can start at the top is when digging a hole."

Hammering hardens steel but crushes putty. Can you take it?"

## SUNDAY SCHOOL LESSON

**Jan. 5. The Church's One Foundation. Matt. 16:13-19; Eph. 2:19-22. Background Scripture: Col 1:15-20.**

MEMORY VERSE: "He is the head of the body, the church; he is the beginning, the first-born from the dead, that in everything he might be preëminent." Col. 1:18 (R. S. V.)

This quarter's series of lessons is designed to set forth the origin, nature and mission of the Christian church.

The logical start in such studies is with Jesus' own words. The passage suggested, Matt. 16:13-19, is a most controversial one, and difficult to interpret. The comments and exposition to be found in *The Interpreter's Bible* may be helpful.

Perhaps it will be profitable to emphasize the personal challenge which is presented by Jesus' words, "Whom do men say that I am?" Can we answer with Peter, "Thou art the Christ, the Son of the Living God"?

I. When faith makes the answer it bursts into song, "The Church's one foundation is Jesus Christ her Lord." See the memory verse.

II. Apostles and prophets, according to Paul, share with Christ, as foundation stones of the "Holy Temple."

III. It is a thrilling teaching of the Apostle Peter that we ourselves may be "living stones, built up a spiritual house, . . . to offer up spiritual sacrifices, acceptable to God by Jesus Christ." Each has his place in the Church whose foundation is Jesus Christ. I Pet. 2:4-10.

# SUNDAY: JANUARY TWELFTH

## MORNING SERVICE

**Theme: When the Ark Sets Forward or The Mercy Seat**

SUGGESTED SCRIPTURE READING: Exod. 25:10-22.

SELECTED HYMNS: "The Church of God is stablished."—Lucius H. Thayer. "Blest be the tie that binds."—John Fawcett. "Father Almighty, bless us with thy blessing."—*Berwick Hymnal.* "Take the name of Jesus with you."—Lydia Baxter. "They who seek the throne of grace."—Oliver Holden.

CALL TO WORSHIP: Lift up your hearts unto the Lord! And the purpose of lifting up our hearts is that we may truly give thanks unto God. Whatever is worthy in the offering of our hearts comes from God's love which draws our human love away from ourselves and unto him.

INVOCATION: Let the beauty of thy holiness shine into our hearts, that we may grow more steadfast in our faith and in our love of thee and of our fellow men. Amen.

**Theme: When the Ark Sets Forward or the Mercy Seat**

TEXT: "I will appear in the cloud upon the mercy seat." Lev. 16:2.

Once God spoke unto Moses from a bush burning in the wilderness. Again

God spoke to him on the top of a great mountain. Now God communes with him from between the cherubim of the ark.

I. It is marvelous to have a place where you know that God is. To find God everywhere is too often to find him nowhere.

According to the ancient Israelitish religion a shining cloud, called the *Shekinah,* rested between the winged creatures on the ark. This *Shekinah* was "the Divine Manifestation through which God's presence was felt by man."

The place of God's presence is a shining place, either actually or figuratively so.

> Down in the meadow spent with dew
> I saw the Very God
> Look from a flower's limpid blue.
> —Alice Brown.

> The round moon hangs like a yellow lantern in the trees
> That lie like lace against the sky,
> Oh, still the night! Oh, hushed the breeze—
> Surely God is nigh.

In the morning some have seen

> God at his anvil, beating out the sun.

In the evening

> God is at his anvil, welding golden bars.

The presence of God is associated with glory and light—God is light and in him is no darkness at all.

It is marvelous to have a shining place where God is, "to be aware of Reality behind reality and to be sensitive to the word of the Everlasting God."

Yes, it is a marvelous thing to know where God is. The ark was placed in the Holy of Holies of the tabernacle, and a veil was drawn before it. The people did not enter. There was no din and clatter, no talk, no gossip. Wherever you discover talk and chatter and bickering, there God is not. God is found in silence. Even when a man is walking the street where hundreds of people are passing and he prays—there is a silent place in the man's soul. Be still and know that I am God. Where only two or three are gathered in my name there am I in the midst of them.

It is marvelous to know where God is, to see his shining, to hear the still small voice in the silence.

II. It is a marvelous thing to find God upon the mercy seat.

Let us look at that ancient ark. It is a box and within the box is placed the law of God—the Ten Commandments. The law in the ark is the token of the law written in the human breast. By that law every man has a bad conscience. By that law every man is sinful.

It is law. It is hard. It is terrible. No man can break it, but it breaks every man.

Men have gone to every extremity to escape that law and appease it. They have scourged themselves with whips. They have become hermits. They have tortured themselves. They have tried to escape the law in drink and narcotics. They have tried to escape by rationalizing with their minds, by running here and there about the earth, by plunging into pleasure, by denying God and his laws. Who can find even one that has succeeded?

But behold this wonderful thing! Above the box is a mercy seat. Look at the word—mercy seat. The law is covered over with mercy. Above the law is the loving-kindness of God.

On the mercy seat are winged creatures, swifter than the wind, able to fly to any man in his despair and need, quick to hear the cry of any sinner in the world. Such are the creatures of the mercy seat of God.

And there on the mercy seat is the Presence of God, the *Shekinah,* the shining of God in his mercy.

Many know the marvel of finding the presence of God on the mercy seat. David felt the marvel of it when he wrote: "Blessed is the man whose transgression is forgiven, whose sin is covered." The law is covered by mercy.

Thus we see the deed of Christ—for the Cross was God's mercy coming down and covering and resting upon the law which revealed man's terrible sin.

Paul puts it well. "Where sin abounded; grace did much more abound."

III. It is marvelous when the ark sets forward.

When the ark moved forward, then the people moved. They had a shining cloud directing the way. I don't know how Moses knew when the *Shekinah* was restless and began to move forward; I suppose by the way that a good man now knows the guidance of God.

It is a fascinating story how the ark led the way. We have such passages as these: Num. 10:33; Josh. 3 and 4. See also II Sam. 6.

When at last the Israelites with the ark leading came to the Jordan river, then Joshua, who had succeeded Moses, commanded the people: "When ye see the ark of the Covenant of the Lord your God and the priests bearing it, then ye shall remove from your place and go after it." What are difficulties when the Presence of God goes before you? They carried the ark around the city of Jericho and the walls of the city fell.

Where the ark is, blessing is—except that only holy hands should try to steady it.

It is marvelous to have the Presence of God point the way forward.

IV. It is marvelous to be a priest before the ark. It is marvelous to enter the Holy of Holies—where God is, where God covers sin, where the cherubim, the messengers of God, are active; where God speaks in the silence. This was the High Priest's privilege and duty.

When Jesus came he became our great High Priest, and it was he who entered into the presence of God and made atonement for us.

When Jesus was upon the Cross there was a great earthquake and the veil of the temple was broken in twain from the top to the bottom. The significance of that is that there is no Holy of Holies where you and I are not permitted to enter. I, too am a priest. You are priests. We believe in the priesthood of believers. It is permitted us to enter where God is, where the *Shekinah* rests upon the mercy seat.

By the token of the ark a church building like this is an ark, or should be.

The altar is a place where God is.

The altar is a place where God's mercy is above God's law.

This altar directs men forward toward God's promised land.

This altar can be approached in humility, in reverence, in awe, in love, in holiness.—H.

A Prayer for the Day: Grant us, O Lord, the shining light of thy presence. May we always find the altar of this house a source of light, an oracle of beauty, the abiding-place of thy glory, a mercy seat. How wonderful to find upon it the tokens of the sacrifice of Christ—the broken bread and the cup of wine!

Help us to approach the altar with reverence; with repentance and humbleness of heart may we receive its grace; and in peace may we go forth from it ourselves to abound in mercy and loving-kindness. Amen.—H.

Offertory Sentence: "And they came every one whose heart stirred him up, and every one whom his spirit made willing, and they brought the Lord's offering to the work of the tabernacle of the congregation." Exod. 35:21.

Offertory Prayer: Prompt our hearts, O God, and make willing our spirits, that we may bring the Lord's offering cheerfully unto thine altar. In Jesus' name. Amen.

Seed Thoughts: Holy Places. One holy place may be a locality rich in wondrous and uplifting associations. Another holy place is the thought or memory of a person whom we have come to know through reading or personal contact. Your holy place may be a verse or a chapter of the Bible. It may be some classic of the devotional life. Some fine souls find their holy place in one of the great prayers of Newman, or Martineau, or John Hunter. or Robert Louis Stevenson, or the *Book of Common Prayer.*—J. N. F.

"The Throne of Grace." Heb. 4:16. It is a royal throne; it is a throne of divine glory. "The *Shekinah* was supposed to dwell between the cherubim; in the new Covenant the Word was made flesh and tabernacled among us, and we beheld his glory." John 1:14.

### Choice Illustrations on the Theme

TREASURE IN THE ARK. Legend tells us that a Roman emperor once stormed into the Temple at Jerusalam and demanded from the high priest the treasures of the Jews. The priest took the emperor to the Holy of Holies, the room containing the ark, and told him the treasure was inside. The emporer greedily opened the ark, hoping to find precious jewels or gold. Instead, he found the sacred scrolls of the Law. When he realized that the Jews regarded a spiritual possession as their most precious treasure, he was so moved that he left the Temple and Jerusalem in peace.—*Christian Friends.*

SANCTUARY. Every soul needs a place where it can find sanctuary. A sign on a London church must have helped many a one terrified by the thought of sudden death from the skies: "If your knees knock, kneel on them." Religion gives a man a holy place where he can find help in meeting and conquering his fears. We hear over and over again that there were no atheists in the foxholes of Bataan. To men face to face with brutal death, the quick extinguishment of young lives, the blighting of all hope and promise in one small moment of time, religion offered a holy place where one could grasp the actuality of immortality, and the ongoing of unconquerable truth and right. A woman, after enduring ten years of hard times, said: "I have been arunning." Others have felt the same way; and to such, religion offers a place of rest for running feet, a moment of quiet in which loose ends might be caught up, a time for prayer in which a larger perspective breaks through.—John N. Feaster.

## EVENING SERVICE

### Theme: Hearing God's Voice Today

TEXT: "Today, if ye will hear his voice." Heb. 3:7.

The word of promise there is the word "today." For that is surely what a real and living religion means, hearing God's voice today, not merely from the far-off centuries, nor only when Jesus was living on this earth, but today, in the midst of all our besetments and our problems.

I. For far too many people, religion has a constantly backward look, and seems to be living on its past. It looks back to Bible days as the time when men did really hear God's voice, and to the years of our Lord's life in Galilee as the time when the Eternal did really concern himself with this world of men. Compared with that, these days of ours seem to many like an unlit street, or a stage from which the chief actor has departed. Many earnest people, therefore, try to hark backward in time for a contact with Reality, and religion for them means living in the past as much as possible. If that is the truth, it means that the Christian religion is like an expedition that is always getting further and further away from its base of supplies.

II. But it isn't the truth and the Easter gospel is the witness against it. For the fact of the living Christ means that God is still speaking as really as ever he did, and cares for this mad world of his children today as truly as when Jesus was visible to men's eyes, and they could grasp his warm living hand.

There is nothing, perhaps .that thinking men and women need more today than a fresh assurance that all the spiritual reality and the invisible resources on which men have ever drawn are as available for us now. Ancient book as the Bible is, we have everything precious that it holds today, because God still is. God, who sent Jesus to live among his brethren, has not himself gone away since then. Real religion, then, must mean looking for him in the world of today, hearing his voice today, living in fellowship with him today, loving and serving him in the world of today as we love and serve our neighbor. Religion isn't only looking back, it is looking around, and looking within, and looking up.

It is the greatest of all mistakes to live as if we had left the God of Jesus in the centuries behind us. It is in him we live. Life is his doing and every growing thing is his handiwork. Love everywhere is the sign of him, and whoso liveth in love liveth in God. All that is good anywhere is the shadow of his presence; all that is true is a word of his speech; all that is beautiful is as his garment. He is near to every one of us, so that we can have true fellowship with him even in our heart. How foolish, then, to look only back for him, when we can hear his voice, and meet with him, and give ourselves to him today!—Archibald Alexander.

**Suggested Texts and Themes**

The Narrow Way to the Life Abundant: "Straight is the gate, and narrow is the way, which leadeth unto life, and few there be that find it." Matt. 7:14.

Formula for Happiness: "Godliness with contentment is great gain." I Tim. 6:6.

Wings—Running Shoes—Boots: Isa. 40:31.

The Surrender of the Heart: "My son, give me thine heart, and let thine eyes observe my ways." Prov. 23:26.

A Spiritual Goal: "That ye would walk worthy of God, who hath called you into his kingdom and glory." I Thess. 2:12.

The Last Word, Not Retribution, Redemption: "For God sent not his Son into the world to condemn the world; but that the world through him might be saved." John 3:17.

## MIDWEEK FELLOWSHIP MEETING TOPIC

(Church Night or Suggested Sermon) Subject)

**Theme: Never Walk Out on Your Dream**

TEXT: "Demas hath forsaken me, having loved this present world." II Tim. 4:10.

We fight that a dream may come true, and the faultier the organization the harder we must fight. "I don't go to church," said a man recently; "I don't like this and I don't like that and I don't get anything out of it." Can you imagine an Englishman saying, "I won't fight for England and liberty, I don't like the way the food is served, and I don't like the language of the sergeant-major"? He who goes into war to get something out of it must be half-witted. You fight and serve to put something into it, to make a dream come true.—Leslie Weatherhead.

Never walk out on your dream. Suppose Peter had. Suppose Isaiah had. Suppose Paul had. Suppose Jesus had.

We have our dream. A church permeated by Christian love. A church requiring simplicity of faith. A church which shall be a house of help. A church where the end in view is the glory of God. Never walk out on your dream.—H.

## SUNDAY SCHOOL LESSON

**Jan. 12. The Church's Power. Acts 1:4-8; 2:1-11. Background Scripture: John 16:1-15; Acts 1:1-14; 2:1-41.**

MEMORY VERSE: "You shall receive power when the Holy Spirit has come upon you; and you shall be my witnesses in Jerusalem and in all Judea and Samaria and to the end of the earth." Acts 1:8 (R.S.V.).

1. The Promise of the Spirit's Power.

II. The Experience of the Spirit's Power. 1. A Spirit-filled people. 2. A Spirit-filled Church.

III. The Continuance of the Spirit's Power. The enduring power of the Christian Church. The energizing power of the Christian Church.

IV. The Need of the Spirit's Power now for the Church to be the Church. The Need of the Spirit's Power for the Church to communicate the Gospel and transmit its power.—H.

# SUNDAY: JANUARY NINETEENTH

## MORNING SERVICE

### Theme: Creative Worship

SUGGESTED SCRIPTURE READING: Isa. 6: 1-8.

SELECTED HYMNS: "Holy, holy, holy! Lord God Almighty."—Reginald Heber. "Worship the Lord in the beauty of holiness."—J. S. B. Monsell. "Praise ye the Father, praise the Lord most holy."—M. Cockburn-Campbell. "We gather together to ask the Lord's blessing."—Anonymous.

CALL TO WORSHIP: "Give unto the Lord the glory due unto his name: bring an offering, and come before him: worship the Lord in the beauty of holiness." I Chron. 16:29.

INVOCATION: Heighten our powers of appreciation, O God, that we may more fully profit by the privilege of this hour of worship, and that we may dedicate our lives more fully to thy service.

Help us to remember the sacrificial labors of those who have given us the open Bible, the welcoming door of the Church, the right to worship thee according to the dictates of our own consciences.

Grant unto us a deeper experience of spiritual blessings wrought out for us by the life and death and resurrection of Christ. Amen.—H.

### Theme: Creative Worship

TEXT: "But as many as received him, to them gave he power to become the sons of God." John 1:12.

INTRODUCTORY: If offered the opportunity to become happier, healthier, more constructive, useful, and radiant, would anyone refuse? That opportunity we all have. With patience and persistence, success is certain. The effort required, however, is where most of us fail. A simple choice we are ready to make, but we weary at the thought of continually striving.

Most of us are willing to put forth great effort to reach less worthy goals. A youth will work hard for many years to acquire an education. A musician will practice many hours a day most of his life to become a master. A young couple will work diligently to establish a home. These earthly goals are ever before us, and we exert ourselves to reach them.

Striving to widen, deepen, and enrich the quality of our spiritual lives is more difficult for most of us. While the reward is greater, it seems less definite and immediate. With persistence, however, our perception focuses on the distant scene and we become increasingly eager to "lay aside every weight" and "run with patience the race that is set before us" (Heb. 12:1).

I. Our Capacity for Spiritual Development. Let us then take stock, see what is involved, and how and where to begin. We know we are made in the image of God with capacity for spiritual development. The question is what are we doing about that capacity? St. John tells us: "But as many as received him, to them gave he power to become the sons of God. . . ." Here we find an astounding promise and a shining goal of unimaginable splendor.

II. The Creative Power of Worship. Men tend to become like that which is the chief interest of their lives—to be transformed more and more into the image of whatever they treasure in their hearts as most sacred. Our ideals gradually become bone and sinew of our existence. To worship God sincerely and persistently is to grow in grace and to take on more of his attributes. Seeking oneness with God is central in the experience of worship. As we seek to know his will we gain a clearer perception of right and wrong, a more sensitive conscience, and a new and better understanding of our own duties and responsibilities.

Between times of concentrated worship, the vision tends to fade, but as we return to worship, it is renewed again and again. Each time it becomes stronger, lasts longer, and integrates itself a little more into the warp and woof of our character. This is creative worship. In time it will transform the life of anyone who practices it.

III. The Experience of Creative Worship. Having entered into this quest, we shall find it becoming more and more absorbing. There is less resistance to the time required. We shall note changes in our lives. Gradually evil loses its appeal. Selfish desires seem progressively less important. The mean, the cheap, and the tawdry lose their attractiveness. The unreal, the dross, and the counterfeits of life appear in their true light and fall away like iron filings from a magnet when the current is turned off. Conversely, the real and the good, the pure and the noble, the beautiful and the upright acquire increasing attractiveness and assume their proper value in our scheme of things.

IV. Attainments through Creative Worship. Worship is the process of piercing the veil of flesh, with its appetites and passions, and revealing the glory and effulgence of spiritual life. When successfully accomplished, it brings the experience described by Luke: "And the glory of the Lord shone around about them." The good in man is raised up and appears beautiful, whereas evil becomes unattractive and loses its appeal.

Worship is the process of becoming more like God. It is the way to implement the great promise which is our text. It is the means of making that power available to us. It illumines and glorifies the whole of life. It straightens out the crooked paths. It substitutes beauty for ashes. It changes sorrow into gladness. It is the process by which man increases his spiritual stature. It is the way ethical ideals are formed. In short, it raises man above the level of the brute and fulfills the statement that he is created in the image of his Maker.—*Christian Economics.*

Prayer for the Day: Our gracious Father, we bless thee for our communion in the ministries of intercession and praise. We thank thee that the solitary life can meet its fellows, and we can get together in the Presence Chamber of the Lord. We thank thee that those who are strong in faith can be the helpers of those who are trembling, and that those whose hopes are burning dim can be encouraged by the spirits of those who are full of joy and expectation. Wilt thou help us to be real companions in worship. May we be very willing to hold our strength in the service of one another. We rejoice in the confidence that all things are now ready, that the table is spread with provisions, and that the Saviour is waiting for his guests. May we come to thee with a great hunger for the best things which thou are waiting to give. May we be ambitious to possess the unsearchable riches of Christ. Wilt thou graciously give us thy strength, so that we may use it in unselfish service. Help us all to believe in thee in difficult times. May we have the faith which can sing songs in the night. May we be believers in the dawn even when the darkness is round about us. May we fight the good fight of faith, and be more than conquerors through him that loved us. Amen.—John H. Jowett.

Offertory Sentence: Ps. 116:17-19.

Offertory Prayer: Help us, O Lord, to redeem this part of our service from mere form. Enable us to add ourselves to our gifts—may we follow them with interest, with prayer, and with expectation that through them the Kingdom will come in the world. Amen.—H.

Seed Thoughts: What is Worship? I. The adoration of God. II. Fellowship with God. III. Commitment to God's eternal purposes.

Worship Releases Energy. As certainly as the closing of an electric current does. I. It heightens all human capacities. II. It refreshes and quickens life. III. It unlocks reservoirs of power.

IV. It opens invisible doors to larger life.—Adapted from Rufus Jones.

Worship. I. It purifies. II. It enlightens. III. It transforms. It does this for every life submitted to its influence.—Evelyn Underhill.

**Choice Illustrations on the Theme**

ACCORDING TO ARISTOTLE. According to Aristotle, as phrased by the Quaker philosopher Rufus Jones, "The true nature of a thing is the highest that it can become." If this be true, as I believe it is, then the true nature of a man is to be a spiritual being.—C. E.

DOES IT SEEM REAL? Two young men were coming out of a church service. One said to the other: "What was the matter with that service? Somehow it failed to get me." The other replied: "I was just thinking of that. Did it seem real to you?" And they agreed that it did not, and that the failure lay at just that point. The young men were recently enough from overseas to carry still the impression of religious gatherings among the soldiers. Worship and preaching there had seemed real at least, however unconventional. What was said had been said not because it was proper to say it but because it needed to be said. What was sung was sung because it expressed something that was to be expressed.

A SUPREME VALUE. For a few dollars we can get a book on religion; for a few more dollars we can get someone to talk to us about the things of religion; but what we cannot get for dollars, however high we heap them, is this experience which is the very heart of religion, this experience of God, this practice of the divine presence, this joy of being ourselves in the Holy of Holies. —Rufus Jones.

## EVENING SERVICE

**Theme: The Conversion of St. Paul**

TEXT: "From henceforth let no man trouble me: for I bear in my body the marks of the Lord Jesus." Gal. 6:17.

January 25 has special significance for all Christian people. On that day we celebrate the conversion of St. Paul. As we give thanks to Almighty God for the life and witness of the Apostle, it is good to remind ourselves that through conversion St. Paul was called upon to suffer greatly for his Lord. Wherever he went on his missionary journeys, there were always those who tried to undermine his influence and counteract his preaching. Nevertheless, the Apostle remained undaunted. The fire of conviction was unquenched in his soul, for he had seen the Lord. Whatever accusations were brought against him, his faith remained firm, for it was founded upon a rock.

I. Accusations against Him.

1. He was accused of being a persecutor. This he admitted for at the stoning of Stephen he had been a consenting party. Before King Agrippa he openly confesses that at one time he did many things contrary to the name of Jesus of Nazareth. St. Paul never denied that he was a persecutor. He never contradicted this accusation of his enemies.

2. He was accused of being an imposter, a renegade follower of the Twelve, a man who knew nothing of Christianity except what he had learned from the apostles at Jerusalem. St. Paul stoutly denies this, and vindicates his apostleship by showing that he received his gospel not from the Jerusalem apostles, not from the Church, not from any man at all, but by direct revelation from God.

3. He was accused of being insincere, of not practicing what he preached. Paul had taught that the way of salvation lay in faith in Christ, and had warned his listeners that it could not be found in the works of the Jewish Law. Yet at Lystra when he met Timothy, the son of a certain woman, which was a Jewess, Paul "took and circumcised him because of the Jews which were in those quarters." His enemies, therefore, could claim that this was inconsistent with his teaching. Paul, however, insisted that "neither circumcision availeth anything, nor uncircumcision,

but a new creature." He proclaims that the one gospel may be presented in different ways according to local and national requirements, and goes on to say that this distinction was recognized by James and Cephas and John, the pillars of the Church.

II. Marks upon Him.

Fortified by a clear conscience Paul could face his enemies and dismiss them with "Let no man trouble me," for he can confidently affirm that he bears in his body "the marks of the Lord Jesus." These were the marks of conversion, commission, consecration.

1. Whatever else his enemies could say about him, they could not deny the fact of his conversion. Time and time again he alludes to his unforgettable experience on the road to Damascus where he became a changed man. From henceforth all his energy was expended in proclaiming the good news of the Christian faith.

Being a Christian means that Christ has left his mark upon us. We become changed. Our Christian profession makes a difference to us. Our thinking, conversation, and conduct testify to our having been with Jesus. Conversion means at least that. It may be sudden, immediate, as it was with Paul, or it may be gradual, as it was with Peter; the imperceptible result of a lifetime of real effort. But there can be no mistaking the true Christian.

2. After his conversion the Apostle was ever conscious that he was distinguished by the marks of commission. He realized for the first time that he was sent to preach, serve, and bear testimony to the Kingdom of God. He had been conscripted into the army of the living God. He had heard the clarion call to arms, and had been commissioned by the King of kings and Lord of lords. God had a purpose for him to fulfill, and Paul was ready to fight the good fight of faith.

Into that battle each of us is called upon to enter, for we too are commissioned by the Prince of Peace to act and serve on his behalf. Ours is the privilege to bear Chirst's name before men. Sometimes this privilege is given early in life, sometimes later, but the important matter is the quality of our obedience to the heavenly vision.

3. The quality of St. Paul's vision never faltered for he bore the marks of consecration. He threw himself unreservedly into his new religious convictions and spread them without fear or favor. His life was dedicated to God, set apart, declared to be sacred. His personal consecration was shown in his devotion to the word of God, his internal passion for souls, and his holy living. He confirmed by his life what he believed with his mind.

That is the type of Christian we need today. People who will live their lives on the principles that what they have and are is dedicated to God, so that anything that may contaminate their lives, impair the purity of their thoughts, or hinder the purposes of God, they courageously and steadfastly avoid.

The Festival of the Conversion of St. Paul is a reminder of the power of the Holy Spirit. We are celebrating not only a past event, but also a present power and reality. The Saviour who spoke to Paul can also speak to men and women today, and of course is doing so. —Norman Haddock.

**Suggested Texts and Themes from I Thessalonians**

An Ideal for a Church: "Remembering without ceasing your work of faith, and labour of love, and patience of hope in our Lord Jesus Christ. . . ." I Thess. 1:3.

A First-century Broadcast: "For from you sounded out the word of the Lord not only in Macedonia and Achaia, but also in every place your faith to God-ward is to spread abroad." I Thess. 1:8.

Magnificent Conversions: ". . . ye turned to God from idols to serve the living and true God." I Thess. 1:9.

Entrusted with the Gospel: ". . . we have been approved by God to be entrusted with the gospel. . . ." I Thess. 2:4 (R.S.V.).

A Two-handed Giver: I Thess. 2:8.

In a Noisy World: "And that ye study

to be quiet, and to do your own business, and to work with your own hands. . . ." I Thess. 4:11, 12.

## MIDWEEK FELLOWSHIP MEETING TOPIC

(Church Night or Suggested Sermon Subject)

**Theme: Unsalted Salt**

TEXT: "But if the salt hath lost its saltness. . . ."

I. Has the saltness gone out of the life of the Christian Church? Is the Church dominating the life of the world, or of the nations; are Christian ideals being incorporated into international law, industrial codes, economic administration, or personal lives? (Discussion point.)

II. Is it the simple fact that great masses of the people who belong to the Church have lost confidence in the effectiveness of spiritual forces? (Discussion point.)

III. The unsalting of the salt in the modern Christian Church is a result of our effort to live in two worlds at the same time.

IV. In emphasizing the love of God we must never fail to realize that just as his love is great so his moral demands are strict and exact.

Any Christian who allows his spiritual resources to be depleted betrays his country, himself, and his Christ.—Adapted from R. L. S.

## SUNDAY SCHOOL LESSON

**Jan. 19. The Church is a Fellowship. Acts 2:42-47; Rom. 15:1-9a. Background Scripture: Eph. 4:17-32.**

MEMORY VERSE: "Be kind to one another, tenderhearted, forgiving one another, as God in Christ forgave you." Eph. 4:32. (R.S.V.).

What, then, is the Church of Christ? We look back to its arrival of self-consciousness and classic self-expression in the New Testament. It is a *fellowship*—that is its distinctive note. It is a *divine* fellowship whose members are in living union with Jesus Christ, with his God and Father, and corporately possess his Holy Spirit. It is a *distinctive* fellowship, aware of its differentiation from the world of men by barriers as marked as those of race and nationality—"an elect race, a holy nation," with their citizenship in a heavenly commonwealth. It is an *inclusive* fellowship, embracing every life to which Jesus is Lord—a single living organism, from which it is impossble for a disciple of Christ to be severed as for foot or ear to dissociate itself from the body. It is a *visible* fellowship and a *realized* fellowship whose members show their oneness with one another in Christ by many tokens—the breaking of bread in communion with their Lord and with one another, right hands of fellowship for kindred tasks, hospitality to visiting believers, the use of personal gifts for the enrichment of the whole group, the attempt to embody brotherhood in a community life ruled by the spirit of love. It is a *priestly* fellowship, all of whose members have direct access to God as his friendly sons and daughters, and in whose collective life, as in a hallowed temple, God himself dwells. It is a *gifted* fellowship. The Holy Spirit bestows upon every member somewhat with which to serve, and it is his charism of leadership, recognized by the spiritually discerning Church, which impels the brotherhood to set apart a man for any distinctive ministry. It is an *authoritative* fellowship, in which as a theocracy God governs, through which as a brotherhood his will is discovered by the judgment of the whole fellowship, and by which that will is set forth to the world.

This fellowship, the Church of Christ, you and I are to build up, to serve, and to lead for the world's rebuilding.—Henry Sloane Coffin.

# SUNDAY: JANUARY TWENTY-SIXTH

## MORNING SERVICE

**Theme: Never Run Away**

SUGGESTED SCRIPTURE READING: Amos 5:1-20.

SELECTED HYMNS: "Give to the winds thy fears."—P. Gerhardt. "Fight the good fight."—J. B. S. Monsell. "True-hearted, whole-hearted, faithful and loyal."—F. R. Havergal. "Christian, seek not yet repose."—C. Elliott. "Awake, my soul, stretch every nerve."—P. Doddridge.

CALL TO WORSHIP: "One thing have I desired of the Lord, that will I seek after; that I may dwell in the house of the Lord all the days of my life, to behold the beauty of the Lord, and to inquire in his temple."

INVOCATION PRAYER: Eternal God, our heavenly Father, under the canopy of thy goodness we gather into thy house in faith and fellowship, lifting up our hearts in praise and thanksgiving and adoration. As each prays for all, grant that all may escape from the loneliness in which we live into the freedom of a common aspiration and the joy of a common communion. To thy greatness we bring our littleness; to thy power we bring our weakness; to thine abundant grace we bring our hearts to be healed and cleansed and made pure. Lord, the days are thine; the work is thine, we are thine. Teach us to adventure in thy name and to trust in thy truth. Amen.

**Theme: Never Run Away**

TEXT: "As if a man did flee from a lion, and a bear met him; or went into the house, and leaned his hand on the wall, and a serpent bit him." Amos 5:19.

INTRODUCTORY: What is this message? It is this: there is no security in running away. There is no satisfaction in running away. There is no sense in running away. Running away from a lion you get attacked by a bear. Running from the bear you get stung by a serpent. Here Amos is warning the rulers. The country was threatened by the enemy. Indecision, delayed action, appeasement, was their characteristic attitude. Amos rams home his message and his warning by this striking picture of the lion, the bear, and the serpent. All this is true to life. There is no security in running away, there is no satisfaction in running away, there is no sense in running away.

When we are speaking like this of running away we are thinking, of course, of the moral issues of life.

I. We run away usually because we are afraid, and life is full of things that frighten us. That is the testing time. What are we going to do, run away or stand our ground? Our text would tell us that if we shirk one responsibility we shall find another awaiting us around the corner. How true that is! Yes, life is full of things that frighten us. Responsibilities, crises, dangers real and imaginary. Here, then, is the message of Amos: Don't run away from the things in life that frighten.

II. Life, again, is full of things that threaten. There is no need to amplify this, for during the past few years we have experienced many threatening things. Our homes, our churches, our cities, even the very existence of the nation, have been threatened by the engines of war.

A parallel to all this may be found in the individual experience. Among the ingredients of life are those things which threaten our honor, our integrity, and our faith. Threats are sometimes used when people want to force us to do something which is dishonorable. Threats are also used sometimes to try to prevent our doing what is right.

Now to all this Amos would give one answer, and it is the same answer. As we must take our stand against the things that terrify, so we must stand out against the things that threaten. If we don't it will be a case again of the lion, the bear, and the serpent.

III. Life, again, is full of things that tempt us. This is the most insidious and deceptive aspect of all, for the amazing thing is that, though temptation can have an appalling and devastating effect upon character, it very seldom appears to terrify or threaten. On the contrary, it nearly always assumes a pleasing and fascinating appearance. The snare of the temptation lies in the fact that we want to do it, and do it in spite of our better nature. Everyone lies open to this. There is not a single soul upon God's earth who is exempt. Different kinds of temptation, of course. It would take too long to go through the whole catalogue. But the point is: what are we going to do about it? And Amos would say "Face up to them. Look them straight in the face. Remember the lion, the bear, and the serpent."

Here is where the example of Jesus points the way. In the wilderness he met his temptations face to face, looked at them straight, and smashed each one in turn as it came along. There is no other way.

IV. I don't want to overemphasize the somber aspects of life. On the other side of the picture, I know (and thank God, too), life is full of things that strengthen, encourage, uplift, things that make for peace, happiness, and beauty, but for all that it is well to remember that there are things that terrify, threaten, and tempt, and the old prophet Amos was right when he said that the only security and satisfaction came when we stood up to them.—W. J. L.

THEME PRAYER: Restrain us, our Father, from making flimsy excuses for lack of faith and action. Seal with thy blessing our worship here this day. Clothe us about with thy love. Protect us with thy grace. Keep our feet in the path of honorable service. And give us thine abiding peace. We ask in Jesus' name. Amen.

OFFERTORY SENTENCE: "Give, and it shall be given unto you: good measure, pressed down, and shaken together, and running over, shall men give into your bosom."

OFFERTORY PRAYER: Help us all to be great men and good, finding more joy in giving than in receiving, and always ready to prepare ourselves to help our fellow men. Bless us all, and bless our offering. Amen.—H.

SEED THOUGHTS:

Amos 5:19. It is said that a wilderness bear was more ferocious than a Jordan lion, the serpent's sting most deadly. Flee, and the worst is yet to come.—H.

This reinterpretation of the Day of the Lord was presented in a forceful simile rather than in words of precise description. Drawing upon his years of experience in the Judean wilds, Amos compared the happenings on that future day to an unsuccessful encounter with natural enemies. The element of inevitability was foremost in the illustration. Even though there had been several escapes in which the Israelites had taken satisfaction, a nation which had committed transgression so persistently was due to meet destruction. There also was a second point of emphasis in this figure, the observation that the doom would come when least expected. As the individual in question met it in the supposed safety of his own home, annihilation likewise would descend upon Israel in an unguarded moment.

Amos, as well as later prophets, envisioned the Day of the Lord as a time of victory for the Lord but not for the nation. Instead of a war in which the deity would annihilate Israel's enemies, the divine glory of the day would lie rather in the Lord's execution of judgment upon his own supposedly chosen people who had gone against him and wished to know nothing of right or morals.—Adapted from Rolland Emerson Wolfe.

### Choice Illustrations on the Theme

HOW RESIST TEMPTATION. In the annals of France is the story of the son of Louis XVI. As a young prince he was handed over to vicious men with the express command that they should wreck his character. The purpose was that he might, a child of royalty, become the mockery of the court. No boy, prince or pauper, has ever been brought face to face with such shamefulness as that to which the young prince was exposed. Unmentionable were the temptations placed in his path, indescribable the company into which he was thrown. But to all the young prince had only one answer to make: "I cannot do that for I am the son of a king." Make yourself a sharer in the aristocracy of God.—O. G. Herbrecht.

COURAGE AND FAITH. The great Baptist pioneer in Germany, Pastor Oncken, suffered much in his younger days for the truth's sake, both fines and imprisonment. One of his great stories was that of the burgomaster of Hamburg, who held up his finger and said: "You see that finger? So long as that can move, I will put you down." "Sir," said Oncken, "I see your finger, but I also see an Arm which you do not see, and so long as that is stretched out you cannot put me down."—*Christian Herald.*

## EVENING SERVICE

### Theme: Open the Eyes to See

TEXT: "And Elisha prayed, and said, Lord, I pray thee, open his eyes that he may see," etc. II Kings 6:17.

INTRODUCTORY: Elisha had often been in peril, but never so hard besed as now. He was alone with his servant on the hill encompassed by the Syrian Army. His servant was sore afraid. Escape seemed to be impossible. He cried out in despair, "Alas! Master, how shall we do?" And then the prophet prayed, and the servant's eyes were opened, and he saw that the mountain where they stood was full of horses and chariots of fire. Round him was an unseen world, though he had never known it till that moment. Between him and the Syrian Army was the flaming chariotry of heaven. It is a picture of that spiritual environment which encircles every one of us, though we never see it till our eyes are opened.

I. One immediate effect of such a vision would be to make the place where he was wonderful. He would feel, like Moses at the burning bush, that it was holy ground. It was only a bare hilltop, swept by every wind, and very desolate. It was rough and wild and rude, with boulders tossed as by a giant's hand. And then the vision came to his blind eyes, and that so dreary and depressing place was filled with the wonder of heaven. It is always so with spiritual vision. It redeems and glorifies the commonplace. It illuminates the daily round, sheds the radiance of hope on suffering, touches as with the light of heaven the daily cross we have to carry.

II. But not only did it irradiate his station; it filled his trembling heart with hope and courage. It assured him he could be more than conqueror, though everything was dark and difficult. When he saw nothing but the Syrian Army, he was brought to the extremity of fear. The encompassing hosts appeared to be invincible. Then broke on his vision the spiritual environment, and in a moment he was a different man. Hope returned like the dove into the ark. He plucked up heart again and was a man, where an hour before he had been cowardly. And whenever you and I, with opened eyes, realize that God is round about us, the same thing happens to this day. We begin to see that "they who are with us are greater than they who are with them." We begin to see we can do all things through Christ who strengtheneth us. So peace returns, and quiet confidence.

III. One should notice that this vision came in the hour of that young man's extremity. It was given when the worst came to the worst. Not when everything was well with him did this rescuing and redeeming vision come. And how often has God used that season to give the soul that vision. When vain is the help of man and human hope is gone; when we have made an utter tangle of our lives and there seems no eye to pity and no arm to save, how often are men wakened to feel that God is near, as with horses and chariots of fire.

IV. Nor must we forget that this uplifting vision was bestowed on one who was a servant. It is the splendid democracy of heaven. There are visions of the beauty of the world that are only granted to the poet. There are visions of the wonder of creation that are only witnessed by the man of science. But the vision of God and of his saving might, and of the unseen powers that guard and guide, that was given to the prophet's servant. You may have it, though no one calls you clever, though you know little science, and were not born a poet. You may have it though your lot be commonplace and your work a constant round of petty things—the sense of God, the assurance of his nearness, in the love and conquering power of the Lord Jesus—the vision of the chariots of fire. That makes all the difference to us, as it did to the young servant of Elisha. Lord! open the the blind eyes that they may see.—M.

**Suggested Texts and Themes**

The By-products of Life: "And I have also given thee that which thou hast not asked." I Kings 3:13.

The Obligation of Opportunity: "By reason of the time ye ought to be teachers." Heb. 5:12.

Omnipotence Limited: "And he did not many mighty works there because of their unbelief." Matt. 13:58.

Love's Delay: "Now Jesus loved Martha, and her sister, and Lazarus. When therefore he heard that he was sick, he abode at that time two days in the place where he was." John 11:5, 6.

The Illumination of a Crisis: "In the year that King Uzziah died I saw also the Lord sitting upon a throne, high and lifted up, and his train filled the temple." Isa. 6:1.

## MIDWEEK FELLOWSHIP MEETING TOPIC

(Church Night or Suggested Sermon Subject)

**Theme: Worship and the Good Life**

TEXT: "They that wait upon the Lord shall renew their strength; they shall mount up with wings as eagles; they shall run, and not be weary, and they shall walk, and not faint." Isa. 40:31.

"They shall mount up with wings as eagles"—they shall meet with adequacy the extraordinary mountain-peak experiences of life; "they shall run and not be weary"—they shall handle without wilting life's unusual demands; "they shall walk and not faint"—they shall face with radiance the routine details of daily life. Such is the contribution of worship to life and service for those who have learned its art.

I. A life grows *inwardly*. "Life begins from within." And worship is one of the needed experiences for this growth. A person of disciplined resourcefulness is required to respond to human need. Only an all-round person can render permanently effective service. To give oneself through service is part of the difference between social welfare professionally done and Christian service personally rendered. The gift without the giver is bare. But to have a real self worth giving is our consideration at this point.

II. A good life grows *outwardly*. "A man is the part he plays among his fellow men." Life is a matter of relationships from cradle to grave. So a man to be truly useful must get on with people—not merely get by. His service, therefore, rests in large measure upon his capacity for fellowship, for understanding, for co-operation. Among the experiences that may awaken and enlarge this capacity is worship.

III. A good life grows *upwardly*. This dimension deals with his reverences which early or late fix the texture of his daily work and service. Worship is the cultivation of these reverences. These reverences are another way of describing the center of gravity in a man's soul. And there seem to be but three possible centers.

One may be *crowd-centered*. One may be *self-centered*. Or a man may be *God-centered*.

To practice the presence of God in Jesus Christ through private and public worship is the most effective way to touch life at every possible point and let God touch us at every point. Thus the big word of life is not *requirement* but *resource*. And God has made is so that we may tap his resources in worship for strong character and effective service.—Adapted from Oscar F. Blackwelder.

## SUNDAY SCHOOL LESSON

**Jan. 26. The Church Organizes for Service. Rom. 12:3-8; I Tim. 3:1-10. Background Scripture: Acts 6:1-7.**

MEMORY VERSE: "Take heed to yourselves and to all the flock, in which the Holy Spirit has made you guardians, to feed the church of the Lord which he obtained with his own blood." Acts 20:28.

I. What is the purpose of church organization? Is the correct answer given in the title of the lesson? Does our church organization fulfill its purpose?

II. What should be the qualifications for church leadership? Do the qualifications given in the Scripture lessons apply today?

III. What is our local church doing to develop adequate and efficient leadership? Our church requires a minister or ministers; have we ever raised up a minister or ministers for the church?

# SUNDAY: FEBRUARY SECOND

## MORNING SERVICE

**Theme: To Learn the Joy of Living**

SUGGESTED SCRIPTURE READING: Matt. 5:1-16.

SELECTED HYMNS: "For the beauty of the earth."—F. S. Pierpoint. "Dear Lord and Father of mankind."—J. G. Whittier. "Jesus the very thought of thee."—Bernard of Clairvaux. "Rejoice, ye pure in heart."—Edward H. Plumptre.

CALL TO WORSHIP: "Rejoice in the Lord alway: . . ." Phil. 4:4-7.

INVOCATION: As we come into thy house, O God, we would render unto thee praise and thanksgivings because of thy kind providence, thine unceasing goodwill, thy great and abundant salvation, and thine own presence through thy Holy Spirit.

By means of song and reading from thy Word, through offering and sermon, by our fellowship with one another and by the manner of our daily lives, help us to show our devotion unto thee —a devotion not forced from us by thy power, but won from us by thy love.—H.

**Theme: To Learn the Joy of Living**

TEXT: "I am come that they might have life, and that they might have it more abundantly." John 10:10.

"I am come," said Jesus, "that they might have life." By these words he did not mean a barren, empty, profitless existence. He meant a special quality of life, the life more abundant. Jesus was constantly talking about life and how to live it. "Life" was one of his favorite words. "I am the way, the truth, and the life." "Ye will not come to me that ye might have life." "He that saveth his life shall lose it."

I. The desire for life is strong in human beings. Everyone longs for life. They want really to live. People will cling to life even in the midst of squalor or of constant pain. Tennyson sings:

'Tis life of which our nerves are scant
'Tis life not death for which we pant
More life and fuller that we want.

Yes, everyone longs for life, and yet how sadly we blunder and fumble with this precious gift of God. We are often poles removed from the kind of life which Jesus has shown us how to live. Here is the distinction as Jesus made it: Life is not to be measured by years, by its duration, but by its quality.

This is the central theme of Jesus' Sermon on the Mount. The purpose of that sermon was to teach men and women how to live. He said: "Blessed are the meek"; "Blessed are the merciful." That word "blessed" can with equal accuracy be translated "happy" or "joyous." It means this as well as signifying "holy" or "consecrated." So what Jesus said was "Happy are the meek"; "Happy are the humble"; "Happy are the merciful." He was affirming that life may be lived joyously. He saw people around him every day eagerly searching for happiness. They were all looking in the wrong direction. They were looking everywhere but in the place where true happiness may be found. They were unable to see that it is not what you have that produces happiness, but what you are. The happiness produced solely by what you have is a short-lived happiness. Only the satisfaction and happiness produced by what you are endures.

II. Now let us look at the characteristics which Jesus says produces the joy of living. They are not such as most people would enumerate. Freely translated they are these. "Happy are the humble"; "Happy are the spiritually hungry, for they shall be satisfied"; "Happy are the merciful, for they shall obtain mercy"; "Happy are the pure in heart, for they shall see God"; "Happy are the peacemakers, for they shall be called the children of God"; "Happy are they who are persecuted for their uprightness, for God himself shall be their reward."

III. "I am come," said Jesus, "that they might have life." He leads us into a finer, deeper, richer quality of life that death is powerless to end. Life is very precious, because in a way it is the only thing we really possess. We have other things. We call them possessions—property, investments, wealth—but we don't really possess these things. We have a temporary lease of them. There is no one who really owns any of these things. A lot of people think they own them, yet these things are not a part of the real self. A day will come when they will be divested of them all, like the man in Jesus' parable who heard echoing through the chambers of his soul the voice of God: "This night thy soul shall be required of thee. Then whose shall those things be which thou hast provided?"

The only real thing we possess is the self, the personality, the soul. All other things are temporary. Those who live for temporal things with neglect of the eternal are forgetful of the fact that one day they will stand in the presence of the eternal God who will ask: "What did you make of it?" "He will not be talking of things; he will be talking about your life. What did you make of life? Are your fellowmen any happier or better because you passed this way?"

IV. What have you made of your life? What have you done with it? What have you contributed to the world? Have you lifted the world ever so little toward God or have you pushed it down toward hell? Have you been self-centered, self-seeking, self-indulgent? Has your little ego been in the center of the stage? If so, God help you. You will feel pitifully small in eternity when the real values of life will shine like burnished gold.

Whether we have lived or half lived, life is passing swiftly by. Let us follow the advice of St. Paul and redeem the time. Whatever is left to us of life let us invest in the things that do not perish by the using. Let us seek first God's Kingdom. Schweitzer says that the love of Christ can sweep a man and a woman into a new course of life. Yes, it can do that for us now.

So I leave now this message with you: "Let God have your life. He can do more with it than you can." Then you will know the joy of living, the poise and the peace that come to those whose lives are surrendered to him. Then you won't need to worry about those twin enemies of man, worry and fear. You will never be anxious for the morrow. You will let yesterday go, and you will be satisfied to wait until tomorrow comes, because everything beyond your control will be yielded into the hands of God. Let God have your life. You will be amazed at what he can do with it. Then at last when the sun is beginning to set and the shadows are lengthening from the west, and the earth and earthly things are drifting forever from your sight, you will have the unspeakable happiness of seeing the Master come to welcome you and will hear him say, "Well done, good and faithful servant, enter thou into the joy of the Lord."—John S. Bonnell.

A Prayer for the Day: Our loving Father, as we gather together to worship on this first day of the week, bring unto our remembrance the fact that every Sabbath is a token of Easter and proclaims the glad news that ours is a living Christ.

Help us to remember, too, O God, that our worship is a proclamation of our faith, a testimony to others that Christ is their Lord and Saviour, as well as our own. Help us to worship so sincerely and effectively that our proclamation may be heard and accepted by those who have never given him their loyalty.

We bring unto thee, O Lord, all our human affairs, the matters that pertain to our personal lives, our homes, our vocations, our responsibilities as citizens of the state, the country and the world, and in them we pray thy Spirit to guide us, to teach us, and to bless us. In our experiences of joy or sorrow, loss or gain, success or failure, fortune or misfortune, grant us thy presence and blessing. Amen.—H.

Offeratory Sentence: "Remember the words of the Lord Jesus, how he said, It is more blessed to give than to receive." Acts 20:35.

Offeratory Prayer: Ever blessed God, Source of all light and truth, Giver of every joy, we lift glad hearts to thee, as we remember that thou dost call us to be fellow workers with thyself in the salvation of the world; and to that end dost entrust us with material possessions, that we may use them as stewards of thy love. Grant that the devotion of our lives may follow the gifts we now make in this house of thy worship, and grant also that these gifts may accomplish much in bringing thy light, thy truth, and thy joy to all mankind, through Jesus Christ our Saviour. Amen.—J. G. K. M.

Seed Thoughts:

Life: How Long? or How Much?

"The Inexhaustible Interest of Life." —Phillips Brooks.

Some Qualities of the Abundant Life: I. It admires more eagerly; II. It hopes more persistently; III. It loves more ardently.

"Our Lord claims: I. To inspire the minds of men; II. To enrich the emotions of men; III. To bring abundant life in terms of action."—Hugh T. Kerr.

And when we come into communion with the Lord, who came that we might have life, and that we might have it more abundantly, we know it, we know it as a reality which cannot be questioned. We know it in richer fullness of being. We know it in new avenues of relation. We know it in new discernments. We know it in new delights. We know it in new griefs. We know it in the new goals and the new roads to reach them. We know it in new points of view and in new outlooks. We know it in new correspondences with God, and man, and the natural world. We know it because we have a new heaven and a new earth.—J. H. Jowett.

**Choice Illustrations on the Theme**

LIFE IS NOT DURATION. A few years ago in the State prison in Trenton, New Jersey, there was a familiar personality whose first name was Archie. He was known to everyone there, having spent thirty-three years in that institution. The newspapers gave him considerable publicity on his eighty-third birthday. The reason for all the notoriety was a consuming fear which dogged him—the fear that he might contract a cold and die. Consequently there were two things he would not do. First, during all his years in the penitentiary he would never take a walk in the yard to get fresh air and sunshine, lest he might pick up some germs. In the second place, he received no visitors through all those years. They might be carriers of bacteria.

No one could recall that he had ever done anything constructive or that in his whole lifetime any human being had become better or happier because Archie had passed that way. He managed to live fourscore and three years. His whole achievement was the duration of his life.

Of course, he had plenty of rivals for that form of greatness. I recall that in the Tower of London the guide pointed very proudly to a raven that was perched on a turret. It looked rather seedy and the worse for wear. He said that the bird was probably over a hundred years old. Archie was only eighty-three. They both had endured. They both could boast of longevity. Contrast for just a moment Archie's eighty-three years with Henry Drummond's forty-six or Raphael's thirty-seven or Jesus' thirty-three! —John S. Bonnell.

LET GOD HAVE YOUR LIFE. In the year 1894 a young man fourteen years of age attended college in Louisville. One day he attended a public meeting. There were thousands of people there. It was an evangelistic service. The youth looked at the speaker on the platform. He was a heavy-set man wearing a Prince Albert coat. His brown beard was beginning to be flecked with gray. His eyes were bright and searching. He began to speak, and his words went right into the heart of this fourteen-year-old young student. "Let God have your life." The speaker was Dwight L. Moody. These same words Moody had uttered in a hall in London where Wilfred Grenfell, the young medical student, was seated. Grenfell said to one of his fellow students: "I am going to see what a Yankee evangelist looks like." Moody said: "Let God have your life. He can do more with it than you can." Out of that meeting Grenfell passed a new man, completely dedicated to God, and destined to become the great Sir Wilfred Grenfell of the Labrador.

Moody used the same words in Louisville, Kentucky. The found lodgment in the heart of this fourteen-year-old boy, and he said: "Here am I God. I give my life to you." That fourteen-year-old youth became the Rev. Joseph Fort Newton, whose life's service in the ministry of Christ has brought spiritual enrichment to multitudes on both sides of the Atlantic Ocean.—J. S. B.

## EVENING SERVICE

**Theme: "Speak unto Us Smooth Things"**

TEXT: ". . . children that will not hear the law of the Lord: which say to the seers, See not; and to the prophets, Prophesy not unto us right things, speak unto us smooth things, prophesy deceits." Isa. 30:9-10.

Human nature changes slowly, Isaiah might have been speaking to our generation when he spoke of those who say to the seers, "see not" and to the prophets "prophesy not unto us right things, speak unto us smooth things, prophesy deceits."

I. It is a natural human desire to hear smooth, easy, pleasant things. It is a severe test continually to ask ourselves, "Do I really want to know the truth with all that it implies of conviction and action on my part, or do I want to hear smooth things that will justify me in an easier, more selfish course?" When our seers see, and our prophets tell us of right things, if these truths do not square with our own programs, it is much easier to say, "Oh, he's a crank and a trouble-maker." And so we bid our prophets tell us of smooth things, and if they will not do so, we stone them and seek false prophets who will.

II. It is easy to find men and women of place and authority who will tell us smooth things. No matter what form of wickedness or selfishness one wishes to engage in, there are plenty of so-called prophets and seers who will rise up and justify it both by spoken and written word. Magazines and books teem with plausible doctrines to justify every form of human degradation. We say to our prophets, "Tell us only smooth things." Unless these prophets are made of iron, they succumb to this universal demand.

III. Not only in the realm of material things, but in the spiritual realm, we demand prophets who will tell us what we want to hear: "One can worship just as well on the golf course, in the woods, or at the shore." Smooth words, these, that help to empty our churches.

As a nation we have not listened to the truth about the degrading influence of many motion pictures, television and radio programs, but to the smooth words, "You can't do anything about it—don't bother—and anyway it's better for people to be primitive and get their emotional release vicariously than personally." So the false prophets continue to justify weakness and make us comfortable.

IV. We shall never recover from the long moral decline in which we have bogged down until we stop rewarding the false prophets who tell us "smooth things" and "prophesy deceit" and listen to the prophets of God who preach repentance, forgiveness, salvation, and restitution. When men and women are born again, they no longer demand "smooth things" but face the facts with resolute determination to live in accordance with the moral laws as illuminated by the love of our Lord Jesus Christ.—*Christian Economics.*

**Suggested Texts and Themes**

Two sources of Strength: ". . . in quietness and confidence shall be your strength." Isa. 30:15.

The Pre-eminence of Human Values: "How much then is a man better than a sheep?" Matt. 12:12.

Our Lost Sense of Sin: "Were they not ashamed when they had committed abomination? nay, they were not at all ashamed, neither could they blush." Jer. 6:15.

Can You Take It?: "If thou hast run with the footmen, and they have wearied thee, then how canst thou contend with horses? . . ." Jer. 12:5.

Faith's Daring: "And straightway the father of the child cried out, and said with tears, Lord, I believe; help thou mine unbelief." Mark 9:24.

## MIDWEEK FELLOWSHIP MEETING TOPIC

(Church Night or Suggested Sermon Subject)

**Theme: Love Conquers Sin**

TEXT: "He was manifested to take away our sins." I John 3:5.

Sin is represented in the Bible as an active, malignant, blighting, death-dealing force in human life. Our experience with sin and our observation of its workings confirm the charges brought against it by the Bible. Sin enters the heart of man and contaminates his emotions; it invades his intellect and warps his judgment; it masters the will and determines the decisions and choices; it degrades the physical senses until they hunger for the satisfactions of sinful delights.

I. John gives us the only remedy that has ever been provided to remove sin from the human heart and life: "He was manifested to take away our sins." The purpose was not merely to curb sin, limit its activities, or even punish its deeds, but to remove it and cleanse the life of its blight. A young man once remarked: "My brother has a sin which only the grace of God can cure." Only the grace of God through Christ can conquer sin in us and free us from its domination.

II. This word "manifested" calls attention to our part in becoming free from our sins. Jesus died for our sins; that was a work which he alone could do. He arose for our justification; no one else could do that. He is now at the right hand of God interceding for us; no one else can fill that place. These functions belong exclusively to him.

But he was manifested, made known, for the purpose of taking away our sins; and he alone can do that. But in the word "manifested" the emphasis is upon our seeing what is revealed and the response we make to that vision. There can be no manifestation unless there is an eye to see what is made plain and a response of appreciation for what the eye sees. Hence the vision of Christ is intended to loosen us from allegiance to sin and awaken in us a desire for the life which we see in him.

III. In the manifested Christ we see: Love wounded by our sins, the kind of man or woman we may become without sin, the power which will enable us to be like him.

"Whosoever committeth sin transgresseth also the law; for sin is the transgression of the law. And ye know that he was manifested to take away our sins; and in him is no sin: I John 3:4, 5. —B. H. Duncan.

## BULLETIN BOARD SLOGANS FOR THE MONTH

Pitch life high.

Time is a ship that never anchors.

Let your anchor firmly grip the truth.

He failed! He left God out of his plans.

He succeeded. He let God into his plans.

He has bad food who feeds on others' faults.

"With malice toward none, with charity for all."—Abraham Lincoln.

"A nation is great, and only as great as her rank and file."—Woodrow Wilson.

"I will let no man drag me down so low as to make me hate him."—Booker T. Washington.

"Show not yourself glad at the misfortune of another though he were your enemy."—George Washington.

## SUNDAY SCHOOL LESSON

**Feb. 2. The Privilege of Church Membership. I Pet. 2:9-10; II Cor. 9:6-8; Gal. 6:1-5; Heb. 4:14-16; 10:23-25.**

MEMORY VERSE: "You are a chosen race, a royal priesthood, a holy nation, God's own people, that you may declare the wonderful deeds of him who called you out of darkness into his marvelous light." I Pet. 2:9 (R.S.V.)

Most interesting comment can be made on this lesson by noting the change from the King James Version, in which I Pet. 2:9 contains the phrase "a peculiar people," to the Revised Standard Version which has "God's own people." In fact both phrases mean the same thing. Back in King James' time "a peculiar" was a private possession. A man's peculiar was a man's own private property; God's peculiars were those who belonged to him. Note that the Latin word for money is *pecunia*.

I. Church membership should mean the privilege of being God's own possession. We are in "peculiar" relationship to him as his children. What other privileges are involved in this?

II. Such privileges carry with them responsibilities. A man may be very strong on his privileges but rather weak in taking up responsibilities.

III. What are the ways by which a church member can express his gratitude for his privileges and discharge their accompanying responsibilities? (It should be noted that the lesson of Feb. 23 stresses "Worship" and that of March 30 the "Sacraments"; they need not be mentioned here.)

# SUNDAY: FEBRUARY NINTH

This is the Sunday before the birthday of Abraham Lincoln, the sixteenth President of the United States of America. He was born on February 12, 1809. Many ministers in the United States preach annually, on the Sunday nearest Lincoln's Birthday, on a theme related to the life of Lincoln. Below is a suggestion for a Lincoln sermon.

## MORNING SERVICE

### Theme: A Man of Faith

SUGGESTED SCRIPTURE READING: Selected verses from Heb. 11. Ecclus. (Apocrypha) 44 is a reading appropriate for the day.

SELECTED HYMNS: "God of our fathers, whose almighty hand."—Daniel C. Roberts. "In Christ there is no East or West."—John Oxenham. "My country, 'tis of thee."—Samuel F. Smith. "O beautiful for spacious skies."—Katharine Lee Bates. "Be strong! We are not here to play."—Maltbie D. Babcock.

CALL TO WORSHIP: "Let us now praise famous men, and our fathers who begat us. The Lord manifested in them great glory, even his mighty power from the beginning."

INVOCATION: We praise thee, O God, for thou dost hear and answer prayer. We rejoice this day to worship with memories in our hearts of men who lifted their voices in prayer unto thee. Because they prayed and because thou didst grant thy favor unto them and those for whom they prayed, we enter into our marvelous heritage.

Especially do we thank thee for that heroic figure whose birthday we remember at this season of the year. We are glad for the name of Abraham Lincoln to hand down to our children and children's children. We rejoice in his exemplification of kindness, honesty, humility, and love of humanity. We pray that we may be enabled to emulate him in all his virtues. In Jesus' name. Amen.—H.

### Theme: The Faith of Lincoln

TEXT: "What shall we then say to these things? If God be for us, who can be against us?" Rom. 8:31.

When American democracy is being tested the faith of Lincoln may well guide leaders and people. Lincoln's faith combined a tough realism and a sane liberalism.

I. Despite the long years of struggle that threatened to dissolve our nation, Lincoln never lost faith in the essential goodness of men. It was a faith in the "equality before God of all his creatures." It was a faith that God created man in his own image. It led Lincoln to recognize the free will of the people as the medium of divine revelation.

In the midst of the terrible conflict, Lincoln never despaired. He always knew that the cause of God would be carried out by his earthly emissaries, the people. In his First Inaugural Address in 1861, he said: "If the Almighty Ruler of nations with his eternal truth and justice, be on your side of the North or on yours of the South, that truth and justice will surely prevail, by the judgment of this great tribunal, the American people."

"He was a tough-minded liberal realist. The liberal must have a stout heart. It demands a facing up to hard realities and a moral force that is proof against discouragement."

II. The evidence shows that Lincoln unhesitatingly put all his trust in God. This faith came from his boyhood training, for as he says: "I was early brought up to the reflection that nothing in my power would succeed without the direct assistance of the Almighty."

When Lee at the time of military successes for the South crossed the Potomac, Lincoln went to his room, got down on his knees and prayed. He tells us himself: "Never before had I prayed with so much earnestness. I wish I could repeat my prayer. I felt I must put all my trust in Almighty God. He gave our people the best country ever given to man. He alone could save it from destruction. I had tried my best to do my duty and had found myself unequal to the task. The burden was more than I could bear. I asked him to help us and give us victory now. I was sure my prayer was answered. I had no misgivings about the result of Gettysburg."

Lincoln knew that we cannot face life alone and without faith. A friend tells of coming on Lincoln on his knees and in complete submission, praying earnestly. On another occasion he was overheard praying: "I cannot guide the affairs of this Nation without Thy help . . . O God! who didst hear Solomon when he cried for wisdom, hear me and save this Nation!"—George R. Grose.

A Prayer for the Day: Hear our prayer, O Lord, for this country, so marvelously served by Abraham Lincoln, and which as citizens we hold in our hearts. We are glad to review thy Providence in preparing this land to become the dwelling-place of our people, in the events of its discovery and settlement by men and women who put their trust in thee. We believe it to be thy will that we should be a free people, a righteous people, and a people destined to serve the nations of the earth. The prayer of our hearts is that we may know and follow thy will. Amen—H.

Offeratory Sentence: "The liberal deviseth liberal things; and by liberal things shall he stand." Isa. 32:8.

Offeratory Prayer: As we bring our offering today we thank thee, O God, for the happiness of our earthly life, for peaceful homes and healthful days, for our powers of mind and body, for faithful friends and for the joy of loving and being loved. We pray that these blessings may come to abound throughout all the world and to all people. In the name of Christ. Amen.

Seed Thoughts:

"God designed us for greatness."

"Some men become magnificient under pressures of necessity."

God wants us to be great, for there is another world which lies ahead of this one in which greatness will be required of us if we are to enjoy the full favor of God and all the blessedness of communion and fellowship with him.—Roy L. Smith.

They Will Survive. True greatness survives. There are qualities of the human spirit that are indestructible. "Courage and sacrifice glow with a new light in the midst of the blackouts of hope. Faith gallantly rides the whirlwind sweeping the earth. You cannot cut down the clouds."

## Choice Illustrations on the Theme

OUR RELIANCE AND DEFENSE. What constitutes the bulwark of our liberty and independence? It is not our frowning battlements, our bristling seacoast, our army and navy. These are not our reliance against tyranny. All of these may be turned against us without making us weaker for the struggle. Our reliance is in the love of liberty which God has planted in us. Our defense is in the spirit which prizes liberty as the heritage of all men, in all lands everywhere."—Abraham Lincoln.

NEW NATIONAL HEROES. As long as wars were small affairs, our national heroes were often the men who had led us to victory. But now with the enlargement, multiplicity, and diversity of atomic weapons, war is a vast all-consuming enterprise, and as in a plane wreck at 500 miles per hour—with little chance for survival. Any fool can become arrogant, impatient, and declare that now is the time for action and no more sense in talking things over.

The courage needed today is actually much greater than in the past, for it is a lonely kind of courage that can hear the strident cry of the self-seeking politicians and not become confused or impatient; that can hear the demands of the populace, realizing they are not aware of the consequence of their passion.

There were times when President Eisenhower stood more alone, more beset by terrible pressures, more needful of courage—than he ever was in battle. The courage to seek peace is sometimes greater than that which wins battles. With God's help we must win the peace, for no one can win a modern war.—C. A. Wells.

WE WILL MAKE PEACE. A British officer had been sent forward in some fighting with the Zulus leading a contingent of men. The Zulus sent out a messenger of peace. By an unhappy blunder the British outposts shot him. The British officer was greatly distressed. So he handed over the contingent to the second in command, and walked straight out, unarmed, to the Zulu lines. He was led to the chief.

"I have come," he said, "to give myself up because we shot your peace messenger by mistake. It is a thing brave warriors never do. I am very sorry. To make amends I place my life in your hands; do with me as you will."

The Zulu warrior chief was silent for a moment, then he said: "You are a man, and your people are men, and the sons of men; we too are men. We will make peace."—Quoted by J. H. Oldham from Sir Frank Benson.

## EVENING SERVICE

### Theme: Prayer and Action in Race Relations

TEXT: "And he said unto them, This kind can come forth by nothing, but by prayer and fasting." Mark 9:29.

The disciples had tried to cure the lad (Mark 9:17-29) but had failed. Jesus appeared upon the scene and cured him. When they had opportunity in private the disciples asked him, "Why could we not cure the child?" Jesus answered, "This kind can come forth by nothing, but by prayer and fasting."

All will admit that the problem of race relations is a most serious one in the world. To solve it will require wisdom and patience and creative imagination far more than we seem to have at the present time. We can scarcely take it for granted that all Christian people desire equality and liberty and justice for all. But let us assume that we have Christian goals. What can we do to reach them?

I. First, we can pray. 1. We can pray as individuals. We can carry this matter into our secret places of meditation and petition and intercession. It is there that we receive wisdom, patience, and grace. There, too, we may receive a discipline of mind and heart and soul which will prepare us for effective action.

2. We can pray together in our churches. But how can we pray, really pray, in spirit and in truth, when men and women of other races than our own are barred from the church or are ungraciously received?

3. We can pray with the men and women of other races. We can welcome them and be welcomed by them in their churches, in our churches, and bow together in humble prayer. Here is an example of a prayer we might pray together. It is adapted from a prayer by Harry Emerson Fosdick.

"For the brotherhood of many races and peoples that exists among us, we praise thee, O God. From the ends of the earth thou hast brought to our land the children of many nations. Help us more worthily to blend them into one family, to love them as one fraternity, to serve them without prejudice, and to make of them one people whose God is the Lord. Through Jesus Christ, our Lord. Amen."

II. Secondly, we can exercise self-discipline. "This kind can come forth by nothing, but by prayer and fasting," said Jesus. Let us take fasting as suggestive of self-discipline. 1. Many will need self-discipline more worthily to blend ourselves and others into one family. It requires self-discipline to make the brotherhood of man more than a phrase.

2. Self-discipline may be needed that we may love all our fellows, whatever kind or color, as one fraternity. A cer-

tain type of romantic sentimentalist may laugh at the suggestion of learning to love by self-discipline. But read concerning love, concerning *agapé,* as described in I Cor. 13, and realize that love in many respects can be learned and made a personal attainment.

3. "To serve without prejudice" is another phrase from Dr. Fosdick's prayer. It is here that we have the most difficulty with ourselves. It is here that we must take ourselves in hand. It is a hard road that lies ahead, but we must walk in it until we come through.

4. Self-discipline is needed to make of us all one people whose God is the Lord. Self-discipline leads to self-denial, to self-sacrifice, unto the building of the Kingdom throughout the whole world, the world near by and the world far away. In this modern age there is really no world far away. We must become Christian world-brotherhood people, all of us children of God.

III. Thirdly, we can act. How futile our prayers, if we do not seek to answer them ourselves! God acts through us. What purpose in self-discipline if we do not exert ourselves where our achievement of character and ability is needed? Self-discipline for its own sake is of doubtful value. In fact it is almost impossible.

1. How shall we act? What shall we do? Some need to begin with the practice of just ordinary decency and courtesy toward men and women of other races.

2. We can be careful of our speech.

3. We should show no discrimination against another race or people and we should seek to break down all discriminations and all barriers between the races.

4. We should use positive means to answer the prayer given above.—H.

**Suggested Texts and Themes**

Their Pains Are in Our Hearts: "Remember them that are in bonds, as bound with them; and them which suffer adversity, as being yourselves also in the body." Heb. 13:3.

Those with Their Backs to the Wall: "Out of the depths have I cried unto thee, O Lord." Ps. 130:1.

The Art of Noticing: "But a certain Samaritan, as he journeyed, came where he was: and when he saw him, he had compassion on him." Luke 10:33.

The Sin of Indifference: "And by chance there came down a certain priest that way: and when he saw him, he passed by on the other side." Luke 10:31.

Dissipating the Moral Haze: Isa. 32:1-8.

## MIDWEEK FELLOWSHIP MEETING TOPIC

(Church Night or Suggested Sermon Subject)

**Theme: An Emergency of Embarrassment**

TEXT: John 2:1-11.

The Midweek Themes for this and the six following weeks are taken from the Gospel of John. They are related to the seven miracles of the Gospel and are stated as emergencies which were met by Jesus. The first is that of the wedding at Cana of Galilee—*an emergency of embarrassment.*

I. Did Jesus perform this miracle only to relieve the embarrassment of a wedding party? Perhaps there was more to it than that, but this was indeed a serious matter, the failure of the wine, in this Oriental household. It was a serious matter to the servants of the household and to Mary. How did she come to learn about it? Fortunately the word had not been passed to the governor of the feast, and certainly not to the bride and groom.

II. It was a "sweet miracle." Hospitality in those days was a sacred thing and for Jesus to turn water into wine was to save that household from a disgrace that they could never live down nor forget.

III. It was a miracle performed that men might keep the joys of life. Jesus shares our joys and adds to them.

IV. Jesus is the transformer of life.

He may find our embarrassments occasions to transform ordinary water into extraordinary wine. How often has he changed dull, boring, insipid, tasteless life into shining, satisfying, salted life, life full of the flavor of meaning and purpose!

V. The wonder of this miracle is expressed in the eleventh verse: "This beginning of miracles did Jesus in Cana of Galilee, and manifested his glory, and his disciples believed on him." Has Jesus ever been asked, been permitted, to make of your embarrassing need an occasion for manifesting his glory?—H.

## SUNDAY SCHOOL LESSON

**Feb. 9. The Church Teaches the Word. I Tim. 4:6-16; II Tim. 2:1-2; Background Scripture: II Tim. 3:10-17.**

MEMORY VERSE: "Take heed to yourself and to your teaching; hold to that, for by so doing you will save both yourself and your hearers." I Tim. 4:16.

I. Teaching is enjoined by Christ in his Great Commission. Matt. 28:19-20.

II. Teaching early became an activity of the Church. New converts "continued steadfastly in the apostles' doctrine." Acts 2:42. The word *doctrine* implies teaching.

III. The teaching ministry of the Church has brought about the establishment of the Christian schools and colleges throughout the world.

IV. The local church has a teaching function. In connection with this lesson the local church might be given some study. 1. How is it organized for teaching? 2. What is the content of its teaching? 3. Whom does it teach? 4. Is it effective in its teaching function? Does it train its teachers? 5. What about its alliances with the home and the public schools? There are many pertinent questions which can be asked with profit, if the issue is not mere discussion but action to improve the situation.

# SUNDAY: FEBRUARY SIXTEENTH

## MORNING SERVICE

**Theme: As Regards Brotherly Love**

SUGGESTED SCRIPTURE READING: I Cor. 13.

SELECTED HYMNS: "Love divine, all loves excelling."—Charles Wesley. "O Master, let me walk with thee."—Washington Gladden. "When thy heart, with joy o'erflowing."—T. C. Williams. "At length there dawns the glorious day."—Ozora S. Davis.

CALL TO WORSHIP: "Behold, bless ye the Lord, all ye servants of the Lord, which . . . stand in the house of the Lord. Lift up your hands in the sanctuary, and bless the Lord. The Lord that made heaven and earth bless thee out of Zion." Ps. 134.

INVOCATION: We thank thee, O God, for the gracious initiative given by thy Spirit unto the men and women who founded this church. We thank thee for the genuine support which has been given to it by consecrated members and friends. We thank thee for the glorious incentive which is ours to build thy Kingdom in this place.

In all this we have enjoyed a marvelous fellowship. Continue thy work among us, we pray. And grant us thy blessing during this hour of worship. Amen.—H.

**Theme: As Regards Brotherly Love**

TEXT: "As regards brotherly love, you don't need any written instructions. God himself is teaching you to love one another, and you are already extending your love to all the Macedonians. Yet we urge you to have more and more of this love." I Thess. 4:9-10 (Phillips).

It is delightful to read in Paul's letter concerning the attainments of the Christians of Thessalonica. He remembers their "work of faith, and labour of love, and patience of hope"; or as J. B. Phillips puts it in his translation: "We never forget that your faith has meant solid achievement, your love has meant hard work, and the hope you have in our Lord Jesus Christ means sheer dogged endurance. . . ."

To read in this letter about these early Christians is a tonic for any modern Christian. Their lives were a "breath of life," "a tonic," to the Apostle Paul; they are the same to us.

I. They had made attainment in brotherly love. "Love had been engraved on their hearts so that there was no need to write about it on paper."

1. Brotherly love was the significant mark of the early Christians. Their loving was a means of their "outliving" the pagan world about them.

2. Brotherly love was not only a mark of character; it was a compulsive power. The early church grew by the magnetism of men loving one another.

3. This same brotherly love might well become our own badge of our Christian allegiance. Taken separately we are not much different from our neighbors who profess no Christian faith, but a recognizable feature of our lives might well believe a great friendliness. This should become most conspicuous in the fellowship of the church.

II. As regards brotherly love, God himself was the teacher of this early Christian church.

1. In the first place this was a teachable church: these were teachable Christians.

2. Teachable men and women who are taught of God are bound to learn that God himself is love. They would see God's love revealed in Christ. And what an inspiration it was for them to have as their minister one like Paul who to a great degree exemplified the love concerning which he wrote.

3. Then, too, God has a way of dealing with our inner lives so that we feel his commendation when we do well. These Thessalonians were not unlike ourselves who know the divine condemnation of the spirit of hatred in us; who know, too, the commendation which God gives secretly to loving men and women. Thus we learn what God teaches.

III. "As regards brotherly love, . . . we urge you to have more and more of this love."

1. They were examples of faith to all who believed in Macedonia and Achaia, I Thess. 1:8; their love should have the same extension, and go even beyond such boundaries. There should be no national or social or racial barriers to the exercise of Christian love.

2. "More and more of this love"—surely this means love deeper in the human heart, love that is the synonym of one's personality as when we say God is love. "More and more" might also refer to finer quality of love. It suggests loving-kindness. Love may become an abstraction, an abstract word; kindness is a concrete word, manifest in deed. Combine the two in loving-kindness. Shall we go forward under the urge to have more and more loving-kindness in our lives?

3. How shall we attain our goal? Love is a divine reality. It belongs to God and is ours by the mercy of God. We cannot have it in all its fullness unless we are willing to share it.

It is in fellowship with Christ that we learn the lessons of sincere affection. When we realize how small are our resources of spiritual energy, then we turn to Christ and refresh ourselves with his undying truth, and find strength again in his inexhaustible love.—Adapted from William Hodgkins.

Prayer for the Day: Our loving Father, we rejoice that we belong to thy family, that we are thy children. As we gather together in thy name we are before thee kinsfolk. And when we leave this house we shall be brethren, and next week when we meet one another it shall be with brotherly greetings. Even death itself cannot sever this bond of relationship for thou hast overcome death for us, and we thank thee that our bonds of brotherhood shall never be broken.

Grant, O God, that we may so live that our fellowship may become a fine and beautiful experience. Keep our minds and hearts pure. Forgive our sins. Cause the Christian virtues and the Christlike graces to appear in our lives.

Enable us to manifest in speech and action our spirit of fellowship. Help us to spread the spirit of brotherhood over the face of the earth. Give us power of intercessory prayer. May we not deny to others a portion of our wealth and time and talent. And help us not to deny the appreciative word and the kind deed and the sympathetic touch to those nearby. Amen.—H.

OFFERTORY SENTENCE: "Thou shalt love the Lord thy God with all thy heart, and with all thy soul, and with all thy strength, and with all thy mind; and thy neighbor as thyself."

OFFERTORY PRAYER: Whatever we do, O Lord, help us to put our whole heart and soul into it, as into work done for thee, and as an expression of our love toward our fellow men. In this manner may we now make offering. In Jesus' name. Amen.—H.

SEED THOUGHTS:

As Regards Brotherly Love. I. Its patience. II. Its power. III. Its permanence. IV. Its supremacy.

Love and Ethical Command. "The Christian system is founded on the fact that there are things which men will do for love which they are unable to do (as the New Testament repeatedly points out) by the external pressure or the tedious insistencies of mere ethical command."

The Character of Love. "Nor can that endure which has not its foundation upon love. For love alone diminishes not, but shines with its own light; makes an end of discord, softens the fires of hate, restores peace in the world, brings together the sundered, redresses wrongs, aids all and injures none; and who so invokes its aid will find peace and safety and have no fear of future ill."—Inspired by the Queen Ladwiga of Poland, A.D. 1413.

**Choice Illustrations on the Theme**

THE MORE EFFECTIVE WAY. There is a story of the various tools which set about to cut a piece of iron.

"I will master it," said the ax. His blows fell heavily, but each blow made his edge more blunt until further striking was useless.

"Leave it to me," said the saw, and with relentless teeth he drew back and forth on the surface, but the teeth were only broken.

Then the hammer laughed and said, "I knew you couldn't do it. I will show you the way." But after a few hard strokes its head flew off, while the iron remained unchanged.

"Shall I try?" asked the small flame. All despised the flame, but it curled itself around the iron and did not leave until the iron melted under its irresistible influence. Some persons use the ax of correction and the cutting saw of criticism to conquer the heart as hard as iron, but God's way is more excellent. Love, "which hath a more vehement flame," is the only effective way.—*Union Signal.*

THE KEY. Edgar Dewitt Jones tells of a young lady who had a rich and benevolent friend. As Christmas drew near, she naturally expected a fine present from one so able and so well-disposed. So with trembling hands she opened the expected gift. But lo! in the package was only a door key. She was almost too disappointed to look at the inscription on the card, but finally she read, "The key to the door of the house of a friend. It is yours to use. Use it every day if you wish." She had great joy when she realized that the piece of shaped metal was the symbol of a great love and the gift of a great right.

## EVENING SERVICE

**Theme: The Gospel of the Grace of God**

TEXT: ". . . the gospel of the grace of God." Acts 20:24.

What is this gospel which is committed to us as it was to Paul?

I. First of all it is the Good News that

mankind can get out of its present moral mess. Everyone agrees that man needs some sort of salvation, though there's not so much agreement as to what kind of salvation is needed. And Christianity is good news about salvation for mankind as a whole.

1. It has to be salvation for mankind first of all and not merely for individuals. God so loved the world—all mankind—and not merely a few chosen individuals here and there. But why that stress on mankind as a whole? Because when you come to think about it you realize that God has so made mankind that there is a certain solidarity about the race that involves every man, woman, and child in the moral condition of the race as a whole.

2. Now the gospel of the grace of God is Good News because it is the revelation that God has done something for this plight of mankind. It's the declaration that the saving of the race doesn't depend upon the cleverness or the goodness of men, nor still less, on reliance upon some automatic process of getting better and better.

No, there must be something more than mere cleverness, something more than reliance upon some automatic improvement year by year. That's not a gospel at all. But if you know that God has done and is doing something to alter the whole moral situation, and that when man responds to that doing of God he finds himself—quite beyond his own power of planning or achievement—releasing mighty powers of God, that surely is Good News.

II. Surely it is Good News that you and I and the man in the street can get out of our own individual moral mess.

Once again it's not a question of our finding some new technique, or of our being encouraged to struggle a bit harder. If that were all, it really would be a gospel of despair. If all you've got to say to defeated men and women is "Never mind, struggle a bit harder"—then you haven't got a gospel for them at all. But if you know and can tell them—yes, tell them out of your own experience—that God has done and is doing something for them and that he's simply waiting to take effective control of their lives, and give them victory over their habits and weaknesses, as soon as ever they are really prepared to allow him to do so, and that they need not be hopelessly defeated any more—that is Good News.

III. But, third, it is the gospel of the *grace* of God.

Can we put our definition of grace as "God's willingness to strengthen and inspire you without your first doing anything to deserve it"?

One of our failings—and I believe it's a failing of many of us—is that we can't really believe that God will do anything for us unless somehow we can qualify. We imagine that we must somehow earn God's help. And—bother it!—we can't. It's because we can't be good that we need God's help.

IV. Fourthly, it is the gospel of the grace of *God*. God! Not some vague spiritual essence; not someone you read about in books, or hear about in sermons, but the God and Father of Jesus. I wish we could make this come alive. Do you believe that God is in this church? In the pew with you enduring with you this sermon? Have you ever thought that either you must cease believing in God in any sense that really matters, or else you must believe that God is here? He is offering you his help—free and without your having first to qualify for it, so that the only thing that prevents your life being set free and being made triumphant, is your own insistence on keeping a tight grip of the handlebars and not letting him have control.

So may I urge that sometime today you will go to your own room where you can be undisturbed and say—really meaning it—"Lord God, I can't run my life successfully, but I am willing that you should run it. Show me how! Lord, I believe that you can make a better job of me than I can of myself. Lord, I believe; help thou my unbelief."—Adapted from Barnard H. Spaull.

**Suggested Texts and Themes**

The Mark of Greatness: "But he that is greatest among you shall be your servant. And whosoever shall exalt himself shall be abased; and he that shall humble himself shall be exalted." Matt. 23:11, 12.

The Pre-eminent Loyalty: "If any man come to me, and hate not his father, and mother, and wife, and children, and brethren, and sisters, yea, and his own life also, he cannot be my disciple." Luke 14:26.

The Creative Minority: "The kingdom of heaven is like unto leaven which a woman took, and hid in three measures of meal, till the whole was leavened." Matt. 13:33.

Men of Beneficent Shadow: "They brought forth the sick into the streets, and laid them on beds and couches, that at least the shadow of Peter passing by might overshadow some of them." Acts 5:15.

Chillun of Quality: "Now therefore ye are no more strangers and foreigners, but fellow citizens with the saints, and of the household of God." Eph. 2:19.

## MIDWEEK FELLOWSHIP MEETING TOPIC

(Church Night or Suggested Sermon Subject)

**Theme: An Emergency of Sickness**

TEXT: John 4:46-54.

I. Jesus is the Lord of Life. According to this Gospel Jesus is the Lord of Life. He is the author of life. Without him there would be no life. All things were made through him. It is the water of life that he pours. It is the bread of life that he gives. Whosoever believes in him is to receive eternal life. He asserts that he is the Life.

II. Jesus is decisively and effectively on the side of health. Jesus accepts the assumption that every good physician makes, that disease or sickness is against nature, against wholeness, against health. He stands ready to do something in behalf of the sick one.

The modern physician who is eager to cure does not attack the disease from without; he attacks from within. He interprets symptoms; he attacks causes. The causes of disease are subject to spiritual influence. "It is a dictum of the *British Medical Journal* that there is no tissue of the human body wholly removed from the influence of spirit."

III. Jesus uses the leverage of another's faith in his cure. A factor in the situation is the faith of the father. It seems that in exerting his spiritual power for the cure of the sick Jesus always demanded faith, the faith of some other, if not the faith of the patient. Without faith he could not heal the sick when on one occasion he returned to Nazareth. Great faith enables great deeds to be done. Even little faith does impossible things. Effective prayer must be charged with faith, as well as with hope and love. It seems to be established that faith is a principle of the inner spiritual realm in which Christ works his cures. —H.

## SUNDAY SCHOOL LESSON

**Feb. 16. The Church Preaches the Word. Rom. 10:14-17; Eph. 3:7-19. Background Scripture: I Cor. 1:18-31.**

MEMORY VERSE: "Faith comes from what is heard, and what is heard comes by the preaching of Christ." Rom. 10:17 (R.S.V.).

I. The *importance* of preaching is stressed by the passage in Romans.

II. The *content* of preaching, "the unsearchable riches of Christ," is emphasized by the Ephesian passage.

It will be interesting to the class to inform them how a minister is trained in the seminary for preaching; to note how many preachers follow the Christian Year; to point out the kinds of sermons that are preached, expository, topical, biographical, etc.; to explain how a preacher prepares his sermon; and the relation of preaching to teaching and pastoral work.

# SUNDAY: FEBRUARY TWENTY-THIRD

## MORNING SERVICE

**Theme: The Gospel of the Bruised Reed and the Smoking Flax**

SUGGESTED SCRIPTURE: Ps. 51.

SELECTED HYMNS: "Every morning mercies new."—Greville Phillimore. "There's a wideness in God's mercy."—Frederick W. Faber. "Just as I am, without one plea."—Charlotte Elliott. "O Love, that wilt not let me go."—George Matheson. "O Love of God, most full." —Oscar Clute.

CALL TO WORSHIP: "Come unto me, all ye . . ." Matthew 11:28-30.

INVOCATION: Down through the centuries, O God, we hear thy loving call to come. Our Saviour calls us to come. The Spirit calls us to come. The Bride which is the Church calls us to come. We come this morning. We come in thy name and at thy call—and we claim fulfillment of Christ's great promise that he will come and be where two or three are gathered in his name.—H.

**Theme: The Gospel of the Bruised Reed and the Smoking Flax**

TEXT: "A bruised reed shall he not break, and the smoking flax shall he not quench." Isa. 42:3.

In the earlier verses of this chapter we have a description of the character and qualifications of "the Servant of Jehovah." Among other splendid, striking, unique qualities, we are told in touching and impressive metaphors that he shall lack harshness, ruthlessness, severity; that he shall be considerate, gentle, compassionate in dealing with the frail, the weak, the unfortunate, the unpromising. "A bruised reed shall he not break, and the smoking flax shall he not quench." Whoever may be "the Servant of Jehovah" as depicted by the prophet, we are sure that Jesus alone realized, in an absolute and supreme sense, this remarkable prophetic picture.

The messages of other religious systems are for the strong; Christianity alone has a message for the weak. Its distinctive glory is its regressiveness. It is the only religion which goes back to gather up the lost things—the things which have fallen by the way and have been left behind, ready to perish. In the divine program there is a place, there is hope, there is a ministry of tenderness, of helpfulness, of recovery for the unfit.

I. The gospel of the bruised reed and the smoking flax brings to us the comforting suggestion that God remembers our frailty in disciplining us.

1. Discipline occupies a large and important place in our lives. Nearly all the best things have come to us by its pathway. Almost every step of progress, every bit of growth, every inch of development, involves discipline. And this is one of the means which God uses to lead men up the path of greatness.

2. The comforting suggestion of our text is that God takes account of our frailty as he disciplines us. "A bruised reed"—symbol of helplessness, incarnation of fragility! "The smoking flax"—emblem of spent energy, apt figure of expiring hope! Is not this a picture of humanity?

Deeply conscious of our frailty, we are fearful lest the strain and stress of life should prove too great and severe for us, and we be crushed beneath the weary burden of it all. But however stern and severe this may be, God never carries it to the breaking point.

3. There are those who do not take this view of things. For many the universe does not seem friendly toward weakness; there is no beneficent intent.

Those who endeavor to see life steadily and see it whole are convinced that this opposite view, however it comes to be, has no justification in the light of all the facts so far as they can be seen; that we live in a friendly universe; that those who face life with courage and the determination to make the most of it come to find that they that are for us are more than they that are against us; and that our frailty enlists the tender mercies of our God and effectually engages his compassions which fail not.

II. This gospel further indicates the spirit and temper underlying the divine dealings with erring and sinful men.

1. Our text is the prophet's way of saying that the Lord deals with wayward and sinful men in a spirit of tenderness. The reed at its best is fragile enough; you can hardly imagine anything more so. But such a reed bruised! A rude wind will fracture it, the slightest pressure is enough to snap it. And yet, such a reed he does not break. Why? Because he is not rash and pitiless; but infinitely tender, and moved by an inextinguishable pity. "The dimly burning wick"—there it is on the verge of extinguishment; its light has been gradually declining until, at last, a few tiny embers, fast expiring, and a streak of curling smoke are all that remain, the vanishing witnesses of the vanished flame. Why does he not put it out and be done with it? Because he is the Infinite Lover and the supreme optimist.

2. He is eternally hopeful. Divine love knows all the shameful possibilities, as well as the glorious potentialities, of human nature; knows the abounding, domineering might of sin, and the superabounding, invincible efficacy of grace; knows the awful, enthralling, tragic power of evil, and its own redeeming purpose, passion, and power. Hence the bruised reed is not broken and the smoking flax is not quenched.

3. The Lord's practice of mercy is not a sign of his weakness. We must not think that tenderness and hopefulness are the only qualities which mark the divine dealings with his sinful creatures. Whatever we do, let us not regard the words of the text as an index of weakness, or as the expression of empty sentimentality or indifferent tolerance. Gentleness is not weakness. How gentle, and yet how powerful, is the sunbeam!

Jesus was moved with compassion when he saw the multitudes, "because they were distressed and scattered, as sheep not having a shepherd"; but he scathed with his burning philippic and scourged with his righteous indignation the scribes and Pharisees for their sinister hypocrisies. He extended that gracious invitation to the weary and heavy-laden, but he also pronounced impending judgment on certain proud and unbelieving cities.

III. The text sugegsts certain indispensable qualifications for all who aspire to be servants of God, helpers of men.

If we are to be his followers, his servants, if we are to be true helpers of our fellows, we need the spirit that will not break the bruised reed, nor quench the smoking flax; we need tenderness and hopefulness.

This is what we need, if we are to reach and save the outcast and the fallen, the unfortunate and the despairing. We must have this unwearying compassion, this yearning tenderness, this unconquerable hopefulness—all of them born of a mighty love and nurtured by an unwavering faith in the immeasurable reach and matchless power of the grace of God. —William Orlando Carrington, *Carry a Little Honey*, Fleming H. Revell Co.

A Prayer for the Day: Most gracious God, we bless thee that we have access into thy grace by faith. We know that door is open to every penitent soul and we can bring the needs which we can take nowhere else. May thy Holy Spirit guide us in all our sinfulness and burden-bearing to the secret place of rest. We thank thee if we are weary of sin. We thank thee if we are growing tired of the far country. We bless thee if we are homesick and longing for the Father's face. Thou wilt more than meet us on the way. When we begin to hunger for thee the blessing has already arrived. May we hasten to the table of thy love and sit with thee at the gospel feast. Wilt thou graciously commune with us, and may our souls be forgiven in order that thy fellowship may be welcome and sweet. Pardon and cleanse and save us, we beseech thee, and may this day's worship make us stronger for all the duties and tests and service of the coming week. Amen.—Adapted from John H. Jowett.

OFFERTORY SENTENCE: Ps. 103:1-5.

OFFERTORY PRAYER: With these gifts we would render unto thee, our Father, the praise of our lips, the devotion of our hearts, and the consecration of our lives. Wilt thou bless them unto the increase of thy gospel of peace and goodwill in the world. In Christ's name we ask. Amen.—H.

SEED THOUGHTS:

The Saving Power of Kindness. "Kindness has saved more sinners than either zeal, eloquence or learning."—Faber.

The Bruised Reed. I. Today, a bruised reed. II. Tomorrow, a tower of strength. III. In the Larger Tomorrow, a pillar in the temple of God.

The Dimly Burning Wick. I. Today, a dimly burning wick. II. Tomorrow, a burning and shining light. III. In the Larger Tomorrow, as a sun in the Kingdom of our Father.

A Bunch of Bruised Reeds. I. Mary Magdalene. II. The Prodigal Son. III. Simon Peter.

### Illustrations on the Theme

DISCIPLINE. The diamond wins its unequaled luster through the exercise of the lapidary's grinding tool; the gold attains its supreme purity through the process of the refiner's fire; the vine yields its richest clusters under the pressure of the pruning knife in the vinedresser's hand; the marble assumes forms of grace and beauty under the weight of the sculptor's chisel and mallet. So God would develop our latent possibilities, leading us from stage to stage, from glory to glory, chastening us into holiness, touching us into saintship, shaping us into godlikeness, crowning us with perfection, and at the long last presenting us "faultless before the presence of his glory with exceeding joy."—W. O. C.

THE EXAMPLE OF GENERAL BOOTH. Some years ago a writer in one of our magazines related how the late General Booth, founder of the Salvation Army, went forth "to snatch broken bodies and scorched souls from the ash-heaps of humanity." He said of him, "He knows all filth, all grief, all horrors yet he sees the sunrise. Surrounded by dust of defeat and degradation, smoke of sin, fog of falseness, and clouds of crime, he has shown men a patch of Christ's clear morning on the horizon of hopelessness, as he marched on through the wide world dragging them out of darkness and death into light and life." He had caught the spirit and temper of his Master.—W. O. C.

TENDERNESS QUALIFIES FOR SERVICE. There is a beautiful tradition of the Rabbis, which illustrates the estimate God places upon tenderness as qualifying for service. When Moses was tending Jethro's flocks in Midian, a kid strayed away, and Moses went in search of it. He found it drinking at a spring and, saying to it, "Thou art weary," he took it up and bore it back on his shoulders. And God said to him, "Because thou hast had pity on a man's beast, thou shalt be shepherd of Israel, my flock."—W. O. C.

## EVENING SERVICE

### Topic: What Is Conversion?

TEXT: See texts under Part I.

INTRODUCTORY: Conversion is something so great and vast that it can neither be defined nor confined within the limits of a single word.

Conversion is the result of two kinds of activity in the soul of a sinful man—it is the happy combination of both human and divine action. The man's activity is described in Scripture as repentance and faith in the Lord Jesus Christ.

But it is God's part in conversion that overwhelms one. Here the unsearchable riches of God's grace and glory are so vast that it takes a great number of terms in Scriptures to describe them. Simply to enumerate some of them gives one a sense of awe and adoration.

I. How Scripture Describes Conversion.

1. Scripture calls conversion a passing from death unto life. "Verily, verily, I

say unto you he . . . hath passed from death unto life."

2. It is a spiritual resurrection. "And you hath he made alive who were dead through your trespasses and sins."

3. It is a birth into eternal life. "Except a man be born again he cannot see the kingdom of God."

4. It is a reconciliation with God. The appeal of the gospel to sinners always is, "Be ye reconciled to God." The accomplished fact in every Christian is, "And you, being in time past, alienated and enemies in your minds . . . yet now hat he reconciled."

5. It is a definite, personal receiving of the Lord Jesus Christ for time and for eternity. "As many as received him to them gave he the power to become sons of God."

6. It is the shining of a divine light into the dark mind and soul. "But God who commandeth the light to shine out of darkness hath shined in our hearts to give us the light of the knowledge of the glory of God in the face of Jesus Christ." The divine commission to all preachers is to call sinful men "out of darkness into his marvelous light."

7. It is also putting off of the old man and putting on of the new man in Christ. "Ye have put off the old man with his doings and have put on the new man."

8. It is eating bread from heaven. "He that eateth this bread shall never hunger."

II. What is in Conversion?

These are not all of the scriptural descriptions of conversion, but they are enough to show that this grace of God is so great that no one word can confine it. A resurrection of the soul, a new birth that means new destiny, a reconciliation to God, the entering into a personal relationship with Jesus Christ for time and eternity, the lighting of the light of a spiritual understanding of the things of God within one's soul, a radical change in one's character—all these can never be put within the limits of a single word any more than the waters from the fountain of life can be put in one or two or a dozen buckets.

III. What Follows Conversion.

Sanctification follows conversion, but there can be no sanctification unless one is first justified by faith. Christian growth follows conversion, but there can be no Christian growth unless there is first the Christian birth into the "life that is eternal." The peace of God which passes all understanding follows conversion, but there can be no peace with God unless one is first reconciled to God "through the blood of his cross." There must be the building up of believers in the knowledge of the truth, but before that is possible there must first be the putting away of the carnal mind which is enmity against God and to which all the truth of God is foolishness.—Thomas C. Pollock.

**Suggested Texts and Themes (Lenten Season)**

Series Suggestion: The Stirring Drama of the Soul. Text for Series: "Satan hath desired to have thee to sift thee as wheat." Luke 22:31.

The Fugitive: "Adam and his wife hid themselves from the presence of the Lord God amongst the trees of the garden." Gen. 3:8.

The Angel Athwart the Path: "He saw the angel of the Lord standing in the way, and his sword drawn in his hand." Num. 22:31.

Entangled Feet: "And another said, I have married a wife, and therefore I cannot come." Luke 14:20.

Those Tyrant Fears: "I was afraid, and went and hid thy talent in the earth." Matt. 25:25.

The Wrestle with Pride: "What shall I do? . . . I cannot dig; to beg I am ashamed." Luke 16:3.

Dreams True and False: "And the devil, taking him up into a high mountain, showed unto him all the kingdoms of the world in a moment of time." Luke 4:5.

Winning Eternal Life (Easter Sunday): "What shall I do to inherit eternal life?" Luke 18:18.—Albert Edward Day.

## MIDWEEK FELLOWSHIP MEETING TOPIC

(Church Night or Suggested Sermon Subject)

**Theme: An Emergency of Failure**

TEXT: John 5:1-9.

This man was in a desperate situation. Thirty-eight years was a long time in which to endure such an unhappy state. It added to his plight that he was so near to the pool through which he expected cure and that he could never reach it when it was medicinally active. This is an emergency of failure. The man just couldn't make it. He had failed again and again. Others had failed in their compassion, for there was no one when the water was troubled to put him into the pool. Then Jesus passed that way.

I. The Discernment of Jesus. "Jesus with his deep discernment quickly discovers the worst case in the crowd."

II. The Challenge of Jesus. "Do you wish to get well?" We can read between the lines and catch the man's feelings as he heard this "foolish question." He might have replied, "Don't you see that I've been trying to get into the pool?" But the interrogation of Jesus is justified. There are people, plenty of them, who do not want to get well. There are people who have quit failing. They take no steps that may result in either success or failure. They are thoroughly defeated. A failure is often an indication of faith and hope. There is hope for failures.

"This man's healing depended in large part upon his will to have it. In the physical realm the will plays a very considerable part, as all medical men will testify. In the spiritual realm it is the determining factor, and is called faith. If either a sick man or a sinner acquiesces in his condition there is no hope for him."

III. Jesus Meets the Emergency. "The impotent man is shown that he does not require the pool, or any other external remedy. The Master cries, "Rise, take up thy bed and walk." Three things are thus shown to be necessary: 1. Instant obedience to the call, which will be followed by strength. 2. Immediate trust, which will enable him to abandon all other means of healing. 3. Readiness to use the strength obtained forthwith. The result is an instantaneous cure."—H.

## SUNDAY SCHOOL LESSON

**Feb. 23. The Church Worships. Matt. 18:18-20; John 4:23-24; Acts 1:12-14; Col. 3:16-17.**

MEMORY VERSE: He said to them, "It is written, 'My house shall be called a house of prayer.'" Matt. 21:13 (R.S.V.).

A very practical approach to this subject might be to take up for comment and discussion the several items in the order of service which is in use by the local church. 1. The call to worship. A related subject for discussion would be Preparation for Worship. 2. The invocation. This points out the certainty of Christ's presence. Two or three are gathered in his name. 3. The hymns. The value of the hymnbook as an aid to worship. What kind of hymns should be chosen for the different parts of the service? 4. The responsive reading and the Scripture reading. Consideration of these may link up this Sunday's lesson with that of Feb. 9. 5. The prayers. The priestly function of the minister when he prays; the prophetic function when he preaches. Do the people *pray* the Lord's Prayer, or do they merely *say* it? 6. The offering. The use of the church offering envelopes may have a very vital relation to the service of worship. There is a value in having the package of envelopes in the home. Some men make the writing of the weekly check for the envelope, or the insertion of the money, a religious exercise. 7. The sermon. The preaching ministry of the church was the lesson subject for Feb. 16. There may be some leftovers to be cleared up. 8. The benediction. What is a benediction? What should be its effect? 9. The spirit of worship that should pervade the church. 10. How can we enrich the worship experience of our church fellowship?

# SUNDAY: MARCH SECOND

## MORNING SERVICE

**Theme: The Miracle of Myself**

SUGGESTED SCRIPTURE READING: Luke 18:10-14; I Cor. 15:9, 10.

SELECTED HYMNS: "Beneath the cross of Jesus."—Elizabeth C. Clephane. "My faith looks up to thee."—Ray Palmer. "Grace! 'tis a charming sound."—Philip Doddridge. "How sweet the name of Jesus sounds."—John Newton.

CALL TO WORSHIP: Enter into this service of worship in great confidence "that he who has begun his good work in you will perform it until the day of Jesus Christ." ". . . go on completing it . . . " (Moffatt).

INVOCATION: We thank thee, O God, for this high privilege of worship and for the perfect worthiness of thy being and character to receive the adoration of all men. Our deep concern is our own unworthiness. We beseech thee to forgive our sins, to bring our lives to rich fruitage through thy Spirit, and to give us the will and power to achieve thy purpose, becoming the sons of God. In Jesus' name. Amen.—H.

**Theme: The Miracle of Myself**

TEXT: "By the grace of God I am what I am." I Cor. 15:10.

Paul quite often draws attention to his own character, and to the things he has done. It looks a little bit like self-advertisement. It is redeemed from all that, of course, by the fact that he gives credit for it all to God: "By the Grace of God I am what I am."

There is a true and a false humility. It is no true humility to depreciate our own gifts and qualities, if these are real. It is a false humility not to acknowledge facts. The shadow of pride falls on the picture only when we take the credit for anything good about us to ourselves. Nothing can so effectively keep us out of the Kingdom of God as that kind of pride. When the Pharisee thanked God that he was not as other men, he was probably stating a fact. He had his virtues and some of them were admirable. But the trouble was that he was proud of them. He felt they did him credit. He did not see the other side. He did not realize that all that he was, had come out of the pity and grace of God.

I. It is a healthy thing to remember this, when pride of our own goodness lifts its head. This may happen when we see someone who has failed or fallen. There is a temptation to make other people's sins an inverted picture of our own virtues. Our judgments of others are often colored with pride in ourselves. If we could trace out the real roots of our own goodness, we should be very humbled. We should find that we are nothing but what the grace of God has been allowed to make us. We should say, "By the grace of God I am what I am."

II. If we could see all that the grace of God has done in us and for us, it would bring a new sense of God into our life. Most people have more experience of God than they recognize. Perhaps our biggest need is to become aware of God, present and active, and often where we least imagine. In one of his soliloquies, Kagawa says, "It is not necessary to go far afield in search of miracles. My physical birth and my soul's existence are miracles. I am myself a miracle. The fact that I am still alive, despite my weakened body, is a miracle. Yet the greatest miracle of all is the reality of my soul. That I should be made victorious in temptations, be the object of God's care in a ruined world, is to me a master miracle." Those who know the story of Kagawa's life will agree with him. His is a life which it takes Christ to explain. Nothing else can do it.

III. But all of us have things in our lives which only God's grace can explain. It is a useful thing, sometimes, to sit down and look for these traces of God's love at work. We can all find them somewhere. Some of them are points of guiding. Why did we take this step or that? What was it that kept us from this or that temptation? Where did we get the impulse that led us to say the word that changed life for a friend? And when we look on the other side of the picture, what do we find? When we did things of which we were ashamed, were we not resisting a persuasion that would have restrained us? When some good spirit took hold of us for a moment and we think back on it, we know it was not ourselves. It came from some deeper spring than our own selfish hearts. It was the grace of God. Great artists and writers have confessed that when they were at their best they felt that some power was using them. It is the same with all goodness. It comes from a power not ourselves that makes for righteousness. We are none of us bereft of the grace of God, if only we look deep enough to see the working of his Spirit. It was a gift of God, not an achievement of their own.

IV. The secret was that they had let God's grace have its way with them. They had let it shape and transform their lives at every point. There are many forces that have a part in the shaping of our lives. Ambition has a hand with many of us. The desire of comfort or success plays its part All the time secret forces are at work on the clay. The result is a very composite character. Only here and there can we trace the Hand of the great Artist. It need not be so if we realize the wonder and the power of the grace of God in Christ.

We are not ourselves till Christ has won his victory in us in everything. The meaning of the Christion life is that we should become what we really are. It is that our true self should be set free. That deliverance he is waiting to bring. —James Reid.

Prayer for the Sabbath Day: Eternal God, may the restfulness of thy Sabbath steal into our souls and give us peace. Deliver us from all the noise and tumult of the world. May our souls have power of wing, that they may rise above everything that is transient into heavenly places in Christ Jesus. Reveal unto us some new wonders of thy glory. May we discover new treasures in the unsearchable riches of Christ. Lead us into the deeper mysteries of thy truth. Let in the light as our eyes are able to bear it. Strengthen us, we humbly beseech thee, in holy living, in order that we may be able to discern the things which thou hast prepared for them that love thee. Sanctify our fellowship with thy presence. Graciously receive all who are inclined to begin a new life. May the old life be richly forgiven, and may the new life begin in the lowliness of quiet faith. Help us all to turn over a new leaf, and may the record be such as thou canst enter in the Lamb's Book of Life. Amen. —J. H. Jowett.

Offertory Sentence: "Do you remember the generosity of Jesus Christ, the Lord of us all? He was rich beyond our telling, yet He became poor for your sakes so that His poverty might make you rich." II Cor. 8:9 (Phillips).

Offertory Prayer: Thou hast been exceedingly good to us, O Lord, for we abound in the riches of thy grace. In appreciation of thy loving-kindness may we desire to give no meager token of our gratitude, but that which is in some measure a worthy gift. In Jesus' name. Amen.—H.

Seed Thoughts:

The Miracle of Others. Under such a heading there is opportunity to preach a series of sermons; for example, "The Miracle of Paul," "The Miracle of Augustine," "The Miracle of Luther," "The Miracle of John Newton," etc.

The Miracle of Christ. Dwell on the wealth of his person more than its mystery, on his irresistibility rather than his gentleness, on his steadfast energy of concentration upon his one work more even than his elemental force of passion or his depth of suffering—dwell on such things if you would come near the center and secret of this personality and its root in coequal God. His effect on the human soul is greater than any human cause can explain, whether you think of the extent of his effect in history, or, still more, of the nature of his effect in a Church and its experience.—P. T. Forsyth.

**Choice Illustrations on the Theme**

THE SUPREME MIRACLE. The Gospel miracles can light up the whole question of man's deliverance from sin, precisely because this deliverance is itself the supreme miracle. The mastery over nature and the mastery over sin are two aspects of one and the selfsame power. Did not Jesus say so himself? "Whether is it easier," he demanded of the scribes, "to say to the sick of the palsy, Thy sins be forgiven thee; or to say, Arise, and take up thy bed, and walk?"—J. S. Stewart.

MIRACLES SEEN: When a man asks me why I believe in miracles, I answer, "Because I have seen them." He asks, "When?" I reply, "Yesterday." "Where?" "In such and such a place I saw a man who had been a drunkard redeemed by the power of an unseen Christ, and saved from sin. That was a miracle." The best argument for Christianity is a Christian. That is a fact which men cannot get over. There are fifty other arguments for miracles, but none so good as that you have seen them. Perhaps you are one yourself. Show a man a miracle with his own eyes, and if he is not too hardened, he will believe.—Henry Drummond.

## EVENING SERVICE

**Theme: Reconciliation**

TEXT: "Be ye reconciled to God." II Cor. 5:20.

It is indeed reconciliation that the world needs. Never was this more evident than today. The great curse of the world is the want of the spirit of reconciliation. The great enemy of mankind is the spirit of strife, hatred, envy, and jealousy. Nations go to war with one another because there is enmity between them. Estrangement between social classes makes life narrow and bitter, and wastes a people's strength. One of the chief causes of industrial distress is the want of good feeling and co-operation between employers and employed. And it is being discovered that to secure the best prosperity some co-operation between business leaders for the good of the public must take the place of unrestricted competition. The domestic paradise is turned into a hell when husband and wife and the children do not know how to make up their quarrels. The joy of friendship is lost when men become too proud to ask for pardon and to give it. The world, then, badly needs genuine, active goodwill, between nations, classes, and individuals.

But there is a greater need than to be reconciled with one another; and that is, to be reconciled to the great Father of us all. For we cannot look on one another as brothers and sisters unless we believe that we have one Father. And we cannot be at peace with all the other members of the family unless we are at peace with the Head of the family. So this is the gospel message: "Be reconciled to God."

I. God wants our reconciliation. But does God want to be reconciled to us? Or have we too deeply offended against him for this to be possible? The good news of Jesus Christ is that God wants very much to be reconciled to us, so much so that there is nothing said about the need of his being reconciled to us.

There is no difficulty on his side. There is no irreconcilability there, no reluctance to be friendly. We have no need to plead with him in this matter. The spirit of enmity never entered his heart. There was never any room for it there. His heart was always full of love. God never broke away from us. We broke away from him. We rejected his friendship. We became estranged from him.

Our Heavenly Father never accepted man's estrangement from him. From the moment of man's lapse from him, he began to take steps to restore the harmony. Through all the ages he has worked for this. He has never given man up. And his reconciling activity reached its climax in Jesus. "God was in Christ reconciling the world unto himself." It is in Christ that God proves that he wants to be reconciled to us.

II. God Offers Reconciliation. What, then, do we see in Jesus? We see a complete absence of revengefulness or bitterness toward the sinner for all the outrages he has committed against him. Instead of bitterness we find a love that will suffer all insults and injustices and injuries rather than retaliate, though he felt all this as no other could. We find a love that will give itself to the utmost to win the estranged ones to friendship and loving fellowship.

Christ let sin do its worst to him, even to the extremity of the Cross. And yet his love was unabated. Thus he proved that his love was proof against all sin, all hatred, all injury, and disgraceful treatment. And this is the love of God. It is a love deathless, unconquerable. It is quite certain, then, that, in spite of all evil we have done, God wants to be friends with us. He is ready to forgive us.

We see that sin is not just breaking the laws of a Ruler, but a personal offense against a Father who loves us; and our Father at the foot of the Cross of his Son brings us to repentance and assures us of his pardon.

III. What Response? God cannot make us accept his offer. We must accept it freely. Friendship can only be offered, not enforced. See, then, God in Christ holding out the right hand of reconciliation to us. We *can* keep our hands glued to our breasts. But *shall* we? Shall we not grasp the outstretched hand? "Be reconciled to God." In view of the fact that sin nailed him to the Cross, let us repent of our sin, and let us put all our trust in the friendship of him who has done so much to prove it. And let us prove that we are at peace with God by being at peace, as far as in us lies, with everybody else, seeng that all are his children and our brothers and sisters. Be reconciled to God and so to all the family.—W. Powell.

**Suggested Texts and Themes**

Series on The Christian Way of Understanding: 1. The Christian Answer to the Question, "What Is Man?" 2. The Christian Way of Thinking about Moral Evil. 3. The Christian Way out of Moral Distress. 4. The Christian Way of Understanding Jesus Christ the Saviour. 5. The Christian Way of Understanding the Church. 6. The Christian Way of Understanding History.—Suggestion from "Christian Doctrine" by J. S. Whale.

The Urgency of Today: "Boast not thyself of tomorrow; for thou knowest not what a day may bring forth." Prov. 27:1.

The Primacy of the Soul: "For what is a man profited, if he shall gain the whole world and lose his own soul." Matt. 16:26.

After the Deluge: "And I will restore to you the years that the locust hath eaten." Joel 2:25.

## MIDWEEK FELLOWSHIP MEETING TOPIC

(Church Night or Suggested Sermon Subject)

**Theme: An Emergency of Hunger**

TEXT: ". . . he himself knew what he would do." John 6:6.

INTRODUCTION: The Story of John 6:1-14.

I. Christ meets human need with what we have.

II. Christ uses little to accomplish much. 1. Compare using much to accomplish little. 2. Compare using something to get an equivalent. 3. The Kingdom principle, as in the Parables of the Mustardseed and the Leaven.

III. Christ provides an excess for later demand.

IV. Christ makes the gift sacramental. He makes the breaking of bread a sacramental thing.—H.

## BULLETIN BOARD SLOGANS FOR THE MONTH

Be Strong in the Lord!
What does God want me to do?

Back to Church—Forward to God!

True religion is spiritual living.

You are as good as you want to be.

Christ in the heart is Heaven on earth.

Real prayer may become a joyful experience.

What Christ puts first we must not put last.

Swearing is the crutch of conversational cripples.

Only he who can see the invisible can do the impossible.

### SUNDAY SCHOOL LESSON

**Mar. 2. One Lord, One Faith. Eph. 4: 1-17; 11-16. Background Scripture: Luke 9:49-50; John 17:20-26; Eph. 4:1-16.**

MEMORY VERSE: "He is our peace, who has made us both one, and has broken down the dividing wall of hostility." Eph. 2:14 (R.S.V.).

I. The essential unity of the Church. In what does it consist? How can this unity be deepened? The problem of the unity of the Church today may be considered in the light of the deeper unity of Christ.

II. The various gifts of the members of the Church. See Eph. 4:11-13. What other gifts are used in the modern church? See how all activity is to work toward one end. Eph. 4:13-16.

III. Discussion of ecumenicity. The meaning of the word. In what does real ecumenicity consist? How can our denominational differences be pointed up to realize unity of spirit?

Christian unity in practice may be illustrated from the use of hymns, many of which are sung in the churches of various denominations and types. "Lead, Kindly Light" was written by one who became a Roman Catholic. "A Mighty Fortress" was written by Luther, founder of the Lutheran Church. The writer of "In the Cross of Christ I Glory" was a Unitarian. "How Sweet the Name of Jesus Sounds" is by John Newton; he was a minister of the Established Church of England. Isaac Watts, whose hymns are found in every hymnbook, was pastor of the Independent Church in Mark Lane, London. "O Little Town of Bethlehem" is from the pen of an Episcopalian. "Immortal Love, Forever Full" is from the pen of a Quaker. "Beneath the Cross of Jesus" was written by a devout member of the Free Church of Scotland. "Hark, the Herald Angels Sing" is Methodist; "O Master, Let Me Walk with Thee" is Congregational; "Rise up, O Men of God" is Presbyterian.

---

# SUNDAY: MARCH NINTH

---

## MORNING SERVICE

**Theme: The Touch of the Master's Hand**

SUGGESTED SCRIPTURE READING: Matt. 8:1-15.

SELECTED HYMNS: "Worship the Lord in the beauty of holiness."—J. S. B. Monsell. "We may not climb the heavenly steeps."—J. G. Whittier. "Jesus, the very tho't of thee."—Bernard of Clairvaux. "O Master, let me walk with thee."—Washington Gladden. "Lord, speak to me, that I may speak."—Frances R. Havergal.

CALL TO WORSHIP: It would fit into the theme of this service to use certain stanzas of John Greenleaf Whittier's hymn, "Immortal Love, Forever Full," as a call to worship. The stanzas suggested begin, "We may not climb the heavenly steeps," and "But warm, sweet, tender, even yet."

INVOCATION: We turn our minds unto thee, O God, expectant that thy touch upon them will give us deeper insight into truth. We turn our hearts unto thee that through them thy love may flow. We bring our wills unto thee that thou mayst guide us in all that we speak and do. As we make our prayer of confession before thee help us to receive the cleansing of our lives; then may we go forth to proclaim by word and deed and life the salvation of Christ.—H.

**Theme: The Touch of the Master's Hand**

TEXT: "And Jesus put forth his hand, and touched him." Matt. 8:3.

Two things Christ did which changed men's lives. He looked upon them, and something in his eyes brought about a transformation. But his look was not all. He touched men—and when his hand was laid upon the little children, the weary, sick, or discouraged folk, his touch had miraculous powers.

Jesus put forth his hand and touched a leper, and the diseased body was cleansed. Simon's wife's mother lay sick of a fever. He put his hand on her and the fever left her. Two blind men came to him as he went along the way, and cried, "Thou, Son of David, have mercy on us." He touched their eyes and they were opened; their darkness disappeared. . . .

The crowning act in the touch of the Master's hand was when he laid his hands on those from whom life had departed—the daughter of Jairus, and the son of the widow of Nain—and new life flowed into their bodies. All of these were instances of physical healing.

Of far greater importance were the transformations wrought by the spiritual touch of Jesus. Timid souls were made bold, fearful hearts were made courageous. Sinful hearts that had given up hope of restoration felt his purifying touch and found new life. Those in the grip of habits that fasten themselves with devastating effect upon the personality, found freedom and release, and were born anew into a life of hope.

Life does get messed up! We do lose the way! We weaken in our loyalties! We become cold and cynical! We run out on our responsibilities! We need to become changed men. Can we not pray in the words of an old hymn?

> Thy touch has still its ancient power;
> No word from Thee can fruitless fall;
> Stretch out Thy hand this sacred hour,
> And in Thy mercy heal us all.

Christ works today, of course, through his disciples, and one of the greatest forces for good is a Christian man or woman who has found peace and can communicate it to others.

I. The Tap on the Shoulder. Sometimes the touch of the Master's hand is that which Peter Marshall calls "The Tap on the Shoulder." Those of you who have read his first book, *Mr. Jones, Meet the Master,* will remember how he bares his own life story and tells the incidents that led up to that moment when he felt a tap on his shoulder, and knew that it was his Master's hand—setting him aside for Christian service.

I want to guard always against giving the impression that it is only those who are in the professional Christian vocations who are called of God. There is no group of whom I am more proud than the Christian men and women who are teachers in our public schools. They have felt the touch of the Master's hand. . . . I care not primarily what your vocation is, be it business, professional, or political. But I am concerned that you know that you, too, felt the tap on your shoulder, that you heard his voice saying, "This is the way; walk ye in it."

II. The Restraining Hand. Have you ever been grateful for some experience of your early life that, in God's wisdom, may have given you a sense of direction or even a warning against taking the wrong way?

I recall a story that John Brown, the well-known evangelist, told over the radio: Two young men had been walking idly along the street, looking into the shop windows as they strolled. One of them was wearing a diamond ring. Carelessly, he pressed it against the glass, and was about to scratch his initials thereon. His companion sensed what he was about to do and put out his hand to deter him, saying: "Don't write there! You can't rub it out!" I can still hear the ringing voice of Mr. Brown as he said in the Master's name: "Don't write there! You can't rub it out!"

III. The Touch of the Master's Hand. You cannot think of the touch of the Master's hand without remembering the scene when little children are brought to the church for dedication. "They brought young children to him, and besought him to lay his hands on them."

The church in every generation extends the touch of the Master's hand and says: "Let the little ones come unto me." An old Scottish minister once said: "Every time you lay your hand on the head of a bairn, you place it on the heart of the parents."—David John Donnan.

PRAYER FOR THE DAY: Our Father, we humbly pray thee to reveal unto us the unsearchable riches of Christ. May thy grace and light be given unto us so that we may come into the liberty of purity and truth.

Impart unto us a deep dissatisfaction with everything that is low, mean, and unclean. Create within us a pure desire so that we may be able to appreciate the things which thou hast prepared for them that love thee.

Nourish our spiritual powers; help us to delight in such things as please thee. Give us strength to fight the good fight of faith and to obtain the Crown of Righteousness.

May thy will be done among all peoples, so that in common obedience to thee all the nations may have abiding peace. Amen.—George S. Paull.

OFFERTORY SENTENCE: "Let your light so shine before men, that they may see your good works, and glorify your Father which is in heaven." Matt. 5:16.

OFFERTORY PRAYER: Our heavenly Father, give us eager hands and willing hearts to do thy will. May we not shirk the hard task nor grow weary in well-doing. Bless this offering unto the sowing of the seed of the Gospel that it may bring its yield to thy name's honor and glory. Amen.

SEED THOUGHTS:

His Hands: I. Tested by toiling. II. Mighty to heal. III. Lifted up to be pierced for our sakes. IV. Uplifted in blessing.—A. Ian Burnett.

His Hands: I. They touch. II. They transform. III. They transfigure.—A. I. B.

Sermon Theme: "Thy Touch Has Still Its Ancient Power."

Compassion, the Motive for Miracle: "And Jesus, moved with compassion, put forth his hand, and touched him. . . ." Mark 1:41.

### Illustrations

ANYTHING CAN HAPPEN HERE. A church in New York had the faith and courage to put up a sign in its sanctuary which read: "Jesus Christ is in this church! Anything can happen here." A young woman came down to New York City from upstate and went to church on a Sunday morning. Her life was all askew; she was bitter about some things; ashamed of others. Life was messed up. She had left home trying in vain to get away from herself, a self she did not like. She came to church that Sunday morning not really expecting that a miracle might happen; but it did. I will let her tell her own story:

"Strangely enough, the moment I entered I felt an atmosphere of quietness and peace, and as the service progressed the feeling deepened. The minister spoke of an occasion when he had heard Dr. Grenfell tell of his work in Labrador, and said that as the physician was speaking his face was so transfigured with the love of Christ that for a moment he seemed to have vanished, and in his place stood One 'whose form was like unto that of the Son of God.' In that instant," said the woman, "I felt that Christ himself was present in the congregation, moving through our midst, touching men and women one by one, and saying, 'Peace be unto you.' I felt that his hands had been laid in benediction upon me. Then I knew that my problem had been solved, and that I would take back to my home the answer that I had found."—D. J. D.

FROM "MY LADY OF THE CHIMNEY CORNER," Alexander Irvine's volume about his mother. Do you remember what she says about hands? "God takes a han' wherever He can find it, and jist doz what He likes wi' it. Sometimes He takes a bishop's and lays it on a child's head in benediction; then He takes the han' of a docther t' relieve pain; the han' of a mother t' guide her chile; and sometimes He takes th' han' of an auld craither like me t' give a bit of comfort to a neighbour. But they're all han's touch't by His Spirit, an' His Spirit is everywhere lukin' fur han's to use."

OUR LORD HELD UP HIS HANDS. Dr. Hubert Simpson has told of a little girl who, returning from school one day, caused consternation in her home by saying that she had been punished by her teacher for the first time in her life. Pressed to give the reason for the punishment, she confessed to a particularly grave fault. "But you never did a thing like that!" her mother protested. "No, of course I didn't," came the answer, "but no one would own up, and something had to be done about it, so I held up my hand." That is what happened on Calvary. Something had to be done about our human sin and sinfulness and our Lord held up his hands for our sakes.—A. Ian Burnett.

## EVENING SERVICE

### Theme: Say "Shibboleth"

TEXT: "Then said they unto him, Say now Shibboleth: and he said Sibboleth: for he could not frame to pronounce it right." Judg. 12:6.

INTRODUCTORY: The story. Judg. 12:1-6. Almost Christians.

I. The Micah Type of Almost Christian—Contact Christians. Judg. 17.

II. The Ananias Type—Withholding Christians. Acts 5:1-10.

III. The Barren Fig Tree Type—Fruitless Christians. Mark 11:12-14, 21-23.

IV. The Isaiah's Vineyard Type—Wild Grape Christians. Isa. 5:1-7.

V. The Foolish Virgin Type—Formal, No-Fire Christians. Matt. 25:1-13.

VI. The Promising Son Type—Irresponsible Christians. Matt. 21:28-31.

VII. The Between-the-Porch-and-the-Altar Type—Near Christians. Ezek. 8:16.

Almost Christians! The door almost shut is open. The plate almost clean is dirty. The examination almost passed is failed. Almost bravery is cowardice. Almost victory is defeat. Almost gain is loss. . . . Almost "Shibboleth" is "Sibboleth."—H.

### Suggested Texts and Themes

Series: Consider His Questions.

I. A Question of Decision: "Jesus said therefore unto the twelve. Would ye also go away?" John 6:67.

II. A Question of Recognition: "And Jesus said, Who touched me?" Luke 8:45.

III. A Question of Ambition: "What would ye that I should do for you?" Mark 10:36.

IV. A Question of Confession: "He said unto them, But who say ye that I am?" Matt. 16:15.—Glenn Randall Phillips.

Inadequate Righteousness: "For I say unto you, That except your righteousness shall exceed the righteousness of the scribes and Pharisees, ye shall in no case enter into the kingdom of heaven." Matt. 5:20.

Do We Worship Idols? "Little children, keep yourselves from idols." I John 5:21.

Our Lives Are Open to God: "Thou compassest my path and my lying down, and art acquainted with all my ways." Ps. 139:3.

## MIDWEEK FELLOWSHIP MEETING TOPIC

(Church Night or Suggested Sermon Subject)

### Theme: An Emergency of Danger

TEXT: John 6:16-21.

The experience of the disciples was full of shifting scenes, difficulties on land and storms at sea. All had to be faced as followers of the Lord Jesus, to try their faith, to test their love, and perfect their education as witnesses for Christ. This was a special experience.

I. It was a time of darkness. "And it was now dark," v. 17. Darkness is the symbol of sin. Sin upon the soul makes it dark; the veil upon the heart makes it dark.

II. It was a time of danger. "And the sea arose," v. 18. There are all kinds of winds and storms for the followers of Christ, the rough wind of persecution, the sharp wind of sorrow, the bitter wind of bereavement, the strong wind of opposition.

III. It was a time of distress. "And they were afraid," v. 19. Fear blinds our minds, blunts our faith, and fills us with alarm, while superstitious fear is the worst of all fears.

IV. It was a time of discovery. "It is I; be not afraid," v. 20. There is a star of promise and hope in the darkest experience. Reveals Christ.

V. It was a time of deliverance. "Then they willingly received him," v. 21. We cannot be lost for Jesus has undertaken to bring us safely to land. There is no experience so dark that he cannot see through. Let us toil and trust, for Jesus is always near.

The experiences of the disciples were pictures of our Christian life today. The sea is a type of world. The ship is a picture of the Church. The journey is a symbol of our lives. The storm illustrates our experiences. The deliverance tells of our salvation. The safe landing points to the power of the Captain of our salvation who has power to comfort and to save.—C. E.

## SUNDAY SCHOOL LESSON

**Mar. 9. The Church's Influence on Society (Temperance). Matt. 5:13-16. I Thess. 5:4-8; James 2:14-17. Background Scripture: Acts 19:21-41.**

Memory Verse: "Let our people learn to apply themselves to good deeds, so as to help cases of urgent need, and not to be unfruitful." Titus 3:14.

I. The background Scripture in Acts shows the Apostle Paul confronting the Ephesians with the Gospel and arousing the opposition of a powerful segment of society. Does the Church today arouse the opposition of any segment of society? Give examples. Examples in America. Examples abroad. If the Church does not arouse opposition, why not?

II. The passage from Matthew may be taken to show the way in which the Church influences society.

III. The passage from Thessalonians gives the temperance emphasis. See *Morning Service* for Nov. 26 in this *Manual*.

IV. The James passage suggests practical aspects of Christian service.

# SUNDAY: MARCH SIXTEENTH

## MORNING SERVICE

**Theme: Immortal Longings**

Suggested Scripture Reading: Ps. 84.

Selected Hymns: "Be still my soul; the Lord is on thy side" (Finlandia).—Katharina von Schlegel. "As pants the hart for cooling streams."—Tate and Brady. "O thou, to whose all-searching sight."—Zinzendorf. "Jesus, where'er thy people meet."—William Cowper.

Call to Worship:

Unto the House of God our steps have led,
And we would share once more the common Quest
For things unseen that do not fade
Nor perish with the passing day.
Here in the place of prayer we fain would know
The mind and heart of Him Who is the Lord.

Come, worship in the name of Christ
That God may bless us with His love,
His peace.

—Francis C. Ellis.

INVOCATION: There is a deep-seated need in our lives, O God, for thee. "Our hearts are restless until they rest in thee." We want to understand better what life is and how to live it. We grope after truth and perfection. We always feel that there is something higher which we ought to attain.

This is thy way with us. By this we know that thou dost care for us and dost ever seek the nurture of our higher manhood, until we all attain unto thy will and purpose for us.

Grant us this hour thy presence and make us aware that thou art dealing with our lives. In Jesus' name. Amen.—H.

**Theme: Immortal Longings**

TEXT: "My heart and my flesh crieth out for the living God." Ps. 84:2.

In the closing scene of Shakespeare's great tragedy *Antony and Cleopatra* there occurs a striking phrase. The Egyptian queen, having witnessed the death of her lover Mark Antony, feels that now she has nothing to live for, and resolves to take her own life. Conscious as she is that her earthly course is finished, and that death is at hand, she says to her maid Iras: "Give me my robe, put on my crown; I have immortal longings in me."

Immortal longings! Surely we may lift from their context these words of a pagan queen, and apply them to that desire for the Eternal which is described in our text. "My soul longeth, yea, even fainteth for the courts of the Lord: my heart and my flesh crieth out for the living God." That verse of scripture is an expression of the perennial emotions of devout souls; the psalmist's words are as enduring and universal as the aspirations which they so perfectly convey. One is reminded of the wistful cry of Job: "Oh that I knew where I might find him!" The quest of our spirits after God is universal; it is the cry of humanity.

I. Man's Universal Desire. All men are alike in this—that not one of us, desiring to live a complete and satisfied life, can do without God. The need for him is a universal need, as John Oxenham has reminded us in his parody of Kipling's famous lines:

The East is Christ's, and the West is
Christ's,
And so the twain shall meet;
The East still East, and West still
West,
At Christ's nail-pierced feet.

But just as no stretch of space can divide longing hearts that reach out after the God of the whole earth, so no passage of time can terminate the need for the God who is the dwelling-place of every generation. Indeed, as the realization of men's brotherhood in God will doubtless become the greatest unifying factor in geography, so the outworking of God's wise plan will also emerge as the "one increasing purpose" undergoing all history. It is faith in God which gives to the centuries their cohesion and meaning.

II. Man's Ageless Desire. But why do men thus seek the Lord, if haply they may feel after him and find him? The answer to that question is in our text. "My heart and my flesh crieth out for the *living* God." God is the source of these lives he has given us.

As God is the source of our life, so he is its only adequate resource. How helpless we are unless we have God to sustain, strengthen, and support us! In sorrow, it is his consolation that helps us to endure; in bereavement, it is his loving hand that wipes the tears from our eyes; in temptation, it is his grace that enables us to overcome; in loneliness, it is his friendship that cheers us; in sickness, it is his strength that heals us; in doubt, it is his truth that guides us; when we fall, it is his mercy that lifts us up. Who is sufficient for these things? Our sufficiency is of God, and only of him.

III. "In the Hour of Our Death." But supremely is God alone the one on whom we can rely when the days of our earthly pilgrimage are drawing to a close. If

God is the only adequate resource for our life, even greater is our need of him in death; and if, while dwelling amid things seen and temporal, we are constrained to seek his aid, greater still is the urgency of our need when we come to contemplate those things which are unseen and eternal.

Not only are all the springs of our life in God; to him also belongs the ocean of eternal life and love into which all the rivers of our human lives are meant to empty themselves. As God is the author of our life, so is he the finisher; the alpha and omega; the beginning and the end. That is why we have immortal longings in us. That is why our hearts and souls cry out for the living God.

IV. The Need is Answered. But the Bible declares that God will satisfy the longing soul. Our holy Christian religion tells us that God has in fact come to answer our need, in the person of his Son. God has replied to the cry of humanity for himself by sending Jesus to show us what he is like. "He that hath seen me hath seen the Father." What a claim for any individual to make! And yet—both by the testimony of believers in every age, and by the witness of God's Spirit to our own hearts —we know that it is true. All the riches of heaven are made available in Jesus to the needy hearts of men. What is the blessing for which you are longing now? Is it forgiveness, a conscience set free from the guilt and power of sin? He is a God ready to pardon! Is it joy that you need? In his presence is fullness of joy! Does your heart crave peace, a peace which this world can neither give nor take away? The peace of God passes all understanding, and that peace he gives to us! Are you hungry for love? God is love, and his love can be shed abroad in our hearts! Not one of us need remain unsatisfied, unhappy, or unblest. Whatever your sin may be, God will forgive it; whatever your need, he will supply it; whatever your prayer, he will hear it; whatever your cry, he will answer it. May you know his blessing now. For his name's sake. Amen.—W. Francis Gibbons.

PRAYER FOR THE DAY: Our minds, O Lord, grope for the truth; "Our hearts are restless until they rest in thee"; our works are futile until they serve thy Kingdom; be thou, O Lord, the center of our lives, the magnet toward which we turn, the Master whom we love and serve. Let no false god beguile us. Let no idol subvert us. Let no selfish passion turn our hearts from thee.

We are grateful, O God, for thy greatness, thy completeness, thy perfection of wisdom, power, and love. Thou dost ever fulfill our quest, yet ever draw us to further quest. We thank thee for the immortal longings of our souls, and for their satisfaction through Jesus Christ. In Jesus' name. Amen.—H.

OFFERTORY SENTENCE: Rom. 10:13-15.

OFFERTORY PRAYER: We dedicate, O God, our tithes and offerings unto the broadcasting of the glad tidings of Jesus Christ. May thy Spirit open the hearts of men to receive them. And in receiving them may they, too, rejoice to tell them abroad, until the gospel of peace shall have passed throughout the whole wide earth. Amen.—H.

SEED THOUGHTS:

Three Beatitudes. Ps. 84. I. Blessed are they that dwell in thy house." II. "Blessed is the man whose strength is in thee." III. "Blessed is the man that trusteth in thee."

The True Object of Yearning. ". . . for the living God."

"Athirst for the Living God." Ps. 42:2.

'Tis life, whereof our nerves are scant,
Oh life, not death, for which we pant;
More life, and fuller, that I want.
—Tennyson.

### Choice Illustrations on the Theme

THE UNIVERSAL NEED. The following incident happened some years ago, during the Sino-Japanese war. A number of Chinese Christians were gathered together in a church for worship, when to their surprise a Japanese soldier entered and sat down among them. His presence created misgiving and alarm, so that the congregation became very restless. At length the soldier stood up and said: "I am a conscript soldier, but I am also a Christian. I feel I must worship with you." So he was made welcome, and at the close of the service he spoke to the minister, asking if he would sign his name in the Bible he had brought with him from Japan. Then, in Chinese characters, the minister wrote: "In Christ there is neither Jew nor Greek." God calls into his Kingdom people of every tribe and nation. The need for him is a universal need.—W. F. G.

GOD IS ADEQUATE RESOURCE. Goodness without God may last a long time; but its roots are severed. It is only awaiting its end. It has no continuence. The second trouble about it is suggested if we raise the other question, If we fail, what then? The grim answer is that nonreligious goodness can never speak the word "pardon." If we fail, we are forever a failure: we carry the stigma eternally. And we know that we *shall* fail. If we are setting our standards even moderately high, in our own strength we can never hope to achieve what we ought. As men say when they have ruined their own life or someone else's, "I can never forgive myself!" They are right. But that which we cannot do for ourselves, God has done in Jesus Christ.—Edgar P. Dickie.

FAITH IN IMMORTALITY. "I don't know what I have done to make people feel like that toward me, except that I have always kept my faith in immortality." These were the words of Alfred Tennyson, uttered after he had read one of many letters which reached him on his eightieth birthday, and in which his friends freely expressed their great love and warm admiration.—W. J. Hart.

## EVENING SERVICE

### Theme: The Divine Reasoning

TEXT: "Come now, and let us reason together, saith the Lord: though your sins be as scarlet, they shall be as white as snow; though they be red like crimson, they shall be as wool. . . ." Isa. 1:18-20.

SUGGESTED SCRIPTURE READING: Isa. 1:10-20.

I. God's Argument.

1. The contrast of scarlet and whiteness. Scarlet is the color of blood, the symbol of passion, the emblem of wrath. White is the color of light, the symbol of purity, the emblem of peace. Livid red *vs.* dazzling whiteness. "Though your sins be as scarlet."

2. The contrast is not one of black *vs.* white. Black suggests negation. Sin is not only negation. Sin is not ignorance. Sin is a terribly positive thing. Sin hurts. Sin destroys. Sin sheds blood. Sin drenches the garments of a man's soul. Sin is rebellion. Sin is anarchy. Sin is red like crimson. Sin is a blood-red garment.

3. There is no mention of gray or pink. Here is no compromise. Here is no excusing of oneself. Falsehood is not compared with gray half-truth, but with the white truth. Lust is not just off-color; lust is scarlet.

4. The transformation. Not by blotting out ignorance. Not by polishing with culture. Not by the use of any ritual. Not by purchase. Not by works. Wash! "Wash you, make you clean." I must wash in the blood of the Lamb. That red sacrifice can wash out the deep red stain. After washing, "cease to do evil; learn to do well."

II. God's Deed. How God backs up his argument.

1. The demand of men is for deeds to back up arguments.

2. God's deed is Christ. The incarnation. The works of Christ. The Christ of Gethsemane. The Christ of Calvary. The Christ of the Resurrection. Christ as the deed of God is a mighty argument.

III. God's Interpretation. The argument must be understood to be effective. The deed must be interpreted.

1. "Without shedding of blood there is no remission." Heb. 9:22. "So Christ was once offered to bear the sins of many." This is an idea suggested by the Jewish ceremonials. It seems to be written upon the human heart, and upon the pages of history.

2. "Behold the Lamb of God, which

taketh away the sin of the world." John 1:29. I must wash in the blood of the Lamb.

IV. God's Proclamation. The argument, the deed, the interpretation must be proclaimed. "How shall they hear without a preacher?"

1. Proclamation through Christ's disciples, Paul, the early Christians, missionaries, the Church, many witnesses.

2. We have no excuse for not accepting God's argument. We have heard. We know.

V. God's Pressure of His Argument and Deed.

1. Not by coercion.

2. Through the inspiration of the Bible; through the inspiration of great music, art, literature, architecture, etc.; through human lives; through the Church; through agencies of mercy, etc.

3. Through the Holy Spirit using these, convicting the world, convincing the world.

VI. God's Condition.

1. "If ye be willing and obedient. . . ." "But if ye refuse and rebel. . . ."

2. God's ultimatum. "For the mouth of the Lord hath spoken it."

3. "Come!" "Wash!" "Cease to do evil." "Learn to do well."

4. John 3:16.—H.

**Suggested Evangelistic Texts and Themes**

At Peace with God: "There is therefore now no condemnation to them which are in Christ Jesus, who walk not after the flesh, but after the Spirit." Rom. 8:1.

Cheer Up! "Why art thou cast down, O my soul? . . ." Ps. 42:11. Someone has pointed out that Jesus gave us "three cheers." First, the cheer of forgiveness: "Be of good cheer, thy sins be forgiven thee." Second, the cheer of companionship: "Be of good cheer; it is I; be not afraid." Third, the cheer of victory: "Be of good cheer; I have overcome the world."

God's Manifested Love: "In this was manifested the love of God toward us, because that God sent his only begotten Son into the world, that we might live through him." I John 4:9.

The Approachable Christ: "For she said within herself, If I may but touch his garment, I shall be whole." Matt. 9:21.

The Test: "Jesus answered and said unto him, If a man love me, he will keep my words: and my Father will love him, and we will come unto him, and make our abode with him."

## MIDWEEK FELLOWSHIP MEETING TOPIC

(Church Night or Suggested Sermon Subject)

**Theme: An Emergency of Despair**

SCRIPTURE: John 9:1-12.

I asked a blind friend concerning his blindness. He said, "Most people shut their eyes to simulate blindness, but that is not the way to do it. Try to see with the back of your head; that will be more like it." Blindness is a condition of despair. Such an emergency Jesus met.

I. To the man himself his blindness was a cause for despair. John 9:32.

II. To the disciples it posed a passing problem.

III. To Jesus it became a glorious opportunity to do the works of God. What wonders Christ and his followers have done for the blind!

"As those who are born blind cannot make themselves see, so the work of Redemption must be performed by Another. We either remain in the darkness of despair or we stand in gratitude before an immeasurable gift."—Edgar P. Dickie.

## SUNDAY SCHOOL LESSON

**Mar. 16. Evangelism in the Home Community. Mark 5:18-20; Luke 10:1-2; Acts 5:42; I Thess. 1:6-10.**

MEMORY VERSE: "The harvest is plentiful, but the laborers are few; pray therefore the Lord of the harvest to send out laborers into his harvest." Luke 10:2 (R.S.V.).

I. Does my church have any obligation for the evangelization of this community? Is it not enough to have a church;

people can come if they want to? Has the church then no evangel, no good news, to pass on to others? What really undergirds fine community life, its morality, its fellowship, its character-building institutions, if not the characters of men and women who have accepted the Gospel? Should their number be increased? What brings individuals the most happiness and peace; what gives them victory over temptation and sin; what brings the wholeness and peace of an integrated life, if not the Gospel of Jesus Christ? Does anyone really have the Gospel who is not willing and ready to share the Gospel?

II. The scope of community evangelism. 1. The new generation. 2. The old, middle-aged, and young who have not yet given their lives to Jesus Christ.

III. Our individual responsibility.

IV. Where shall we begin? What shall we do? (This lesson should issue in more than talk.)

---

# SUNDAY: MARCH TWENTY-THIRD

---

## MORNING SERVICE

### Theme: The Illimitable Love of God

Suggested Scripture Reading: Eph. 3:14-21.

Selected Hymns: "Joyful joyful, we adore thee."—Henry van Dyke. "God is love; his mercy brightens."—John Bowring. "There's a wideness in God's mercy."—F. W. Faber. "Thou hidden love of God, whose height."—Tersteegen and John Wesley. "O Love that wilt not let me go."—George Matheson.

Call to Worship: "For thus saith the Lord God, the Holy One of Israel; In returning and rest shall ye be saved; in quietness and in confidence shall be your strength: and ye would not." Isa. 30:15.

Invocation: We turn unto thee, O Lord, in the midst of our days, thankful that by thy Providence we know thee as a God of wisdom and power and love. In the midst of perplexing days help us to come unto thy wisdom. In our weakness may we find thy power. And always amidst all our various activities of life may we live in thy love and receive thy grace. Amen.

### Theme: The Illimitable Love of God

Text: "What is the breadth, and length, and depth, and height; And to know the love of Christ, which passeth knowledge." Eph. 3:18, 19.

What is the biggest thing on which the human mind can be exercised? There are the vast lone spaces of the stellar fields . . . with stars as the pilgrims, ever moving on their unknown journeyings. We can lose ourselves there. There is "the dark backward and abysm of time," and we can lose ourselves there. There is the appalling wilderness of human need. And we can lose ourselves there. And then there is the deadly, ubiquitous presence of human sin.

All these are stupendous themes. But there is something more majestic than the heavens, more wonderful than the far, mysterious vistas of time, more pervasive than human need. and more abounding than human sin. The biggest thing with which the mind can cope is the infinite love of God.

I. Let us reverently gaze into the "height" of the love of God. In love the scale of height is measured by the degree of purity. A diamond is of the "first water" when it is without flaw or tint of any kind. And love is lofty in proportion to its brilliance. Love can be deteriorated and degraded by the tint of jealousy. It can be debased by the tint of envy. It can be vulgarized by a strain of carnal passion.

1. Now it is here that the scriptures begin in their revelation of the love of God. They begin with its brilliance, its

holiness. "In him is no darkness at all." How would that be as a description of a diamond? "No darkness at all!" Nothing sinful in his love! But more than that. Nothing shady in it, nothing questionable, nothing compromising or morally indifferent! "No darkness at all": no blackness of faithlessness; no twilight of forgetfulness: "no night there"!

2. And thus it is that when the Book guides us in the contemplation of the eternal love, it first of all leads us into the contemplation of the eternal light. We are led away into the light, into the unshadowed brilliance, into the holiness of God. If therefore God's love be symbolized by a mountain, its heights will be clothed in the dazzling whiteness of the everlasting snow. Love's heights are found in love's holiness. "God is light," "God is truth," "God is love."

3. From this primary teaching I wish to adduce an inference. The force of love always depends upon its height.

4. And another inference—that the ultimate ministry and goal of life is also determined by the height of its holiness.

II. Let us gaze into the depths of the love of God.

1. It is only the really lofty that can truly reach the really deep. The arm that can reach far upward is the only arm that can reach far downward. It is only holy love that can deal with humanity's deepest needs.

2. God's love is deeper than human sorrow.

3. God's love is deeper than death.

4. God's love is deeper than sin.

III. Let us gaze into the breadth of the love of God. Here again I want to say that the breadth of love is determined by its height.

IV. And what of its length? There is no end to it. To what length will it not go? "Greater love hath no man than this, that a man lay down his life for his friends." To that length! "Becoming obedient unto death; even the death of the cross!" To that length! God's love is as long as the longest road. God's love is as long as the longest day. God's love is as long as the longest night. God's love is as long as life. God's love is as long as eternity. "I have loved thee with an everlasting love." "I will never leave thee nor forsake thee." "Love never faileth." O love of God, how long! —Adapted from John Henry Jowett.

PRAYER FOR THE DAY (This can be used as a Prayer of Confession): Our Heavenly Father, who by thy love hast made us, and through thy love hast kept us, and in thy love wouldst make us perfect, we humbly confess that we have not loved thee with all our heart and soul and mind and strength, and that we have not loved one another as Christ hath loved us. Thy life is within our souls, but our selfishness hath hindered thee. We have resisted thy Spirit. We have neglected thine inspirations.

Forgive what we have been; help us to amend what we are; and in thy Spirit direct what we shall be; that thou mayst come into the full glory of thy creation, in us and in all men, through Jesus Christ our Lord. Amen. From *The Methodist Hymnal.*

OFFERTORY SENTENCE: "And though I bestow all my goods to feed the poor, and though I give my body to be burned, and have not love, it profiteth me nothing." I Cor. 13:3.

OFFERTORY PRAYER: Accept, O Lord, our morning offering. Bless it that it may serve men as Jesus served them. May it heal the sick and open the eyes of the blind and cause the lame to walk. May it carry comfort and help to human souls in need. May it carry far and near the story of the love of Christ.

We know that its intrinsic value cannot accomplish this, but thy blessing upon it can bring these things to pass. In Jesus' name we pray. Amen.—H.

SEED THOUGHTS: The Breadth of God's Love. I. No limitations. 1. No social limits. 2. No national limits. 3. No ecclesiastical limits. 4. No creedal limits. II. The love of God is as broad as the race. Nowhere is there a single man in any clime, or of any color, in congested city, in tropical jungle, or on a lonely frontier line where a pioneer has built himself a primitive home—nowhere is there a single man, woman, or child who is orphaned of a place in the eternal Father's heart.—J. H. J.

The Perfecting of Our Love: By dwelling in the (1) height, (2) depth, (3) breadth, (4) length of the love of God.

"Sunbeams can move among sewage and catch no defilement. The brilliant, holy love of God ministers in the deepest depths of human need."—J. H. J.

**Choice Illustrations on the Theme**

AN ANALOGY—WATER AND LOVE. The force of love always depends upon its height. We find the analogy in water. The force of falling water is determined by its height. If your shower bath is lazy and loitering, chilling you rather than bracing you, your remedy is to raise the source of your supply, and in the increased height you will get the requisite tingle. The tonic is born in loftiness. It is even so with love.—J. H. J.

ANOTHER ANALOGY—WATER AND LOVE. Water rises no higher than its source. Water can lift no higher than its source. It is even so with love. Our love can never raise a loved one higher than the love itself. There are aspects of that law which are altogether staggering. Take the love of a parent for his child. Our own tainted love will not lift our child into purity. Our own jealous love will not lift our child into an unembittered disposition. Our own envious love will not lift out child into moral serenity. Our love will not lift above its own level.

"O Love of God, Most High!" I have been spending part of my holiday on the island of Arran. From the supreme height of the Fells there comes rolling down the granite slopes a gloriously alive and vitalizing stream. They call it "The White Water," and it is well named! It gleams on the slopes like the whitest foam! Out at sea, when everything else was obscure, I could see the white water running on its ceaseless errand! And oh, the loveliness of its bequests, and the unutterable beauty of its dells and glens! It feeds the bracken, it nourishes the stalwart heather, it moistens the retiring fern. The White Water endows its haunts with its own loveliness. And the white water of the eternal love, ceaselessly flowing from the holy heart of God, brings with it power to make everything lovely, and at last to present everything spotless before the throne. "O love of God, most high!"—J. H. J.

## EVENING SERVICE

**Theme: God's Altar Stairs**

TEXT: "I beseech you therefore, brethren, by the mercies of God, that ye present your bodies a living sacrifice, holy, acceptable unto God, which is your reasonable service." Rom. 12:1.

INTRODUCTORY: A friend has called these familiar words "St. Paul's Altar Call." They suggest more than

The great world's altar-stairs
That slope through darkness up to God

as Alfred Tennyson put it. They are God's altar stairs that bring the soul in dedication to divine transformation and to an experiential proof of what is "that good and acceptable and perfect will of God." We may clear the field for our thought by asking this question.

I. Who are to consecrate? The Apostle's recognition of the Christian brotherhood in Rome is as tender as it is tactful. He introduces strong incentives in his appeal for dedication, but one of the most persuasive is that it is an obligation of brethren in Christ. The inclusiveness of the brotherhood, Gentile and Jew, makes the presentation of the body upon God's altar by all who have entered the "Charmed Circle" a privilege as great as the obligation is strong.

We have here, too, the New Testament foundation for what in later years has been called "the priesthood of all believers." What greater sacrifice can be made? What priestly function can take unto itself greater meaning or higher significance than the offering of oneself as a living sacrifice unto the Lord?

II. The nature of consecration. The Christians at Rome were called upon to present their bodies a living sacrifice. We should not be taking from the passage if we paraphrased it to say: "I beseech you . . . that you present your life in the body a sacrifice unto God." We see, do we not, that such a presentation involves the will and the love and loyalty of the heart? It means that we devote all that living means here and now to God. It takes into its embrace all that stewardship of time and talent and substance and personality can mean.

III. The motives to consecration. We have emphasized the persuasion to dedication of life which belongs to the Christian brotherhood. The Apostle enforces such an obligation on prior grounds: "by the mercies of God." The fact of mercy becomes an incentive to consecration and the greatness of mercy makes an entire consecration altogether reasonable.

We remember the setting of this passage. It points back to "the riches both of the wisdom and knowledge of God" and to the Apostle's proclamation that "where sin abounded grace did abound more exceedingly."

We today have been blessed when we knew not we were blessed. We have been blessed when sometimes we thought we were cursed. In the language of the great Apostle and in the name and for the sake of the Christ, "I beseech you therefore, brethren, by the mercies of God."

IV. Consecrated to God. We have not dealt in thoroughness with the call to consecration until we give positive attention to its direction. Hear the text again: "Present your bodies a living sacrifice . . . unto God."

That is more than consecration to service—though a living sacrifice is to have its outward expression in service. Consecration is unto God to be what he wants us to be, first of all, and then to go or stay, to speak or keep silent, to serve or to suffer. Our consecration is not primarily to the Church but rather to the Head of the Church. Then to the Church that is the bride, we will give our love. Through the Church we will channel our service.

Do we find God when we climb his altar stairs? Does God make answer to the consecration of his people? He answers with acceptance. He answers with an inner transformation and renewal. He answers with an experience that brings us into a knowledge of his will, even "the holy and acceptable and perfect will of God."—Joseph Owen.

**Suggested Texts and Themes**

How Love Cancels Hate: "Bless them that curse you, and pray for them which despitefully use you." Luke 6:28.

A False Alignment: "Then said Jesus unto him, Put up again thy sword into his place; for all they that take the sword shall perish by the sword." Matt. 26:52.

Your Identification Tag: "By this shall all men know that ye are my disciples, if ye have love one to another." John 13:35.

What the World is Waiting For: "The creation waits with eager longing for the sons of God to be revealed." Rom. 8:19 (Moffatt).

Tired of Doing Right? "Never let us grow tired of doing what is right. . . ." Gal. 6:9 (Moffatt).

## MIDWEEK FELLOWSHIP MEETING TOPIC

(Church Night or Suggested Sermon Subject)

**Theme: An Emergency of Death**

TEXT: John 11:1-46.

This last miracle in John's Gospel is linked with the first (see Midweek Topic of Feb. 9.) by Jesus' statement in v. 4, "This sickness is not unto death, but for the glory of God, that the Son of God might be glorified thereby." Note John's comment in 2:11, "He manifested his glory." This sentence binds all the miracles of the Gospel together. In each "he manifested his glory."

I. Jesus meets this emergency of death with his presence, v. 28.

II. Jesus meets this emergency of death with his sympathy, v. 35. "He knows the wrench and the heartbreak. He sympathized; he understood; and so he wept. Is no work of grace effected by such tender tears?"

III. Jesus meets this emergency of

death with prayer, vv. 41, 42. A thanksgiving! He gives thanks for what he is "about to receive."

IV. Jesus meets this emergency of death with power. "He commands, clothed in sovereign power: 'Lazarus, come forth!' That is the same voice which in the beginning created the heavens and the earth."

## SUNDAY SCHOOL LESSON

**Mar. 23. The Church and World Evangelism: Matt. 28:18-20; Acts 13:1-3; Rom. 1:14-18.**

Memory Verse: "Go therefore and make disciples of all nations, baptizing them in the name of the Father and of the Son and of the Holy Spirit." Matt. 28:19 (r.s.v.).

The man who owns a 160-acre farm with his home at one corner does not cultivate only the acres which are near his house. The farthest acres are cultivated to bring a harvest, as well as the acres nearby. In fact the farthest acres may be the most productive acres.

The Church in Europe and America had its beginnings in the missionary enterprise. Once these were uttermost parts, farthest acres; their evangelization came because of missionary zeal.

Some motives for world evangelization:

I. Christ's Great Commission and Promise. These have never been revoked.

II. Thanksgiving for what we have received.

III. A sense of world brotherhood.

IV. Missions promote freedom and honor human personality, thus there is no better way to combat the false isms and panaceas of our day.

V. There is no surer way of bringing peace to our world than by helping to reach all men with the name of Jesus.

VI. There is a present urgency for a world-wide preaching of the Gospel.

See Section VI of this *Manual.*

# SUNDAY: MARCH THIRTIETH

## MORNING SERVICE

**Theme: The Tragedy of Ignorance (Palm Sunday)**

Suggested Scripture Reading: Luke 19:29-48.

Selected Hymns: "Fairest Lord Jesus." —From the German. "Joy to the world." —Isaac Watts. "Ride on! Ride on in majesty!"—H. H. Milman. "Fling out the banner."—G. W. Doane.

Call to Worship:

Once to every man and nation comes the moment to decide,
In the strife of Truth and Falsehood, for the good or evil side;
Some great cause, God's new Messiah, offering each the bloom or blight,
Parts the goats upon the left hand, and the sheep upon the right,
And the choice goes by forever 'twixt that darkness and that light.

—James Russell Lowell.

Invocation: Our Father, we open with joy the gates of our souls to let the King come in. Not for a passing hour of triumph would we receive him, to send him hence away with a broken heart and a frustrate purpose; but we welcome him to abide forever as our Lord and King. Prepare us for his coming. May our hearts be cleansed of sin and our purposes purified from all evil. Create in us clean hearts, and renew right spirits within us. Then with gladness and the voice of praise we shall greet him, whose right it is to reign. Amen.

**Theme: The Tragedy of Ignorance (Palm Sunday)**

TEXT: Luke 19:42-44.

INTRODUCTION: The road which Jesus followed on the Sunday of his so-called Triumphal Entry into Jerusalem runs from the village of Bethany, across the shoulder of the Mount of Olives, then down into the valley of the Kidron, and sharply up through a gate in the city wall into the city of Jerusalem.

As one comes from Bethany there is a sudden turn in the road where the walled city bursts into full view. It is a fascinating spot. Today as one stands there and looks across the intervening chasm to the city set upon a hill, considering its historical associations, it is the most striking scene in all the world.

In Jesus' day he could seee the gleaming gold and marble temple, with smoke rising from the burning sacrifices. And near the temple were the palaces of Caesar's friends. Round about these great buildings were the dull gray houses of the poor. All stood close together within the city wall.

It was at this turn in the road that Jesus burst into tears. There are tears which only a strong man can weep. There are tears which only a man who knows a situation can weep. There are tears which only a prophet, the man who sees, can weep. There are tears which only a Saviour can weep. Jesus, the hero, the man of knowledge, prophet, Saviour, there wept bitterly. Luke 19:41 reads: "And when he was come near, he beheld the city, and wept over it."

"Thou knowest not the time of thy visitation," said Jesus. It is the *Tragedy of Ignorance.* "If thou hadst known . . . the things which belong unto thy peace." And again, "Thine enemies shall cast a trench about thee, and compass thee round, and keep thee in on every side. And shall lay thee even with the ground, and thy children within thee; and they shall not leave in thee one stone upon another; because thou knewest not . . ."

This prophecy was all so terrible and horribly fulfilled in A.D. 70. The narrative of Titus' siege is told in awful detail upon the pages of Josephus. It is said that when Theodore Roosevelt was making a campaign tour through the country he went early one night to his berth in the train and took up a copy of Josephus to read the story. The next morning at breakfast time he was still reading. He had not slept. It is a history of horror, as is the story of Hiroshima, which, too, may have been a tragedy of ignorance.

I. As Jesus looked across from Olivet he could see the dome of the temple. How well he knew its precincts! There he had often encountered Sadducean priests and the Pharisees, ever binding the people under the ceremonial and moral law. *They knew law, but they did not know grace.* That was their ignorance. Therein was tragedy.

Even the sacrifice upon the temple altar was only a legal thing. A prophet had said that God desires mercy and not sacrifice. Legal sacrifice they knew; loving mercy they knew not.

It is no wonder that he who personified love and mercy stood on Olivet and wept as he looked across to the temple, aware that legalism was doomed, that only love is eternal.

This tragedy of ignorance is a tragedy of today. High priests and elders teach hatred and the power of force. Heavy burdens are placed upon the backs of the people. With the passing of time inevitable, with the future related to the present, ignorance moves toward catastrophe. Are the things which belong unto peace hidden from their eyes? Do they not know the time of their visitation? Love weeps!

Ignorance of grace is the tragedy of many lives. How many live lives of defeat and guilt under the law! They do what they hate and what they deeply desire of good they do not. They are unaware of the victory that a man may have through the grace of Christ.

Each man has his day of visitation when Christ stands ready to give him peace. Blessed are they who know that day. How tragic the lives of those who do not know it! Is this your day? your hour?

II. Jesus looked across to the dull and drab houses of the poor. How well he knew them! These common people were looking for a Messiah. *They knew prophecy, but they did not know the fulfillment of prophecy.* Their ignorance was tragic. A few knew. A few of those Galileans waving branches and shouting must have had true knowledge of him. The masses did not. "He came unto his own, and his own received him not." Someone says that that was the greatest blunder in history.

Jesus wept! Here is insight into the heart of God. He was feeling the hurt of the world. By this insight and compassion he would go to the Cross. "O Jerusalem, Jerusalem, thou that killest the prophets, and stonest them which are sent unto thee, how often would I have gathered thy children together, even as a hen gathereth her chickens under her wings, and ye would not!"

III. And there within the view of Jesus stood the palaces of Roman power in all their magnificence and pride. They were symbols of the Roman empire. Perhaps Jesus could see the soldiers standing guard. *They knew a king, but they did not know the King of kings.* They knew the sovereignty of Caesar, they did not know the sovereignty of God. There was a Pax Romana, but the peace which begins in the hearts of individuals, the peace which is without understanding, the peace which became the legacy of Christ, the peace which bindeth societies and nations and peoples together in mutual good will, that peace they did not know. It is a terrible tragedy not to know the things that belong unto peace. This is the tragedy of ignorance.

Oh, the glory of knowledge! "I know whom I have believed. . . ." "That I may know him, and the power of his resurrection. . . ." "They shall not hurt nor destroy in all my holy mountain; for the earth shall be full of the knowledge of the Lord, as the waters cover the sea." How we thrill to these texts! Does Christ look out over our own city in our day and weep bitterly? —H.

PRAYER FOR THE DAY: We come before thee, O God, on this anniversary day and at the beginning of a Holy Week with mingled feelings of joy and sadness.

As we join with those who greeted Christ with shouts of gladness we realize that the shouts of a following Friday called for his crucifixion. We wonder about ourselves—we question our own loyalty to our Master. In days of stress and strain our allegiance, too, might be weak. Caught up by the passion of the crowd we, too, might crucify our Lord. We pray that this may not be so. In thy strength alone shall we be able to stand. By thy grace shall we be strong. Grant us then thy grace to empower us. And grant thy forgiveness wherein we have ever proved disloyal. Amen.—H.

OFFERTORY SENTENCE: The earth shall be full of the knowledge of the Lord, as the waters cover the sea.

OFFERTORY PRAYER: We dedicate these gifts, O Lord, to the cause of peace—peace in human hearts, peace among the nations of the world. We dedicate them in the name of the Prince of Peace and his coming Kingdom. Amen. —H.

SEED THOUGHTS: The Inevitability of Time: "For the days shall come upon thee." Luke 19:43. "The night cometh."

The Relatedness of Days: ". . . this thy day . . . for the days shall come upon thee." On a certain day Abraham Lincoln was born. On another day a shot was fired in Serbia. On a certain day a bomb was dropped on Hiroshima. Significance of certain days for choice, for venture. Every man sometimes meets "a present crisis."

The Tragedy of Ignorance: I. The tragedy of ignorance is the tears of Christ. II. The tragedy of ignorance is the sufferings of men. III. The tragedy of ignorance is the delay of peace.

### Choice Palm Sunday Illustrations

JOSEPHUS CONCERNING JERUSALEM. "Yet hath not its great antiquity, nor its vast riches, nor the diffusion of its nation over all the habitable earth, nor the greatness of the veneration paid to it on a religious account, been sufficient to preserve it from being destroyed. And thus ended the siege of Jerusalem."

THE DAYS SHALL COME UPON YOU. It was not a great war by modern reckoning, but it was brutal and bloody enough. Civilians falling into the hands of the enemy were crucified before the walls of the besieged city within sight of its defenders, or sent back with their hands cut off, in an effort to undermine morale. From first to last more than a million men, women, and children were slaughtered or died of stravation. And when the fighting ended the city was a complete and ghastly ruin with hardly *one stone upon another*. Thus destruction came in 70 A. D. to Jerusalem. Since that time many a city has been destroyed, including Rome whose mighty legions brought death to Jerusalem. Would that we today "*knew the things that make for peace*."—Ernest Fremont Tittle.

## EVENING SERVICE

### Theme: The Hope of the Cross

TEXT: "But far be it . . . Lord Jesus Christ." Gal. 6:14.

INTRODUCTORY: Men think and live by symbols. Symbols constitute a convenient way of expressing in small compass complex and far-reaching ideas. The world is full of symbols. We have today the hammer and sickle, Old Glory, and the Union Jack, for example, as symbols of nationalisms; in medicine there is the caduceus; in law, the scales of justice. The early Christians used a fish as their secret symbol, since the letters of the Greek word for fish furnished the initial letters for the expression "Jesus Christ, Son of God, Saviour."

But the most meaningful symbol the world has ever known or will ever know is the cross. Crowded into that emblem is the whole significance of the universe and the world, of human life and destiny.

I. Consider some of the eternal truths symbolized by the cross. The cross tells us about God, and it tells us about him in such an emphatic and conclusive way that any man zealous for truth, and obedient and teachable in spirit, cannot fail to discover something of what is in the mind and the heart of the Heavenly Father.

He hates sin. That is the meaning of the blood. God is an ethical God, a God of uncompromising morality. God loves man with an everlasting love. That also is what this symbol the cross says. Calvary is just the measure of the distance God will go to encourage, to help, to save you and me. He gave his Son. He gave himself. The cross tells what happened in Palestine two thousand years ago, and it likewise tells what is happening now, two thousand years later. Fod God is here the suffering, loving God, the invisible Spirit at work in each of us.

II. The cross tells us about man. It proclaims that man is not just a sinner. He was and is created in the image of his loving Heavenly Father. That thorn-crowned, bleeding figure on Calvary's hill is I. He is the eternal humanity revealing to the light of day the deep inner nature of man, his insatiable idealism, his never-ending struggle with the flesh.

III. The cross has still another story to tell, a story of forgiveness and healing of body, mind, and soul, for men and women and children everywhere. The cross has a message for all sin-burdened, fear-obsessed, sick and afflicted men and women. That message is forgiveness, and a new start backed by the invincible power, wisdom, and love of the Creator and Father of all mankind. All this the cross means, and much more. Someone has pointed out that the cross on which Christ was crucified had an upright and cross-piece, signifying the meeting of two worlds—the visible and invisible. The horionztal bar stands for our human life lived in time; the vertical bar is the life of the Eternal coming down from above to pierce our material existence with a new spirit and a new power. The cross, then, is the focal point in human history, marking a new order of things, proclaiming a God of righteousness and love, the godlikeness of man, and the possibility of forgiveness and a new start. A new start! That is the inspiration, the power, the hope of the cross.—*Zion's Herald.*

**Suggested Texts and Themes**

The Gospel of the Resurrection: "That I may know him, and the power of his resurrection. . . ." Phil. 3:10.

Thwarted: "Yet thou shalt see the land before thee; but thou shalt not go thither unto the land which I give the children of Israel. Deut. 32:52. (Can be used as a Palm Sunday text.)

The Day of Palms: Mark 11:1-11.

The Kingship of Christ: "Behold, the world is gone after him." John 12:19.

The Impossibility of Neutrality: "He that is not with me is against me." Matt. 12:30.

## MIDWEEK FELLOWSHIP MEETING TOPIC

(Church Night or Suggested Sermon Subject)

**Theme: This Week in the Life of Jesus**

It is helpful to meditate each year upon the events of Holy Week. The people like to have them put in chronological order and to ponder upon the significance of each day. The days and the passages which give the narrative follow.

Sunday. The Day of Triumph. Matt. 28:1-11; Mark 11:1-11; Luke 19:29-44; John 12:12-19.

Monday. The Day of Authority. The cursing of the fig tree. Matt. 21:18-19 (20-22); Mark 11:12-14. Second cleansing of the temple, Matt. 21:12-17; Mark 11:15-19; Luke 19:45-48. Read also John 2:13-22.

Tuesday. The Day of Conflict. Christ's authority challenged. Matt. 21:23-27; Mark 11:27-33; Luke 20:1-8. See also the portions of scripture which follow those given here. The record of this day is quite full.

Wednesday. The Day of Silence. No record. The significance of the silence.

Thursday. The Day of the Last Supper. Matt. 26:17-30; Mark 14:12-26; Luke 22:7-30; John 13:1-30. Christ's farewell discourses: John 13:31-16:33. The intercessory prayer, John 17.

Friday. The Day of Crucifixion. The passages begin with Matt: 16:36; Mark 14:32; Luke 22:39; John 18:1.

Saturday. The Day in the Tomb. Matt. 27:62-66.

Sunday. The Day of Resurrection. Matt. 28:1-15; Mark 16:1-14; Luke 23:-56-24:43; John 20:1-25.

## SUNDAY SCHOOL LESSON

**Mar. 30. The Church Observes the Sacraments (Ordinances). Rom. 6:3,4; I Cor. 10:14-22. Background Scripture: Matt. 26:26-29; John 6:35-59; Acts 8:26-39; Rom. 6:3-11; I Cor. 11:23-29.**

MEMORY VERSE: "As often as you eat this bread and drink the cup, you proclaim the Lord's death until he comes." I Cor. 11:26 (R.S.V.).

I. Baptism. The origin, meaning, and significance of this sacrament are not clear in the minds of many church members. This lesson gives opportunity to deal with these important matters. The background scripture Rom. 6:3-11 points up the climax of the whole matter in the new outlook which comes to those who are baptized in Jesus Christ—death unto sin, aliveness unto God through Jesus Christ.

II. Communion. By discussing the various names by which this sacrament is called the teacher can open up the subject interestingly and profitably. 1. It is a *Sacrament.* 2. It is a *Eucharist,* a giving of thanks. 3. *Communion,* a fellowship with Christ and his followers. 4. *The Lord's Supper,* a means of partaking of the grace of Christ through the symbolism of the bread and the cup. (See Section V of this *Manual.*)

## SUNDAY: APRIL SIXTH

### MORNING SERVICE

**Theme: Not Seeing but Believing (Easter)**

SUGGESTED SCRIPTURE READING: John 20:19-29.

SELECTED HYMNS: "Christ the Lord is risen today."—Charles Wesley. "The day of resurrection."—John of Damascus. "O for a thousand tongues to sing."—Charles Wesley. "Life is good, for God contrives it."—Percy Dearmer. "All hail the power of Jesus' Name."—Edward Perronet.

CALL TO WORSHIP: Now is Christ risen from the dead, and become the firstfruits of them that slept. If ye then be risen with Christ, seek those things which are above, where Christ sitteth on the right hand of God.

INVOCATION: O thou who makest the stars, and turnest the shadow of death into the morning; on this day of days we meet to render thee, our Lord and King, the tribute of our praise; for the resurrection of the springtime, for the everlasting hopes that rise within the human heart, and for the gospel which hath brought life and immortality to light. Receive our thanksgiving, reveal thy presence, and send into our hearts the Spirit of the Risen Christ. Amen.

**Theme: Not Seeing but Believing (Easter)**

TEXT: "Jesus saith unto him, Thomas, because thou hast seen me, thou hast believed: blessed are they that have not seen, and yet have believed." John 20:29.

At times the story of the Resurrection seems incredible to us, and we find ourselves with Thomas, full of honest doubt, and saying, "Unless I can see for myself, I cannot believe."

We are between belief and unbelief, wondering which part we should take, on which side we should stand. There are many, trained in the scientific method, who say, "If I can't see a soul in my laboratory, I cannot believe there is a soul. Except I see in his hands the print of his nails and touch his wounded side, I will not believe."

Suppose you could see. Suppose you had the kind of proof that ends all doubt. Would it not also end all thought, all discovery, all trust, all serving of goodness for its own sake, all great adventure in the realm of the spirit: Suppose that you could prove God and immortality. Suppose the rewards for goodness were spelled out in black and white. Then virtue would become mere obedience to the traffic light and the corner policeman, and all dedication and heroism a calculation of self-interest, a kind of down payment on a mansion in the life to come.

Here we see through a glass darkly. Here we know in part. And there are good religious reasons for what we don't know and what we can't prove. "Blessed are they that have not seen and yet have believed."

I. What can we see that supports the bold affirmations of Christianity about God and life eternal? God is love, says Christianity, and he that dwelleth in love dwelleth in God and God in him. But how can you say that, and where can you see it, even through a glass darkly.

You find love in letters that young men write to their parents halfway round the world. You find it, a glad and grateful love, when fathers and mothers bring their little ones to be baptized. You find love bearing all things, believing all things, hoping all things, enduring all things, as a woman waits and prays near a hospital bed while a husband struggles for his life.

You see love when you look inside a

little tent in the Antarctic. It was Scott's expedition, and they were out of food and fuel, and Seaman Oates had frozen feet, and they had to drag him on a sled. He knew he was slowing them up. Without him they might make it. Somehow he managed to stand up and say good night, and stumbled out into the blizzard. They were to weak to stop him, but they knew it was the act of a gallant gentlemen. Surely greater love hath no man than this, that a man lay down his life for his friends.

Where do you think it comes from? What is your scientific explanation? Is this just a problem of physics or chemistry—atoms or cells that divide and rearrange themselves in patterns that are fixed by law? Or will you say that man is just an animal and self-preservation is his highest law? But you have something more than just an animal when a person laying down his life in love fulfills a higher law.

Faith is just the persuasion that what is highest in man is deepest in nature; that what comes out of the process is somehow within it and behind it; that God must be at least as good as the best that we see in man. How can a fountain rise higher than its source? And when we see the Saviour dying on a cross, we say the secret of such perfect love is hidden deeply in the universe that brought him forth. There is love at the heart of all things from which such love appears.

This is the central word of the Gospel, the good news of the love of God, and the Resurrection throws light on it, for what we see dimly we see more clearly in the brightness of Easter morning.

II. And because we believe that God is love, we see more clearly the reason for the Christian hope in everlasting life. It has always been the hope of mankind, however strangely expressed. The urge to go on beyond the grave, according to the best opinion, has been deep and universal among the primitive peoples of the earth.

That doesn't make it true. Of course not. But man has always been in rebellion against his death, brooding wistfully and hopefully about his fate, and therefore in a sense above his fate.

As long as life is precious, there is something within us that cannot be reconciled to death.

I don't know how it is with you. I can only speak for myself. If you say we must all die and that ends it, speak for yourself. That is your world. It is not mine. I am a square peg in that kind of a hole, and to try to force myself into it is to fight against my own nature, and I think against the truth of God.

Now bring these two great thoughts together. Put this human life, hoping, aspiring, seeking for more understanding and comradeship than earth affords, into the framework of the love of God. You cannot say that your life does not matter. You have no right to say it. It may not matter to you. But it matters to God, and his love will be seeking you always, and will never let you go.

This we believe, though we cannot see the print of his nails, nor touch his wounded side. Blessed are they that have not seen and yet have believed.—Harold E. Nicely.

Prayer for the Day: O God, our Father, we thank thee for this day of days in the history of the world, the Resurrection Day of our Lord, this day of his victory over sin and death.

Make this a day of days in the life of the Church, a day of remembrance of his rising, a day of experience of his presence, a day of expectation that we shall see him face to face.

Make this a day of days in the secret history of our souls. May there be a resurrection within us, a glorious springtime bursting into bloom. May any darkness in our inner lives be dispelled by the light of the morning. May the desert places, by the rising of the Sun of Righteousness, bloom and blossom as the rose. May the seeds of the Christian virtues and graces, planted long ago perhaps, begin to spout and to grow in us making of our lives the very fields of God. Amen.—H.

Offertory Sentence: "Go ye therefore, and teach all nations, baptizing them in the name of the Father, and of the Son, and of the Holy Ghost: . . . and, lo, I am with you alway, even unto the end of the world."

Offertory Prayer: From our pocket purses, O Lord, we dedicate a portion of our wealth as a token of our Easter praise. But our heart purses hold the true riches. We open them to render unto thee our faith, our allegiance, and our love. Wilt thou bless these offerings of our hands and our hearts. In the name of the Risen Christ. Amen.—H.

Seed Thoughts:

Doubt and Belief. "Nothing is so firmly believed as that which has once been doubted." A. B. Bruce.

"Jesus Is Lord." The finality of Jesus is summed up in the confession of the early Christian Church, "Jesus is Lord." These words imply I. Illumination; II. Authority; III. Salvation; IV. Security.—Edgar P. Dickie.

The Blessing! John 20:29. There is no nook or cranny of life which is not crowned with light and flooded with sunshine, no dull stretch of the road which does not grow romantic, no common task or lonely way which is not transfigured, no human friendship which is not hallowed, no heavy cross which does not begin to shine with glory, when once Christ and his glad tidings have gripped the heart.—James S. Stewart.

### Choice Illustrations on the Theme

Pascal's dilemma. Three centuries ago Pascal wrote, "I look on all sides and see nothing but obscurity. Did I see nothing there which marked a Divinity I should decide not to believe in him. Did I see everywhere marks of a Creator I should rest peacefully in faith. But seeing too much to deny and too little to affirm, my state is pitiful. I have a hundred times wished that nature would say all or nothing, that I might see which part I should take."

Quotation from Frederick W. Robertson. There is an inward state of heart which makes truth credible the moment it is stated. It is credible to some men beause of what they are. Love is credible to a loving heart: purity is credible to a pure mind; life is credible to a spirit in which life beats strongly: it is incredible to other men. Because of that such men believe. Of course that inward state could not *reveal* a fact like the resurrection; but it can *receive* that fact the moment it is revealed without requiring evidence. The love of St. John himself never could discover a resurrection; but it made a resurrection easily believed, when the man of intellect, St. Thomas, found difficulties.

## EVENING SERVICE

### Theme: Eternal Life Now (Easter)

Text: "This is eternal life, that they know thee the only true God." John 17:3 (R.S.V.).

Nowhere in the Gospels can we find Jesus talking about immortality. Instead we hear him talking about "eternal life."

Immortality carries with it primarily continuous existence. Eternal life stresses and means quality of life. Immortality is merely going on and on; eternal life means life so rich in the experience of the forgiveness and reality of God, that going on and on is desirable. Immortality is post-mortem; eternal life is now.

I. One practical aspect of this emphasis is that we must cease postponing eternal life. Our living now must be focused, not on the distant future, but on the here and now.

When the Scotch Presbyterian was told "Now is the time to go to heaven," he replied, "That is where I am living now." Eternal life is here in the Gospel. It is here in the gift of God's Son to us, whom we crucified, but whom God raised from the dead. It is here in all the moral and spiritual values that make up the Kingdom of God. It is here in good causes waiting to be served and in whose service there is perfect freedom and eternal life.

II. Another aspect of this matter is

to make eternal life desirable. "Immortality without eternal life, so far from being desirable, is terrible." Merely to go on and on in a static, never-ending existence, so far from being desirable, would be unendurable.

This is Christ's gift to the race: "I am come that you may have life and have it in abundance." Jesus brought into life a deeper and richer experience of the forgiveness of God and personal friendship and partnership with him, opening new dimensions to life's meaning and purpose and so making going on and on and on with God desirable and exciting. So Paul said that it hasn't entered into the heart of man the things that God has prepared for those who love him.

III. Consider, finally, that this emphasis is to make eternal life inevitable for some. Peter in his sermon on the day of Pentecost said to Jesus: "But God raised him up, having loosed the pangs of death, because it was not possible for him to be held by it." When through surrender and obedience we build into our life the quality of God's life we call "eternal life," death is powerless.

If everything we participate in here is transient, ephemeral, passing, and earthy, then it is a spiritual law that in the end we shall be like the chaff which the winds drive away, but when we participate in goodness and truth and righteousness and justice, serve sacrificially the Gospel, belong to God in Christ as our lord and Master, we are deathless by nature of what we belong to and love.—H. Richard Rasmusson.

## Quotable Easter Poetry

### Easter Hymn

'Tis Easter morn. Again we see
The garden path where women tread;
The open tomb. We hear the words:
"Lo, He is risen as He said."
Rejoice, be glad, praise and adore:
He lives, Christ lives forevermore.
'Tis Easter morn. Like angels here
Let lilies stand in heaven's array.
Let music's holy incense rise:
This is His second natal day.
Rejoice, be glad, praise and adore:
He lives, Christ lives forevermore.
'Tis Easter morn, May every soul
To Him complete allegiance give.
For us His cross. His empty tomb:
Because He lives, we too shall live.
Rejoice, be glad, praise and adore:
He lives, Christ lives forevermore.

—Frank P. Fletcher.

### His Dream Is Coming True!

He lives! He lives! His dream is coming true!
His sojourn among men was not in vain.
His perfect plan and purpose cannot fail;
He shall not lose the world He came to save.
His truth shall bring true freedom to mankind.
The kingdom He established shall endure;
His glory shall illumine every soul.
His love abides, His victory is sure!

—Author unknown.

## Suggested Easter Texts and Themes

The Reasonableness of Immortality: "Why should it be thought incredible with you, that God should raise the dead?" Acts 26:8.

The End and the Beginning: "When Jesus therefore had received the vinegar, he said, It is finished: and he bowed his head, and gave up the ghost." John 19:30.

The Most Haunting Idea in the World: "The idea of immortality has given life to virtue, holiness to love, hope to bereavement, even sweetness to sorrow."

If the Dead Rise Not: "If after the manner of men I have fought with beasts of Ephesus, what advantageth it me, if the dead rise not?" I Cor. 15:32.

I Believe in Immortality: "Because I live, ye shall live also." John 14:19. I believe in immortality. I. I believe in immortality because of the world in which I live—the air, the water, the bounty of nature. II. I believe in immortality because of the love I have found in my home which good days have made even greater and dark waters could not quench. III. I believe in immortality because of people—the good ones who do not deserve to be blotted out, and the bad ones who may yet come to know their Heavenly Father's redeeming love. IV. I believe in immortality because of Jesus Christ, who lived on earth a life of heavenly dimensions, who said that in his Father's house there are many rooms and that he went to prepare a place for us. V. I believe in immortality because I believe in God—God whom I know not through what the world calls knowledge but through a faith which has revealed his love and care. By faith I know him whom to know is Life Eternal.—Roy M. Pearson.

## MIDWEEK FELLOWSHIP MEETING TOPIC

(Church Night or Suggested Sermon Subject)

**Theme: After Easter—Pentecost**

TEXT: "It is expedient for you that I go away; for if I go not away, the Comforter will not come unto you; but if I depart, I will send him unto you." John 16:7.

Divisions of the Church Year: World-wide Communion Sunday to Christmas; Christmas to Easter; Easter to Pentecost; Pentecost to World-wide Communion Sunday.

I. The date and season of Pentecost.

II. Pentecost is based upon a condition and a promise. See text. "Only by departing from the vision of the privileged few could he reign by his Spirit in the hearts of all." "His departure was expedient for the spiritualizing of religion, for the universalizing of the Gospel, for the energizing of evangelism, for the fortifying of the faith." James S. Stewart.

III. The spectacular fulfillment. Acts 2.

IV. Our needs of Pentecost.—H.

## BULLETIN BOARD SLOGANS FOR THE MONTH

God believes in you!

God is near to help and bless.

Daily prayer lessens daily care.

God is tested by fire; man, by gold.

Only "new" men can build a new world.

Prayer is the greatest enemy of worry.

Most of those who drink to be sociable aren't.

There has always been a sunrise after a sunset.

The path of least resistance usually leads downhill.

He who has immortality in his soul never fears dying.

Welcome the Cross of Christ and bear it triumphantly.

"Be of good cheer: I have overcome the world."—Jesus.

## SUNDAY SCHOOL LESSON

**Apr. 6. The Church's Assurance of Victory. John 20:26-29; Eph. 1:15-23. Background Scripture: Rev. 7:9-12.**

MEMORY SELECTION: "Now to him who by the power at work within us is able to do far more abundantly than all that we ask or think, to him be glory in the church and in Christ Jesus to all generations, for ever and ever. Amen" Eph. 3:20-21 (R.S.V.).

The Church's Assurance of Victory lies in the opening of our minds, the illumination of our understanding. We must have what Chad Walsh calls "double seeing." Paul prays for the Ephesians, Eph. 1:18, that they may be "enlightened," eyes and heart. With insight we shall be aware of three wonders wrought out for us in Christ by his resurrection from the dead.

I. We may realize "how great is the hope to which he is calling us."

II. We may see "the magnificence and splendor of the inheritance promised to Christians." Eph. 2:7, 8.

III. We may know how "tremendous is the power available to us who believe in God," "the exceeding greatness of his power." It is the power of the resurrection which changes both the quantity and the quality of life. "Abundance," "length of life," "breadth," "depth," are terms of quantity. "Happiness," "hopefulness," and "holiness" are terms of quality.

Eph. 1:20-23. "Nowhere else in the New Testament is the exalted Christ, head over all things for the Church, so gloriously portrayed."

## SUNDAY: APRIL THIRTEENTH

### MORNING SERVICE

**Theme: The Adequate Christ**

SUGGESTED SCRIPTURE READING: Luke 24:13-35.

SELECTED HYMNS: "Fairest Lord Jesus." —German, 17th Cent. "Ye servants of God, your Master proclaim."—Charles Wesley. "We may not climb the heav'nly steeps."—J. G. Whittier. "Jesus call us o'er the tumult."—Cecil F. Alexander.

CALL TO WORSHIP: "Jesus saith unto Thomas, because thou hast seen me, thou hast believed: blessed are they that have not seen, and yet have believed."

INVOCATION: Grant unto us, our Father, that blessing which was promised unto those who put their faith in Christ, even without the testimony of their eyes that they have seen him.

We thank thee for our recent experience of Easter joy. Help us to remember that our worship together on the first day of the week is in remembrance of the fact that on the first day of the week Jesus rose from the dead. We rejoice in our living Lord. Amen.

**Theme: The Adequate Christ**

TEXT: "After that he appeared in another form unto two of them, as they walked, and went into the country." Mark 16:12.

INTRODUCTORY: 1. Jesus is the unchanging and unchangeable One. 2. Yet he is not a stereotyped Saviour. 3. It is a wonderful fact that Christ has an appeal for each and all. 4. How do you account for his universality? How do you account for him?

Here are two aspects of Christ which the skeptic cannot gainsay. Each carries abundant evidence of his uniqueness, but taken together they make an irresistible appeal. He is big enough for a world! On the other hand, he is specific enough to fit the yearnings of a little child. He transcends the largest conception the mind of man can hold. See human need in the infinitesimal, still he fits it perfectly. Extremes meet in him. You will find every variety of life at his cross. Go into the hall of learning whose shelves are crowded with products of the brightest minds and ask for the best book and they will place in your hands the story of Jesus. Go into the tenement where there is little time and perhaps little taste for books, ask the same question and you will gain the same repsonse. The artist with his masterpiece and the peasant who knows nothing of perspectives and tints and tones both gaze with raptured eyes into the face of Christ. The musician and the mechanic acknowledge together that his voice is the sweetest sound that ever fell upon their ears.

I. Each of us may expect to find in Christ that which will satisfy his deepest longing and challenge his noblest capacities.

He came to meet your need—yours and mine. And whatever the need is he meets it adequately.

It was said of him, "He knew what was in man." He did and he does. He knows the wretched mess we have made of things. He knows how we have played fast and loose with life—the dearest treasure that humans possess. He knows our defilements. He knows our humiliation. He knows our timidity. He knows our difficulties and our fears. He knows our latent possibilities.

He holds the key. He and only he can unlock the glories that are dormant within the soul.

II. If he appears to men in different forms, we have no right to question the validity of our brother's experience, simply because it does not parallel our own.

Shall Lydia doubt Paul's conversion because it came with a splendor which blinded his eyes? And shall Nicodemus discredit Matthew because Matthew answered the Master's call without conflict of soul?

He manifests himself in different ways. Sometimes he comes through the mind. Sometimes he comes through the imagination. Sometimes through the emotions. Sometimes through the sympathetic outlook upon human need. How he comes matters not if only he comes.

The emphasis should not be upon the process, but upon the big glad fact of his presence in the life. Your brother's creed may differ from yours; his forms of worship may differ from yours; what matter if only you and he trust and love and seek to serve the same matchless Christ!

III. And surely we shall not belittle this universal Christ by withholding him from the world. Among all the religions which have appealed for the faith of men the message of Christ is the only one which carries the real marks of universality.—Edwin F. Hallenbeck.

A Prayer for the Day: Help us, O God, to walk on high levels. Give us moral attainment, eager and able to discriminate between right and wrong, with a will to do the right. Give us spiritual attainment—help us to lay hold on that for which we were laid hold on by Jesus Christ. May we achieve the mind of Christ. May we submit our lives unto the power of thy Spirit for cleansing, for fruit-bearing, for becoming channels of power. We desire to live under the ministry of thy love, accepting thy grace for our weakness, thy forgiveness for our sins, thy comfort for our grief, and thy sympathy for our sorrow and our joy. May the very stature of the manhood of Christ become the measure of our manhood. Amen.—H.

Offertory Sentence: Hear the advice of Paul to the Church at Corinth, setting us a good example: "Now concerning the collection . . . upon the first day of the week let every one of you lay by him in store, as God has prospered him. . . ." I Cor. 16:1, 2.

Offertory Prayer: It is the desire of our hearts, O Lord, to be faithful in all things. Bless us then with a spirit of sympathy and love, and remove from us all inferior motives which impede and inhibit our benevolence. Accept this offering and bless it as a token of our desire. Amen.—H.

Seed Thoughts:

Christ's Gospel transcends the differences which set man at variance with man. I. The discord of race and nationality. II. The differences between the old and the young. III. The differences between conservatives and progressives. IV. The differences between the institutionalists and the independent.—W. R. Bowie.

An Adequate Theme: "I determined," Paul told the Corinthians quite frankly, "not to know any thing among you, save Jesus Christ." "To me," he wrote to the Philippians, "to live is Christ"—life means Christ to me. That was his one theme, given to him straight from God himself, and if ever a time should come when that is no longer the central theme of the Christian Church, then the day of the Church will be finished. The one thing that can justify the Church is a great passion for Christ.—James S. Stewart.

## Choice Illustrations on the Theme

THE UNIVERSALITY OF CHRIST. Translate the words of Jesus into whatever country's language you will, he might have been the offspring of that country. Date them by whatever century of the world you will, they belong to that century as much as to any other. He was not the Asiatic. He was not the European. He was not the Jew. He was not the type of that century stamped with its peculiarities. He was not the mechanic. He was not the aristocrat. He was the man. He was the child of every age and every nation. He was a heart pulsating with the blood of the human race. He reckoned for his ancestry the collective myriads of mankind. He was the Son of man."—Robertson of Brighton.

HE MEETS THE WORLD'S NEED'S.

Thine is the mystic life great India craves,
Thine is the Parsee's sin-destroying beam,
Thine is the Buddhist's rest from tossing waves,
Thine is the empire of vast China's dream.
Thine is the Roman's strength without his pride,
Thine is the Greek's glad world without its grave,
Thine is Judea's law and love beside,
The truth that conquers and the grace that saves.

—Author Unknown.

THE ALPHA AND OMEGA. The early Church had a strange name for Jesus. It called him "the Alpha and the Omega"; which means, to put it in the language of today, that Jesus is simply everything in life from A to Z.—J. S. S.

## EVENING SERVICE

**Theme: Why We Miss God**

In his familiar and moving poem, "The Hound of Heaven," Francis Thompson confessed that he had run away from God—"I fled Him . . . I hid from Him." For how many of us did this sensitive poet speak? We may be quite certain that if a man misses the divine, it is not because God has eluded him, but because he has hidden from God. Behind what do we hide?

I. First, man hides behind his mask. Hypocrisy spoils communion with the Infinite. Refusing to be honest with ourselves, pretending we are better than we are, we evade the humble confession of our needs which must surely precede a religious experience. Then, of course, there are our modern sophisticates who pretend that they are worse than they are. In a day when hardness and cynicism are popular men simulate these qualities. When we deny our urge to idealism and tenderness we deny God, for the very word which best describes the God of Jesus—love—connotes the emotional qualities which this new hypocrisy has banned.

II. Many people are hiding from God behind prejudices and preconceptions. We have grown up with quite definite ideas of what it means to find God. We have read in a book or heard in someone's testimony that a religious experience involves some strange accompaniments such as hearing a voice, seeing letters written across the sky, or feeling some unusual ecstatic thrill. Or we have accepted the necessity of passing through the gateway of some creed or doctrine, and to date that creed or doctrine does not seem credible. After reading the history of the Christian Church one is surprised to note how Jesus went about winning his disciples. As I read the record, Jesus set up no creedal or experimental test. Instead his test was a very practical one—"Follow me." If we are expecting God only in the wind, earthquake and fire, we may miss him in "the still small voice."

III. Third, a man may miss God because he is hidden in a mass of preoccupation. Perhaps there is no danger in our modern world greater than this. One's wee twenty-four hours to the day have not lengthened one bit, but how terrifically have the duties and interests increased which fill those hours!

Someone has said, "If the devil cannot make us bad, he will make us busy: too busy to accomplish many of the good and effective things we are capable of." Wilberforce, a man who was both good and religious, became involved and burdened in his struggle to emancipate slaves. He made this reply to a woman who asked him how he ever found time to look after his soul: "Madam, I had almost forgotten that I have one!" Religion, like friendship, love and home, requires some time for quiet, thought, and devotion. But we are too busy.

IV. Last, most men who miss God are hiding behind their sin. Indeed, that is what makes a thing sin! It stands between you and God. In so many ways man in his selfishness builds a wall between himself and God. He does so with his resentments. You will never find God while your heart is fouled by bitterness. The unforgiving spirit is sin; it separates man from man and therefore man from God. More than once Jesus said or implied that forgiving others is prerequisite to being ourselves forgiven by God.—Frank B. Fagerburg.

**Suggested Texts and Themes**

The Look That Changes Life: "And the Lord turned, and looked upon Peter. . . ." Luke 22:61, 62.

Blessed Assurance: "I know whom I have believed." II Tim. 1:12.

True Security: "But seek first his kingdom and his righteousness, and all these things shall be yours as well." Matt. 6:33 (R.S.V.).

Potentialities: "I am not come to call the righteous, but sinners to repentence." Matt. 9:13.

Religion is the Answer: "Commit thy way unto the Lord; trust also in him; and he shall bring it to pass." Ps. 37:5.

## MIDWEEK FELLOWSHIP MEETING TOPIC

(Church Night or Suggested Sermon Subject)

**Theme: Christ Precious to Believers**

TEXT: "Unto you therefore which believe he is precious." I Pet. 2:7.

"Precious, precious, more than precious" were the dying words of Bishop Simpson. To her class of children a teacher said, "You have been reading that Christ is precious; what does that mean?" After a pause in silence one boy replied, "Father said the other day that mother was precious 'for whatever should he do without her?'" That is a great feature of the preciousness of Christ, Whatever could we do without him?

I. Christ is precious to the believer on account of what he is in himself.

II. Christ is precious to the believer on account of what he has done for him. 1. He has redeemed us with his precious blood. 2. He loves us with a precious love. 3. He justifies us through precious faith. 4. He comforts us with precious promises. 5. He sanctifies us with a precious union.

III. Christ is precious unto them who believe on account of what he has done in them.

IV. Christ is precious unto them who believe on account of what he is still doing both for them and in them.

V. Christ is precious to them that believe on account of what he has promised and pledged himself to do for them hereafter.

## SUNDAY SCHOOL LESSON

**Apr. 13. God's People in Bondage. Exod. 1:7-22. Background Scripture: Exod. 1.**

MEMORY VERSE: "With the Lord on my side I do not fear. What can man do to me?" Ps. 118:6 (R.S.V.).

This Sunday's lesson begins a second unit in the studies of the year. The lessons cover the time span from the Hebrews' slavery in Egypt and the Exodus up to the time of Samuel. This may be explained to the group, pointing out that three periods of history are included: (1) the slavery in Egypt, (2) the nomadic life following deliverance from Egypt, and (3) the settlement in Canaan and the time of the Judges. Since the lessons are centered in significant events, it is important to refer to the connected history of the period frequently during the quarter.

The lessons emphasize the purpose of God in selecting and training a people to become witnesses to his revelation.

I. Review of the circumstances which brought the children of Israel into Egypt.

II. The cause and condition of the exploitation and enslavement of the people.

III. God's providential purpose in the disciplines of suffering.

IV. The difficulties that confront God's people in our day, recognizing his claims on their obedience in every circumstance.

# SUNDAY: APRIL TWENTIETH

## MORNING SERVICE

**Theme: The Cross of Circumstance**

SUGGESTED SCRIPTURE READING: Luke 23:20-26; Phil. 4:4-13.

SELECTED HYMNS: "Spirit of God, descend upon my heart."—George Croly. "O for a faith that will not shrink."—W. H. Bathurst. "Must Jesus bear the cross alone?"—Thomas Shepherd. "Am I a soldier of the cross?"—Isaac Watts. "Soldiers of Christ, arise."—Charles Wesley.

CALL TO WORSHIP: "When he, the Spirit of truth, is come, he will guide you into all truth: for he shall not speak of himself; but whatsoever he shall hear, that shall he speak: and he will shew you things to come. He shall glorify me: for he shall receive of mine, and shall shew it unto you." John 16:13, 14.

INVOCATION: Holy and Eternal Spirit of God, brood thou over us in all thy creative power. Create in us clean hearts and renew a right spirit within us.

Inspire our minds that we may know God. Touch our hearts that we may love him and love one another. Energize our wills that we may go forth to serve the cause of Christ in the world. Amen.—H.

**Theme: The Cross of Circumstance**

TEXT: "And as they led him [Jesus] away, they laid hold upon one Simon, a Cyrenian, coming out of the country, and on him they laid the cross, that he might bear it after Jesus." Luke 23:26.

Have you ever pondered upon these words from the Fourth Gospel? "No man taketh my life from me, I lay it down of myself." The heroism of Jesus and his cross lies largely in the fact that the cross was for him a conscious choice. It was not forced upon him against his will. He could have refused it. In the Father's will the cross had a redemptive purpose. But in this purpose Jesus could have been unfaithful. Calvary was a free, voluntary, consciously accepted strategy on Jesus' part.

But not all crosses are of this kind. In the case of the man we read about in the Scripture lesson, Simon of Cyrene, far from the cross being something consciously chosen, it was something forced upon him. He did not choose it. Had he been free to run away, very likely he would have done so. But circumstances conspired otherwise and Simon was impressed to bear a heavy cross. We call it the cross of circumstance.

Here was Simon, having come from Cyrene to participate no doubt in the Passover festivities. On a particular day he stopped to watch a man called Jesus carry a heavy cross down a dusty road. Then suddenly without any warning, he was compelled without his consent to carry this same heavy cross. There are crosses we do not willingly choose. There are crosses of circumstance.

I. Consider, first of all, that we have here a fearful truth that life is illustrating all the time. How suddenly sometimes a cross we never could have consciously chosen is impressed upon us.

Without warning sometimes we find ourselves under a heavy cross.

How vividly this thing I am talking about came a few years ago to some of you. Many of you had the direction of your lives changed and that unwillingly by war. Some of you in the future will have your lives changed and against your will. Whatever plans you have will be laid aside and you will assume a burden, a responsibility, a cross that you would never have consciously chosen.

In many homes across our land during the last war—and in other countries too —gold stars replaced blue stars. What parent consciously chose that cross? It was a sorrow impressed upon them against their will. "And on him they laid the cross."

II. Consider next that when the cross of circumstance is forced upon us, if we are not to be utterly deflated and sink into despair, we must take it up as a cross of conscious choice and make our burden redemptive. I do not mean that we should see it as the will of God. But when through foolish choices, inadequate diet, poor housing, illogical diplomatic actions, crosses of circumstance are impressed upon us, only the redemptive spirit can save us from defeat and despair.

Crosses of circumstance can be made redemptive. To rail at the crosses of circumstance that fall upon us is only self-defeating. Only as we consecrate our talents and strength to a ministry of love for all men, making the labor of our brief existence here redemptive, can we be saved from despair when blind powers hurt us on the way.

III. Consider, finally, that not only must the cross of circumstance be embraced in a redemptive spirit, be made a cross of conscious choice; it often becomes in retrospect our crown of glory, something that we come to know as having made all the difference.

Tradition says about Simon that he became a Christian. And now far from the cross being a bitter disappointment it is his crown of glory. What had been at first a cruel experience, ended by becoming a medium of service. Through his cross of circumstance he found something about life that apart from this experience he might never have found. Life is full of strange surprises and paradoxes. Here is one of them. So hardships may be a thing of love and suffering and have uses far beyond what we now can understand.—H. Richard Rasmussen.

PRAYER FOR THE DAY: Eternal Spirit, we have been placed in a strange school, where many difficult lessons need to be learned. Help us not to spend our days complaining at circumstance or fretting at discipline, but to grow in the grace and knowledge of Christ and his purposes. Amen.

OFFERTORY SENTENCE: "Therefore, my beloved brethren, be ye stedfast, unmovable, always abounding in the work of the Lord, forasmuch as ye know that your labour is not in vain in the Lord." I Cor. 15:58.

OFFERTORY PRAYER: Help us, O Lord, to find our wealth a means of expressing our loyalty to thee. Both of that which we distribute and of that which we keep help us to be faithful stewards. Multiply the usefulness of this offering by giving it thy blessing. Amen.—H.

SEED THOUGHTS:

Simon of Cyrene's Cross: I. A compulsory cross. II. An unexpected cross. III. An honorable cross.—J. T. Woodhouse.

Bearing the Cross. In the act of bearing the cross we increase our strength. That is the heartening paradox of grace. Virtuous energies pass from our very burdens into our spirits, and thus "out of the eater comes forth meat." We bravely shoulder our load, and lo! a mystic breath visits the heart, and a strange facility attends our goings! The dead cross becomes a tree of life, and a secret vitality renews our souls.—J. H. Jowett.

## Choice Illustrations on the Theme

THE EXPERIENCE OF WILLIAM ROBERTSON NICOLL. At the age of 35 after twelve years of fruitful work in the Christian ministry, William Robertson Nicoll was compelled to resign his charge because of tuberculosis. Writing about it he said: "Spitting a little blood may change for me the face of earth and sky. The remote horizon of 70 is replaced by near and nearing walls. To realize that one is fallen out of the race when as yet hardly in—to feel the shadow of the prison house upon us in youth—that is hard." To be sure that was hard. It was something he never would have consciously chosen. It was something forced upon him from without. We call it the cross of circumstance.—H. R. R.

EXPERIENCE OF JOHN BRIGHT. Those of you who are familiar with English history will recognize the name of John Bright, one of England's great statesmen. When John Bright's young wife died after a brief, but happy marriage, the cross of circumstance rested heavily on his spirit. He was desperately lonely and his heart ached for her companionship. It seemed to him that the only heart of life had ceased to beat and that God himself was dead. Then a friend came to him and after speaking a few words of consolation said: "There are homes in England bereaved and in poverty through no fault of their own. I advise you, after the first shock of your grief is passed, to come with me and we will not rest until the Corn Laws of England are repealed." And how Cobden and Bright worked together, doing a great work of social justice, is now immortal history. Taking up the cross of conscious choice, John Bright overcame the cross of circumstance.—H. R. R.

FROM "THE GREAT HUNGER." John Bojer, the great Norwegian novelist, has written a novel entitled *The Great Hunger*. The principal character is Peter, a blacksmith who had lost his wealth and position and was now eking out a meager existence. Two of his children were sent to live with a relative. The one remaining child, kept at home, was killed one night by a wolf dog let loose by a neighbor. It was a year wherein a late frost had killed everything that the farmer had planted. Peter knew that his neighbor's field was barren—the man whose dog had killed his child. But Peter Holm had a half-bushel of barley and early one morning he rose and left the house quietly, took his half-bushel of grain, and, crossing to his neighbor's field, sowed it there. His wife had silently followed him and watched his act of forgiveness with tears of joy. "Standing upon the ruins of my life," says Peter, "I felt a vast responsibility. Mankind must arise and be better than the blind powers that order its way; in the midst of its sorrow it must take heed that the godlike does not die."—H. R. R.

## EVENING SERVICE

### Theme: The Things You Can't See

TEXT: "The things which are seen are temporal; but the things which are not seen are eternal." II Cor. 4:18.

It is about a year since we came to stay in the house where we are now staying. It's quite an old house, and since we came into it a good deal has had to be done to it in one way or another. When jobs have to be done on the woodwork an old craftsman, who is a bit of a character, and who is also a magnificent workman, comes to do them.

One day he was fitting new sills to the windows because the wood of the old sills was rotten. He was telling us how if we did not get these sills fitted the water would get in and ultimately it would get right down to the foundations and do all kinds of damage although we could not see it.

And then he said: "Aye, it's the bits of a house that you don't see that matter most." He was profoundly right. You don't see the beams, but if the beams have dry-rot, it's a grim lookout.

You don't see the foundations, but if there's anything wrong with them the house won't last for long. And it is not only true of houses, it is also true of lives that it's the bits you don't see which really matter.

I. It is the things which you can't see which make a man. A uniform doesn't make a soldier, and a football suit doesn't make a football player, and expensive clothes and external possessions don't make a man.

You can't see a man's character, but that's the bit of him that matters, and although you can't see it, you won't be long in discovering what it's like.

II. It is the things you can't see which make a man happy. It is not in the power of things to buy happiness.

III. It is the things which you can't see that last the longest. There is an end to every material thing in life; the material things belong to the world which changes and passes away. It is love which is immortal. "Love is strong as death. . . . Many waters cannot quench love, neither can the floods drown it" (The Song of Sol. 8:6, 7).

It is a man's relationship with God which lasts forever, through life and beyond death. "Thou shalt guide me with thy counsel, and afterward receive me into glory" (Ps. 75:24).

It is the things we cannot see that make a man what he is; it is the things we cannot see which bring happiness and peace of mind; it is the things we cannot see which last when the things we can see have passed away forever. And it is on these things that we should set our hearts and base our lives.

Paul knew a lot about life, for Paul was a man who had really lived, and Paul had a way of being right. And he was right when he said: "The things which are seen are temporal; but the things which are not seen are eternal."—William Barclay.

### Suggested Texts and Themes

Some Poor Men Are Rich: "Hath not God chosen the poor of this world rich in faith, and heirs of the kingdom which he hath promised to them that love him?" James 2:5.

The Test: "Wherefore by their fruits ye shall know them." See Gal. 5:22, 23.

Living Creatively: "So run, that ye may attain." I Cor. 9:24.

The Secret of Self-Government: ". . . so did not I, because of the fear of God." Neh. 5:15.

The Kindliest Word Ever Spoken: "Neither do I condemn thee: go, and sin no more." John 8:11.

## MIDWEEK FELLOWSHIP MEETING TOPIC

(Church Night or Suggested Sermon Subject)

**Theme: "The Motive Power of All Christian Men"**

Belief in the Resurrection of Jesus is the motive power of all Christian mankind. From what did this faith spring? From five or six remarkably vivid hallucinations? To think so is just as absurd as to suppose that five or six sparks would make water boil in a huge caldron.—D. Merezhkowsky.

Between Easter and Ascension Day is a good period in which to consider the appearances of Jesus after his Resurrection.

I. The appearances. 1. On Resurrection Day morning: to the women, Matt. 28:9-10; to Mary Magdalene, Mark 16:9, John 20:14-18; to Simon Peter, Luke 24:34. 2. On Resurrection Day afternoon: to Cleopas and another, Luke 24:13-35. 3. On Resurrection Day evening: to the disciples in Jerusalem, Luke 24:36-40, John 20:19-25. 4. The appearance to Thomas and the other disciples, John 20:26-29. 5. The appearance to seven disciples by the sea of Galilee. John 21:1-24. 6. The appearance to the eleven on a mountain in Galilee, Matt. 28:16-20. 7. The appearance to 500, I Cor. 15:6. 8. The appearance to James, I Cor. 15:7. 9. The final appearance, Luke 24:44-53, Acts 1:1-9.

II. His purposes. "I see the risen Jesus, inspiring and equipping as many men and women as possible to be the invincible pioneers, in the wide world, of God's Gospel and Kingdom. It is thrilling to watch him making, like all strong personalities, straight paths for his feet, and for the achievement of his purposes." —S. Pearce Carey.

1. He had corrections to make in the personalities of his disciples. 2. He had certain clinching experiences to give them. 3. He had a final commission to give them. 4. He had certain instructions to give them. 5. He was giving

them a message. 6. He was giving them power.

III. The motive power of the disciples. The motive power of all Christians.

## SUNDAY SCHOOL LESSON

**Apr. 20. God Prepares a Leader. Exod. 3:1-7; 10-15. Background Scripture: Exod. 2-4**

Memory Verse: "By faith Moses, when he was grown up, refused to be called the son of Pharaoh's daughter. . . . He considered abuse suffered for the Christ greater wealth than the treasures of Egypt, for he looked to the reward." Heb. 11:24, 26 (R.S.V.).

In this tremendous experience Moses was given that which he needed for the task of delivering his people from bondage.

I. An experience of *awe*. Goethe said, "Awe is the best in man." It was Moses' response to the holiness of God. Note that he had the capacity to experience awe. Does this capacity belong to every man? Have we moderns lost this capacity to any extent?

II. An experience of *destiny*. Moses belonged to the line of Abraham, Isaac, and Jacob. Their God was his God. This line was his father's line. It makes a far-reaching difference in life to what line a man belongs, and whether he is aware of this relationship.

III. An experience of *call*. "God called unto him out of the midst of the bush." Ever after he had a sense of vocation: He could make life an answer to a word previously spoken by God himself.

IV. He felt the compassion of God. "And the Lord said, . . . I know their sorrows."

V. He was overwhelmed by his own sense of inadequacy. He was humbled before God, v. 11.

VI. He became aware of the purpose of God. He was to share that purpose and was to become God's agent in accomplishing it.

VII. He was given a promise and a token to sustain him in the midst of his task, v. 12.

VIII. He was granted revelation of the nature of God, his holiness, and his eternal unchangeableness.

# SUNDAY: APRIL TWENTY-SEVENTH

## MORNING SERVICE

**Theme: The Holy Habit of Prayer**

Suggested Scripture Reading: Matt. 6:5-13; Matt. 7:7-11.

Selected Hymns: "This is my Father's world."—Maltbie D. Babcock. "Come ye disconsolate."—Thomas Moore. "Sweet hour of prayer."—W. W. Walford. "Lord, dismiss us with thy blessing."—John Fawcett.

Call to Worship: "Let us come boldly unto the throne of grace, that we may obtain mercy, and find grace to help in time of need." Heb. 4:16.

Invocation: O Lord, our God, it is with no sense of worthiness, with no awareness of merit or achievement that we bow in prayer unto thee. We come because thou hast made us so that we are restless until we rest in thee. We come because in the silence of our hearts we hear a trumpet call unto a higher allegiance. We come because thy goodness and loving-kindness has kindled a spark of gratitude in our natures. We come because we have the Christ to be our Saviour and our Friend. We come because we must bow in worship in order to find the deepest and fullest expression of ourselves.

Accept, O God, thy worshipers. Hear our petitions. Give heed to our intercessions. Receive our praise. Amen.—H.

**Theme: The Holy Habit of Prayer**

TEXT: "Pray without ceasing." I Thess. 5:17.

If, out of the pages of history, the saints of Christendom were to come walking before you, you would marvel at their certainty, their assurance, and their devotion. If you had the privilege of asking them from whence they received the quality of sainthood, they would answer with one accord. "It came from the constant prayer life." When we examine the life of Jesus from any viewpoint, be it critical, historical, devotional, or otherwise, we always find that his power lay in his prayer life. I am sure that it was through prayer that he overcame the temptations in the wilderness. It was through prayer that Jesus was able to face death upon the cross for the redemption of mankind.

Certainly if our lives are to contribute anything toward the building of God's Kingdom, they must be conditioned through prayer. The holy habit of prayer conditions one so that he may serve God in four ways.

I. If prayer does nothing else, it provides an association with God. We do a lot of talking about God, and we create theories about God. But we never know God until we come face to face with him through prayer.

II. Prayer also provides an opportunity for one to be associated with his better self. Most of us are better Christians than we once thought we could be. But most of us have room for constant improvement in the life of the spirit. Hidden away among life's nonessentials are good qualities which we uncover through prayer. We need desperately to know more about ourselves and to realize that we are capable of being much better than we really are.

III. Prayer conditions one's mind and causes one's thoughts to be placed in right channels. Some of us are confused by our particular way of thinking. We let our lives become filled with prejudices which breed upon ignorance. In our stubborn stupidity we refuse to see light or to give light. Our thinking becomes muddled, and we get off-focus perspectives. But through prayer our minds become tuned to the mind of God.

IV. Prayer also inspires one to Christian service. It was Isaiah who went into the temple to pray. There he met God. There God spoke to him, saying, "Whom shall I send, and who will go for me?" Because of his devoted praying, Isaiah heard the Lord and was able to answer, "Here am I, send me." And so it is with all praying. If we wait upon the Lord, the Lord will speak and send us out into avenues of service.—W. A. Tyson, Jr.

PRAYER FOR THE DAY: We bow, O Lord, before the mystery of thy Presence. Our faith tells us that thou art with us in no sense less really than when thou didst walk upon this earth in human form. Thou art by our sides to help us in our human need. Thou didst promise to come unto us as Comforter—one who is like a fort, a high tower, a rock—sure and steadfast and strong. And so as we come before thee to worship we praise thee for all that thou art; we remember thy goodness; we rejoice in thy loving-kindness; we open our lives to receive thy grace.

By thy grace forgive our sins, grant us victory over temptation, in our weakness perfect thy strength, give us vision high and clear, fill our hearts with love, inspire our wills to serve thee and thee only. In Jesus' name. Amen.—H.

OFFERTORY SENTENCE: "Where your treasure is, there will your heart be also."

OFFERTORY PRAYER: Nothing is common in thy sight, O Lord, and this portion of wealth is significant before thee as a token of our faith and love and life. Bless it, we pray, that it may accomplish great and lasting good. Amen.—H.

SEED THOUGHTS:

Emerson's First Sermon. Ralph Waldo Emerson's first sermon was on the text, "Pray without ceasing." It had three points, which shows that it was true in form, whatever we may think of its teaching. The three points are as true as they are startling. First, men are always praying. Second, all prayers are answered.

Third, be careful what you pray for, lest you get it and it be your undoing.—Joseph Fort Newton.

The Habit of Sincere Prayer. If you make a habit of sincere prayer your life will be profoundly altered. Prayer stamps with its indelible mark our actions and demeanor. A tranquility of bearing, a facial and bodily repose, are observed in those whose inner lives are thus enriched. Within the depth of consciousness a flame kindles, and man sees himself. He discovers his selfishness, his silly pride, his fears, his greeds, his blunders. He develops a sense of moral obligation, intellectual humility. Thus begins a journey of the self toward the realm of grace.—Dr. Alexis Carrel.

**Choice Illustrations on the Theme**

A GOOD REMINDER. In a native African village, with small mud huts closely crowded, there was no place for quiet prayer, so the Christians there chose, each for himself, a tree in the forest where he could be alone for prayer and devotion. If one became discouraged or careless, the path to his tree became overgrown and lost to sight. Then another would remind him: "Brother, the grass grows in your path."—Inez Brasier.

ENDURING FELLOWSHIP. How often we meet an old friend whom we haven't seen for years. Enthusiastically we talk for some minutes but after a half hour there isn't much left to say. We have not let our friendship grow through the years. Some of us find ourselves in a similar relationship with God. We knew God when we were children, but we have not grown spiritually with him. We can talk with God for a few moments but we have little common ground upon which to build an enduring fellowship. Such fellowship is possible only through the constancy of prayer.—E. Paul Hovey.

BEGIN WITH PRAYER. My watch was not keeping good time. I took it to a watchmaker. "Please tell me why this timepiece is so irregular," I said. He put his magnifying glass to one eye, opened the back of the case, and peered intently at the works for a moment.

"When do you wind your watch?" he said.

"When do I wind it? Why, when everybody else does, of course."

"When is that?"

"Just before I go to bed."

"Well, you are mistaken if you think eevrybody winds his watch then. You should wind it the first thing in the morning, and I'll tell you why. All through the day your watch will be getting a succession of jars. Every step you take on the hard pavement will jar that delicate mechanism. You ought to begin the day on a strong spring."

My watchmaker was talking about watches, but he might as well have been speaking of the human spirit. "Begin the day on a strong spring" may with perfect appropriateness be applied to a man's prayer life.—William S. Abernethy.

## EVENING SERVICE

**Theme: When God Breaks Through**

TEXT: "Can there any good thing come out of Nazareth?" John 1:46.

There is a fragment of conversation in the first chapter of the Gospel of John. It is an exchange between two men, Philip and Nathanael. Philip, who has just accepted Christ, seeks out Nathanael and tells him that he has found the one of whom Moses and the prophets wrote. It is Jesus of Nazareth. Then Nathanael responds with a surprising question, touched with skepticism and flavored with cynicism. "Can anything good come out of Nazareth?" he asks.

Nathanael did not question the need for a Saviour to come nor did he doubt the possibility that God was going to do it. It was just such an unbelievable way for God to bring it about—out of Nazareth! To him Nazareth was so commonplace. Fortunately Philip had great wisdom. He did not argue the point. He just said, "Come and see."

Nathanael's question seems to fit almost every part of Jesus' earthly life. Can anything good come out of a manger, out of a carpenter's shop . . . ?

It isn't hard to see how God is in

these things which are made up of truth and beauty and goodness. But what of the other areas which seem so commonplace and sometimes the objects of contempt? Can anything good come of these?

I. God breaks through average lives. We are bound to ask ourselves, Can anything good come out of a life so average? Unfortunately we preachers too often talk about the dramatic men and women, the geniuses of faith. In our desire to make the Christian life vivid we inevitably look to the extraordinary and the outstanding. I am sure that some must go away saying that all this may be true for these spectacular lives, but what about ours which run so to the average? Or we may look at those who profess their Christian faith and see that they still have their shortcomings, their problems, their failings. Where is God in lives like these which are so average?

We ought to be reminded that God has entered into life on every level, the commonplace as well as the spectacular. This was, in fact, one of the remarkable marks of Christ's life. He went among the outcasts, the taxgatherers, the sinners. Common sense would say that he lowered himself by coming to such people. But this is the miracle of Christ. By such contact he never lowered himself, he only lifted them. So, when God touches the common experience of every day he hasn't cast off all his majesty, he has only lifted all things into it.

II. God breaks through adversity. Or again, there is the almost inevitable question, can anything good come out of adversity so deep? We are not talking here about the difficulties and inconveniences of every day. We mean real adversity: when your back is against the wall, when it is touch and go as to whether you will make it at all, when all the things you cherish most seem challenged by the things you fear most. Can any good possibly come out of such times? The answer comes back from voices that have a right to speak, saying that some of the deepest assurances come out of just those times. You didn't learn it by logic, but you found it so. The God who brought Christ out of Nazareth brought new life out of your adversity.

III. God breaks through responsibility. Some would ask the question in another way, "Can anything good come out of responsibility so heavy?" Day by day it's there, seemingly demanding more strength than you have. You look down a long road and see no end to it. What possible good can come from this kind of situation?

The very responsibility that is with us day by day may be the call to the divine partnership, the ministry of compassion and concern. It is a sobering but a dignifying truth, you, indeed, may be the very instrument by which God is fulfilling his promise of care and compassion in the life of another.—Gene E. Bartlett.

**Suggested Texts and Themes**

I Am Strong: "God is the strength of my heart, and my portion for ever." Ps. 73:26.

Hope Dispels Tension: "Why are thou cast down, O my soul? and why art thou disquieted in me? hope thou in God: for I shall yet praise him for the help of his countenance." Ps. 42:5.

Our Vital Breath: "Pray without ceasing." I Thess. 5:17.

The Silent Partner: "And, behold, I am with thee, and will keep thee in all places whither thou goest, and will bring thee again into this land; for I will not leave thee, until I have done that which I have spoken to thee of." Gen. 28:15.

Fruitful Failures: "But the Lord said to David my father, Forasmuch as it was in thine heart to build an house for my name, thou didst well in that it was in thine heart." II Chron. 6:8.

## MIDWEEK FELLOWSHIP MEETING TOPIC

(Church Night or Suggested Sermon Subject)

**Theme: Forgiveness**

TEXT: Matt. 18:21, 22.

INTRODUCTORY: 1. When Christ tells us to love our neighbor we say "Amen," because we like to be on good terms with people and to live peaceably with all men. 2. When he enjoins us to go the second mile we know it is a hard lesson to learn. 3. When he talks about forgiving "until seventy times seven" we find ourselves hesitating, perplexed. What did Jesus mean?

I. Jesus meant that we were to forgive to the extent that we would normally seek revenge. Read of Lamech and Cain in Genesis, chap. 4. If Cain was avenged sevenfold truly Lamech shall be avenged seventy and sevenfold. Such is the attitude of the unregenerate man. Vengeance to the last ounce. Compare the section on forgiveness in the Sermon on the Mount.

II. We are to forgive because God has forgiven us. The Parable of the Unforgiving Servant. We fail to appreciate the magnitude of God's forgiveness. We fail to appreciate the pettiness of the wrong which others do to us.

III. We must forgive in order that God might forgive us. Recall the words of the Lord's Prayer. The law of love.—A. Gilmore.

## SUNDAY SCHOOL LESSON

**Apr. 27. God's Mighty Deliverance. Exod. 11:1, 12:23-28, 14:27-31. Background Scripture: Exod. 11:1-15:18.**

MEMORY VERSE: "He saved them for his name's sake, that he might make known his mighty power." Ps. 106:8 (R.S.V.).

A God of Deliverances. I. The mighty deliverance of the Hebrews from Egypt. Liberation a motivation to fidelity. II. The mighty deliverance of men from sin. This liberation is also a motivation to fidelity.

Stories of Deliverance: Deliverance of the family of Jacob, Gen. 45:7; Deliverance of the Jews from captivity, Ezra 9:13, David's deliverance at a time of rebellion, II Sam. 15, 16, 17; Ps. 3; Daniel's deliverance from the den of lions, Dan. 6:22, 23; and many others. Our God is a God of Deliverances.

# SUNDAY: MAY FOURTH

## MORNING SERVICE

**Theme: Everything Begins at Home (Christian Home Sunday)**

SUGGESTED SCRIPTURE READING: Col. 3:12-25 or Deut. 6:4-15.

SELECTED HYMNS: "For the beauty of the earth."—F. S. Pierpont. "How gentle God's commands."—Philip Doddridge. "Jesus calls us, o'er the tumult."—Cecil F. Alexander. "Happy the home when God is there."—Henry Ware.

CALL TO WORSHIP: "Take diligent heed to do the commandment and the law, to love the Lord your God, and to walk in all his ways, and to keep his commandments, and to cleave unto him, and to serve him with all your heart and with all your soul." Josh. 22:5.

INVOCATION: As we come into thy house, O God, the recollections of other Sabbaths which we cherish in our memories return unto us. We praise thee for our privilege of worship and pray thee to grant unto us, as thou hast done in the past, the refreshing, cleansing, empowering and illuminating blessings of grace, which make life so joyous, so holy, so useful and so full of beauty. Amen.—H.

**Theme: Everything Begins at Home**

(It is not expected that any minister will use all the headings given below for his sermon on Christian Home Sunday. They are given for their suggestive value. Under each heading will be found comment or illustration.)

I. Love begins at home. "The home circle is the nursery of affection; it is the Eden of young attachments, and here should be planted and tended all the germs of love, every seed that shall ever sprout in the heart—and how carefully should they be tended, how guarded against the frosts of jealousy, anger, pride, vanity. We cannot honor with too deep a reverence the home affections; we cannot cultivate them with too great a care; we cannot cherish them with too much solicitude.—N. M. Dellinger.

II. Honesty begins at home. Some consider honesty to be the first Christian virtue. It includes absolute fairness without partiality. No deceit should be shown toward anyone inside or outside the house. Children know whether or not their parents are honest. Sham is easily detected.

III. Worship begins at home. In many homes this is not a fact, but it should be. "We are not only parents; we are ourselves children of God. If that truth has really gripped us and God's love has laid hold of us, we will be manifesting toward him the trust and loyalty and worship which are his due. And the child's love and trust and understanding of the issues of life, which began in the narrow compass of his relations to us, his parents, will widen and grow if caught up into association with our own."—*Daily Devotions.*

IV. Faith begins at home. "The home has the child in the most impressionable years—the years that count the most for shaping attitudes, habits, character, religious understanding, and a living faith."

V. Education begins at home. "The home is the fountain of civilization. Our laws are made in the home. The things said there give bias to character far more than do sermons and lectures, newspapers and books. No other audiences are so susceptible and receptive as those gathered about the table and fireside. No other teachers have the acknowledged and divine right to instruct that is granted without challenge to parents."—N. M. Dellinger.

VI. World Peace begins at home. The Methodist General Conference of 1952 said, "The most effective education for world peace lies in the attitudes and ideas expressed in daily conversation." Parents build around their own firesides the peace for which all families pray.

VII. Abstinence from alcohol begins at home. Once when attending a banquet, a friend invited a young woman from a Christian home to have a cocktail before dinner. She courteously but firmly refused. "Oh, come on," said the friend; "you're a big girl now. One has to be modern nowadays." She was, indeed, a big girl, big enough to know that accepting a cocktail would be turning her back on her Christian training. And it would hurt her parents, both devout Christians. She would not accept.—Ada C. Davison.

VIII. Sane attitudes on sex begin at home. "Parents, if properly instructed, are best fitted to help growing children understand the facts regarding the origin of life and the nature of their personalities as it relates to sex."

IX. Respect for law and order begins at home. Out of her experiences with 45,000 children who were brought before her through more than twenty years, Judge Camille Kelley observed, "The child's richest heritage is a well-ordered home. If every child had such an opportunity, delinquency would fade from court records. There would be no need for juvenile courts or juvenile judges."

X. Culture begins at home. "A true family is a cultural unit, it must make its own culture, with songs in which all can join, stories all can enjoy, games all can play; without its own social life the role of the family degenerates into something subhuman. . . . The Christian family exists for the perfection of each of its members, as an individual soul rejoicing in the freedom of the sons of God; if it is anything less, it is to some degree a failure."—H. L. Binsse.

PRAYER FOR THE DAY: O God, our Heavenly Father, who hast set the solitary in families: Look in favor, we beseech thee, upon the homes of thy people. Defend them against all evil, and supply all their needs according to the riches of thy grace. Make them sanctuaries of purity and peace, love and joy. Bless all dear to us wheresover they are, and grant that they and we may follow thee at every step of our daily life, that, though our paths may lead us far from one another, we may all abide within the safe shelter of thy love; through Jesus Christ our Lord. Amen.—*The Book of Common Worship.*

Offertory Sentence: "Honour the Lord with thy substance, and with the firstfruits of all thine increase: so shall thy barns be filled with plenty, and thy presses shall burst out with new wine."

Offertory Prayer: Bless us and guide us, O Lord, in all our human relationships. Help us in days of crisis to render sacrificial service to our brethren in the world. Multiply the usefulness of these gifts which we lay before thee in the name of Christ. Amen.—H.

Seed Thoughts: Planning Your Home for Better Living. I. If it is a home, not just a house, we are planning, we had better plan for an altar. II. If we are planning a home for better living, it must be a place of fellowship. III. Better living—that is living on the highest level—comes when a home is not merely a shelter from the world to which we retreat, but also a place from which we go out to service.—H. E. Luccock.

The Real Home. I. The real home is a playground. II. The real home is a workshop. III. The real home is a forum. Honest, open discussion of life's great problems belongs originally and primarily to the family circle. IV. The real home is a secret society. Loyalty to one's family should mean keeping silent on family matters. V. The real home is a co-operative league. Households flourish in peace where the interest of each is the interest of all. VI. The real home is a haven of refuge. The world makes us hunger for sympathy.—E. E. Puriton.

### Choice Illustrations on the Theme

where love is. Visiting in the Southern Mountains, a Sunday school missionary was entertained in a small home. The house was made of logs. It had two rooms, a larger front room with an open wood fireplace, and a lean-to kitchen and dining room combined.

On entering the dining room the missionary saw a floor of rough boards with no covering, a home-made table, a wooden bench on either side of the table for seats, and a chair at the end which was given to him.

Hanging on the wall behind the table was a card on which were these words: "Jesus the unseen Guest at every meal." As he read those words the missionary asked himself, "Can that be true? Is Jesus here in this humble home?" Becoming acquainted with the father, mother, and four children, he discovered that Jesus was there.

For home is not on granite wall, nor art, nor luxury, nor all the glittering robes that pomp may wear to hide the signet of despair. Where Love is, Home is ever there. God is Love.—Louis E. Black.

the meaning of home. Recently I picked up a dictionary and looked up the word "Home." This definition says that Home is an Anglo-Saxon term which originally meant dwelling. Then it goes on to say that home has come to mean an endeared dwelling, the scene of domestic love and a happy, cherished family life. Obviously then, a house is not a home. A home is a set of intimate personal relationships within a house. We build a house of wood, stone, brick, and cement; we create a home out of intelligence and understanding and love. The house may be destroyed; the home goes on.—Marie Dean.

## EVENING SERVICE

### Theme: A Basket of Summer Fruit

Text: "Behold a basket of summer fruit." Amos 8:1.

These are the words of a prophet familiar with country life. Amos was a dresser of sycamore trees and a herdsman; a true child of nature. (See his prophecy for other striking figures.) The ultimate purpose of the Christian life is fruit. "By their fruits ye shall know them." Turn to the familiar catalogue of fruits in Gal. 5:22,23.

I. The first three fruits, virtues, graces, express our relationship to God. 1. The fruit of the Spirit is Love. It is significant that the word translated "love" in Galatians is the same that we have in that superb chapter, I Cor. 13.

2. The fruit of the Spirit is joy. We are to "serve the Lord with gladness," not like slaves in chains.

3. What is peace? It is not the quietness and unanimity of the cemetery. It is the stillness of the engine room, where the machinery moves but does not creak; it is the perfect motion of wheel within wheel; it is frictionless activity. Peace is the perfect communion of the soul with God. God takes possession of the Christian, and the divine peace which passeth all understanding keeps his mind and heart and will. "Peace I leave with you," said Jesus, "my peace I give to you."

These are the first three Christian virtues. They describe our relationship to God: Love, Joy, Peace.

II. The second three fruits. Our relationship to our fellow men is described in a second trinity of graces: Longsuffering, Gentleness, Goodness. 1. Longsuffering: "Good temper" is Dr. Moffatt's translation. The power to bear with irritating people without becoming irritated; the ability to tolerate even the intolerant; it is long temper as contrasted with short temper. It is a fruit much harder to cultivate in some soils than in others.

2. Gentleness: "Kindliness" is Dr. Moffatt's translation. We are to be courteous and gentle, not because it is rude to be discourteous, but because we are followers of the "Gentle Jesus" of whom we sang in our childhood. "Kindness" is the Revised Version word. Kind words and kind ways are the marks of a Christian. Some very good people are like prickly pears; others are "sweet briar Christians," a curious combination of fragrance and thorns.

3. Goodness: "Large-heartedness" is Dr. Moffatt's translation. Goodness is generosity. "If we would get the full wealthy content of the word 'goodness,'" said Dr. J. H. Jowett, "we must call to our aid that fascinating list of words beginning with the syllable 'bene.'" In goodness we find benediction, benefits, benevolence, beneficence.

III. The third three fruits. These graces require little more than naming: Faithfulness; Meekness; Self-control. 1. Faithfulness: That is the Revised Version rendering. Dr. Moffatt says "Fidelity," the Authorized Version "Faith."

2. And then, Meekness. Meekness is one of the least popular of all the graces and yet one of the most beautiful. It does not mean want of spirit; it must never be confounded with weakness and cowardice. Meekness and courage are often seen together. Moses was "meek above all the men which were upon the face of the earth," and yet he was a man of the sublimest courage.

3. Last in the list is Self-control. Temperance is the word often used. The word signifies having the mastery. Self-restraint, not merely in relation to drinking and eating, but in every relationship of life; the suppression of all excess.

Toward God: Love, joy, peace. Toward one another: Longsuffering, gentleness, goodness. Toward ourselves: Faithfulness, meekness, self-control. Would we produce such a cluster of fruit, we must be "rooted and grounded" in Christ. "Abide in me and I in you," said Jesus. "Herein is my Father glorified that ye bear much fruit; so, shall ye be my disciples."—Adapted from G. H. Clothier.

**Suggested Texts and Themes**

Housework or Homework: "Martha, Martha, thou art careful and troubled about many things: But one thing is needful: and Mary hath chosen that good part, which shall not be taken away from her." Luke 10:41,42.

Six Requisites for a Happy Home: "Six things are requisite to create a happy home; Integrity must be its architect and tidiness the upholsterer. It must be warmed by affection, lighted up with cheerfulness, and industry must be the ventilator, renewing the atmosphere and bringing a fresh salubrity every day; while over all, as a protecting canopy and glory, nothing will suffice except the blessing of God."

A Summons to Dine: "Bring these men home, . . . for these men shall dine with me at noon." Gen. 43:16.

Learning from the Children: ". . . and a little child shall lead them." Isa. 11:6.

Worth Remembering: "When I call to remembrance the unfeigned faith that is in thee, which dwelt first in thy grandmother Lois, and thy mother Eunice; and I am persuaded that in thee also." II Tim. 1:5.

## MIDWEEK FELLOWSHIP MEETING TOPIC

(Church Night or Suggested Sermon Subject)

**Theme: Jesus Cleansing the Temple**

TEXT: Matt. 21:12, 13.

Jesus is the great purifier. He does not disdain to use force. He is no coward, no slacker in the face of danger. Some of the temples Jesus would cleanse:

I. The Temple of the Body. He would cleanse the temple of the individual in respect to his mind, affections, personality. He cleanses of moral rottenness, physical weakness, mental wrongness, personal evil.

II. The Temple of the Home. He would cleanse the temple of the family in respect to its thoughts, speech, habits. He purifies the home of selfishness, disobedience, infidelity, and intemperance; of petulance, impatience, and abuse. Jesus overturns the false relationships that have taken up residence in the family circle, and sets up in the temple the altars of love and faith and restored confidence.

III. The Temple of Business. He would cleanse the temple of commerce in respect to dishonest dealing, unfair competition, exorbitant profits. He drives out false weights and measures, lying advertising, and misrepresentation. He cleanses the temple of trade and commercial dealing of all that undermines and destroys confidence, and sets up honesty, industry, and sound principles.

IV. The Temple of the Church. He would rid the temple of religion of any false worship, of materialism, and of wrong teaching. He rids the sanctuary of hypocrisy, make-believe, and commercial invasion.—G. H.

## BULLETIN BOARD SLOGANS FOR THE MONTH

"Open your home to God."

Making Home is "Big Business."

Blessed is the home when Christ is there.

Prayer should have a place in every family.

Integrity is the architect of the home beautiful.

"God is love, no matter which way the wind blows."

"One former is worth a thousand reformers."—Horace Mann.

The Christian home and the Church have a common cause and mission.

"Blessed are the homemakers: for they are the builders of mankind."

"The future marches forth on the feet of little children."—Phillips Brooks.

## SUNDAY SCHOOL LESSON

**May 4. God's Law in a Nation's Life. Exod. 19:3-6; 20:1-4, 7-8, 12-17. Background Scripture: Exod. 19-20; Deut. 5.**

MEMORY VERSE: "If you will obey my voice and keep my covenant, you shall be my possesion among all peoples." Exod. 19:5 (R.S.V.).

This lesson gives opportunity to choose from many points of emphasis, for example: I. God's law is a revelation of his character.

II. God's law reveals his concern for men and nations.

III. God's law is given in connection with a covenant relationship between him and his people.

IV. Obedience to God's law brings true freedom.

V. When a nation cherishes God's law, that nation will receive his blessing and guidance.

VI. It is a function of the home to teach God's commandments.

VII. The Ten Commandments are fundamental to the social and spiritual world.

# SUNDAY: MAY ELEVENTH

## MORNING SERVICE

**Theme: "Take a Child to a High Place" (Mother's Day)**

SUGGESTED SCRIPTURE READING: Deut. 4:9-10; I Kings 2:1-4.

SELECTED HYMNS for children and adults to sing together: "We gather together to ask the Lord's blessing."—Netherlands Folk Song. "Faith of our fathers! living still."—Frederick W. Faber. "I would be true."—Howard A. Walter. "O beautiful for spacious skies."—Katharine Lee Bates. "Let all the world in ev'ry corner sing."—George Herbert.

CALL TO WORSHIP: "A woman that feareth the Lord, she shall be praised. Give her of the fruit of her hands; and let her own words praise her in the gates." Prov. 31:30-31.

The glory of the whole world is mother-love: which began in the beginning and has continued unchanged to this present time—the conspicuous beauty of the fabric of life: the great constant of the problem.—Norman Duncan.

Mother love at its best, and its best is very common, is the nearest thing on earth to the love divine.—William Lyon Phelps.

INVOCATION: We praise thee, our Father, for all the sacred memories and hallowed associations of this Sabbath day. We remember that it was upon the first day of the week, early in the morning, that our Lord arose from the dead. Help us on this first day to honor him by our worship.

We are glad, too, to set apart this special Sabbath on which to render honor to our mothers. From their lives and lips and faces we first learned of thee. We thank thee for revealing thyself so beautifully and so wonderfully. Amen. —H.

**Theme: "Take a Child to a High Place"**

TEXTS "Tell ye your children of it, and let your children tell their children, and their children another generation." Joel 1:3.

Hand in hand, father and mother and child, go to a high place together. Let the father and mother tell the child. Look up! Show him the heavens. Let him see the greatness of God.

Look abroad! "Show him the country." Tell him the story of his heritage.

> Tell him the stories of the two great births of history—
> A child in Bethlehem,
> In Independence Hall, a nation—
> And fuse these into common moral sentiment;
> His birthright is of flag as well as altar.

What shall the parents tell the child?

I. Tell him the story of the birth of Jesus at Bethlehem.

1. How God loves the world. How God loves him. Tell him that God is a loving Father.

2. Tell him how Jesus came into the world; how a little child comes into the world; about fatherhood and motherhood and sonship.

3. Tell him how Jesus grew; how a child can grow "in wisdom and stature, and in favor with God and man."

4. Tell him that Jesus is his Friend and Saviour.

5. Tell him how a child, and a man, can follow Jesus, going about doing good.

6. How the home may be the abiding place of love and loyalty and peace, a place of worship and of prayer.

7. Reveal his destiny as a child of God.

8. Point out his right to belong to the People of God.

II. Tell him concerning his American birthright.

1. "The right to self expression—the freedom to worship, to study, to listen, to make independent judgments, and to speak. . . ."

2. "The right ot participate—the opportunity for communion and assembly; the privilege of public opinion and of free elections. . . ."

3. "The right to a choice of labor—the liberty to choose and to change jobs, to work with people or with things—or even not to work; to employ men, or to employ learning or money. . . ."

4. "The right of contract—the wonder of a man's word becoming his bond. . . ."

5. "The right to own property—the title a man has to set his seal upon the land, to furrow his own name into a field, or to a plant a hill with the seeds of his own orchard; his right to buy, and to build, and to call a thing his own. . . ."

6. "The right to a heritage—the right of one man to leave to another, tangible and intangible fruits, so that the personality of his labor and his learning will not be alienated or lost; to receive of forbears and to leave for posterity, the uninjured meaning of words of tradition. . . ."

7. "The right to belong—not as a child belongs to a parent, but with knowledge and intent, with right born of responsible being. As a man gives himself to faith, to principle, or to deeds of a high cause. . . ."

Tell him these rights are his,
And the greatest is the most incidental,
For, the right to belong
Is an offshoot of belief,
And a circumstance of loyalty—
And those are the essence of allegiance.

Take a child to a high place . . .
Tell him the stories of the two great births of history—
A child in Bethlehem,
In Independence Hall, a nation—
And fuse these into common moral sentiment;
His birthright is of flag as well as altar.

(The quotations given above are from a poem entitled "American Birthright" by Jo Bingam, published in *The P. E. O. Record.)*

A Prayer for the Day: "Heavenly Father, we thank thee for our homes and for all their holy influences. We remember in tenderness those who bore us and nurtured us, whose lives have left their impress upon all the days of our years. We pray that the virtues in motherhood that have helped to make us a strong people shall abide: that thy grace may be upon all who bear the responsibility of rearing children in these times. Make our homes a foretaste of the home above. In Jesus' name. Amen."—*Today.*

Offertory Sentence: "Thou shalt love the Lord thy God with all thy heart, and with all thy soul, and with all thy strength, and with all thy mind; and thy neighbor as thyself."

Offertory Prayer: May human need stir our compassion, O Lord; may the wealth in our hands encourage our generosity; may the love which we have received inspire the love which we show toward thee and our fellow men. Bless this offering, we pray, in the name of Jesus. Amen.—H.

Seed Thoughts: From Emerson: "A sufficient measure of civilization is the influence of good women."

A Spiritual Succession: "The unfeigned faith that is in thee; which dwelt first in thy grandmother Lois, and thy mother Eunice." II Tim. 1:5 Motherhood is not a general or impersonal institution. It is a glorious reality that individualizes itself every time a newborn babe comes into the world. Mothers have names to identify them: names like Lois and Eunice. These names represent more than titles; they represent qualities transmitted by heritage and training to the generations following.

Happy is the one who, like Timothy, is in the line of a spiritual succession. Thank God for grandmothers who are mothers grown, not only older, but wiser as well. This day we all may well evaluate anew the treasure of a sturdy, God-fearing ancestry—*Today*.

### Choice Mother's Day Illustrations

A MOTHER MILLIONAIRE. The other day when I received a cleaned garment from a young woman at the counter, I said, "How much money do you want?"

"A dollar, please," she replied.

Then I said jokingly, "You didn't quite catch my question; I said, 'How much money do you *want*?' I did not ask the cost of the cleaning."

"Oh!" she exclaimed, "I am now worth four million dollars!"

"How does that happen?"

"I have a husband and three children," and she challenged me to deny her affirmation that she was a millionaire.—H.

WHEN MOTHERS ARE RICH. All mothers are rich when they love their children. There are no poor mothers, no ugly ones, no old ones. Their love is always the most beautiful of the joys. And when they seem most sad, it needs but a kiss which they receive or give to turn all their tears into stars in the depths of their eyes.—Maurice Maeterlinck.

THE PIONEER WOMAN. Near Ponca City, Oklahoma, stands the famous statue of "The Pioneer Woman." It stands thirty-five feet high, the figure of a mother with a Bible in one hand and the hand of her young son who walks at her side in the other. Bravely she is going out into an unknown future, an inspiring picture of confidence and determination. The Bible in her hand speaks of her love for God and her readiness to submit to his will and guidance. The way she holds the hand of her son reveals her love for her child and her determination to have him walk God's way with her.—Armin C. Oldsen.

### Quotable Mother's Day Poetry

TELL HER TODAY

My grandfather did not express
His deeply buried tenderness.
But after grandmother passed away,
When I tidied up his room each day
I'd find her little knitted cape,
All crumpled up and out of shape,
Upon the pillow of his bed
Where he had laid his lonely head.
He'd loved her well since long ago
But did not think to tell her so.
—Clara Johnston Pierce.

MOTHER

Words can be coined, and they will ring as true
As those long grown accustomed to the ear,
But I have only simple words for you,
Whose hands were gentle and whose ways were dear.
All has been said a thousand times before,
And yet I cannot hope to find
A better language than I learned from your
Own lips, though years ebb slowly out of mind.

This I can tell you: I have tried to build
As you would have me; I have tried to keep
Your eyes before me, clear and laughter-filled,
Carried your love from waking into sleep,
Living your pattern, strong in the belief,
This is a better monument than grief.
—Dorothy Quick.

TO A TIRED CHILD

Argue with sleep, my darling, quarrel with rest—
I know beforehand which will have the best
Of such an argument. I am too wise
For anger in such heavy-eyed disguise
Only the stupid join the righteous league
Who take to heart the tirades of fatigue.
Tired children, like tired men, need sufferance—
Few words, soft beds and patient deference.
Which probably is why each mother billows
And gives a little, like the best of pillows.
—Virginia Brasier.

## EVENING SERVICE

### Theme: The Place of Human Recovery

TEXT: "But as for me, my feet were almost gone; my steps had well nigh slipped. . . . Until I went into the sanctuary of God." Ps. 73:2, 17.

I. Before he went into the sanctuary. The dire and desperate condition of this man is graphically confessed in verses two to sixteen of this Psalm. "What's the use?" might well have been announced as his life's motto. 1. What's the use? Look about you. See that the wicked prosper. When they get into trouble they can buy themselves out of it. They never need to draw in their belts because of hunger. They can satisfy any desire with money. When they go to the hospital they can occupy the best rooms and pay the fees of the finest physicians. Of course, they are corrupt, but what of it? They set their mouths against heaven itself, and nothing happens. They get away with anything and everything.

2. What's the use? I've tried to live a clean life. What is the good of it? I've refrained from dishonesty andy impurity. I've "washed my hands in innocency." With all that every day I am plagued with trouble and chastened. What's the use?

3. What's the use? Of course, I know I should not let this get me down, because of my children. I must keep a stiff upper lip for their sakes. But that's not easy. It's too much, too hard! What's the use?

II. Then he went into the sanctuary of God. The sanctuary became for him the place of his recovery.

He didn't mince matters there; the psalm suggests that he poured out his anguish before God.

1. In the sanctuary God restored his judgment. He gave him a true perspective. His steps had well nigh slipped before, but now he is aware that these wicked whom he had envied are the ones who stand on slippery places. He himself has a firm foothold. God is the rock, the "strength," v. 26, of his heart.

2. In the sanctuary God lifts him out of his stupidity. He had been stupid as a beast. v. 22. The "beast" he had in mind was most likely the hippopotamus, "a plump colossus of flesh, the symbol of plain stupidity." He was lifted out of the stagnant water, the mud, the filth, by the right hand of God.

3. In the sanctuary God restores the man to fellowship with Himself. It is to a communion never to be broken; "I am continually with thee." It is not to be interrupted by death; "Thou shalt receive me unto glory." Flesh and heart may fail, but never again shall he slip into the slough of despond from which he had been delivered. God is now the strength of his heart.

He now experiences the goodness of the nearness of God. He now has assurance of God's presence and power. He will now declare the works of God. This psalm which begins "Truly God is good to Israel, even to such as are of a clean heart," is such a declaration.

The sanctuary is the place of human recovery because it is here that man is brought into the experience of the divine, into communion with God. It is in God alone that man finds recovery. —H.

**Suggested Mother's Day Texts and Themes**

"What Have They Seen in Thine House?" II Kings 20:15.

Household Religion: II Kings 20:15 or Isa. 39:4.

Mary, the Ideal Mother: "But Mary kept all these things, and pondered them in her heart." Luke 2:19.

Loving Deeds Are Recorded: Matt. 25:31-40.

The Faith of a Mother: "Then Jesus answered and said unto her, O woman, great is thy faith: be it unto thee even as thou wilt. And her daughter was made whole from that very hour." Matt. 15:28.

## MIDWEEK FELLOWSHIP MEETING TOPIC

(Church Night or Suggested Sermon Subject)

**Theme: The Smallest Church in the World**

TEXT: "Fear not, little flock, for it is your Father's good pleasure to give you the kingdom." Luke 12:32.

What is said to be the smallest church in the world is situated in a little village in North Yorkshire, England. It dates back to A.D. 840, has a tiny tower, and seats only about fifteen people. The building is small indeed; but let it bring thought of a church as a spiritual institution. In that sense some small churches are big and some big churches are very small. Any church that is too small for God to get into is too small.

I. The absence of the sense of God makes a very small church. It may be a bustling secular institution, priding itself on the seven-day-a-week, nonstop quality, but if it never brings the mood, "Be still, and know that I am God," it is too small to be a Christian church. We sometimes hear the criticism that the church is too otherworldly. Is not the truth in the other direction, that the church is not otherworldly enough? The ministering church is a soul-saving church.

II. A further fact is that one of the smallest churches on earth is one in which Jesus' vision of the welfare of the people finds no place. Some such churches are far too much concerned with their own little life.

III. Then, too, in a deep sense, the smallest church on earth is one in which lines of caste and race run their little fences through what ought to be a fellowship in Christ. The church in which all the brothers in Christ are not welcome is too small for Christ himself.

How big is your church?—Abridged from H. E. Luccock.

## SUNDAY SCHOOL LESSON

**May 11. When God's People Worship. Exod. 35:20-26; 40:34-38. Background Scripture: Exod. 35-40.**

Memory Verse: "Ascribe to the Lord the glory due his name; bring an offering, and come into his courts!" Ps. 96:8 (R.S.V.).

See the Evening Service Theme of this date in this *Manual* for a discussion of some of the values of worship.

Exod. 35:20 to 36:7 is a graphic and inspiring narrative. I. Here is a spirit of giving that any church might well emulate. II. Here is the endowment of workers by which any church might profit. III. Here, Exod. 40:34-38, is the blessing of God by which any church might go forward.

Some may wish to point out the importance of this focus of worship for the political, social, and religious life of the wilderness wanderings. Exod. 35:20-26, 36:5-7 is a striking stewardship illustration.

# SUNDAY: MAY EIGHTEENTH

## MORNING SERVICE

**Theme: Why the Church Never Gives Up**

Suggested Scripture Reading: Eph. 5:15-33.

Selected Hymns: "Glorious things of thee are spoken."—J. Newton. "I love thy kingdom, Lord."—T. Dwight. "Head of the Church triumphant."—C. Wesley. "Christ is made the sure foundation."—Anon.

Call to Worship: "Enter into his gates with thanksgiving and into his courts with praise; be thankful unto him, and bless his name, for the Lord is good; his mercy is everlasting and his truth endureth to all generations."

Invocation Prayer: Almighty God, may thy gracious Spirit give us this day deliverance from all that is formal and external, and may we be led into the full and glorious liberty of the children of God. Lead us into the inner rooms of spiritual communion. May the Light Divine shine upon our souls. Refine our discernments so that we may be able to discriminate between the transient and the eternal. Subdue our hearts to pure inclination so that we may love the lovely and may appreciate the things that please thee. Knit us together in the fellowship of holy worship. May our sympathies be so pure and full that we shall be able to apprehend one another's sorrows and share one another's joys. And graciously lead us through the fellowship of praise into the aspirations of prayer and sacrificial service. In Christ's name we ask. Amen.

**Theme: Why the Church Never Gives Up**

TEXT: "Son of man, I send thee to the Children of Israel, to a rebellious nation . . . and thou shalt speak my words unto them, whether they will hear or whether they will forbear."—Ezek. 2:3-7.

INTRODUCTORY: It needs more than ordinary courage to be a Christian in a world like this. At times we lose heart and have serious misgivings about the Christian future of the world. Now the prophet Ezekiel found himself in a similar situation. He was sent out into a bitterly hostile world. He is not promised that his message will be popular. He must preach; he must witness; he must fulfill his God-given commission whether they will listen or refuse to listen.

There can be no denying the fact that our Christian faith comes somewhat awkwardly into this modern world. But I am quite sure that Jesus Christ has a word to say to us all at this time. It is just this: "Keep at it! Be faithful to the truth you have seen and embraced. Go on witnessing whether they will listen or refuse to listen!"

Consider the significance of this persistent, courageous witness to Christ and his truth in a rebellious world.

I. By such witness we provide men with an opportunity to be saved.

Throughout the New Testament the gospel and its proclamation are always thought of as opening out a great new opportunity and men are urged to grasp it with both hands. When Jesus let loose his Gospel upon the world, a new day had dawned; the world's great chance had come. It was the "accepted time"; "the day of salvation."

What if the church were not in this town? What if there were no consecrated, Christian personalities here and there throughout this community keeping its life sweet and clean? Many who never darken the church's doors would shrink from such a prospect. Whether we listen or refuse to listen we know that a society with no church, no gospel, no Christian personalities, would be a society with no hope. But so long as there is somewhere in the heart of this community a witness to God and his Christ, and a gospel that can change human nature and create fellowship, there is still a chance, and there is still hope for the world.

II. By such witness we leave men without an excuse if they are not saved.

St. Paul, speaking of the rebellious world of his day, and of God's revelation of himself to that world, said: "They are without excuse."

The light of the gospel has shone forth, but if men close their eyes to it, the responsibility for the consequences is theirs and theirs alone. In the church of Christ there is fellowship; a fellowship that transcends differences of nation, race, and tradition. In the Family of Christ the brotherhood of man is achieved. But if the world, with this redeemed community in its midst, pursues selfish, nationalistic policies that breed only suspicion and hatred, and, in the end, lead to war, who is to blame for this tragedy? If we will not hear and heed, and accept God's way of life, we are wtihout excuse. We are responsible.

III. By our patient, persistent, courageous witness to Christ we affirm our faith that, by the power of God, men will ultimately be saved. Whether they will listen or refuse to listen, we go on, for we believe that as every little wave on the sea beach had the throb of the mighty ocean in it, so every word spoken for Christ, every bit of Christian influence we shed abroad, every uncompromising stand we make, has the power of God behind it. It will not die. It will remain in some heart, and, in after years, it will bear fruit, perhaps in a lonely hour.

So we work; so the church keeps at it, believing that no effort is finally in vain in God, and that his power, working through our weakness, will ultimately save the world.—S. A.

THEME PRAYER: Thanks be to thee, O Lord Jesus Christ, for all the benefits which thou hast given us: for all the pains and insults thou hast borne for us. O merciful Redeemer, Friend, and and Brother, may we know thee more clearly, love thee more dearly, and follow thee more nearly. And when trouble comes, may be bear it triumphantly. In thine own name we ask. Amen.

OFFERTORY SENTENCE: "Lay not up for yourselves treasures upon the earth, where moth and rust consume, and where thieves break through and steal: but lay up for yourselves treasures in heaven, where neither moth nor rust doth consume, and where thieves do not break through nor steal: for where thy treasure is, there will thy heart be also."

OFFERTORY PRAYER: O God, the Father of mercies, receive thou the offering which we bring thee at this time as a part of the worship of thy house. May these gifts be symbols of a consecration that holds nothing back from thee, who givest all. In Christ's name we ask. Amen.

SEED THOUGHTS: Fearless Preaching: It is said that when a Roundhead in St. Andrew's, Holborn, leveled a musket at the breast of the venerable prelate Hacket, and bade him desist from preaching, he never hesitated for one moment, but simply said, "Soldier, do your duty; I shall continue to do mine." —W. Denton.

Helps against Fear: I. Let your fear be exercised about God. II. Set faith to work. III. Labor for purity and holiness. IV. Value not life too much. Be willing to spend and be spent for God and his Church.—W. G.

Ministry to the Unresponsive: "We may preach and preach," said a great bishop to his ordinals, "and our words will seem to fall upon stone, and not upon a man's heart." Under any such trials of patience Ezekiel's experience will prove helpful.

### Choice Illustrations on the Theme

CHURCH A CITADEL. In pioneer days people lived in settlements around the edge of which were farms. Within the circle of farms was a stockade surrounding homes, stores, a church, and a school. In the center of the stockade was the blockhouse. Essential supplies, in the event of an emergency, were stored there. This was the fortress and place of last resort in time of danger. Under attack by a strong enemy the pioneers gave up their farms if necessary. If severely pressed they surrendered their homes, stores, the church building, and the schoolhouse. But the blockade they never yielded. There they took their stand though it might mean struggling to death. There they had at hand supplies to see them through a crisis. The church is a kind of blockhouse. It is the shelter for the essentials of life. These it holds ready for call. These it defends to the last.—J. Gordon Howard.

THE CHURCH INDESTRUCTIBLE. After the famous old church "All Hallows" had been totally destroyed in London the rector and his people started immediately on a program of ministering to the people both as to their physical and spiritual needs. In writing of the work done since the church's destruction, the rector headed his account: "The Indestructible Church." The true church is not one composed of bricks and mortar. It is made up of those whose loyalty to Jesus Christ and to one another constitutes a holy fellowship. Such a spiritual church knows no destruction.—Arthur Wallace.

THE NECESSARY CHURCH. At the approach of many of our cities we pass a large structure emblazoned by night and day in huge letters—LIGHT, HEAT, AND POWER COMPANY. The church is the fellowship that believes that we possess in the God and Father of our Lord Jesus Christ—Light, the interpretation of our puzzling existence, Heat, the love which warms men's hearts with the sense of a friendly universe and fuses them into a friendly society, Power, conferring mastery over fear and selfishness. Only an appreciative church, giving God his worth, can resinstate him in the minds and hearts of a generation to whom he seems unnecessary.—H. S. Coffin.

## EVENING SERVICE

**Theme: Have You Seen Any Miracles Lately?**

TEXT: "Master, we would see a sign from thee." Matt. 12:38.

INTRODUCTORY: It was not a facetious question, "Have you seen any miracles lately?" My friend was sincere, and I knew what he meant.

I. "Certain of the scribes and Pharisees answered Jesus, saying, Teacher, we would see a sign from thee. But he answered and said unto them, An evil and adulterous generation seeketh after a sign," etc. There is a kind of miracle that we have no expectation of seeing, and for which in our better moments we do not express desire, or at least not until we are in deepest extremity, and then our expectation is not of water being poured into water pots and dipped out in wine.

II. There are, however, miracles which we should see. "The healing of His seamless dress is by our beds of pain" is a line which we should take seriously. We believe in doctors and nurses. We believe in the skill which gives the right medicine and practices a correct surgery. We believe in influencing the patient psychologically so that the mind may have good influence upon the body. We believe that another's cheerful heart may be good medicine. We believe that the right man with the right word at the right moment can tremendously help a sick person. And we believe too that the spiritual presence of the Christ can give the extra strength needed in a moment of crisis, the extra endurance required for hours of ordeal, a grace of healing during weeks of convalescence, and restoration of power through many years of life.

III. "Have you seen any miracles lately?" He was thinking about the miracles of character. And my answer was, "Yes, there are always three miracles near by." Miracle No. 1, Myself. Every Christian man is his own miracle of grace. "There, but for the grace of God, lies John Bunyan." Miracle No. 2, Yourself, my Christian friend. He who began a good work in you is perfecting it. Miracle No. 3, the Christ himself, the ever-living, ever-present Christ. He is the great miracle, the greatest miracle, the only miracle that matters.—H.

**Suggested Texts and Themes**

"Together in Unity": "Behold, how good and how pleasant it is for brethren to dwell together in unity!" Ps. 133:1.

The Basis of Christianity: Matt. 22:15-22, 34-40.

"Other Sheep I Have": "And other sheep I have, which are not of this fold." John 10:16.

In the Golden City: Isa. 52:1. "So these are the glories of the golden city. I. There is wakefulness. II. There is strength. III. There is beauty. And these glories will be our defence. A positive virtue is our best rampart against vice."—J. H. Jowett.

Real Co-operation: "They helped every one his neighbor; and every one said to his brother, Be of good courage. So the carpenter encouraged the goldsmith. . . ." Isa. 41:6, 7.

## MIDWEEK FELLOWSHIP MEETING TOPIC

(Church Night or Suggested Sermon Topic)

**Theme: The Art of Witnessing**

TEXT: "Now when they saw the boldness of Peter and John, and perceived that they were unlearned and ignorant men, they marvelled; and they took knowledge of them, that they had been with Jesus." Acts 4:13.

I. "Unlearned." Witnessing is not a matter of the use of grammer. See this verse in the Greek. This word probably had special reference to Rabbinic culture, the absence of which was conspicuous in Peter's address. Think of the witness that has been borne for Christ by uncultured men. Also by cultured men.

II. "Ignorant." See the Greek. This word suggests one in private station, rather than one in public affairs. Without professional knowledge. The professional may have only secondary contact with religious reality. The layman's contact may be primary.

III. "They took knowledge of them, that they had been with Jesus." See Acts 2:32 and Acts 4:33. Here was primary contact with religious reality. Four tests of primary contact: "Inward reinforcement of personality, a transcendent happiness, a deep serenity, an outgoing love."

IV. "Boldness." The boldness of conviction. The boldness of positive action. They spoke. They acted. They showed forth their witness in what they were. —H.

## SUNDAY SCHOOL LESSON

**May 18. God's People Tested or Giants and Grasshoppers. Num. 13:30-14:3, 19-24. Background Scripture: Num. 13:17-14:45.**

MEMORY VERSE: "Today, when you hear his voice, do not harden your hearts as in the rebellion, on the day of testing in the wilderness." Heb. 3:7-8.

The Grasshopper Complex. "And we were in our own sight as grasshoppers, and so we were in their sight." Num. 13:33.

I. These spies to the promised land were suffering from what we would designate by using the well-worn phrase "inferiority complex." A man who is obsessed by fear feels exceedingly insignificant.

II. A knowledge of the fears of an individaul is the key to the understanding of his personality. There are few of who do not allow ridiculous fears to impede our effectiveness and darken our souls.

III. That which undermines a person's faith in himself is to be avoided as a noisome pestilence. Lowell makes Hosea Biglow say: "Folks thet's afeerd to fail are sure o' failin'." Fear is invariably a handicap to efficiency. The grasshopper complex vitiates one's intellectual honesty. We are afraid of our thoughts.

We are disloyal to the right because of our fear of the criticism of some human grasshopper whom we take to be a giant. Some of the most essential work for human betterment is being left undone because those who should be doing it are afflicted with the grasshopper complex.

IV. In mastering the art of right living it is imperative that a person get rid of his irrational fears. Stonewall Jackson's motto was, "Do your duty and leave the rest to providence." He who remembers that if we do our part, God will not fail in his, will not dissipate his energy and his talents in cowering in the shadow of fancied fears.—Lewis H. Chrisman.

# SUNDAY: MAY TWENTY-FIFTH

## MORNING SERVICE

**Theme: The Consequences of Pentecost (Pentecost)**

Suggested Scripture Reading: Acts 2:1-21.

SELECTED HYMNS: "Come, thou Almighty King."—Anon. "Holy Spirit, Truth Divine."—Samuel Longfellow. "Our Blessed Redeemer, ere he breathed."—Harriet Auber. "Breathe on me, Breath of God."—Edwin Hatch. "Spirit of God, descend upon my heart." —George Croly.

CALL TO WORSHIP: "The Spirit and the bride say, Come. And let him that heareth say, Come. And let him that is athirst come. And whosoever will, let him take the water of life freely." Rev. 22:17.

INVOCATION:

Come, Holy Spirit, heav'nly Dove,
With all thy quick'ning pow'rs;
Kindle a flame of sacred love
In these cold hearts of ours.

**Theme: The Consequences of Pentecost**

TEXT: "And they were all filled with the Holy Ghost." Acts 2:4.

The experience of the Holy Spirit was basic to the vital Christianity of the early Christians and was a distinctive factor in the life of the church of the first generation.

The history of essential Christianity from the Day of Pentecost until now is the history of the operation of the Holy Spirit in the believer and in the church.

The operation of the Holy Spirit is ageless yet always contemporary. Its gifts and ministries are manifold. Yet the consequences of the coming of the Holy Spirit are basically the same as they were in Jerusalem on the first Christian Pentecost.

I. We are greatly impressed by the marked change which took place in the lives of those who came under the influence of the Holy Spirit on the Day of Pentecost. Individuals became conscious that the Holy Spirit had entered into them, and their lives were thereby tansformed. These people found themselves in a new world. They were brought into a new and living relationship with Christ, they felt his presence in their lives, and they knew that he was with them counseling and comforting them. They enjoyed the fellowship of the Spirit with spirit and received an inward witness that they were in communion with their Lord.

II. This was reflected in the new authority which came to those under the influence of the Holy Spirit. They were now able to testify that they knew the truth of Christ at first hand, and that they had not received their authority to witness to the things of Christ from any secondary source, either from man or community. Their authority was of the Holy Spirit. The Spirit gave them a new confidence.

III. They also knew that with the coming of the Holy Spirit they received the gifts of Christ himself. Not that they received more life, but they received new life, life that was joy, peace, love, patience, and longsuffering in the Holy Spirit. The whole of their living was lifted on to a new level of meaning and purposefulness. Life was conceived in a new light. There was an eager seeking after holiness, and things which once had seemed to matter were now seen in a new perspective so that Christ might be all in all.

IV. The consequence of the coming of the Holy Spirit was also seen in that all-embracing unity which possessed those who received it. We read that those who received the Spirit were together in one place and had all things common. It was not only material things they had in common, but a common spiritual experience. Those who were gathered together felt themselves to be a living company, enjoying unbroken fellowship with their exalted Lord and with one another. Together they prayed and supped as a brotherhood united in the new faith. So, in accordance with the will of their Lord, they ordered their lives together. In this Spirit-created fellowship each member continued to be himself, and the claims of the fellowship never stood over against the individual. But it was known and felt that the Spirit was in the believer and in the fellowship. All knew what it meant to be in the unity of the Spirit and in the bonds of peace and love among themselves.

V. The transformation brought about through the agency of the Holy Spirit in the individual and in the Christian fellowship was evident also in the new missionary concern which followed the experience of Pentecost. Those who had themselves been changed by the Spirit worked for the ultimate transformation of the whole of life, because they knew that nothing short of this was the purpose of the Lord whom they had come to know in a new way. The Christian fellowship became in effect an outreaching fellowship. Christians could not keep to themselves what they had heard and seen and known.—J. G. Harris.

Prayer for the Day: O thou Holy Spirit of God, who inspireth the minds of men, who burneth like living fire in their hearts and moveth their wills to do thy purposes, be in the midst of this assembly of people and brood over the life of each individual unto the forgiveness of sin, the endowment with power, the application of comfort, the giving of peace, and the liberation of Joy. Amen.—H.

Offertory Sentence: "And the Lord spake unto Moses, saying, Speak unto the children of Israel, that they bring me an offering: of every man that giveth it willingly with his heart ye shall take my offering." Exod. 25:1, 2.

Offertory Prayer: We lay before thee, O God, a token of our gratitude for thy lovingkindness. Bless our token of gratitude.

We bring unto thee, O Christ, a token of our love for thy salvation. Bless our token of love.

We lay before thee, O Holy Spirit, a token of service, and pray for thy direction in its use, that it may carry the Gospel of Christ unto the hearts of men. Amen.—H.

Seed Thoughts: Perpetuating Pentecost: "Someone has well said that the first Pentecost cannot be duplicated but it can be perpetuated. One of the things about the first Pentecost, which can and should be perpetuated, is evangelism."

A Dramatic Picture: "And they were all filled with the Holy Spirit and began to speak with other tongues, as the Spirit gave them utterance." Act 2:4. See Acts 2:1-47. This is one of the most dramatic pictures in the Bible—the meeting of the little band of disciples; the rushing, flaming sense of God's presence and their excited response; the quick criticism of the onlookers; Peter's great sermon knitting together Old Testament vision with the good news that had come to men in Christ; the call to repentance; baptism of three thousand souls into the new fellowship—and then the daily sharing of their praises and their bread "with glad and generous hearts." The impact of the story, if we took it seriously enough today, would be tremendous.—Georgia Harkness.

## Choice Illustrations on the Theme

TOGETHERNESS AND POWER. It is said that when D. L. Moody was once talking to a man who claimed that he was on fire for Christ but had little room for the churches, the missioner took from the fire, before which they were sitting, a live coal, and, as they watched it lose its heat and glow, he pointed the lesson that a solitary Chistian is ever in danger of losing the spiritual glow from his life. Again and again the power of the Spirit has come to the gathered community. Togetherness is one condition of our receiving the promised power.—E. A. Buxton.

WAITING FOR POWER. While we should certainly wait in preparation for the Spirit's coming, we should be on our guard against the perils of waiting for power. Mr. Beverly Nichols has put on record a conversation he once had with Sir Winston Churchill on the subject of writing. Mr. Nichols confessed that he often had to wait for inspiration. Sir Winston's report was: "Nonsense; you should go to your room every day at nine o'clock and say, 'I'm going to write for four hours.' " When Beverly Nichols raised objections, Sir Winston said, "You've got to get over that. If you sit waiting for inspiration you will sit waiting until you are an old man. Writing is like any other job—like marching an army, for instance. If you sit down and wait until the weather is fine, you won't get very far with your troops. Kick yourself; irritate yourself; but write; it's the only way." How often we have found that when we make the effort the power is there to hand! . . . A men's meeting had listened to an address on "Christianity and the Community" and the discussion that followed had got round to the problem of drawing the outsiders into the churches. The speaker suggested that the church was not ready for the task but must wait and prepare. A retired minister sitting in the corner retorted, "They were saying that forty years ago." There are perils in waiting against which we must beware. We shall only know the greatness of the Spirit's power when we obey our Lord's commands.—E. A. Buxton.

## EVENING SERVICE

**Theme: Memory's Gateway (Memorial Day)**

TEXT: "A book of remembrance was written." Mal. 3:16.

Remembrance enriches life by bring- into focus the hazy, indistinct, silent past, and making it vivid and vocal. For this reason Books of Remembrance were kept in very ancient times, both by the Jews and the Persians. The Book of Remembrance to which Malachi refers was one of Jehovah's most valued treasures, a book inscribed with the names of his most heroic and loyal worshipers, whose deeds were to shine with eternal luster never to be tarnished by the breath of forgetfulness.

With justifiable feelings of pride and deep gratitude we not only keep books and scrolls and plaques of remembrance, but we set aside special Days of Remembrance. Such a day we shall celebrate during the coming week, our American Memorial Day. It is therefore fitting that we should consider memory as a Gateway to Destiny. This is our evening theme.

I. Remembrance has a very great impact upon thought and mind. Its power and influence are felt by us all. It is one of our greatest incentives to action, and as a determining and controlling factor in life it is almost unrivaled and supreme.

The memories we cherish in the heart become an active power working out a destiny in accord with its own character and our relationship to it. No impression the mind receives remains quiescent and dormant. It becomes an active agent in the formation of conduct and character. And character is destiny.

The first essential in determining our mode of life is to guard well our relationship to these Books of Remembrance we all write and the Days of Remembrance we all keep. Our relationship to them determines whether they shall become the copybook of life by which we model all our character writing. It determines whether memory shall be an uplifting ennobling power or a degrading influence in life.

II. The source of Christianity's power to revolutionize men's lives and the life of society and nations, is centered in the memory of a Cross of sacrifice erected nearly two thousand years ago. When Jesus, by instituting the Lord's Supper with the words "This do in remembrance of me," concentrated men's minds on his sacrificial death, he set free a life-giving power of sacred memory that has changed the course of history and become in the hearts of men a purifying flame. And it is ever so. As we look back upon the past with its high-souled struggles and sustaining strength, its sacrifices issuing in glorious triumphs, and its victories over evil, confidence for the future, however dark the present, awakes in the heart. We know that the God who has been our help in ages past is also our hope for years to come, and the future is bright with hope.

Optimism is born of happy memories. Pessimism cannot live in an atmosphere of sacred remembrances. The cynic is a man with a short, distorted, and biased memory. He never lifts his eyes to the distant hills of glorious achievement and triumphant success.

III. We as a nation and as individuals are rich in memories with power to inspire every confidence in the future. There may be little in the present to inspire hope and confidence. We may be discouraged by the widespread indifference to religion, oppressed by our feelings of impotence, troubled and perplexed by the dark clouds of fear both in our own lives and on the distant horizon, tormented with an aching sense of insecurity that shatters our peace of mind and heart, and bewildered by the complexity of the present position. All this is true. But let us recall the past with its glow of religious fervor in the great spiritual unheavals that transformed the lives of thousands, the triumphs over social evils and oppressions revealing an ever-increasing emphasis upon the sanctity of human life, miraculous deeds of valor and self-sacrifice, courage that nothing could subdue and powers of endurance that amazed the world.

IV. But there is another kind of Book of Remembrance that we must not pass over. All memories are not of this inspiring character. Some Books of Remembrance are not only distressing but degrading to read. They leave an evil influence on the whole of life. It seems surprising that we should give such memories a place in life. But the human mind seems biased in that direction, and we find it easier to retain evil memories than those of an uplifting character.

Because the memory of oppressive conditions or injustices inflicted make men bitter in spirit and revengeful in action, yesterday's clouds are allowed to darken today's sky, and life is often completely spoiled by such dark memories. The future, too, is mortgaged by them, because we cannot build the future on a foundation of past grievances. They may become incentives to actions not unrelated to the spirit of revenge, and wreck all hopes for future welfare.

Only the Book of glorious and sacred memories affords us strength for our journey, inspiration for the hour of difficulty and frustration, and power to tread the path of light that the star of hope and Christian idealism sheds on our way. Let us free life from the power of every memory that militates against our future welfare, and foster only those remembrances that make possible the divine purpose for us all. Let us never forget that our Book of Remembrance may aslo become our Book of Destiny. And in simple trust in God let us commit our future to him.—Adapted from R. Shepherd.

**Suggested Texts and Themes**

Clouds of Witnesses (Memorial Day): "Wherefore seeing we also are compassed about with so great a cloud of witnesses, let us . . ." Heb. 12:1.

Christian Witness: "But ye shall receive power, after that the Holy Ghost is come upon you: and ye shall be witnesses unto me . . ." Acts 1:8.

Waiting for Power: "And, behold, I send the promise of my Father upon you: but tarry ye in the city of Jerusalem, until ye be endued with power from on high." Luke 24:49.

Tides of the Spirit: "For I will pour water upon him that is thirsty, and floods upon the dry ground: I will pour my spirit upon thy seed, and my blessing upon thine offspring . . ." Isa. 44:3, 4.

The Strengthener: "And I will pray the Father, and he shall give you another Comforter [Strengthener], that he may abide with you for ever." John 14:16.

## MIDWEEK FELLOWSHIP MEETING TOPIC

(Church Night or Suggested Sermon Subject)

**Theme: Looking Up and Lifting Up**

TEXT: "In the name of Jesus Christ of Nazareth rise up and walk. And he took him by the right hand, and lifted him up." Acts 3:6, 7.

I. That is surely the order in which those "greater things" are done which are to distinguish the faithful disciple of Christ. It is no use enjoining the impotent man to rise. It is no use taking him by the hand and lifting him up. The word and the act must have their roots in the infinite energies which are hidden in "the name of Jesus Christ."

II. And what is implied in naming the sacred Name? It is infinitely more than the mere utterance of a talisman prior to the performance of some wonderful trick. No one can name the name without reverence, and aspiration, and prayer, and communion, and reception. To name him is humbly to seek fellowship with him, so that through the channels of vital union his wonder-working power may flow into all our words and deeds. To name the Name is far more than the utterance of the lips; it is the act of the soul flinging itself back upon the unlimited resources of grace.

III. But while we cannot do anything without the Lord, he will not do everything without us. His communion demands co-operation. We can ensure the needful endowment by looking up, and naming the sacred Name; but the endowment is only revealed when we address ourselves to our tasks, and lay hold of the burden, and lift with all our mind and heart and strength. We are to look up, and then we are to lift up, and the miracle will be wrought.

IV. And what is the blessed issue in this story? What happened to the impotent man? "He, leaping up!" That is the issue. And that is always the divine order; the look up, the lift up, the leap up! In that order God will reveal his glory to us in our own day, and we shall do impossible things in the name of his holy Child Jesus.—J. H. Jowett.

## SUNDAY SCHOOL LESSON

**May 25. Living by God's Laws. Deut. 6:1-3; 11:18-21, 26-28. Background Scripture: Deut. 6; 11.**

MEMORY VERSE: "Hear O Israel: The Lord our God is one Lord; and you shall love the Lord your God with all your heart, and with all your soul, and with all your might." Deut. 6:4-5 (R.S.V.).

An interesting approach to this lesson can be made by telling the group about the *mezuzah* (Lit. door post, Hebrew), which is the name given to a piece of parchment inscribed with the passages Deut. 6:4-9 and 11:13-21 rolled up like a scroll and placed in a container fastened to the upper right-hand posts of the entrances of Jewish buildings as a sign of faith in God. The biblical source of this rite is Deut. 6:9 and 11:20.

The *mezuzah* is often found today at the doors of the homes of Orthodox Jewish families. The members of the family touch the *mezuzah* with their fingers on leaving or entering the house.

The phylacteries (see Matt. 23:5) which in present Orthodox Jewish practice are worn by adult males on week days at morning worship, were in Jesus' day worn by the Pharisees and rabbis all day. These are two small boxes of black leather, containing parchment slips on which are inscribed the four texts, which prescribe the use of "frontlets"; Deut. 6:4-9, 11:13-21; Exod. 13:1-10, 13:11-16, and are bound on the forehead and on the left arm by straps.

Presented as "sign" and "memorial" of God's deliverance from bondage, they also aimed to direct the heart of the Jew to God and his commands.

With such introduction the teacher can go on to stress the mission of the home in religious teaching; also to show that spiritual prosperity and stability depend upon fidelity and obedience to God's laws. The promises and warnings of God to Israel have urgent significance for individuals and nations today.

# SUNDAY: JUNE FIRST

## MORNING SERVICE

**Theme: Is Our Religion Big Enough?**

SUGGESTED SCRIPTURE READING: II Tim. 1:1-14. (Suggestion: Read from J. B. Phillip's translation.)

SELECTED HYMNS: "How firm a foundation."—Rippon's Selection. "Rock of Ages, cleft for me."—A. M. Toplady. "Strong Son of God, immortal Love."—Alfred Tennyson. "I heard the voice of Jesus say."—H. Bonar. "My faith looks up to thee."—Ray Palmer.

CALL TO WORSHIP: "I will bless the Lord at all times: his praise shall continually be in my mouth. My soul shall make her boast in the Lord: the humble shall hear thereof, and be glad. O magnify the Lord with me, and let us exalt his name together." Ps. 34:1-3.

INVOCATION: Almighty God, the Father of our Lord Jesus Christ, deliver us now from the vain things which have power over us, and enable us to rest our souls in thee and yield ourselves to the guiding of thy loving Spirit. Make us ready to offer thee the joy that is thy gift, and worship thee with glad and thankful hearts. Amen.—Source unknown.

**Theme: Is Our Religion Big Enough?**

TEXT: "For the bed is shorter than that a man can stretch himself on it." Isa. 28:20.

When in 1650 Oliver Cromwell sent his famous message to the General Assembly of the Church of Scotland: "I beseech you by the tender mercies of Christ, think it possible that you may be mistaken"—a brave man was Oliver to send that message to a company of Scotsmen—he counseled them to read the 28th chapter of the prophecies of Isaiah, and learn therefrom the feebleness and futility of clever human schemes which leave God out. In this chapter the prophet uses a homely figure to drive home his point: "The bed is shorter than that a man can stretch himself on it." "The bed" referred to the shrewd devices of Isaiah's time which gave men a false sense of security.

Is your religion, and mine, big enough for the times in which we are living? That the times are testing to courage and faith, no one will question.

I. Many kinds of religion are not big enough. I am quite sure that certain rather common types of religion are not big enough for our times. There is a religion, for instance, which concerns itself mainly with the extremities of life. On the rolls of our churches are not a few persons who are sensitively careful that babies are christened when they come into the world, and that proper rites are sympathetically said for those who pass from it; but in the great throbbing midway of life as churchmen we never see nor hear of them.

1. A religion reserved for the greater crises of life is a short bed for a man to lie on, a narrow covering to bring warmth and peace. A man's faith is just like his muscles, or his music, or

his golf game—if he does not exercise it, he loses it. If he does not take care of it in the sunshine, no wonder he cannot find it in the storm.

2. Again, a religion of opinion is not big enough for the times in which we live. Alas, that in a challenging period of history like this Christians should still dispute and divide over secondary questions of doctrine or of church government, while the people are wondering whether there is a God. Belief in the great realities of our faith is supremely important; unless a man has within him some vivid world of ever-expanding conviction in which he finds refuge in days of storm and stress, unless he is able to say of the Saviour of his soul, "I know whom I have believed"—God help him.

3. Once more, a religion which concerns itself mainly with preparation for a future life, or with a man's life with God without regard to his everyday life with his fellows, will not do at this time. Religion must touch with transforming power every bit of life, or it is fiction and fraud. The great enemy of Christianity today is Christianity confessed but inactive—Christianity floating like a flag on the far horizons of life, but not permitted to interfere with business, pleasure, or statecraft. Unless a man is saved as an employer, as an employee, as a husband, as a citizen, as an investor, as a trustee, as a public servant, his salvation is a perilous illusion.

II. What, then, on the positive side?

1. A religion big enough for our times must meet adequately the needs of the individual. And how tremendous these needs are! So many broken, baffled men and women, the old securities in which they have trusted, gone, not knowing where or to whom to turn. A religion big enough for our times must look disaster, sickness, and death fearlessly in the face without a quiver.

2. A religion which is to be big enough for the times must not only meet the needs of the individual, but beginning there, working through the individual, must provide a solution for the tremendous needs of the world. Has Christianity ever failed to show the way where it was given free scope?—Adapted from A. MacColl.

PRAYER FOR THE DAY: As the heavens are higher than the earth, so are there ways higher than our ways, and thy thoughts than our thoughts, O God. For every gleam of light from thee, for every revelation of thy mind, for every expression of thy love toward us, for every indication of thy purposes we thank thee. Forgive us for dullness of mind, unresponsiveness of heart, blindness of eye, and deafness of hearing. We stand bewildered and perplexed sometimes as we look out upon our world and inward into our lives. But help us to hold fast our faith in thee, our God of infinite wisdom, unfathomable love, almighty power—our Father.—H.

OFFERTORY SENTENCE:

Jesus calls us from the worship
Of the vain world's golden store,
From each idol that would keep us,
Saying "Christian, love me more!"
—Mrs. Cecil F. Alexander

OFFERTORY PRAYER: Dear Father, thou givest all: the breath of life, the pulsing heart, the power of thought, the skill of hand, the will to do, the happy home, the love of friends, the beauty of life, the peace of Christ; all are gifts of thy boundless love. In gratitude we bring unto thee our gifts, sacrifices of human love, the purest gold that we possess. Use them, we pray, unto thy divine purpose. In the name of Jesus. Amen.—T. Haines.

SEED THOUGHTS:

Minimum Religion Is Not Enough: Isa. 28:20.

Adequate Religion. No religion is equal to the strain of life unless it is able to make us sure of God's love so that we meet sorrow without rebellion, loss without self-pity, adversity without whining, temptation without surrender, death without fear.—G. G. D. Kilpatrick.

Christianity is a creed for heroes. Constantly the New Testament points us to a God whose resources are far beyond any human emergency. From its pages let the little word "able" ring in the ears of all troubled folk as they face their personal problems.

**Choice Illustrations on the Theme**

JOHN WESLEY CONCERNING OPINIONS. "I am sick of opinions." said John Wesley; "let my soul be with Christians of whatsoever opinion they be. I have no more right to object to a man for holding a different opinion from mine than I have to differ with a man because he wears a wig and I wear my own hair; but if he takes his wig off and shakes the powder in my eyes, I shall consider it my duty to get quit of him as soon as possible."

A BIGGER IDEA. Sir James Barrie once told this lovely story: He had been calling, he said, on the most gracious lady in the land. She was celebrating her third birthday. It was the little Princess Margaret, younger daughter of the King of England. She was looking with delight at one of her gifts—a tea table with painted flower pots on it, each about the size of a thimble. "Is that really yours?" asked Sir James Barrie. With the sweetest smile, she answered at once: "It is yours and mine."

## EVENING SERVICE

**Theme: Marriage is For Keeps**

TEXT: "And walk in love." Eph. 5:2.

The damaging effects of high divorce rates are increasingly felt in our culture. Serious proposals have been made to the effect that no marriage licenses be issued after the third divorce. However, the cure is not in legislation. It lies in overcoming the current casual attitude toward marriage with the true Christian ideal that marriage is for keeps.

Many marriages don't last simply because people don't enter into them with the idea of making them last.

Romantic love is not enough to hold marriages together in our kind of a world. It takes a stronger, tougher, more durable kind of love. It is love that Paul talks about in Ephesians. He is not applying it to married life. But it fits perfectly. "Let all bitterness, and wrath, and anger, and clamor, and railing be put away from you, with all malice: and be ye kind to one another, tender-hearted, forgiving each other . . . and walk in love even as Christ also loved you."

This kind of love is the basis of enduring marriage.

I. Couples that walk in love *are wise enough to allow for frequent adjustments.*

Most marriage counselors and clinics agree that the biggest single cause of marriage trouble is emotional immaturity. It is sometimes called "adult adolescence." It may come to light in one of many forms: selfishness, lack of patience, absence of courtesy and consideration for the other, insecurity, attempted domination of one by the other, unfairness, or poor money management. In other words, plain, ordinary human adjustments are the groundwork of lasting marriages.

Love that is real and lasting is sensitive enough to make such adjustments with good will and good humor.

II. Couples that walk in love *are co-operative enough to be companions.* Plain everyday selfishness is a big cause of much unhappiness in marriage, to say nothing of many broken homes. The marriage that lasts is a two-way partnership. It grows on co-operation.

A successful and lasting marriage takes co-operation all along the line. It means that there can be no secrets. It means that both partners will confide in each other and will trust each other completely. It means that all money matters be kept open and above board. It means mutual agreement and mutual effort to live within the family income. It means a complete sharing of plans and hopes as well as fears and failures. It means respect for the dignity of personality. It means respect on both sides for friends and in-laws, hobbies and recreation. It means that either one may count on the other to hold them up when they are down. It means a common agreement and emphasis on what is essential and a common willingness to overlook the trivial.

Much has been said in recent years about sex compatibility as the most important single factor in lasting marriages. This is not so. The late Henry C. Link, director of the Psychological Service Center in New York, said that "sexual maladjustment is one of the less frequent causes of unhappy marriages." Dr. Link adds: "In other words, character and unselfish personality and the many good habits they involve, are far more important than the details of sex, and require infinitely more practice before they can be mastered."

Partners in marriage need to mature with age. The perennial playboy can become a bore in time. The ageless beauty queen finally succeeds only in being tiresome. But an understanding and cooperative comradeship is a lifetime need and a lifelong benediction for it makes marriage keep sweet and good all the way.

III. Couples that walk in love *are strong enough to withstand any crisis.* Conflicts and differences between man and wife are bound to arise in every home. We have made divorce so easy and popular that it seems a way of escape at the slightest sign of so-called incompatibility, to say nothing of an actual family crisis. But marriage can be a sturdier institution than this. And in most cases (though not all) the threatening crisis, whether emotional, financial, or physical, can and must be resolved. Mutual faith in God, mutual devotion to the spirit of Jesus Christ, and mutual dedication to the ideal of a Christian home are the binding ingredients that can make any marriage strong enough to live through most crises that arise.—Charles M. Crowe.

**Suggested Texts and Themes on Marriage**

Growth through High Thinking: Phil. 4:8.

The Christian Conception of Married Love: "Husbands love your wives, even as Christ loved the Church, and gave himself up for it. . . . Even so ought husbands also to love their own wives as their own bodies. . . . For this cause shall a man leave his father and mother, and shall cleave to his wife; and the two shall become one flesh." Eph. 5:25 ff.

The Roots of Harmonious Living: "Love is very patient, very kind. Love knows no jealousy; love makes no parade, gives itself no airs, is never rude, never selfish, never irritated, never resentful; love is never glad when others go wrong, love is gladdened by goodness, always slow to expose, always eager to believe the best, always hopeful, always patient. Love never disappears." I Cor. 13:4-8 (Moffatt).

The Unseen Partner: "Happy is the family in which God is an Unseen partner, and the religion of the home is to treat one another as God wills."—Leland Foster Wood.

Inner Ties: "Happy is the family that is bound together by inner ties stronger than marriage laws."—L. F. W.

## MIDWEEK FELLOWSHIP MEETING TOPIC

(Church Night or Suggested Sermon Subject)

**Theme: Gentleness**

TEXT: Ps. 23:1-2.

I. The grace of gentleness. "The Lord is my shepherd." There are words which carry meanings no dictionary can contain. "Shepherd" is one of them. It is native to hillside pastures and sheepfolds old as history. There is tenderness in it—for sheep are so helpless; strong defense—for they are easily imperiled; wisdom—for they are very foolish; and overtones of gentleness which make a music of its syllables.

"The Lord is my shepherd." His shepherding care is the revelation of his gentleness.

Gentleness is no weak or insubstantial quality. It has the power to dissolve enmities; cushion contacts, transform relationships, and, in the long, long last, even penetrate iron curtains. It is a way of using strength without irritation and with winning power.

II. The compulsion of gentleness. "He

maketh me to lie down in green pastures." "Make" is a hard word, but none of the translators soften it—nor does life.

They are not always easy to bear, these compulsions of gentleness. They halt us in our foolish ways, rebuke our headstrong attitudes, and shut alluring doors in our faces. But when the administrations of the gentleness of God have had their full and revealing way with us, we know that they were best and are ourselves taught that when the accounts of life are cast up, the gentle are not only the strong, but the victorious.

III. The restoration of gentleness. "He restoreth my soul." Souls need so many and so various restorings. They get worn and weary, earth-stained and sin-stained; frustrated, confused. They lose courage, force, and faith, and suffer all sorts of inside entanglements.

Consider what understanding gentleness is needed to restore a soul—for harshness only deepens its hurt—and what loving patience is needed with the estranged, with the wrong and the wronged!

We, ourselves, may share this almost divinest of God's offices, when others can say of us, "He or she restores my soul." —Gaius Glenn Atkins.

## BULLETIN BOARD SLOGANS FOR THE MONTH

Love speaks in all languages.
Make friends with your children.
Homes that pray are built to stay.
Character may be forged, but is never inherited.
Encouragement is twice as effective as correction.
Happy marriages don't just happen; they are earned.
The sins of the fathers are imitated by the children.
It is not so much where we stand as in what direction we are going.
We make a living by what we get, but we make a life by what we give.
The future always holds something for the man who keeps his faith in it.

## SUNDAY SCHOOL LESSON

**June 1. Leadership Requires Character. Num. 27:18-20. Josh. 1:1-9. Background Scripture: Num. 27:12-23; Deut. 34:9-12; Josh. 1.**

MEMORY VERSE: "Be strong and of good courage; be not frightened, neither be dismayed; for the Lord your God is with you wherever you go." Josh. 1:9 (R.S.V.).

I. An evaluation of Moses' character would be fitting. Discussion point: As a leader whom would you prefer to follow, a strong man or a weak?

II. What qualities of character make for strong, courageous, Christian leadership? Num. 12:3 is a parenthetical sentence, " (Now the man Moses was very meek, above all the men which were upon the face of the earth.)" What is meant by meekness? Recall Jesus' beatitude, "Blessed are the meek: for they shall inherit the earth." Discussion point: What were the qualities of Joshua which qualified him for leadership?

III. May the blessing, help, and presence of God be expected by those who strive for such qualities? Discussion point: Can you give examples of those who were especially helped of God when they were in positions of leadership?

# SUNDAY: JUNE EIGHTH

## MORNING SERVICE

**Theme: Jimmy Asks, Daddy Answers (Children's Day)**

SUGGESTED SCRIPTURE READING: Mark 10:13-16.

SELECTED HYMNS FOR CHILDREN AND GROWNUPS TO SING TOGETHER: "Fairest Lord Jesus."—Silesian Melody. "Jesus loves me! this I know."—Anna B. Warner. "Lord, I want to be a Christian."—Negro Melody. "We are climbing Jacob's ladder."—Negro Melody. "Let all the world in ev'ry corner sing."—George Herbert.

CALL TO WORSHIP: "And when the chief priests and scribes saw the wonderful things that he did, and the children crying in the temple, and saying, Hosanna to the son of David; they were sore displeased, and said unto him, Hearest thou what these say? And Jesus saith unto them, Yea; have ye never read, Out of the mouth of babes and sucklings thou hast perfected praise?" Matt. 21:15, 16. (With children present, J. B. Phillips' translation may be more effective.)

INVOCATION: O God, our heavenly Father, whose blessed Son was heartened on the first Palm Sunday by the singing of little children, grant that our songs today may be pleasing unto him.

Help us human fathers and mothers to teach our children to sing praises from the heart, and from the depths of their hearts to say "Our Father." Amen.

**Theme: Jimmy Asks, Daddy Answers (Children's Day)**

(Suggesting a Children's Day sermon for both children and adults.)

I. "Where is God?" asked Jimmy, on his knees after his evening prayer and looking up earnestly into his father's face.

"God is everywhere," replied his father, opening Jimmy's bedcovers.

But in typical four-year-old fashion, Jimmy refused to be content with abstract generalities.

"Is he right here in this room?" he persisted.

"Yes."

"Is he in the woods where we had the picnic?"

"Yes, he is there, too."

"Is he where Cousin Mary is?"

"Yes, God is in Iowa with Cousin Mary. God is everywhere," said Jimmy's father, a little wearily. He knew that thesee questions could go on endlessly while the boy delayed getting to bed and the evening paper still lay unopened downstairs. But the next question startled him into wide-awake attention.

"But, Daddy, how?"

The paper could wait. Taking the little pajama-clad boy on his knees, the father smiled and said, "That is hard to understand, isn't it? But let's try."

Gently pinching the lad's nose, he asked, "Is Jimmy there?"

Jimmy thought it was funny that his dad should ask that. But he laughed even more when he felt him pinching one of his toes and heard him ask, "Is Jimmy there?" When he said he was there, too, his father protested, "But I thought you said you were up here!"

"I am!" Jimmy answered, laughing. Then came his dad's clincher:

"But, Jimmy, how?"

Perhaps this did not explain very much, nor could, since even the most learned men do not understand clearly and completely how consciousness is related to the human nervous system, much less how God's purpose is related to the physical universe. But at least the mystery beyond Jimmy's experience was explained in terms of a mystery within his experience.

The ground was laid, too, for his later understanding that, when we say God is everywhere, we mean that he is immediately aware of and concerned with what goes on everywhere, and that he is able to act directly everywhere. Jimmy was also impressed with the thought of a God vastly greater and much more wonderful, even, than himself.

What if there were dangers of his imagination picturing arms and legs stretched out over thousands of miles across the earth? Any such mistakes could be corrected now or later. A boy does not have to learn all his theology when he is four.

Yet he can get started if his parents are on easy, loving, happy terms with him and they answer his questions when he asks them—answer as accurately and fully as they can in relation to his limited but marvelously exciting experience.

II. It was six-year-old John who, after his prayer one night, asked his father, "Why doesn't God ever talk to me?" and added reproachfully, "I talk to him every night, but he never says anything to me."

A parent needs to have a sustained prayer life of his own and to have clear thoughts, too, if he is going to answer that question helpfully. But what an opportunity he has!

Now he can tell how God speaks to us through the beauty of stars and bird songs, the love of parents and friends, the quiet sense of his presence and love, the approvals and warnings of conscience (the feeling that someone is saying, "Better not!"), the wise prophets of old and our Lord Jesus Christ—all these and who knows what other wonderful ways which he uses to speak to one who eagerly listens for his voice!

A few minutes after that conversation, as his father bent over his bed, John looked up with his eyes dancing and said, "I'm already learning to hear people talking to me when I can't hear anything with my ears. Like now, I know what you are saying."

"What am I saying?" asked his father, eagerly.

A little shyly, but with unforgettably sweet sincerity, John replied, "You're saying, 'I love you, John.'"

Six weeks later it was near Christmas and it was again night.

"You know it will soon be Christmas. You know what Christmas is? It's Jesus' birthday. Everywhere I go now I hear God singing 'Happy birthday' to everybody!"

Some will complain that they have themselves been so poorly taught in these matters that they cannot instruct others. I am convinced that thousands are eager to make up this deficiency so that they can both know and teach the deep insights of our faith. (Here some books in addition to the Bible may be suggested.)

III. It was ten-year-old Frankie who looked up one day and said, "Daddy, my Sunday School teacher said that God speaks to us; does he also talk to Japanese and Chinese people?"

"Yes, God's love goes out to all men. He speaks to Japanese and Chinese boys and girls just as he speaks to you."

"But, Daddy, how does God know all the languages of the earth?"

This time it was an easy question to answer. "God speaks to us in our minds and in our hearts, not with words for the ear."

"I can understand that," replied Frankie, and then added, "I'm glad that I don't have to send my questions to Dr. F. who answers questions over the radio. I can just bring them to you."

The wicked are not the only "blind leaders of the blind." Loyally devoted men and women can lead the children entrusted to their care into many a ditch if they do not take the trouble to learn the meaning of faith. We should not think of letting our children grow up without being introduced to the accumulated mathematical or historical knowledge of the race. Do we think less important the accumulated wisdom of faith by which millions have learned the steep but shining path to life eternal?—Adapted from L. Harold DeWolf.

Prayer for the Day: O God, our Father and Friend, whose spirit is ever at work in the world, we thank thee for the beauty of the world in which we live. May we ever be on the search for that beauty—in the world of flowers, rivers, and woods, in the world of books, pictures, and music, in the world of friendship with those near to us and with the many children of other races, all members of thy family. Amen.—Horace M. Hollister.

OFFERTORY SENTENCE: "Then Andrew, Simon Peter's brother, . . . put in, 'There is a boy here who's got five little barley loaves and a couple of fish, but what's the good of that for such a crowd?' . . . Then Jesus took the loaves, gave thanks for them, . . . and the disciples passed them on to the people sitting on the grass. They distributed the fish in the same way, giving them as much as they wanted." John 6:9,11 (J. B. Phillips' translation).

OFFERTORY PRAYER: Bless our offerings, O Lord, as thou didst bless the boy's gift of loaves and fishes so long ago in Galilee. Multiply their usefulness so that they may feed many with the Bread of Life. We thank thee for the privilege of giving. Amen.

SEED THOUGHTS: Children and Parents. There are two things in their relationship to parents that all normal children wish to feel: they want to be wanted and they want to be trusted. They must know that they have their parents' love and faith. These are as essential to their growth as rain and sunshine are to the growth of a tree. Reared in an atmosphere of rejection, a child will doubt its own worthiness. Confronted by an attitude of distrust, it will fail to develop confidence in its own competence.—Louis Binstock.

Another Gift from God. Years ago, when a baby was born, our grandfathers and great-grandfathers used to write in the family Bible the name of the baby, and the words, "Another gift from God." Of course, our forefathers were dead right! A child is a gift from God. A man and a woman are agents of its making, but the gift of its life is the gift of God. Its life is a sacred trust in the hands of the father and mother. —R. W. Hugh Jones.

**Choice Illustrations for Children's Day**

OBSERVATION. A sixth-grade teacher in a small town was pleading with an eleven-year-old boy recently to do better school work. "You are a bright boy but you are lazy," she said. "If you would study you would be the best student in your class. With your personality and intelligence you could easily become one of the leaders in this community."

With a look of pity for her naïveté, the boy replied, "Miss Burton, from what I have observed of the leaders of this community, I'm not interested in being one of them."—*Union Signal.*

TAKING LIBERTIES WITH ROYALTY. In Australia some years ago a tiny girl outwitted guards, parents, and bystanders by dodging under a rope and jumping into the lap of Queen Elizabeth. Consternation prevailed. Humiliated guards were apologetic. They had failed to prevent a desperately naughty little abstraction from doing an unheard of thing.

But the Queen saw the child's face. She hugged her little admirer to her for an instant and then gave her a kiss that the child will treasure as long as she lives.

That is not the first time a child has taken liberties with royalty. When the King of kings walked the earth, the children, on one occasion, pressed near him in the crowd and were rebuked. But Jesus knew them as individuals. He looked into their faces, took them in his arms, and blessed them.

## EVENING WORSHIP

**Theme: We Gather Together**

TEXT: "I had rather be a doorkeeper in the house of my God, than to dwell in the tents of wickedness." Ps. 84:10.

An old-fashioned story with a timely point comes to us from the days when organs were supplied the needed oxygen through the bellows by the pumping of a bellows boy. A great artist was playing the organ most skillfully, and when the intermission came he was roundly applauded. As he left the stage, he was met by the little bellows boy. "Say, mister, we certainly went over all right, didn't we?" he beamed. The organist replied rather stiffly, "What do you mean, 'we'? I'm doing the playing."

After the intermission, the organist came forward to play again. But to his amazement and disgust no sound was forthcoming from the organ. Exasperated, he whispered to the boy: "What's the matter back there? Why don't I get any sound?" Not a word in reply. The organist started fingering the keys again. Still there was no music. "Come on, boy, let's get going," he whispered hoarsely, while beads of perspiration broke out on his brow. Then came the shrill voice from behind the organ, "Say 'we,' mister, and she'll play."

I. Today, as never before, you and I must learn to say "we." If daybreak rather than midnight lies ahead for the world it will be because we are learning to say "we" in the nick of time, realizing that mankind is a unit. If deeper darkness awaits us, it will be because we stubbornly insisted on saying "I" when the time to say "we" was overdue. On the world scene, as on the personal scene, ruthless individualism that treads roughshod on the heads of neighbors is doomed.

II. As in toil, so in every mood and activity men are held in community. We sorrow alone and together. The Apostle writes to the Galatians: "Every man shall bear his own burden." Yet he has just finished these words: "Bear ye one another's burdens and so fulfill the law of Christ." Joy is a deep secret, profoundly personal. Yet the woman who has found the coin calls her neighbors to rejoice with her. A bitter psalmist found his bitterness scattered when he went into the sanctuary with the people. The 73rd Psalm tells about it. Do we not feel that the best friend is the one who can share with us our joys and sorrows? Would we not long "to live in a house by the side of the road and be a friend to man"? Heaven, I believe, is a community of such spirits, a place where everybody's friendly, where all accept the fact of togetherness and rejoice in it.

III. A soul is not mature until he has learned how to work with another. An athlete may be good, but he's better if he's played on a team. A skillful violinist is better for having been a part of a great symphony orchestra. But it makes a great deal of difference whether you belong to a good or evil group as you work together. We often disparage crowds, but there are many different kinds of crowds. There is the hate-filled mob, wallowing in half-truths. There is the crowd that watches the game. There is a crowd listening to a symphony, living through the community of appreciation. And there is the worship crowd, lifted from self to the Everlasting Arms. In drawing thus together, life should find its meaning and fulfillment.

IV. It is necessary that we learn to say "we," but something further is needed. To say "we thieves" or "we liars" but multiplies the evil that I as a thief or liar can do. Togetherness itself must be redeemed. It must be "we" at our best. One of the finest hymns begins with these words: "We gather together to ask the Lord's blessing!" A worship crowd in harmony—there is the picture. They are united in a common goal and purpose. A church fellowship presents a body of sinful people, but people who have felt the power of the great redemption. The true worship of one God makes the people one. It enables them to say in truth, "Our Father."

In the great fellowship, international and universal, of the Christian church there is hope. It is the basic fellowship and unity found among those who are known of God and lifted from the power of sin through Christ. From the perfecting and extension of that fellowship a saving remnant may prevail as leaven in the lump until all is leavened. God grant the abolition of all that mars or halts the communion of those who in the spirit of Christ would gather together—M. C. Allen.

### Suggested Texts and Themes from the Life of David

MAGNIFICENT CONTROL: "And David put his hand in his bag, and took thence a stone, and slang it, and smote the

Philistine in his forehead . . ." I Sam. 17:49.

The Strong Friendship of Strong Men: "I am distressed for thee, my brother Jonathan: very pleasant hast thou been unto me. . . ." II Sam. 1:26.

A King's Kindness: "And David said, Is there yet any that is left of the house of Saul, that I may shew him kindness for Jonathan's sake?" II Sam. 9:1.

Thou Art the Man: "And Nathan said to David, Thou art the man." II Sam. 12:7.

Cherishing the Dream: "And it was in the heart of David my father to build an house for the name of the Lord God of Israel. . . ." I Kings 8:17, 18.

## MIDWEEK FELLOWSHIP MEETING TOPIC

(Church Night or Suggested Sermon Subject)

**Theme: Honoring God**

TEXT: ". . . them that honour me I will honour, and they that despise me shall be lightly esteemed." I Sam. 2:30.

Eli, the priest of Israel, was a good man, but his sons were wicked. They did much evil and "made the Lord's people to transgress." "The sin of the young men was very great before the Lord; for men abhorred the offering of the Lord." There came, therefore, a man of God to Eli with the message that his sons should not succeed him in the priestly office, for only those who honored God would be honored by him. His sons had dishonored God and profaned his holy institutions. Therefore they would be set aside. Already God had, in the boy Samuel, one who was responsive to his voice and would be faithful.

Let us think of some of the ways in which we of the present day can honor God.

I. We can honor God in his day. Christians who worship on the Lord's Day are doing more than maintain a testimony, though that is much. They are honoring God.

II. We can honor God in his Word. If we believe that God has given us a revelation which is contained and secured in the Bible, then we ought to honor God by reading it with attention, not to say reverence.

III. We honor God by accepting the moral standards set forth in the Law, especially as that Law is confirmed and made more spiritual by our Lord, who came not to destroy, but to fulfill.

IV. We honor God by associating openly with his people, thus showing on whose side we are.

How God will honor those that honor him we may safely leave to his wisdom and his love.—Adapted from Gilbert Laws.

## SUNDAY SCHOOL LESSON

**June 8. A People Must Choose. Josh. 11:16-20, 23; 24:14-18. Background Scripture: Josh. 4; 11:16-23; 23-24.**

MEMORY VERSE: "Put away the foreign gods which are among you, and incline your heart to the Lord." Josh. 24:23 (R.S.V.).

I. A nation's choice in some distant past may become directive for the present and the future. It may present good argument for a present choice. But it is not enough.

II. Each generation must make its own choice, whether or not to serve the Lord, the true God.

"To ask *whether* a man believes in 'God' is to misunderstand the issue. The proper question, as the biblical writers never forget, is rather: What (or *who*) is his god? . . . Life's most urgent question is 'Which is the *true* God?' "—E. LaB. Cherbonnier.

Many persons are confused by the misunderstanding that since every man has *a* god, all men therefore acknowledge the *same* God under different names. . . . The fallacy of this position consists in the assumption that, since the rival deities all wear the same functional label ("god"), they are at bottom identical. This is like saying that, because Henry VIII and Louis XIV were both kings, they are fundamentally the same.—E. LaB. C.

III. The real choice of the God that is served is made at the grassroots. "As for me and my house, we will serve the Lord."

# SUNDAY: JUNE FIFTEENTH

## MORNING SERVICE

**Theme: A Sense of Significance or A Man with a Shovel (Commencement Season)**

SUGGESTED SCRIPTURE READING: Ezek. 2:1-8a.

SELECTED HYMNS: "The Son of God goes forth to war."—Reginald Heber. "Courage brother, do not stumble."—Norman Macleod. "Go forth to life, O Child of earth!"—Samuel Longfellow. "Father in heaven, who lovest all."—Rudyard Kipling. "Hark, the voice of Jesus calling." Daniel March.

CALL TO WORSHIP: "Ask, and it shall be given you; seek, and ye shall find; knock, and it shall be opened unto you: for every one that asketh receiveth; and he that seeketh findeth; and to him that knocketh it shall be opened."

INVOCATION: O Lord our God, who art always more ready to bestow thy good gifts upon us than we are to seek them, and art willing to give more than we desire or deserve; help us so to seek that we may truly find, so to ask that we may joyfully receive, so to knock that the door of thy mercy may be opened unto us; through Jesus Christ our Lord. Amen.

**Theme: A Sense of Significance or A Man with a Shovel**

TEXT: "And he said unto me, Son of man, stand upon thy feet. . . ." Ezek. 2:1.

We were driving along the highway, and we came to a place where the old road was blocked off. The new one was not yet surfaced and we bounced and crawled along for some distance. Dump trucks rumbled by; gigantic earth removers shook the ground as they bit into the mountainside and carried it off; bulldozers and graders were busy.

And then we came upon a single solitary workman who was wielding a shovel.

The incongruity of it startled us and my wife remarked, "What can he do?" What indeed? A man with a shovel on a job that involved the moving of hundreds of tons of dirt and rock! A man with a shovel surrounded by machinery that was moving mountains ten cubic yards at a time! How futile! How insignificant!

The twentieth century seems almost to have entered into a vast conspiracy to deny us any individual sense of significance.

Not only is this an age of mass movements, but also of the concentration of power, and that tends to reduce the importance of the average individual. The vast problems, movements, forces of our time, tend to make every thoughtful person feel pretty insignificant. He is like a man trying to build a highway with a shovel.

It is a psychological commonplace, however, that we must have a sense of significance. Once a man is convinced that he is worthless, or that he cannot do anything anyhow, then he is licked. But let him feel appreciated or respected and he cannot be stopped.

One of the great glories of the Christian faith has been its power to save people from a sense of insignificance. There is that marvelous line spoken to the prostrate prophet Ezekiel by the Most High, "Son of man, stand upon thy feet."

The problem we face is this: Can we preserve a sense of individual significance in times like ours? I think it will help to keep us from being intimidated by our times if we'll bear in mind three things.

I. First, there is the *power of ideas.* We are tempted to think that one man's ideas, or those of a minority group like the Christian church, cannot have much effect upon the whole. Nothing could be farther from the truth. "There is nothing so powerful as an idea whose time has come." Oliver Wendell Holmes used to say that "a valid idea is worth a regiment any day."

What can we do in the face of the movements and forces which threaten to overwhelm us? We can hold to Christian ideas in the conviction that, although the majority has scorned them as wrong, they will yet see them turn out to be right.

II. Second, let's remember that *everyone has a circle of influence greater than he thinks.* We never know what results from even the most fleeting of our deeds. And that is something to hearten us when it seems that we are trying to build a highway with a shovel.

Dwight L. Moody used to say that "a loving deed costs very little but, done in the name of Christ, it will be eternal." And it was Moody's Master who taught us all that the smallest thing we did for the very least of persons was done for him. Everyone has a circle of influence greater than he thinks.

III. A third fact to remember is that *it is one's motives that makes one's life finally significant.* You remember that Jesus said that the one penny the woman put in the offering was more than that dropped in by all the others. It was her motive that made it great.

Jesus himself was a man with only a shovel. He was a small-town laborer. He never saw a city of 50,000 people. The only traveling he ever did was on foot. His Sermon on the Mount can be read in ten minutes. He spent most of his time with a handful of folk. . . . But was he significant? Even so secular and sophisticated a modernist as H. G. Wells called him "the most famous failure in the world." More than that, as the New Testament puts it, "God has highly exalted him and bestowed upon him the name which is above every name"! Why? Because his motive was as high as heaven, his influence will be as lasting as eternity.—Raymond E. Balcomb.

A Prayer for the Day: Our Father, whose life is within us and whose love is ever about us, grant that thy life may be manifested in our lives today, as with gladness of heart, without haste or confusion of thought, we go about our daily tasks, conscious of ability to meet every rightful demand, seeing the larger meaning of little things and finding beauty everywhere. In the sense of thy presence may we walk through the hours, breathing the atmosphere of love and seeking by love rather than by anxious striving to quicken and bless the lives of others. Amen.

Offertory Sentence: "Cast thy bread upon the waters: for thou shalt find it after many days."

Offertory Prayer: We thank thee, O Lord, for the privilege of sending a part of ourselves beyond our immediate horizon to build thy kingdom in the uttermost parts of the earth. Bless this offering that it may do much good as it carries to those near by and to those far away the message of the grace of Christ. Amen.—H.

Seed Thoughts:

Ezek. 2:1, 2. Ezekiel, Man of Influence. I. His dramatic call. II. His revealed mission. III. His unique methods. "His peculiar nature was used of God to make a valuable contribution to the life of Israel in exile." IV. His fearless character. V. His distinctive doctrine: the moral responsibility of the individual soul.—Kyle M. Yates.

The Least and the Greatest. The least may influence the greatest. It was St. Andrew that influenced St. Peter to "come and see" Jesus. One least spoken of among the apostles influenced the one who took the foremost place among them as if to show that such power is independent of personal superiority. It is not the great and gifted alone who exercise the mysterious power of influence. It is a universal law of life. Those personal influences, first of Jesus on Andrew, then of Andrew on Peter, were the beginning of the conversion of the world.—C. W.

### Choice Illustrations on the Theme

Individual Significance. There is the promise of the Revelation that God himself will write his name on our foreheads—not in the mass, but individually, one by one. There is the sublime confidence of Christ that not even a sparrow falls to the ground without God's concern, and that the very hairs of our heads are numbered. One of the most famous sermons ever preached by an American was that by Horace Bushnell, "Every Man's Life a Plan of God."—Raymond E. Balcomb.

THE POWER OF AN IDEA. Did you ever hear of a lawyer named William Clapp, of Ephrata, Washington? I never had. But along about 1918 he got an idea. The idea was that a dam could be built at Grand Coulee to furnish power and irrigate a million and more acres. Practically everyone laughed at it. But its time came.—R. E. B.

INFLUENCE THAT REACHED TO TRAGEDY. Do you remember the great circus fire at Hartford, Connecticut, in 1944? A total of 168 people died in it; 487 others were seriously injured. Damages were in the millions.

It was not an accident. It was set afire by an arsonist. More than six years later they found the man who did it. He confessed to three murders and nine other arson cases.

What had made him turn against his fellow men? "All my life," he said, "for any little thing I done [the grammar is his] I was beaten. If you had a bunch of brothers who called you 'dopey' all the time, maybe you'd understand. I never had a happy day in my life." Do you see? A mother and father, brothers and sisters and playmates all unconsciously had a circle of influence that eventually reached to tragedy.—R.E.B.

## EVENING SERVICE

**Theme: Our Intangible Allies (Commencement Season)**

TEXT: The outline below suggests material for a baccalaureate sermon. The idea *What have we got?* may be introduced by the text, "The house of Jacob shall possess their possessions." Obad. 1:17.

There is a saying among people, "What has he got that I haven't got?" I'd like to reverse that and ask: "What have *we* got that they haven't got?" Thinking of the contemporary enemies of all that education stands for, if there are powerful assets that will stand by us in this time of difficulty, we had better take note of them.

I. *Wisdom.* Without an awareness of certain insights, sensitivities, and values that usually emerge through education there is no creativity. One does not find wisdom altogether in the practical contacts of life. One discovers wisdom by wandering purposefully through the labyrinths of science; by living with the minds of sages treasured up in books; by sharing the beauties of art, as well as the disciplines of science. Out of this experience we should have with us the intangible ally, wisdom.

II. *Culture.* But we have also something called culture. How can one live unless one can have the overtones of music, unless one can catch something between the lines in art, unless one can become aware of the essence of human culture? We should become people of culture, with intangible assets stocked up for the years ahead of us.

III. *Consciousness of interdependence.* We have associated with people in living centers, with the usual give and take of human relationship. Out of that should have come a social consciousness, leading to a sense of obligation. This world is chaotic because it is torn by people who have little regard for the necessities and rights of their fellow men. In such a world our consciousness of interdependence of all people is a major asset.

IV. *Perspective.* We should, likewise, have gained perspective. As educated people we should possess the ability to adapt to a difficult situation, to draw on all our resources, and to turn liabilities into assets. With this sense of perspective should come a consciousness of what is most important. An educated person should have that perspective so that he knows what counts; he knows what abides; he has allies to fight for him when life crashes about him.

V. *Freedom.* We are here as citizens of the United States of America. We should point out immediately that we have that intangible freedom. We mean the freedom of the individual, with certain inalienable rights, whether he be Jew or Gentile, Roman Catholic or Protestant, Hindu or Buddhist, black or white.

VI. *Government under law.* We have something else rather precious, too, which is definitely under pressure now: Government under law. In Russia they do not have it. In America we still have the privilege, regularly, of going to the ballot box.

VII. *The value of the human individual.* Underneath all this is a deeper idea: The value of the human individual. Human beings in many places are just something to be liquidated if they get in the way. We say that the human individual is a child of God and therefore infinitely to be respected. In our efforts to defend freedom, we must not completely abrogate the rights and dignity of the individual. We must not let the individual be betrayed.

VIII. *A mighty faith.* Finally, we are the heirs of a mighty faith. We believe in God. And we believe that everybody, whether he is conscious of it or not, is an offspring of the eternal. Because of that, we believe that life should be so ordered here and ultimately across the world that every human being's dignity will be preserved.—Charles C. Noble. The P. E. O. Record.

**Suggested Texts and Themes**

A Fatal Lack: "My people are destroyed for lack of knowledge." Hos. 4:6.

Value Judgments: "Woe unto them that evil good, and good evil; that put darkness for light, and light for darkness; that put bitter for sweet, and sweet for bitter!" Isa. 5:20.

The Paradox of Growth: "For unto every one that hath shall be given, and he shall have abundance: but from him that hath not shall be taken away even that which he hath." Matt. 25:29.

Prospectors of Life: "And he that seeketh findeth." Matt. 7:8.

Proving Out the Ideals of Christ: "Only let your conversation be as it becometh the gospel of Christ. . . ." Phil. 1:27.

## MIDWEEK FELLOWSHIP MEETING TOPIC

(Church Night or Suggested Sermon Subject)

**Theme: Walking with God**

TEXT: "And Enoch walked with God: and he was not; for God took him." Gen. 5:24.

"Born," "lived," "died," is the way most of the Bible characters are mentioned. Enoch is an exception. Of him the sacred writer says: "And he was not; for God took him."

I. Ancestry. There are those who make much of ancestry, not for any moral worth of character it may convey, but simply that they may say they are connected with some sprig of greatness. The ancestry really worth mentioning is that which enables a man to become a child of God.

II. Enoch was not; for God took him. The words suggest 1. Duty gloriously met. Life nobly lived. 2. That the age in which a man lives has but little to do with his greatness. The age in which Enoch lived was not remarkable nor conductive to greatness. 3. It is the life that makes some great.

III. The source of Enoch's greatness: He walked with God. This implies a close intimate relationship characterized by absolute trust.

IV. Walking with God necessitates. 1. Agreement. To walk in peace and friendliness. 2. The putting away of sin.

V. Greatness and goodness are not dependent on years. Enoch lived not as many years as his son Methuselah, but he lived a nobler, diviner life.

VI. Walking with God insures a quiet, calm, victorious ending to life.—W. C. B.

## SUNDAY SCHOOL LESSON

**June 15. The Times of the Judges. Judg. 2:16-19; 4:4-9; 5:6-9. Background Scripture: Judg. 2:11-23; 4-5; 21:25.**

MEMORY VERSE: "Let the wicked forsake his way and the unrighteous man his thoughts; let him return to the Lord, that he may have mercy upon him, and to our God, for he will abundantly pardon." Isa. 55:7.

I. The background picture. 1. No central government. 2. Social confusion. 3. Moral decadence. 4. Spiritual instability—a recurring cycle of waywardness, judgment, repentance, and deliverance.

Here in the Book of Judges are living examples of what happens to a nation, tribe, or clan that forgets the Lord. Note the significance of the first half of the memory verse: "Let the wicked . . . return to the Lord."

II. God is in the picture. As a God of guidance, justice, and mercy in dealing with his people. Note the last half of the memory verse: "Return to the Lord, . . . for he will abundantly pardon."

# SUNDAY: JUNE TWENTY-SECOND

## MORNING SERVICE

### Theme: High Visibility

Suggested Scripture Reading: Gen. 13.

Selected Hymns: "Now thank we all our God."—Martin Rinkart. "God is my strong salvation."—James Montgomery. "Open my eyes, that I may see."—Clara H. Scott. "Lord, speak to me, that I may speak."—Frances R. Havergal.

Call to Worship: "This then is the message which we have heard of him, and declare unto you, that God is light, and in him is no darkness at all. If we say that we have fellowship with him, and walk in darkness, we lie, and do not the truth: but if we walk in the light, as he is in the light, we have fellowship one with another, and the blood of Jesus Christ his Son cleanseth us from all sin."

Invocation: Almighty God, author of eternal light; illumine our hearts by the light of thy grace, that our lips may praise thee, that our lives may bless thee, that our worship may glorify thee: Through Jesus Christ our Lord. Amen.

### Theme: High Visibility

Text: "And the Lord said unto Abraham, after that Lot was separated from him, Lift up now thine eyes, and look from the place where thou art. . . ." Gen. 13:14-18.

What you are and what you will become depend in large measure upon what you see. What you see depends upon whether your visibility is high or low. Low visibility is a phrase used by aviators and military men. It is the condition which exists when they find it impossible to look out over a wide area because of atmospheric conditions such as fog or rain or even certain conditions of clear weather. When visibility is high one sees farther, more clearly, more relatedly, and with truer perspective.

Three examples will contrast high visibility with low.

I. Abraham and Lot. Gen. 12:1-5; 13:1-18. 1. The story. Two men are standing upon a high place in ancient Palestine. Abraham is a sturdy old pioneer who had left his ancestral home, crossed a desert, and entered a new country. He looks like weather-beaten sailcloth. The other is his nephew Lot, young, ambitious, with life almost all before him. He has the texture of thin and flimsy silk.

Both are cattle raisers and prosperous. They are so prosperous that they face an embarrassing situation. (Continue the narrative.) The contrast is between a man of high visibility, Abraham, and one of low visibility, Lot.

2. The Contrast. (a) "lust of the eye" (Lot) *vs.* "Venture of faith." (b) Lot

pitches his tent *toward Sodom.* (Note its wickedness.) Abraham builds an altar *in Hebron.* (c) Lot's action blasts the lives of his children; Abraham blesses his posterity. (d) Lot says "I'll make my way." Abraham says, "I'll let God make me."

II. Elisha and Gehazi. II Kings 6:8-23.

1. The story. 2. The contrast. (a) Low visibility sees the foes; high visibility sees the friends. (b) Low visibility has fear; high visibility has confidence and serenity. Daily dread *vs.* calm mastery. (c) Low visibility sees the instruments and chariots of iron; high visibility sees chariots of fire. Power *vs.* omnipotence.

III. Jesus and a Passer-by. Matt. 27:38-44.

1. Sensation *vs.* Saviour. In his essay on "Sensation or Sacrifice" Hubert L. Simpson points out that had Jesus come down he had been a nine-days' wonder instead of a nineteen-centuries' worship. "He would have been Jesus the juggler instead of Jesus the Christ. He would have been the sensation of the world, but not its Saviour." With low visibility he might have gotten into the headlines of *The World,* but his high visibility brought him into the heart of the world.

2. Surrender the ideal *vs.* die for it. "Come down!" cries this passer-by. "Give up that spiritual kingdom that you talked about, and you'll be given a kingdom like Caesar's." High visibility replies, "Never. I'll die for my kingdom."

It is the men of high visibility that have truly saved the world—men like Abraham, Elisha, Jesus. Are you a Lot or an Abraham? Do you live on the basis of God? Are you a Gehazi or an Elisha? Do you live in the presence of God? Are you a servant of the race or do you belong to the passing crowd? Do you live with the passion of God throbbing in your heart? For great living we must have high visibility.—H.

Prayer for the Day: We catch inspiration, our Father, from those who in times past kept the windows of their chambers open toward Jerusalem, and whose custom was to kneel in prayer. We follow an old, old habit of our race as we, too, open the windows of our lives toward the Eternal City and receive strength and courage for our earthly pilgrimage.

We thank thee for the infinite spiritual horizons of our lives, the visions of faith and hope and love that break upon our souls, telling us that we are not meant to gauge our lives by the measure of an hour or day, but that we are meant for life abundant, life that is full of meaning, even life that is eternal. We thank thee for the horizon of beauty all about us, for the horizon of truth, and that of goodness. Help us to be adventurous and ever cross these that even greater and higher things may break upon our souls. Amen.—H.

Offertory Sentence: "Every man to whom God hath given riches and wealth, and hath given him power to eat thereof, and to take his portion, and to rejoice in his labor; this is the gift of God."

Offertory Prayer: Accept our offering, O God, and accept the prayer that goes with it. So bless this money that it may buy truth for those in error, and love for those whose lives are loveless, and peace for those who have restlessness of spirit. In Jesus' name. Amen. —H.

Seed Thoughts:

For the higher a man looks, the farther he sees. . . . The very gesture of faith bestows upon the mind a breadth of view. The man, who lifts his faith to God in heaven, is he whose eyes sweep simultaneously the farthest prospect of earth, and bring to him a sense of the proportion of things.—Geo. Adam Smith.

Jesus and the Passer-by. The passer-by sees the cross as penalty, defeat, death. Jesus sees it as reconciliation, victory, eternal life.

It does make a difference how far one sees. "Think of Lot," says Dr. Jowett, "then think of Abraham. Think of the feverishness of the one, and of the graceful beauty of the other. The one is self-made, guided by vicious impulses; the other is the handwork of God. The one is rooted in self-will; the other is rooted in the power of divine grace. So one becomes big and ugly; the other grows in strength and beauty."

### Choice Illustrations on the Theme

VISIBILITY ON SAN FRANCISCO BAY. Some years ago each week I crossed San Francisco Bay on one of the ferry boats that shuttled back and forth within the Golden Gate. The passengers were always restless when visibility was low. When visibility was high they took delight in looking far out through the Gate to the ships at sea. Then Berkeley's Campanile appeared through the clear air as a heaven-pointing gray arrow in the gray Stadium's bow. One could see all little bays and inlets within the inland sea in their relatedness. Deep-wooded ravines between the ridges increased the beauty of Mt. Tamalpais. In the morning one was inspired for the day's task. In the evening one was filled with quietness and peace. When visibility is high one sees not only farther and more clearly, but more relatedly and with truer perspective.—H.

ON A BATTLE FRONT. On the fifteenth day of October, 1918, between St. Juvin and St. Georges in the Argonne the visibility was low. The American infantry had dug in along the road, but three times a German plane was able to fly low above the line, drop lights, and thus give the range to the German gunners. That afternoon many American boys were killed and wounded. It made a tremendous difference whether visibility was high or low.—H.

A WORKMAN'S VISIBILITY. When the Columbia River Highway, one of the most picturesque drives in the world, was in process of building, a passer-by noticed an Italian workman going to the utmost pains to fit a stone into one of the walls which are now a marvel to the traveler. The observer lost count of the number of times that the workman lifted the heavy stone into place only to remove it again and shape it more perfectly. Finally he ventured a question, "Why do you go to so much trouble to shape and fit the stone?" "Well," replied the Italian, "you see I got little boy. Sometime my boy, he grow up. Then he come, see the highway, and say, 'My papa, he build the highway.'" The man saw his task in its true relation; the fitting of one stone was ennobled by the whole wonderful enterprise of the highway.—H.

## EVENING SERVICE

### Theme: The Treasure of a Quiet Mind

TEXT: "Be still, and know that I am God." Ps. 46:10.

This Psalm has always been most popular in times of crisis and upheaval. When you sit down quietly, forgetting everything, and read this Psalm it has a most wonderful effect.

The stillness and poise of spirit that come from giving in and admitting that God is round about us!

I. The need for stillness. Perhaps you are not feeling too well, but you have not told anyone; you feel that you have so much to do but you are not grumbling. The demands are just more than you can cope with for the present. So, in the hurly-burly, you go to see your doctor because you feel that there must be something wrong with you. He looks you in the face and at that moment you are convinced without further examination that the doctor has appreciated what was wrong with you; it was something which you, quite honestly, knew too but you would not admit it and you would not give in. He tells you to go home to bed and rest for a few days—to be still—to be quiet. There was nothing wrong with you except that you could not be still; you felt that the world depended on you.

II. The difficulty of being still. It is difficult to be still and to realize that the world will go on pretty well much the same! Placidity of spirit is a great gift and a great possession. In some senses, it is such a pity that we are not ready to believe that "they also serve who only stand and wait."

One pleasant Sunday afternoon found me in the company of a saintly old Welsh farmer returning from a service held at a small and quaint chapel in the more remote hills. He asked me, "What's wrong with the world—what's wrong with us all?" as though to suggest that he intended answering the questions. Then he added: "We are too busy *to live*." He was quite right. We just cannot be still. Dr. Moffatt translates our text: "Give in, . . . admit that I am God.". We will not admit and we will not give in.

III. Christ's own need for stillness. There were times when even Christ himself stood still and apparently did nothing. There were times when he was inactive and silent. How often do the Gospels report that "he did no mighty work there"—"that he answered them not a word"—that he left the city, the town, and the village—that he went into a mountain or that he crossed the sea! And he did it for the sake of peace and poise, for the sake of calm and spiritual comfort; he did it that he might be still.

IV. Sometimes stillness is misunderstood. A quiet, stilled mind is difficult to acquire; and what makes this tranquillity even more of an effort is that people will think that because you are still, quiet, poised, and at peace, you are doing nothing. I read once a story concerning Charles Darwin when he was engaged in his epoch-making book, *The Origin of Species.* Hour after hour he would be seen standing in his greenhouse observing various plants to no apparent purpose. His health was far from good, and an old domestic servant suggested in confidence one day to Mrs. Darwin that she thought "Master would be a good deal better if he could find something useful to do." She thought he was idle when he was thinking out quietly a theory that shook the scientific world to its foundations.

Be still! It is difficult. You will be misunderstood; that is certain. But what a treasure the possession of a quiet mind must be! A mind that has made the supreme admission that God *is* and that this is his world.—Adapted from G. Llewelyn Griffiths.

**Suggested Texts and Themes**

The Motivation of a Christian: "Seekest thou great things for thyself? Seek them not." Jer. 45:5. "Seek ye first the Kingdom of God." Matt. 6:33.

You Can't Be a Christian Alone: "So we, being many, are one body in Christ, and every one members one of another." Rom. 12:5.

The Gospel of Liberty: "Stand fast therefore in the liberty wherewith Christ hath made us free, and be not entangled again with the yoke of bondage." Gal. 5:1.

The Grace of Adaptability: "To the weak became I as weak, that I might gain the weak: I am made all things to all men, that I might by all means save some." I Cor. 9:22.

By-paths: "And he said unto them, Come ye yourselves apart into a desert place, and rest a while." Mark 6:31.

## MIDWEEK FELLOWSHIP MEETING TOPIC

(Church Night or Suggested Sermon Subject)

**Theme: Meeting Life's Tasks**

TEXT: "I take pleasure . . . in necessities." II Cor. 12:10.

Some people fail in life not because they cannot do what they want to do, but because they will not do what they have to do.

St. Paul said, "I take pleasure in necessities." If so, he knew the secret of sound living, for each and every man has the job of living within his means, of living with his limitations and handicaps and of accommodating himself to tedious tasks.

Quite frequently it is pointed out that religion helps a person to do what he ought to do. Would not religion mean more if we knew it as a factor in helping us to do what we have to do?

1. Religion's first law is humility in the presence of the inevitable. Freedom

is only one side of experience. Compulsion is the other. Life, as a college course, is a combination of electives and basic requirements. Much unhappiness has its origin in rebellion against things which must be accepted. The self divided between life's unyielding demands and tempting desires is condemned to frustration and defeat.

II. Something is needed, however, beyond supple resignation before the inevitable. To do effectively what we have to do we need a sound philosophy regarding life's compulsions. Such a philosophy is summed up in the much-neglected precept of Jesus, "And whosoever shall compel thee to go a mile, go with him twain."

III. Paul's motivation in the presence of necessities is expressed in the fuller text than that quoted. He says, "I take pleasure in necessities . . . for Christ's sake." Therein lies a secret which we might well make our own.—Adapted from W. Ralph Ward, Jr.

### SUNDAY SCHOOL LESSON

**June 22. Wasting God-given Strength. Judg. 15:11-15; 16:15-21. Background Scripture: Judg. 13-16.**

Memory Verse: "If you live according to the flesh you will die, but if by the Spirit you put to death the deeds of the body you will live." Rom. 8:13.

I. God entrusts every man with great responsibilities.

II. Samson is an example of a man of great powers and possibilities, who wasted his strength. 1. Physical strength is meaningless without spiritual strength. 2. The Christian ideal of the body as the temple of God.

III. Life is a success in God's sight only when its God-given responsibilities and powers are used in terms of self-control and obedience to God's law.

IV. In this connection the teacher might wish to point out the physical and moral effects of beverage alcohol. It wastes God-given strength.

---

# SUNDAY: JUNE TWENTY-NINTH

## MORNING SERVICE

**Theme: Democracy—What Is It? (Independence Day)**

Suggested Scripture Reading: Isa. 62.

Selected Hymns: "God of our fathers, whose almighty hand."—Daniel C. Roberts. "My country, 'tis of thee."—Samuel F. Smith. "O beautiful for spacious skies."—Katharine Lee Bates. "Not alone for mighty empire."—William P. Merrill.

Call to Worship: "And many nations shall come, and say, Come, and let us go up to the mountain of the Lord, and to the house of the God of Jacob; and he will teach us of his ways, and we will walk in his paths: for the law shall go forth of Zion, and the word of the Lord from Jerusalem." Micah 4:2.

Invocation: Almighty God, who hast given us this good land for our heritage; we humbly beseech thee that we may always prove ourselves a people mindful of thy favor and glad to do thy will. Bless our nation with honorabe industry, sound learning, and pure manners. Save us from violence, discord, and confusion; from pride and arrogancy, and from every evil way. Defend our liberties, and fashion into one united people the multitudes brought hither out of many kindreds and tongues. Endue with the spirit of wisdom those to whom in thy name we entrust the authority of government, that there may be justice and peace at home, and that, through obedience to thy law, we may show forth thy praise among the nations of the earth. In the day of trouble, suffer not our trust in thee to fail; all of which we ask through Jesus Christ our Lord. Amen.

**Theme: Democracy—What Is It?**

In this sermon I am looking at democracy as we who are a part of Western culture look at it and see it.

I. This means that democracy is something that we can experience and practice every day of our life. It is literally "a way of life—a way of everyday life." It is freedom of discussion; and as Wendell Phillips, of Abolitionist fame, said: "If there is anything in this world that can't stand discussion, let it crack." It is the belief that my neighbor, irrespective of his origin or color, is as good as I am. It is equality of opportunity for all men and the practice of it. It is a majority without tyranny and a minority without fear. It is all this and more.

And because it is a way of everyday life, it can be lost. We can be duped by demagogues and the yelow press into race hatred, class fears, feelings of superiority, and antagonisms of many kinds. This is why every local community should take seriously its democratic pretensions.

II. Again, democracy for us means the rule of law, not the rule of men. Because many people exercise no part in the choice of those for whom at election time we vote, it is only in part the rule of law and also in part the rule of men. But in principle democracy is "the rule of law and by men we have the right to play a part in choosing."

One of the major themes of the history of England and America and one of the most thrilling is that of the slow triumph of the idea of the rule of law as over against the arbitrary rule of king or despot.

The dictatorship of the Fascist and Communist type is a denial of the progress and meaning of law. Under these regimes the despot rules by arbitrary power; there are no laws that bind the despot as there are laws in our democracy binding on both president and subject, officer of the law, and citizen. We tend to take this for granted. Let us not be unaware of our heritage of freedom under law. Ours is in principle and ideal a government of all the people, by all the people, for all the people. May we never lose it.

III. Consider again, that democracy is more and more being envisaged as a tool, by means of which the elected representatives of the people do for the people what they could not do at all—or do so well alone. This is viewing democracy functionally.

According to our Constitution, the government was set up "to provide for the common welfare." This is subject to many interpretations. But it is becoming agreed pretty generally now that government must in many instances arbitrate among the forces in our society and see that the good earth and human intelligence provide every member of society with the "minimal basis for decent health, housing, education and recreation." The Declaration of Independence said that "to secure these rights"—life, liberty, the pursuit of happiness—governments are established among men. Here government is seen not as man's enemy, but his friend and helper.

IV. Finally, democracy is a faith. Harry A. Overstreet has written that "our American Republic can best be described as . . . the formuation of an hypothesis: Namely, that average human beings can become capable of self-government." He goes on to say that this is in all likelihood "the most complimentary hypothesis regarding the nature of man that has ever been given political expression."

Also it is faith in truth. Democracies in the West do not believe that they have all the truth. We believe in the "free trade of ideas" because more truth can break forth from God for our life and growth.

Some people would stop all untrammeled discussion and free trade in ideas among us. They would fight communism by imitating her and so become like her. They forget that it was diversity of opinion, the fact that we have no one fixed economic creed, no one-man definition of patriotism, no prison camp for dissenters among us, that has made us great. When we lose this faith in the free mind among us, we have surrendered our democratic faith for another and betrayed the Fathers who gave us birth. —H. Richard Rasmusson.

THEME PRAYER: O God, our Father, make us worthy of the trust which thou hast placed in us. May we have bravery and devotion which befit these times. As a nation may we have the warm courage of unity and the clear consciousness of seeking tried and precious moral values. As citizens may we have the clean satisfaction that comes from the stern performance of duty. May we have faith in the future of democracy, and may we build for a world of lasting brotherhood and peace. Amen.—H. R. R.

OFFERTORY SENTENCE: "Seek ye first the kingdom of God, and his righteousness; and all these things shall be added unto you." Matt. 6:33.

OFFERTORY PRAYER: Remember in thy love, O God, those who have brought this offering and those for whom it is given. So follow it with thy blessing that it may promote peace and goodwill among men, and advance the kingdom of our Lord and Saviour, Jesus Christ. Amen.

SEED THOUGHTS:

Democracy, Possible and Necessary. "Man's capacity for justice makes democracy possible; but man's inclination to injustice makes democracy necessary."—Reinhold Niebuhr.

Two Cheers. E. M. Forster, in his book of essays, *Two Cheers for Democracy,* explains that he considers democracy worthy of two cheers only—one because it permits variety and two because it permits criticism. His third cheer, he declares, is reserved for what he calls "Love, the Beloved Republic."

The thought is significant. Democracy is not an end in itself. It is valuable for what it permits. But to love one's neighbor as oneself—here is the principle that gives positive content to the permissive freedoms of democracy, that points the way from competitive struggle, to cooperative order, that lifts the free individual into the universal republic of man and reflects the Love that is God.—*Christian Science Monitor.*

**Choice Illustrations on the Theme**

THE BIBLE AND AUTOCRACY. Victor Hugo, pointing to a Bible and mentioning an autocratic institution, said, "This will kill that."

THE BIBLE A DEMOCRATIC BOOK. When King Robert of Sicily heard the words pronounced in a religious service. "He hath put down the mighty from their seats, and exalted them of low degree," he remarked, "It is well that was sung only in Latin." The Bible is a democratic book and wherever it has gone and has been understood, it has made for freedom.—E. B. P.

WHAT DOES AMERICA STAND FOR? What is the meaning of that Statue which is built at the mouth of New York harbor, and which looks out with frank and earnest face, toward the old world? It is a Statue of Liberty. But that great emblem does not carry the significance that man has liberty to do as he likes, but liberty to do as God likes, an ample opportunity to obey God's holy will. Liberty carries in her hand a torch and not a firebrand—a torch which is the symbol of enlightenment, and rectitude, and truth. It is liberty in the service of light, it is liberty finding hersef in the ministry of everything which is lovely and of good report. That is the national emblem as this country has built it on the very frontiers of the new world.—John H. Jowett.

## EVENING SERVICE

**Theme: The Forests of God**

TEXTS: "And out of the ground made the Lord God to grow every tree that is pleasant to the sight." Gen. 2:9. "O Lord, to thee will I cry: for the fire hath devoured the pastures of the wilderness, and the flame hath burned all the trees of the field." Joel 1:19.

SCRIPTURAL BACKGROUND: The book of Joel contains an allegory in which the Judgment of God takes the form of a fire. Joel describes accurately the appearance and the terrible effect of forest fires. See Joel 1:18-2:10.

These passages are worthy of study today because we are learning anew that conservation of the natural resources with which the Divine Providence has blessed us is essential to the continued welfare of our people and of our nation. Dissipation and waste of these resources today will bring punishment in the form of loss and misery just as described in the Bible.

I. God's Gift of Trees. 1. In the Bible God is represented as ordaining that man should wake to life embowered in a garden of trees. Gen. 2:8-9.

2. The troubled spirit of man finds renewed faith in God and man, new strength and peace and courage in the quiet and beauty of the forest.

II. Man's Devastation of Trees. 1. In ancient times and now. In past centuries when man's civilization was given time enough and scope enough, he produced in an entire region like Palestine or a vast area like China, a state of things in which the once fertile land was stripped bare and left defenseless against soil erosion and so became a prey to recurrent floods, drought, and famine.

Everywhere man as he begins to practice the acts of civilized life or undertakes to establish a home and a settlement on a new frontier lays with a light heart a heavy hand on the primeval forest, and finds that the by-products of his clearings make for agricultural purposes and supply the means of shelter and of fuel for his cooking and his warmth. He may be encouraged by the spectacle of the natural regeneration in his abandoned clearings to think that the forest can take care of itself. He does not worry himself as to the effect that this reckless felling or burning may have on the fourth or fifth or even fiftieth generation.

2. Joel's vivid allegory. Joel 1:18-2:10. Isaiah and Ezekiel liken the punishment for evil-doing and turning away from worship of God to the ravages of forest and field fires: Isa. 5:24, 10:16-19, 9:18-19; Ezek. 20:47.

III. Our Stewardship of the Forest. 1. We should stop an idle waste. In the neighborhood of 150,000 forest fires occur each year in the United States of America. Ninety per cent are man-caused, less than 10 per cent by lightning.

2. We should stop our carelessness. Of the number of fires, 35 per cent are due to carelessness.

This is not very good stewardship of the bounty of God has placed at our disposal.

3. Our Presidents have encouraged conservation.

Any nation which in its youth lives only for the day, reaps without sowing, and consumes without husbanding, must expect the penalty of the prodigal, whose labor could with difficulty find him the bare means of life. A people without children would face a hopeless future, a country without trees is almost as hopeless. Forests which are so used that they cannot renew themselves will soon vanish and with them all their benefits.—Theodore Roosevelt.

The handling of our forests as a continuous, renewable resource means permanent employment and stability to our country life. The forests are also needed for mitigating extreme climatic fluctuations, for holding the soil on the slopes, retaining the moisture in the ground, and controlling the equable flow of water in our streams. The forests are the lungs of our land, purifying the air and giving fresh strength to our people. Truly, they make the country more livable.—Franklin D. Roosevelt.

4. Rules of Stewardship. (a) In brush burning for land clearing, notify your neighbors and the nearest Forest Ranger or Forest Warden; build the piles small; choose a quiet day; don't leave until the fires are dead out. (b) Extinguish campfires or warming fires completely before leaving them. (c) Crush out your cigarette or pipe ash before you throw it aside. (d) Break your match in two before you throw it away.—(These suggestions for a sermon have been taken from a bulletin of the U. S. Dept. of Agriculture, Forest Service, entitled "Forests and Forest Devastation in the Bible.")

## Suggested Independence Day Texts and Themes

A Light to the Nations: "I the Lord have called thee in righteousness, and will hold thine hand, and will keep thee, and give thee for a covenant of the people, for a light of the Gentiles." Isa. 42:6.

Freedom in Fellowship: "For, brethren, ye have been called unto liberty; only use not liberty for an occasion to the flesh, but by love serve one another." Gal. 5:13.

They Remembered: "And they remembered that God was their rock, and the high God their redeemer." Ps. 78:35.

"Patriotism Is Not Enough"—Edith Cavell: "Love your enemies, bless them that curse you, do good to them that hate you, and pray for them which despitefully use you, and persecute you." Matt. 5:44.

The Bible and Christian Citizenship: "Except the Lord build the house, they labour in vain that build it: except the Lord keep the city, the watchman waketh but in vain." Ps. 127:1.

## MIDWEEK FELLOWSHIP MEETING TOPIC

(Church Night or Suggested Sermon Subject)

**Theme: The "Inasmuch" Parable**

TEXT: Matt. 25:31-46.

I. This "Inasmuch" parable has reference to the nations being brought together and the Lord confronting them with their achievements and shortcomings as nations. I had always imagined that the sheep and the goats of the parable were individual persons.

II. I see now that while the passage does not neglect individuals, it is not limited to them. The gospel of compassion is for nations, too.

There is a startling standard for nations here. They are not to be judged by their size or history, their climate or culture, but by their sensitiveness to human need. They are not to be rated by their wealth, or their trade, or their natural resources, but by their ability to meet the needs of people. Compassion, not military might, is the measure by which nations are to be separated into those on the right hand and those on the left.

III. And to say that is to start some long thoughts about our beloved land. What we Americans have done for others in comparison with what others have done is really beside the point. And so, I suppose, is what we have done when measured against what we had to do with. These are the most common comparisons, and the least valid.

Of far more moment is what we have done alongside what needs to be done. That stretches our minds and troubles our hearts. That stirs our imaginations. That saves us, as a nation, from both hateful selfishness and prideful selflessness, because it centers out attention not on ourselves, but on others.

Happy is the nation whose God is the Lord!—Adapted from T. Otto Nall.

## SUNDAY SCHOOL LESSON

**June 29. Called to Speak for God. I Sam. 3:10-20. Background Scripture: I Sam. 2:12-3:21.**

MEMORY VERSE: "Samuel grew, and the Lord was with him and let none of his words fall to the ground."' I Sam. 3:19 (R.S.V.).

I. Israel's need for a new leader, and God's awareness of the situation. When a people, a nation, the world is in need of a great man, the hope rises that God has one ready to call or in preparation. How important is it that great leadership be found within the nation, in the church, and elsewhere in human affairs? Advanced classes might wish to discuss the so-called "Great Man Philosophy of History."

II. God's call to responsibility and Samuel's response. Here is opportunity to discuss that call of God which gives a man a sense of vocation. But what if God calls and no response is given?

Samuel was sensitive to God's call. Are there those who miss God's call because of insensitivity? Note that Samuel was in the house of God when the call came. Is that a task of the Christian church—to make boys and girls, men and women, sensitive to the call of God? How can this be done?

# SUNDAY: JULY SIXTH

## MORNING SERVICE

### Theme: Faith and the Natural World

Suggested Scripture Reading: Ps. 19.

Selected Hymns: "This is my Father's world."—Maltbie D. Babcock. "My God, I thank thee, who hast made."—Adelaide A. Proctor. "O, worship the King, all glorious above."—Robert Grant. "We thank thee, Lord, for this fair earth."—George E. L. Cotton.

Call to Worship: "He shall be as the light of the morning, when the sun riseth, a morning without clouds, when the tender grass springeth out of the earth, through clear shining after rain." II Sam. 23:4.

Invocation: Open wide the window of our spirits and fill us full of light, O Lord. Open wide the door of our hearts, that we may receive and entertain thee with all our powers of adoration and love. Amen.—Christina G. Rossetti.

### Theme: Faith and the Natural World

Text: "And he said unto them, Come ye yourselves apart into a desert place, and rest awhile." Mark 6:31.

The Sunday exodus from city to coast and countryside has began. With the majority of the escaping multitudes I have real sympathy. Many of them have been confined in house and hospital, in office, warehouse, and factory. Can anyone reproach them for seeking renewed vitality of mind and muscle and nerve in the open spaces? Few would prefer to remain in a gloomy, airless room, or a dusty, smelling street, when the bright banners of summer are beckoning and the birds are calling. I can appreciate the point of view of those who decline to forsake the sunshine and the breeze for the shadows and stuffy atmosphere of a place of worship. Yet two, or, at the most, three hours devoted to the public worship of God seem a trifle when a week has 168 hours.

I. But the question arises, What can nature do for the spirit of man? Can nature bestow the spiritual stimulus and stability which public worship offers? Some, indeed, affirm that nature gives them God. They assert that in viewing "the varied field of nature, the delightful scenery, the mountains, and the resplendent rivers," the desire to worship is satisfied. In the spacious cathedral of natural beauty they find God as they cannot find him in any church. They sense a Presence and find peace. Has nature so great gifts to hold out, then?

I believe that my love for nature is as deep and ardent as any man's. I delight to lift my eyes to the hills and to the far horizons of land and sea and sky. The beauty of a landscape, the beauty of the meanest flower that blows, excites my wonder and joy. I love everything almost that is nature's. Yet I cannot trace in nature "the *unambiguous* footsteps of God." Nature offers me no evidence of a God who is adequate to the real, deep needs of men. It has no word of salvation or of a Saviour, no gospel of a redeeming love. It cannot forgive my sins nor empower my will to goodness.

II. Nature may compel belief in an August Creator with an amazingly artistic mind and a sublime love for the details of little things. Whoever has examined the perfect form and delicate shading of color in a butterfly's wing or the petal of a wild pansy may easily be led to ask some such question as Thoreau's, "How did those beautiful rainbow tints get into the shell of the fresh-water clam, buried in the mud at the bottom of our dark river?" But nature is not universally beautiful, sweet, and gentle. It does not everywhere whisper, "The hand that made us is divine."

In my garden I observe a blackbird swallowing an innocent and useful worm and a cat preparing to bury its teeth in the bird. The newspaper tells of lightning, volcanoes, earthquakes, tidal waves, and tornadoes, striking, smothering, drowning, crushing men, women, and children. The sea, which is the children's paradise in summer, is, to many, a cold, callous, treacherous monster which has swallowed their beloved. Many a believer has marshaled certain natural facts to prove his thesis. Many an unbeliever has appealed to other natural facts to demonstrate that either God is not, or he is impotent, or he lives careless of mankind.

III. Nor is there in nature any power to compel the soul to virtue. Someone wrote:

> The kiss of the sun for pardon,
> The song of the birds for mirth,
> We are nearer God's heart in a garden
> Than anywhere else on earth.

If that were true would it not follow that those who live in the heart of nature's loveliest gardens would be conspicuous for virtue, since nearness to God implies approximation to his nature. The inhabitants of many a Pacific island gorged themselves with human flesh and indulged in bestial excesses hardly to be conceived, while all around them was nature's most equisite beauty. But there is no need to go so far afield to find localities where "every prospect pleases and only man is vile." To live in intimate association with nature is not guarantee of beauty and sweetness of spirit.

IV. And nature cannot satisfy the desire to worship. What response can nature make to adoration? Worship is not the admiration of a Creator's craftsmanship. At its best, worship is fellowship with a God who draws close to men in their desperate needs. Can nature lead guilty man to a cleansing stream? Has it a voice to tell of love like that of Calvary? The God who can meet the sovereign necessities of the human soul is revealed alone in Jesus Christ, his words, his work, his life, his death. Can nature introduce us to Christ? It cannot.

V. Yet one remembers how Jesus walked amid the natural beauty of Galilee and saw almost everywhere messages which read, "This is My Loving Father's world." "Behold the wild birds!" He said, "Look at the lilies of the field!" Jesus drew continually on nature for parables, similes, metaphors. and illustrations, and when the disciples were overdriven and weary, the tonic he prescribed for them and shared with them was the quiet and the open air of a "desert place." Jesus certainly met God in nature. But (and this is the point) nature did not lead Jesus to the Father. He took his knowledge of God and his faith in him into the fields, and there he saw his knowledge and faith confirmed, exemplified. Nature *illustrated,* but did not reveal.

Nature can never give God to men. That is the peculiar office of the Son, the Book, the Church. They who neglect these deprive themselves of that which is essential to the soul, and which is not in the power of nature to impart. —A. Crichton Barr.

A Prayer for the Day: Our lives rejoice today, our Father, in the loveliness of the earth and sky after they have been cleansed and refreshed by rain.

> Thy loving-kindness, O Lord, is in the heavens;
> Thy faithfulness reacheth unto the skies.
> Thy righteousness is like the mountains of God;
> Thy judgments are a great deep.

Our greater joy is in the Christ who has made thy loving-kindness, thy faithfulness, thy righteousness, and thy justice as personal and intimate. In him we find thee. In him we find thy greatness and goodness brought close to us in grace and truth. And though we do not see thee, we live as seeing the invisible. Amen.—H.

Offertory Sentence: "Offer unto God thanksgiving; and pay thy vows unto the most High: and call upon me in the day of trouble: I will deliver thee, and thou shalt glorify me." Ps. 50:14, 15.

Offertory Prayer: The cattle on a thousand hills are thine, O God, the gold and silver of the earth are thine also, and we, too, belong to thee. In thine infinite goodness thou hast given us, in trust, gold and silver and cattle. Help us to honor thee with what is placed in our hands. Take what we bring to thy house just now, and sanctify it for use in thy service, and to the honor of thy name. Amen.

SEED THOUGHTS:

The Ministries of Leisure. Mark 6:31. I. Rest which is richly earned. II. The rest of mutual intercourse. III. Rest in the fellowship with nature. IV. Rest in the fellowship of Christ. V. Rest which fits for further service.—G. H. Morrison.

Theme: The Ministry of Summer.

Theme: What Shall I Take on My Vacation? "They never leave their fishing-rods at home. They often leave their religion at home."

Theme: Your Happiest Holiday. Take Christ with you when you go.

**Choice Illustrations on the Theme**

HOLIDAYS. There are people who tell you they do not need a holiday. Such people are always to be pitied. They are like men with some malignant trouble, who tell you that they do not a doctor. It is one thing to need a thing; it is quite another to feel the need of it; and perhaps there is no man who so needs a holiday as the man who assures you that he does not want it. We need a holiday that we may rest, and we need a holiday that we may see. There is nothing so fatal to a kindly vision as an unceasing and unvarying routine. To understand anything we must not only look at it; we must learn the art of looking away from it; and holidays are given us for that end, that we may see things in their right proportions.—G. H. Morrison.

LINES FROM COWPER. William Cowper denotes the necessary qualification for discerning moral meanings and spiritual promptings in nature in the lines:

Acquaint thyself with God, if thou would'st taste
His works. Admitted once to His embrace
Thou shalt perceive that thou wast blind before;
Thine eye shall be instructed; and thine heart
Made pure shall relish with divine delight,
Till then unfelt, what hands divine have wrought.

LINES FROM TOLSTOY.

No blade of grass that glistens yonder
But seems a star from heaven's height,
God's boundless love to His creation
Speaks through this beauty to my heart!
Fain would I in rare exaltation
Sound through the world the wondrous message
Of boundless love to all creation
To all His love and joy impart!

## EVENING SERVICE

**Theme: The Dimensions of a Deed**

TEXT: "Who shall render to every man according to his deeds." Rom. 2:6.

My purpose is to show how we may measure our deeds.

I. First, the length of a deed—its beginning and end and all the distance between—in short, its career. It was conceived in the mind, born in the act, and will come of age on the Judgment Day, and it will live on through the eternal ages.

II. Second, the breadth of a deed—in other words what influence is it going to wield? People judge our profession by our deeds and are attracted or repelled accordingly. "How far that little candle throws its beams; so shines a good deed in a naughty world!" Our deeds are making a stairway by which others climb.

III. The height of a deed is to be found in its purpose—an unworthy purpose means a leaking roof. Your life and deeds should reach God's throne and win all heaven's approval.

IV. The depth of a deed is its motive. An unworthy motive means a rotten foundation just as an unworthy purpose predicts a rotten roof. "The motive is the largest part of the deed," so consider your motive, and test it by comparing your life with that of Christ's. We must serve our fellows out of love for God and to please the Saviour.

V. The weight of a deed depends entirely upon the character of the doer. "The ungodly are like the chaff which the wind driveth away." And their work is like a house built upon sand, the sand of a dry riverbed which will be swept away when the next storm brings down the river.

VI. The bulk of a deed is to be established in terms of publicity. "Let your light so shine before men that they may see your good works and glorify your Father which is in heaven."

VII. The shape or form of a deed stands for the manner in which it is done. The Christian should not only be polite but courteous.

VIII. Now we come to the eighth way to measure a deed—by its cost, i.e., the sacrifice put into it. The good man is ever ready to render every service gladly, and every sacrifice willingly.

Let us now apply these measurements to several matters—the marriage tie for instance.

Worship is another act to measure up.

Finally, let me ask you to measure up the greatest deed of all the ages—the Saviour laying down his life to redeem the world.

Let us, then, ever pray that the works of our hands as well as the words of our mouth and the meditation of our heart may be acceptable in the sight of him who is our strength and our Redeemer, who will surely render to every man according to his deeds.—F. Lowell Lloyd.

**Suggested Texts and Themes from Philippians (Phillips' Translation)**

Whatever Happens: "But whatever happens, make sure that your everyday life is worthy of the Gospel of Christ." Phil. 1:27.

Awe and Responsibility: "Be keener than ever to work out the salvation that God has given you with a proper sense of awe and responsibility." Phil. 2:12.

Spiritual Ambition: "How changed are my ambitions! Now I long to know Christ and the power shown by His Resurrection: now I long to share his sufferings, even to die as He died. . . ." Phil. 3:10.

Go Straight for the Goal: "But I do concentrate on this: I leave the past behind and with hands outstretched to whatever lies ahead I go straight for the goal." Phil. 3:14.

Where to Fix Your Minds: "Fix your minds on the things which are holy and right and pure and beautiful and good." Phil. 4:8.

## MIDWEEK FELLOWSHIP MEETING TOPIC

(Church Night or Suggested Sermon Subject)

**Theme: Overcoming Disgrace with Grace**

TEXT: "If we confess our sins, he is faithful and just to forgive us our sins, and to cleanse us from all unrighteousness." I John 1:9.

I. The disgrace of individuals and their need of grace.

II. The example of the woman of Samaria. John 4:1-42. 1. She was brought face to face with her own past. There is no such thing as finding God when the whole life is wrong. Jesus demanded that this woman, with all her charms and her camouflage, should "externalize her own rottenness."

2. She seeks to avoid the issue. She is ready to discuss religion, to debate theology, rather than face reality. There are people like that.

3. The disclosure of her life led her into faith. John 4:29.

4. The transformation of her personality. The woman had allowed her life to express itself on a low level. In the presence of Jesus something happened. All her powers were lifted, raised, elevated, sublimated. Her personality was transformed and all the driving vitality that had well-nigh ruined her, now impelled her to a service that was sublime. The same energies, the same instincts, the same personality, now moved in the channel of spiritual power.

III. Modern examples.

IV. Think of all the strong men and women we know, who need only to be converted, transformed, sublimated, lifted up, to have the world around us enriched and ennobled. We covet them for the Christian church and for the Kingdom of God.—Adapted from Hugh T. Kerr.

## BULLETIN BOARD SLOGANS FOR THE MONTH

Even a spark is fire.

If men would think, they would not drink.

The wages of sin have never been reduced.

To worship is to keep life at a high level.

I'd rather see a sermon than hear one any day.

A candle loses nothing by lighting another candle.

True patriotism means a peaceful and united nation.

Appropriate coincidence: the word "American" ends in "I can."

Every rose is an autograph from the hand of God.—Theodore Parker.

Faith makes all things possible, and love makes them easy.

## SUNDAY SCHOOL LESSON

**July 6. The Justice and Mercy of God. Deut. 10:12-15, 17-11:1; Rom. 5:6-11. Background Scripture: Deut. 10:12-11:1; Ps. 145; Mic. 6:6-8.**

MEMORY VERSE: "But the steadfast love of the Lord is from everlasting to everlasting upon those who fear him, and his righteousness to children's children." Ps. 103:17 (R.S.V.).

The justice and mercy of God are mentioned together in a text in which some have found the perfect ideal of religion. This is Mic. 6:8.

God has shown us by his own nature the character of justice and mercy. A study of the Old Testament words for justice and mercy is rewarding.

I. Justice is a quality of personality, "a presupposition which makes healthy, wholesome, and harmonious personal and community life possible." It is a virtue exercised by God toward his people in a covenant community. It carries with it the idea of restoring bonds when they have been broken.

II. Mercy: the Hebrew word is variously translated in different versions of the Old Testament. Mercy, loving-kindness, steadfast love, are some of the variants. Add these translations together and note that thus added together the quality and meaning of the word is revealed in Christ.

How wonderful it is that God requires his people to deal with one another and with all men on the basis of justice and mercy. By obedience to God's call for justice and mercy we shall develop a better society and become good and gracious men and women.

# SUNDAY: JULY THIRTEENTH

## MORNING SERVICE

**Theme: The God of Hills and Valleys**

SUGGESTED SCRIPTURE READING: Deut. 11:1-21.

SELECTED HYMNS: "O worship the King."—Robert Grant. "Saviour, like a shepherd lead us."—Dorothy A. Thrupp. "Children of the Heavenly King."—John Cennick. "How firm a foundation."—Rippon's Selection.

CALL TO WORSHIP: Ps. 121.

INVOCATION: Fill our hearts with joy, O Lord, that joy may escape from our lips. Fill our hearts with love that by our loving we may awaken the divine spirit in others. Fill our hearts with peace, that we ourselves may bring peace to others and the world and thus become sons of God. We render unto thee now our sacrifice of praise. Amen.—H.

**Theme: The God of Hills and Valleys**

TEXT: "But the land whither ye go to

possess it, is a land of hills and valleys, . . . , a land which the Lord thy God careth for. . . ." Deut. 11:11, 12.

INTRODUCTORY: 1. In the days when the world was young they did not know that God was the God of the whole world. We scarcely know that now. Sometimes we speak of "God's Country," meaning our own, with a narrowness and snobbishness that is far removed from a true conception of God. 2. We place untrue and unworthy limitations upon God. Some make of him a tribal God. In early days men put geographical limitations upon God. Examples: Jonah, Naaman. 3. God as a God of the hills. Story of Benhadad—I Kings 20:23 and context. 4. The God of the 139th Psalm. Note the contrast with previous conceptions.

I. The God of Hills and Valleys. 1. Now may we take our text as a figure of speech: "The land whither ye go over to possess it, is a land of hills and valleys." Make this symbolical of life. Life is a land of hills and valleys. One day is a day of exaltation, the next is one of depression. In common speech we say, "We have our ups and down." One day has new and exciting experiences, the next is one of deadly routine. Yesterday was full of success crowning years of effort, today spells disaster. Or it may be yesterday was defeat and today is victory. Yesterday's song was a lilting dance tune, today's is a dirge. Yesterday was lingering summer, today is premature winter. Yesterday, vision; today, I can't see ahead.

2. God is a Both-And God. Now if our God is only a God of the hills then he is only the God of half of life; or if he is the God only of valleys, that limits him to half. He is the God of both hills and valleys. He is a both-and God. He is a God of both here and there; both winter and summer; both sunshine and cloud; both storm and calm; both North wind and South wind; both upland and lowland; both mountain and plain.

3. We differ in temperament. God is present in the hills to those who temperamentally find him in the valleys. Make use of the valley experience in the hills.

God is present in the valley to those who temperamentally find him in the hills. Make use of the hill experience in the valley.

It is a great thing to stand upon a mountaintop of happiness or vision and looking down be able to say, "I went through that valley where every yard had the smell of death in it and I did not flinch, thank God."

"I went through that valley of temptation, and I came through clean, thank God."

"I went through that Gethsemane and shed my tears and was able to say, 'Thy will be done.'"

"I carried my cross and I hug it to my bosom as my chief joy."

How the hill experience is enhanced by experience in the valley!

The two do go together. "My friend had his hour of waiting and said, 'It's a pity there is nothing to look at.' Then his eye caught the shimmer of sunlight on the gray-blue water of a pond. And for twenty minutes he studied the view to etch it on his memory so that he could hang it, at some later day, on an officewall, or perhaps the wall of a hospital room." It was on the wall of a hospital room that he hung it.

Let us not forget when we are on the mountain that once we were in the valley, and had God not helped us then we might not be upon the height. And when we are in the valley we might remember the words of the Psalmist, "I will lift up mine eyes unto the hills. . . ."

II. Little Journeys in the Valleys. 1. The Valley of Eshcol—the valley of abundance. See Num. 13:23, 24 and context. 2. The Valley of Shaveh. Shaveh: the plain, the dead level, the dull routine, the drab drudgery. Gen. 14:17 and context. "The Valley of Shaveh which is the king's dale." The reference is not to a king's experience; it refers to Abraham's experience. In the Valley of Shaveh he met Melchizedek, the King of Salem, the King of Peace. There you have it! The valley of the daily routine, the long drag, the drudgery, it is in that valley that you meet the King of Peace —and it is transformed into the King's Vale.

3. The Valley of Achor. This is the valley of trouble. Josh. 7:25, 26 and context. Isa. 65:10. Hos. 2:15. "The valley of Achor is a door of hope."

4. The Valley of Jehoshaphat. The valley of God's judgment. The valley of decision. Joel 3:12, 14.

5. The Valley of the Shadow. Ps. 23:4.

6. The Valley of Vision. Isa. 22:1.

And so you will go out to possess life. Then possess the hills and the valleys which the Lord thy God careth for: Eshcol, the Valley of Abundance; Shaveh, the Valley of Routine, where the King walks; Achor, the Valley of Trouble, in which a door of hope is opened; Jehoshaphat, the Valley of Judgment, Deliverance, where the lily grows, where the eyes are lifted to the Cross; the Valley of the Shadow, where one knows the presence of God by the hand touch; the Valley of Suffering which becomes a mountaintop of vision.—H.

PRAYER FOR THE DAY: O God, our Father, we do now fix our attention upon thee, our Maker, Defender, Redeemer, and Friend, and we do now seek to enter into that communion with thee, through Jesus Christ, which is stronger than temptation or sin or death.

In the midst of what seems like unending confusion and tumult in the world we find thee, alone, to be strong and sure, steady and unchanging, without variableness or shadow that is cast by turning. Help us to rest upon thy righteous will and eternal goodness and to find our peace in thine everlasting love. In Christ may we appropriate all thy loving-kindness. Amen.—H.

OFFERTORY SENTENCE: "Whatsoever ye do, do it heartily, as to the Lord, and not unto men; knowing that of the Lord ye shall receive the reward of the inheritance; for ye serve the Lord Christ."

OFFERTORY PRAYER: Shed abroad in our hearts, O Lord, a spirit of gratitude. And may our thanksgiving not be limited to this moment, this hour, this day, but may a spirit of gratitude be the deep and permanent spirit of our lives.

Bless our offering, O Lord, unto the good of others and the upbuilding of thy Church. Amen.—H.

SEED THOUGHTS: The Partial Exclusion of God. I Kings 20:28. Historical setting of the text. I. There are scenes with which we naturally associate God. II. We are often blind to God just where he is most active. III. To exclude God always spells disaster.—G. H. Morrison.

"I to the Hills Will Lift Mine Eyes." That heart must be cold as a stone which has never sung with David, "I to the hills will lift mine eyes." It was on a hill that the God of Israel, in the wilderness, gave to Moses the tables of the law. It was on a hill that our Saviour blessed the world with the priceless teaching of the Sermon on the Mount. On a hilltop Jesus was transfigured till his garmetns shone so that no fuller on earth could white them. And on a hilltop, having said farewell, he ascended to the mansions of his Father. Somehow right through the Bible story there clings to the hills the thought of the divine. Somehow, though the earth be God's, the Bible gives the hills a double blessing. —G. H. M.

### Choice Illustrations on the Theme

A VALLEY EXPERIENCE. If only I could get away for a little while—away from the hurry and confusion, from the unceasing round of duties, from the worries, criticisms, tensions, and unpleasant surprises! Oh! Where can rest be found!

But I cannot get away. To get away now would be to add still further anxiety and stress to the lives of others. It is base to refuse to face facts, to escape from action, to fly from reality. . . . But I must get away! The facts are too much with me. Let me not fly from reality, but let me fly to reality, to the living and real God. Let me fly to him without moving one inch or losing a second. The lines of an old Gospel song steal into my mind:

> In the secret of his presence,
> How my soul delights to hide.

Where is the secret of his presence? Where can rest be found? In God who is Righeous Will, Eternal Goodness Everlasting Love? Let me get away to him. Let me get away to him now in this very moment of tension. Why, he is near! "In him we live and move and have our being." He will hear. "And it shall come to pass that, before they call, I will answer." He will give quietness and confidence in the heat and burden of the day, at the moment of fainting. "In returning and rest shall ye be saved; in quietness and in confidence shall be your strength." I will now take refuge in the living and real God, my Creator and my Redeemer, the God and Father of our Lord and Saviour Jesus Christ.—Harold McAfee Robinson.

FOR VALLEY USE. After I had quoted a bit of hilltop poetry in a sermon a woman said, "Will you write it out and give it to me?" "What will you do with it?" I asked. "Commit it to memory, and when my dark day comes I will use it." —H.

IN THE VALLEY LAND. Once I stood in a valley in that Eastern country and I stooped to pluck a flower. It was a scarlet anemone. It was "the lily of the valley." I catch the symbolism. It is the lovely symbol of the Christ. And the Valley of Judgment becomes the Valley of Redemption, and I look up unto the hills and see a Cross and have peace.—H.

## EVENING SERVICE

### Theme: The Divine Shoemaker

TEXT: "Thy shoes shall be iron and brass; and as thy days so shall thy strength be. Deut. 23:25.

Passing along the main street, I saw a notice in a shoemaker's shop window which read, "We make shoes especially for this district." I crossed to see what type of footwear was indicated and found them to be shepherds' shoes. They were strongly made and had steel plates across the welts to give them durability when climbing.

That incident spoke to me of God as the Divine Shoemaker in the world. The text leapeth afresh to my mind: "Thy shoes shall be of iron and brass; and as thy days so shall thy strength be." That promise made to the sons of Asher, dwellers in a hilly district, is a timeless one in its application to the needs of men. The Shoemaker is always adapting shoes for those whose ways of life are along the hard roads.

A friend tells with horror in his voice that he had never realized how essential shoes were until he had, as a prisoner of war, bartered them away for a few biscuits. The Negro sings of the great joy which will be theirs when they can walk around God's heaven in their shoes. Throughout the ages symbolism has been associated with shoes. To cast a shoe over land meant ownership; they were used to denote life's pilgrimage; they were associated with rank, as emphasized by Jesus in the story of the lost son who returned and was found shoes for his feet. In war days the best of material was utilized for the footwear of the army. "Every critical battle," said a famous general, "has been won by soldiers' boots."

I. Rough places are everywhere. Today things are disquieting, dismaying, discouraging, but experience indicates that God is still in his world and that he will fashion footwear suitable to the needs of our times. In that faith we never need lose heart and may face life's inevitabilities with assured poise. Truly, "the Almighty has his own purpose."

II. The rough roads. Our response to the challenge of the difficult places determines both our destination and our destiny.

1. The road of awakening.
2. The road of frustration.
3. The road of misunderstanding.
4. The road of temptation.
5. The road of loneliness.
6. The road of suffering.

The battle is ours, but God is in it with us. To the lonely fighter he bids us remember: "Lo, I am with you even unto the end of the world." To the hopeless fighter God says: "My grace is sufficient for thee." Trust God to equip you and he will.

III. God fashions our shoes by the material we furnish. God fashions our shoes by the material of our prayers.

Most of our prayers to God deal with requests that he should remove the hard places, but so often, to our dismay, we find them left. Yet greater equipment comes into our lives, and with courage we go ahead hopefully, realizing that God's shoes are never misfits.

IV. Wearing God's shoes enables us to turn a minus into a plus. Read for inspiration Milton on his blindness; R. L. Stevenson on his tuberculosis; the amazing letters of Scott of the Antarctic, written while death stared them in the face; how Stanley Jones took a fresh grip upon life as related in *The Christ of the Indian Road.* So often the spirit of adventure is deadened by what are wrongly termed the "hard facts of life." Don't be afraid of the shoes God offers. The novel Quo Vadis ends with a picture of Peter trying to run away because God's shoes were hurting his feet, but when he met Jesus he put them on again and retraced his steps. Tempted to shirk our responsibilities to God, let us discern Jesus sharing with us life's hard road.

Listen again to the old promise, and let God made it true of you: "Thy shoes shall be of iron and brass; and as thy days so shall thy strength be."—Bert Wright.

**Suggested Texts and Themes**

Father and Sons: "And Jacob called unto his sons, and said, Gather yourselves together, that I may tell you that which shall befall you in the last days." Gen. 49:1.

Results of a Good Vacation: "But they that wait upon the Lord shall renew their strength. . . ." Isa. 40:31.

The Common Weariness: "Oh that I had wings like a dove! for then would I fly away, and be at rest." Ps. 55:6.

Patio Gardens: "The wilderness and the solitary place shall be glad for them; and the desert shall rejoice, and blossom as the rose." Isa. 35:1.

Mountain Climber or Mountain Gazer: "And the Lord came down upon mount Sinai, on the top of the mount: and the Lord called Moses up to the top of the mount; and Moses went up." Exod. 19:20.

## MIDWEEK FELLOWSHIP MEETING TOPIC

(Church Night or Suggested Sermon Subject)

**Theme: Overcoming Doubt with Certainty**

SCRIPTURE: John 20:24-29.

I. Contrast Thomas in a condition of doubt with Thomas in a condition of certainty, expressing his conviction, "My Lord and my God."

II. The evaluation of doubt. 1. Honest doubt.

There lives more faith in honest doubt,
Believe me, than in half the creeds.
—Tennyson

Where doubt, there truth is,—'tis her shadow.
—P. J. Bailey

Doubt is the beginning, not the end, of wisdom.
—George Iles

2. Doubt may end in despair.

Doubt indulged soon becomes doubt realized.
—Frances Ridley Havergal

Our doubts are traitors
And make us lose the good we oft might win
By fearing to attempt.
—Shakespeare

Uncertain ways unsafest are,
And doubt, a greater mischief than despair.
—Sir John Denham

III. The value of personal experience. (See Evening Service for Oct. 26.) 1. One must make some venture of faith, though it be small indeed. At least one may visit the Upper Room as did Thomas on the second Sunday evening.

2. Personal experience brings proof.

3. Personal experience confirms faith and hope more than sermons and arguments.

IV. The arrival at assurance, certainty, knowledge, conviction, wisdom. John 20:28. II Tim. 1:12.—H.

## SUNDAY SCHOOL LESSON

**July 13. Social Justice and the Gospel. Matt. 5:17-20, 46-48, 23:23-26; Matt. 5:13-48.**

MEMORY VERSE: "Whatever you wish that men would do to you, do so to them; for this is the law and the prophets." Matt. 7:12 (R.S.V.).

This is the second basic lesson in the series. The first lesson strongly emphasized the fact that the basis for social justice lies in the nature of God.

I. This lesson tells us that the teaching of Jesus demands justice in human relationships.

II. This leads into the discusson of the differences between the profession and practice of justice. Give examples. How easy it is for one to conform to the outward trappings of religion without reaching to its central core!

III. In the selection from Matt. 23 the teacher can note the severe condemnation Jesus pronounces upon those who pretend to be what they are not.

# SUNDAY: JULY TWENTIETH

## MORNING SERVICE

**Theme: The Romance of the Road**

SUGGESTED SCRIPTURE READING: Isa. 35.

SELECTED HYMNS: "Praise ye the Father."—M. Cockburn-Campbell. "Through all the changing scenes of life."—Tate and Brady. "He leads us on by paths we did not know."—Hiram O. Wiley. "He leadeth me: O blessed thought!"—Joseph H. Gilmore.

OPENING SENTENCE: "Forgetting those things which are behind, and reaching forth unto those things which are before, press toward the mark for the prize of the high calling of God in Jesus Christ." Phil. 3:13, 14.

INVOCATION: Lead us, O God, with high courage along the varied way. May we walk boldly in trouble and humbly in achievement, but always as in thy presence.

Implant thy Holy Spirit within our hearts that we may move forward in purpose, striving to do thy will, ever guided by thy Word. If we turn aside from the straight path, forgive us, and set our feet again in the paths of righteousness. Amen.—Mrs. J. N. Jackaway.

**Theme: The Romance of the Road**

TEXT: "And an highway shall be there, and a way, and it shall be called The way of holiness; . . . and sorrow and sighing shall flee away." Isa. 35:8-10.

INTRODUCTORY: It is a distinctive mark of man that he makes roads. No other creature does precisely that. Only men make roads.

And what roads they have made down the centuries—from the great thoroughfares of imperial Rome to the magnificent highways of modern Europe and America! Roads! What romance is in them! To what enthralling adventures do they beckon us! With what wooing visions do they lure us on! Half the happiness of life is linked with roads.

But beyond all the roads that man has made, and infinitely far surpassing them, is the great road which God has made for his people. "And an highway shall be there."

Passing over in silence the historical situation which gave rise to this outburst of prophetic rhapsody, let us take the text as a parable of the Christian life, a picture of the road along which the feet of God's folk are forever traveling.

There are four features of the road, here brought before us, of which I wish specially to speak. First, it is a High Way; next it is a Harmless Way; again, it is a Happy Way; and finally, it is the Homeward Way.

Let us consider them briefly in that order.

I. A High Way. We will start with that. A high way! Every man in his passage through the world is confronted by two ways—a high way and a low way—and compelled to make his choice between them. The high way is the way of probity, of purity, of idealism, of heroic self-commitment and self-sacrifice; the low way is the way of avarice and sensuality, of self-seeking and self-indulgence. And the human soul stands ever at the fork where those two roads divide.

Constantly we are faced with these moral alternatives, and there is no escaping the responsibility of the decision.

Yet the tragedy is that so many take the wrong road. Every way which is not God's way is no way. That is a conclusion to which, sooner or later, we all have to come. Nevertheless God in his loving wisdom does not suffer us long to pursue a false course in life without giving us frequent and forcible warnings.

The road on which the Lord wants us to travel is never a dead end. It is a high way, free and wide and open to the sky, rolling on and on toward the infinite horizon. No other way is worth taking. "This is the way; walk ye in it." "I am the Way," said Jesus. Is it not, then, bound to be a high way, the way of holiness? Hugh T. Kerr puts the point finely in a piquant epigram: "The right of way belongs to those who are in the way of right." For all others it is "No thoroughfare"! It is a high way, not a subway, and none but those of holy and humble heart are fit to tread in it. The way to the highest is a high way.

II. A Harmless Way. "No lion shall be there, nor any ravenous beast shall go up thereon." A harmless way! It is strange to find savage monsters in God's fair world—the lion, the tiger, the leopard—with their rough roar and terrific teeth. It is strange, too, to discover that these savage creatures have their counterparts in the moral world—fierce temptations that leap out upon us, like a lion from a thicket, threatening to destroy our souls. Such moral monsters we all meet. Some of us are surrounded by a positive menagerie of them! But here the Bible has a heartening message for those of us who are on the royal high way. "No lion shall be there," it declares. That does not mean that these savage beasts may not come near the high way. It does not mean that we may not hear them growling. It does not mean that they may not creep so close to us that, as Whyte used to say, we may feel their hot breath on our very necks! But it does mean that, so long as we are on the high way, so long as we keep close to the crown of the royal road, we have nothing to fear. There is always a way through for those who live a holy life. "Keep sound wisdom and discretion," counsels the Book of Proverbs, "then shalt thou walk in thy way safely."

III. A Happy Way. "And the ransomed of the Lord shall return, and come to Zion with songs and everlasting joy upon their heads: they shall obtain joy and gladness, and sorrow and sighing shall flee away."

Never before in human history have people felt, as they feel today, that happiness is an elemental human right. Men and women in the modern world have rewritten the first article of the *Westminster Shorter Catechism* as follows: "Man's chief end is to enjoy himself for ever." But the old divines knew better. Their rendering was the right one: "Man's chief end is to glorify God and to enjoy Him for ever." The fact is, we cannot really enjoy ourselves in the highest sense unless we enjoy God. He is the source of every true happiness we have, and the way on which he bids us journey is a way of joy.

Is not that a lovely picture of the Christian life, the life of the pilgrims to the City of God? It is a happy way leading to a Happy Land. There is no road in all the world nearly so joyous as the high way of the Lord.

IV. The Homeward Way. Every road is good, however long and rough and steep and winding, if it leads home at last. And there is no doubt that this royal road leads Home. For centuries it has been trodden by the feet of countless travelers and no one who has taken it has ever failed to find the open door and the light burning in the window at the end. "And the ransomed of the Lord shall return, and come to Zion."

But now in conclusion may I ask you a personal question? Are you sure that your feet are on this road, that you are a pilgrim on the Homeward path? It is a matter about which you cannot afford to be indifferent or careless. Upon it your eternal destiny depends. To have the right of way you must be in the way of right.—Ian Macpherson.

THEME PRAYER: Our Father, we thank thee that thou hast revealed to us, in Christ, the perfect way of life. Grant us, we pray, the wisdom and strength to walk unfailingly in the King's Highway. For thy glory. Amen.

OFFERTORY SENTENCE: "There is that scattereth, and yet increaseth; and there is that withholdeth more than is meet, but it tendeth to poverty." Prov. 11:24.

OFFERTORY PRAYER: O God, save us from wasting precious time and energy in fruitless activity. Save us, too, from wasting our wealth for trivial purposes. Teach us how to invest our wealth in human life and for thy Kingdom's sake. Bless this offering unto the good of our fellow men. In Jesus' name. Amen.—H.

SEED THOUGHTS: Walk in the Good way. "Thus saith the Lord, Stand ye in the ways, and see, and ask for the old paths, where is the good way, and walk therein, and ye shall find rest for your souls." Jer. 6:16. It may be that someone has been thinking it is too late to turn back onto the main highway of life. That is never true! This word from Jeremiah is for all of us.

The Triumphant Way. I. Safe despite danger. II. Peaceful in the midst of turmoil. III. Trustful through trials.

The Homeward Way. "The time of my departure is at hand. I have fought a good fight. . . ." II Tim. 4:6-8. There is a most valiant pilgrim nearing home! By the mercy of Christ he can look back upon a brave day, and there's a fine hopeful light in the evening sky. I. He has fought well! *"I have fought a good fight."* II. He has run well! *"I have finished my course."* III. And well he had guarded his treasure! *"I have kept the faith."*

And now the day is nearly over. "Henceforth there is laid up for me a crown of righteousness which the Lord will give me at that day." —J. H. Jowett.

**Choice Illustrations on the Theme**

THE WAY OF THE UNGODLY. "The Lord knoweth the way of the righteous; but the way of the ungodly shall perish." That word "perish," said G. Campbell Morgan, is extraordinarily suggestive in the original. It means literally to "run out," to "fade away," to vanish like a sheep track on the hills.

THE HIGH WAY. There are two trails to the summit of Mount Adams in the White Mountains. One is called the "valley way." You cross a meadow, then plunge suddenly into a forest. Lofty shoulders of the mountain compass you about. There is a feeling of being hemmed in, cramped, narrowed by the valley walls. Many hikers turn back, we are told, before they come to the head-wall which lifts to the summit of Adams, the second highest peak of the Presidential Range.

But there is another trail to the summit called the "air line." The very name suggests freedom, liquid air, broadness of view, far horizons. And so it is, for I have taken it. Immediately you clamber to the top of a shoulder leaving the valley behind, and what a vision of loveliness spreads out before you! For the one who has attained the "knife edge" of Durand Ridge is no longer bound by stifling walls. The goal looms clearly ahead; the whole world appears to be at his feet; and buoyantly he marches on.

The valley way and the air line! The high way and the low! You and I select which way we will go. If we take the valley way, we grope among uncertainties, rimmed about with fears and futilities. But there is another open to us, the high way, which is the life lived always on the heights of spiritual oneness with God. If we take this way, fears fall away, the goal stands always in bold relief before us, and we are buoyed up by the rarefied atmosphere of the heights.—Carl S. Weist.

## EVENING SERVICE

### Theme: Look Here!

TEXT: "The eyes of a fool are in the ends of the earth." Prov. 17:24.

He is a poverty-stricken man in his spirit and experience who never looks beyond his own home or his own church. "Where there is no vision the people perish." We must be conscious of the whole world in these days when time and distance mean almost nothing. But don't we occasionally need someone to remind us that we may be equally impoverished if our eyes are always on the distant things? Don't we need someone to say to us now and again, *"Look here!"*? Without this reminder we are in danger of missing the greatness of humanity.

I. Look here! There is heroism on our doorsteps.

Not long ago there was reported a magnificent story, from Eastern waters, of two sailors who had been forced to abandon their bombed ship. One of the men, with a lifebelt, and unharmed, was swimming steadily toward the far-distant shore. Then, near at hand, he saw a comrade who was wounded, and who could hardly keep afloat. Without any hesitation he passed over his lifebelt. "I'll make it without that," he said. He *didn't* make it. The shore was too far away. But the man to whom he had given his lifebelt was saved. People who read that story on their way to work or over the breakfast table remarked: "There's a lot of goodness in men, after all, you know."

Yet, surely, it shouldn't take a war correspondent from the other end of the earth to assure us of that fact. Isn't there heroism much nearer at hand? Is it so closely at hand that we don't recognize it for what it is? Perhaps a minister comes upon it more often than other folk, but it is there for all to see. The daughter who devotes her life to the constant service of an ailing mother, sometimes without much gratitude; the man, suffering from a disease that is incurable, who keeps the whole ward peaceful by his own example, and never lets the nurse go off duty without feeling she has done something worth while; the calm acceptance of disappointment, of loss, of tragedy, which is something more than stoicism; the rebuilding of a life that has been all but shattered. There is greatness here. It is to be found in your own church, in your own street, and in your own office. It comes from God.

II. Look here! Our real task is close at hand.

How often—and how inappropriately—have we heard that song about "My Task"! Often enough, at any rate, to sigh when the first chord is struck—and sit back without noticing the words. The song is trite enough, certainly, but at least it doesn't pretend that our task is at the end of the world.

Two things stand out clearly. 1. We shall most of us find our real task very close at hand, and shall only unfit ourselves for it by too much dreaming of the tasks which someone else must do.

2. Even if we *are* called to the distant field, to the more demanding work, it is in the immediate task that we must prove our fitness for other work. The disciples were told to begin first in Jerusalem, not to begin at the world's end and work back home. It was only in the discipline of working among those who knew them that they learned the lessons that were to serve the Kingdom in Africa, Asia, and Europe.

III. Look here! There is inspiration in the local church.

With our eyes in the ends of the earth, we may easily miss the source of our inspiration. We live at a time when the "World Church" is on everyone's lips. Now and again the local church is thrilled with the story of world travelers who have seen the church at work in a dozen different countries, and we say: "How wonderful it must be to see such things for yourself, and what an inspiration!"

Have you ever thought what such a

man may miss, if he is nothing more than a traveler? A traveler whose work for the church took him constantly from country to country recently said something you may care to ponder. "I would give anything, at times, for the fellowship of the local church, however small it is. The interest of seeing the World Church doesn't compensate a man for the inspiration of the local fellowship which he has to forego."

There is interest and inspiration in the far horizons. But the source of inspiration for each of us must be in the local church, with its consecrated fellowship of men and women, tiny though it may be, meeting week by week, seeking the will of God in prayer and trying to do it by his power.—Adapted from Cyril J. Davey.

**Suggested Texts and Themes from Philippians (Phillip's Translation)**

What Does Living Mean? "For living to me means simply 'Christ,' and if I die I should merely gain more of Him." Phil. 1:21.

Whatever Happens: "But whatever happens, make sure that your everyday life is worthy of the Gospel of Christ." Phil. 1:27.

Lights in a Dark Place: "Do all you have to do without grumbling or arguing, so that you may be God's children, blameless, sincere and wholesome, living in a warped and diseased world, and shining like lights in a dark place." Phil. 2:14, 15.

Genuine Righteousness: "God has given me that genuine righteousness which comes from faith in Christ." Phil. 3:9.

Genuine Christians: "Let me be your example here, my brothers: let my example be the standard by which you can tell who are the genuine Christians among those about you." Phil. 3:17.

## MIDWEEK FELLOWSHIP MEETING TOPIC

(Church Night or Suggested Sermon Subject)

**Theme: Overcoming Evil with Good**

TEXTS: Rom. 12:21; John 16:33.

Christ's final word to his eleven disciples who, against hope, clung to him with the tenacity of love: "In the world ye have tribulation: but be of good cheer; I have overcome the world."

I. The certainty of conflict between good and evil. In this world we are surrounded with subtle invisible forces that are opposed to everything for which Christ stands.

II. It is over this world of evil that Jesus claimed victory. "I have overcome the world." And it was a present conquest he claimed. The victory was in his hands.

The victory of Jesus was the victory of the Cross, where love at its best meets sin at its worst and not only survives but conquers.

We know now that goodness is mightier than evil, that love is stronger than death, that forgiveness can outthink and outlive and outlast sin, that truth can endure the shock of defeat, that faith is the victory that overcometh the world, that God never abdicates.

III. Because of his victory Jesus issued his call to courage: "Be of good cheer." Sharing in the victory of Christ, we too can overcome evil with good.

IV. If we answered Christ's call to courage, in what practical ways would we seek to overcome evil with good? What evils now assail us? What evils have insidiously crept into our modern society? Can we find any evils in our church life? In our personal lives? What is the good which would drive out each evil? How can we establish that good? Dare we claim the victory of Christ over these evils? Just how can we do that?—Adapted from Hugh T. Kerr.

## SUNDAY SCHOOL LESSON

**July 20. Justice Begins at Home. Eph. 5:21-31, 6:1-4; I Tim. 5:8. Background Scripture: Lev. 19:32; Mark 10:2-16.**

MEMORY VERSE: "Let each of you look not only to his own interests, but also to the interests of others." Phil. 2:4 (R.S.V.).

Let each one tabulate the relationships of the home and of kinship. Each one is a grandson or granddaughter, a son or a daughter. In most families each one is a brother or sister. In the family there is a husband and a wife. The husband may be a father and the wife a mother. They may even be grandparents. Each member of a family has in the family four or more relationships.

Suppose each of these relationships were idealized. I'll be the best son, brother, husband, father, that it is possible for me to be. Justice seems too weak a word to express such idealization. Love, in the true Christian meaning of the word, expresses it.

In the atmosphere of love justice will be learned and practiced. In the family practical problems arise, in solving which fairness is valued, known, and exemplified. Boys and girls need help in understanding the part God has in making home a place where fairness is the rule.

Nothing seems to rankle in the human soul as does an experience of injustice. How much delinquency has had its beginning in a youth's feeling that he has been the victim of an injustice perpetrated toward him by a member of his family!

This lesson may treat some practical and typical problems in which fairness can be learned and practiced.

# SUNDAY: JULY TWENTY-SEVENTH

## MORNING SERVICE

### Theme: Moods and Attitudes

SUGGESTED SCRIPTURE READING: Mark 4:1-20.

SELECTED HYMNS: "When morning gilds the skies."—From the German. "The Lord our God alone is strong."—Caleb T. Winchester. "Jesus, thy boundless love to me."—Paul Gerhardt. "Take the name of Jesus with you."—Lydia Baxter.

CALL TO WORSHIP: "Behold, God is my salvation; I will trust, and not be afraid: for the Lord Jehovah is my strength and my song; he also is become my salvation." Isa. 12:2.

INVOCATION: Almighty God, from whom cometh down every good and perfect gift, and who pourest out on all who desire it the spirit of grace and supplication; deliver us, when we draw nigh to thee, from coldness of heart and wanderings of mind; that with steadfast thoughts and kindled affections we may worship thee in spirit and in truth; we ask it through Jesus Christ our Lord. Amen.

### Theme: Moods and Attitudes

TEXT: Mark 4:26-29.

One of our recurring perplexities in life is that of our changing moods.

The best way to master a mood, which is a particular and often a temporary state of mind, is to cultivate an attitude which is deeper and more permanent and on which we can depend as a steady and reliable resource.

This is easier said than done, but for this there is unfailing help in the teachings of our Lord. We shall consider the teachings of our text.

There are three central attitudes suggested, drawn from the experiences of the farmer, and reflected in the character and outlook of Christ.

I. Notice that the farmer, when the planting is finished, sleeps and rises night and day, as though in calm reliance on a power beyond himself. There is no restlessness, no feverish effort, no forcing of results. To be sure, there is work to be done each day. There is never any escape from responsibility. But he is never vain enough to think that it all depends on him with the flurry and the worry of those who think the world would stop tomorrow morning if anything happened to them. It is plain enough that apart from the seed and the soil, the sun and the rain, he could do nothing. The earth bringeth forth fruit of itself. On that simple fact he puts his whole reliance, as he sleeps and rises night and day.

II. Consider, moreover, the attitude of wonder which belongs with a sense of reliance. "The seed groweth up, he knoweth not how." Here is a mystery which no farmer can explain, which no expert in soil or plant life can comprehend. Simple, familiar, multiplied many times over, are these first green blades appearing where yesterday a farmer scattered the seed. There is the unfolding answer to our simplest prayer, "Give us this day our daily bread." And not one of us knows how.

III. Always we are to live eagerly, as those who have hope for the future. For the earth bringeth forth first the blade, then the ear, then the full corn in the ear. Always in the background of the farmer's mind is the thought of the ripening grain. For while there is mystery in life, there is meaning, too, and to those who look for it, God makes his purpose plain.

Perhaps a further line should be appended to the parable from the farmer's experience. What does he do when his fields are covered with the swirling waters of a flood, the seed washed out, his labor vain? He plants again with the confident belief that the fields were made to bring forth grain. They have no other meaning.

And men also plant again in faith that the earth was designed to bring forth the fruits of the spirit—truth and justice and liberality and freedom—in the life of man. Apart from that it has no meaning—only a wasteland remains.

So the farmer sleeps and rises night and day, in calm reliance on a power beyond himself. The seed groweth up, he knoweth not how, but wonder fills his mind. And with an eager spirit he watches first the blade, then the ear, then the full corn in the ear. This is his hope for years to come. For our Lord speaks as one who holds all the ages in the hollow of his hand.—Harold E. Nicely.

PRAYER FOR THE DAY: Heavenly Father, we thank thee for our knowledge that all our springs are in thee. Wilt thou deliver us from any sense of self-dependence, and lead us into an intimate fellowship with the ministries of thy grace. If any triumph has made us self-confident, if any earthly success has made us proud, may thy Holy Spirit lead our spirits into the lowliness which is the beginning of true wisdom and strength.

We humbly ask that thou wilt deliver us from the sins which have become our masters, and in which we find unholy delight. Incline our hearts unto thy law, and help us to find pleasure in obedience to thy holy will. Graciously redeem us from every care which fetters our souls, and give us such an assurance of thy providential love that we may exult in the glorious liberty of the children of God. Amen.—J. H. Jowett.

OFFERTORY SENTENCE: "Trust in the Lord, and do good; so shalt thou dwell in the land, and verily thou shalt be fed. Delight thyself also in the Lord; and he shall give thee the desires of thine heart."

OFFERTORY PRAYER: We dedicate unto thee, O Lord, this offering. Bless, we pray thee, that part which is offered as a result of self-denial and sacrifice. Follow it with thy favor as it releases energies to build thy Kingdom.

Bless that part which is a token of devotion, that part which is an affirmation of belief in God, and that part which may have been idly given as a matter of course. By the warming of our hearts in thy presence and by the gift of thy grace may we learn that there is no giving or withholding without significance. Amen—H.

SEED THOUGHTS: The Mystery of the the Kingdom. I. The Kingdom is a *vital force.* II. The Kingdom is one of *wondrous adaptations.* III. The Kingdom of God moves through *orderly development* to a resistless harvest.—George A. Buttrick.

We Like to Get Results. I. The farmer. Mark 4:26-29. II. Parents like to get results with their children. III. We like to get results when someone is ill. IV. We would like to get results in other fields. We would like to destroy hunger, poverty, injustice, and war. We would like to gather the fruits of God's harvest here and now. And isn't there something that we can do about it tomorrow morning at eight o'clock?

Well, the good seed has been planted, and through the ages, despite reluctant soil, it has been growing, and there is work for each of us to do. But for its fulfillment we must still depend on something beyond ourselves. It is still the quiet working of God's spirit in nature and in the souls of men on which we finally depend, and to which we look in calm reliance for the fulfillment of every good hope. The Father worketh hitherto and henceforth, while we work. Our part is to be faithful in the field assigned, living night and day in calm reliance on a power beyond ourselves, as we pray, Thy Kingdom come, Thy will be done on earth.—H. E. N.

### Choice Illustrations on the Theme

CALM RELIANCE. Our knowledge and skill have tended to obscure our real dependence on a power beyond ourselves. We seem to have taken control of the energies of nature. We store up the precious waters in great reservoirs, harness the power of the swift torrent, give back to the soil the food that plants require, and even drop magic seeds in rain clouds to produce the needed shower. But even as, in the springtime, a fleet of tractors churns up the broad fields so swiftly and efficiently, the farmer's true relation to nature is no different from that of a peasant with a wooden plow. It is still the earth that brings forth fruit of itself, and the proper attitude of man, not only in farming, but in all of his labors is one of calm reliance on a power beyond himself.—H. E. N.

OUR KNOWLEDGE ENDS WITH QUESTIONS. An eminent physicist remarked that when scientific enigmas die, they give birth to twins. Even in the midst of simplest things, we know not how.

FOLDED IN THE SEED. Quietly and without haste the moral and spiritual powers resident in human life unfold. The tender green of spring, the pledge of the summer's ripening wheat, the reaper's song, and the bursting granaries are all stored within the seed. Unhurried but sure, the hidden vitality evolves through its full cycle of development. What a history of Puritan achievement was hidden in the seed of the *Mayflower*! What centuries of Christian growth were folded vitally in the seed of the Apostles' band!—George A. Buttrick.

## EVENING SERVICE

### Theme: Finding God in the Dark

TEXT: "My grace is sufficient for thee." II Cor. 12:9.

We should be amazed to learn how many men and women have found God in the dark. When life danced along in light and song the sense of God was dim; but when the clouds gathered and the thunder and lightning of trouble encompassed them, then something happened which opened the doors of their closed hearts. Trouble does not always have this effect. Sometimes it leaves hearts more closed, hard, and bitter than they were before. Nevertheless, history's record is crowded with instances in which people did not recognize the highest values nor experience God until the light was put out.

I. Adversity may drive a man to a new appreciation of other people. In the day time we can be fairly comfortable alone, but when night comes, then it is so good to have someone near. One can get along quite well by himself when light and prosperity bless his way; but when it grows dark and his path is dogged by adversity he feels the need of human fellowship. God reaches us through persons, so human fellowship is a pathway to the divine.

II. In the second place, trouble stops

a man short and makes him sober. Some people are sobered in no other way than by adversity. When you go out at night you do not see anything but the big things. The overarching sky, the encircling horizon, are stupendous; against them one may see dimly the outlines of big things such as a mountain peak. But squirrel holes and molehills are lost against the background of the tremendous. So in the hour of trouble one is driven to the big things. It is when one begins to see life in true perspective—first things first—that he begins to recognize God as most important of all.

What light does to the eye carefree prosperity may do to the soul. It distracts; it tempts to absorption in a dozen lesser interests. Things—plenty to eat and drink and wear—bulk large when one is well and happy; but in the dark days one becomes thoughtful and certain that there are more important values. A Detroit newspaper reported that an expectant mother clad in a shoddy cotton dress, who had come up from South Carolina, when asked why she had joined a certain religious group, said, "Honey, when you ain't got nothin', God looks good." Yes, there is something sobering about hard times.

III. Something else happens in the dark: It not only makes a man sober, it makes him humble. Who has not had the experience of feeling utterly fearless, buoyant, confident, while the sun was shining; but in the same place with no change except the coming of the dark, feeling apprehensive, depressed, and utterly inadequate? It is a symbol of one's moral and spiritual experience. In days of health and prosperity a man is easily tempted to be proud and self-sufficient. Someone has defined wealth as stilts that make a little person look big. That is not the worst of it. Prosperity not only makes a little man look big to misapprehending neighbors; it sometimes makes him feel big. But adversity knocks away the stilts and makes one feel his real pigmy size.

Adversity forces a man to find strength beyond himself. So long as his own strength is adequate he never thinks to search for surplus power. Is not that the personal experience which Paul describes? He tells of a thorn in the flesh. What it was we do not know—perhaps illness, epilepsy, or eye trouble. It was so exasperating and humiliating, however, that he called it a "messenger of satan," and prayed three times that it might be taken away. It was not taken away; but in his extremity he found a new and rich experience. The answer came back from God, "My grace is sufficient for thee." Paul found God very real in the dark. Driven to recognize his own utter inadequacy he learned of the complete adequacy of the Infinite.

The instances are legion in which men like Paul have in the dark found what had never come in sunny days of self-sufficiency. Rufus Jones related this story: A young man went to the physician and was told by him that in a year's time he would be blind and deaf. He was staggered by the announcement. He felt as if he had reached a blank wall at the end of a blind alley.

Out in the street he stood holding on to a pole for support. As he waited he felt the surge of God's love going through him. There was then a door in the seemingly blank wall; through it he found a glorious release. He became calm, met his predicted fate a few months later, and lived a radiant life until his death when still a young man. —Frank B. Fagerburg.

**Suggested Texts and Themes (from the Psalms)**

Religion in the Laboratory of Life: "O taste and see that the Lord is good: blessed is the man that trusteth in him." Ps. 34:8.

Homesickness for God: "My soul longeth, yea, even fainteth for the courts of the Lord: my heart and my flesh crieth out for the living God." Ps. 84:2.

God, the Ever Dependable: "Before the mountains were brought forth, or ever thou hadst formed the earth and the world, even from everlasting to everlasting, thou art God." Ps. 90:2.

The Perils of the Noonday: "Nor for the pestilence that walketh in darkness;

nor for the destruction that wasteth at noonday." Ps. 91:6.

God's Beckoning Skyline: "I will lift up mine eyes unto the hills, from whence cometh my help." Ps. 121:1.

## MIDWEEK FELLOWSHIP MEETING TOPIC

(Church Night or Suggested Sermon Subject)

**Theme: Overcoming Death with Life**

TEXT: "I am the resurrection and the life." John 11:25.

I. Man is utterly incapable of overcoming death with life.

II. It is Christ alone who challenges death. "Jesus and death belong in two different realms. Jesus is life. Death is death.

III. As believers in our Lord we can look at death through his eyes. Life is the true hope and the heart of our Christion faith—life, abundant life, everlasting life.

IV. The nearer we get back to the fountain springs of the life of the early church, the closer we are to this faith that challenges death. "For me to live is Christ," said St. Paul, "and to die is gain."

During the excavation of the catacombs in 1856 three inscriptions, prepared by the same hand, were discovered at different places. Some man had written them for his beloved wife or mother or sister or betrothed, whose name was Sophronia. He had gone to the catacombs of St. Calixtus to pray and to seek comfort, and there he wrote the words we still read. Underground and near the entrance he wrote, "Sophronia lives in peace." Farther on, in a little chapel where the bodies of twelve popes lie side by side, he waited to pray, and then he wrote, "Sophronia lives in the Lord." He did not write of sleep or death, but of life. Farther on, in the chapel of St. Cecilia, he knelt in prayer, and there he wrote, "Dear Sophronia lives for ever in the Lord." Yes, she lives, she is not dead. She is alive. In Christ there is no death.—Adapted from Hugh T. Kerr.

## SUNDAY SCHOOL LESSON

**July 27. Justice in Community Life. Lev. 19:15-18; James 2:1-9. Background Scripture: Lev. 19:11-18; Deut. 15:7-8; Rom. 13:8-10; James 2:1-13.**

MEMORY VERSE: "Love does no wrong to a neighbor; therefore love is the fulfilling of the law." Rom. 13:10 (R.S.V.).

I. Refer to last Sunday's lesson, "Justice Begins at Home." The attitude toward, and practice of, justice in community life is largely a reflection of life in its homes.

II. Focus the problem of class distinctions and social injustices in terms of the local community.

III. Stimulate an active concern to secure equal opportunities for the peoples of the local community. The principles involved may be applied in the areas of school, church, and social life.

IV. Discuss ways and means by which Christians may exhibit justice to neighbors in personal relationships as well as in club, civic, political, business, and church affairs.

# SUNDAY: AUGUST THIRD

## MORNING SERVICE

**Theme: On Being Worthy of the Gospel or a Wonderful Way of Living**

SUGGESTED SCRIPTURE READING: Phil. 1:27-2:11.

SELECTED HYMNS: "Come, let us tune our loftiest song."—Robert A. West. "Go, labor on! spend and be spent."—H. Bonar. "Fight the good fight with all thy might."—J. S. B. Monsell. "Rise up, O men of God."—Wm. P. Merrill.

OPENING SENTENCE: "Wherefore also God highly exalted him, and gave unto him the name which is above every name; that in the name of Jesus every knee should bow, of things in heaven, and things in earth, and things under the earth, and that every tongue should confess that Jesus Christ is Lord, to the glory of God the Father."

INVOCATION: We who have heard the good news, the Gospel of Christ, gather in his name, O God, to worship thee.

Grant unto us the presence and ministry of thy Holy Spirit that our minds may be quickened to know thee, our hearts to love thee, and our wills to serve thee.—H.

**Theme: Being Worthy of the Gospel or A Wonderful Way of Living**

TEXT: "Only let your manner of life be worthy of the gospel of Christ." Phil. 1:27 (A.R.V.).

INTRODUCTORY: "Philippians—a letter written by a brave man in a gloomy time to friends that he trusted and loved." Many passages to underline in this letter. Some of them are . . . Here is another, Phil. 1:27.

This text consists in the original of five Greek words translated: 1. "Only"; 2. "Let your manner of life be"; 3. "Worthy of"; 4. "Gospel"; 5. "Christ." These head the five divisions of the sermon.

I. "Only." Dr. Goodspeed gives us the translation, "Whatever happens." "Whatever happens let your manner of life be worthy of the gospel of Christ."

1. Paul was writing out of his own experiences. Many things had happened to him. He was not writing out of theory. He had endured beatings, thrashings, stonings . . . That word "Whatever happens" had real significance to him.

*The Gospel will keep you steadfast in your time of crisis.* He was sure of this.

2. Paul saw that little church at Philippi immersed in a pagan world. It is just this that paganism cannot do —it cannot keep a man steady in his day of crisis. Its characteristic is "an inner emptiness, resulting in an inadequacy to meet outward contingencies and situations."

3. Are we ourselves not immersed in paganism? Round about us are many who cannot keep steadfast in a time of crisis, "the impact of circumstances places a tension in the mind which the inner resources cannot bear effectively." Personality in fragments *vs.* steadfastness.

4. Something is going to happen. It always does. Whatever happens, don't live like a pagan; live like a Christian. If what happens seems to be ill, don't cry like a baby; don't whimper like a child; don't frazzle out like a neurotic; don't join some silly cult that has no center; don't grit your teeth like a Stoic; don't disvalue life like the Epicurean; don't chew the cud of bitterness; don't get hard; don't be a pagan.

5. Be a Christian! The Gospel will keep you steady in your day of crisis.

II. "Let your manner of life be." The Greek word which is thus translated in the same word in its root form from which come our English words, "politics" and "police." It really means "being a citizen." Therefore,

Dr. Goodspeed translates as follows. "Whatever happens show yourself citizens worthy of the Gospel."

1. A little later in this letter Paul uses the word again. See 3:20. (Compare the different versions.) The American Revised Version reads, "Our citizenship is in heaven." Or as Dr. Moffatt indicates, Paul is taking advantage of the fact that he is writing from Rome, the capital, to a group who are residents in a colonial city—"You are a colony of heaven."

He is saying, "Even as you go about your daily walk and occupations as colonists of Rome, belonging to a fairer city than Philippi and obedient to a higher culture and law, remember that you have a citizenship in heaven. Be true to that."

*The Gospel will help you to live above the common level.*

2. You are citizens of the commonwealth of God immersed in a pagan world. This being so, one is always troubled by the level of the standards of the place where one lives.

3. Whatever happens, be sure that your everyday life is worthy of the Gospel of Christ.

III. "Worthy." "Whatever happens show yourselves citizens worthy. . . ."

1. Worthy of something. Worthy of the Gospel. Paul made sure that they would understand. He tells what the Gospel is in the letter. See Phil. 2:5-11.

2. Live worthy of the coming of Christ *to* the world. Worthy of Bethlehem. Worthily receive him.

Live worthy of the service of Christ *in* the world. Worthy of Galilee. Worthily follow his example.

Live worthy of the death of Christ *for* the world. Worthy of Calvary. Worthily accept his salvation; worthily enter into his sufferings.

Live worthy of the victory of Christ *over* the world. Worthy of the empty tomb. Worthily live in the power of the resurrection.

Live worthy of the reign of Christ *throughout* the world. Worthy of his universality. Worthily go to the uttermost parts.

Live worthy of the glory of Christ *above* the world. Worthy of the heavenly places. Worthily share his glory.

3. It can't be done! Paul knew that it couldn't be done. Paul knew that the secret of victorious living lies in doing what can't be done. See Phil. 3:13-14.

"I press toward the goal." *I go straight for the goal.* Worthiness does not rest in attainment; worthiness rests in the aspiration and the struggle, the reach exceeding the grasp.

4. Live worthily—you'll aspire to reach the goal.

IV. The fourth word of our text, "Gospel," "Good News." "Whatever happens . . . the Good News of Christ."

1. Now let our first three points throw light on the fourth. Suppose that we Christians proved steadfast in time of crisis; suppose that we lived above the common level; suppose we went straight for the goal; what would be the effect of that? Suppose that a Christian citizen in Philippi had done that in that pagan city. He would have been an evangelist. He would have been a witness of and for the Gospel of Christ. He would have been a missionary in that pagan world.

2. Now just suppose that today in your home, in this community, you lived out these three thing: steadfast in the day of crisis; life above the common level; aspiring toward the goal, the character of Christ. What would you be? You'd be not only an evangelist; you'd be Good News itself. You'd not only bear good tidings; you'd be good tidings.

3. Emphasize the word "Gospel" in the text: *You'll be a witness to the Good News.*" "You'll be as lights in the world." Phil. 2:16.

V. The fifth word is "Christ." "Whatever happens . . . Christ."

1. There is much to say here but I point out only one idea which pervades this Pauline letter. He writes, "Christ is proclaimed and therein I rejoice, yea, and will reojice." The word "joy" pervades the letter.

"What a climax." Only let your manner of life be worthy of the Gospel and *you'll rejoice in your Lord and Saviour Jesus Christ.*

What a wonderful way of living!—H.

PRAYER FOR THE DAY: O God, our Father, we find it a great privilege to have knowledge of the Gospel of Jesus Christ. It is in the name of Christ and by the power of the Gospel that we worship thee and bind ourselves together in praise and aspiration and prayer.

We worship humbly because we are not worthy of the Gospel—that Christ should have humbled himself, lived a lowly life of service, endured the Cross, achieved victory over sin and death for us. We can only thank thee for him, consecrate our lives to him, let him be our Ideal and Example, accept him as our Saviour, and acknowledge him as our Lord. Amen.—H.

OFFERTORY SENTENCE: We are stewards of the Gospel of Christ. We are stewards also of our wealth. It is a prime requisite in a steward that he should be worthy of his trust.

OFFERTORY PRAYER: We desire, O Lord, in all our ways to acknowledge thee. Help us to look upon our wealth as a sacred trust related to the building of the Kingdom. May we be faithful to our trust. Amen.—H.

SEED THOUGHTS: The Text in Various Translations. "Only let your conversation be as it becometh the gospel of Christ" (K.J.V.). "Only let your manner of life be worthy of the gospel [good tidings, *margin*] of Christ" (A.R.V. and R.S.V.). "Only, do lead a life that is worthy of the gospel of Christ" (Moffatt). "Only let the lives you live be worthy of the gospel of the Christ" (Weymouth). "Whatever happens, show yourselves citizens worthy of the good news of the Christ" (Goodspeed). "But whatever happens, make sure that your everyday life is worthy of the Gospel of Christ" (Phillips).

"A Colony of Heaven." Phil. 3:20. "Our conversation is in heaven" (K.J.V.). "Our citizenship is in heaven" (A.R.V.). "Our commonwealth is in heaven" (R.S.V.). "We are a colony of heaven" (Moffat). "We are free citizens of heaven" (Weymouth). "But the commonwealth to which we belong is in heaven" (Goodspeed). "But we are citizens of heaven" (Phillips).

### Choice Illustrations on the Theme

ABOVE THE COMMON LEVEL. The other day a lady aged eighty-five called me on the phone and asked whether I could do something about a certain obscene magazine which was on sale at the newsstand. Since then the Postmaster-General has prohibited its sale. But I am asking now, Why should that old lady care? It meant nothing to her. It would have no evil effect upon her life. Yet she did care. She belongs to the Commonwealth of Heaven and she is deeply concerned about the standards of the city where she lives. She lives above the common level.

THE NATURE OF PAGANISM. Jeremiah wrote concerning the paganism of his day that it was *inane* and that the pagans met any unusual circumstances with dismay. Halford Luccock, commenting upon this, says: "Certainly, a life inane at the center will be dismayed at the circumference. Where there is fatty degeneration of character at the heart of life, there will inevitably be panic and rout on the field of action."

LIVING WORTHILY. When taveling in the Orient how important to remember that one is an American, to live worthy of the name. During World War I an American captain in France spoke for himself and the three lieutenants of his company: "We were gentlemen in America; we have decided to be gentlemen in France."—H.

## EVENING SERVICE

### Theme: Come Ye Apart

TEXT: "And Jesus said unto them, Come ye yourselves apart into a desert place, and rest a while." Mark 6:31.

One of the things that strikes us about

Jesus is his concern for every aspect of human need. The disciples had come back from a preaching tour, a little tired and strained. On the top of this had come the news of the death of John the Baptist at the whim of a dancing girl. They were naturally depressed, and doubts began to overshadow their minds. It was the kind of mood in which we are all likely to see the black side of things and to wonder if the spiritual conflict is worth while. Jesus did not argue with them. He knew that they were physically tired. The fatigue of body and nerves had reacted on their minds. Sheer fatigue can lower our spiritual resistance and open the gate to an attack of fear and futility. A few days' rest of body may sometimes enable us to get back our poise. So Jesus took them away by themselves into a quiet place to rest.

I. But the great point was that he was with them. It was his presence that enabled them to relax. Under his influence the tension was relieved. They could let go. They could leave their burdens to him. Spiritual resources will enable a man to do amazing feats of toil or endurance. Most of us, we are told, work a long way below our potential capacity. But to keep touch with these resources of the spirit, which are of God, we must take time to make and to restore the contact with him. That can only be done as we take time to come apart from the world with him.

II. In that quiet hour several things will happen. 1. For one thing, we recover a sense of proportion. We see the things that worry us in their true perspective. We realize how small they often are.

2. It is in the quiet place with God that doubts are often best put to silence.

3. In the quiet hour, the reality of God's love in Christ has power to reach the heart. We know afresh that he lives and that his love is the reality which can never be defeated or destroyed.

III. Our great need today is to open our minds and hearts to the other world, the world that is unseen and eternal. Most of us live too much in the world of time. Passing events absorb the mind. We listen to news bulletins one after another. Our minds become a prey to rumors that breed false hopes and lying fears. It is all very exhausting to the spirit. It is so easy to lose perspective and to forget that the supreme reality is God and his Kingdom. Our real business is the same as it always was. It is to do his will. The greater the strain and perplexity, the more we need his inner guiding and power. The more things pass, the more we need to fix our anchor in his abiding love.

We cannot live without inspiration of some kind—something to cheer or encourage or kindle hope. I remember, during a walk in the country, seeing a reservoir full of water. There had been a long time of drought from which the whole countryside had suffered, but now the rain had come and it seemed as if all would be well. The reservoir was filling up. But a frined who was with me was not satisfied. He told me the authorities were very concerned. The reason was that the hidden springs were not yet active. They had not begun to flow. The water that filled the reservoir was only from surface streams. It would not meet the need. So many people are like that. They live on surface inspirations, little bits of cheer of friendship which carry them through. But the deeper springs in the heart have never been set flowing. These only rise within us when we take time to come apart with God.—James Reid.

**Suggested Texts and Themes**

Series: Questions God Asks. 1. Where art thou? Gen. 3:9. 2. Where is thy brother? Gen. 4:9. 3. What is that in thine hand? Exod. 4:2. 4. What doest thou here? I Kings 19:9.

Series: Three Looks of Jesus. 1. He looked upon a young man. "And Jesus looking upon him loved him." Mark 10:21. 2. He looked upon the multitude. "And Jesus looked round about and saith unto his disciples. . . ."

Mark 10:23. 3. He looked upon his disciples. "Jesus looking upon them, saith. . . ." Mark 10:27.

God's Extras: "I do set my bow in the cloud." Gen. 9:13.

## MIDWEEK FELLOWSHIP MEETING TOPIC

(Church Night or Suggested Sermon Subject)

**Theme: Near yet Unaware**

TEXT: ". . . between the porch and the altar, were about five and twenty men, with their backs toward the temple of the Lord." Ezek. 8:16.

On a certain summer Sunday it was estimated that seven hundred thousand persons visited a sea beach resort. How many of them missed seeing the great ocean?

I. How many were near, yet unaware? Some carried not back to the narrow walls of their accustomed task the broad horizon of a boundless sea.

II. Near the mountains, how seldom do we lift up our eyes! How desperately easy it is to be near and yet unaware! Is there one of us without regret and heaviness of heart because some time or other we were near a great experience and missed it? We were in the neighborhood of the burning bush but did not turn aside to see.

III. The judgment of nearness is indeed startling. Here were these five and twenty men within the temple of God. The very God was present in his sanctuary. There was proximity but not contact.

IV. The church tower sends its gleam of invitation out across the neighborhood. How many are near, yet unaware. There spirits are restless while peace is near by.

Nearness, not to a church, not to a building, not to a minister, not to an organization, but nearness to Christ who frequents the temple. How many are like those who stood between the porch and the altar!—H.

## BULLETIN BOARD SLOGANS FOR THE MONTH

Love often dies of neglect.

"It isn't the whistle that pulls the train."

Are you lonely? Then go to church next Sunday.

Weather that is always fair becomes depressing.

For a happy vacation—good will and sportsmanship.

A stubborn man may be a slave to his own opinions.

Going on vacation? Keep your eyes and your mind open.

"You cannot steal second and keep one foot on first."

"The toughest form of mountain climbing is getting out of a rut."

Face God and you will find it easier to face circumstances.

## SUNDAY SCHOOL LESSON

**Aug. 3. Guarding Our Freedoms. Amos 7:10-15; Gal. 5:1, 13-18, 25. Background Scripture: John 8:31-38; Acts 4:15-20, 5:27-32; Gal. 3:23-28, 5:1-25.**

MEMORY VERSE: "If you continue in my word, you are my disciples, and you will know the truth, and the truth will make you free." John 8:31-32 (R.S.V.).

I. How did we acquire our freedoms, such as freedom of speech, worship, assembly, press, and so forth?

II. What forces within society now threaten these freedoms?

III. To whom are we responsible for the preservation and continuance of these freedoms?

IV. Does loyalty to Christ help make these freedoms secure?

V. What can we do here and now for the cause of freedom?

# SUNDAY: AUGUST TENTH

## MORNING SERVICE

### Theme: What Your Faith Makes Possible

SUGGESTED SCRIPTURE READING: II Thess. 2:13 (Phillips' translation).

SELECTED HYMNS: "Praise to the Lord, the Almighty, the King of creation!"—Neander. "Take time to be holy."—W. D. Longstaff. "Breathe on me, Breath of God."—Edwin Hatch. "How firm a foundation."—Rippon's Selection.

OPENING SENTENCES: "Never damp the fires of the Spirit, and never despise what is spoken in the Name of the Lord. By all means use your own judgment, and hold on to whatever is really good. Steer clear of evil in any form. Never stop praying. Be thankful, whatever the circumstances may be." I Thess. (Phillips' translation).

INVOCATION: We are thankful for the day, O Lord, for thou hast chosen us to be children of light. We are thankful for the beauty of the day; may the beauty of the Lord God be upon us. We are thankful for thy providence whereby the needs of our bodies, minds, and souls are satisfied. We thank thee for the privilege of worship on this Sabbath Day. Let our hearts be glad, and our lives be joyful, in the name of our Lord Jesus Christ. Amen.—H.

### Theme: What Your Faith Makes Possible

TEXT: "He will effect in you all that his goodness desires to do, and that your faith makes possible." II Thess. 1:11, 12 (Phillips' translation).

INTRODUCTORY. 1. The Church at Thessalonica was exemplary in many respects. It had become twisted because of an obsession concerning the Second Coming of Christ. Paul applies discipline in his letters. He suggests a far better outlook upon their destiny. He said: "In view of this great prospect, we pray for you constantly, that God will effect in you all that his goodness desires to do, and that your faith makes possible."

2. Certainly a man ought to think about his destiny. Personal destiny is a matter of fundamental importance. Now, facing human destiny, our own future, let us look at Paul's prayer for these destiny-minded Thessalonians, which I take rather as a declaratory statement of fact: "God will effect in you all that his goodness desires to do, and that your faith makes possible."

The natural and immediate question to ask is, "What is it that God's goodness desires to do for me and with me?"

Paul answers precisely in the second chapter of his letter. This is best brought out by Phillips' translation. Three things God desires to do for you. First, "He has chosen you from the beginning to save you." Second, "He has chosen you from the beginning to make you holy." Third, "He has set before you the prospect of sharing the glory of our Lord Jesus Christ." There is your destiny, if your faith makes it possible.

I. He has chosen you from the beginning to save you. 1. He is not going to lose you. 2. God's salvation was made manifest to us in Christ. It is in him an implemented salvation. 3. This salvation which is ours is a process, not just an incident. We cannot see the infinite reaches of it. The process includes forgiveness, justification, call to service, growth in grace, becoming a child of God, "and it does not yet appear what we shall be."

4. Now look at the text: "God will effect in you all that his goodness desires to do, *and that your faith makes possible.*" There's an *if* to be considered, or the little conjunction *and*. This process of salvation, active and effective because of the passionate goodness of God, is

made possible by our faith. A man doesn't have to be saved. A man has the choice of linking himself with the life-destroying processes.

In other words faith must gear into God's desires. (See Illustrations.)

II. What is it that God's goodness desires to do for you? "He has chosen you from the beginning to make you holy." 1. Now all that we have said concerning salvation applies also to holiness. Holiness is our destiny. Our holiness is implemented by the Holy Spirit. By faith we may "gear in" to God's desire for us.

2. There are some who are prejudiced against this word "holy." They do not like self-righteous attitudes, holier-than-thou speech and demeanor.

Let not unpleasant experience lose the word. It is a great word; it expresses a high ideal; it designates something that God wants to do for us and in us. Its opposite is "profane." Holiness is a process. Holiness is health. Holiness is wholesome. Holiness is integration of personality. Reconciliation with God is holiness. The experience that within you God is working is holiness.

3. Faith must gear in, that God's purpose may come to pass.

III. What does God's goodness desire to do for you? "He has set before you the prospect of sharing the glory of our Lord, Jesus Christ." 1. Our destiny includes the prospect of sharing the glory of Christ.

2. Some need to shift from the fear-of-eternal-death attitude to the sharing-the-glory attitude.

3. Some need to shift from an other-worldly attitude to "I-got-a-glory" attude. (See Illustration from Archibald Rutledge.)

4. Recall the emphasis, "God is utterly to be depended upon. . . ."—H.

A Prayer for the Day: We thank thee, O god, for the blessed memories which come to us as we gather for worship on the Lord's Day. The associations of thy house are of kinsfolk and friends whose memories we lovingly cherish, old scenes where in years past we lived and labored, where we worshiped and aspired. We recall the songs and sermons of other days. We recall how thou didst support us in our days of crisis, and lead us in our hours of darkness, and make full our days of gladness. We thank thee for the rich ministry of memory.

For this present day, so wonderful in its provision for our bodies, our minds, our hearts, and our souls, we thank thee.

We thank thee, too, that our lives look forward. We have faith to believe that the good work thou hast begun in us will be perfected, that we shall grow in grace and into the likeness of our Lord Jesus Christ, that all the things which thy goodness desires for us will come to pass. In Jesus' name. Amen. —H.

Offertory Sentence: "Every man according as he purposeth in his heart, so let him give; not grudgingly, or of necessity: for God loveth a cheerful giver."

Offertory Prayer: Help us to give, O Lord, unto thee as thou dost give unto us, out of the good desires of our hearts. Help us to give liberally and joyfully. And may thy rich blessing rest upon our offerings that they may do much good.—H.

Seed Thoughts:

Living Encounter. I. Faith brings me into the presence of God. II. The prayer of faith gives me personal communion with God. III. Through faith I receive his salvation. IV. By faith I appropriate his promises.—John G. McKenzie.

What Faith Means. I. Assured position in relation to God. II. Bold exploration of God's resources. III. Firm belief in the presence of Christ in the heart and soul of the Christian.—J. B. Phillips.

## Choice Illustrations on the Theme

gearing in. We ought to become great Christians, if gearing into God's good desires for us is the secret of our destiny. We have become so skilled at gearing in.

In the morning I go to the garage, take my seat in a high-powered car, turn on the ignition. It runs in neutral. Then I gear in—and away I go.

We sit before our radio or television set—the programs are in the ether; they're ready; they're released. Then we turn the knob and dial. The program unfolds before us.

Now wouldn't it be wonderful if God had endowed us with some kind of antennae and apparatus in our heads so that we could dial in or channel in or gear in without the use of a radio or television set? Those ethereal vibrations are in our heads, in our bodies; they go through us. Why not provision in our personal make-up for that?

This idea is not so foolish. We have antennae in our heads for the light waves that come from the sky and the stars, from the mountains and the trees. We have eyes constructed as receivers that respond to the rays of light. We have ears constructed to receive sound waves. They are antennae, one on each side of our head, with a very intricate mechanism.

Then why shouldn't there be some spiritual organ of response toward God's good desires for us? Why shouldn't we dial in to God's program? Why shouldn't we channel in to God's purposes? The text suggests that we can. The text says that *faith* makes God's good desires possible.

God made the beauty of the earth; it seems reasonable that God should give man eyes to see it. God effects man's salvation; it seems only reasonable that God should also give a man capacity to receive it.—H.

"I Got a Glory!" Archibald Rutledge once told of how he climbed into a tiny tugboat, which he had often used to cross a southern river. There was a new Negro engineer in charge. Rutledge noticed that the engine room was immaculate. The strong odors heretofore evident in that area were gone. The engine itself shone. The brass was gleaming. Clothes were hanging on the wall instead of being strewn around on the floor and the benches.

When Rutledge asked the stolid Negro engineer how it happened there was such a change in the boat he replied, "Mister, it's just this way: I got a glory!" Said Rutledge, "Making that engine the finest engine on the river was his glory in life, and having a glory, he had everything."

Do you have a glory? Each of us needs a glory—something that challenges and inspires us, that pulls us out of ourselves and keeps alive our joy in living. Perhaps this is what we mean by the *glory of God* in human life—the glory that enables us to take common, everyday experiences and make them magnificent in the service of the Kingdom.—Kenneth A. Carlson.

## EVENING SERVICE

### Theme: The Look that Changes Life

TEXT: "The Lord turned and looked at Peter . . . and he went out, and wept bitterly." Luke 22:61, 62.

There are different ways of looking at things and at people. We can look without seeing. We can travel miles through the country and not notice how lovely it is.

We can go among people in the same blind, impersonal way, even those in the home or the worship. We notice nothing of the trouble, the frustration, the longing that may be registered on their faces; for "faces," as Bacon says, "are but a gallery of pictures, where there is no love."

It was different with Jesus. When he looked at people he "marked each want, each weakness clear." He saw things in Zacchaeus, the squalid little taxgatherer, that no one else had ever seen or believed could be there.

He looked at Peter passing out of the room where he had miserably denied the friendship Jesus had given him. There was only time for one look, but it was enough. It reduced Peter to that abyss of self-despair from which new life can spring. "The Lord looked at Peter, and he went out, and wept bitterly."

I. What was it that Jesus saw when he looked at Peter?

Peter had a façade of strength concealing an inner insecurity. Jesus saw through this. But he saw also all the hidden gold—all that the world's eye fails to see. He saw the ardent love, the latent courage, the faith that on other occasions had conquered doubts and hesitations. He saw in Peter's volatile nature that which could become rock on which he could build.

What did Peter see? He saw himself mirrored in those eyes of Jesus. That is what we can always see if we let ourselves come face to face with him. The first reaction was a sense of shame and self-loathing. How could he have been so base? That question must have stabbed at his heart.

His self-assurance had never before been broken and only now did he realize how unfit he was to be a disciple. Sometimes it needs a "killing sin," as Stevenson calls it, to break those hidden roots of self-confidence and to force us to throw ourselves in utter dependence upon the mercy of God.

II. In that look of Jesus was the love that never lets us go, an infinite compassion. It was always there when Jesus looked at people. To us a crowd is often a very unattractive thing. Sometimes it is menacing. The worst passions may come to the surface and take control of many who by themselves are kindly, reasonable men.

But when Jesus looked at a crowd he was filled with compassion. He saw how blind and helpless they were in their frustration. We are told that "when he saw the multitude he was moved with compassion because they fainted, and were scattered abroad, as sheep having no shepherd."

Even while they were crucifying him he prayed, "Father, forgive them, for they know not what they do." This compassion was in his eyes as he looked at Peter. He saw him in the grip of forces that Peter did not understand and could not control.

III. But there was more in the compassion of Jesus as he looked at Peter. There was hope and the assurance of an indestructible friendship. This must have helped to keep Peter near the cross when Jesus died. It held him from going out into the darkness. He still visited the upper room and later went with John to the empty tomb of Jesus.

It was a glimmer of faith and a tiny ray of hope that sent him there. He could not forget the Last Supper when Jesus had broken bread and given it to them and said, "This is my body broken for you." It was as if he had said to them in effect, Remember, whatever happens, nothing is going to separate me from you. Nothing will ever make me give you up, not even my death, not even your sin.

The bond between us and Christ when we have accepted his love is forever—the one thing in all the universe which is finally indestructible. Whatever may befall us at the hands of life, or tempt us from the road, whatever darkness may gather round us, this love will hold.—Adapted from James Reid.

**Suggested Texts and Themes**

Divine Oxygen: ". . . and his windows being open in his chamber toward Jerusalem. . . ." Dan. 6:10.

Fruit in Its Season: "We should bring forth fruit unto God." Rom. 7:4.

The Homing Instinct of the Soul: "The Spirit itself beareth witness with our spirit, that we are the children of God." Rom. 8:16.

Rocks on Either Side: "And between the passages, by which Jonathan sought to go over unto the Philistines' garrison, there was a sharp rock on the one side, and a sharp rock on the other side. . . ." I Sam. 14:4.

A Beautiful World: Isa. 35:1, 2.

## MIDWEEK FELLOWSHIP MEETING TOPIC

(Church Night or Suggested Sermon Subject)

**Theme: Silences**

TEXT: "Be still, and know that I am God." Ps. 46:10.

When the sun goeth forth in the morning, when the moon riseth in the evening, when the stars come out one by one and go back one by one, the movement of star and sun and all heavenly bodies is in silence.

I. Growth is silent. Without noise a great tree lifts itself into the air. Without noise a garden clothes itself with beauty or an orchard with fruitfulness. The human body grows without the creaking of joints or the rattle of bones. Growth is silent.

II. Nature is to a great degree silent. "I will lift up mine eyes unto the hills," yet when I incline mine ear they are mute. "The hills are mute: yet how they speak of God!"

III. The depths of the sea are a great silence. The air above us and the stratosphere are silent. The earth itself is not noisy. It is only city streets and highways that drown out silence. The mountains and the deserts, the heights and depths, are silent.

IV. Love in its deeper expression is silent. The unspoken word is often more eloquent than the spoken. When love is on the wire it can easily be drowned out with inconsequential chatter. We remember that the divinest Gift that love ever made was on a quiet night at Bethlehem underneath the silent stars. A bomb did not explode at Bethlehem; a Baby was born!

V. We must keep silent spaces in our hearts where in the stillness God may become known. "Be still, and know that I am God."—H.

## SUNDAY SCHOOL LESSON

**Aug. 10. Justice in Government. Deut. 16:18-20; Amos 5:12-15; Rom. 13:1-7. Background Scripture: Deut. 17:14-20; I Kings 3:5-13.**

Memory Verse: "Teach me to do thy will, for thou art my God!" Ps. 143:10.

I. Just government is a divinely imposed obligation. This was so with the ancient Israelites. Does this idea still hold?

II. Does just government impose any duties upon citizenship? Distinguish between rights of citizenship, duties, and privileges. Can a man be strong for his rights and weak toward his duties? What about the man or woman who does not vote on Election Day? If justice in government is the responsibility of both the leader and the electorate, does this responsibility carry with it the obligation to work against injustice? to withstand injustice? to rebel against injustice? even to go to war that justice may be established?

III. It is the ideal that those who rule do so as servants of God. This being so, a man should not withdraw from political responsibility just because he doesn't want to get into "dirty politics." He should keep sensitive to God's call in this as in all other matters.

---

# SUNDAY: AUGUST SEVENTEENTH

---

## MORNING SERVICE

**Theme: What Your Hope Makes Possible**

Suggested Scripture Reading: Rom. 5:1-5, 8:24-28, 15:4; or Col. 1:1-14.

Selected Hymns: "Our God, our help in ages past."—Isaac Watts. "Spirit of God, descend upon my heart."—George Croly. "Blest be the tie that binds."—John Fawcett. "Love divine, all loves excelling."—Charles Wesley.

Opening Sentences: "Blessed is the man that trusteth in the Lord, and whose hope the Lord is." Jer. 17:7. "It is good that a man should both hope and quietly wait for the salvation of the Lord." Lam. 3:26.

Invocation: Almighty God, who hast walked with us along every pathway of daily duty and hast given us strength to do our tasks, meet with us, too, as we gather for fellowship and worship.

Release in us holy desires and high aspirations that by these thou mayst bless us, and send us forth to let our lights shine before men, that they may see our good works, and give glory to thee. In the name of our Lord and Saviour, Jesus Christ. Amen.—H.

**Theme: What Your Hope Makes Possible**

TEXT: "Rejoice in your hope." Rom. 12:12 (R.S.V.). "Let your hope be a joy to you" (Moffatt). "Base your happiness in your hope in Christ" (Phillips).

INTRODUCTION: 1. The Definition and Illustration of Hope.

(a) Hope is not just wishful thinking. "I wish to go to Spain" and "I hope to go to Spain" are very different in their meaning as anyone will recognize.

(b) It is difficult to distinguish faith and hope. I find them like identical twins. They look very much alike. Yet each stands alone. Paul places them side by side: "And now abideth faith, hope, love." Faith is at the left hand of hope, and hope at the right hand of faith; they support each other. Faith that is linked with hope brings the greater confidence; hope that is attached to faith brings the greater joy. Faith gives a man a foundation; hope gives him a goal. The opposite of faith is doubt; the opposite of hope is despair.

(c) It is easier to illustrate hope than to define it. I said to a little girl, "How old are you?" She replied, "I'm five, going on six." Those words "going on six"—that's hope.

2. The Present-day Need for Hope. As regards hope we belong to a disillusioned generation. All our easy hopes, akin to wishful thinking, have disintegrated.

(a) Two great wars, a lot of little wars, false philosophies and inadequate ideologies, tyrannical leaders, the imperialistic aims of nations, have brought millions to despair.

(b) When you read the daily paper and glance at the stories of suicide, murder, often both, do you ever stop to think of the deep human despair out of which these come?

(c) Think of the stagnant lives, the men and women trying to escape their hopeless states, those who drown their lack of hope by absorption in the trivial and the unworthy.

(d) "The hunger of every heart is for hope. We cannot live without hope. Sometimes we go along without consciously thinking of it, in the tranquil times. But in the hour of crisis we see what has been there all the time; hope is as essential to living as breathing and food and rest."—J. B. Phillips. It is not only essential that individuals have a genuine hope. It is the need of peoples, of nations; look abroad and see that this is true.

What then does your hope make possible? Why can we base our happiness upon hope? Hope does something for us. Hope does something in us. Hope does something through us.

I. Hope Does Something for Us. 1. It leads us on. (a) Time pushes us on. (b) Circumstances may push us around.

2. Hope carries a man through. Give me tomorrow and I can go through anything today. Consider Paul's going through. It was written of Jesus that for the joy that was set before him he endured the Cross. Christ's hope carried him through and that was the basis for his joy.

3. Hope lifts a man up. Often the way up is through. The goal which genuine hope gives a man is always an elevation. Life becomes an ascent. He may have to go through a valley, but the narrow valley leads to a mountain. If you press toward the prize you will generally find it an uphill road.

Hope lifts. To a mountain climber there is something magnetic about the summit of a mountain. There is something magnetic about a goal.

4. Hope places a man above. Hope gives a man a sense of attainment. Did you ever hear a person say when tempted, "I'm above that!"? Hope places a man above the petty, the trivial, the sinful. There is purer air where hope places a man. There is wider outlook. There is deeper peace.

II. Hope does something in a man. 1. It gives him an indomitable optimism. 2. It gives him "dogged endurance." 3.

It gives him a joyful temper.

III. Hope does something through a man. Consider all the things that have been done by men when their hope was kindled. By hope the *Mayflower* crossed the Atlantic and all the consequences of that may be credited to hope.

By hope the Founding Fathers of our nation gave us the Declaration of Independence, the Constitution with its Bill of Rights. . . .

By hope all that we dream of good comes to pass.

What then shall men hope for? I suppose that a man should have three kinds of hope: basic hopes, creative hopes, "little" hopes. A man should have great basic fundamental hopes, like the old Greek hopes—the attainment of truth, the appreciation of beauty, the achievement of goodness. Or the hope which was Hebrew: "Blessed is the man that trusteth in the Lord, whose hope the Lord is." Or the hopes which are Christian: the hope of salvation, the hope of holiness, the hope of glory, the hope which is laid up for us in heaven, the hope of eternal life, the hope of becoming that which it hath not yet appeared that we shall be. In such hopes men have their being. By such hopes they live. These are the basis of joy.

There are also hopes by which we build a better world. These are creative. These are the hopes which we share with one another and in which we co-operate for the common good. By such hopes we bring health and strength and beauty and goodness and the Christian spirit to the social order. These are the hopes to which we dedicate our vocations, our time, our talents, our wealth.

Then we should have little hopes which make life rich and sweet. It is the hope of the little girl, "I'm going on six." The instinctive hope of the older girl as she plays with her dolls, of the boy as he tinkers with his tools. It is the hope expressed in a hope chest, in passing an examination at school. It is the dream of owning a home, of becoming a better man or women, of being a good example to John and to Jane, of gathering strength and beauty for old age. What could we do without our little hopes?

By hope we become men. By hope we are saved. By hope we attain glory. By hope we become happy and joyous men and women.—H.

A Prayer for the Day: O God, who rulest the world from end to end and from everlasting to everlasting; speak to our hearts when courage fails, and men faint for fear, and the love of many grows cold, and there is distress of the nations upon the earth. Keep us resolute and steadfast in the things that cannot be shaken, abounding in hope and knowing that our labor is not in vain in thee. Restore our faith in the omnipotence of good; renew in us the love which never faileth; and make us to lift up our eyes and behold, beyond the things which are seen and temporal, the things which are unseen and eternal; through Jesus Christ our Lord. Amen. —*A Free Church Book of Common Prayer.*

Offertory Sentence: "Even so faith, if it hath not works, is dead, being alone."

Offertory Prayer: May we show our faith, our Father, not only in word but also in deed. May it be a joy to us that we have opportunity to give ourselves and of our substance to thy service. Amen.

Seed Thoughts:

The Function of Hope. I. Hope is a door. Hos. 2:15. II. Hope is a helmet. I Thess. 5:8. III. Hope is an anchor (especially a kedge anchor). Heb. 6:19.

The New Vision. During the last half-century men have become aware of the possibility that every person may reasonably hope for such a freedom from disease, destitution, and ignorance that he can take a responsible share in the great human enterprise. Man's new vision is that *every* person is important, and that we should turn our great new powers toward giving *every* person his proper chance. The growth of this new vision is itself one of the most significant changes in modern society.—Arthur Compton.

### Choice Illustrations on the Theme

HOPE SEES A STAR. In the sight of death, hope sees a star and listening love can hear the rustle of a wing.——Robert G. Ingersoll.

MEN CANNOT LIVE WITHOUT HOPE. From Novgorod to Cadiz, from Jerusalem to the Hebrides, steeples and spires raised themselves precariously into the sky because men cannot live without hope.—Will Durant, *The Age of Faith.*

GIVE ME TOMORROW. One bitter cold morning in Korea, according to Margaret Higgins who tells the story, a group of marines just back from combat were clustered around a truck trying to eat some breakfast. Breakfast consisted of cold beans eaten with a trench knife. A correspondent walked up to one of the men who was showing all the evidence of battle fatigue, his face covered with a heavy beard, his clothes encrusted with mud, and himself stiff with the cold. The correspondent asked a very strange question. I can't imagine what prompted him to phrase it in this way. But he did. He said to the marine, "If I were God and could grant you anything you wanted, what would you like most?" The man stood motionless as though he hadn't heard for a moment, and then gave a strange yet revealing answer, "Give me tomorrow," he said. It is a hunger rooted in every heart. We cannot live without hope.—Gene E. Bartlett.

## EVENING SERVICE

### Theme: Recovery of Righteousness

TEXT: "Blessed is the man that walketh not in the counsel of the ungodly, nor standeth in the way of sinners, nor sitteth in the seat of the scornful. But his delight is in the law of the Lord; and in his law doth he meditate day and night." Ps. 1:1, 2.

A famous historian lists nineteen civilizations which have flourished and disappeared. He points out that only three of these were overcome by outside forces; sixteen of them decayed from within. The outward manisfestations of this inner decay have been threefold; namely, drunkenness, idleness, and immorality. This means that strong civilizations have been characterized by sobriety, industry, and clean moral living.

If this be true of civilizations it is also true of individuals, for personality also decays from within. Men can withstand almost any outward pressure so long as the inward character is intact and strong. We break outside because we have first broken inside.

There is, therefore, no greater need before us today than the recovery of plain, everyday righteousness.

What are the roads that lead to the recovery of righteousness?

I. We must realize that tolerance of sin destroys personal character and undermines good society. We live in a time when sin has become respectable. It has moved out of the gutter into the drawingroom. It comes dressed up in the popular novel, the seductive advertisement, the technicolor movie.

We need to learn again one of the stern facts of life. Sin destroys! Sin kills character, betrays homes, blights personality, undermines society. Sin is not old-fashioned nor out of date. It is a real and living threat to men and nations, and to tolerate sin in any form is to invite it to take over.

The moral laws of God can't be broken without suffering and we must know it. We must recover a sharp sense of right and wrong.

II. We will move in the direction of the recovery of righteousness when we recognize the drink evil as the chief cause of crime and depravity. We have a public conscience against every other major evil except this one which is itself at the root of so many of the others. No man nor nation will walk the road of righteousness until this ugly menace is recognized and renounced.

III. The recovery of righteousness is dependent on the recovery of Godliness. Morality cannot be divorced from religion. When our codes of behavior have no other roots than the habits and customs of the people we are headed downhill. It is when we forget God that our ethical ideals and moral disciplines weaken, and give way. The good man is the basis of the good society.

God-centered righteousness is not a dull and negative thing. It is the source of happiness and security. "Mark the perfect man, and behold the upright: for the end of that man is peace."

Here, then, is the very heart of our problem and the key to its solution. We need to know that this is a moral universe and that right and wrong have eternal significance. We can't do as we please on moral issues without paying the penalty in personal unhappiness and social degeneration. Right and wrong are not decided by majority vote.

We don't make our own rules of conduct. We get them from God. The moral commandments of God have not been outgrown. And men and nations who try to sidestep or ignore them will be broken upon them.—Charles M. Crowe.

**Suggested Texts and Themes**

I. Looking at Me: "And take heed to yourselves. . . ." Luke 21:34.

An Isle of Safety: "The sabbath was made for man, and not man for the sabbath." Mark 2:27.

The School of Silence: "Be still, and know that I am God."

Magnifying the Commonplace: "And the Lord said unto him, What is that in thine hand? And he said, A rod." Exod. 4:2.

Advertisements of God: "The heavens declare the glory of God; and the firmament showeth his handiwork." Ps. 19:1.

## MIDWEEK FELLOWSHIP MEETING TOPIC

(Church Night or Suggested Sermon Subject)

**Theme: Truth from a Tree**

I walked through a forest glade and stood before a patriarch of pines. There it stood, bearing the scars of flame and flood, centuries old in Abraham's day, its life half lived when the Star of Bethlehem led the Wise Men to the manger.

I said, "Tree, you've lived wisely and well. Be my teacher. Teach me the truths you have learned."

For a moment there was silence. The wind rustled in the high branches of the forest. A hawk paused, then wheeled in its flight. Then it seemed I heard the old tree speak.

I. "O mortal man, you who are so easily impressed with the immense, we can teach you the art of contentment, the satisfaction of the timeless with small beginnings: Behold our seed!"

II. "You who worship action and strive for quick results, we can teach you patience, the tremendous truth that all that is great develops slowly."

III. "You who stoop to conquer, who so often sacrifice principle for prestige, we can teach you to stand straight and unashamed."

IV. "You who strive and compete, who visit famine and fire upon one another, commit violence beyond brutality of the beast—we of the forest know that we need one another. We can teach you the meaning of brotherhood."

V. "You so often satisfied with your present state, we can teach the meaning of growth, a vitality increasing in stature."

VI. "You who so often affirm God in your heads but deny him in your hearts, as we thrust our roots deep into the soil which gives us nourishment, and our branches toward the light which gives us life, we can teach you the meaning of faith, of hope, of love."—Donald E. Roberts.

## SUNDAY SCHOOL LESSON

**Aug. 17. Justice to Minorities. Lev. 19:33,34; Deut. 24:14,15; Matt. 9:9-13; Gal. 3:28. Background Scripture: Lev. 19:33-37; Deut. 23:7,8; John 4:7-9, 39-41; Gal. 3:26-28.**

MEMORY VERSE: "Let brotherly love continue. Do not neglect to show hospitality to strangers, for thereby some have entertained angels unawares." Heb. 13:1-2 (R.S.V.).

I. In this lesson the members of the class should become acquainted with the injustices suffered by minority groups because of color, race, nationality, or religion.

II. Young people especially might face up to the injustices suffered by members of their own groups because of personality defects, cliques, snobbishness, physical handicaps, etc.

III. Look then at the problem of social justice from the standpoint of racial and other minority groups in society: immigrants and displaced persons (Lev. 19:33-34; Deut. 24:14-15); oppressed and exploited people (Matt. 9:9-13); racial and cultural minorities (John 4:7-9, 39-41; Gal. 3:28); ill-treated persons (Heb. 13:1-2).

IV. It is the duty and privilege of Christians to seek out these minority groups and help them to secure justice and equal rights. Positive means and methods of implementing the teachings of the Bible in view of these injustices should be suggested.

# SUNDAY: AUGUST TWENTY-FOURTH

## MORNING SERVICE

**Theme: What Love Makes Possible**

SUGGESTED SCRIPTURE READING: I Cor. 13 or I John 4:7-21.

SELECTED HYMNS: "For the beauty of the earth."—F. S. Pierpont. "God is love, his mercy brightens."—John Bowring. "O Love, that will not let me go."—George Matheson. "Ye servants of God, your Master proclaim."—Charles Wesley.

CALL TO WORSHIP: "A new commandment I give unto you, That ye love one another; as I have loved you, that ye also love one another. By this shall all men know that ye are my disciples, if ye have love one to another." John 13:34, 35.

INVOCATION: We worship thee, our Father, because thou art a God of love. When we have forgotten that we are thy children, thou didst continue mindful of us. When we turned our hearts from thee, thou didst turn thy heart toward us. When we were busy following our own ways, thou wast watching over us and caring for us. We thank thee for thy loving providence.

Grant us again thy presence, and may our hearts be responsive unto thee, showing toward thee that divine passion which thou dost manifest toward us. Amen.—H.

**Theme: What Love Makes Possible**

TEXT: ". . . but the greatest of these is love." I Cor. 13:13.

INTRODUCTORY: Dealing with Superlatives. "The *greatest* of these is love." In considering love you are dealing with ultimates and superlatives, and these are hard to handle. Here are some of the superlatives related to love. (Of course, we mean love in the highest Christian sense.)

The finest pronouncement or essay concerning love seems to have been written. Paul's essay, I Cor. 13.

The best sermon seems to have been preached—Henry Drummond's *The Greatest Thing in the World.*

The most fundamental fact has been established—God is Love.

The most poignant drama has been played upon the stage of time—the Drama of Love: Creation, Redemption, Destiny.

The sublimest deed has been done—Calvary, the Cross.

The ultimate energy has been released—the love-energy. "We love, because he first loved us."

The uttermost failure is known—"the uttermost failure is not to love." (See illustration.)

What does love make possible? I. Love does something for us. What does love do for us? Love gives us infinite value. 1. Examples of love giving value: a mother values her babe; a man values his friend.

2. God is love: he gives us value. (a) He gives us intrinsic value; he makes us in his own image. (b) He gives us relative value; in this wonderful world in which we live, man is the highest and noblest of God's creations. (c) Man is the recipient of God's providence. He gives us care value. Can God's care be less than an expression of his love? God's discipline is God's care, God's love. (d) Redemptive value of man. The redemption wrought out by Christ is a revelation of God's love. When a man has been died for, redeemed, what infinite value it places upon him! (e) Man's destiny value is a value given to him by God's love. "It does not yet appear what we shall be. . . ."

II. What does love do in a man? Above, the functional value of man has been deliberately omitted, because we need to look at it separately. The function of a man is to love and be loved. That is the nature of God, to love and be loved. That is the function of Christ.

Then what does love do in a man. Love makes him loving. That is the process that you and I are in.

1. God's love makes loving men. (a) There are differences in response. Some men are pliable. Some are recalcitrant. Some are like shifting sand—Peter. There is necessity for discipline.

2. Examples of God's love making loving men.

3. The changes in men which take place in the process. See the character of love in Paul's essay. God makes us patient, kind, generous, humble, courteous, unselfish, good tempered, guileless, sincere. Then we shall become saints? Yes. Recall the African chief's remark when he became a Christian: "I'm condemned to be a saint."

4. We must not misunderstand this matter. God does not make us loving by sprinkling holy water upon us. Love is not applied by putting us into a perfumed bath. There is a line of an old Gospel hymn that is nearer the truth. It asks, "Are you washed in the blood of the Lamb?" It must not be forgotten that to put us in the process of becoming loving men and women Christ died upon the Cross. We are obstinate, sinful, hard material to endue with love-energy. God's method cannot be entered into here. We are considering only what love makes possible. It is possible that you will become a loving person.

III. Love does something through us. It spreads love in the world. 1. As a kind of divine contagion. 2. Like a flow of water. Love is like a river that flows from its source in God. It refreshes, purifies, empowers, beautifies, transforms the desert into a garden, gives buoyancy and joy. Love is not like a dry western river; "love never faileth." See Rev. 22:1. 2.

The river of love flows from its source in God. It flows into the world through men and women, through you and me, a trickling stream in some, a mighty flow in others; but wherever love goes something happens; hope is nourished, faith is enlarged, homes are sweetened, human relations become kinder, men cease hurting one another, men forgive one another, old wounds are healed, and all antagonisms, great and small, are ended. Sympathy prevails. Men take up their crosses. Men lay down their lives for their fellow men. Even the healing of the nations will come to pass under the tidal flow of love.—H.

A Prayer for the Day: We thank thee, our Father, for the many and various ways in which we experience thy love. For the light of each new day wherein we can live and labor; for the bountiful provision for our daily needs; for those about us who share their lives with us in friendship; for the grace which forgiveth our sins and healeth our diseases; for the strength that overwhelms our weakness and the comfort that assuages our sorrow; for the hopes that carry us through difficulties and lift us into the heavenlies; for the blessed sleep that restores our wearied bodies and revives our spirits—for these and all the other tokens of thy love, we give thee thanks. Amen.—H.

OFFERTORY SENTENCE: "If ye fulfill the royal law according to the scriptures, Thou shalt love thy neighbor as thyself, ye do well." James 2:8.

OFFERTORY PRAYER: Help us, our Father, to give our offering as an expression of our love toward thee and toward our neighbor. In Jesus' name. Amen. —H.

SEED THOUGHTS:

The Foundation Truth: God is love.

The Failure of a Loveless Life. Our first impression as we read what Paul wrote to the Corinthians so long ago is that a loveless life is sure to be a failure. There may be the gift of brilliant and compelling speech, but if there is no love back of it, the eloquence is metallic and without true life. There may be the sharpest intellectual discrimination, but without love it is impotent. There may be a very definite faith; if loveless, it may move mountains, but it cannot move hearts. There may be a perfect asceticism of self-sacrifice; but a loveless, self-conscious sacrifice is most unprofitable. These other things have no soul unless love dwells within. Then they are great indeed. Eloquence has not only light but heat when it is the speech of love. Knowledge is warm and vivifying when the man who knows is also a man who loves. Faith glows with new meaning and potency when love shines through it. And self-sacrifice is the most creative thing in the world when it is the self-abandon of love.—Author Unknown.

### Choice Illustrations on the Theme

QUOTATIONS. "If I have not love, I am nothing."—Paul.

"He who loves not lives not."—Ramon Lull.

"Not where I breathe, but where I live, I love."—Robert Sothwell.

Life with all it yields of joy and woe,
And hope and fear . . .
Is just our chance o' the prize of learning love.
— Robert Browning.

THE UTTERMOST FAILURE. A letter once appeared in The London *Times,* written by a young woman. The letter was found upon her body after she had killed herself. The letter read:

"I am killing myself because I have never sincerely loved any human being in all my life. I have accepted kindness and friendship and even love without gratitude and give nothing in return."

The letter was followed in the newspaper with this sentence: "The coroner recorded a verdict of 'Suicide while of unsound mind.'"

I think it was Harry Emerson Fosdick who made the following comment: "I read that verdict of the coroner with a shock, for surely no more rational statement of the failure of life was ever made."

GOD'S GREAT LOVES. Edward Irving went to see a dying boy once, and when he entered the room he just put his hand on the sufferer's head and said, "My boy, God loves you," and went away. And the boy started from his bed and called to the people in the house, "God loves me! God loves me!" It changed that boy. The sense that God loved him overpowered him, melted him down, and began creating a new heart in him.

INFLUENCE OF LOVE. What we love we shall grow to resemble.—Bernard of Clairvaux.

## EVENING SERVICE

### Theme: The Lost Beatitude

TEXT: "Blessed are they that have not seen, and yet have believed." John 20:29.

When we think of those who must believe even when they cannot see, it makes us think of needs which are very evident in this present hour. It has a special word for twentieth-century people like us.

I. The Experience Waiting for Completion. First, it speaks to those of us whose religious experience is incomplete. There are many whose experience is good as far as it goes. But it has not yet come to that fulfillment to which Christ invited the soul of every man.

Has not God invited us to fullness of life and fellowship with him? And the world does carry its own evidence that he lives. Here is the warmth of loving hands that welcomed us to the world. Here are the things of beauty. Here is the orderliness and the work of those who serve in his name. And now you must have faith that if you will wait in confidence and expectation, he will come to you as he promised, and you shall know him, as it were, face to face.

This is what I mean by the experience waiting for completion; there is sufficient evidence to give our hearts confidence to wait, that he, indeed, will come to us face to face. It is to those who have gone so far but not far enough that this word comes with pointed reality, "Blessed are those who have not seen and yet believe."

II. A word for the Wistful. Again, this speaks with special meaning to those who are wistful. If the Gospel is to reach hearts of men as they are today, we must not leave out those who have searched and not found, listened but not heard, knocked but waited in vain for faith to be opened to them. Jesus said it truly when he called the believer, blessed, which means happy. There are so many of us who would be so grateful to be blessed that way, but who, having done all that we know, find ourselves outside looking in, wistful and hungry, but not knowing how to overcome our wistfulness.

It is interesting to consider how much we live in other realms of life by things we have not and never will see. We are totally dependent upon the things unseen. At this moment our lives are sustained by oxygen. If the supply were cut off, we should die in moments. Yet it is unseen. We shall never be able to see it. We shall only have to live by it. Physically every moment of the day a thousand silent processes go on within our bodies that make life possible. We do not ask for them. They were the gift of God, and they go on without our direction.

When Christ called upon us to believe where we could not see, he was standing in the midst of a world which God had already made upon this law and this necessity.

If there are some here today, wistful, searching, and hoping, why not open your heart to another great unseen force which is here by the gift of God, the living, loving, and available spirit of Jesus Christ, ready at your decision to enter into your life with healing and hope? It is to the wistful that the word of Christ comes with such meaning.

III. Spiritual Need of the Suffering. We could not deal with this matter without touching a third modern need. It is the spiritual need of those who are passing through suffering. The spiritual side of suffering is often the most acute part of it. It is exactly to these who pass through suffering, both known and unknown, that this beatitude speaks.

We should be amazed beyond words if we could know how many souls await in spiritual hunger and suffering for a comforting and saving word. If that should be you, I beg you to hear that word today, for your suffering can be lifted by one who said, "Blessed are those who have not seen and yet believe."

IV. Meaning for lives without Purpose. Finally, in this modern world there are those who feel their lives to be without any purpose. They are like the lost coin in Jesus' parable.

But the coin was found. Jesus lays his claim upon us. We are needed. He has work for us to do. Blessed are those who are willing to be found by the Christ. Blessed are those who hearing this believe where they cannot see.—Gene E. Bartlett.

**Suggested Texts and Themes (G. H. Morrison)**

The Failure of the Brook: "And it came to pass after a while, that the brook dried up, because there had been no rain in the land." I Kings 17:7.

Drink from the Depths: "He clave the rocks in the wilderness, and gave them drink as out of the great depths." Ps. 78:15.

The Ministry of the Sea: "The sea is his, and he made it." Ps. 95:5.

The Tidings of the Breeze: "The wind bloweth where it listeth, and thou hearest the sound thereof. . . ." John 3:8.

The Message of the Rainbow: "I do set my bow in the cloud, and it shall be for a token of a covenant between me and the earth." Gen. 9:13.

## MIDWEEK FELLOWSHIP MEETING TOPIC

(Church Night or Suggested Sermon Subject)

**Theme: The Double "If"**

TEXT: "If ye know these things, blessed are ye if ye do them." John 13: 17.

Our blessedness is thus doubly conditioned. We must both know and do that we may receive the Master's commendation.

I. Knowing and doing are the twin pillars, Joachin and Boaz, on which the house of happiness is built.

II. The familiar legend of service told by Dr. Henry van Dyke in poetry carries a great lesson. The city of Lupon was blessed with three men of great piety, one very wise, one very eloquent, and one very loving. An angel inquired of the Lord which of the three loved God best. To obtain an answer, the angel was sent bearing a message to each of the men. To each was given the same commission, to go across the snows to Spiran's huts, to perform a task which was not yet revealed. The angel delivered his message. The great preacher received the summons with the question, "Why?" The wise man answered "How?" The loving man started up eagerly crying "When?" "Now," said the angel, and added:

Thou hast met the Master's bidden test,
And I have found the man that
loved Him best.

III. Our actions must be the ultimate test of our love. We may know—and we do know—but unless we act upon this knowledge, we may find ourselves among those of whom the Christ spoke when he said: "Not every one that saith unto me, Lord, Lord, shall enter into the kingdom of heaven, but he that doeth the will of my Father who is in heaven."—J.A.M.

## SUNDAY SCHOOL LESSON

**Aug. 24. Justice among Nations. Mic. 4:1-7; Acts 10:34-35; Eph. 2:13-16. Background Scripture: Isa. 30:1-5, 15-18, 31: 1-3; Mal. 2:10; Acts 10:25-35; Eph. 2:13-3:21.**

MEMORY VERSES: "Great and wonderful are thy deeds, O Lord God the Almighty! Just and true are thy ways, O King of the ages! Who shall not fear and glorify thy name, O Lord? For thou alone art holy. All nations shall come and worship thee, for thy judgments have been revealed." Rev. 15:3-4.

I. The Isaiah passages point out the folly of military alliances which take the place of trust in God and righteous conduct on the part of a nation. II. The prophet Micah envisions a warless world based on international justice and good will under the rulership of God. III. Acts 10:25-35 is a plea for international friendship. IV. Eph. 2:13-3:21 exalts Christ as maker of peace between people at enmity.

# SUNDAY: AUGUST THIRTY-FIRST

## MORNING SERVICE

**Theme: The Life Worth Living (Labor Sunday)**

Suggested Scripture Reading: Luke, 19:12-26 or Rom. 12.

Selected Hymns: "Lead on, O King Eternal."—E. W. Shurtleff. "Jesus calls us o'er the tumult."—Cecil F. Alexander. "A charge to keep I have."—Charles Wesley. "Soldiers of Christ, arise."—Charles Wesley.

Call to Worship: May this service of Worship influence our lives throughout the coming days. This week may we go to work knowing that we serve both God and man, and that we are no longer living in two different worlds, diverse in their aims and purposes, but rather knowing that we live in our Father's world, where in serving God we are serving man, and in serving man we are serving God."—Quoted from a Workers' Study Group Report.

Invocation: We come before thee, O God, to worship thee. We bring unto thee for blessing our working days, with all their economic and social production, in terms of goods and services and human relations and personal experiences. In Jesus' name. Amen.

**Theme: The Life Worth Living (Labor Sunday)**

Text: "Think soberly, according as God hath dealt to every man the measure of faith." Rom. 12:3.

There is a native desire in each one of us to live a life worth living. What is it that drives some to miserliness, some to drink, and some to a thousand-and-one other abnormalities but an urge to find something satisfying, some sense of adequate living? Is there anyone who wouldn't like to be able at the age of eighty-four to look back on it all, as Sherwood Eddy recently did in writing his autobiography, and say, "It seems one glorious adventure"? I believe that Christianity has something to say about the life worth living and I propose that we think a little about it.

I. One ingredient of a life worth living is a *work fit to live for.* I was talking with a man once and he told me that one of the things he liked most about his particular business was its social by-products. I thought he was talking about the interesting people he met, "important" social contacts he made, and so on. Not so. He was speaking of the valuable effect his particular line of work had on the economy as a whole, the contribution it made to the community's life. A feeling like that about one's work—says Christianity—is every man's privilege. And if he does something for a living which does not or cannot yield that return he will never find a life worth living at all.

The word "vocation" literally means calling. God calls every man to work fit to live for. Vocation is not synonymous with occupation. There are lots of occupations not fit to be vocations. Only socially useful work faithfully performed can be a vocation.

II. A second is a *self fit to live with.* You can never get away from yourself. You are your own constant companion and if you aren't fit to live with life isn't going to be worth living. A cartoon once showed a physician facing his patient with an anxious look, saying, "This is a very serious case; I'm afraid you're allergic to yourself."

Jesus once declared that a man is accountable for every careless word he speaks. What is the careless word? It is the unguarded word. It is the word we speak off the record. What I say in this pulpit is not necessarily a revelation of what I am; I am on guard here. The unguarded word, the careless word, is the one that reveals my true self. What is the self that your careless words reveal? Is it one fit to live with?

The good news of Christianity is that this so un-ideal self can be transformed under the inspiration of Christ into one fit to live with. You have heard of doing something so often that it becomes "second nature" to us. So Christianity says that under the tutelage of Christ we can learn of him until Christlikeness is "second nature" to us. With his help we put off the old man and put on the new. As Paul puts it, we are transformed by the renewal of our minds.

III. A third ingredient of the life worth living is *a faith fit to live in.* There is a sense in which it can be said that we each make the house of faith in which we live. Many of us throw up such an improvisation of miscellaneous feelings and notions that when the real test comes it collapses.

Maybe our house of faith collapses before the onslaught of criticism; maybe it's not big enough to include all truth and we dare not expose it to the findings of geology or biology. Charles Clayton Morrison has told how as a student with his first church he was sure that the doctrines of evolution and higher criticism would fatally undermine Christianity. Then he read some of Henry Drummond's writings and found a faith fit to live in in the twentieth century.

For everyone whose house of faith has been smashed by new ideas, however, there are a hundred whose faith is not adequate for personal disaster and misfortune. Again, the good news of Christianity is that there is a faith fit even for tough times. Sickness closes in on a man. The doors shut on every side; his active life is gone; he seems little more than a rat in a trap. And then the amazing resources of vital faith begin to show. Opportunities restricted but insight deepened, he becomes as inwardly radiant as he was once outwardly active, and men and women are drawn to him sensing the reality of the spiritual life. The northeast winds seem to strengthen the fiber of the man with a faith fit to live in; hardship leaves him a better man; bereavement makes him gentler and more sympathetic than he was before.

Be sure your faith is one fit to live in!
—Raymond E. Balcomb.

PRAYER FOR THE DAY: Almighty Lord, who hast commanded that no man should be idle, uphold us in the duties of that state of life to which thou hast been pleased to call us; and let thy blessing be upon us, our labors, and upon all that belongs to us. Give us grace that we may honestly improve the talents which thou hast committed to our trust, and that no wordly business, no worldly pleasures, may ever divert us from our preparation for the life to come. And this we pray through our only Mediator, Jesus Christ. Amen.

OFFERTORY SENTENCE: "The earth is the Lord's and the fulness thereof." "It is he that giveth thee power to get wealth."

OFFERTORY PRAYER: Eternal Father, Maker of heaven and earth, who didst reveal thyself to mankind as the carpenter's Son, help us to see the value of all our labor. We acknowledge thee as the creator of strength for labor, capital for industry, and the natural wealth of the earth. Receive our gifts today in recognition of our dependence upon thee and all of mankind as co-laborers in the work of thy Kingdom. We pray in Christ's name. Amen.

SEED THOUGHTS:

From a Workers' Study Group Report. We regard work as a God-given instrument which man must use to enable him to grow in grace and wisdom, and so enter into the more abundant life, wherein lies his salvation. This abundant life, the gift of God in Jesus Christ, demands that through work man shall be able to express his love toward God and man.

Therefore, the development of men as living souls depends upon these divine-human relations being realizable through the instrument of work, otherwise a large part of man's life is existing undedicated and alienated from its true source of joy and happiness.

Given this spiritual priority in the use of work, we believe that the social and economic sides of industry will gain immeasurably. Dividends, wages, living standards, will be looked at from the point of view that industry produces men as well as goods.

And if we can conceive of a Christian doctrine of work in such terms, we shall be able to state that production is for man and not man for production; and we shall have gone some distance in solving this problem of the divorce between the worker as a person and the work he performs. Such an outlook upon work would demand an entirely new approach to work by workers and employers; and just as work comes under the conversion of the Word of the Living God, so must all who participate in work come under the conversion of the same Word.—Group of Aberdeen, Scotland, Corporation Transport Workers.

**Choice Illustrations on the Theme**

MEANING IN LIFE. When life becomes meaningless, nothing really matters.

We are like the man hired by a psychologist for an experiment. He was taken to the back yard and given an ax.

"Do you see that log lying there?"

The man nodded.

"I want you to make like you're chopping wood; only I want you to use the *back* side of the ax, not the blade. I'll give you three dollars an hour."

The hired man thought the psychologist was crazy; but the pay sounded fine, so he set to work.

After a couple of hours he knocked on the back door. The psychologist came and asked what he wanted.

"Mister, I'm quitting this job!"

"What's the matter; don't you like the pay you're getting? If it isn't enough, I'll raise your wages."

"No, Mister, the pay is good enough; but *when I chop wood, I've got to see the chips fly!*"

Unless we see meaning in the things we do, we can't continue long without cracking under the strain. A priceless gift of our religion is the meaning it gives to all of life.—Herman J. Kregel.

SOMETHING GOOD BEFORE I DIE. Some time ago there was a riot at the Massachusetts State Prison in Charleston. I have visited prisoners in that jail and I could have understood it if they had protested against the food or the filth or the discipline. Doubtless many of them were protesting. But it was something different that drove one of the leaders at any rate. "Ted Green's eyes," we read, "filled with tears as he tried to explain . . . 'I've done a lot of bad things, evil things, in my life. My only wish is that sometime I might do a good thing, like giving my eyes so that a blind child might see, or my body so that men could understand disease better. The trouble is, isn't there some way that I could do something good before I die?' " —R. E. B.

HE FORGOT HIMSELF INTO IMMORTALITY. On the lawn of the post office in a little Ontario town on the shore of Lake Huron, I saw a monument honoring a physician. It had been erected in honor of a man who for full fifty years had served in the spirit of Christlikeness as family doctor to the neighborhood. The inscription did not claim that the doctor became rich or famous as the result of the practice of his profession. It simply stated that for two generations he had been at the service of that community in its times of greatest need. He lost himself in service and forgot himself into immortality.—Jesse H. Arnup.

## EVENING SERVICE

**Theme: Vision and Duty. From Seeing to Serving**

TEXTS: "The Lord called Samuel." I Sam. 3:4. "And Samuel lay until the morning, and opened the doors of the house of the Lord." I Sam. 3:15.

INTRODUCTORY: This was the great hour of Samuel's life. It was both his conversion and his call. We can imagine the intense excitement it must have stirred within that boyish heart. Hitherto Samuel had been a child. His farthest horizon had been his mother's home. He had been happy, as any child would be, doing his little tasks within the sanctuary. Now God had spoken to him, and called him by his name, and come into living personal contact with him, and the world of childhood had vanished like a dream. Old things had passed away; all things had become new. He had heard the voice that alters everything, so that life never could be the same again. And the beautiful thing is that having heard it, Samuel lay quiet until the morning, and then "opened the doors of the Lord's house."

I. It was a strange task after such a night. It accorded ill with the vision in the darkness. Was it for him, who had been favored so, to sweep the floor and draw aside the curtains? It is characteristic of this faithful soul that, after an hour that changed the world for him, he went back again to lowly menial duty. It is a splendid trait in Samuel's character that, after the most thrilling hour of his life, he opened the doors of the Lord's house in the morning. The beatific vision must not keep us from our common duties. We must pass from the seeing to the serving.

II. The same fidelity to the appointed task shines through the life of the Lord Jesus. Think, for instance, of the Transfiguration. For him that was an hour of vision. He was glorified in the fellowship of heaven. He saw his Cross in the light of law and prophecy—for Moses and Elias spake with him. Could we have wondered had he lingered there, in the ectasy of heavenly vision, disdainful of the lowlier tasks of love? What a contrast between the glorious hour and the spectacle of the epileptic boy at the foot of the mountain. What a change from the voices on the Mount to the uncertain voices of the crowd. And yet our Blessed Lord came down the hill, and mingled with the common crowds again, and resumed his patient ministries of tenderness. That was his duty and his task.

III. Now that is a lesson everyone must learn who wants to handle well the trust of life. It is hard, often, to get back to drudgery after enriching or unsettling hours. When spring has come, with its strange, disturbing voices; when holidays have broadened our horizon; when love arrives, calling us by name, and casting its beautiful witchery on everything, how often do the drudgeries of life, which yesterday we wrought in dull content, begin to seem repellent and intolerable. Sometimes, too, when a great sorrow comes, it has a like effect upon our hearts. Nothing is harder after a time of sorrow than to resume the interrupted duty. And in such hours we should remember Samuel who, when all the deeps were broken up, went quietly back to his apportioned task. To take up our common work again, to set ourselves quietly to the old drudgeries after some hour has changed the world for us so that nothing shall be the same, that is one of the victories of life, for us just as it was for Samuel, when in the morning he opened the doors of the Lord's house.

IV. Nor must we forget this when the great vision comes of the redeeming love of God in Jesus Christ. Conversion always has its roots in vision. That vision is so wonderful that we crave something bigger than the tasks of yesterday. And often God has a larger service waiting, nor can we doubt the pointing of his will. Great services reveal our possibilities; little services reveal our consecration. The first task of the converted man is to do better than ever what he did before.—M.

### Suggested Texts and Themes for Labor Sunday

Servant or Son? "Wherefore thou art no more a servant, but a son; and if a son, then an heir of God through Christ." Gal. 4:7.

Recompense: "He that tilleth his land shall be satisfied with bread." Prov. 12:11.

Yokes Rest on Two Shoulders: "Bear ye one another's burdens, and so fulfil the law of Christ." Gal. 6:2.

Power Shortage: "And I besought thy disciples to cast him out; and they could not." Luke 9:40.

Builders: "He is like a man which built a house. . . ." Luke 6:48-49.

## MIDWEEK FELLOWSHIP MEETING TOPIC

(Church Night or Suggested Sermon Subject)

**Theme: Seven Days and Seven Ways**

Here are seven constructive ways, suggested by Wallace C. Speers, a businessman, in which you can put religious faith to work every day in your business or in your home.

I. Have faith in God, in man, in yourself—faith in the ultimate victory of right over wrong. Have faith in our leaders and in God's ability to use them for his purpose.

II. Be an island of calm confidence in a world of turmoil—not blind wishful thinking, but belief in the power for right of a God who cares.

III. Be friendly to everyone you meet. Throw a pebble of kindness into the pool of human relations to help overcome hatred.

IV. Pray repeatedly, realizing that you are using an overwhelming power for good. Use spot prayers more and more frequently during the day to try to condition beneficially destructive situations as they are reported.

V. Practice the exclusion of doubt and fear from the mind. Keep a record of constructive thoughts put into words during the day and of destructive thoughts not uttered. Be sure the balance at evening is on the positive side.

VI. Develop the consciousness that there is a constructive answer no matter how depressing events may seem.

VII. Look upon yourself as a child of God, made in his image. Then love your neighbor as yourself.

## SUNDAY SCHOOL LESSON

**Aug. 31. Temperance and Social Justice. Rom. 13-11-14:4, 15-21. Background Scripture: Prov. 23:29-35; Hab. 2:9-16.**

MEMORY VERSE: "So each of us shall give account of himself to God. Then let us no more pass judgment on one another, but rather decide never to put a stumbling-block or hindrance in the way of a brother." Rom. 14: 12-13.

Beverage Alcohol Damages Society. I. Because of its cost. The Charlotte, N. C. *Observer* made a thorough and factual study of the cost of drinking in Mecklenburg County, population 175,000, in which Charlotte is located. The study showed that direct costs were 23 million dollars a year. Indirect costs, estimated with the help of informed agencies and businessmen, reach at least 50 million a year. Figure out the liquor cost per individual. The *Observer* pointed out that this does not set any price on the "unaccountable cost in broken homes, broken hearts, broken minds and broken spirits."

II. Because it causes crime. The FBI's annual uniform crime report for 1954 showed that drinking figured in 60.9 per cent of all arrests. Clinton T. Duffy, warden of San Quentin prison, declares that alcohol is a major factor in crimes committed by 65 per cent of the inmates of San Quentin prison.

III. Because it increases juvenile and parental delinquency. Mr. Hoover of the FBI declares that the greatest single factor in the rapid increase of delinquency and crime among youth is the drinking habit of either the youths or their parents.

III. Because of the death toll it takes on our highways. Frank H. Andrews, chief of the Evanston, Ill, traffic police and a national authority on the subject, declares that alcohol is involved in from 40 per cent to 60 per cent of America's highway accident deaths.

The argument that this vast social evil should be tolerated because of the returns it brings is completely false. Dr. Lester Breslow of the Department of Public Health of California found that California's alcoholics cost that state 12 times the total liquor tax revenue. Massachusetts authorities estimated the costs there at 8 times the total tax revenue. (See Sunday Morning Sermon for Oct. 26.)—Charles M. Crowe.

# SUNDAY: SEPTEMBER SEVENTH

## MORNING SERVICE

**Theme: Let His Cross Inspire You**

SUGGESTED SCRIPTURE READING: Rom. 8:14-18, 28.

SELECTED HYMNS: "Come, we that love the Lord."—Isaac Watts. "In the Cross of Christ I glory."—John Bowring. "Saviour, thy dying love."—S. D. Phelps. "In the hour of trial."—James Montgomery.

CALL TO WORSHIP: "O come, let us worship and bow down; let us kneel before the Lord our Maker. For he is our God: and we are the people of his pasture, and the sheep of his hand."

INVOCATION: O Almighty God, from whom every good prayer cometh, and who pourest out on all who desire it the spirit of grace and supplication; deliver us, when we draw night to thee, from coldness of heart and wanderings of mind; that with steadfast thoughts and kindled affections we may worship thee in spirit and in truth; through Jesus Christ our Lord. Amen.

**Theme: Let His Cross Inspire You**

TEXT: "We know that all things work together for good to them that love God." Rom. 8:28.

These words were not written, as you might suppose, by an inexperienced youth, nor by a dreamer sitting in an armchair by a warm fire, but by an elderly, experienced man of action, who was also one of the world's greatest sufferers.

Writing as an elderly man he gives as his considered judgment that everything that ever happened to him worked out for the best because he never lost his faith that God could bring good out of evil.

Let us think of some of the wonderful ways in which God brings good out of evil and uses even the troubles of life for our enrichment.

I. Character. For one thing, when trouble comes to a Christian it has a curious way of building character. We can all think of men and women whom we have known for years who were singularly fortunate in health and wealth and success. Fortune smiled on them, and to be honest, we sometimes envied them; though there was a complacency and shallowness of character about them.

Then suddenly, out of the blue, like a thunderbolt, trouble came; and we held our breath to see how they would take it. To our astonishment they rose to the occasion and displayed qualities of strength, heroism, and tenderness that amazed us. In every way they became larger, finer, more generous persons.

We shall never be our best selves until we have suffered. Trouble makes men and women out of us. "To them that love God all things (even trouble) work together for good."

Another wonderful thing about trouble is that when it comes into the life of a real Christian it makes him much more sympathetic toward other people and consequently a very much more useful Christian. Almost without exception, the people we turn to in times of trouble are the people who have suffered themselves.

II. Sublimation. Some years ago a missionary and his young wife went out to India and there was born to them a little daughter (an only child) who at the age of five contracted leprosy and died.

It would have been very natural and easy for that mother and father to have become cynical and rebellious. They might have said, "God is unjust and ungrateful. We have left all to come out here and serve him. We don't seek wealth, comfort, or prestige; all we asked was the privilege of serving Christ and here he goes and allows our little child to die of this foul disease."

But because they were Christians, and remembered that at the heart of their religion was the Cross, they did not argue like that. Instead they said, "Because our child suffered and died we will do something to save other children from the same disease"; and so they lectured, wrote books, and collected money until at last they were able to erect one of the finest leper hospitals in the world, in which thousands of children have been cured of the disease from which their child died.

They did not merely endure the agony of bereavement (that is not Christianity but Stoicism). They sublimated their sorrow; they did something creative with it.

III. Discovery. But the most wonderful thing about trouble I have kept to the last. Trouble can teach us more about love and power of God than any other experience in life. When life goes well and the skies are blue and the sun shines it is easy to forget about God.

It may be very wrong of us, but let's face the fact that many of us pray only when we are in trouble. We seek God's help only when our own strength has entirely failed. For this reason many of our biggest discoveries concerning God have come when we were desperately in need and when there was no one else to whom we could go.

There are countless thousands of men and women all over the world who could say that they never knew how loving and how dependable God was until they were in trouble.

IV. Supreme Example. The supreme example of how God can bring good out of evil is the Cross of Christ. We cannot realize the horror of sin till we can see what sin did to the Son of God.

Yet Jesus so handled that situation, approaching it in prayer and regarding it as an opportunity to be used rather than a burden to be borne, that in his hands the Cross became a shining instrument for the saving of the world; and a world-wide symbol of God's love for man.

Let the Cross inspire you. Every cross may be one of two things; either a tragic burden or a great opportunity. —W. Rutherford Basham.

A Prayer for the Day: We come unto thee, O God, because we cannot walk alone along the ways of our earthly pilgrimage. We are dependent upon thy favor for the common necessities of life, and for the spiritual blessings we rely upon thy grace. It is especially for the higher blessings that we pray this morning, for a spirit of wisdom and of love to be given unto us and unto all others. It is by our lack of wisdom and by a selfish spirit that with an abundance of physical blessings we often find ourselves in distress. Deliver us we pray from every evil state and in the midst of prosperity and good will and peace may all men learn to honor thee and serve thee and live together as brethren under thy Fatherhood.—H.

Offertory Sentence: "Honor the Lord with thy substance, and with the first fruits of all thine increase."

Offertory Prayer: We make our offering, O Lord, with desire that it may do good in the world. Help us in word and deed to evercome evil with good, and thereby bring glory to thee. Bless these gifts, we pray, that they may accomplish that for which they were given. Amen.—H.

Seed Thoughts:

Victory. God is in it with you and you and you are in it with God—that is the message of the Cross on the mystery of suffering. And that message means victory. There was victory at the Cross of Christ: and God wants you to know that there can be victory at every cross for you.—J. S. Stewart.

Calamity as Revealer. Apparent calamity is often the minister of revelation. The great storm clears the air, and luminous vistas come into view. The howling wind of adversity drives away the earth-born clouds and we see the face of God. Our sorrows prove the occasions of our visions. We see new panoramas through our tears. Bereavement gives us spiritual surprises, and death becomes the servant of life. And so it happens that days which began in gloom end in revelation, and we keep their recurring anniversary with deepening praise.—J. H. Jowett.

**Choice Illustrations on the Theme**

SONG AND SORROW. In a play of Ibsen's one of the characters asks another, "Who taught thee to sing?"

And the answer comes, "God sent me sorrow."

THE CLUE TO SOLVE THE RIDDLE. There was a day when Thackeray was walking out the Dean road to the west of Edinburg, with three companions; and as they went, they passed a quarry, and saw, standing out against the sky above it, a great wooden crane—just like a cross. Whereupon Thackeray stopped and pointed, and murmured one word: "Calvary." Then they moved on, all suddenly grown silent, and pondering deeply.

Why did Thackeray do that? Why should a novelist in the eighteen hundreds, and not a very spiritual one either, hark back instinctively to that death on the Judean hill long ago? Why should a Roman gallows, and the strange Man who hung there, haunt the imagination and the conscience of the race? How is it that we today are able without any sense of imcongruity to sing.

> In the Cross of Christ I glory
> Towering o'er the wrecks of Time.

It is because man, in the depths of his spirit, has always been conscious that there, in that Cross, God has spoken, and eternity has intersected history. It is because we know that, past all our fumbling human attempts to answer the problem of evil and suffering, here is God's answer. Here, if anywhere, is the clue to solve the riddle.— J. S. Stewart.

TROUBLE AND CHARACTER. Marie Antoinette, the young French aristocrat, was one of those whose folly and levity helped to bring on the bloody terrors of the French Revolution. She was a silly, frivolous girl, full of grace and charm she flitted through life like a butterfly, and you would have said she was shallow and characterless.

Then came the Revolution and all her world collapsed around her like a house of cards and she was imprisoned and put to death. But at the end she turned out to be a strong, courageous woman. Character had been there all the time but it required trouble to bring it to the surface.

## EVENING SERVICE

**Theme: Where God is to be Met**

TEXT: "In all places where I record my name I will come unto thee, and I will bless thee." Exod. 20: 24.

The many sanctuaries scattered up and down the land were so many memorials of the occasions on which God had revealed himself to the fathers and therefore so man assurances that their children in their turn might hope to meet him so. Alas, we live today in a world from which God seems to be absent; in the whir of machines we miss his voice. Yet there are still certain points in our experience at which he meets with us, and I would speak particularly of two of these.

I. The first is where God says "No" to us, in some acute suffering or shattering disappointment, when we find ourselves at the end of our own resources and then go on to find that we are only at the beginning of his.

Or the crisis in which God meets a man may be one of shame. Like the prodigal son, he realizes with acute distress that he has forfeited life's truest happiness, and he longs to return home. He repudiates, not only his past actions, but his very self; he wants to become another man, and to achieve this he is ready to surrender everything, yes, even the pride it is so hard to give up.

At such a time God comes to a man with the offer of hope where he himself can see no hope. God finds him in bondage and flings open the prison door that he may go forth free.

Countless souls have met with God under circumstances of pain and trial, loss and frustration. When the heart aches he comes in an offer of consolation, and where they were afraid once they now walk secure, because they have met with him.

II. In the second place, God meets us

at the point where life says "Yes" to us, where it offers with open hands the desire of our hearts or even more than we had dared to desire, where some floodtime of happiness bears us to a haven beyond our imagination. Have we not all of us known at some time an incredible joy, a joy that we could only accept with wonder and offer again to God in heartfelt gratitude?

Or there are moments of achievement in which our powers are strained to the uttermost and we prove capable of what we had hitherto not thought possible. As we look back on the deed done, we cannot well imagine how it came to be done. This may happen in the grand scale or only on a small but very real scale, when a man asserts his mastery over circumstances, so that they take on the shape he requires of them. Alike when our powers break down and when they come to full expression he offers himself to us. And we are free to accept or reject that offer.

III. God meets us therefore at these two points, when life says to us "No" and when it says to us "Yes." But of course there are long periods in which life seems to say now one thing and now another, when we pass from discouragement to elation and back again to discouragement. God reveals himself amid the sunlight on the mountain peaks and by the gloom in the low-lying, shut-in valleys. But where is he when a flat, unbroken plain stretches as far as the eye can see?

I would answer that if God is to train us to be his servants, he must conceal himself as well as reveal himself; for only so can we learn to be faithful even when there is no sign of his presence. Our service must learn to be independent even of God's self-revelation. God does not want us to remain always children who have to be led; he wants us to grow up into men and women who can find the way for themselves, and with that in view he must sometimes withdraw and leave us alone.—E. L. Allen.

**Suggested Texts and Themes**

At Ease in Zion: "Woe to them that are at ease in Zion. . . ." Amos 6:1.

Faith is Power: "Ask, and it shall be given you; seek, and ye shall find; knock, and it shall be opened unto you." Matt. 7:7.

Room to Live: "In my Father's house are many mansions." John 14:2.

The Liberating Word: John 8:31, 32.

The Weapons of Our Warfare: "For the weapons of our warfare are not carnal, but mighty through God to the pulling down of strong holds." II Cor. 10:4.

## MIDWEEK FELLOWSHIP MEETING TOPIC

(Church Night or Suggested Sermon Subject)

**Theme: Jesus Kept the Feasts**

Scripture Background: Luke 2:41; John 2:23; John 7:37-38; Luke 22:14-20.

The Midweek Fellowship Meeting Topics until the second week in October will be under the general heading, "How Jesus dealt with Tradition, Custom and Ancient Things." It is a hard experience to get caught between the millstones of the Old and the New. Changing the figure, the middle-of-the-road man does not always find the way delightful. To know when to conform and when not to conform requires great wisdom. A study of Jesus' methods and customs may help some of us to walk quietly and unobtrusively along our way with the prayer that we may be wise as serpents and harmless as doves.

The themes given may be followed as a series or as separate topics.

I. Jesus kept the feasts. Have you ever walked along Oriental roads when the pilgrims were going up to the great city to participate in a festival? At no other time is a journey there so pleasant. Friends meet who have not seen one another for months. There is the exchange of courtesies and felicitations. Good spirits prevail.

We see Jesus mingling with the crowds going up to the feasts at Jerusalem. The Pilgrims sing the Songs of Ascent: "I will lift up mine eyes unto the hills"; "If it had not been the Lord who was on our side"; "Except the Lord build the house." Does he join the pilgrims in song? We hear him singing.

II. The feasts were different because he was there. Something new was added, something unique and hopeful. The feast days were occasions for him to be about his Father's business; or to busy himself in his Father's house. When a boy he amazes the doctors there; later he cleanses the temple of unholy traffic; while attending the feast of tabernacles he teaches the multitudes, and when on the last day of the feast they come to the place in the temple ceremony when the priest pours the water from the golden pitcher and the great "Hallel" is chanted, then we hear him cry out, "If any man thirst let him come unto me and drink. . . ."

How thankful we are for the record of that last Passover in the upper room.

III. Consider the feasts and festivals of the local church.—H.

## BULLETIN BOARD SLOGANS FOR THE MONTH

Faith in God is never out of season.

Let good men do nothing and evil wins.

Alcohol is a little slower than arsenic.

The man who loves his work is a rich man.

Return to God is the secret of moral victory.

Life returns what we put into it—with interest.

Men occupied in useful service are seldom unhappy.

A good name is rather to be chosen than great riches.

The kindly word that falls today may bear its fruit tomorrow.

The greatest city is that which has the greatest men and women.

## SUNDAY SCHOOL LESSON

**Sept. 7. Justice in Daily Work. Exod. 20:9-10; Eccles. 9:10; Eph. 4:28; Col. 3:22-4:1. Background Scripture: II Thess. 3:6-12.**

Memory verse: "Whatsoever your task, work heartily, as serving the Lord and not men." Col. 3:23 (R.S.V.).

I. Daily work should be performed as a service to God. Daily work and sabbath rest are divinely commanded in Exod. 20:9-10.

II. The workman should practice faithful, conscientious workmanship. Eccles. 9:10.

III. The workman should give honest labor: stealing and loafing on the job are condemned. Eph. 4:28. The sin of idleness is condemned in II Thess. 3:6-12.

IV. The motivation for honest toil, as well as the responsibility of employers for just treatment of employees, is stressed in Col. 3:22-4:1.

---

# SUNDAY: SEPTEMBER FOURTEENTH

## MORNING SERVICE

**Theme: Return to the Word of God**

Suggested scripture reading: Selected passages from II Kings 22, 23.

Selected hyms: "Praise ye the Father."—M. Cockburn-Campbell. "Dear Lord and Father of mankind."—J. G. Whittier. "How firm a foundation."—Rippon's Selection. "O Word of God incarnate."—W. W. How.

Opening sentences: "For what nation is there so great, who hath God so nigh unto them, as the Lord our God is in all things that we call upon him for? And what nation is there so great, that hath statutes and judgments so righteous as all this law, which I set before you this day?" Deut. 4:7-8.

Invocation: We worship thee today, O God, with a sense of thy greatness and our own littleness. It is marvelous unto us that we should be permitted to speak unto thee even as a subject speaks unto his lord, but much more that we may come unto thee as a child comes to his father.

In humility and awe we come. In confidence and trust we come. Deal with our lives, O God, that they may be more pleasing unto thee, more vital in service, more valuable unto others, and more satisfactory to ourselves. Amen.—H.

**Theme: Return to the Word of God**

TEXT: "For thus saith the Lord God, the Holy One of Israel; In returning and rest shall ye be saved; in quietness and confidence shall be your strength." Isa. 30:15.

(For Sept. 14, 21 and 28, the sermon themes are in series. They do not need to be treated in this manner. Each theme can stand alone. Or one sermon may be preached under the subject. *Return to God* with the discussion headings as follows: I. Return to the Word of God; II. Return to the Grace of God; III. Return to the Man of God.)

Introduction. 1. A man and his times. (a) It is quite easy to keep up with the times in which we live. We have the radio, telegraph, newspaper, etc.

(b) It is always difficult to interpret the times in which we live—interpretation waits for the future.

(c) It is wisdom to be ahead of the times in which one lives and become an agent to direct them rightly.

2. Turn to the ancient prophets to get ahead of the times. Turn especially to the prophecy of Isaiah. Here is an example of what we discover in such reading. (It will not be difficult to find a parallel in American history.) (a) Isaiah writes about the Kingdom of Judah with its capital at Jerusalem. He tells about an alliance which Judah made with Assyria, an alliance that went bad—a kind of oil and water alliance.

Then Isaiah tells about Assyria becoming the enemy of Judah and threatening her with war. The initiative is with Assyria, and Judah is afraid.

Under the threat of Assyria the politicians of Judah seek to make an alliance with Egypt. They load the shoulders of young asses with riches, and put their treasures on the humps of camels and send them down to Egypt. (Isa. 30.) This Egyptian policy would make sure, they thought, that Egypt would be on the side of Judah. It was a policy devoid of intelligence and faith. "When the sole motive is fear, whether uneasiness or panic, force may be displayed, but neither sagacity nor any moral quality." It is bad politics.

Isaiah, in this emergency, strides ahead of his times. "If you wish to reform the politics, you must regenerate the people; and it is no use to inveigh against a senseless policy, such as this Egyptian one, unless you go farther and expose the national temper which has made it possible."

(b) The situation in Judah called for a regeneration of the people—by that idea Isaiah stepped ahead of his times. What does the situation call for? Isaiah's word to the people was this: "Thus saith the Lord God. . . . In returning and rest shall ye be saved; in quietness and confidence shall be your strength."

Return to what? Return to whom? Return to God! Salvation and strength is what we want. Then return to God! This is better than an alliance with any Egypt. Return to the Word of God.

I. Return to the Word of God brings revival. I. The story of the revival in Judah when the book of the law was found in the house of the Lord is found in II Kings 22, 23.

2. In the fourteenth and fifteenth centuries when the Bible was translated into English and German so that the common people could read it a thrill went through the countries of northern Europe. This was the Reformation. It was followed by the evangelism of Wesley and Whitefield.

II. A return to God's Word brings reform. 1. In the days of Josiah when the book of the law was read, it is recorded that "all the abominations that were spied out in the land of Judah and in Jerusalem, did Josiah put away, that he might perform the words of the law which were written in the book that was found in the house of the Lord."

2. Isaiah said that if the people return to God they will go to the images of false gods, the images of silver and the molten images of gold, and they will defile them and cast them away as an unclean thing. Reform will begin.

3. What about reform in America? When in our generation has greed not been rampant? The liquor traffic is bold and blatant. The authorities seem unable to curb criminality. The spectacles before our eyes are those of materialism. How does reform come about? In national life? social life? family life? personal life? Does not the beginning of reform come with a return to the Word of God?

III. Return to the Word of God brings reliance, reliance upon God.

1. We have reliance because we now understand history. We are endowed with the insight which reads history in the light of the divine purpose. Every event has moral significance.

2. We know that God is sovereign in the earth. His hand is over every event. His judgment rests upon every act. He rides upon the storm. Peace is not a vacuum. His providence stands astride every event. Battles are not always won by the biggest battalions.

3. We find God to be both a Rock and a Refuge. He is a stance for your feet and a rest for your soul.

4. Returning to the Word of God we will pray. Our prayer will not be the prayer of despair, of superstition, or of duty. It will be prayer which comes from a revived personality and a revived Church, which comes out of reformation of life and character, prayer of reliance and trust.

5. Return to the Word of God and God will answer prayer. "When God hears he will answer."

(In conclusion, definite instruction might be given to the people how to return to the reading and use of God's Word).—H.

A PRAYER FOR THE DAY: Almighty God, "who made of one every nation of men to dwell upon the face of the earth, who determines their appointed seasons, and the bounds of their habitation," by thy providence and grace we are men and women alive in this year of our Lord. We find it a difficult time in which to live—not that thou hast not dealt with us lavishly in giving us material goods, but we have not used well our blessings. We are repentant, perplexed, and unable clearly to see our way.

Thou hast blessed us with every spiritual blessing in Christ Jesus and yet we know ourselves to be spiritually impoverished. We have often refused to accept thy blessings.

We are aware of our condition. We have been sufficient unto ourselves and now find ourselves in confusion. We find it difficult to be humble. Perhaps we have lost our capacity to pray. Or we pray to gods of wealth or well-being or force. We say our prayers to thee, but we do not pray to thee.

We desire deep in our hearts to return unto thee, O Lord. Help us in this service to learn how we may return. By the return of thy people may we be saved. In quietness and confidence may we become strong. In returning may we become a people of wisdom and understanding, of loyalty and devotion, of service and sacrifice, of serenity, and peace. Amen.—H.

OFFERTORY SENTENCE: "Remember the words of the Lord Jesus, how he said, It is more blessed to give than to receive."

OFFERTORY PRAYER: We pray, O Lord, that these offerings may be as seed sown upon good soil bringing forth even an hundredfold. May they carry thy saving Gospel to the people and bring forth in their lives the fruits of the Spirit.

We would add to our offerings our thanksgivings, and sent our intercessions throughout the whole earth. In Jesus' name. Amen.—H.

SEED THOUGHTS: National Salvation. Let us ponder the four words which the prophet uses to indicate in what direction their salvation lay, and upon what terms they might be sure of the divine interposition and abiding protection. I. "Returning." II. "Rest." The meaning is, of course, such a resting in God as would prove the genuineness of their return to him. III. "Quietness." How the very word rebukes the haste, excitement, and trepidation with which they had prepared for the siege of their city! IV. "Confidence."—J. G. M.

Time for Returning. There is a time for going forth and a time for returning. There is a time for going out and a time for coming in, and the Lord shall be thy providence in both (Ps. 121:8). There is a time for venture and a time for rest. There is a time for scattering the seed and a time for bringing in the harvest. There is a time for the ships to sail for distant ports and a time for them to seek the joy of the home harbor. Always the venture, if only it is good venture; always the return, if only it is good return; and the Lord is the Lord of both. Out on the wings of the morning; home again under the evening stars.

**Choice Illustrations on the Theme**

LUTHER'S COMFORT. Luther's house in the city of Wittenberg is entered by a richly-carved portal. On either side is a stone seat, and, over the seat, a canopy. On the one canopy you see a portrait of Luther; on the other his arms are engraved. Round the arms are the five letters V.I.V.I.T.—He lives! They reflect Luther's exultant faith in the living presence and ultimate triumph of his risen Lord. On the opposite canopy, round the portrait, is this text: "In returning and rest shall ye be saved, in quietness and in confidence shall be your strength." "These words," Luther used to say, "were an exceeding comfort to me."—Frank W. Boreham.

THE INFLUENCE OF THE BIBLE. J. R. Green in his *A Short History of the English People* includes this word about the influence of the Bible: "No greater moral change ever passed over England during the years which parted the middle of the reign of Elizabeth from the meeting of the Long Parliament. England became the people of a book, and that book was the Bible. It was as yet the one English book which was familiar to every Englishman; it was read at churches and read at home, and everywhere its words, as they fell on ears which custom had not deadened to their force and beauty, kindled a startling enthusiasm. The whole temper of the nation was changed. A new conception of life and of man superseded the old. A new moral andl religious impulse spread through every class."

A LEAD FROM GOD HIMSELF. Bishop Eivind Berggrav, Primate of Norway and inspirer of Norwegian resistance during World War II, was for two years a Nazi prisoner of war. For months he was in solitary confinement. Later he said to a select London audience: "The Bible was the weapon of our souls . . . it was with us in our sufferings and it fought for us. . . . The Bible spoke to us as a voice closer to our trembling hearts than any other voice. . . . There is a lead from God himself in the Bible . . . This small book is the charter of peace, the charter of freedom, the charter of the future life of mankind."

## EVENING SERVICE

**Theme: Thirty-seven Mighty Men**

SCRIPTURE: II Sam. 23:8-39. "Thirty and seven in all." II Sam. 23:39.

We have the names of all thirty-seven, such names as Uriah the Hittite and Gareb the Ithrite. These are the last two on the list. All were warriors. They lived in the days of hand-to-hand conflict. Some of them had a record of brave exploits; all were mighty.

Adīno is first on the list. "He lift up his spear against eight hundred whom he slew at one time." It seems impossible, but there it stands in the old records. Eleazar smote the Philistines until his hand clave to the sword. His fingers were stiffened. They would not unbend. Through him a great victory was wrought.

After Eleazar was Shammah who stood his ground against a troop. Abishai lifted up his spear against three hundred and slew them. Benaiah went down into a pit and slew a lion in time of snow. And once in hand-to-hand conflict with an Egyptian he plucked the spear out of his opponent's hand, and slew him with his own spear.

The best story: II Sam. 23:13-17.

Now it is not because I am in a warlike mood that I turn to these ancient records of combat and bloodshed. I see in them some simple lessons by which we might profit.

I. How fortunate was David, the King, to have thirty-seven tried, trusted, courageous, loyal, and sacrificial men attached to his person! David was a great man and a great king in his own right; but how much greater when surrounded by his thirty-seven! When one man could win victory over eight hundred, then thirty-seven such men was a large number. We recall how Buddha gathered about himself a group of monks with which to evangelize India. Jesus chose twelve. The Apostle Paul had his Timothy, Silas, Luke, and others whom he could trust. Many a campaign has been won by the thirty-seven stalwarts, which could not have been won with ten thousand weaklings. What would happen in any church or community that had thirty-seven thouroughly consecrated and sacrificial Christian men?

II. It should be noted, too, that these thirty-seven had a great leader. David himself stirred their hearts and spurred their actions. We recall the story of Napoleon sitting in his tent before a battle while his generals passed through to shake his hand. Something of Napoleon entered each man's soul.

Think of the thirty-seven in a church all directed by the heroic Christ!

III. A connecting phrase attracts our attention in this account of the thirty-seven: "And after him." "And after him [Adīno] was Eleazar . . . and after Eleazar was Shammah." Adīno was an example to Eleazar, and Eleazar's exploit filled the heart of Shammah with courager. The power of example.

Each man belonged to a line of heroes. It is a great thing to belong to a line of spiritual heroes. If that line be also a physical heredity line, surely that is good. When a boy can look back and say, "My father, grandfather and great-grandfather were stalwart Christian men," he haas triple incentive to pass on their character and lengthen the line.

But a line does not need to be one of physical heredity. There is social heredity. There is spiritual heredity. What is your spiritual heredity?

Recall the story of Gideon's band, Judg. 7:1-8.—H.

**Suggested Texts and Themes**

Christ's Deep Therapy for Anxiety: Matt. 11:28-30.

Not Forgotten and Not Forsaken: "I will never leave thee, nor forsake thee." Heb. 13:5.

Wonderful Words of Life: "Then Simon Peter answered him, Lord, to whom shall we go? thou hast the words of eternal life." John 6:68.

Winning Possession of Our Souls: "We, however, are not the ones to shrink back and perish, but are of those who believe and so win possession of our souls." Heb. 10:39 (Weymouth).

Singing at Midnight: "And at midnight Paul and Silas prayed, and sang praises unto God: and the prisoners heard them." Acts 16:25.

## MIDWEEK FELLOWSHIP MEETING TOPIC

(Church Night or Suggested Sermon Subject)

**Theme: Jesus Frequented the Synagogue and Temple**

SCRIPTURE BACKGROUND: Luke 4:16; John 2:13-22; Luke 21:1-5; Matt. 24:1-2.

The temple of Jesus' day had been restored by Herod, murderer of his wife, his sons, his brothers—slaughterer of innocents. Over its chief entrance he had placed a golden eagle, symbol of Roman supremacy.

Jesus' estimate of the priesthood of his time is suggested in the parable of the Good Samaritan; the priest passed by on the other side.

The practices in the temple courts, the selling of beasts for the sacrifices, and the changing of money were offensive to Jesus. He knew that the temple was not permanent—"here shall not be left one stone upon another."

With all this, it was his Father's house, and as such it received his reverence. He told a leper whom he had cleansed to present himself to the priests and to fulfill the law of sacrifice. He paid the temple tax. He had a sense of the holy character of the sanctuary. He frequented the temple. We often find him in his Father's house.

How uttely absurd are the excuses which people give for not attending church!

What happens in a church at the time of worship. As William Temple told us, the holiness of God quickens the conscience; the truth of God feeds the mind; the beauty of God purges the imagination; the love of God opens the heart; the purpose of God subdues the will.—H.

### SUNDAY SCHOOL LESSON

**Sept. 14. Justice in Economic Life. Exod. 20;15; Amos 8:4-7; James 5:1-5; I Pet. 4:10-11. Background Scripture: Lev. 25:35-38; Deut. 25:13-16; Prov. 11:1.**

Memory verse: "He who is faithful in a very little is faithful also in much; and he who is dishonest in a very little is dishonest also in much." Luke 16:10 (R.S.V.).

I. There is a basic conflict between the gospel of Jesus Christ and dishonest, unfair, shady, and sharp business practices. (Give modern illustrations of the evil practices set forth in Amos 8:4-6.)

II. Christianity is not only critical and condemnatory of many business practices and economic relations, it has just principles to apply. These are found in the doctrine of Christian stewardship. I Pet. 4:10-11.

III. Christianity teaches that the mercy and love of the Saviour reaches and changes people who engage in dishonest business. Luke 19:1-10.

IV. It is a great thing to be known as a forthright, scrupulously honest and genuinely charitable man in all the relationships of life.

## SUNDAY: SEPTEMBER TWENTY-FIRST

### MORNING SERVICE

**Theme: Return to the Grace of God**

Suggested scripture reading: Isa. 30:1-3,7, 15-21, or other selected portions from Isa. 30 and 31.

Selected hymns: "Let all on earth their voices raise."—Isaac Watts. "There's a wideness in God's mercy."—F. W. Faber. "Return, O wanderer, return."—W. B. Collyer. "Lead us, O father, in the paths of peace."—W. H. Burleigh. "God of grace and God of glory."—Harry Emerson Fosdick.

Call to worship: ". . . the Lord waits to be gracious to you; . . . he exalts himself to show mercy to you. For the Lord is a God of justice; blessed are all those who wait for him." Isa. 30:18 (R.S.V.).

Invocation: Hear us, O Lord, and give answer. Our prayer riseth unto thee. It riseth from the deep restlessness of our souls, which cannot find peace except in thee. It riseth out of the guilt of our spirits which canot find forgiveness except of thee. Our prayer riseth out of the ignorance of our minds which cannot find knowledge except in thee. It riseth from the confusion of our wills which come to thee that we may know what to do. It riseth from the loveless-ness of our hearts, which need thy touch upon them that they may become tender and warm and gracious.

Answer our prayers, O Lord, the spoken and the unspoken prayers. Quiet our restless souls. Forgive our sins. Lift us out of ignorance and confusion. Grant unto us hearts of love. Amen.—H.

**Theme: Return to the Grace of God**

TEXT: "Thus saith the Lord God, the Holy One of Israel; In returning and rest shall ye be saved; in quietness and in confidence shall be your strength." Isa. 30:15.

(Connection may be made with last Sunday's sermon, "Return to the Word of God.")

I. When we return to the grace of God we return to an authentic thing, proven, tested, something we can be sure of

1. Authenticated in Jewish history. A Hebrew could never forget that God by the hand of Moses delivered his people from the tyranny of Pharaoh in the land of Egypt. God had his hand in the history of the tribes and that for good. Illustrate from Hebrew literature—Pss. 103, 105, 124, etc.

2. Authenticated in American history. Note how God made America, the land itself, as a dwelling place for a great people. Note how God here fashioned a people (see "Choice Illustrations" for quotation from George Washington's First Inaugural). When we return to the grace of God we return to that which is well-authenticated in our national history.

II. When we return to the grace of God we return to the Greatness of God. 1. The ultimate greatness of God does not rest in his power. Compare Islam which exalts a God of power. 2. The ultimate greatness of God does not rest in his wisdom. Compare Zoroastrianism, which exalts a God of wisdom. 3. The ultimate greatness of God rests in his love. (a) Isaiah, "mercy that exalts." (b) Hebrew literature, "lovingkindness." (c) The love of God as manifest in the Man of God; his life, his death, his victory, his presence.

III. When we return to the grace of God we return to the rightness of God. 1. Isaiah was not a sentimentalist—"therefore will the Lord wait that he may be gracious; and therefore will he be exalted that he may have mercy upon you; for the Lord is a God of judgment." Isa. 30:18. Compare Amos 7:8.

2. What men and nations do is try to rationalize their own crooked lines of action. Instead they should experience a sense of evil; they should return with a sense of repentance and make a venture of faith.

3. Return and receive grace. See Isa. 30:19-26.

4. God's grace is shown in the rightness of God, in his justice and his judgment. His judgment is sometimes severe. Isa. 30:27. When Assyria comes God's presence is in the coming. Napoleon said, "The Almighty is too strong for me." God's judgment sifts the nations. He will not keep the evil; he will not lose the good. His anger is under control.

God's judgment spares. Isa. 30:29.

God smites; God sifts; God spares.

How shall we return to the grace of God? When Israel remembered, when the Jews returned to God, they always gave token of their return by keeping the feast of the Passover. Thus might we return, by keeping our Sacrament, by entering with deep repentance, increased faith, and devoted love into the Sacrament of the Lord's Supper. Then in our daily lives of prayer and of service we can return, vicariously bearing before God the evils of our nation, that thereby we may save the nation and the world. —H.

A PRAYER FOR THE DAY: O thou God of deliverances, whose ways are righteous and just and full of loving-kindness, who hath power over all men and nations to lift them up or cast them down, who hath wisdom to establish purposes toward which all things move, help us to cast aside all lesser gods and our idolatries that we may worship thee and thee alone.

May we scorn alliance with all evil and place our reliance on thee. Help us to return unto thee that out of the confusion of the present hour there may come righteousness in the world and peace.

May we return to thy Word, to hear it and obey it. May we return to thy grace that our iniquities may be forgiven, our diseases healed, our lives redeemed from destruction. Then thou wilt crown our lives with loving-kindness and tender mercies and satisfy our mouth with good things. Amen.—H.

OFFERTORY SENTENCES: "The cattle upon a thousand hills belong unto the Lord; the world is his and the fullness thereof. Offer unto God thanksgiving; and pay thy vows unto the most High."

OFFERTORY PRAYER: We accept the wealth in our hands as a gift from thee, O Lord. We have received in material and spiritual blessings far more than we have deserved. We thank thee for thy goodness expressed toward us.

Having received, we give. Help us to give in the spirit of thine own giving, remembering the words of Jesus who said that God loveth a cheerful giver. Amen.—H.

SEED THOUGHTS: Return to the Grace of God. I. In the day of fear. II. In the day of confusion. III. In the day of moral debacle.

Return to the Grace of God. I. To the greatness of God. II. To the judgment of God. III. To the deliverance of God.

Quietness and Confidence. I. Quietness and confidence are strength of character. II. They are strength for work and achievement. III. They are strength for endurance. IV. They are the strength of spiritual advancement.—C. M. M.

### Choice Illustrations on the Theme

GEORGE WASHINGTON'S FIRST INAUGURAL. After a reverent acknowledgment of God's guidance in the development of this country and a statement of his own conviction that this nation was born under God, he writes this: "In tendering this homage to the great Author of every public and private good, I assure myself that it expresses your sentiments no less than my own; nor those of my fellow-citizens at large, less than either. No people can be bound to acknowledge and adore the Invisible Hand, which conducts the affairs of men, more than the people of the United States. Every step by which they have advance to the character of an independent nation seems to have been distinguished by some token of Providential agency."

A GLORIOUS TRANSFORMATION. Some years ago a phenomenon occured in Death Valley, that torrid region in Nevada, one hundred and fifty miles long and from ten to thirty-five miles wide, far below the sea level. In the summer even the lizards and horned toads disappear, and the parched ground is bare of vegetation.

Wonderful to relate, showers fell in this district for nineteen consecutive days, and seed which had been hidden there for years suddenly came to life, so that the whole valley burst into a riot of gorgeous colors.

That marvel may never happen again in Death Valley, but in the world of the spirit it happens constantly. It is always foolish to give up any life as barren and dead, however forbidding it may appear. Let the showers of divine grace fall on it, as in some blessed revival, and seeds of beauty and goodness planted long ago will suddenly spring into loveliness, and the entire life will be gloriously transformed. This applies as well to communities and nations.

## EVENING SERVICE

### Theme: The Particularity of Jesus

TEXT: Luke 9:57-60.

One of the most striking things in the gospel narrative is the way in which

Jesus adapted his teaching to the needs of individuals. He never addressed himself to a merely abstract or typical man, but always to the particular man or woman with whom he was in contact at the moment, and he dealt with each according to his special circumstances and limitation.

Here are two men who come to Christ. They have been confronted by his claims and they are on the verge of discipleship. How does Jesus treat them? Does he present them with some general form of subscription which each must sign? Does he prescribe the same treatment for both? He dealt with each according as his special temperament and situation required.

I. The first man of our text—Matthew tells us he was a Scribe—was an enthusiastic, impulsive, almost reckless individual. Jesus realized that his well-intentioned enthusiasm would most likely peter out when he came up against the hard and exacting demands which following him involved.

We are familiar with the saying which advises us to look before we leap. The scribe was the kind of man who leaps before he looks. He was a man of impulse. I am not going to decry impulse or condemn it wholesale. The world owes a lot to impulsive people. Some spend all their time looking and never leap. They are forever considering alternatives, balancing probabilities. They forget that life is slipping past and if they are ever going to do anything worth while they must proceed. A generous impulse to sweep them off their feet might not be the worst thing that could happen to them. But there is peril in acting from impulse alone. An act should be the result of thought and will as well as emotion and impulse.

The last thing Jesus would do is to exploit one's emotional nature, or hypnotize us into faith. When this man came to him he at once saw danger ahead. The scribe's effervescence was scarcely equal to the realism of the situation. So Jesus confronted him with the stern reality, in order that his will and reason, as well as his emotions, might be brought into play.

II. The second aspirant for discipleship erred on the side of caution. This man was playing for time. He was making home duties an excuse for not making an immediate decision. So Jesus proceeded to apply the spur. Other things can be done without you, but this cannot. You are urgently needed for this particular work, and there is no time to be lost.

This prospective disciple didn't require to be told of the austerity of the Christian calling as the other did. What he needed to be impressed with was its urgency, the fact that it demanded immediate decision and action. On his decision and the decision of others who were prepared to throw in their lot with Christ without delay momentous issues hung.

We read that at certain stages of Jesus' ministry many turned back, but some few went on and the world's hope lay in those few. Unless they had been willing at the outset to break with their old life there and then and to follow him who so surprisingly summoned them, that hope would never have arisen for the world.

We must take the tide at the flood, or "lose our ventures." "Seek ye the Lord while he may be found. Call ye upon him while he is near." And for the sake of the world and our influence upon its life, our contribution to the Cause and Kingdom of Christ, we must not delay.

Jesus Christ does not deal with everybody in the same way, but he deals with everybody in the right way.—Adapted from A. Stanley Hill.

**Suggested Texts and Themes**

Sunday is the Day when . . .: "Remember the sabbath day, to keep it holy." Exod. 20:8.

Life: Anchorage or Voyage: "Now when he had left speaking, he said unto Simon, Launch out into the deep. . . ." Luke 5:4.

Do We Worship Idols? "Little children, keep yourselves from idols." I John 5:21.

The Christian's Guiding Principle: I Cor. 13.

Shining Christians: "Ye are the light of the world."

## MIDWEEK FELLOWSHIP MEETING TOPIC

Church Night or Suggested Sermon Subject

**Theme: Jesus Hallowed the Sabbath**

SCRIPTURE BACKGROUND: Luke 6:1-11.

I. Are we perplexed about the Sabbath, what we may do on that day and what we may not do? Here at least is one thing that we may do—Do good! And the good itself has an object: we may do good to others.

Jesus hallowed the Sabbath by using the day for higher purposes than it was used by others. In these modern times the Sabbath is often used for low purposes, and still lower purposes. It seems that one can scarcely help being enmeshed in the weekend orgy, but the better way is still open, that of doing good.

II. Are we still perplexed? Then here is a principle to apply: "The Son of man is lord of the Sabbath." Make him indeed Lord and many of the questions about the Sabbath which cause friction or tensions in our lives will disappear.

The happiest men I know are the men who have made Jesus Lord of the Sabbath. One is a wholesale druggist, another a steel worker, another a manufacturer. They are men of poise and peace, of patience and sympathy, well known for their good works. This is their secret, Jesus is lord of their Sabbath and of their weekdays as well.—H.

## SUNDAY SCHOOL LESSON

**Sept. 21. Justice for the Needy and Neglected. Isa. 58:6-8; Luke 4:16-22; I John 3:17-18. Background Scripture: Deut. 15:7-11, 24:19-21; Matt. 9:35-36; Heb. 13:1-3.**

MEMORY VERSE: "If any one has the world's goods and sees his brother in need, yet closes his heart against him, how does God's love abide in him?" I John 3:17.

"It may be noted that there are actually millions of people on the earth who are throughout their lives desperately hungry." That is a true statement. We have heard it often; callous as many of us are it makes little impression. But let us try a different tack today.

I. Place *one* hungry person in your imagination and thinking. Don't let the ones get lost in the millions. It may be that you are acquainted with one hungry person. Perhaps you can name the person. Now you are face to face with a task commensurate with your capactiy to help. You can do something about one. From this you will catch the perspective which will take in the millions.

II. Place *one* lonely person in the foreground of your thinking.

III. Place *one* sorrowful person in your thinking . . . one mentally ill person . . .

If each Christian would help one, millions would be helped. "Inasmuch as ye have done it unto *one* of the least of these my brethren, ye have done it unto me." Matt. 25:40.—H.

# SUNDAY: SEPTEMBER TWENTY-EIGHT

## MORNING SERVICE

**Theme: Arresting the Drifts (Note: the sermon may be adapted to follow the theme "Return to the Man of God," concluding the series of three sermons which began Sept. 14)**

SUGGESTED SCRIPTURE READING: Ps. 91 or Isa. 32:1-8.

SELECTED HYMNS: "I heard the voice of Jesus say."—Horatius Bonar. "From every stormy wind that blows."—Hugh Stowell. "Beneath the cross of Jesus."—Elizabeth C. Clephane. "How firm a foundation."—Rippon's Selection.

CALL TO WORSHIP: "I will bless the Lord at all times: his praise shall continually be in my mouth. O magnify the Lord with me, and let us exalt his name together."

INVOCATION: We come unto thee, O Lord, as unto a "strong refuge," as unto a shelter in the time of storm. We shall go forth in thy strength. Our lips shall greatly rejoice when we sing unto thee; and our souls which thou hast redeemed.

**Theme: Arresting the Drifts (See note above)**

TEXT: "And a man shall be as an hiding place from the wind, and a covert from the tempest; as rivers of water in a dry place, as the shadow of a great rock in a weary land." Isa. 32:2.

In *The Book of Isaiah* (The Expositor's Bible) Sir George Adam Smith gives an outline based upon this text which has become a classic in sermonic literature. "The prophet here has no individual specially in his view, but is rather laying down a general description of the influence of individual character, of which Jesus Christ was the highest instance. Taken in this sense, his famous words present us, *first,* with a philosophy of history, at the heart of which there is, *secondly,* a great gospel, and in the application of which there is, *thirdly,* a great ideal and duty for ourselves."

INTRODUCTORY: The Figure of Speech. The "weary land." 1. The desert. "Where the first day's travel is the happiest—fullest of laughter." "Afterward, under the spell of a merciless sun and of awe-inspiring monotonous distance, will come desperate fatigue and silence." "Tighten your belt and go forth as a giant." "There is no lying down in comfort; for there is no medicine for the sun by day nor for the great winds at night." Sand. Wind. Sun. Want. 2. Thirst. In the regions of Palestine, Arabia, and Egypt, thirsts are classified; the worst is known as Sudan thirst. It is caused by hot sand which the wind pockets blow into the throat of the traveler. There is no saliva to relieve it. The symbolism of the parched tongue. 3. Tempest. The sand blast is cruel. 4. Mirage. A torment of the spirit. "The mirage is the child of the heat." The mirage is an enticement to destruction. 5. The Rock in a weary land. In the shadow of a rock there is safety, an oasis—a spring of water, protection from the wind, coolness—cool outlook and cool vision, shade—cool shadow.

I. A Philosophy of History. Here we have the statement of the Great-Man Theory, which says that the great drifts which threaten nations, mankind, civilization, true religion, are stopped by men of outstanding character and ability. "Great men are not the whole of life, but they are the condition of all the rest; if it were not for the big men, the little men could scarcely live. The first requisites of religion and civilization are outstanding characters."

Examples: Moses, Martin Luther, Abraham Lincoln.

The call of every crisis in human history is the call for a man like the shadow of a great rock in a weary land.

II. This text contains a gospel. These great men who were as rocks and the men who are as rocks now "are but pale shadows of the great spiritual fact with which this text will be forever associated; namely, the work of the man Jesus Christ, the great, immovable, heavy Rock of Ages."

He is a rock to stop the longest, heaviest drifts of human history. These are the drifts of sin and death.

What did Jesus do to stop these drifts? We quote from R. J. Campbell's sermon on this text: "What did Jesus do? He brought God into human life with a force and intensity never before known. He gave men something worth living for and dying for; he showed them how to save their souls; he rekindled within them the consciousness of the eternal. He did more, he linked the human and divine in a unity of experience which could never more be dissolved. It is not too much to say that whatever doctrines may come and go, Jesus will always live to human apprehension as the being, bone of our bone, and flesh of our flesh, in whom deity and humanity were realized as one. From the day on which this new revelation came into the world, and a new spiritual experience was born of it, the process of decay was arrested and the whole race began to move forward again toward its distant goal. The Christian church was the one live thing, the one institution that stood firm, amid the shock af falling empires and the vast inundation of barbarism in the first few centuries of our era. All would have been lost but for Jesus. He appeared at just the right moment in the order of divine providence. He breathed a new spirit into a few simple men who began immediately to lay the foundations of a new and nobler order than that which was passing away. What the old Israelitish prophet had seen on the tiny scale of the fortunes of his own country now became true on the scale of the world itself—'A man shall be as an hiding place from the wind, and a covert from the tempest . . . as the shadow of a great rock in a weary land.'"

III. In this text we find a duty and an ideal for ourselves. "*A man* shall be as the shadow of a great rock"—in each crisis *a certain man*; to stop the great drifts of sin and death, *A Man, That Man Jesus Christ*; this is *any man's* duty and ideal.

The call is for men and women who will stand as rocks. It is these who keep back the unclean and bitter drifts, save us from the sand blast, protect us from the tempest, shelter us from the east wind, give us refreshing water to drink, restore our true discernment, dissolve the mirage, shade our eyes from the fierce glare of the sun, keep us cool in the midst of the fierce heat of the day.

It is *any* man's duty and ideal, *every* man's duty and ideal.—H.

A Prayer for the Day: We come unto thee, O God, because we cannot walk alone along the ways of our earthly pilgrimage. We are dependent upon thy favor for the common necessities of life. For spiritual blessing we rely upon thy grace. It is for the higher blessings that we especially pray this morning, for a spirit of wisdom and love to be given unto all men. Deliver us, we pray, from every evil state and in the midst of prosperity and good will and peace may all men learn to honor thee and serve thee and live together as brethren under thy Fatherhood.

Guide us, O Lord, along our individual ways. From hard experience may the water of life begin to flow as the spring gushed from a rock in the wilderness. May bitter springs by the way become sweet water. In our night of darkness may a pillar of light guide us, and by thy sign in the skies may we be kept in the straight road during the day. Grant us strength to overcome all enemies that assail us. Enable us to face all hard circumstances. Give us courage in the presence of danger.

Give us a spirit of compassion with our fellow travelers on the road. May we have deep awareness of thy presence by our sides. In Jesus' name. Amen.—H.

OFFERTORY SENTENCE: "To do good and to communicate forget not: for with such sacrifices God is well pleased." Heb. 13:16.

OFFERTORY PRAYER: Help us, O Lord, to lift the level of all our service in thy name. May we serve thee with higher motives, with greater skill, with broader vision, and with deeper consecration. Accept this offering unto the spreading of the Gospel throughout the world. Amen.—H.

SEED THOUGHTS:

The Sheltering Manhood: Isa. 32:2.

The Need of the Age—for men who can stop the drifts.

A Cooling Presence. Such a cooling presence changes I. passion into quietness; II. prejudice into vision; III. trembling into peace.—J. H. Jowett.

The Heaviest Drift in Human History. What is sin? Sin is simply the longest, heaviest drift in human history. It arose in the beginning, and has carried everything before it since. "The oldest custom of the race," it is the most powerful habit of the individual. Men have reared against it government, education, philosophy, system after system of religion. But sin overwhelmed them all. Only Christ resisted, and his resistance saves the world.—George Adam Smith.

### Choice Illustrations on the Theme

ARRESTING THE DRIFT. In the East the following phenomenon is often observed. Where the desert touches a river valley or oasis, the sand is in a continual state of drift from the wind, and it is this drift which is the real cause of the barrenness of such portions of the desert at least as abut upon the fertile land. For under the rain, or by infiltration of the river, plants often spring up through the sand, and there is sometimes promise of considerable fertility. It never lasts. Down comes the periodic drift, and life is stunted or choked out. But set down a rock upon the sand, and see the difference its presence makes. After a few showers, to the leeward side of this some blades will spring up; if you have patience, you will see in time a garden. How has the boulder produced this? Simply by arresting the drift.—G. A. S.

THE SHADOW OF ALFRED LORD TENNYSON. A man approached Mr. Tennyson as he was passing on the street, and said: "You're Mr. Tennyson. Look here, sir, here am I—I've been drunk six days out of seven; but if you'll shake me by the hand, I'll never get drunk again."

THE SHADOW OF HENRY DRUMMOND. An elderly woman once came to the home of Henry Drummond and expressed her request in these words: "My husband is dyin', sir. He's no able to speak to you, and he's no able to hear you, and I dinna ken as he can see you; but I would like him to hae a breath o' you aboot him afore he dees."

THE SHADOW OF CLERK MAXWELL. Of the late Clerk Maxwell it was said, "He made faith in goodness easy for other men."

## EVENING SERVICE

### Theme: What I Want My Church to Be

TEXT: "Christ also loved the church, and gave himself for it." Eph. 5:25.

I. First of all, I want my church to be a Christ-centered temple, the place where we are to catch a vision of Jesus and so come to know God, the Father and the Holy Spirit.

II. I want it to be a spiritual storehouse from which I gather for every moment of every day comfort in sorrow, courage in trial, help in temptation, calm in life's tempests, sympathy in suffering, solace in bereavement, the essential supply for my soul's need at every step of the journey.

III. I want it to be a happy family. We are children adopted into the family of God, brothers and sisters of our Heavenly Father. Jesus is our elder brother. As brethren we are to dwell together in unity, endeavoring to keep that unity in the bond of peace; wrangling and contention are to be unknown; consideration is to rule our actions, and forbearance and forgiveness to cover our mistakes; no clannishness is to dominate, and democracy of spirit is ever to obtain.

IV. I want it to be a haven of hope,

where the lost may find safety; where the distressed and downcast may find help; from which the gospel light is ever shining that the way of Jesus may be seen. And in its revelation of this hope I want it to be world visioned, recognizing the fact that Jesus is for all mankind.

V. I want it to be a community asset—to have an influence so powerful for right and righteousness; to have a ministry so worth while and helpful; to have a courage so beautiful and noble, and a conviction so sterling and worth while, that the community shall be ennobled, uplifted, and enriched by its presence and Jesus be revealed as the Way, the Truth, and the Life for individuals and for the world.—John Van Lear.

**Suggested Texts and Themes**

Tumbleweeds: "That we henceforth be no more children, tossed to and fro, and carried about with every wind of doctrine. . . ." Eph. 4:14.

God Be in My Mouth and Understanding: "Now therefore go, and I will be with thy mouth, and teach thee what thou shalt say." Exod. 4:12.

Passing Through: "Who passing through the valley of Baca made it a well." Ps. 84:6.

In Touch with Reality: I Sam. 5:2-4.

Using Talents to the Full: "For unto whomsoever much is given, of him shall much be required: and to whom men have committed much, of him they will ask the more." Luke 12:48.

## MIDWEEK FELLOWSHIP MEETING TOPIC

(Church Night or Suggested Sermon Subject)

**Theme: Jesus Rejected the Bondage of Tradition**

Scripture Background: Mark 7:1-16.

"Jesus was a man born into a past that was too small for him. The Jewish religion was narrow and restricting but Jesus reverenced it. He frequented the Jewish synagogues and read the Scriptures and obeyed the temple laws, and yet he could break that religion in 'the greatest revolution the world has ever known.'"

The elders say so and so; what of it, if God says something different? Which shall it be, the grip of dead men or the guidance of the living God? Follow the elders and become static; follow the Spirit and become dynamic. Obey the elders, a life imitative; obey God, a life creative. Obey the elders, a life of outward practice; obey God, a life of inward power. The life of inward power will break through to determine the outward practice. The life of outward practice will curb and kill the powers of the soul. It is conformation over against transformation. It is lip service over against service from the heart. The traditions of the elders mold a man into someone else; the power of God develops a man into his greater self.

Here is the secret of the originality of Jesus. He was not original because he sought for originality. He was original because he thought about things and felt about them with the mind and heart of God.

What do people think about it? Ask that question and one becomes a copyist. What does God think about it? Ask that question and one becomes original.—H.

## SUNDAY SCHOOL LESSON

**Sept. 28. Justice and Judgment. Matt. 25:31-46. Background Scripture: Isa. 1:10-20; Amos 7:7-9; Mic. 2:1-3, 6-8; Matt. 7:15-27.**

Memory Verse: "The Lord knows the way of the righteous, but the way of the wicked will perish." Ps. 1:6 (R.S.V.).

Paul Tillich calls our attention to two forms of justice: I. Calculating Justice. The ideal here is expressed in the golden rule.

The golden rule, however, is not ultimately valid. "Except for him who knows what he *should* wish and actually wishes it, the golden rule is not ultimately valid." For example: "We wish to receive a fortune which makes us secure and independent. We would be ready to give a fortune to a friend who asks for it, if we had it. But in both cases love would be violated. For the gift would ruin us and him." Love is needed to transform calculating justice into creative justice.

II. Creative Justice. It is love that makes calculating justice into creative justice. Our lesson lies in the realm of creative justice and the lack of it.

III. Men who practice injustice become unjust; if they practice selfishness, they become selfish, shriveled, small of soul and spirit. Men who do not love make the uttermost failure. The uttermost failure is not to love. "If I have not love, I am nothing."

---

# SUNDAY: OCTOBER FIFTH

---

## MORNING SERVICE

**Theme: The Dimensions of This Church**

SUGGESTED SCRIPTURE READING: Isa. 56:1-2, 6-7.

SELECTED HYMNS: "Holy! holy! holy! Lord God Almighty!"—Reginald Heber. "In Christ there is no East or West."—John Oxenham. "Fling out the banner! let it float."—George W. Doane. "Hail to the brightness of Zion's glad morning."—Thomas Hastings. "No form of human framing."—Henry van Dyke.

CALL TO WORSHIP: The Call to Worship comes to us from Africa sounded to the rhythm of the drums:

Come everybody, come everybody
Prepare to come to the house of God
Come, come, come—
The hour of worship is near
Prepare your bodies, prepare your hearts
Come, let us worship the Lord.

In more than one hundred countries today people of many tribes and nations will gather at the Communion Table. In the early dawn the Christians of the Fiji Islands will gather. As the day wings its way westward their brethren in other lands will join them and the keeping of the Sacrament will continue for twenty-four hours until finally it is concluded on St. Lawrence Island in the Arctic regions.

Come everybody, come everybody
Come, let us worship the Lord.
—*Call to Prayer*, United Church Women.

INVOCATION: We bow in worship before thee, O God, the Father of our Lord Jesus Christ and our Father. Thou art Light and in thee is no darkness at all. Shine into the hearts of thy children throughout the whole earth, we pray thee. Grant that by thy grace and by obedience to thy Spirit, we may be true followers of Christ. So may thy kingdom come and thy will be done—and thus may there be peace among the nations. We ask it in the name of Christ. Amen.—Council of Church Women.

**Theme: The Dimensions of This Church (World-wide Communion)**

TEXT: "Mine house shall be called a house of prayer for all people." Isa. 56:7.

INTRODUCTORY: The physical dimensions of a church may have symbolic significance. The upward thrust may suggest aspiration. The breadth may suggest the scope of its fellowship. Our text, however, gives us the spiritual dimensions.

I. *My house*. Though built and used by man, this church is indeed the house which belongs to God. The laws of the land may require human ownership; but we must ever remember that our tenure is a trusteeship, a stewardship.

By this fact the care of the house becomes a matter of sacred importance. All activity within the church should be carried on with reverence, as though in the presence of God.

A minister was turning the key in the lock of the church door. A little child who was watching him said, "Is that your house?" "No," replied the minister, "this is God's house." Then asked the child, "Did God tell you to lock the door?" Our house is God's house.

II. *A house of prayer.* On this World-wide Communion Sunday as we think of the Christian Church throughout the world we may feel no unity because of any particular belief or doctrine. Theological beliefs and doctrines may have a tendency to divide us rather than unite us. Rituals, too, may be divisive. But the humble act of prayer draws us together. Prayer unites us. Think of the mighty company in all lands with whom we join in the Lord's Prayer today.

The distinctive note of the house should be that of prayer.

III. The breadth of this church is that it is for all people. It is surely not the will of God that it should be locked for anyone's exclusion.

There is considerable pathos in our text in that it was spoken by the prophet to the Jews when they were in exile, when their temple in Jerusalem lay in ruins. But he looked forward to the return and the rebuilding when the restoration should come—then the new temple should be built as a house for all peoples. This did not come to pass. Ezra, a conservative, an exclusionist, limited the house unto the worship of those who had Jewish blood. It was only with Christ that the veil of the temple was rent in twain, the lock was broken, the glory of God escaped, as it were, into the world to shine above the altar of every truly Christian shrine, whether humble chapel or great cathedral.

And so this which is God's house, a place of prayer for all peoples, fulfills the ancient prophecy. We see ourselves joined with millions of Christians in the world as we take part in this communion. It is as though they were here in our midst, in our house of prayer, brethren of every clime and nation, of every race and color, of every station whether high in the eyes of the world or low. We are all equal here; we are all children of God. Our church cannot contain them, our temple made of wood and stone cannot hold the mighty company. But there is another temple which is more expansive—the temple of our hearts, which has no limitations made by wood and stone. Our hearts can be like the heart of Christ—as broad, as inclusive as his, open to all God's children.—Adapted from Harold G. Jones.

Prayer for the Day: Infinite God, yet tender Father of us all, we who are Christian brethren throughout the world bow before thee in adoration. In differing speech we utter our praise, confess our sins, renew our vows of consecration. Thou understandest all.

Forgive us wherein we have sinned toward one another. Forgive us for not helping one another. Forgive us the sin of walled-up thinking, and give us grace to expand our caring from narrow domestic and national walls to the vast human family.

As thou dost bind us today in unity about thy table grant us strength to melt our pride into humility, to change our race and class prejudice into fellowship, to turn our selfishness into sharing, to change our behavior that wars may cease and thy Kingdom come. Rewrite into our hearts the sure knowledge that thine is the Kingdom and thine the power. In Jesus' name. Amen.—United Council of Church Women.

Offertory Sentence: Matt. 28:19-20.

Offertory Prayer: Help us, O Lord, to extend our vision unto the uttermost parts of the earth. Help us there to extend our prayers. And may these gifts of our hands there have influence. We thank thee that in thy service we are not subject to limitations, but find ourselves bound up in the bundle of the whole race of men and with thee. Bless, we pray, this offering for Jesus' sake. Amen.—H.

Seed Thoughts: Unity means interdependence, and interdependence demands co-operation.

The world was meant to be a family. If you treat it as a battleground everybody loses.—G. A. Studdert-Kennedy.

The Tentacles of Our Imagination:

"Where there is neither Greek nor Jew, circumcision nor uncircumcision, Barbarian, Scythian, bond nor free: but Christ is all, and in all." Col. 3:11.

The World's Hope is a new sense of community.

If, in this troubled time, we are ever to have "One World," that world is foretold and prefigured in the bread and wine of this sacrament.—Willard L. Sperry.

**Choice World-wide Communion Illustrations**

A WORLD-WIDE COMMUNION SERVICE. It was Communion Sunday. Eleven of us foreign students, newcomers in Washington, D.C., went to church. The minister used as his text the words of Isaiah, "They shall beat their swords into plowshares, and their spears into pruninghooks. . . ."

The choir sang, "Let us break bread together on our knees." The invitation was given to partake of the Lord's Supper. We knelt together—Americans, both white and Negro; a boy from Austria; a Japanese beside a girl from the Philippines; and other nationals from Africa, Uruguay, Argentina, Malaya, Korea, and India.

The hymn "In Christ there is no East or West" held a deep meaning for all the worshipers in that church that morning as they sang and prayed together—a world-wide community of God's children.—Remedios Asencio (Philippines).

THE SAVIOUR OF THE WORLD. In the sanctuary of our church there is a beautiful and unusual memorial window. Jesus stands with a globe of the world in his hands. Above his head are the towers of the Golden City, the new Jerusalem.

Our young people recently led a vesper service, training a spotlight on this window in a darkened sanctuary. In all its beauty and meaning the figure of Christ stood out—the Saviour of the world. Now, in the darkness of this hour, he lifts our broken and weary world up to God. May we realize that always.—Edward J. Vorba.

CYPRIAN'S LETTER TO DONATUS. Written from Carthage in the third century. "This is a cheerful world as I see it from my garden under the shadows of my vines. But if I were to ascend some high mountain and look out over the wide lands, you know very well what I should see: brigands on the highways, pirates on the sea, armies fighting, cities burning; in the amphitheaters men murdered to please applauding crowds; selfishness and cruelty and misery and despair under all roofs. It is a bad world, Donatus, an incredibly bad world. But I have discovered in the midst of it a quiet and holy people who have learned a great secret. They have found a joy which is a thousand times better than any pleasure of our sinful life. They are despised and persecuted, but they care not. They are masters of their souls. They have overcome the world. These people, Donatus, are the Christians—and I am one of them."

## EVENING SERVICE

**Theme: This Is the Life!**

TEXT: "All [things] are yours; and you are Christ's." II Cor. 3:22-23 (R.S.V.).

At the news counter at the airport a voice beside me said to the salesgirl, "*Life*, please." Now, anyone knows that he was asking for a magazine. In fact, the names we have given to our magazines are surprising—*Life*, *Time*, *Fortune*! I see there is another one added called *Wisdom*. It is quite a day when you can buy all of these at a newsstand! But somehow those two words have remained in my mind because they summarize a desire very deep in the heart of us all, "Life, please."

But today I turn with this request to the deepest answer anyone can find. The answer that is in Jesus Christ. For in the New Testament when men talk about him they are always talking about life—life abundant, life received, life brought to its full in him.

"All things are yours; and you are Christ's." Here is the answer to that deep search for life at its fullest.

I. "All things are yours." First, what a freedom there is in those words. This means for one thing that all the unfolding discoveries of life are yours.

Somehow when you realize that this is our Father's world it all becomes yours—all the beauty, all the power, and all the mystery—making you realize how great God must be who has made a world like ours.

Sometimes the unfolding discovery is not in our world but in ourselves.

Moreover, all the fellowship of the Christian family is yours. How important it is that we have a deep sense of belonging. Of all the gifts which Christ brings this is one of the most real.

II. Responsibility as well as Privilege. Also, all the responsibilities are yours. It isn't all privilege, nothing worth while ever is. We are bound together in the whole bundle of life, and we must take our share of responsibility and even suffering for the cause of Christ.

How true this is! All things are yours, all the responsibility as well as the privilege, all the pain as well as the peace; all the struggle as well as the reward. But for every testing there is a hope and a help.

It is a heart-warming truth to see how God has set before us the whole scope of life and invited us to its fullness. To that deep inner quest which says, "Life, please," the answer comes back, "All things are yours."

III. "You are Christ's." But standing by itself this is not the whole story. The deeper part of it is this, "And you are Christ's." It seems strange but true that at the very time we are offered the whole great freedom of life we are called to obedience, but there is no lasting freedom without it any more than a wheel can revolve without the hub that is firm at the center.

Isn't this the way in which we become known as persons, that is, by our relationships? What is it that distinguishes you from everybody else? For one thing, you have a name, the name of your family. This is a relationship to which you belong. Moreover, you have a citizenship. That's a relation to your country. Again, most of us are known by the work we do. This is a relation to our daily task. But it leaves unanswered the deepest question of all, "To whom does your basic loyalty belong—the loyalty that comes not by birth nor by chance but only by choice? Can you really say, "I am Christ's"?

Now that is a decision that everyone has to make. You cannot forever be neutral. Someone once said to a young man, "Have you decided for Christ?" He replied quite honestly, "No, but I haven't decided against him either because no one ever asked me." And the other came back, "Will you decide now?" The answer was, "Yes, I will, completely and gladly."

We could wish so deeply that some of you might come to that decision today. . . .—Gene E. Bartlett.

**Suggested Texts and Themes for World-wide Communion Sunday**

Broken Walls: "For he is our peace, who hath made both one, and hath broken down the middle wall of partition between us." Eph. 2:14.

One World—One Kingdom—One Family: "And they shall come from the east, and from the west, and from the north, and from the south, and shall sit down in the kingdom of God." Luke 13:29.

The New Spirit: "Be reconciled to your brother." Matt. 5:24 (R.S.V.).

The Savior of the World: "And we have seen and testify that the Father has sent his Son as the Savior of the world." I John 4:14 (R.S.V.).

Crossing the Frontier: "We know that we have crossed the frontier from death to life because we do love our brothers." I John 3:14 (Phillips).

## MIDWEEK FELLOWSHIP MEETING TOPIC

(Church Night or Suggested Sermon Subject)

**Theme: Jesus Outflanked Ancient Evils**

SCRIPTURE: Mark 12:28-34.

I. One marvels at the great evils of Jesus' day which are unmentioned in the gospel records. T. R. Glover in *The Jesus of History* carries us back into the first century and shows us what a hard, hard world it was.

He points out that the pagan world took it for granted that a man and his wife might put away their girl baby if they wished to do so. Visualize a crucifixion scene in all its details—a world that could pass by where men hung upon their crosses was a hard and cruel world. Remember, too, that slavery, robber of the natural rights of men, was prevalent everywhere. Yet these three great evils, infanticide, crucifixion, slavery, as such are unmentioned by Jesus. He was aware of them. He denounced hypocrisy. He attacked the profanation of the temple. Murder and cruelty seem worse than hypocrisy. The desecration of living temples seems far more flagrant than bartering in the temple made of stone.

II. Jesus used grand strategy. He knew where and when to employ the method of direct attack. Some great evils he outflanked. Infanticide, crucifixion, slavery, may still be practiced in out-of-the-way corners of the earth, but they are no longer the expression of the character of the age. They have been outflanked by means of the strategy of Jesus.

III. The practice of Christian love might be discussed as a method of outflanking evil. In July, 1918, we looked across the German lines to Mt. Sec, then held by the Germans. The French had lost thousands of men trying to take this strong point by direct attack. In the St. Mihiel drive the Americans outflanked the position and took it with comparative ease.

Discussion points: What present-day evils should be attacked directly? What evils might be outflanked? Is there a danger that outflanking strategy might become do-nothing strategy?

## BULLETIN BOARD SLOGANS FOR THE MONTH

Daily prayer lessens daily care.

Speak kind words: hear kind echoes.

Consistent Christians always command respect.

The Church of Christ is the world's only hope.

Success tip: "Start at the bottom and wake up."

Are you in good company when you're by yourself?

We can be deceived by ourselves as well as by others.

Would I rear my children where there are no churches?

Cast all your care on God! That anchor holds.—Tennyson.

Small deeds done are greater than great deeds planned.—Peter Marshall.

## SUNDAY SCHOOL LESSON

**Oct. 5. Introducing the Gospel. Luke 1:1-4; 3:1-14.**

MEMORY VERSE: "When the time had fully come, God sent forth his Son." Gal. 4:4.

The purpose of the lesson is to provide the background for the quarter's study. This is the beginning of a six-months' study of the life of Jesus Christ.

The treatment of the lesson might include:

I. A description of the source material on the life of Jesus. The material for the lessons has been taken from Matthew, Mark, and Luke.

II. A description of the kind of world into which Jesus came and how desperately it needed him. The parallel need of our world today for his gospel might be indicated.

III. Since this is World-wide Communion Sunday, the fact that the gospel is for all mankind, and how it has been slowly "making paths straight" in the world, may be emphasized.

# SUNDAY: OCTOBER TWELFTH

## MORNING SERVICE

**Theme: Lamps that Christian Men Set Burning**

SUGGESTED SCRIPTURE READING: James 1:17-18; 22-25.

SELECTED HYMNS: "Christ, whose glory fills the skies."—Charles Wesley. "O Word of God incarnate."—W. W. How. "Ye servants of God, your Master proclaim."—Charles Wesley. "Brightly beams our Father's mercy."—Philip P. Bliss. "Onward, Christian soldiers!"—Sabine Baring-Gould.

OPENING SENTENCES: Matt. 5:14-16.

INVOCATION: We turn our minds unto thee, O Lord, expectant that such contact will give us deeper insight into truth. We turn our hearts unto thee that through them thy love may flow. We bring our wills unto thee that thou mayst guide us in all that we think and speak and do. As we make our prayer of confession unto thee help us to receive the cleansing of our lives. Then send us forth to proclaim by word and deed and life the Gospel of Christ. Amen.—H.

**Theme: Lamps That Christian Men Set Burning**

TEXT: "Let . . . your lamps be burning." Luke 12:35.

John Ruskin sat at the end of life's day watching a lamplighter with torch in hand lighting the lamps on a distant hill. The man himself could not be seen, but a long line of lights came on behind him. By and by Ruskin said to a friend, "That is what I mean by a real Christian. You can trace his course by the lamps he sets burning."

What are some of the lamps which Christian men set burning, and which by the grace of God they are to keep burning brightly?

I. The Lamp of Faith. In the first place there is the lamp of faith. "That man's dark doubts have quenched his great lamp of faith" is one of the most tragically pathetic words ever uttered by one individual of another. In fact these words could be said of a vast multitude in the world. There are those who so doubt the dependable quality of the very life of God that they live their lives in a world of darkness and fear. They are afraid of their foes. They are afraid of their friends. They fear what may come in the world. They are afraid of the future. They are even afraid of themselves. They fear death.

It is in a world like this that the Christian sets the lamp of faith burning in such a fashion that men everywhere may emerge from the darkness of their doubts into the full light of faith.

II. The Lamp of Hope. Then there is the lamp of hope. The hopelessness and despair of many lives is one of the most startling spectacles of our time. Men are all the while rushing from one frustration to greater frustration. They move from one hopelessness to a vaster despair. They look to science to redeem the world only to discover that science may come not only to destroy the last possibility of the New Jerusalem but also to banish the dream and the dreamer. They look to the nation to secure a safe and dependable life for the world only to discover that the nation has lost its ideal amid the conflicts of a distraught and frightful age. They look to their own virtues for salvation only to discover that a number of those virtues have already turned into vices and are bringing their own dark harvests of despair. They may shout from the housetop that "hope springs eternal in the human breast," but such words only reveal the depth of their despair. They may cry, "Why art thou cast down, O my soul, and why art thou disquieted within me?" But until they come to light the lamp of hope in God there can be no sure and dependable sense that all things will work together for good.

It is in a world like this and to such that Christian men come to minister. They have long since set their lamp of hope burning and are keeping it lighted. They know that to be Christian is never to despair and to keep their lamp of hope burning is never to need to despair. They are confident in life and equally confident for the life to come.

III. The Lamp of Love. Then there is the lamp of love. There is a very definite sense in which we would not want it said that we live in a friendless world. There is even a greater sense in which we would not want it said that we live in a loveless world. But when we come to think of it the apostles of hate are always with us. They live in the little community where we live. They dwell in the vast city of which we are a part. They move through the nation and out into the great world of all peoples. In no end of ways they are responsible for our broken and torn and troubled age. It is in such a world that Christian men come to set the lamp of love burning so brightly that its deep shining will at last envelope all the darkness of the hatreds of evil men.—Harold C. Vernon.

A PRAYER FOR THE DAY: O God, our Lord, who hath set our lives in the world that they may do good and serve thy righteous will, so work in them through thy Spirit that they may accomplish thy purposes. Grant that our lives may be made whole and wholesome and holy. Endow them through thy grace with the virtues which appear in the life of Jesus. Motivate our lives with faith and hope and love. So control them that in all their activities they may bear witness to thee and thy Gospel. Amen.—H.

OFFERTORY SENTENCE: "For Zion's sake will I not hold my peace, and for Jerusalem's sake I will not rest, until the righteousness thereof go forth as brightness, and the salvation thereof as a lamp that burneth." Isa. 62:1.

OFFERTORY PRAYER: We pray, O God, for Christian men to set the lamps of love burning so brightly in the world that their deep shining may dissipate all darkness and all evil. Help us by our offerings to kindle love in human hearts. —H.

SEED THOUGHTS: Tracing the Course of a Man. What lamps did he set burning?

That Light. A secret unobserved religion cannot be the religion of Jesus Christ. Whatever religion can be concealed is not Christianity. If a Christian could be hid, he could not be compared to a city set upon a hill; to the light of the world; to the sun shining from heaven and seen by all the world below. Never, therefore, let it enter the heart of him whom God hath renewed in the spirit of his mind to hide that light, to keep his religion to himself; especially considering it is not only impossible to conceal true Christianity, but likewise absolutely contrary to the design of the great Author of it.—John Wesley.

Offer the Lamp. "If we offer the lamp our Lord will give the flame."

**Choice Illustrations on the Theme**

LET YOUR LAMPS BE BURNING. One of the most moving passages in Lord Grey's autobiography *Twenty-five Years* is that in which he describes the night of August 3 on which Great Britain issued a declaration of war on Germany. After the historic debate in the House of Commons had been concluded and the vote taken, he went to the Foreign Office in Whitehall and spent the early morning hours there. As dawn broke over the city he looked out of the window and watched the street lamps being extinguished one by one. Quite suddenly he turned to a friend and said, "The lamps are going out all over Europe, and we shall not see them lit again in our life time."

THE DARKNESS OF PARIS. On one occasion, after addressing a most distinguished audience, M. Sarcy, at that time head of the *Académie française,* said to the *maréchale* of the Salvation Army, "I cannot understand why you should come to Paris with your ideas which we have eclipsed long ago. You should go to the South Sea Islands or the heart of Africa, but never to Paris. Paris is the city of light. We march toward the light."

"Monsieur Sarcy," she replied, "in the poor quarter of the city where I live a man lies dying. During my last visit he said, 'I am afraid! Oh, I am afraid to die. It is all so dark.' Has Paris found a light for that man? A light which will illuminate the valley of the shadow of death where we must all pass one day?"

Monsieur Sarcy looked at the *maréchale,* dropped his head, turned away, and was gone.—*Prophetic Word.*

DO LIKEWISE. A recent young convert was asked if he had done anything for Christ since he had believed.

"Oh, I am a learner," he replied.

"Well, when you light a candle, do you do it to make the candle more comfortable, or to give light?" his friend asked.

"To give light, of course."

"Do you expect it to give light after it is half burned, or when you first light it?"

"As soon as I light it."

"Very well; go and do likewise. Begin at once."

Shortly afterward there were fifty more Christians in that town as a result of the young man's testimony.—*Bible Expositor.*

## EVENING SERVICE

### Theme: Barnabas, Son of Encouragement

TEXT: "And Joses, who by the apostles was surnamed Barnabas, (which is, being interpreted, The son of consolation,) a Levite, and of the country of Cyprus, having land, sold it, and brought the money, and laid it at the apostles' feet." Acts 4:36-37.

His real name was Joses, but the apostles called him Barnabas. Three meanings have been given to the name by translators. It means either son of consolation, son of exhortation, or son of encouragement. The last meaning is the best, for most things that we know about Barnabas are keyed to that word.

Barnabas encouraged the apotsles. The rapid growth of the Church brought together many poor and needy people for whom the apostles felt responsibility. The anxious strain on the leaders was relieved by the generosity of Barnabas.

I. He encouraged a convert. When Saul was converted he sought to join himself to the disciples; but they were afraid of him, and believed not that he was a disciple. Barnabas took him and brought him to the apostles. Barnabas affirmed the reality of Saul's conversion. Who can say what would have become of Saul if the chilly suspicions of the mother Church had not been overcome by the noble-hearted Barnabas?

It is a great thing to encourage new converts. By that we may be doing far more than we know. A Barnabas may encourage a Paul.

II. Barnabas encouraged a new adventure. In Acts we read how certain private Christians broke through what had been the previous practice, and preached the gospel to the Greeks in Antioch, the heathen, and a community of Christians was gathered in that pagan center. When tidings of this unheard-of proceeding came to the ears of the mother Church they felt they ought to inquire into the matter. Whom should they send? Surely they were God-guided when they sent the noble Barnabas. He was the very man to handle sympathetically this new venture.

III. Barnabas encouraged a worker to enter a larger sphere. The work at Antioch so developed that Barnabas could not cope with it. What should he do? Suddenly he thought of Saul, who had gone down to Tarsus. "Then departed Barnabas to Tarsus, for to seek Saul. And when he had found him, he brought him to Antioch." Then followed the glorious year of gospel work in that city.

The Spirit of God falls on this new church in Antioch; and its leaders, Barnabas and Saul, are called to a wider adventure for God and the gospel. Under direct guidance of the Holy Spirit they set out on the Gentile mission.

IV. Barnabas encouraged one who had failed. The Gentile mission being ended and reported to the church at Antioch, an unhappy dispute arose. Should Mark, who had turned back, be given another chance? "Barnabas took Mark, and sailed unto Cyprus." Mark overcame his failure under the kindly support of Barnabas. Instead of being lost to the cause he became an important worker in it.

Many who have served God nobly in the end made an uncertain start. The intervention of some encouraging Barnabas dissipated their fears and gave them confidence.

Let no one be daunted by one failure. Let the wise and experienced take diffidence by the hand and let such befriend the faint-hearted. There is place for lesser men in so great a cause.

The cousin of Barnabas must have made a great recovery, for he later became the companion of Peter. The last we hear of Mark in the Bible is that Paul himself, now aged and a prisoner expecting death, asks for Mark to come to him before the end. "Take Mark and bring him with thee, for he is profitable to me for the ministry."

The companion of Peter, the first evangelist, the desired friend of the dying Paul, was a man worth saving. What shall we say but "Well done, Barnabas"? —Adapted from Gilbert Laws.

**Suggested Texts and Themes for World Order Day**

Love Worketh No Ill: "Love worketh no ill to his neighbor: . . ." Rom. 13:10.

Impossible Co-existence: "Ye cannot serve God and mammon." Matt. 6:24. "Christ and Caesar cannot ever co-exist."

The Acceptance of Peace: "My peace I give unto you." John 14:27.

God's Peace Terms: "Mercy and truth are met together; righteousness and peace have kissed each other." Ps. 85:10.

When Shall This Be? "They shall not hurt nor destroy in all my holy mountain: for the earth shall be full of the knowledge of the Lord, as the waters cover the sea." Isa. 11:9.

## MIDWEEK FELLOWSHIP MEETING TOPIC

(Church Night or Suggested Sermon Subject)

**Theme: Jesus Re-evaluated Ancient Ideas**

Background Scripture: Matt. 5:20; John 8:39, 14:7-11.

I. Jesus caused his disciples to rethink many ideas. His clash came with the Pharisees because they were unwilling or unable to change their minds. They were unteachable. Woes were pronounced upon them. A man unteachable is a man doomed.

How much of Jesus' time was spent trying to lead that little group of disciples into new and deeper ways of thinking about things! How much was accomplished when they finally grasped the new conception of God as taught and manifested by his own self! He is not willing that they should feel that their knowledge was complete because they had been with him. Among his last words were these, "I have yet many things to say unto you. . . ."

II. We must forever seek to have the mind of Christ. How different all everyday things, flowers, trees, children, friends, loved ones; all virtues, love, joy, peace, kindness, meekness; all nations, America, India, China; the continents, Asia, Africa, South America, Europe; how different the world—could we think of them with the mind of Christ!

I suppose that the idea which must change most continuously is our idea of God. Our finite minds must reach out more and more to grasp the idea of an infinite, all-powerful, all-wise, everywhere present, all-loving Father. With each greater appreciation of God our ideas of all other things large and small will be changed, taking on greater significance.—H.

## SUNDAY SCHOOL LESSON

**Oct. 12. The Messiah—Fulfillment of Hope. Luke 2:25-35. Background Scripture: Luke 2:1-40.**

Memory Verse: "Mine eyes have seen

thy salvation which thou hast prepared in the presence of all peoples, a light for revelation to the Gentiles, and for glory to thy people Israel." Luke 2:30-32.

This lesson comes in that season of the year when many churches include in their programs some reference to the United Nations and to World Order. What Christ's coming means for the ultimate realization of world peace is a possible emphasis in this lesson.

I. God's purpose to save mankind.

II. God's purpose made visible in Christ. "Mine eyes have seen thy salvation." Luke 2:3o.

III. Our only dependable hope for world peace lies in the salvation which Christ makes possible.

# SUNDAY: OCTOBER NINETEENTH

## MORNING SERVICE

**Theme: God Recruits Men (Laymen's Sunday)**

SUGGESTED SCRIPTURE READING: Exod. 3:1-12.

SELECTED HYMNS: "Not alone for mighty empire."—William P. Merrill. "Jesus calls us, o'er the tumult."—C. F. Alexander. "Lord, speak to me, that I may speak."—Frances R. Havergal. "O Master-workman of the race."—Jay T. Stocking. "Rise up, O men of God!"—William P. Merrill.

OPENING SENTENCE: "But ye are a chosen generation, a royal priesthood, an holy nation, a peculiar people; that ye should shew forth the praises of him who called you out of darkness into his marvellous light." I Pet. 2:9.

INVOCATION: It is with deep joy and gratitude, O God, that we read these words (I Pet. 2:9). We feel in our hearts that we are a people for thine own possession; for thou hast created us and redeemed us. We are thine. Help us, our Father, in all our strivings for goodness, and bring it to pass that our lives may indeed show forth the excellencies of him who called us out of darkness into his marvelous light.—H.

**Theme: God Recruits Men**

TEXT: Texts will be found in the body of the outline.

I. *God is calling men today!*

Exod. 3:4, "God called unto him out of the midst of the bush . . . 'Moses, Moses.' And he said, 'Here am I.' " God takes the commonplace of our existence and makes it speak for him. God took a bush on a hillside where the sheep were grazing. He made it a means of making clear to Moses that he wanted him to lead the people of God out of Egypt. God may call a man today from some burning bush which is not consumed. He is forever calling us from a world in turmoil to do his bidding. He is calling men today. What about you?

II. *God is seeking men today!*

"Whom shall I send, and who will go for us?" Isa. 6:8. King Uzziah had died. The times were turbulent and chaotic. Nothing was certain. A young man came to pray in the church of his day. There in the house of God he saw a King of kings upon the throne which changes not with the changing times of men. The young prophet realized his own inadequacy, but he also found the forgiveness of God. He was overwhelmed with the claim of God upon him. We live in the midst of change. The vision is still there for those who will lift up their heads to see.

III. *The necessity of witnesses.*

"Understandest thou what thou readest? . . . How can I except some man should guide me?" Acts 8:30-31. This question of Philip to the Ethiopian points up the possibility of a great tragedy. What if Philip had not been there? Tradition tells us that it was through him that the message of Christ came to Ethiopia. In fact, here may have been the beginnings of the great Coptic church. How many others are waiting for a Philip to introduce them to Christ? You can be God's man. You can be the man who speaks the right word at the right time for the right purpose to win others to Christ.

IV. *Do you have hearing ears?*

God wants a hearing in the lives of men. Nothing gladdens the heart of God more than to hear the such words as the boy Samuel spoke in the night in the temple of old when the voice of God spoke unto him. "Speak; for thy servant heareth." I Sam. 3:10. So many have ears but do not hear. Their ears are closed to God's voice by ambition, by a desire for a place in the social world, by a desire to get things. God wants us to see life as he sees it, not as the world sees it. God seeks men who will hear and heed his call to tell others of the Christ who died for them.

V. *The answer God is seeking.*

"Lord, what wilt thou have me to do?" Acts 9:6. How strangely personal is this question. Such a response indicates a heart that means business. God can do much with such a heart. He can take a Saul and make him into a Paul, but only when that Saul is willing to ask God his bidding. Such words indicate an aroused soul. The man who speaks them must know surely where the issues of life lie. Such a response points up the fact that the man thus awakened is ready to serve God. Most important of all it manifests a surrendered will. Such a one has caught the spirit of the words, "I'll go where you want me to go, dear Lord." They are the ingredients of unselfish service. You can be very certain that if a man responds in this way God has called him to serve Christ and his church.

VI. *Men of Decision.*

When Christ called the disciples, "Straightaway they forsook their nets, and followed him." Mark 1:18. The church needs such men today, men who will take him seriously, men who will give him all their life, men who will take the initiative for the church and risk their lives for their Saviour. This involves surrender, sacrifice, and service. Christ will take nothing less. Real Christian faith involves all these things. Nothing less will satisfy. Christ can use that kind of men.—George C. Ames.

A Prayer for the Day: We thank thee, our Father, for the manifestation of thyself in special ways to chosen men. We thank thee that some have heard thy voice speaking in the miraculous and extraordinary. We thank thee for the influence upon the world and upon our own lives of men and women who have been called out to do great deeds in thy name. For all who have achieved greatness and goodness we give thee thanks.

We are grateful, O Lord, that we, too, are called unto our tasks, humble though they may be, yet part of the world's work, and necessary to be done. We thank thee that in our work we can achieve skill and satisfy our instinct for workmanship. We thank thee that each task we do is a threshold to larger vistas of life, that we can achieve character while doing our daily work, thus making it eternally significant. We rejoice that our tasks are a means of serving others, a means of doing good. We pray for inspiration and strength to do well, heartily as unto the Lord, the things which we have to do. Amen.—H.

Offertory Sentence: "Whatsoever ye do in word or deed, do all in the name of the Lord Jesus, giving thanks to God and the Father by him." Col. 3:17.

Offertory Prayer: We lay before thee, O God, a portion of the labor of our hands. It is a token of our desire that all our labor may be dedicated to high and noble purposes, the service of our fellow men, and the upbuilding of thy kingdom. Grant unto this offering thy special blessing that it may accomplish much good. Amen.—H.

Seed Thoughts: The Heart of Religion. The divine-human encounter from which one goes out under orders with a great vocation is the very heart of the Bible's religion.—Harry Emerson Fosdick.

The Overalls Sainthood (I Sam. 30:20-25). In the past we have clothed sainthood in the stole and cassock. The new sainthood will be the sainthood of the overalls, that is, the sainthood of common service. The canonized will be those who devote their own trade and their tools, whether hammer, pruning hook or pen, to the common task of building the Kingdom of God. David honored those who tarried by the stuff as much as those who went down to battle. Often the captain who goes down with his ship standing upon the bridge is counted a hero, while the coal stoker who stood by his job down in the hole is quite forgotten, though perhaps, measuring the conditions, it took more courage and genuine loyalty to duty to stay down the hole than it did to refuse to leave the bridge.—Guy L. Morrill.

### Choice Illustrations on the Theme

I'LL BE THAT MAN. Dwight L. Moody, the great evangelist, said, "The world is waiting to see what God can do with a wholly yielded man. I'll be that man." See what great things God did with this humble shoe salesman. If God can do it with others, he can do it with you. Christ needs men who can take a stand and mean it. Christ can use you.—G C. A.

MAPS WITHOUT MEN. General Montgomery, the famed British military strategist, was giving a preview of a forthcoming battle in his famous map room somewhere in North Africa. When he had finished, his field officers agreed that the battle plan was sound. Montgomery then put the matter before them rather sharply when he said, "The plan is sound, but maps without men mean nothing." There you have it. The church possesses a grand strategy, but it needs men, men of decision. Are you that man?—G. C. A.

WHAT IS A CALL. Keith-Falconer, a young man of brilliant attainments, rich and influential, the son of a British peer, said: "What is a call? A call is a need, a need made known, and the power to meet that need."

MATTHEW'S CALL. In *The Man Born To Be King* (Harper, 1943) Dorothy Sayers lets Matthew or Levi) tell about his call:

"And I looked up—and there he was. 'Hello!' I thought. 'Here's the Prophet. I suppose he'll start calling me names like the rest of 'em. Let him. Hard words break no bones.' So I stared at him, and he stared at me—seemed as though his eyes was going straight through me and through me ledgers, and reading all the bits as wasn't for publication. And somehow or other he made me feel dirty. That's all. Just dirty. I started shuffling me feet. And he smiled—you know the way he smiles all of a sudden—and he says 'Follow me.' I couldn't believe my ears. I tumbled out of my desk, and away he went up the street, and I went after him."

### Alternate Theme: The Mind We Need for Peace (World Order Day)

The mind we need for peace will be:

I. A realistic mind, which sees things as they are, which recognizes that the price of peace may be sacrifice.

II. An idealistic mind, which knows facts yet is not afraid to dream of what might be, though the goal may seem to be distant.

III. A flexible mind, which can change its viewpoint, if necessary, when circumstances have altered.

IV. A mind unafraid and willing to find out the causes of wars, to trace the acts of the past that have culminated in the condtions we now face, to see ourselves in relation to other nations in a world grown small.

V. A resolute mind which acts with decision to use its influence for the thing in which it believes.

VI. A co-operative mind which acknowledges that both personal and national isolationisms are dead, and which is willing to share in the give and take of co-operative thinking.

VII. A mind which accepts the golden rule and the Ten Commandments as guides in all decisions, believing that national and international morality are as necessary as personal morality for a decent and good life.—*War Cry*.

A PRAYER FOR THE DAY: Almighty God, who in these days hath bestowed upon our nation great power; give us the grace to consecrate our resources to the well-being of the world. Save us from complacency or self-righteousness which set us apart from the sufferings and needs of mankind. Help us to commend democracy through the sincerity of our brotherhood and the integrity of our government. May we play our part in hastening the day when the nations shall dwell together in unity, and the world shall know thy righteousness and peace. Through Jesus Christ our Lord. Amen.—National Council of Churches.

## EVENING SERVICE

### Theme: Broken Nets Must Be Repaired

TEXT: Mark 1:16-20.

When Jesus passed by the Sea of Galilee he saw two men of action, Simon and Andrew, casting their net into the sea. Immediately he called them into his service. He also saw two repairmen, James and John, mending their nets. With equal promptitude he called these repairmen to follow him. Today every railroad has two general departments—the operating department and the maintenance department. One is for action, the other for repair. Behind the train crew are the linemen, the car whackers, the section gangs. Without constant repairs the streamline trains could not speed across the continent. To be a fisherman a person must cast his net; to be a successful fisherman he must mend his net. For nets, like tracks and trains, like boats and men, like bodies and souls, like enthusiasms and inspirations, wear out in time. Back of continued action there must always be repair.

I. As the pounding of traffic wears out the track, so the floundering of a heavy draft of fish wears out the net. Cords are snapped and holes are rent by the game and fighting fish that fishermen delight to catch. In the human body activity burns out cells that must be repaired in sleep. And so success wears down a man, as Elijah found when he had triumphed over the prophets of Baal. The giving off of power drains a man's strength, as Jesus felt when the afflicted woman was restored by the healing touch of his garment's hem. A sermon, if it comes from the central fire of an earnest soul, burns out a man. Any "big day" or unusual effort is likely to exhaust a church, as the attendance on the Sunday after Easter so often shows. Nets are broken by the success of the catch, and broken nets must be repaired.

II. Nets are broken by the snags they meet—the jagged rocks they must be dragged across, the rough and splintered surfaces of the sides of the boat, the submerged obstructions which are hidden from view. In like manner, the souls of men are rent by the snags they meet—the disappointments, the discouragements, the interruptions, the oppositions, the detractions, the exactions, the nagging, dragging grind of it all, with now and then a foreboding sense of frustration due to some submerged and unseen obstruction which tears the net and dissipates the catch. If any man should know the meaning of this, surely that man is the pastor of a church. Nets are broken by the snags they meet, and broken nets must be repaired.

III. And nets are broken by disuse. They are left lying idly on the shore and their fiber is dried and made brittle by the sun, or rotted by mildew in some damp boathouse, and their strength is gone. Look at a disused railroad track, and see the rotted ties and rusted rails. It has gone to waste, not by the pounding of the traffic but by the inevitable law that decay follows disuse. Who will dispute that talents hidden away in a napkin are lost? Who can say how many ministers have lost their pulpit power by disuse of the study? Who does not know that the sweetness and the power of prayer are lost by disuse of prayer? Who will deny that men called to be fishers of men have lost the knack by disuse of the evangelist's net? Who is not aware that churches have lost their strength and joy by their neglect of the living mission they were appointed to fulfill? It is a law of life that nets are broken by disuse and that broken nets must be repaired.

When Savonarola was invited to preach before Lorenzo de' Medici, he said in the course of his sermon: "I am here in the waters of Tiberias. . . . We must fish, therefore, in these waters with nets that let not even the little fish escape." Not even the little fish! Though called to fish in deep waters, though dealing with the important issues which affected the moral welfare of the state, he still recognized that his nets should be perfect enough to catch the smallest fish.

Such was the wish of Christ, who sent men forth to minister, not in the mass and not to the great and powerful alone, but also to "the last of the least of the lost." It takes good nets to be used by fishers of men, and Jesus, knowing this full well, called both casters of nets and menders of nets, and he surely meant that the casters of nets should keep them in repair.—John C. McCoy.

### Suggested Texts and Themes for Laymen's Sunday

Having a Great Cause: "I am doing a great work, so that I cannot come down." Neh. 6:3.

Magnifying the Commonplace: "And the Lord said unto him, What is that in thine hand? And he said, A rod." Exod. 4:2.

The Will to Win: "Fight the good fight of faith, lay hold on eternal life, whereunto thou art also called." I Tim. 6:12.

Men Have Different Gifts: "Now there are diversities of gifts, but the same Spirit." I Cor. 12:4.

Appreciating the Things that are Excellent: "Finally, brethren, whatsoever things are true, whatsoever things are honest, . . . think on these things." Phil. 4:8.

## MIDWEEK FELLOWSHIP MEETING TOPIC

(Church Night or Suggested Sermon Subject)

### Theme: God's Thoughts toward You

TEXT: "I know the thoughts that I think toward you, saith the Lord, thoughts of peace, and not of evil." Jer. 29:11.

God's thoughts are like God. They are wonderful as himself and worthy of himself. His ways are the results of his thoughts. These words were addressed to the Jews when they were captives in Babylon.

I. The words should have been to them as a sunbeam bursting through dark clouds. Some of them may have found difficulty in reconciling the goodness of God with earthly dangers and trying circumstances. That is a human weakness that persists to the present time.

II. And surely it is to meet such weakness that this assurance is given. We may not be able fully to understand God's ways, but it should be enough to know that God lives, that God is good, and that his thoughts toward his children are thoughts of peace, "and not of evil."

III. We, therefore, can look forward with hope, for God is for us and he is more than all that can be against us. It is this faith that enables us to hold up our heads even when we cannot see the way ahead.

IV. In that faith we may not only rest upon the Master's assurance of the many mansions in our Father's house, but we can look for a better world in the future for struggling humanity. What is our religion for but to comfort and to give assurance for a time like this! Indeed, God still lives; God is good, and God is all-powerful. What more can we want? —R. T.

### SUNDAY SCHOOL LESSON

**Oct. 19. The Meaning of Jesus' Baptism. Luke 3:15-22. Background Scripture: Matt. 3:13-17.**

MEMORY VERSE: "I have come to do thy will, O God." Heb. 10:7 (R.S.V.).

I. Jesus' baptism may be understood in the light of John's message that the Messiah's ministry was to be one of spiritual power and reality.

II. John's prediction was verified in the descent of the Spirit upon Jesus at his baptism and in the words of divine approval.

III. This event marks the transition from Jesus' private life to his public ministry.

IV. Since Jesus dedicated himself in doing the will of God, so students may be led to a dedication of themselves to the will of God.

## SUNDAY: OCTOBER TWENTY-SIXTH

### MORNING SERVICE

**Theme: To Drink or Not to Drink (World Temperance Sunday)**

SUGGESTED SCRIPTURE READING: Prov. 23:23-35.

SELECTED HYMNS: "We gather together to ask the Lord's blessing."—Anonymous. "I need thee every hour."—Annie S. Hawks. "I would be true."—Howard A. Walter. "Christian! dost thou see them?" —Andrew of Crete. "Soldiers of Christ, arise."—Charles Wesley.

CALL TO WORSHIP: "Who shall ascend into the hill of the Lord? or who shall stand in his holy place? He that hath clean hands and a pure heart; who hath not lifted up his soul unto vanity, nor sworn deceitfully. He shall receive the blessing from the Lord, and righteousness from the God of his salvation."

INVOCATION: Almighty God, unto whom all hearts are open, all desires known, and from whom no secrets are hid; cleanse the thoughts of our hearts by the inspiration of thy Holy Spirit, that we may perfectly love thee, and worthily magnify thy Holy Name; through Christ our Lord. Amen.

**Theme: To Drink or Not to Drink (World Temperance Sunday)**

TEXT: "Abstain from all appearance of evil." I Thess. 5:22.

In modern-day America the practice of drinking, as a result of tremendous advertising pressures, has become a commonplace and accepted social custom. The question comes to almost everyone, To drink or not to drink? The answer for the Christian lies in the extent of one's own personal desire to exemplify the spirit of Christ. Is drinking wrong? The test always is, that any activity that degrades the human body, human personality, character and society, is morally wrong and cannot be countenanced by Christian people. If the answer is still not clear, Paul gives us a pointed principle: "Abstain from all appearance of evil."

The appeals to personal freedom and social custom in this matter need to be measured by a frank consideration of at least three factual propositions.

I. Beverage alcohol is harmful to the human mind and body, personality and character. 1. These facts are well authenticated and well known. (Gather supporting facts from authoritative sources.) 2. These facts are ignored by the average drinker in the thought that harmful results come only from excessive drinking. This is not so. (Substantiate this statement.) 3. The end result is that alcoholism has become a national health problem. It is more prevalent than cancer, tuberculosis, and polio. 4. Alcohol is the Number 1 moral problem of the nation. Should the Church lift its voice against this monstrous thing? The answer is unmistakable for the Christian conscience.

II. Beverage alcohol degrades human society.) See Sunday School Lesson for Aug. 31 in this *Manual*.)

The evidence is overwhelming. An FBI annual uniform crime report showed that drinking figured in 60.9% of all arrests. These figures do not include the offenses of assault, rape, and offenses against the family and children in which alcohol is often a major factor. The problem is increasing every year. J. Edgar Hoover reports that since 1950 the crime rate has outstripped the nation's population growth almost four to one.

III. Beverage alcohol and not "alcoholism" is the root of the drinking problem. The words "alcoholic" and "alcoholism" refer to the problem drinker, that is, to the person who has apparently lost control over his drinking. Dr. P. S. Vitullo of the Chicago Police Dept. says that there are 135,000 problem drinkers and alcoholics in Chicago. Even the liquor industry warns against excessive drinking which sends people to skid row or the equivalent.

But the fact is, the problem drinker is the least of the problem. It is the habit-forming, poisonous nature of alcohol consumption itself that causes the most trouble all along the line. There is a popular school of thought that excuses alcoholism as a disease. If this is so, why is it that public health authorities tolerate the source of the disease, which is beverage alcohol? In the case of no other "disease" do we treat only the results and at the same time actually advertise and promote the cause.

A recognized authority, Dr. Anton J. Carlson of the University of Chicago, declared: "There is no question about its people today are drinking far too much. . . . The tendency today is to blame alcoholism on everything else but alcohol—frustrations, unhappiness, anything. The truth is that perfectly normal people can become addicted to alcohol through chronic consumption: or, in plainer words, too much social drinking."

It is this seemingly innocent social drinking that is by far the biggest cause of the crime, sex immorality, delinquency, divorce, accidents, and human failure brought on by beverage alcohol. The chief cause of widespread social drinking is the terrific social pressure exerted by the industry and by drinking people.

This vicious social pressure is the concern of the Christian. Few temperance groups are working toward the idea of national prohibition. What they and the church are concerned about is the right of the people to know the facts about the destructive influence of beverage alcohol. And we are insisting on the right of the individual to his freedom not to drink. It is a freedom that those who say they are free to drink do not seem to want to recognize. Since when have the customs of society dictated the moral standards of the Christian?

To say that social drinking is necessary to social acceptability or to business success is pure rationalization. There is abundant evidence against it. There are many social measures proposed to cope with the liquor traffic. But there is only one sure and positive way for the individual to hand the alcoholic beverage problem for himself. And that is to let it alone. "No thanks, I don't drink." Let this be the slogan of the Christians of America and the evil tide would turn. —Charles M. Crowe.

Theme Prayer: All-wise and all-loving God, Creator of all things, for the bounties of the earth and their usefulness unto thy children we give thee thanks. Thou hast exalted us by giving us dominion over thy works and a stewardship responsible to thee. We rejoice in the enrichment of our lives when we have used thy bounties well.

Forgive us, we pray, for any lack of responsibility, for inefficiency and sinfulness in our handling of thy gifts to us. Use has often become misuse and abuse. Thy blessings have often been used by us to curse our fellow men and ourselves. May thy Spirit move us to repentance and turn us to righteousness.

Especially do we repent for the sinful abuse which is seen in the traffic in, and addiction to, alcoholic liquor and beverage alcohol. Let the knowledge that this has ruined millions of homes, cursed innumerable lives, degraded the social life, and become a national scandal—let this cause us to bow in shame, and rise up with courage to end this grievous condition and usher in a better day. Deliver us from mere wishful thinking. Strengthen our hands to fight and make us valiant and sacrificial unto the end that our country and the world may be delivered from this great evil. In Jesus' name. Amen.—H.

Offertory Sentence: "Righteousness exalteth a nation: but sin is a reproach to any people." Prov. 14:34.

Offertory Prayer: Bless our offering, O Lord, that it may be used to cast down evil and extend righteousness in the land. May all agencies to promote temperance and right living in our beloved country be blessed of thee. Amen.—H.

Seed Thoughts:

It Doesn't Make Sense. I. Consider the fact that the highways are lined with appealing advertisements in an all-out effort to sell the very stuff that causes the most accidents on the road. It doesn't make sense. How stupid can we be?

II. We raise millions of dollars to fight cancer, polio, and tuberculosis and at the same time spend billions to buy and promote the sale of alcoholic beverages, which in turn cause one of the most serious health problems of the country. It doesn't make sense. How stupid can we be?

III. In the case of no other disease do we treat only the results and at the same time actually advertise and promote the sale of the cause of that disease. It doesn't make sense. How stupid can we be?

IV. We permit this vicious enemy of home life and of youth to parade in our very living rooms through the glamorous allure of television. To invite into the home the very thing that would tear it down just doesn't make sense. How stupid can we be?

V. There are those who argue that the tax on liquor sales is important revenue. However, in a recent survey, Dr. Lester Breslow of the California Department of Public Health found that California's alcoholics (not counting the enormous costs to the courts and institutions of ordinary drinking) cost the state twelve times the total liquor-tax revenue. Yet the liquor industry is the one sacred cow against which no voice dare be lifted except at the risk of being labeled a killjoy. It doesn't make sense. How stupid can we be?

VI. The one thing that contributes most to crime enjoys not only the immunity but the respect of the law and the people. It doesn't make sense. How stupid can we be?

Shall the intelligent person who knows something of the damaging effects of beverage alcohol and doesn't like it anyway continue to be a victim of a highly overrated social custom which he knows is against his own best interests? Let him declare his personal freedom not to drink! How stupid can we be?—Charles M. Crowe.

### Choice Illustrations on the Theme

An example for the Christian conscience. Witness this letter from a college student to Donald Kuhn, a Methodist student leader: "As I was preparing to write to you this afternoon, I was interrupted by a student. She came to tell me that one of our girls has just left for home. She was pregnant because one night she drank three pitchers of beer to show that she could. The father is a sixteen-year-old, and the girl is engaged to a student at the state university."—C. M. C.

A senator testifies. Senator Richard L. Neuberger is not a prohibitionist but he is a teetotaler. He said: "I am never called upon to explain why I don't eat oysters or calf's liver or Swiss kale. I don't have to give an account of why I never go hunting or play polo. But wherever I turn down a Martini or whisky sour, the host is likely to ask sympathetically, 'Ulcers?' And if I shake my head and say, 'Never use the stuff,' explanations are immediately and persistently demanded." Yet the Senator went on to say that whenever he asked for a limeade or tomato juice instead of a highball, invariably others would change their orders to soft drinks also.—C. M. C.

## EVENING SERVICE

**Theme: The Value of Personal Experience**

TEXT: "Prove all things; hold fast that which is good." I Thess. 5:21. "By all means use your judgment, and hold on to whatever is really good" (Phillips).

We may prove a machine by trying it. Will the watch keep time? Will the locomotive travel on the track by its own energy and draw a train of cars over the mountains? Will the telegraph deliver my message and bring me a reply in a few moments? These things are open to trial. One may prove them for himself.

I. We may prove a science. Take astronomy. Will it do what it is intended for? Make a calculation of an eclipse to take place three years hence, according to the rules and tables of the book, and if the event verifies the prediction we know the astronomer is not a cheat.

II. One may prove a friend. He makes great professions of faithfulness, saying, "Call upon me at any time for any service I can render, and you will find me ready. Trust me." Is he a genuine friend? Try him. If he will stand by you through evil report as well as good you need no endorsement, no argument. He is worthy.

Will God submit his love, his truth, his grace, to practical tests? This is one beauty of the religion of the Bible. The Lord of the whole earth has sent out his challenge, "Prove me."

III. We may prove the existence of God. Let us not claim too much for our religion. We shall gain nothing by making statements which are not warranted. But we are safe in saying that anyone who will, may prove that there is a God. Some say there is no God. Others believe that the evidences for and against the existence of such a Being are about equal. Others still insist that this is a subject about which no one knows and no one can know anything. Many tell us that the Bible assumes the existence of God without trying to prove it, and we must do the same. Is this true?

If you ask for a mathematical demonstration or a scientific demonstration which will satisfy the intellect, we confess that it is impossible. If you insist that this proposition must be proved by philosophical reasoning, which will satisfy every thinking mind, we acknowledge that it cannot be done.

But there is in every soul a religious feeling, or instinct, or capacity, or hunger, which reaches out after God as eagerly and peremptorily as the hunger of the body demands bread. And as surely as the hunger of the body finds something without answering to this inner craving so surely does the soul find God and satisfaction. There is something in us akin to God that demands communion with him, and enjoys him when he is found.

IV. We may prove the friendship of God. Many say they believe there is a God, but is he friendly? They doubt. Everyone feels the need of a friend, a powerful friend, a wise friend, a safe friend, who will not mock those who trust him with flattery nor crush them with criticism, who will never leave them nor forsake them. The Bible tells us that God is just such a friend.

V. You may prove his salvation. You may prove that he will dwell in the heart of a mortal. You may prove that he will answer prayer.

One's own experience is worth more to one than all the books on religion that ever were written. We must not ignore the testimony of others. We must not undervalue the Bible and great religious books. Read them. They are full of light. But above all, try your own religious experiments. Your personal experience will do more to confirm your faith and hope than all sermons and all arguments.—Author Unknown.

**Suggested Themes for World Temperance Sunday**

A Covenant with Sin and Death: "Our

revenue may derive some unholy benefit from the sale of alcohol, but the entire trade is nevertheless a covenant with sin and death."—Lord Bacon.

Poisoning for Profit.

The Shame of Skid Row.

Legalized Tragedy.

His Majesty Alcohol: "His Majesty Alcohol is a dictator beside whom William II and Hitler seem but pygmies."—M. André Monnier, Paris, France.

## MIDWEEK FELLOWSHIP MEETING TOPIC

(Church Night or Suggested Sermon Subject)

**Theme: Religion is Modern**

TEXT: "Jesus Christ the same yesterday, and today, and for ever." Heb. 13:8.

It is a great comfort to believe in a religion in whose brow Time can cut no furrow, nor chisel hard lines upon its countenance. A religion that tyrants cannot destroy, suffering cannot tarnish, and the anger of mobs cannot flatten to the ground.

I. By believing in Jesus Christ as my Lord and Saviour I have a religion as dateless as its Author, "the same yesterday, and today, and for ever."

II. Give us a religion that is effective in this day. Proclaim a religion capable of grappling with wickedness that is eating the heart out of society. Give us a religion that is as modern as the sorrow and grief that stains every cheek and cuts down the fond hope of the aged and youth alike.

III. Give us the religion of God's love for all mankind. The religion that proclaims its eternal antagonism to modern hate: hate that drives the knife into the heart of a brother; that robs a sister of food for her starving children. Give us a religion that proclaims a remedy that is as old as the race and yet is as modern as the morning. There are no new situations, no new dilemmas for which he is unequal. This religion, as modern as your need, is found in Christ.—Oliver G. Wilson.

## SUNDAY SCHOOL LESSON

**Oct. 26. Victory in Temptation. Matt. 4:1-11.**

MEMORY VERSE: "Because he himself has suffered and been tempted, he is able to help those who are tempted." Heb. 2:18 (R.S.V.).

The Tense Struggle. The fight began within himself, the fight that makes a man worth something, for temptation is a possibility for a sinless nature, but a necessity for a holy one. He could not think it well to ask to be lifted out of the normal experience of his fellows.—S. Pearce Carey.

I. In the tense struggle knowledge of the Scriptures helps a man to win victory over temptation. Note the example of Jesus.

II. In the tense struggle a firm faith in God helps a man to win victory.

III. Victory in the tense struggle is the means to high character and broad service. See James 1:2-4 and the memory verse.

---

# SUNDAY: NOVEMBER SECOND

---

## MORNING SERVICE

**Theme: A Vital Tradition (Reformation Sunday)**

SUGGESTED SCRIPTURE READING: Ps. 118.

COMMENT: This is a great Psalm, full of human nature and rich in historic associations. Basil in Pontus sang it at the dawn of every day. Luther said of it: "This is my psalm, my chosen psalm . . . This psalm lies nearest to my heart, and I have a familiar right to call it mine. . . . It is my friend, dearer to me than all the honors and the power of the earth." It was sung on the battlefield by the Huguenots under Coligny and

Henry of Navarre. At the landing of William of Orange, it was sung by the troops before their encampment standing along the English beach.—John Kelman.

SELECTED HYMNS: "A mighty fortress is our God."—Martin Luther. "Faith of our fathers, living still."—F. W. Faber. "O for a faith that will not shrink."—W. H. Bathhurst. "How firm a foundation."—Rippon's Selection. "Lord, dismiss us with thy blessing."—John Fawcett.

OPENING SENTENCES: Nor are we only kings and the freest of all men, but also priests for ever, a dignity far higher than kingship, because by that priesthood we are worthy to appear before God, to pray for others, and to teach one another mutually the things which are of God. —Martin Luther.

INVOCATION: We thank thee, O God, for the open and welcoming doors of the church, for the open Bible upon its pulpit, the good fellowship of our brotherhood, the liberty with which we worship, the presence of thy Holy Spirit, and the opportunities which tomorrow will afford us for witnessing in the name of Jesus Christ. Amen.—H.

**Theme: A Vital Tradition (Reformation Sunday)**

TEXT: To a people whose energies had been drained by long years of captivity, who had lost all hope of liberation, even though the hour of their deliverance was near, Isaiah spoke as follows: "Look unto the rock whence ye are hewn. Look unto Abraham your father, and unto Sarah that bare you. For the Lord shall comfort Zion, and make her wilderness like Eden, and her desert like the garden of the Lord. . . . Awake, awake, as in the ancient days, in the generations of old." Isa. 51:1-3, 9.

To look backward is always dangerous, and the perils are summarized in what happened to Lot's wife, when she looked back on the city from which she was fleeing and turned into a pillar of salt. But there is an important benefit to be gained by looking backward, and that is to recover from old traditions new courage and vitality for present tasks. It is good to look to the rock from which we are hewn, if in looking, we wake up as in the ancient days.

This first Sunday in November is called Reformation Sunday, commemorating October 31, 1517, when Martin Luther began the Protestant movement by nailing his ninety-five theses on the door of the castle church at Wittenberg.

I. Luther's Discovery. Luther was a Roman Catholic monk. As a young man he had an uneasy conscience, and he was searching within the walls of the monastery for peace of mind. He found no answer in the rigorous disciplines of an ascetic life, intensive study, prayers, fasting, penance, and long vigils. Somehow, all he did to achieve merit did not relieve the tension of his soul. Turning at last from philosophy, church history and Catholic theology to the Bible itself, to his wonder he found in the gospels and in Romans and Galatians that the salvation which he sought was not to be achieved as a reward for merit, but was already given him by the grace of God, and was to be received by faith. With this discovery came the long-sought peace of mind, and the beginning in his soul of a conviction that was to launch the Reformation.

II. Luther's Protest. As this idea was developing in his mind, he was deeply disturbed by the sale of indulgences by Johann Tetzel, and in protest he nailed his theses to the door of the church. He had no desire at this time to break with the Roman Catholic Church, and no idea that his action would drive him from the Church. He was concerned in his protest with the honor of the Church.

An indulgence was a special form of grace, bestowed by the bishops or by the Pope, relieving men of the necessity of full penance for their sins. It was a kind of executive clemency, granting absolution for infractions of the canon law, or for more serious sins in recognition of mitigating circumstances. For example, the Crusaders were all granted remission of penance when they undertook the liberation of the Holy Land. It was a natural and further step to grant special indulgences to those who contributed liberally to the cost of the Crusades. It was customary to relax the full measure of penance due when church property was acquired or church buildings, as for example, St. Peter's in Rome, were in process of construction. Instead of the probationary discipline, usually prescribed as penance for sins, special indulgences were granted in return for notable service to the Church, not uncommonly in recognition of liberal gifts. So it was only a step to the purchase of absolution for departed relatives, who died with a few things left undone, to reduce their term in purgatory, and even, as Luther encountered it, to buy indulgences for sins not only in the past, but not yet committed. Such was the profanation of the high doctrine of forgiveness. Such was the exploitation of the soul troubled with its sense of guilt.

Against this practice Luther began to contend, for the honor and purity of the Church. The controversy continued, and he was given an opportunity to repudiate his position as set forth on many central questions. But this was his answer: "Unless I shall be convinced by the testimonies of the Scriptures or by clear reason, I neither can nor will make any retraction, since it is neither safe nor honorable to act against conscience. Here I stand. I can naught else. God help me. Amen." Within a few days he was excommunicated by the Church and declared an outlaw by the state.

III. Luther's Affirmations. From his experience, from his knowledge of the Bible, from reason, and the guidance of God's spirit, he came to three central affirmations of Protestantism.

1. The final authority is the Word of God, as it speaks directly to the mind and conscience of the believer under the guidance of the Holy Spirit, and not the Church, which stands between the believer and the Word.

2. The Grace of God is given freely to the believer who receives it by faith, and not through the mediation of the priest in exchange for penance as prescribed by him. The condition of forgiveness is never penance—something performed that something may be earned—but penitence, that knows that all is given although nothing is deserved.

IV. The true church is the "congregation of the faithful" who remember the words of our Lord: "Call no man Master, for one is your Master, even Christ, and all ye are brethren." The place of worship is "neither on this mountain nor at Jerusalem," for it is not a geographical location but a condition of the heart. "God is a Spirit; they that worship him must worship him in spirit and in truth." —Harold E. Nicely.

Theme Prayer: We thank thee, O God, for the gospel which was wrought out for us by the life and death, the resurrection and spiritual presence of Christ, our Lord and Saviour. We thank thee for the lives of valiant men who stood for truth, and by their stand passed on to us the gospel with its heritage of freedom.

Quicken, O God, our appreciation of our heritage that we, too, may be steadfast and strong, courageous and sacrificial, bearing bravely our responsibilities to thee, our fellow men, and future generations. In Jesus' name. Amen.—H.

Offertory Sentences: Faith is a living, busy, active, mighty thing. It is impossible that it should not always be doing good. It asks not whether good works should be done, but before one asks it does them, and is always doing them.—Martin Luther.

Offertory Prayer: Increase our faith, our hope, and our love, O God, that our works in thy name may increase. With added prosperity may we do greater works. Bless, we pray thee, these offerings unto thy purposes. Amen.—H.

Seed Thoughts: Standing Alone. It has often been the fate of reformers that they had to stand alone. Even the disciples forsook Jesus and fled.

"All Are Yours!" The treasures of Lutheranism should not be kept alone to the followers of Luther—they belong also to me. The treasures of Presbyterianism should not belong alone to the followers of Calvin—they belong also to me. Nor should the treasures of Anglicanism belong alone to the followers of Cranmer, nor those of Methodism belong alone to the followers of Wesley—they belong also to me. "All are yours!" I hear the apostle declare, as if he spoke directly to me.—Charles Clayton Morrison.

### Choice Illustrations on the Theme

MARTIN LUTHER'S OPINIONS. Dr. Whiston, a clergyman of the seventeenth century, was persecuted for his advanced ideas. George II said to him, "However right you may be in your opinions, you had better suppress them." Whiston replied, "Had Martin Luther done so your majesty would not have been upon the throne of England."

BACKFIRE FOR TETZEL. John Tetzel was the agent of the Archbishop of Mayence, primate of Germany, in the traffic in the "plenary indulgence" proclaimed by Pope Leo X in order to raise funds for the rebuilding of St. Peter's Church at Rome. It is reputed that the readiness to sell immunity from penalty even for future sins upon one occasion produced a disconcerting "backfire" for Tetzel himself. A nobleman bought an indulgence for a highway robbery that he intended to commit; he then attacked the indulgence-seller himself and gave him a sound thrashing. And when Tetzel brought complaint against him, the case was dismissed.

THE WORD "PROTESEANT." The word "Protestant" does not mean "To protest against" as is often thought to be the case. It comes from two Latin words, *pro* and *testare* which mean "to testify for." As applied to members of the original movement, therefore, it meant, "One who bears witness to his faith," or "One who testifies that he has had an inner spiritual experience." Luther's own testimony was but the spark that ignited a flame. For his bold declarations found a ready response in the hearts of countless thousands. The early Protestants found for themselves a new, vital, personal faith which freed them at last from the dictatorship of the Roman Church.—Charles M. Crowe.

## EVENING SERVICE

### Our Protestant Worship

TEXT: "I was glad when they said unto me, Let us go into the house of the Lord." Ps. 122:1.

The writer of these sermon notes had not attended a Protestant service of worship, except a most informal service on shipboard on Easter evening, for more than two months. During that time he had passed through many Roman Catholic churches and cathedrals in northern Italy and Spain. Now he was seated in a Protestant church waiting for the service to begin. During the hour our Protestant service of worship gathered a fresh luster and an enhanced value, beyond that which he had previously experienced. Here are some of the glories of that service. They apply generally to worship in Protestant churches.

I. A sense of freedom. I was attending that service under no compulsion except that which existed in my own soul. So it was, I feel sure, with my fellow worshipers. There was no hand forcing our presence. Conscience? Yes. The Spirit of God? Yes. But no priest, no system, no hierachy. We were free.

The service was not attended by persons forced to do penance, though in it many, or even all, may have shown a repentant spirit. The ministry of the ministers was not something bought at a price; it was freely given and freely received. The form of worship was not the imposition of a static tradition. There was no dead hand laid upon either the minster or the congregation. The Spirit of God gave freedom to all.

II. A second inspiring fact was that the service was intelligible and appealed to the intelligence. It could be understood as a whole and in all its parts. No dead language veiled any part. And in this service the sermon on *Christian Love* moved on a level which enabled anyone present to understand.

III. The togetherness of the service was warming. Those present most certainly worshiped in the secret places of their own hearts, but they also worshiped together. In the prayer of confession the minister and the people spoke in unison. The assurance of pardon was accepted by the minister for himself and given to all. In the singing of hymns and in responsive readings the voices of all were blended. At the close of the service the expressions of Christian love were mutual and sincere.

IV. It was a rooted service. The hymns chosen were among those sung by our fathers. The anthem reached back to Paul's letter to the Philippians. The Scripture Reading and text were the thirteenth chapter of First Corinthians. The Lord's Prayer was prayed.

V. It was a service that looked out into the future, the future of eternity. It ended upon the climax of I Cor. 13—"And now abideth faith, hope, love, these three; and the greatest of these is love." One knew that in the immediate future, in fact during the following week, the kindness, the courtesy, the humility, which belong to Christian love, would be more manifest in the homes and places of work of those who had worshiped in this service.

VI. The service rested upon the authority of the Word of God. The Bible lay upon the pulpit desk. God was speaking in the service through his Word. The Holy Spirit through the preacher made the preaching sacramental and God's Word was made contemporary.—H.

**Suggested Themes for Reformation Sunday**

Protestant Basic Convictions.

Protestantism Affirms.

What Protestants Believe.

How to avoid Tyrants. "To avoid tyrants, obey God."—William Penn.

Pulse-beats of the Reformation. I. Not works, but faith. II. Not our merit, but God's grace in Christ. III. Not our own penances and satisfactions, but the merit of Christ only.

**Suggested Texts and Themes for All Saints' Day**

A Source of Comfort: "For if we believe that Jesus died and rose again, even so them also which sleep in Jesus will God bring with him. . . . Wherefore comfort one another with these words." I Thess. 4:14-18.

Kindness to the Living and the Dead: "Blessed be he of the Lord, who hath not left off his kindness to the living and to the dead." Ruth 2:20.

Saintship: "Salute every saint in Christ Jesus." Phil. 4:21.

The Heavenly Home Gathering: "And they shall come from the east, and from the west, and from the north, and from the south, and shall sit down in the kingdom of God." Luke 13:29.

We Have a Keeper: "The Lord is thy keeper." Ps. 121:5.

## MIDWEEK FELLOWSHIP MEETING TOPIC

(Church Night or Suggested Sermon Topic)

**Theme: Love Not the World**

TEXT: "Love not the world . . . for all that is in the world, the lust of the flesh, and the lust of the eyes, and the pride of life, is not of the Father, but is of the world." I John 2:15, 16.

INTRODUCTORY: What is the world that we must not love? What is the pride of life against which we are warned? (Discussion.) Not the world as God created it with its varied patterns of natural loveliness. Not the world of physical phenomena with its obedience to immutable laws. The world organized apart from God. The theater of human activity which Bunyan called "Vanity Fair."

The nature of pride. (Discussion.) It is one of those spices of life of which a little may be all right, even essential, but of which too much may be ruinous. An element of honorable self-respect, yet difficult to handle. We are tempted to "vaunt ourselves, be puffed up, behave ourselves unseemly. . . ."

I. The Pride of Life. Natural and rightful joy in physical vitality *vs.* the pride of life that witholds from God the years of our strength.

II. The Pride of Knowledge. What seems the pure light of the intellect is not immune to pride. The pride of scientific materialism.

III. Spiritual Pride. Are we confident in our health? Are we counting only our material resources? Satisfied with the direction of our lives? These are dangerous attitudes. To be content with our thinking, our prayers, to be no more understanding, no more loving, complacent about our soul's health, what is this but spiriutal pride?

How does one avoid the pride of life? By consecration. By stewardship. Let us quicken our consciences by the thought of God's holiness; nourish our minds on his truth; purify our imagination by the thought of his beauty; open our hearts to his love; direct our wills to his purposes.—Leslie Badham.

## BULLETIN BOARD SLOGANS FOR THE MONTH

Grumbling makes the loaf no larger.

The law of living is the law of giving.

Money often unmakes the man that makes it.

American ideals can't be preserved in alcohol.

The power of the Cross is not a creed but a life.

God has given us abundant reason for thanksgiving.

You do not need bank references in order to borrow trouble.

Those who hope for no other life are dead even in this.

Thanksgiving is possible only to those who have time to remember.

It takes more than a verbal platitude to express genuine gratitude.

## SUNDAY SCHOOL LESSON

**Nov. 2. The Galilean Ministry Begins. Mark 1:14-22. Background Scripture: Mark 1:14-39.**

MEMORY VERSE: "The time is fulfilled, and the kingdom of God is at hand; repent, and believe in the gospel." Mark 1:15 (R.S.V.).

Note: The Evening Sermon notes for Oct. 19 in this *Manual* are based upon Mark 1:16-20.

I. It may be noted that Jesus calls men from ordinary walks of life to follow and serve him. "He rightly first called into his inner circle these obvious representatives of the rank and file, to assure the multitudes that the gates of the Kingdom were wide open for themselves."

II. "The wonder is that such was his quickening power over this plebeian quartet that one, James, became so potent as to be marked by an alarmed king for first martyrdom (James 12:1-2); and a second, Peter, the Kingdom's most effective preacher; whilst to the memoranda and reflections of a third, John, all will agree that we owe the world's most precious Christian book, the Gospel of John."—S. Pearce Carey. Let it be noted, too, that Andrew became the first Christian missionary. The day after his conversion was the day on which he became a soul-winner. John 1:40-42.

# SUNDAY: NOVEMBER NINTH

## MORNING SERVICE

**Theme: A Life Given is a Life Gained (Veterans' Sunday)**

SUGGESTED SCRIPTURE READING: Isa. 2:1-5.

SELECTED HYMNS: "O God, our help in ages past."—Isaac Watts. "O beautiful for spacious skies."—Katharine Lee Bates. "God of our fathers, known of old."—Rudyard Kipling. "My country, 'tis of thee."—Samuel F. Smith. "Fling out the banner! let it float."—George W. Doane.

Opening Sentence: "Not by might, nor by power, but by my spirit, saith the Lord of hosts."—Zech. 4:6.

Invocation: Our God and our Father, clear our imaginations that we may see thee more plainly, and deepen our understanding that we may know thee more genuinely. We would open all the doors and windows of our lives, that the light of thy spirit may come to us in truth and beauty and peace. Amen.—Paul J. Bockhoven.

**Theme: A Life Given is a Life Gained (Veterans' Day)**

Text: "Whosoever will save his life shall lose it; but whosoever shall lose his life for my sake and the gospel's, the same shall save it." Mark 8:35.

The words which most readily come to mind on this day are "Remembrance" and "Sacrifice." At the national level we remember that we live as a people, that we enjoy freedom and toleration, that we are a republic, because of the sacrifice of others. The nation lives because men died for it.

At the personal level there will be individual and family sadness. There are those who will be recalling the death of fathers, brothers, sons, husbands. And we remember that we live, that we can make a living, get married, set up house, and live without fear because of their sacrifice. We live because they died. At the religious level, for the Christian, Sunday is always a day of remembrance. For him the most sacred command is to remember. "This do in remembrance of me"—remembrance of him who died that the world might live through him. The Christian lives because Jesus died.

I. A Law of Life. At all levels it is Remembrance and Sacrifice. The many live because of the sacrifice of the few. That seems to be the way life goes on: the pattern on which life is built. That is part of the price we have to pay for our membership one of the other. One man's decision can plunge a world into war. One man's foolishness can ruin thousands. One man's sacrifice, equally, can save thousands.

II. But a Law Evaded. Today, as you and I look back and remember with gratitude to God those who sacrificed themselves for us, I wonder if we can honestly say that we have learned this lesson: that the way to life is through losing life. Have we taken the matter to heart and tried in our own personal lives and in our own personal relationships with one another, to emulate the example which has been given to us, and by which we live? Isn't it only too true that the law by which a great many people live today is not that they should sacrifice themselves for others, but rather the simple rule of "Look after Number One"—which is just the modern respectable version of "Every man for himself and the devil take the hindmost"? The rule is one of preservation by self-interest. Let every man look after himself—and look after himself at the expense of others. "Number One" first and every time, and the rest where they can get in behind. What suits me is right. What brings advantage to me is right—no matter how it may affect others. As far as they are concerned—well—"I just couldn't care less."

Don't we recognize that as a common rule of life today? And it is a way of life which is gaining adherents daily. But can it lead to life? Self-seeking leads to self-destruction.

III. Proved in Experience. This principle of finding life by losing it may not be easily accepted, but isn't it something which we have all experienced at some time or other? Suppose we have set out to find pleasure or happiness for ourselves—we have sought it by way of our own self-indulgence—but at the end of our search all we had for our seeking was a dreadful, unsatisfied feeling. But some other time we weren't looking for pleasure, we weren't expecting to find it—but it came when in complete forgetfulness of ourselves we were doing something for somebody else. It may even have been that the call came when we were about to set off on our own pleasure—and we were annoyed that we should have to give time to another, and yet, in giving it—and ourselves—we found a pleasure which we wouldn't have found the other way.

The person who gives his life in the service of others, and above all in the service of Jesus Christ, and loses it in him—that person finds the life which is life indeed. The Christian life in all its depth and richness is found by the surrender of our wills to the will of God in Jesus Christ, by the death of our own inclinations to the duty of obeying God, by the consecration of our lives to the service of Jesus Christ. "If any man would come after me," said Jesus, "let him deny himself and take up his cross and follow me."

IV. Remember the Cross. No one would pretend that this is in any way easy. But the great symbol of Christianity is a Cross, and that Cross is the noblest example of just this principle—that life comes through death. For on that Cross hung Jesus of Nazareth who died for the sin of the world. The loving dying for the loveless; the just for the unjust; the sinless one for the sinful many; the one dying for the salvation of the world. Jesus died that the world might live through him.

Nothing touches us quite like the remembrance of Jesus hanging there and the knowledge that is was for us he hung and suffered there. And nothing can move us to follow in just that way of self-sacrifice like the thought that he suffered for us.

Remembrance and Sacrifice—those are the words for today. Remembrance of those who died in war that we might live. Remembrance of him who gave his life a ransom for many.

Let this Day of Remembrance bring us back to this great basic principle of life, that whosoever would save his life shall lose it; but whosoever would lose his life for Christ's sake and the gospel's, the same shall find it.—Adapted from E. T. Donald James.

A PRAYER FOR THE DAY: Our Father who art in heaven, we worship today with thoughts of those who gave their lives upon the battlefields of the earth that we might live. No word or deed of ours has earned this sacrifice, offered up so freely and vicariously, without thought of recompense or price.

Enable each of us to pay the price for peace on earth and a better country. Soberly and in the light of conscience, let use resolve, as a personal convenant with our honored dead and with our veterans and with thee—

To work for righteousness between men, and an end of human bondage.

To work for the right of every child to learn, and to train himself to the full grasp of his powers.

To work for homes which shall be serene, each one the abiding place of love and security and joy.

To work for new regions of health, that the springs of our national life may be ever replenished.

To achieve once more the ancient knowledge of our fathers—that we can go forward only if we put our trust in thee. Amen.—Adapted from David K. Ford.

OFFERTORY SENTENCE: "Thy kingdom come. Thy will be done in earth, as it is in heaven." Matt. 6:10.

OFFERTORY PRAYER: O God, help us not to put "any value upon anything that we have or are except in its relationship to thy kingdom." Bless this offering, we pray, unto the cause of thy kingdom, and by that unto the cause of peace in the world. Amen.—H.

SEED THOUGHTS:

The Needful Offering. The sacrifice of the past must be continued into the present and the future. It is not the sacrifice of blood and limb that is now called for, but the sacrifice of those things which now retard the building of the city of peace—national and personal pride and greed, man's inhumanity to man, racial prejudices, selfishness and stubbornness. We have learned from war that war itself cannot build the city of peace and good will. The sword cannot do it. We must guard against making this Veterans' Day one for military ends. We must live to serve and help forward the cause of peace and good will amongst all men.—J. G. Harris.

Some Comparatives. There is something more noble than peace, if peace means a benumbed indifference to moral issues, and a dead aloofness to the cry and sigh of those who are wronged. There is something worse than the endurance of pain, and that is a callous disregard when pain is unrighteously inflicted by others. There is something worse than death, and that is to be dead to the call of chivalry, dead to the trumpet blast of justice and of truth.—John H. Jowett.

**Choice Illustrations on the Theme**

". . . FOR EXTRAORDINARY HEROISM . . ." ". . . His courageous spirit of self-sacrifice. . . . Gave his life for his country. . . ."

These are official statements, taken from the United States Navy citation, notifying Mrs. Maynard William Tolberg that the Navy Cross and the Purple Heart had been awarded to her husband., Bill Tolberg, killed in action off Guadalcanal on January 30, 1943.

Action off Guadalcanal! A ship hit by a Japanese torpedo . . . shattering explosions and the sudden release of high-pressure steam in the engine room . . . one man left alive there. Bill Tolberg . . . and he blinded, scalded, fatally burned. . . .

Groping his way over the bodies of his dead comrades, Tolberg forced a passage to the upper deck, then used his fast-ebbing strength in an attempt to close an oil valve. He knew scores of his mates were trapped . . . the open valve meant death to them.

He died . . . but his heroism saved three hundred lives!—Moody Bible Institute Bulletin.

FOR OUR SAKES

In grateful love I bow the knee
To nameless men who died for me.

. . . . . . . . . . . . . . . . . . . . . . . . . . . . . . . . .

For be it ever understood
I am a man redeemed with blood.
I must go softly all my days
Down my redeemed and solemn ways.
Christ take the men I bring to Thee,
The men who fought and died for me.
—Author Unknown.

## EVENING SERVICE

**Theme: The Reconciling Loyalty**

TEXT: "But seek ye first the kingdom of God." Matt. 6:33.

From no less reputable a source than the "Life and Work" of the Church of Scotland there comes a tale of two mothers who had an acute difference of opinion regarding the public schools attended respectively by their two sons. One mother became so hot that she declared, "If yours was the only school in Scotland, I would not send my son to it." Within a week after, the two mothers were sitting together in a stand at Murrayfield, watching the Rugby International match. At a critical stage in the game, a fine run by a former pupil of the school in question resulted in a try for Scotland. Both mothers were immediately on their feet, cheering with the crowd, the one who had been so contemptuous of that school no less heartily than the other! A larger national loyalty had swallowed up the school loyalties, in so far as they were hostile to each other.

It is a good, human story, not only because it shows those instincts at work that can so wreck our happiness, but because it gives a thrilling glimpse of how they may actually be reconciled in some bigger devotion.

Man is an inveterate group-former. His history is the tale of his successive groups, and the loyalty they have called out—home, tribe, state, and, someday, please God, a real league of nations.

But besides that general development, each of us all the time is being drawn, by tastes or temperament, into groups, parties, associations, to which we give our allegiance. That is the way God made us. And much good comes of it, for it spells co-operation, and it is so that things get done.

But much harm can come too. For

the difficulty is to be loyal to your own group without being hostile or unjust to others. Think of the tension immediately created by the very labels of groups like Socialist and Conservative; Capital and Labor; Town and Gown; Church and Chapel. So the curse of social group loyalty is class consciousness and snobbery. Political group loyalty easily becomes pure—and therefore blind—party spirit. Love of country may easily degenerate into that spurious form of patriotism whose creed is "My country, right or wrong" or the inflamed nationalism from which the whole world is suffering today.

The trouble about all these causes, in defense of which men and women find themselves in opposition, with consequent unhappiness, is that none of them in itself is big enough to be worth our whole or utter allegiance, although they sometimes get it. It is Jesus Christ who, by example and teaching, has shown the world the truth for which human nature was made; namely, that there is only one object on earth which is worth a man's utter loyalty, the will of God for all mankind. God made us for himself, and there is no other way of living happily. All our group loyalties can and will be dangerous until they are transcended and united in that one. The prescription of Jesus for the only really successful kind of living, whether for an individual or a nation, is "Seek ye first the kingdom of God." Christ's teaching is that a man's first loyalty does not belong either to the state, or its head, or a majority, or any other human authority whatever, though it may demand it. His first loyalty belongs to God and to him only.

A Christian, properly so-called, is one who, having found in Jesus Christ a revelation of God's gracious purpose to him and to all men, is living first of all for the establishment of the Kingdom of God on earth and the doing of God's will in the world today. He is not a capitalist nor a Socialist nor an American, nor a Briton first, and a Christian afterward, but a Christian first, and everything else afterward. In that supreme overarching loyalty to the will of God as Jesus has revealed it, all party and group loyalties are transcended. They do not disappear. Rather they are sanctified and reinforced. But the conflict is taken out of them. They suffer voluntary disarmament. A man does not love his home or his country one whit the less because his supreme allegiance is to the will of God and the Spirit of Christ. But he is delivered from that home-selfishness which makes him blind to the needs of other homes, and from that national pride which counts all other nations cheaper and poorer stuff.

The reason why things are as they are and no better is that we are citizens and adherents of this or that political party first, and Christians afterward, if at all. And it has stood for nineteen hundred years that that is the wrong way round. Seek ye first, said Jesus, the Kingdom of God.

Harry Emerson Fosdick tells that Henry George was once introduced to a New York audience by a chairman, anxious to curry favor with the crowd, as "Henry George, the friend of the working man." George stood up and sternly began: "I am not the friend of the working man." Then, after a strained silence, "And I am not the friend of the capitalist." Then, after another silence, "I am for men, simply as men, regardless of any accidental or superficial distinctions of race, creed, color, class or yet function or employment."

It is that larger loyalty that alone can unite and immunize all our competing small ones. And Paul had the vision of it when he cried: "There is neither Jew nor Greek, there is neither bond nor free, there is neither male nor female, for ye are all one in Christ Jesus."—Archibald Alexander.

Suggested Texts and Themes.

The Future Demands—Courage: "Be strong and of good courage." Josh. 1:6.

The More Excellent Way: "Yet show I unto you a more excellent way." I Cor. 12:31.

Will Spirit Win? "Not by might, nor by power, but by my spirit, saith the Lord of hosts." Zech. 4:6.

Dying for the People: "And I, if I be lifted up from the earth, will draw all men unto me. This he said, signifying what death he should die." John 12:32-33.

Carry On! "Only be strong and very courageous." Josh. 1:7.

## MIDWEEK FELLOWSHIP MEETING TOPIC

(Church Night or Suggested Sermon Subject)

**Theme: Why I Believe in Tithing**

TEXT: Mal. 3:10.

I believe in tithing because it is scriptural, reasonable, and practical. Firmly grounded in the Old Testament, commended by Jesus, validated by the personal experience of thousands of Christians who have tried it, tithing remains the best method for the material support of the church and the progressive realization of the revealed purposes of God for his world.

I. Tithing is scriptural. Only by the most radical application of historical-critical methods of interpretation can it be explained away.

II. Tithing is reasonable. Anyone, rich or poor, can tithe. It asks of no one that which he does not have.

III. Tithing is practical. It works. It works for the individual: it works for the church. There is little doubt that it is the bedrock foundation of the financial system of the most successful churches and denominations.

Our God knew what he was doing when by the Holy Spirit he wrote the principle of the tithe into the Bible. Let no man who is giving less than a tenth to the work of the church say, "I don't believe in tithing." Jesus said, "I came not to destroy the law, but to fulfill it." The only way to escape the law of the tithe is to fulfill it by rising above it; to ignore it as a law by giving more than a tenth out of sheer gratitude and joy. Regardless of when, where, and to whom it was first written, Mal. 3:10 still speaks to the heart of modern man. You can prove that it is the word of God to you, if you will read it and obey.—H. C. Goerner.

## SUNDAY SCHOOL LESSON

**Nov. 9. The Marks of a Christian. Matt. 5:1-12.**

MEMORY VERSE: "You are the salt of the earth. . . . You are the light of the world." Matt. 5:13-14 (R.S.V.).

The marks of a Christian are:

I. A new spirit.

II. New ideals. The Sermon on the Mount describes the ideals for the attitudes and conduct of a true disciple.

III. A new quality of life. 1. Like salt. 2. Like light.

IV. A new inner force. Those who follow this way of life become a permeating influence in various areas of life to stop the corruption of society and to give insights needed for abundant living.

V. A new kind of joy. Such blessedness does not eliminate the possibility of persecution and mockery.

# SUNDAY: NOVEMBER SIXTEENTH

## MORNING SERVICE

**Theme: Where is Our Treasure? (The sermon notes and suggestions given below may be adapted for use on Loyalty Sunday or Every-Member Canvass Sunday)**

SUGGESTED SCRIPTURE READING: Matt. 6:19-34.

SELECTED HYMNS: "The Church's one foundation."—Samuel J. Stone. "Take my life, and let it be."—Frances R. Havergal. "O Jesus, I have promised."—John E. Bode. "Breathe on me, Breath of God."—Edwin Hatch. "Onward, Christian soldiers."—S. Baring-Gould.

CALL TO WORSHIP: "Lord, I have loved the habitation of thy house, and the place where thine honor dwelleth. O taste and see that the Lord is good; blessed is the man that trusteth in him."

INVOCATION: Unto thee, O Lord, we come in the quietness and confidence of this hour of worship. Unto thy strength we bring our weakness; unto thy greatness we bring our littleness; unto thy peace we bring our restlessness; unto thy forgiveness we bring our guilt; unto thy comfort we bring our sorrow; unto thy sympathy we bring our joy. Perfect, we beseech thee, the good work which thou hast begun in us; unto the glory of our Lord and Saviour, Jesus Christ. Amen.—H.

**Theme: Where is Our Treasure?**

TEXT: "Where your treasure is there will your heart be also." Matt. 6:21.

This is a very penetrating statement. We have only to think of it to find how it reveals us to ourselves. A mother's treasure is her little child. Wherever he is, there her thoughts travel and her interests lie. Whatever affects him touches her very life. Her plans and hopes are centered there. In her child you find the key to the understanding of her life.

Or here is a man whose son is in some distant land. The slighest mention of the place in the newspaper will catch his eye, and he will read it with eagerness. His treasure is there and his heart is there also. Here is another whose treasure is in his business. He has given his life to build it up. It occupies all his thoughts. His mind flies back to it in his spare moments. Life may hit him very hard; but so long as it does not touch his business, the wound does not run very deep. He may have other interests, but they are secondary.

I. Our real life is centered in the things we value most. From these we draw our inspiration. In these we find our joy and comfort. In secret and often unconsciously, our purposes and plans are shaped and directed by the things we value most. They have in our hands the making of our life for good or ill. The things that hold our heart shape our character and fashion our spirit. Our treasure is the key to our life. If we can discover what we value most, we shall know what we really are and what is happening to us.

II. It is very important to find this out. Where is our treasure? What are the things we really value? Is it money or reputation? Is it the pleasure which life can bring us? There are two kinds of things that can hold our heart. So Jesus tells us. We can find our treasure in material things, in things that belong to this world. It is often difficult to avoid it. The struggle for daily bread is so keen that it is hard for some people not to be materialists. Much of our mind must be given to the making of money if we are to maintain life at all. But we can center our life on the things of the spirit—on people, on our fellowship with God, on the service of his

Kingdom. This is what distinguishes people from one another in the view of Jesus. The difference is vital. It is the dividing point of life.

III. This is the point of the counsel Jesus gives. "Lay not up for yourselves treasure on earth." He came to show us what the real things are that we may center our hearts on these. The real treasure of life shines in his light like grains of gold in a torrent bed when the sun strikes on it. But we have to claim it. That was what Christ bade the rich young ruler to do when he told him to sell all and follow him. One thing was needed to change the center of his life. It was the step of renunciation for which Christ asked. If only he had taken that step, however hard, the treasure of Christ's fellowship would have come fully to possess and hold his heart.

Is not this what Christ means by bidding us lay up our treasure in heaven? We can change the center of our life if we will. We can do it by deliberately investing in his Kingdom. Interest in his Kingdom grows by what we do for it.

Sometimes circumstances break the chain and help us to find the real treasure. God often works in this way. Moth and rust corrupt our treasures. Business goes down. Misfortune comes. In the emptiness, our eyes are opened to see the real things in life, and seek them in God's fellowship. The passing of a loved one sometimes loosens a man's grip on earth, and opens his heart to prayer and the service of others. But we need not wait for the rude hand of misfortune or bereavement to change the center of our life. We can seek the company of Christ that he may open our eyes. We can invest our lives and our money in what is real by service and prayer that cost, we can lay up our treasure in heaven. Where our treasure is there will our heart be also.—James Reid.

PRAYER FOR THE DAY: O God and Master of us all, teach us to render, day by day, an account of our stewardship to thee. All we have of time and talents and possessions are thine; and we are thine, bought with a price. We come with contrite hearts to acknowledge that we have often wasted time that should have been spent with thee and for thee; we have used thoughtlessly and for our aggrandizement talents that should have been used in thy service; and our possessions have been so little at they disposal. Consecrate us, and all that we have, more truly to thyself. Give us opportunities for serving thee and our fellow men; and grant to us courage and vision to use these oportunities aright. Help us to give gladly the first fruits of all that thou dost give to us, that bringing the tithes into the storehouse, the hungry and needy everywhere may be satisfied and thy blessing may be ours. Teach us the joy of time spent in thy presence interceding for others, and having thee guide us into all truth. In the name of our Redeemer Christ we pray. Amen.—Stewardship Dept. of the Board of Missions, Presbyterian Church, U.S.A.

OFFERTORY SENTENCE: "He which soweth sparingly shall reap also sparingly, and he which soweth bountifully shall reap also bountifully." "The liberal deviseth liberal things and by liberal things shall he stand."

OFFERTORY PRAYER: O thou who openest thy hand in bounties unto thy children, forgive us our foolish wasteful ways. So instruct us in the true wealth of life that, seeking the welfare of all thy children, we may no longer be anxious for our daily needs, having found the secret of the abounding life. Graciously receive and use these offerings of thy people for the support and extension of thy Kingdom in the world. Bless both the gifts and the givers, we ask in the name of Christ. Amen.—G. H.

SEED THOUGHTS:

The Principles of Stewardship. I. God is the owner of all. II. I am his steward and must account for all I have. III. God requires me to give a definite proportion of my income in acknowledgment of his ownership and my stewardship. IV. I should use all the rest—

what I spend and what I save—in ways that are pleasing to him.

Fabricating Character: I. By the stewardship of time. II. By the stewardship of talents. III. By the stewardship of possessions.

The Tither's Surprise. The Christian who begins to tithe will have at least six surprises. He will be surprised: 1. At the amount of money he has left for the Lord's work. 2. At the deepening of his spiritual life in paying the tithe. 3. At the ease in meeting his own obligations with the nine-tenths. 4. At the ease in going from one-tenth to larger giving. 5. At the preparation this gives to be a faithful and wise steward over the nine-tenths that remain. 6. At himself in not adopting the plan sooner.

### Choice Illustrations on the Theme

GIVING IS HAVING. Maybe you have seen that cryptic picture of G. F. Watts, the English painter, which bears the title, *Sic Transit Gloria Mundi*—"So passes away the glory of the world." It is a very strange picture. It represents simply a bier with a shroud thrown over the silent form lying on it. You cannot see the man's face except the outlines of it through the white shroud. All around the picture are the little emblems that tell the story of his life. He was fond of art. He was a man of wealth. He had the best culture of his day. All the world speaks of as riches had entered into his life, and this is all there is of it at the last.

To tell the story the painter has painted around the three sides of the picture these three inscriptions: "What I spent, I had. What I kept, I lost. What I gave, I have."

Someday we shall realize that and know that all we put into this most unselfish enterprise (missions) is all that we shall have to count as our own in the day of judgment.—Robert E. Speer.

TO HOLD FOR A DAY. A prosperous businessman was recalling experiences of his childhood in Sweden where he had grown up in poverty. His special task was to tend the cattle. One day, as he wished to be away, he persuaded his sister to do his work, promising that in return she would be permitted to hold for the day a small coin. To be sure, it had little value, but as money was scarce in the home, she counsented, worked hard all day, and at night returned the coin, well content with her wages.

After the businessman—who was so gleeful over his sister's simplicity—had related the incident, a Chrisitian in the audience replied, "That is all you get; you hold your wealth to the end of the day of your life; then you give it up and have as little as before, and the whole of your life is gone."

A startled look spread over the man's face, for he had never thought of it in that light.

Stewards are we—not possessors.

## EVENING SERVICE

### Theme: Everyone's Servant

TEXT: "I made myself servant unto all." I Cor. 9:19.

I do not know whether it is a common inn-sign in England, but in Cheltenham there is an inn called "The Five Alls." And its sign is most interesting. On the sign there is a *king*, with the motto: "I rule for all." There is a *bishop*, with the motto: "I pray for all." There is a *lawyer*, with the motto: "I plead for all." There is a *soldier*, with the motto: "I fight for all." And there is an *artisan*, in working clothes, with the motto: 'I work for all." There indeed is a program for all.

I. *I rule for all.* If it should happen that we are in control of many people, the motive which should animate us is not our private profit, but the good of all. If we are simple ordinary people, servants and not masters, there is one person whom we can rule, and that is ourself, for only he who is master of himself is fit to be the servant of others.

II. *I pray for all.* That is not the prerogative of the bishop; any man can do that. Jowett, the great preacher, used to tell of a girl who came to join his church. She was a servant girl, not well off, and not well educated. He wished to make sure that she knew what she was doing and that she was in earnest about her profession, and he asked her how she proposed to live the Christian life.

"I haven't much time off, sir," she said, "and I can't attend many meetings or even many services." "Well," said Jowett, "what do you do?" "Well, sir," she said, "I always take the daily paper to bed with me at night." Jowett was puzzled, as well he might be. "What's the good of that?" he said. "Well, sir," she said, "I look at the first page and I read the birth notices and I pray for the babies that have been born; and I read the marriages and I pray that they may be happy and true; and I read the deaths and I pray that God's comfort may come to these sorrowing homes." Is it not a staggering vision—the waves of prayer which went out from that attic beneath the tiles? *I pray for all*—the servant girl did and so can we.

III. *I plead for all.* Surely this takes our vision straight to Jesus Christ. The writer to the Hebrews has the most tremendous vision in the New Testament. He speaks of Jesus in the heavenly places and he says of him: "He ever liveth to make intercession for us" (Heb. 7:25). Even in heaven Jesus is pleading for men.

IV. *I fight for all.* That is what the great lovers of humanity have all done. They saw some wrong, some iniquity, some oppression, some distress, some need, and they fought that it might be removed. Often they themselves were well-to-do and comfortable and lived at ease; the conquest in the struggle of social reformation was not going to profit them; but they spent themselves for the sake of others. Where there was poverty, oppression, sorrow, distress, they must fight their battle.

It is too often the case that so long as things are well with us, we do not much mind what is happening to others. The great men were the men who bore the sorrows of the world upon their hearts, and who were God's crusaders in the battle for the downtrodden and the underprivileged and the oppressed.

V. *I work for all.* Do we? The tragedy of things today is that hardly anyone does. Some of us work for ourselves, a bigger bank balance, a television set, a refrigerator, a new automobile—these are the things for which we work. Some of us go a little further and work for our families, a better chance for our sons and daughters, a better start in life for them, a better job than we have—these are the things for which we work.

Some of us work for the class to which we belong, more privileges, higher pay, shorter hours, longer holidays, better conditions for ourselves and our mates—these are things for which we work.

But there are so few, so very few, who work for *all,* who have the spirit of service which sees beyond the boundaries of self and selfish interest. The social and the economic millenium will come when master and man work, not for self, but for God and for all.

God so loved the *world.* His love is over *all.* And we, who are his servants, must ever seek to be like him.—William Barclay.

## MIDWEEK FELLOWSHIP MEETING TOPIC

(Church Night or Suggested Sermon Subject)

**Theme: Your Greatest Thought**

TEXT: "As he thinketh in his heart, so is he." Prov. 23:7.

(This subject when introduced might lead into vital personal testimony and group discussion.)

Daniel Webster was at one time considered the greatest living American. He was great as attorney, orator, statesman, leader of men. Also he was a candidate for the presidency.

The story has more than one version. But it was something like this: A select banquet was made in honor of the great man. Only twenty-five were present, but these, leaders of the nation—judges of the Supreme Court, eminent Senators —and others.

When seated at the table one man, probably expecting to get a discussion of some subject of state, asked the honored guest, "What is the greatest thought that ever entered your mind?"

Answered Webster: "The greatest thought that ever entered my mind is the thought of my responsibility to my God." Having said this, he wept, excused himself from the table, and went into an outer room the better to get control of his emotions. When he returned to the table he discoursed for half an hour upon "a man's responsibility to God."

I. If men may be judged by the importance of the things to which they give attention—and this is possible—then here is one measure of Webster.

II. But as to ourselves, what are our greatest thoughts? It is too bad if we are chiefly occupied with the cheap or the trivial, or even with the commonplace—though these things are always present with us. These subjects are enough and big enough for creatures which have no immortality. But we are different.

III. What is the greatest thought that ever entered your mind? Does it dominate your whole life? It should.—*Free Methodist.*

## SUNDAY SCHOOL LESSON

**Nov. 16. Christian Concern for Health. Matt. 8:1-17.**

MEMORY VERSE: "Jesus went about all the cities and villages, teaching in their synagogues and preaching the gospel of the kingdom, and healing every disease and every infirmity." Matt. 9:35 (R.S.V.).

I. Christ's concern for health. 1. In the eyes of Jesus the body was not something evil. It is fashioned by God as an instrument of his eternal plans. See John 2:21. See also Paul's statement concerning the body as "the temple of God." I Cor. 3:16.

2. Jesus was very much concerned with sick persons. His interest seems to have been focused on the suffering person rather than on the disease itself.

3. Guilt and anxiety and other spiritual factors were his concern as causes of illness; he was also concerned with forgiveness and faith as necessary elements in the cure.

II. The Church's concern for health. 1. A review of the Church's influence in the development of the practice of medicine and nursing, in the building of hospitals throughout the world, and in stimulating research in the cause and cure of disease. Example, medical missions to lepers. The Church has great interest at the present time in the fostering of mental health.

III. The class might consider how the local church program could be used to foster the physical and mental health of people. What vocations, besides medicine, surgery, dentistry, and psychiatry, are open to young people who wish to devote their lives to a ministry of health?

# SUNDAY: NOVEMBER TWENTY-THIRD

## MORNING SERVICE

**Theme: Think and be Thankful (Thanksgiving)**

SUGGESTED SCRIPTURE READING: Ps. 105:1-7; Ps. 103:1-5.

SELECTED HYMNS: "Come, ye thankful people, come."—Henry Alford. "Not alone for mighty empire."—William P. Merrill. "My country, 'tis of thee."—Samuel F. Smith. "Now thank we all our God."—Martin Runkart.

CALL TO WORSHIP: O give thanks unto the Lord, for he is good: for his mercy endureth forever.

O that men would praise the Lord for his goodness, and for his wonderful works to the children of men!

Whoso is wise, and will observe these things, even they shall understand the loving-kindness of the Lord. Ps. 107:1, 15, 43.

INVOCATION: Be present as we worship, Lord. Release our minds from all attentions and distractions that inhibit our true worship. Cleanse our hearts from all clogging evil that the well-springs of gratitude may flow. Touch our lips to express our thanks in gracious words, and move our hands to show forth our gratitude in loving deeds. In Jesus' name. Amen.—H.

**Theme: Think and be Thankful (Thanksgiving)**

TEXT: "Be ye thankful." Col. 3:15.

INTRODUCTORY: A little prayer has been running through my mind which I would like to pass on to you. Here it is:

We thank thee, Lord, for all the blessings that we can name and count: we thank thee, too, for all the blessings that we cannot name and count.

That misses nothing of good whether known or unknown. Perhaps we might consider it too comprehensive—a generality, an abstraction—but I hope that you will take it home with you and use it. It would make a good grace to be spoken before you sit down at the Thanksgiving table.

Thanksgiving Day provides the preacher with opportunity to say something about his country, the land that we love, and I am sure that all of us are thankful for . . .

I should like to say something which would help us truly to be thankful men and women. "A grateful mind is both a great and happy mind." A grateful heart is a loving and sacrificial heart. A will motivated by gratitude is one of the most dynamic things in the world. So here are three suggestions:

I. *Think* and be thankful. Think and thank are words coming from the same Anglo-Saxon root. A thank is a thought. A good thought is a good thank. So think and be thankful!

1. Think a little more deeply and you will be a little more thankful. We might even think deeply enough to reach beyond the second causes of all that happens, to the first cause.

The other day I was about to read a few verses from my Bible, with a commentary in my hand, when I was amazed by a statement of the commentator. He said, "These verses contain the greatest statement of fact in the world." What could it be? He referred to the great foundation fact—God is working.

God is working! There is a kind of virtuous circle established when a man thinks through to that fact. A deep faith is stimulated. By the leverage which that faith gives God works the more.

How often as we ponder the affairs of our nation and the world we feel that our leaders are missing the most powerful and essential factor in the situation —God is working.

Think of God working and you will be thankful.

2. Think a little more broadly and you will be thankful. It is on the horizontal plane that you meet your fellow men. Perhaps some of them still live who nurtured you, and surely there are some who depend upon you. You will not forget those who trust you and those whom you trust in return; these we call friends. And there is a circle which you cannot measure of those who serve you, body, mind, and spirit. Many of these serve you from long ago, and some from far away. Think widely and be thankful.

3. Think higher and be thankful. "God made the stars also," reads the Scripture. We look up and "the stars *also*" bring us into touch with the extras of life—all the things that didn't have to be that way, but are—such things are color and fragrance and music.

Think higher and we will catch the perspective of the stars. It is the North Star that gives us our directions. Every surveyor's line and every tick of the clock is measured by the stars.

When Louis Agassiz pointed out to his Maine guide some of the geological wonders of his state, the guide remarked, "Maybe it makes no difference whether Blaine is elected President or not." How things change in their relative importance when we get a glimpse of the higher perspectives!

To sum it all up, including a thousand things unmentioned, think. Think deeply, broadly, higher, and be thankful.

II. *Appreciate* and be thankful. Appreciate is a word into which one can sink a shaft and bring up gold. First, it means to esteem to the full worth of, so I appreciate a friend. Second, it means to be sensitive to the aesthetic values of, so I appreciate music. Third, it means to be fully sensible of the significance of a thing, so I try to appreciate Christmas. Fourth, it means to add something to the value of, the opposite of *depreciate*. So I try to add something to the Christmas spirit in the world. To sum these up, it means to show gratitude. There are many ways of being thankful.

1. Appreciation is an art. Appraisal, to estimate the true value of things, is an art. Do not stop with counting your blessings, appraise them. You will have the joy of practicing a fine art. You will be thankful. It is one of the joys of leisure, to appraise, to enter into the worth of a garden, a friend, a child, a sunrise, a sunset, the love of Christ, a great promise of Scripture. How this enhances gratitude!

2. Appreciation is sensitivity to aesthetic value. It is an art to be a good listener. Not everybody sees the beauty in a sunset, a storm at sea, a landscape.

There are persons who do not see the *also's*, God's *also's*—the stars, the God-given extras in life. You see, the Master did not need to come as a little Babe and give us all that marvelous tale of angles and wisemen. Sensitivity to the extra is also a fine art. Cultivate it and be thankful.

3. Appreciate. Be sensible to significance. Be mindful of meanings. Never take anything for granted, neither a loaf of bread nor him who is the Bread of Life; neither a cup of water nor the Living Water of eternal life. Take neither the small thing nor the great think for granted, and you will be thankful.

4. Then wonder of wonders, everything waits for your appreciation. Everything waits for you to add your little extra, too. The rosebush waits for your appreciation, the plucking of its rose, for that is its pruning. The violinist's rendition is not complete without your applause. The leper's curing is not finished by the negation of his disease by Jesus, but only as he gives thanks and a positive blessing thrills through his veins.

The coming Christmas will be the more joyous by your adding something to Christmas—and now I do not mean that you give something to somebody—I mean, for example, by your adding your joy to the Christmas joy, your worship to the Christmas worship, by your giving of yourself to the Christ. Appreciate, that is add something, and you will be thankful.

III. *Give* and be thankful. There is a natural alliance here as expressed by the word "thanksgiving." Think! Appreciate! Giving inevitably follows! When the blessing is received, appraised, given sensual response, weighed for its meaning, or in other words appropriated by the hands, mind, eyes, and heart, the will also desires a share in the appropriation. The will acts outwardly in giving thanks.

Thus it comes about that the thankful spirit is one of the most dynamic things in the world. Thanks are expressed in gracious deeds, consecrated talents, sacrificial gifts. Thanksgivings to God, while often expressed in the quiet ways of communion and prayer, also take form in concrete offerings. Thus it comes about that the coffers of great benevolences are replenished, institutions of mercy are founded, churches are built.

So this is the spirit of the day and hour: think, appreciate, give. And along the channels of your thanksgiving the greater blessings will flow into your soul. You have no possibility of desiring or thinking of all the blessings that God has in store for the truly thankful heart.—H.

PRAYER: Thanksgivings are in our hearts, and praise is upon our lips, O God, because of thy continued loving-kindness unto us. We have received thy mercy; we have lived abundantly; we have experienced thy constant love. Thanks, a thousand thanks! Though how can we measure thanks for thine immeasurable goodness?

By our daily lives help us to express our gratitude—by upright living and by devotion to the cause of Christ. Ever receiving may we be ever giving.

We live in expectation, Lord, of seeing greater things and doing nobler deeds and becoming better men. In Jesus' name. Amen.—H.

OFFERTORY SENTENCE: "Honor the Lord with thy substance, and with the first fruits of all thine increase. Give unto the Most High according as he hath enriched thee, and, as thou hast gotten, give with a generous hand."

OFFERTORY PRAYER: Most gracious God, we know that all that we have comes of thy bounty. Let us not forget then that each thing is included in the all. So may we count our blessings, name and count them. Then from the heart of gratitude may we give thanks, prompting our wills to express our thanks in sacrificial gifts. Amen.—H.

SEED THOUGHTS: How Are We Thankful? "1. A really thankful man it is a pleasure to meet. There is about him a kind of radiance—a genuine gratitude that has in it dynamic power. 2. The thankless man, on the other hand, says that he has nothing to be thankful for. He is right, for we possess nothing except in appreciation. 3. But there is still another kind of man. Long ago a parable was told about him—about how he went up to the temple to pray, giving thanks that he was not as other men, not even like the fellow praying next to him. His thanksgiving was completely sincere, yet it was rejected, nullified by his shallow, disdainful attitude. How are we thankful?"

Thanksgiving is a Soul Force. 1. It admits the sunlight into one's solitude. 2. It burns out bitterness and dross. 3. It reveals the beautiful and valuable. 4. It releases energies for creative living. 5. It awakens kindness.—A. D. Stauffacher.

### Choice Thanksgiving Illustrations

THANK YOU. In a tiny boat tossed about by icy winds and angry waves lay ten exhausted men. Fifty hours before they had seen their ship swallowed up by the cold gray waters of the ocean. Now, weak and hungry, most of them had not even the strength to grasp an oar. But presently their ebbing hopes were rallied by the drone of a plane approaching overhead. Eventually, guided by its pilot, two ships sped to their rescue. In no time they were brought safely aboard. Just as the plane was about to turn for home the pilot espied a flash from one of the ships. "Anything wrong?" he signaled. "No," came back the answer, "Only these fellows we have just picked up want to say 'Thank you.' "—Graham W. Hughes.

RETROSPECT. The king and high priest of all festivals was the autumn Thanksgiving. When the apples were all gathered and the cider was all made, and the yellow pumpkins were rolled in from many a hill in billows of gold, and the corn was husked and the labors of the season were done, and the warm, late days of Indian Summer came in, dreamy and calm, and still, with just enough frost to crisp the ground of a morning, but with warm traces of benignant, sunny hours at noon, there came over the community a sort of genial repose of spirit—a sense of something accomplished, and of a new golden mark made in advance—and the deacon began to say to the minister of a Sunday, "I suppose it's about time for the Thanksgiving proclamation."—Harriet Beecher Stowe.

## EVENING SERVICE

### Theme: The Victory of Praise

TEXT: "He appointed singers unto the Lord, and that should praise the beauty of holiness, as they went out before the army, and to say: Praise the Lord; for his mercy endureth for ever." II Chron. 20:21.

INTRODUCTORY. Has good old Jehoshaphat lost his head? He stands upon the threshold of what promises to be one of the most important battles he has ever waged. Thousands of Moabites and Ammonites with their allies are marshaled against him. It is a critical time.

If ever he needed to exercise military genius, it is now. And he is going into the fight with a company of singers in the front of his army. Why does he not first make the ranks strong with the mighties warriors he can find? What strange freak is this? Singers at the front with instructions to cry when they meet the foe: "Praise the Lord, for his mercy endureth for ever." Nothing about weapons or maneuvers or charges. They are instructed to sing: that is all.

We must admit that this is not the world's idea of things, but let us give the old king a chance. It is not fair to judge a campaign until we behold its results. Follow the hosts of Judah into the fight. Never have they marched with firmer step; never have they entered a fight with more of a foregleam of victory upon their faces. Not a weapon is drawn save the weapon of praise: not a charge is made save this oft-swelling outburst of praise, of holy grateful song. But when they hear it, the enemy is confounded; a strange delusion is fallen upon them, they smite each other until the ground is literally covered with the slain. The triumph of Judah is complete. So whether we approve Jehoshaphat's method or not, he has gained the victory. We must acknowledge him to be more of a philosopher than we thought.

I wonder if he cannot teach twentieth-century Christians some important lessons for the battle of life. Some of us have taken little account of praise as an element in the conflict. We have recognized it as a proper part of our religious exercises. We have allowed it a place in the program of the house of God; but as a means of routing the foe, a method of victory, we have left it out of our calculations. Others of us have counted praise an essential element, but we have kept it in the background. We have taken the singers along, hoping they might have something to do when the fight is over.

I am pleading for the primacy of praise. I am pointing out a mighty weapon for the battle of life. I am telling you that the singers belong in the front ranks. The time to begin the song is before the battle.

I. Let us notice that the man who goes into the fight with praise upon his lips possesses the essentials of heroism. Anybody can sing a *Te Deum* when the fight is over. There will always be plenty of singers looking for a place in the Lord's chorus when the enemy has laid down its arms. But the man who counts, the man who contributes to the triumph, is the man who can praise God in full view of the shining bayonets.

II. The soul who goes forth with a song of praise is prepared for the fight. Praise is a tonic. It stirs the sluggish heart; it sharpens the dull spirit. It revives the tired muscles; it brings latent powers into alertness and activity. It turns our eyes away from ourselves and our surroundings and gives us a vision of the face of God until we are ready to undertake the impossible.

III. Praise on the edge of battle is acknowledgment that victory is the Lord's. Read with care the record of Jehoshaphat's fight, and you will be impressed with his absolute dependence upon God.

They were fighting the battle of the Infinite. He was their strength. They were his soldiers. The issue was absolutely sure.

But not more so than the result of the conflict today. Listen to these words of inspiration: "There hath no temptation taken you but such as is common to man, and God is faithful who will not suffer you to be tempted above that ye are able, but will with the temptation make a way of escape, that ye may be able to bear it." "If God be for us, who can be against us?"

This message is from the throne as truly as that which came to the people through Jahaziel the Levite. It is for you as truly as that was for them. You do not need to suffer defeat. God has made it possible for you to win. The resources of the Infinite are within your reach. Catch the spirit of that old warrior of the long ago who suffered far more than you can ever suffer, and cry with him, "I can do all things through Christ which strengtheneth me." Put the singers in the front ranks. When the foe appears, let him hear the strains of that holy hymn: "Praise the Lord; for his mercy endureth for ever."—Edwin F. Hallenbeck.

**Suggested Thanksgiving Day Texts and Themes**

Thanks for Surprises: "Blessed be the Lord, who daily loadeth us with benefits." Ps. 68:19.

Thanks for Life's Hurts: "Do not reject the instruction of the Almighty. For he wounds, but he binds up; he smites, but his hands heal." Job 5:17, 18 (Goodspeed).

The Great Thanksgiving Psalm: "Bless the Lord, O my soul: and all that is within me, bless his holy name. . . ." Ps. 103.

Thankfulness—and Then What? "What shall I render unto the Lord for all his benefits toward me?" Ps. 116:12.

Thanksgiving in Adversity: Ps. 50:14, 15.

## MIDWEEK FELLOWSHIP MEETING TOPIC

**Theme: Dayspring Mercies (Thanksgiving)**

TEXT: "It is of the Lord's mercies that we are not consumed, because his compassions fail not. They are new every morning: great is thy faithfulness." Lam. 3:22, 23.

It is almost startling to find this tender and inspiring utterance embedded in the very heart of a book of lamentations. Here are mentioned dayspring mercies. "His compassions fail not. They are new every morning." But for God's great mercy his people would be utterly cut off. With many of us every day has its acts of shortcoming. Yet God's forgiveness fails not.

I. Here is suggested the resourcefulness of God's providence. The mercy that is ever fresh to pardon is also ever fresh to guide. God's gracious hand never forgets to make ready its surprise of joy in the morning.

II. Here is suggested the unfailing truth and faithfulness of God in his relation to his people. Dayspring mercies. The return of the day is one of the most perfect symbols of God's constancy. "They are new every morning." No failure. Never ceasing. Dayspring mercies for all God's people.

III. Here is suggested the unfailing promptness of God's ministrations. His mercies are new every morning. That is, just as soon or even before we need them. Prompt. Free. A gift. Wages belong to the evening. God's purpose is of the dayspring. His gifts come to us with the dawn, before we have had time to do a stroke of work.

IV. Here is suggested also the perpetual freshness of the divine nature. God's compassions are new, pure, fair, out of the depths of the divine Fatherhood. They have the ever-renewing and living sweetness of his own springlike nature in them.—T. G. S.

## SUNDAY SCHOOL LESSON

**Nov. 23. Why Men Oppose Jesus. Mark 2:18-28. Background Scripture: Mark 2:1-3:6.**

MEMORY VERSE: "Blessed is he who takes no offense at me." Matt. 11:6 (R.S.V.).

Mark has given us a group of stories which explain the development of opposition to Jesus.

I. The opposition to Jesus. 1. The Pharisees are offended by his claim to have power to forgive sins with its implied assertion of deity.

2. In the call of Matthew, Mark 2:14-16, Jesus violates the accepted social standards of his day.

3. He gives offense also through his healing on the Sabbath Day.

II. In what respect does the gospel of Christ today cut across the generally held ideas and practices of society, and thereby arouse opposition? If the class finds difficulty in answering this question, what is the significance of this? Is the Church so weak and unaggressive that it does not excite opposition? Are its pronouncements and teachings ignored?

III. As followers of Christ are we taking any unpopular stands in his name? If so, what are they? If not, why not?

## SUNDAY: NOVEMBER THIRTIETH

### MORNING SERVICE

**Theme: The Eternal Son (Advent)**

SUGGESTED SCRIPTURE READING: John 1:1-3; John 8:54-59.

SELECTED HYMNS: "Come, thou almighty King."—Anonymous. "Crown him the Son of God."—Matthew Bridges. "High in the heavens, Eternal God."—Isaac Watts. "Watchman, tell us of the night."—John Bowring.

CALL TO WORSHIP: "And he said unto me [John], It is done. I am Alpha and Omega, the beginning and the end. I will give unto him that is athirst of the fountain of the water of life freely. He that overcometh shall inherit all things; and I will be his God, and he shall be my son." Rev. 21:6, 7.

INVOCATION: Eternal God, our Father, we find it a great privilege to have knowledge of the Gospel of Jesus Christ. In the name of Christ and by the power of the Gospel we worship thee today, and bind ourselves together in praise and aspiration and prayer.

We are not worthy of the Gospel—that the Eternal Son should have humbled himself, lived a lowly life of service, endured the Cross for us—this causes us to bend low in humility, while we rejoice in our great salvation. Amen.—H.

**Theme: The Eternal Son (Advent)**

TEXTS: "Unto us a child is born." Isa. 9:6. "Before Abraham was, I am." John 8:58.

At Christmas, in common with all Christendom, our thoughts go gladly journeying toward Bethlehem. A birthday is always a great day, and Christmas is the greatest birthday of the year. We have only to think of all that Christ has been, we have only to think of all that Christ has done, to be thrilled by the ineffable grandeur of the hour, when unto us a child was born.

But the fact is, we are out of touch a little with the apostles' conception of the Saviour. The one thing the apostles never do is to date the career of Jesus from his birth. For them, with all their marked divergencies, he was the eternal Son of God. They knew the gladness of the prophetic message, "For unto us a child is born," but they knew also with undimmed assurance that "Before Abraham was, I am."

It is a singular and indeed inexplicable thing that Christ's pre-existence is apostolic doctrine, and that unquestionably it had its place in the mature consciousness of Christ himself. Christ does not speak of himself as being born. He says, "I am come" or "I was sent." "Father, glorify thou me," he says, "with the glory which I had with thee before the world was." And then there is the second of our texts, a word that should thrill us, "Before Abraham was, I am."

What then are the spiritual values of Christ's pre-existence? Let me indicate the three that are most evident.

I. The first is that when we lost our hold on it immediately the love of God is dimmed. For God so loved the world not that he thought—God so loved the world not that he said—God so loved the world that he *gave* his only-begotten Son for you and me. And the simple fact is that if Jesus Christ began to be in the hour when he was born, then in heaven there was no Son to cherish, and none in the fullness of the time to give. I learn the depth of a true mother's love from her unfailing spirit of self-sacrifice. I learn how dearly the patriot loves his country from his readiness to fight for it and die for it. And so alone do I learn the love of God, not from the beauty of the summer meadow, but from a deed of sacrifice more wonderful than ever mother or patriot achieved.

II. Again, if we lose our hold upon Christ's pre-existence, then the glory of the life of Christ is dimmed. It may still win us as a life of beauty, but it has ceased to awe us as a life of grace. For the grace of our Lord Jesus Christ is certainly *not* the fact that he was poor. The grace of our Lord Jesus Christ is this, that *though he was rich,* for us he became poor.

Remove the pre-existence, and you lose the infinite grace of the Redeemer. There were no riches to be given up if Christ began to be when he was born. And therefore if you would know the joy of Christmas, it is not enough to say a child is born; you must launch out into the deeps and whisper, "Before Abraham was, I am."

III. Lastly, if we lose our hold of Christ's pre-existence, the glory of our humanity is dimmed. We have lost our historical and abiding argument for the nobility and dignity of man.

What is man that thou are mindful of him—a creature of a day upon a distant satellite? What is man whose life is as a vapor, on a far atom of a boundless universe? From all such sense of nothingness, there is no argument so mighty to redeem as the argument that God so loved the world that he gave his only-begotten Son for you and me.

Never again can I belittle man, if the eternal Son became man. Never again can I despise humanity, if he was found in the likeness of humanity. And never again can I be quite so certain of the infinite value of mankind to God, if Christ began to be when he was born. *Unto us a child is born*: yes, the gladness of Christmas is in that. It has hallowed home, and sanctified the child, and given new radiance to the eyes of motherhood. But remember that deep is calling unto deep, where the little infant is crying in the manger—and so go out into the night and say, "*Before Abraham was, I am.*"—G. H. Morrison.

PRAYER: O thou God of loving-kindness, who hath kindled in our hearts the fires of gratitude, we thank thee for the day of festival which we have recently experienced. For the joy that was ours as we gathered with kinsfolk and friends we give thee thanks. The bounties upon our tables were a token of thy Providence. The love in our hearts was a gift of thy grace. We shall remember the day by its afterglow, continuing all through another year.

We now look forward to another day of rejoicing. Across a little stretch of time we see approaching the birthday of our Lord. As prophets and people of old looked forward to the coming of the Messiah, so may we anticipate the day of gladness. By this prospect may we show good will toward all men within the circle of our influence. Help us to plan our time and activities that by no undue anxiety or fretfulness of spirit shall we subtract from the joy of Christmas.

We intercede, our Father, for those, our brethren in the world, who live without a saving knowledge of Christ. On the wings of the Christmas day may many learn about the coming of the Saviour. And hasten the day when the whole world shall be covered with a knowledge of the Lord as the waters cover the sea. Amen.—H.

OFFERTORY SENTENCE: "And I will shake all nations, and the desire of all nations shall come: and I will fill this house with glory, saith the Lord of hosts. The silver is mine and the gold is mine, saith the Lord of hosts." Hag. 2:7, 8.

OFFERTORY PRAYER: Our hearts shall ever praise theee, O God, for the gift of our Lord and Saviour to the world. It is our hearts' desire that the whole world may come to his shining. Unto the building of his Kingdom we make our offering and pray thy blessing upon it. Amen.—H.

**Illustrative Material**

SEED THOUGHTS: "Before Abraham was, I am." I. An Assertion of Existence. II. An Assertion of Personality. III. A Claim to Deity. The apprehension of truth comes through the response of men's souls.

When the Jews heard Jesus say these words, "Before Abraham was, I am," they took up stones to cast at him. Stones were their final argument. By his assertions and claims they believed him a blasphemer. He is either a deceiver or the eternal Son of God. Some men reach for stones in his presence; others bow in adoration.

"He is the eternal 'Now.' This is the plain sense of Christ's language, and perhaps the most instructive commentary on its force is to be found in the violent expedients to which some writers have been driven in order to evade it." —Canon Liddon.

### Choice Illustrations on the Theme

A CHILD IS BORN. Was Christ conscious of that former life of his? Was it present to him when he was a child? As he played in the village street of Nazareth did the glory he had left lie open to him? I think that every one of us must feel that any such consciousness of pre-existence is fatal to the simple human charm of the infancy and youth of Jesus. Doubtless he had his childish dreams of that kingdom where time and space are not. Heaven lay about him in his infancy as it lay about all of us when we were children. But to think that he was vividly conscious as a child that he had lived for ever with the Father, is to pluck the heart of childhood from his bosom, and the innocent wonder of childhood from his eyes. I think that his birth was a sleep and a forgetting, through trailing clouds of glory he had come. I do not imagine that this knowledge reached him by any easy way of reminiscence. I think that it was slowly formed within his mind as the choicest fruit of his filial obedience; that it emerged for him into a perfect certainty out of the depths of his fellowship with God. When he was a child he thought as a child, for unto us, we read, a *child* is born.—G. H. M.

A HARD, SHARP FACT. Consider Christmas, for instance. The hard, sharp fact is that at a point in historic time, the Son of God, as was prophesied of him, came to assume our flesh, walk our ways, purpose the will of his Father, and die for our redemption. That is the reality of belief supposedly held by those who call themselves Christians.

If we consider Christmas merely a pretty legend and Jesus Christ merely a very good man, who went about helping people and preaching some excellent sermons, then we are forced to face the embarrassing question of why anyone bothered to crucify him.—Richardson Wright.

## EVENING SERVICE

### Theme: Rediscovering Christmas

TEXT: "The people that walked in darkness have seen a great light." Isa. 9:2.

How can we say "Merry Christmas," the one word that fits the day, in a world so full of misery and fear? How can we keep a feast that tugs at our hearts with all the pull of playtime, when the Four Horses of doom ride the winds of the world?

Ah, but that is just the secret of Christmas, if we can find it again. Jesus was born in Bethlehem in the days of Caesar, the dictator, in a hard old Roman world. He came, one of the children of the year, among a subject people, living under iron military rule; soldiers everywhere.

The contrast between faith and fact was ghastly, then as now. If there was music in the heavens; alas! there was murder on the earth; the song celestial and the slaughter of little children by Herod, the monster. Yet, somehow, in a way beyond our knowing, Jesus brought a new joy and a new hope to man.

Then Caesar tried to blot out the gospel of Christ. Awful days followed, when the lovers of Jesus were hunted and put to death to make a Roman holiday. Christmas seemed lost beyond recall.

I. St. Nicholas, the boy-bishop, rediscovered Christmas in the fourth century, and made it merry again for a brief time. He slipped into the homes of little children and left presents, without getting caught, making them happy on the sly. Then darkness fell again, and Christmas Day was as somber as Good Friday.

II. Still later, Francis of Assisi recaptured the Christmas spirit. He asked the priest of the village church to let him use the church on Christmas Eve. He filled the chancel with hay, pulled an ox and an ass into the church, and pushed them up the aisle. He induced a young mother to sit beside them with her baby, making a picture of Christmas.

The clergy said he was crazy; the people said he was a saint. An artist, a saint of the order of poets, he wrote the first Christmas carols—simple songs, homey, cheerful, playful—and taught them to the people. They spread from land to land, bearing his gospel of pity, joy, and loving-kindness.

III. Others discover Christmas. The Christmas tree grew in Germany, along with other old and sweet customs, like the burning of the Yule log; both symbols of the life everlasting, as holly was of the Crown of Thorns. In some strange way St. Nicholas returned to Holland as Sankt Klaas, and came with the early Dutch settlers to America as Santa Claus; akin to Father Christmas in England, where Dickens made Christmas merry from castle to cottage.

IV. We must rediscover Christmas. Thus many people, in many ages, helped to discover Christmas and make it merry, each adding beauty to it, all finding joy in it, making it at once a symposium and a symphony. Just so, today, in a world darkened by war and cruelty, we must rediscover Christmas, not merely the picture, but the faith and fact, as deep as the home and family—as deep as love and death—that the human heart can be a Cradle in which the love of God can be reborn in the life of man.

As many folk of many races and ages joined in discovering Christmas, so, at long last, many peoples must work together to create the "peace on earth among men of good will" of which Christmas prophesies. History is a book of surprises, and that day may come with a satisfying suddenness before we know it.

Not a myth, not a divine fairy story, not a fiction woven of stablestraw and starlight, Christmas is both a fact and a faith, a power and a prophecy of a brighter, kinder, happier world, in which pity and joy will join hands and walk, star-led, in the way of the will of God. Only God could have thought of Christmas.

Blessed Christmas! It takes us down from our towering pride, it melts our hard cynical wisdom, and makes us, for a brief time—so swift to come, so swift to go—forget ourselves and our selfishness into happiness, by the kindly, joyous doing of good, which is our real business of earth.—Joseph Forth Newton.

**Suggested Texts and Themes**

Prepare the Way of the Lord: "Prepare ye the way of the Lord, make his paths straight." Matt. 3:3.

God's Reassuring Word: "In the beginning was the Word, and the Word was with God, and the Word was God." John 1:1.

Christmas Cards: "As cold waters to a thirsty soul, so is good news from a far country." Prov. 25:25.

God in Person: Heb. 1:1,2

The Rising Star: "There shall come a Star out of Jacob." Num. 24:17.

## MIDWEEK FELLOWSHIP MEETING TOPIC

(Church Night or Suggested Sermon Subject)

**Theme: The Horizons of Here and Now**

Who does not love horizons? The western horizon when the red ball of the sun descends into the sea and leaves an aftergrow of pulsating light and pastel color becoming a corridor of reverie. The horizon of the mountains seen from the plain when the peaks are cut out of cardboard and stand silhouetted against a deep dark blue. The horizon of the desert when the clouds are piled up like medieval castles standing on the shore of rivers of gold. Have you ever seen the horizon of Kansas which is miles of ripening grain waving in the wind?

There are mental horizons, horizons of interest. How often the mind looks far away to a line brought near by an absent friend. Even heaven itself is glimpsed because a loved one enjoys its light and glory.

I. The Horizon of Christmas. 1. The horizon of little children. Christmas: a fact. 2. The horizon of their elders. Christmas: a Faith.

II. The Horizon of the New Year. 1. What is fact? 2. What is faith?

III. The Horizon of a New Age. 1. A New Age is coming—is this a Fact? 2. A New Age is coming—is this our Faith? 3. Or is the New Age here? 4. What about the translation of faith into fact? —H.

### SUNDAY SCHOOL LESSON

**Nov. 30. Why Jesus Used Parables. Mark 4:1-12. Background Scripture: Mark 4:1-34.**

MEMORY VERSE: "Be doers of the word, and not hearers only, deceiving yourselves." James 1:22 (R.S.V.).

The parable of the sower, or the parable of the soils, may be studied as an example of Jesus' use of parables: I. To hold the attention. II. To present eternal truth in imperishable story. The parables often contained some hidden meaning which is not really understood, a symbol of the mystery of the gospel that can never be summed up completely. III. To teach in a tension-filled situation.

## SUNDAY: DECEMBER SEVENTH

### MORNING SERVICE

**Theme: Included in Christmas (Advent)**

SUGGESTED SCRIPTURE READING: Isa. 9:2, 6-7.

SELECTED HYMNS: "O come, O come, Emmanuel."—Neal Coffin. "Jesus, the very tho't of thee."—Bernard of Clairvaux. "Jesus shall reign where'er the sun."—Isaac Watts. "Joy to the world!" —Isaac Watts.

CALL TO WORSHIP: "Sing and rejoice, O daughter of Zion: for lo, I come, and I will dwell in the midst of thee, saith the Lord." Zech. 2:10.

INVOCATION: Our Father, we thank thee for the Advent of our Lord and Saviour Jesus Christ.

As we stand today in this beginning of this joyful season the Babe of Bethlehem attracts us afresh by the charm of his infancy. We feel our hearts grow tender and loving. Though we may have followed others, from this day forward let the little Child lead us. In him may we find our salvation, our joy, and our peace Amen.—H.

**Theme: Included in Christmas (Advent)**

TEXT: "Unto us a child is born." Isa. 9:6.

Yes, you and I are included in Christmas. Even in the old prophetice text of Isaiah we feel that the us means *us*. Then, too, we cannot limit the announcement of the angel, as given to the shepherds alone—"Unto you is born this day in the city of David, a Saviour." That you is *you*, my friend, and the good tidings for all people are for me. And there is no doubt about it that we are included in the great text, "For God so loved the world that he gave his only begotten Son that *whosoever* . . ."—that whosoever reaches to you and me. We are included in Christmas.

Even if you are a disbelieving pagan, or a stingy Scrooge, or an evil-tempered misanthrope, you are included. You can't get away from Christmas. You can't escape it. You may build yourself a dungeon—Christmas will get in between the cracks. You may seek the loneliness of the Arctic pole—memory will betray you. You'd better give in. Christmas is coming and that includes you.

We're all included, wise men and shepherds—the Babe was born under a token star that withheld its shining from none.

I. And of course we're all included in the *meaning* of Christmas. The significance of a birth lies not alone in the birth but in all that follows in that life. And what follows the birth of Christ is his life of doing good, his death, his resurrection, his spiritual presence. All that he came to do, which was wrought out in the doing—that has influence and bearing in our lives. All that Jesus was and did and said includes us. And what that Babe later did includes you and me. Yes, the Cross; he died for us.

And what that Babe became includes us. His perfection includes our perfection; his Sonship includes our sonship. He came to be like us that we might become like him. A child was born unto us.

II. We're included in the joy of Christmas. Should we have spoken first about the *joy* of Christmas and then about the *meaning*? No, let us keep meaning first, for the deep joy comes from the meaning. Those who keep Christmas without Christ, even these have merriment, but the "great joy" of which the angels sang, that is another experience, Christmas with Christ in the center.

So it is our high privilege to participate in all festivity that is "great joy," all that brings joy to you, and all that gives joy to others. The joy of Christmas, you're included, recipient and giver. No wonder we raise our voices in the carols and hymns. No wonder we give gifts especially to children, that the tide of joy may rise and spread out upon the earth.

III. We're included in the good will of Christmas. We've said that already for the meaning of Christmas is God's good will toward men. The joy of Christmas is man's good will toward God and his fellow man.

Now at Christmas time all hatreds must be erased, all sins against us forgiven, grievances and grudges must be dispelled; it is the time for loving and being loved, for forgiving and being forgiven, for letting the sunshine and the heavenly breeze drive away the smog. In the clear air we shall see the star again, and hear the songs of angels, and make our way to the stable where like the Wise Men of old we shall bow in worship, open our treasuries and make gifts to our King.—H.

A PRAYER FOR THE DAY. Our hearts rejoice, O God, in the "whosoever" note of the Gospel. It is like the shining of a star that never fails us, which back of every cloud is always shining, which addeth joy to the crystal night.

It is beyond our knowledge why we should be included in thy grace. But we are, and we know it, and we rejoice in our salvation. Help us to make this glad evangel known to others. It belongs to all people; make our lips and lives eloquent with the good news. In Jesus' name. Amen.—H.

OFFERTORY SENTENCE: "Prepare ye the way of the Lord, make straight in the desert a highway for our God . . . and the glory of the Lord shall be revealed, and all flesh shall see it together: for the mouth of the Lord hath spoken it."

OFFERTORY PRAYER: For the high privilege, O God, of preparing the way of Christ unto the hearts of men we give thee thanks. May we become good road builders, skillful in our vocation, and faithful to our task. We dedicate our offering today, O God, unto the preparation of the way of the Lord. Amen.—H.

SEED THOUGHTS: Why Did Jesus Come? I. He came to serve. Mark 10:45. II. He came to suffer. John 12:26, 27. III. He came to save. Luke 19:10.

His Unspeakable Gift. John 3:16. I. The life of Jesus was a gift to the world. Human nature deserved no such blessing. It came freely out of God's love. II. The perfect knowledge that Jesus had of his Father was a gift to the world. Man's deepest wisdom and clearest thinking could produce no such insight. III. Jesus' death on the cross was a gift to the world.

### Choice Advent Illustrations

TOO LITTLE TO HATE. Six-year-old Dorothy Smith and I were riding my big white horse, Silver, over the mountains to a remote Sunday school. Dorothy began to tell me about her baby brother, Billy-Roy: "Uncle Sam, he'll soon be a year old." There was so much endearment in her voice that I said, "You must like your little brother very much." To my surprise she replied, "Why, you don't *like* a little baby; you *love* him."

Then she added quickly, "He's too little to hate."—Samuel VanderMeer.

AN AMAZING FACT. If you are inclined to wail because there is so much that is irreligious about Christmas, with all its commercialism, its pagan frivolity and revelry, remember that this outward gaiety is a very ancient practice that began in pre-Christian Rome, when for four days the city in riotous pleasure cast off its cares and worries to celebrate the winter solstice, for the shortest days of the year had come. The sun had reached the end of its journey and was coming back with its promise of longer and warmer days and the brightness and gladness of spring. And into this ancient pagan setting of giving gifts and revelry and song, the Christian gospel made its way with its message that the Son of God has come with his sure promise that the old earth, scarred and worn, would one day be adorned with the beauty of the Lord. What is really amazing is not that Christmas is so pagan, but that a pagan festival has become so Christian, so that even in a Noah's Ark store one can go in for a piece of hardware and hear the music of "Hark, the herald angels sing."—Harold E. Nicely.

## EVENING SERVICE

**Theme: John Milton: a Pulpit Biography**

TEXT: "O give thanks unto the Lord; for he is good: for his mercy endureth for ever." Ps. 136:1. At the age of fifteen John Milton paraphrased the 136th Psalm into the hymn, to be found in most hymnbooks, which begins as follows:

Let us with a gladsome mind
Praise the Lord for he is kind,
For his mercies aye endure
Ever faithful, ever sure.

(Note: John Milton was born on Dec. 9, 1608. Next Tuesday will be his 350th anniversary. Some ministers will find this Sunday evening the occasion to give a pulpit biography of this great Puritan poet, or to preach a sermon based upon or illustrated from the record of his life. Others may wish to preach an Advent Sermon based upon Milton's Ode, "On the Morning of Christ's Nativity." The outline given below may be used for a sermon without reference to John Milton. On the other hand it may be used as a framework for a sermon on John Milton, using illustrations from his life and writings.)

I. It is a great thing for a man to be born in times which stir his finest emotions.

II. It is a great thing for a man to be nurtured in the Christian faith.

III. It is a great thing for a man to give his life to a stupendous task.

IV. It is a great thing for a man to rise above a terrible handicap.

I. His Times. 1608-1674. "He was only seven when Shakespeare died; he was ten when Sir Walter Raleigh was executed; he was twelve when the *Mayflower* sailed. . . . Much of *Paradise Lost* was written whilst London was being decimated by the Great Plague. . . . He lived through the whole of the Civil War; he mingled freely with the principal actors in those stormy and dramatic scenes; he saw the rise and fall of the Commonwealth, the execution of the King, and the death of Cromwell. The pulsations of such momentous happenings stirred the deepest emotions of a singularly sensitive and impressionable spirit; they inscribed themselves indelibly upon his memory; and taking to themselves weird and fantastic shapes, they wove themselves into a splendid fabric of his priceless epic."—F. W. Boreham.

Milton threw in his lot with Parliament against Charles I. He took the side of the Puritans.

II. His Christian Nurture. "John Milton was a tremendous lover of the Bible. He used to say that, if England became a Bible-reading, Bible-believing, Bible-studying nation, its distresses would quickly vanish and its wounds be healed. . . . It is no exaggeration to say that Milton drew the whole of his inspiration from the Bible. And no wonder! For, during the most impressionable years of his life, his character was moulded by the hands of three men; and all three of them regarded the Bible as earth's chiefest treasure."—F. W. B.

These three men were his father, his minister, and his tutor.

III. His Stupendous Task. In Johnson's *Lives of the Poets* the writer refers to certain promises that Milton made to undertake something, he yet knows not what, that may be of use and honor to his country. "This," says Milton, "is not to be obtained but by devout prayer to that Eternal Spirit that can enrich with all utterance and knowledge and sends out his Seraphim with the hallowed fire of his altar to touch and purify the lips of whom he pleases. To this must be added industrious and select reading, steady observation, and insight into all seemly arts and affairs; till which in some measure be compassed, I refuse not to sustain this expectation."

"From a promise like this, at once fervid, pious, and rational," says Johnson, "might be expected the 'Paradise Lost.'"

"Very seldom has a man set himself as deliberately as did Milton to a colossal task, and with so little encouragement, carried it to its completion. He was a callow youth when he conceived the stupendous project; he was an old man when he rolled up the finished manuscript. In the interval he traveled far, learned much, and became engrossed in many cares. But the dream of his boyhood was never forgotten. Like the Temple, erected without beat of hammer or click of trowel, the glorious work was silently growing in the poet's soul. He brooded upon it in secret; his masterpiece was always there at the back of his mind.

"'You ask me,' he writes as a young fellow in the twenties, 'you ask me what I am thinking about? Why, with God's help, of *immortality*! Forgive the word; I only whisper it in your ear! Yes, I am pluming my wings for a flight!'"—F. W. Boreham.

IV. His Handicap. John Milton became totally blind in his forty-fourth year, 1652, and he could go about only with someone to lead him.

**Suggested Advent Texts and Themes**

Watchman, What of the Night? "Go, set a watchman, let him declare what he seeth." Isa. 21:6. "A watchman was set on the walls of the fortified city. He was to announce any lurking dangers, to receive reports from distant messengers, and to herald the coming of the morning light. The watchman is a symbol of our Advent hope."

A Season of Expectation: "My soul, wait thou only upon God; for my expectation is from him." Ps. 62:5.

Prepare Your Hearts: "Prepare ye the way of the Lord, make straight in the desert a highway for our God." I. Prepare by penitence. II. Prepare by expectation.

The Mood of Advent—Hope: "Rejoicing in hope." Rom. 12:12.

Tidings of Comfort and Joy: "And the angel said unto them, Fear not: for, behold, I bring you good tidings of great joy, which shall be to all people. . . . Luke 2:10-11.

## MIDWEEK FELLOWSHIP MEETING TOPIC

(Church Night or Suggested Sermon Subject)

**Theme: Preparing God's Way**

TEXT: Prepare ye the way of the Lord, make his paths straight." Matt. 3:3.

Are we preparing God's way as John bade the people of his day? Or are we waiting with a kind of dull despair for God to break in and take the hearts of men by storm? What does it mean to prepare his way? How can we prepare his way?

I. We can, of course, pray, and prayer is a mighty thing. With all the urgency of his being Jesus bade us to pray and not to faint.

II. We can also prepare God's way by making room for Christ in our own hearts, in our own spirit and actions, so that men can catch some glimpses, however feeble, of the shining of his face.

III. We can prepare God's way by opening minds to knowledge and healing men's diseases. We can remove the obstacles to the Kingdom.

IV. We can prepare God's way by proclaiming the message of his love. "You shall be my witnesses," said Christ to the disciples before his ascension, and a witness is a man who tells what he has seen. He relates his own experience.

To see Jesus Christ and show him to others is the business of every Christian. We can all do something to open the door for the entry of Christ.—Adapted from James Reid.

## BULLETIN BOARD SLOGANS FOR THE MONTH

Love is kind.

Let us be reverent this Christmas.

Generosity is the salt of Christmas.

Some people grow up—others just puff up.

Arrange for pleasant memories in advance.

The pure in heart seldom need a psychiatrist.

The open Bible is an invitation to great adventure.

Kindness is the oil that takes the friction out of life.

God will give his great gifts if we are ready to receive them.

At Christmas consider not so much the gift of the friend, but the friendship of the giver.

## SUNDAY SCHOOL LESSON

**Dec. 7. Jesus' Power in Human Life. Mark 5:1-13. Background Scripture: Mark 4:35-5:43.**

MEMORY VERSE: "Go home to your friends, and tell them how much the Lord has done for you." Mark 5:19 (R.S.V.).

In the stories of Mark 5 Jesus is presented as having power in human life over demon possession, disease, and death itself.

It was the intention of those who prepared the International Sunday School Lessons that this lesson might be related to man's struggle for victory over enslavement to alcohol by presenting Jesus as one who is able to give men freedom from this enslaving habit and to restore them to health and sanity.

The following quotations from the confessions of a reformed alcoholic whose "first drink led to twenty-five years of hell" may be suggestive. "Then one day I decided to quit drinking, but to my dismay I found that I couldn't. . . . I came to the startling realization that I had no mature or adequate conception of God. My thoughts gradually evolved around the word 'power.' I began to think of God as a spiritual power or presence 'in whom we live and move and have our being.'

"I ceased praying to a 'faraway' God; God was near at hand, the kingdom of heaven was within my own heart and soul.

"One morning, after three months of meditation and soul-searching and while I was still in confusion, I heard a bird singing outside my window—singing as though his heart would break. As I listened, the thought came to me that the bird was in tune with God!

"If only I could bring myself to the some mental attitude of that little bird, would I be in tune with God? It was worth a try.

"Fifteen years have passed since that wonderful morning. I have not only been able to let drink alone, but my entire life—my personal life, my home life and my business life—has been completely changed. I can truthfully say it has been the happiest period of my whole life.

"Each day my faith in God and my understanding of his power to remake the lives of men have increased. I have been able to evolve a workable conception of God and spiritual power consistent with my intellect and the teachings of Jesus Christ."

# SUNDAY: DECEMBER FOURTEENTH

## MORNING SERVICE

**Theme: The Bible in Our Day (Bible Sunday)**

SUGGESTED SCRIPTURE READING: II Tim. 1:1-10.

SELECTED HYMNS: "O Word of God incarnate."—William W. How. "Hail to the Lord's Anointed."—James Montgomery. "Break thou the bread of life." —Mary A. Lathbury. "A glory gilds the sacred page."—William Cowper.

CALL TO WORSHIP: Ps. 130:5-7.

INVOCATION: Most gracious God, our heavenly Father, in whom alone dwelleth all fullness of light and wisdom; illuminate our minds, we beseech thee, by thy Holy Spirit, in the true understanding of thy Word. Give us grace to receive it with reverence and humility. May it lead us to put our whole trust in thee alone, and so to serve and honor thee that we may in all things glorify thy name: through Jesus Christ our Lord. Amen.

**Theme: The Bible in Our Day (Bible Sunday)**

TEXT: "Whatsoever things were written aforetime were written for our learning." Rom. 15:4.

What was said of Shakespeare's plays, that they are "not of an age, but for all time," can be said with equal truth of other literary masterpieces. Plato's *Republic,* for example, is conditioned throughout by a particular period in the history of ancient Greece, yet it is amazingly up-to-date. The Bible is not the only book that speaks to our day; what is unique about it is what it has to say to us. It is a book of such a character that when we open its pages to read them with understanding, Christ himself steps out of them, as one who comes from God and brings us to God.

I. The Bible and Freedom. Let us now consider the place of the Bible in our present world situation. If it is asked what is most at stake today, the answer is clear. It is freedom. And freedom is one of the major themes of the Bible. Freedom is grounded in the fact that all human authorities are under God and so can claim allegiance only as they acknowledge themselves subject to his righteousness.

The final source and final guarantee of all authority are with God. Freedom perishes where a mortal man arrogates to himself an absolute right over his fellows and legislates as though there were none above him. But where the Sovereign accepts the highest dignity with the deepest humility and holds it as from God and under him, there freedom is secure.

II. The Bible and Christian Unity. And now we come to the church. Our service is a reminder that, divided as we are over so much, in the Bible we occupy common ground. It is not our common possession. It is the source of the spiritual life on which we draw in common. As long as the Gospels are in circulation, the possibility is open to each person of a direct encounter with Christ. As long as the Bible is preserved in the life of the church, it bears witness to our common origin and common message.

In the ecumenical movement it is becoming of increasing concern that we cannot meet around the Lord's Table. Yet one point of unity remains; we can all gather around the open Bible.

There is an effort in the Roman Church to encourage the reading of the Bible. Fresh translations have been made and new commentaries published, societies are formed and periodicals founded to promote the study of the Bible. Not so long ago the Society for Old Testament Study met in Rome with a Roman Catholic scholar as president, and the Pope in a special audience expressed his appreciation of its work. The Bible is a link between churches which are gravely separated, and from this a fuller understanding may grow in time.

III. The Bible and Ourselves. But what of ourselves? One grave weakness in our church life is the decay of the authority of the Bible, so that it is no longer the sure word of God it was for our fathers. We have learned what the Bible is not: that it is not a textbook of science, not an infallible guide to conduct, and so on. Hence a large number among us no longer read the Bible, or, if they do read it, do not know where to place it nor how to value it. And those of us who teach the Bible constantly find that we are taking too much for granted. We expect our hearers to assimilate what we give without our realizing how disturbing it may be for them.

We need, therefore, some clear statement on what the Bible is and can do, and I would venture such a statement at my own risk. The function of the Bible is to introduce us to the God and Father of our Lord Jesus Christ and to make possible a personal relation to him. Other books may do so derivatively; this book does it originally, and can do it in every language and for every people under heaven. The value of the Bible, therefore, does not lie in itself but in the God to whom it brings me.

The most important fact about the Bible is that in it and through it God makes an offer of himself, to be received in humility, reverence, and obedience. We find the truth in it only as we receive it in willingness to live by it. In it Christ speaks to us personally in the call of duty and the whisper of forgiveness, and it is for us to incorporate into our lives what we hear.

Somehow or other we must bring together the truth of the Bible and the stark actualities, the mechanism and forces of the contemporary world. We must stay ourselves upon the living God and at the same time enter sympathetically into the mood of the time, with its strange mixture of overconfidence and impotence. We have only begun to translate the Bible when we have found equivalents in English for Hebrew and Greek words. The harder task is to communicate the ideas of the Bible in such terms as will come home to men amid the technical apparatus and political obsessions of the day.

The Bible has spoken to us and we are grateful for this. Let us not forget the multitudes around us to whom the Bible does not yet speak. We are told of men in the Malayan jungle who had a Bible with them but who, though they had often promised themselves that they would read it when they had time, never did. We are not bound to reproduce the words of the Bible if we are to convey its message. We should take whatever language men about us can understand and make use of that. So doing, we fulfill the purpose of the Bible—which is to enable Jesus Christ to step out of the past into the present that we may meet with God in him.—E. L. Allen.

PRAYER FOR THE DAY. O God, the Father of Lights, whose word is enduring and whose promise cannot fail, grant unto us the spirit of wisdom that we may understand thy word, and faith that we may keep it unto life eternal. Graciously impart unto us the spirit of meekness that we may receive thy truth. Take away all our pride and all feelings of self-sufficiency, and bring us in hunger to the things which thou hast provided for them that love thee. Incline our hearts to keep thy law. Cleanse our desires from everything that defileth, and help us to drink of the river of thy pleasures. Give us deliverance from the bondage of every evil habit, and guard us lest by any unholy purpose we enter into new bondage. Let everything that is crooked be made straight, and may all that is within us praise and bless thy holy name. Amen.—John H. Jowett.

OFFERTORY SENTENCE: "So shall my word be that goeth forth out of my mouth: it shall not return unto me void, but it shall accomplish that which I please, and it shall prosper in the thing whereto I sent it." Isa. 55:11.

OFFERTORY PRAYER: We rejoice, our Father God, that we are privileged to be fellow workers with thee, in spreading the light of the Gospel of Jesus Christ unto the uttermost parts of the earth. Make us faithful stewards in this Divine Partnership, we beseech thee: and graciously multiply our offerings to the feeding of the souls of men. And to thy holy name shall be the praise, both now and forever. Amen.

SEED THOUGHTS:

Within the Pages of the Bible. Within its pages: 1. we find power for the ordering of our inner lives; 2. is offered a way of escape from those inner perils which threaten our modern life; 3. are found the secrets by which men walk the pathways of light and hope and freedom; 4. assurance is given that man is supremely dear to God; 5. we discover the way to world brotherhood; 6. is information as to whither we are bound and why; 7. is offered a sound philosophy; 8. is the teaching, in the words of Emerson, that "the lesson of life is to believe what the years and the centuries say, as against the hours."—Paul B. Kern.

### Choice Illustrations on the Theme

GIVING THE BIBLE TO A PEOPLE. What happens when an African tribe receives such a book in its own language? It experiences an immense enlargement of its horizon, it enters into a process that is as old as time and as extensive as the world. A great army is marching across the centuries to the drumbeat of the Kingdom of God, and it falls in as one more contingent and marches forward with the rest. To give the Bible to a people is to introduce new participants in an enterprise in which they are workers together in the purposes of God. —E. L. A.

THE PROBLEMS OF THE MACHINE. The problem of the machine cannot be solved by an executioner. It must be solved by a master. If modern civilization is likened to a high-powered automobile we may gaze at the great machine with grave anxiety. But we will see sooner or later that we cannot meet the situation by destroying the machine. What we really need to do is find a new driver. We will scarcely cease to produce machines. We must learn how to produce men who can be trusted to control and use the machinery for the purposes of moral and spiritual order, for the good of the world and the honor of God.

The Book which the Bible societies send about the world contains that secret. It does not tell us how to make machines. It does tell us how to make men that can be trusted with machines. —Lynn Harold Hough.

## EVENING SERVICE

### Theme: Pages of Power (Bible Sunday)

TEXT: "So shall my word be that goeth forth out of my mouth: it shall not return unto me void, but it shall accomplish that which I please, and it shall prosper in the thing whereto I sent it." Isa. 55:11.

Dr. Moffatt puts that last clause into simple straightforward modern English: "My word carries out my purpose."

I. The Word has power to proclaim a purpose of God.

1. A Question Asked. There is a sentence which often falls from careless lips which is one of the deepest questions that a man can ask, "What is it all about?" Galaxies of stars in the heavens, planets swing in their orbits about central suns . . . a stream of generations . . . youth, maturity, old age, death . . . flowers and black-widow spiders, sunsets and rattlesnakes . . . wars and civilization . . . on and on, *ad infinitum*—what is it all about?

Some ask the question nonchalantly to dismiss thinking. We ask it seriously to start thinking—what is it all about? To put it in other fashion, Are we getting anywhere? Is there purpose in the universe?

2. A Question Unanswered. This question "What is it all about?" is largely

unanswered because we often seek the answer in a wrong place. "Fancy trying to find a purpose in the complicated machines, let us say, of a textile mill. Analyze that machinery until doomsday, and the more you take it apart the less purpose you will find there. From watching people use machinery you might learn what machines are for, but no analysis of the machines would give you that knowledge." Purpose resides in mind.

Our text says that purpose resides in the mind of God. The answer to the question "What is it all about?" does not come from the universe itself; it resides in the mind of God.

What are the purposes of God? He says that they are, if known by us at all, only partially known. "My thoughts are not your thoughts. . . . For as the heavens are higher than the earth, so are my ways higher than your ways and my thoughts [plans] higher than your thoughts [plans]."

It behooves all scientists, philosophers, preachers to be humble.

3. A Question Answered. God has purpose. His purposes are only partially known. His Word has power to proclaim a purpose. There is one purpose of God, one at least, implicity and explicity proclaimed in this book of Isaiah; no one can mistake it; it is expressed clearly in the chapter of our text, and it is a crimson thread running through the whole Bible. It is this: It is a purpose of God to pardon men of their sins. The Bible proclaims that. By that proclamation its pages are pages of power.

II. The Word has power to offer the pardon of God.

1. The Book creates desire for pardon. There is just no use to offer a thing to a person who has no concern or interest in it, no felt need for it. Desire must be awakened. The Bible creates desire for pardon. The Word says "Thou art the man!"

2. The Book stimulates aspiration. Men see the things that are honorable and they want them. They see the path of truth and they long to walk in it. They read the story of the Good Samaritan and deep in they feel themselves to be that kind of a man. They see a woman transformed from impurity of life into the matchless loveliness of Mary Magdalene on Resurrection morning and all things pure and lovely become possible. They see an impulsive and shifting character like Peter changed into a personality of granite. They see glimpses of him who walked in Galilee. Then when men desire and aspire—

3. The Book has power to offer the pardon of God. Isa. 55:1-3, 7. The Word is not a charm or fetish, an idol. The word does not compel—it offers.

III. The Word has power to appear in personality. It becomes incarnate. Words and ideas appear on written and printed pages but the Word of God documents itself in flesh and blood.

Thomas Carlyle said that when he thought of "salvation by faith" he thought of Thomas Chalmers.

So God's Word concerning his purpose and his word concerning his pardon become manifest in a living document, the Man of Galilee—the Christ.

The Bible therefore has pages of power—pages which proclaim the purpose of God to pardon, pages which offer the pardon of God, pages which show forth a life which redocuments God's purpose and offer.

These pages are not pages to compel. They find our hearts. They reach our minds. They challenge our wills. But they do not compel acceptance. What responsibility a man takes upon himself when he refuses to heed the proclamation, when he spurns the offer, when he turns aside from the living Christ.—H.

**Suggested Bible Sunday Texts and Themes**

The Indestructible: "Heaven and earth shall pass away: but my words shall not pass away." Luke 21:33.

The Impress of the Gospel: "For our

gospel came not unto you in word only, but also in power. . . ." I Thess. 1:5.

The Textbook of Freedom: "If ye continue in my word, then are ye my disciples indeed: and ye shall know the truth, and the truth shall make you free." John 8:31, 32.

The Enduring Word: "But the word of the Lord endureth for ever." I Pet. 1:25.

The Interpretation of Scripture: Acts 8:26-38.

## MIDWEEK FELLOWSHIP MEETING TOPIC

(Church Night or Suggested Sermon Subject)

**Theme: A Christmas Song**

TEXT: Luke 1:46-55 (The magnificat).

Just where Luke received his information concerning the advent of Christ we cannot tell, but it is a story of beauty, particularly as it gives us the song of Mary, known as the Magnificat.

The song was sung in the presence of Elizabeth. Mary had gone to visit her cousin, aware of the strange thing that was happening to her, yet unable to talk of it to anyone. We can imagine her joy when she was greeted by Elizabeth in such a way that she knew secrecy was now unnceessary. All the wonder, reverence, and joy that had been held in could now break forth in the Magnificat.

I. In Mary's song we notice three things. First of all, the relationship of this song to the Old Testament is notable. In spirit, reference, and even in vocabulary, this is an echo of the Old Testament. One cannot hear the song without remembering the song of Hannah after the birth of Samuel (I Sam. 2:1-10).

There are other reminders of the Old Testament. We notice reference to some of the Psalms, such as Pss. 36, 113, and 124, and to Mic. 7:20. We have said that these are "echoes" of the Old Testament; they are not deliberate quotations. These are the result of a piety that steeped itself in the Old Testament writings and in Old Testament thought.

II. A second point that deserves notice, particularly in the light of later development around the person of Mary, is the attitude of Mary toward herself. If the adoration of the Virgin is to have any real foundation, it must be found in one of two places—either in the claims that Mary made for herself or in the claims that her Son made on her behalf. Since the attitude of the Son, though respectful, strongly indicates that in his position of Messiah his earthly mother has no influence upon his work (Matt. 12:46-50; John 2:4), special urgency has been put on some of the mother's own words. Luke 1:46-48 bears on this question. What do these verses say? They say simply that because God has chosen Mary to be the instrument of a glorious miracle, all generations will regard her as having been blessed. With that no Christian would want to argue. To have been the mother of Jesus Christ was indeed a blessing and a privilege, even though the privilege was mixed with pain and sorrow.

The silence of almost every other part of the New Testament concerning Mary does not take away from her the privilege, but it does reveal that among the first Christians who knew her she was regarded, even as she thought of herself, as the instrument through which God's grace acted, happy and blessed in being used, and neither wanting nor receiving any other position.

III. The third point concerns what we might call the humanitarian emphasis of this song. When we compare it with its contemporary, the song of Zacharias (Luke 1:68-79), we are impressed with the emphasis on the merciful acts of God in comparison with the strife and bloodshed that Zacharias predicts.

Mary sings out of her own experience a song of the poor—she is more concerned with food than with national sovereignty; her complaint against the proud and the mighty is more the outcry of the humble peasant against those immediately above him than of the patriot against the foreign tyrant. National aims were always present among the Israelites, but here they are subordinate. Human needs are primary.

Taken as a whole, the Magnificat is characterized by a spirit of trust. It breathes gratitude to God for a work just begun yet considered as accomplished. It expresses the belief that God not only can but also has and will deal in history with the injustices that we see all around us. In this it speaks to our world, which, perhaps out of impatience because "the mills of God grind slowly," has begun to doubt that the mills of God grind. Let us remember with Mary that the coming of Christ, because it brings with it the beginning of the Kingdom of God, carries with it also the assurance of the victory of that Kingdom.—J. Stuart Dickson.

## SUNDAY SCHOOL LESSON

**Dec. 14. Jesus Works through Disciples. Mark 6:6b-13. Background Scripture: Mark 6:30-44.**

Memory Verse: "He had compassion on them, because they were like sheep without a shepherd." Mark 6:34 (R.S.V.).

I. Jesus does many things *for* his disciples.

II. Jesus does many things *in* his disciples. He reaches their minds, hearts, and wills. He prepares them for active participation in his work. Christians are not to be mere spectators; they are to be active agents. They are to be witnesses.

III. Jesus does many things *through* his disciples. Jesus planned to make his impact on his own generation through his disciples. What things has Christ done in these modern days through his disciples? In the world? Locally? What things does Christ send us out to do now? What is our response?

# SUNDAY: DECEMBER TWENTY-FIRST

## MORNING SERVICE

**Theme: This is a Wonderful Christmas (Christmas)**

Suggested Scripture Reading: Luke 2:1-20.

Selected Hymns: Processional, "O come, all ye faithful."—Latin Hymn (Adeste Fideles), 17th Cent. "There's a Song in the Air!"—J. G. Holland. "O little town of Bethlehem."—Phillips Brooks. "Hark! the herald angels sing." —Charles Wesley.

Call to Worship: "And, lo, the star. . . ." Matt. 2:9-11.

Invocation: Eternal God, our Father, with our hearts all hushed by the mystery and wonder of the birth of the Christ Child, we bow in humble and adoring prayer on this Christmas Sunday morning. Make us truly wise with the wisdom of a little child, that once again the highest truth may be born afresh in our hearts. Let not our souls be busy inns that have no room for him, but this day may we throw wide all the doors of our lives to welcome our Holy Guest. May his presence be very near to us all this day, and especially now as we worship together in thy house of prayer. We ask in his name. Amen.

**Theme: This is a Wonderful Christmas (Christmas)**

Text: "And all they that heard it wondered at those things which were told them by the shepherds." Luke 2:18.

I. The Fact of Christmas. It is

wonderful that we have kept the fact. It is wonderful that the birth of the Babe has escaped oblivion. Nineteen hundred and fifty-eight years after the event our great festival brings us deepest joy. Alexander the Great had a birthday—he conquered worlds—who knows or keeps his birthday? Herod the Great had a birthday, Augustus Caesar had a birthday—Plato, Aristotle, Socrates. Does even Rome, much less the world, keep Caesar's birthday? What Greek, much less an American, remembers Socrates' natal day? But 1,958 years after and on the other side of the world from Bethlehem we remember the scene in the stable and rejoice. The *fact* is wonderful.

II. This is a wonderful Christmas because the *story* is wonderful. At Christmas time we become like little children who listen to bedtime stories. Every mother knows that she must not drop a word from the oft-repeated story. Do not drop a line of this story of Mary and Joseph, the journey from Nazareth to Bethlehem, no room in the inn, the stable with the oxen, the cry of a Babe, angels singing in the hills to shepherds keeping their flocks, wise men from afar following a star, gifts for a King, gold and frankincense and myrrh, the blessing of the Babe in the temple, the flight into Egypt, the return to Nazareth—and on and on—the crucifixion, the resurrection. How he stirred the hearts of artists who painted the mother and the Babe! How he put poetry into the souls of men! How he filled them with music—"O Little Town of Bethlehem." "Silent Night," "There's a Song in the Air"—the story goes on and on—ten centuries, twenty centuries, it may be thirty, forty, a hundred hundred years—and the story of Christmas is continued into eternity!

This is a wonderful Christmas because it is part of the story.

III. This is a wonderful Christmas because of the *contrasts*.

Christmas comes in the dark of the year—it should always come in the dark of the moon—the symbol of Christmas might well be a dark night with a single candle burning. On such a night which would be the more significant, the darkness or the candle?

The contrast of Christmas is darkness *vs.* light. The Child was a light shining in the darkness and the darkness could not put it out—no more than the night could put out the star which the wise men followed. It is good to light candles at Christmas, for light is a token of the Christ.

The contrast of Christmas is hatred *vs.* love. Find a sketch of the life of Herod the so-called Great, that subking who ruled from Jerusalem when Jesus was born at Bethlehem just six miles distant.

You will discover that Herod was the most hateful and hating and hated man that ever lived. Personally, taking all things into consideration, I believe that this is no exaggeration. Herod was the personification of hate. Jesus was the personification of love. Herod murdered; Jesus saved. Herod held little boys under water and drowned them, slaughtered the innocents; Jesus took little children into his arms and blessed them. The child Jesus who became a loving man, with the love of God in every thought and deed, was born in the reign of Herod, the Hateful.

The contrast of Christmas is one of death *vs.* life. It is well that we keep Christmas at the winter solstice—at the dark, dead time of the year. "In him was life," wrote John. He said, "I am the Resurrection and the life."

No matter how dark, how hateful, how death-dealing the day may be—here in the Christ Child is the light and love and life of the world.

This is a wonderful Christmas because of the *contrasts.*

IV. This is a wonderful Christmas because of the *halos.* Every Christmas we must look again for those circles of beauty and light and glory that encircle the brows of the participants in the story.

There is a halo above the head of each shepherd. What is this but a token that common labor and toil—work, tending sheep, tilling land, making things, serving in the kitchen—all toil, labor, work, is honorable, bright, glorious! Seen at his full worth every man that does honest work wears a halo at Christmas.

The Wise Men's halo is a token of glory about the brow of every man on quest for wisdom and truth. Our modern wise men, our scientists and philosophers, might do well to bring their gold and frankincense and myrrh to lay them at the feet of Jesus. He would lead them into all truth and the truth would make us free.

By the Birth there is a halo about motherhood and childhood, and even Joseph gives fatherhood reflected light, which means that a radiance comes to the family on Christmas—there is a strange and mystical light in the home—and that makes Christmas a wonderful day.

The *halos* which encircle us make this a wonderful Christmas.

V. This is a wonderful Christmas because of the *hope* of Christmas. Hope springs eternal in our human breasts. How much of that hope was kindled by the expectation of his coming! The old prophets wrote about swords being changed into plowshares; they named the coming one Prince of Peace; they wrote poetry about the desert blossoming as a rose. And when he came, above the Judean plain was heard the song, "Peace on earth; good will toward men." From that day until now, in the hearts of good men is found the hope of peace. In the hearts of some is the will to peace.

This is a wonderful Christmas because we still keep singing our songs of *hope*.

VI. This is a wonderful Christmas because it is a Christmas of *grace*. Grace came through Jesus Christ. What is grace? Grace is that which binds up our wounded hearts and heals us. The other day I went to a home where there was deep sorrow—this woman as did Mary felt a sword pierce her soul. But she was serene and calm. And what was the secret of her serenity? She held in her hand a book, and she looked up and said, "I am reading the fourteenth chapter of John's Gospel." She was receiving grace through Jesus Christ.

Here is another, and through the years there is the miracle of change—the natural hardness has become tenderness, that bitterness has become sweetness, that coldness has become warmth, that selfishness has become generosity. And how does one account for this? It is by the grace of Jesus Christ.

So the wonder of Christmas is the wonder of grace—Old Scrooge does become generous on Christmas; on Christmas the harsh word becomes a kind one; for one day there is compassion toward the poor; and men enter the Kingdom of God because their hearts become like those of little children.

That is the wonder of Christmas—it is the Christ Child's gift—the gift of grace.

VII. This Christmas is wonderful because of the *revelation*. In the Babe we see God. Did you ever think about the imagination of God? His imagination set the scene of the birth in a stable with a cow and a donkey looking on. I'm glad for the humor of God which made a donkey part of the birth scene. Matthew and Luke missed this point, but I'm glad we found it.

At the birth we see the faithfulness of God. He is being true to his promises to his people. The race of men whom he created are by this Child to be redeemed.

As the Child grows to manhood we see in him the wisdom of God. He reveals also the love of God. By his revelation his followers were enabled to say, "God is love." By his revelation we know that to be true. The very acme of love is revealed by him on the cross.

He is the power of God. He is the presence of God. God walks among us. The same Christ that was born in a manger at Bethlehem—that is the Christ who answers us when we pray,

Come to our hearts, Lord Jesus,
There is room in our hearts for Thee.

The very God! "See the Christ stand!" Here! Now! This is a wonderful Christmas!—H.

PRAYER FOR THE DAY: Our loving Father, we thank thee for our quickened memories today and the pictures they present to our minds. We see the scenes of long ago, a mother and a babe, wakeful shepherds and their sheep, pilgrim wise men and a guiding star; and other nearer scenes of our own childhood.

We thank thee for the touch of love upon our hearts, for the Christ spirit seeking entrance in our lives. Help us to open every door of our hearts unto his full entrance.

God bless us every one, old men and children, mothers and their babes; the high, the low; the rich, the poor. God bless us every one throughout the whole wide world.

And let the joy of our hearts and their peace be unto the praise of him who once was the Babe of Bethlehem. Amen.—H.

OFFERTORY SENTENCE: "And when they were come into the house, they saw the young child with Mary his mother, and fell down, and worshipped him: and when they had opened their treasures, they presented unto him gifts; gold, and frankincense, and myrrh."

OFFERTORY PRAYER: We open our treasures and make our gifts to our King. To gold we would add gratitude, to frankincense faithfulness, to myrrh the devotion of our hearts. Accept, O Lord, that which our hands have brought, and that which our hearts have brought. Bless both of these as means to bring tidings of great joy unto the hearts of men.—H.

## Illustrative Material

SEED THOUGHTS:

The Seven Wonders of Christmas: I. The Fact; II. The Story; III. The Contrasts; IV. The Halos; V. The Hope; VI. The Grace; VII. The Revelation.

The Wonder of the Story: I. The Beginning of the Story—when the morning stars sang together. II. The Development of the Story. III. The Unfolding of the Story. IV. The Continuance of the Story.

Grace for the Healing of the World. I. Grace for sorrow. II. Grace for sin. III. Grace for transformation.

The Wonder of the Hope. I. The Wonder of the Prophets. II. The Wonder of the Angels. III. The Wonder of the Singers. We must keep on singing!

## Choice Christmas Illustrations

CHRIST IN CHRISTMAS. I took twenty-five Christmas cards at random from those which I had received and of the twenty-five fourteen ignored the fact back of Christmas; eleven recognized it. Fifty-six per cent had no relation to the fact, 44 per cent were based on the fact. One of these cards was from a Jewish friend; you would not expect him to refer to the real event. But another was from the president of a theological seminary—the card might have been sent by a Mohammedan in Mecca or a Buddhist in Bangkok. I am not judging my friends, for some of the non-fact cards came from devoted Christian people—I am only illustrating how subtly and gradually we permit the Christ to slip out of Christmas.—H.

THERE'S GOOD NEWS TODAY. For several years a daily newspaper carried on its front page a news feature with this heading: "There's good news today." Under the caption one could read daily a gladdening story.

"There's good news today"—the Christmas story deserves first place under such a headline. The angel was saying, "There's good news today; unto you a Saviour is born, Christ the Lord."

Each Christmas season brings us good news, the good news of Jesus' mission to the world. It brings us the good news of a world-wide Christian fellowship that crosses national boundaries, boundaries of language and race, and brings persons together in a new, common language. This good news is the best hope of mankind.—Ben F. Lehmberg.

THE COMRADESHIP OF CHRISTMAS. There is no area of Christian life in which

Christians are more united than in the hymns we sing at Christmas. In their origin they come from all types and kinds of Christianity: "Silent Night!" is Roman Catholic; "Away in a Manger" is Lutheran; "Hark! the Herald Angels sing" is Methodist; "O Little Town of Bethlehem" is Episcopalian; "It Came upon the Midnight Clear" is Unitarian; "Joy to the World" is Congregational.

And yet how little difference there is among them in their real message to our hearts. Perhaps if we gave ourselves more earnestly to the simple, fundamental things of our religion, we would be less conscious of our differences and could find the comradeship of Christmas lasting throughout the year. —*Daily Devotions.*

**Quotable Christmas Poetry**

THE IDEAL

The roots of the Anglo-Saxon race
Strike too deep within the Christ-Ideal
To be blighted utterly by any fate.
As long as children shall endure,
Or the child-like heart;
No misinterpretations or rejections,
However great,
Shall quite destroy the vision
Of the Word made flesh,
Justice among men,
Truth incarnate.

—Elizabeth La Dow.

THE MAGNIFICENT

We look across the history of years
And always Jesus is magnificent.
The One who loved and wiped away all tears,
Whose deathless words are ever eloquent.
Today hate leads a world—a world gone mad,
And hot-brained rulers stir up deadly strife—
They joke about the Virgin Mary's Lad,
Doubt the divinity of His short life.
But still His glory lives. His lowly birth,
His blessed promises of peace for man.
His parables, His miracles, His plan
To heal the sick and desolate of earth,
Great civilizations have passed away
But still remembered is the Christ's birthday.

—Betty L. Whitsell.

PRAYER ON CHRISTMAS EVE

High on the wind-swept hills the shepherds kept
Their quiet sheep above dark Bethlehem.
The starry night was hushed, the old town slept;
When suddenly a song broke over them,
And all the cradling hills were full of light.
The patient beasts knelt down before the Child
Whose birth the heavens told that Holy Night;
The Wise Men sought Him; and the shepherds mild—
All those of gentle hearts and kindly wills.
Our world is broken by its tale of years,
O, turn our hearts tonight to those far hills,
That we may see, beyond our bitter tears,
The star of hope, alight, and, thru the din,
May hear the angels' song above the Inn!

—Beverly Githens.

## EVENING SERVICE

**Theme: The Tale of Two Inns**

TEXT: "There was no room for them in the inn." Luke 2:7.

"Go out quickly into the streets and lanes of the city, and bring in hither the poor, and the maimed, and the halt, and the blind, and the servant said, Lord, it is done as thou hast commanded, and yet there is room." Luke 14:21, 22.

I. The Inn of the Human Heart.

1. St. Luke says significantly that "there was no room for them in the inn." *For them,* as though for some special reason they were singled out for exclusion. There was room for others—for a gregarious gambling man and his family from Gaza, maybe; for

a talkative taxgatherer from Tiberias; for a wealthy merchantman and his wife from Magdala; for an old Herod-hating bachelor from Bethsaida—but there was no room in the inn *for them.* And what could the reason for exclusion have been, if it were neither the lack of Joseph's wealth, nor his girl-wife's condition, which promised inconvenience to the innkeeper? It seems as though those to whom God had entrusted the care of Jesus was turned away from the inn precisely because they appeared to be so poor.

And—there is no mistaking the fact—Mary and Joseph *were* poor. It was into this status of poverty, which was—and still is—the lot of the world's millions, that the Eternal Word chose to appear and live in his perfect humanity. He chose to be a member of the working classes; he chose himself to be a worker. When he had grown to manhood what did he say of himself, and what was said of him? "Behold I am among you as one who serves"—"Is not this the carpenter's son?"

2. He Comes to Us. When we think of the great God entering the universe which he had created, how utterly enthralling is the true story of the stable and the straw! Clothed in the garment of frail human flesh, God came to take his share in that part of the world's history in which his human life would be spent, and his entry was unnoticed and unknown, except by "the first of the few." Why was it that the majority of those he came to help and to heal, to seek and to save, did not recognize him when he came? Simply because their lives were so crowded with what they styled religion and with all sorts of selfish interests, that they could find no room for him in the inn they called their heart. Here was the most wonderful of all happenings in human history: it was not merely the birth of a baby, though the birth of any baby is a wonderful thing enough, but God contracted to the size of a helpless child—a new all-appealing, all-revealing, and all-redeeming manifestation of the Eternal One, and they did not see him, they had no room for him.

In the circumstances of life, circumstances as menial as the manger, as commonplace as the carpenter's workshop, as happy as the marriage feast at Cana, and as sad as looking upon an inhospitable and even hostile city from the crest of Olivet, as almost agonizing as Gethsemane, and nearly as tragic and awful as the Cross, he comes to us. He comes to seek and to save that which is lost, to bring light into our darkness, strength to our weakness, peace to our war-wounded hearts; and still too many of us crowd him out of our lives. There is no room for him in the inn of the human heart.

II. The Inn of the Heart of God.

1. Room for Our Interests. This is precisely what Jesus pointed out in the parable recorded in the fourteenth chapter of St. Luke's little and beautiful biography. The point of this parable is not so much that the folk who were bidden stayed away from the banquet as their attitude of mind and heart toward the Lord of Life who had asked them to come. In the parallel passage in St. Matthew's Gospel we are told significantly enough that they "made light of" the invitation. It was a silly misunderstanding, on their part, of the mind of God to think that they could not bring to him for consecration those very things that kept them away. The people are roughly of three types—a landed gentleman, a laborer, and a lover. Our Lord says: "If you had only known, you could have asked my blessing on your property! Do you think your oxen are not of interest to me? Do you really believe the tender love of your heart is not precious to me? Your fields won't walk away, and your oxen will be all the better for the rest, and surely you could bring your wife to the banquet. There is room . . . !"

2. Room for All. In the heart of God there is room for all the world. There is room in God's inn for every temperament and type. There is room in this world, as there is in the parable, for everybody, and work enough and food

enough, if the world of men and women were really guided by the truths of Christmas Christianity.

God, at Christmas time, comes again to call all men to him—and he will restore all things in him through "all them that love his appearing." The great door of the Inn of God is unlatched. Can't you hear him calling? "Come in, this moment, at his call. . . ." "It is done . . . and yet there is room" in the Inn of God for more.—Johnstone G. Patrick.

**Suggested Christmas Texts and Themes**

A Dictator Trembles: "When Herod the king had heard these things, he was troubled, and all Jerusalem with him." Matt. 2:3.

There's Good News Today: "And the angel said unto them, Fear not: for, behold, I bring you good tidings of great joy, which shall be to all people." Luke 2:10.

The World's Unforgettable Person: "For unto you is born this day in the city of David a Saviour, which is Christ the Lord." Luke 2:11.

There's a Song in the Air: "Glory to God in the highest, and on earth peace, good will toward men." Luke 2:14.

Christmas Decorations: "Worship the Lord in the beauty of holiness." Ps. 29:2.

## MIDWEEK FELLOWSHIP MEETING TOPIC

(Church Night or Suggested Sermon Topic)

**Theme: Under the Christmas Star (Christmas)**

TEXT: "We have seen his star in the east, and are come to worship him." Matt. 2:2.

I. Underneath the star of Bethlehem lay a visible token of the love of God. "And they called his name Jesus."

II. Power lay beneath the star. And where Christ is, there is power now for us all.

III. Hope lies waiting for us beneath the star of Bethlehem—a new hope of a better life.

IV. Beneath the Bethlehem star lay faith, that first Christmas night. The men from afar saw only a child, yet they knew the child for a King. They had faith—in the years that would bring him to manhood. Have we as much faith in Christ, in ourselves, in other people?

V. Beneath the star lay unselfishness—in the Wise Men; in Mary, the mother; in Jesus, the willingly earth-born Son of God; and in God, the Father of him. And every Christmas that is worthy the name is marked by a spirit of unselfishness—even today.

VI. Beneath the Bethlehem star there was found a combination of sorrow (there was no room for them in the inn) and joy, but the sorrow was quite overwhelmed in the joy. Always it is so for those who find the Lord Jesus.

VII. When we follow the star we find a starting point and a terminus; a beginning of all that is worth while for ourselves and the end of all our longing; the Beginning and the End; the Alpha and the Omega.—Paul Faris.

## SUNDAY SCHOOL LESSON

**Dec. 21: The Significance of the Saviour's Birth. Luke 1:46-55; 2-4-7. Background Scripture: Luke 1:26-56; 2:1-20.**

MEMORY VERSE: "My soul magnifies the Lord, and my spirit rejoices in God my Saviour." Luke 1:46-47 (R.S.V.).

I. Verse 46. "My soul magnifies the Lord." What the soul magnifies makes a vast difference in human life. Here indeed is the secret of true success and of tragic failure.

II. Verse 49. "He who is mighty has done great things for me." This was the grateful confession of the early Christians. They said: God has drawn near to us; he has revealed his love toward us; he has saved us from our sins and from despair; he has filled our hearts with joy and hope; and hast given us the assurance of everlasting life.

III. Verse 52. "He has put down the mighty from their thrones." As fallen empires attest, and will do so again if power is misused. Every imperialism, every political totalitarianism, every racial discrimination, all human exploitation and oppression has resting upon it the judgment of God, and cannot permanently endure.—Ernest Fremont Tittle.

# SUNDAY: DECEMBER TWENTY-EIGHTH

## MORNING WORSHIP

### Theme: The Road to New Life

SUGGESTED SCRIPTURE READING: John 6:48-51; 58-69.

SELECTED HYMNS: "Jesus, thou divine Companion."—Henry van Dyke. "O Master, let me walk with thee."—Washington Gladden. "O God, our help in ages past."—Isaac Watts. "Dear Lord and Father of mankind."—J. G. Whittier.

(Note: Dec. 28 is the 250th anniversary of the birth of Charles Wesley. It would be appropriate on this day to sing hymns which he wrote, and also inform the people by giving a short sketch of his life.)

CALL TO WORSHIP: "Serve the Lord with gladness; come before his presence with singing. Enter into his gates with thanksgiving, and into his courts with praise; be thankful unto him and bless his name. For the Lord is good; his mercy is everlasting; and his truth endureth unto all generations."

INVOCATION: O thou, who art the true Sun of the world, evermore rising, and never going down; who, by thy most wholesome appearing and sight, dost nourish and make joyful all things, as well that are in heaven as also that are on earth; we beseech thee mercifully and favorably to shine into our hearts, that the night and darkness of sin, and the mists of error on every side, being driven away, thou brightly shining within our hearts, we may all our life long go without any stumbling or offense, and walk as in the daytime, being pure and clean from the works of darkness, and abounding in all good works which thou hast prepared for us to walk in. Amen.—A Prayer of Erasmus (1467-1536).

### Theme: The Road to New Life (End of Year)

TEXT: "Lord, to whom shall we go? Thou hast the words of eternal life." John 6:68.

INTRODUCTORY: There is a moving incident in the life of Jesus which comes very close to our situation today. You see, in that first century people were unsatisfied with life; they too were looking for someone or something which could show them the road to a new life. And then came Jesus of Nazareth. At first he seemed to have the answers and eagerly they turned in their thousands to him. But then doubts began to rise. His methods didn't seem forceful enough or likely to produce results quickly enough. So "many went back and walked no more with him," the account says significantly, poignantly. Then Jesus turned to his men, those who knew him best, "Will ye also go away?" But Peter, as usual, had his answer ready, strong and confident. "Lord, to whom shall we go? Thou hast the words of eternal life."

Before the hour is finished I would hope that we might come to that answer just as confidently. But let's first stop at the question: "To whom shall we go?" What alternatives are there open to us? Which roads seem to lead to new life? Which?

I. The Way of Escape. One way, with the mood of yearning for a new life upon us, is to ignore it. It is to plunge into a continual round of business and pleasure and let the world go by, to try and silence the voices of our soul.

1. One trouble with taking the way of escapism is that it leaves the world just as it is. If we do nothing to clear and improve a pioneering tract of land it remains useless and unproductive. If we pass by problems of chaos in our society and the unsolved tragedies of the world, life chaos and tragedy simply continue and get worse. God has so made his world that he will do nothing for us until we are ready to let him do something through us. And then we discover while we may leave the world alone it won't leave us alone.

2. Another difficulty about living an escapist life is that we cannot always escape from ourselves. However full and exciting we make our days, the time comes when somewhere we are alone with ourselves, and that yearning for a better life rises again unbidden within us. We know then we've missed the answer we need. Then too the sudden shock of sorrow or sickness comes and we learn how pitiful are our resources. Then we discover that no man can run away from God and run away from himself forever. And when life catches up with us, what then? Escapism is no road to new life. "Lord, to whom shall we go?"

II. Changing the Environment. Another road to which we all at times trust is that which we believe takes us to a new environment. In our social and world thinking we imagine that by some rearrangement of external conditions of life a new world can be born. And when the way is difficult in our own affairs we yearn for a change of circumstance—a different job, a new house, a better salary.

Why can't we see that it's the spirit that needs changing with the changing of the structure of society? To grapple with one without the other is, in the end, to be—as you were.

III. The Way of the Moralist. We move nearer to the answer of our need when we speak of moral recovery and an ethical revival. We become convinced that by realizing our weaknesses and our perils and by calling upon ourselves and each other to advance moral ideals and standards we shall be saved. The history of nations and the story of most of our lives are dotted with determinations to do and be better men. Every new year we make our vows. On other occasions when things go wrong we set out to change our ways. And in society we take the way of the moralist.

But here we must think clearly and frankly. Men do not rise to higher moral standards merely by being told that they ought to live better lives. Through the centuries this way has been tried and it has failed. The truth is, the way of the moralist does not go deep enough. There is no creative power in being told to be better. And even if we try to respond there is no power on which to draw. We are ourselves tainted with the moral helplessness from which we yearn to escape. The way of the moralist, though it looks like it, is not the road to new life. It is the way to rejection and disappointment. "Lord, to whom shall we go?"

IV. The Christian Answer. Where then, is the answer? Is our longing for better things always to be denied? Is our yearning a cheat? If the answer is not in escapism or in environmental changes or in the way of the moralist where is it to be found? "Lord, to whom shall we go?" The place of renewal and recovery is where it has always been, where alone it is to be found—in the transforming power of God given to us through Jesus Christ. "Lord, to whom shall we go? *Thou* hast the words of eternal life."

There is only one force in all the world which can change the moral tone and atmosphere of a nation; there is only one power in the whole universe which can take any one of us as we are and make us what we ought to be. It is the power of true religion. There is only one set of answers sufficient to meet the needs of our minds and hearts giving purpose to living and goal at the end of the road. It is found in the Christian faith. There is only one figure in all history who can take our highest yearnings and satisfy them. It is Jesus of Nazareth. Men and women, it is the Christian Gospel we need—the full-orbed Christian faith. The world cries out not for morality but religion; not ethics first, but faith—then all other things will be added. There is no other way to new life save the Christian way. "Thou hast the words of eternal life." —Alan Walker, Australia.

PRAYER: O thou who art forever opening doors into a fuller life, from which we turn away; who art eager to give us good gifts, which we are not ready to receive; who hast filled our world with treasures which we have carefully wasted; we lift our hearts to thee, because thou hast made us that we reach up for a Reality higher than ourselves, as the flowers climb toward the sun.

We cannot understand thy love, which can bear our littleness, and care about us through all our sins. We wonder at thy patience, able to wait so long for the fulfillment of thy purposes until we grow enough in grace and wisdom to work with thee for their achievement. We humble ourselves in reverence before such goodness as thou hast revealed to us in Christ, as we remember that insofar as we are his followers, we follow very far off.

We could not believe that thou art mindful of us—except that each day brings us some encounter with a Will that has planned good things for us, each breath links us with a vast and intimate world that we did not create, each quiet moment brings us a Presence of peace and power, and each memory of Christ assures us of a Friend in the unseen.

As thou hast continued in love to seek us out, thy wandering sheep, be thou still the Pursuing Presence telling us that we are not alone; the Voice that speaks in conscience telling us that we are not without sin; the Power that wells up in our hearts making us able for all things; and the Light that shines beyond the far horizon, bidding us be sure that eye hath not seen, nor ear heard, neither have entered into the heart of man the good things which thou hast prepared for them that love thee. Amen.—Author Unknown.

OFFERTORY SENTENCE: "I will remember the works of the Lord, surely I will remember the wonders of old." "I will press toward the mark for the prize of the high calling of God in Jesus Christ."

OFFERTORY PRAYER: Take and receive, O Lord, our memories and our hopes. All that we have thou hast given us, and all that we expect to have will come from thy hand. Help us, we pray, to give all back to thee, to be disposed of according to thy good pleasure. Give us now thy grace and thy love. With these we shall be rich enough, nor need we ask for aught besides. Amen.—Adapted from an ancient prayer.

SEED THOUGHTS:

"To Whom Shall We Go?" John 6:66-68. I. Jesus gave Peter a new God. II. Jesus Gave Peter a new relationship to God. III. Jesus had given Peter a new conception of man. IV. Jesus also gave to Peter an all-sufficient moral dynamic. V. Jesus gave to Simon Peter the glorious hope of immortality.—John H. Jowett.

"To Whom Shall We Go?" I. The confession of a great need. II. The suggestion of a great search. III. The discovery of a great fact.—Hugh T. Kerr.

"To Whom Shall We Go?"—"The Pre-eminence of Christianity."

**Choice Illustrations on the Theme**

A ROAD WHICH LEADS NOWHERE. When I was in America a motor-boat firm was running a national advertising campaign, trying to induce people to buy its boats. One of its advertisements prominently displayed a letter from a satisfied customer. Describing the thrill he was getting from his new outboard motor boat, he said: "I have discovered a new philosophy for living. I'm not any more going to worry about atom bombs, wars, and depressions. I am going to have a lot of fun."

Well, that's one way. It is a very ancient course of action. The Bible knew something about that way: "Let us eat, drink and be merry, for tomorrow we die." The English playwright, Oscar Wilde, tried it. In his undergraduate days he vowed he would throw the pearl of his soul into every glass of wine. But this way has proved to be a certain failure, a road which leads nowhere.—Alan Walker.

CHANGING THE SCENERY ONLY. Studdert-Kennedy put his finger on this truth when, during an election in Britain, he said: "Changing the Government is only putting one lot of sinners out and putting another lot of sinners in."

THE WAY OF THE MORALIST. In England in the eighteenth century many good men became alarmed about the moral deterioration of England. A whole series of societies and organizations aiming at arresting the drift were started. They had such titles as "The Society for the Reform of Manners." But all their efforts were largely useless; the decline continued, the darkness deepened.—A. W.

MAN'S ULTIMATE DESTINY. In the entrance hall of the fabulous Rockefeller Center in New York there is a series of murals. They show the onward march of mankind. First man is shown laboring painfully with his hands, living precariously but with an indomitable will to survive. Then he is depicted as the maker of tools, extending the comforts of his civilization. On the next mural he is the master of the machine, harnessing to his will the forces of the material world. But the final picture shows Christ, delivering the Sermon on the Mount. Underneath are these words: "Man's ultimate destiny depends not on whether he can learn new lessons or mark new discoveries and conquests, but on his acceptance of the lesson taught him close upon two thousand years ago."—A. W.

## EVENING SERVICE

### Theme: For a Season and Forever

TEXT: "But when the fulness of the time was come, God sent forth his Son." Gal. 4:4. "Lo, I am with you alway, even unto the end of the world." Matt. 28:20.

The great poem of Genesis, Chapter One, carries the line: "And God said, Let there be lights in the firmament of the heaven to divide the day from the night; and let them be for signs, and for seasons, and for days and for years." And so it came to pass that man is enmeshed in seasons while God dwelleth in eternity.

But that is not all. This follows: God came to us for a season that we might be with him for eternity.

I. God came to us for a season. Early in December we began to sing, "O come, O come, Emmanuel!" and "Joy to the world, the Lord is come!" And so the Christmas season becomes the token of those days long ago when in the fullness of the time God sent forth his Son. During days and years the Son was upon the earth.

1. How important it was that Christ came to be with us, within the same limitations of time and space as we ourselves are. Missionaries who preach in lands where Krishna or Siva or Amida or Kwannon are worshiped have tremendous advantage when they point to a historic Christ who visited mankind at a definite time and a certain place. Those others are lost in a misty past wherein they are shadowy figures.

There is an enrichment of our lives and culture, even by the dating of our letters 1958 or 1959, in the Year of our Lord; and by the phrases which we use, such as Jesus of Nazareth, the Christ of Galilee, the Carpenter.

2. And so it comes to pass that the token of the Christmas season ushers us

into the Reality of Jesus. We bow before the cradled Babe and at the same time give him room in our hearts. We follow him into manhood and watch him doing good. The words of the Gospel become no longer printed sentences on the page of a Book, but words uttered by a human voice. We go on further and by the Birth we grasp also his death and his resurrection. And all this because he came to us for a season.

3. Because he came to us for a season long ago and entered into our lives during a season now, we know a little better, much better, what God is like. He came to tell us that. By his words we know that God is wise; by his deeds we know that God is good; by his death we know that God is sacrificial and forgiving; by his resurrection we know that God is eternal.

4. Because he came to us for a season we know what we are like. In becoming man he revealed to us our possibilities and potentialities.

II. God came to us for a season, but remains with us for ever. The season ushers us into eternity. We know that it was expedient for him to go away in order that his spiritual presence might be with us forever. The season fades; eternity grows bright.

1. How important it is that Christ should be with us without limitations of time and space. We need to make no pilgrimages to find him. "Lo, I am with you alway" were his words. We appreciate the season of his coming; we appreciate the eternity of his staying.

2. The Reality of Jesus becomes more vivid through his eternal presence, meeting with us not at some rendezvous on the shore of Galilee, but within the experiences of life—experiences of joy, sorrow, repentance, forgiveness, consecration, and sacrifice—making a rendezvous of home, and shop, of city street and country lane, the seaways and the skyways—God with us, always.

III. The Year—the coming year is a season of eternity. To God it is of the nature of eternity; to us it is of the nature of time. But God adjusts his timelessness to time, his eternity to a season. All that Christ is to us by the token of the Christmas season, and all that Christ is to us by the token of the word eternity—that Christ will be to us as we cross the threshold of the coming year, and as we pursue our ways until another Advent season sets us singing, "Joy to the world, the Lord is come!" —H.

**Suggested Texts and Themes for the Year's End**

Life's Storybook: "We spend our years as a tale that is told." Ps. 90:9.

God's tomorrow: Isa. 40:1-11.

We Shall Reap: "Let us not be weary in well doing: for in due season we shall reap, if we faint not." Gal. 6:9.

Has He Ever Gone? "Lo, I am with you alway, even unto the end of the world." Matt. 28:20.

The Certainty of God's Love: John 3:16 or Rom. 5:1, 2,

The Life of the Ages: "For the wages of sin is death; but the gift of God is eternal life through Jesus Christ our Lord." Rom. 6:23.

## MIDWEEK FELLOWSHIP MEETING TOPIC

(Church Night or Suggested Sermon Subject)

**Theme: At the Threshold (New Year)**

TEXT: I Cor. 15:58.

In the afterglow of Christmas we find ourselves at the threshold of a new year about which as yet we know nothing. We have hopes and forecasts but no certain knowledge.

I. Man is a creature who, in the words of the poet, "looks before and after and pines for what is not." He sweeps the past with memory and the future with hope and brings the influence of both to bear on his present experience.

II. Of the past he has much knowledge. He can add survey to survey. He can divide and subdivide his investigations. The evidence of what has been is available and his knowledge of the past rests on facts.

III. But before the future a curtain hangs which is impenetrable. We are confident that the sun will rise, and after winter has passed the springtime will come. The tides and currents that are moving in history will sweep on into the future, but we can only estimate the power and direction of their flow. There will be anxieties, and there will be great hopes. In personal life we can expect some joy, some pain, some achievement, and some disappointment, but how much or in what form we cannot tell.

IV. Even though the future is unknown we have some power over it. We are not accidents of fate. We are not mere victims of chance. God has given us freedom to be or not to be. We cannot of course change our names or our nationality. We cannot choose our parents. Who we are and where we are have been settled, but what we are is still within the zone of freedom which God has given to us.

Let us, therefore, resolve together to make the most of this new year. Whether or not it is a year of notable progress in international relations, in science, in industry, we can make it a year of great discovery, of great faith, of great loyalty, of great love in our own hearts. "Therefore, my beloved brethren, be ye steadfast, unmovable, always abounding in the work of the Lord, forasmuch as ye know that your labor is not in vain in the Lord."—Harold E. Nicely.

## SUNDAY SCHOOL LESSON

**Dec. 28. Jesus Is Christ the Lord. Mark 8:27-35.**

MEMORY VERSE: "You are the Christ, the Son of the living God." Matt. 16:16 (R.S.V.).

How would you feel if someday you should meet John the Baptist walking down the road? There he is, bearded, wearing sandals, camel's hair cloak, the marks of the desert upon him. You would be curious. You might follow at some distance to look at him.

Suppose it were Elijah or one of the prophets that you met. Perhaps you would be more than curious, a feeling of wonder might come over you. You would recall what Elijah did. You would remember the great books that came from the pens of the prophets. You would feel yourself to be in the presence of greatness, or of genius—just as though you met Plato or Shakespeare or Abraham Lincoln.

Suppose that you met Jesus. No, you would not just be curious, not just filled with wonder or awe; you would worship him. You would feel the attractive power of his personality. His words "Come unto me" would pass through your mind. You would kneel at his feet.

Pupils may be led to realize that at the center of Christianity is not one who excites curiosity, not one who evokes wonder, but one who causes us to cry out, "Thou art the Christ," "My Lord and my God," and bow down in humble worship and accept his grace.

# *SECTION VIII. The Junior Pulpit. A Church-School Year of Suggested Sermons for Children and Youths*

## JANUARY 5. How to Walk Straight

A light snow fell on Friday night and blanketed the town where the Babcocks lived, also the surrounding country. It was too dry for snowballing and not deep enough for coasting so the half-dozen boys who had gathered in front of Jimmy's house did not know what to do to take advantage of a Saturday morning, with no school, but with new-fallen snow.

Mary-Jo happened to come out on the porch and immediately she saw the situation. Then she had a happy thought. She stepped down among the boys and said, "Follow the leader!"

All the boys knew that when Mary-Jo started something it was going to be fun, so all followed Mary-Jo closely to the edge of town and on out into a large meadow with a big oak tree standing in the middle of it. All followed so closely that there was really only one track in the white snow.

When they came to the tree Mary-Jo said, "Now all stand with your backs against the tree. Now each boy, when I give the signal, walk to the opposite fence, and then come back on the same track to the tree. Let's see who can make the straightest track."

The signal was given. They started. They reached the fence and returned to the tree. "Who has made the straightest track?" said one of the boys, named Frank Allison.

"Harry Armstrong's is the only one that is straight at all," said Tom Sanders. "I don't see how we all went so crooked, when the meadow is so smooth and there is nothing to turn us out of the way," said one of the boys.

And then looking to their successful companion, they said: "Tell us, Harry, how you managed to make so straight a track."

Harry said: "I fixed my eye on that tall pine tree, on the other side of the fence toward which I was to walk, and never looked away from it till I reached the fence."

"That's the way to do it," said Mary-Jo, "with no particular aim in view, no wonder you other boys walked crooked."

"Say, fellows, tomorrow's New Year, that's a pretty good lesson for the New Year," said Jimmy, Mary-Jo's brother.

"I thought of that," said Mary-Jo.—Adapted from *The Young Soldier, Toronto, Canada.*

## JANUARY 12. Three Rules

Nothing brings Jesus nearer to us than the stories of his boyhood. Like any happy, human boy, Jesus had looked forward to that long-promised visit to Jerusalem. And when he saw the fine buildings, the places made famous by stirring deeds of the past, his heart was filled with interest. But nothing was so attractive as the Temple. Like you, he loved the House of God. All things, however, come to an end! The time came to go back to the quiet Nazareth home. Although the caravan had set off without our Lord, his mother later found him in the Temple. And when she told him that they must now return home, he obeyed her instantly. There were no "Buts" or "Why?" on his lips; only prompt and unquestioning obedience in his heart. We all like to obey when to obey is something we like. For instance, if father says he is planning a surprise for us, and tells us to get ready, we do not need to be told twice. Not we! We are all eagerness to be ready as soon as he is—before him, if we can! But if he asks us to do something for him, or tells us to set about some small service which we fancy is disagreeable, are we as swift to obey? Now we can be sure that Jesus went back to Nazareth with as happy a face as he had when he had gone up to the Holy City.

I. Do Right and Be Blest. That is the secret of happiness. The horses which work in pairs have discovered that if one pulls one way, and the other another way, it makes the work harder for both. When they pull together, there is a certain amount of pleasure in their task. When a skillful musician plays the organ or the piano, the two hands are playing different notes and are on different parts of the keyboard. Yet they are working together, and there is music, both harmonious and delightful. The great world in which we live, moving rapidly through space, is so obedient to the laws which control its motion, that we cannot feel it. And the obedient heart, trying always to do what God has asked us to do in his holy Word, and making the example of Jesus Christ its guide, can know the gladness and music of the Christian life. If the musician's left hand refuses to follow the orders of his brain, while the right hand obeys, you know what happens to the music! If the express train leaves the rails, there is disaster. And so it is with the heart which is perverse, wanting to go its own way, and do what it likes rather than what it ought. So, do right and be blest! That is the fruit of obedience.

II. Hold Tight to the Best. He would be very foolish who would miss the blessing, and lose the happiness of the heart, just for the sake of doing what suited him. And yet, so many of us make that mistake.

There is an old Greek story about a beautiful princess named Atalanta. There were many who wished to win her for their bride, but to do so, they had to race with her. And she was so swift that she always outstripped her wooers. But one took three golden apples, and as he ran, he threw them, one at a time, in front of Atalanta. Each time she stopped to pick one up, or turned aside to get it, he gained on her, and the third time passed her, and won the prize. To turn aside in the heavenly race is to miss the prize. To disobey is to lessen life's joy. So, hold tight to the best.

III. Keep Bright through Each Test. We must do right, but we must do it rightly—and that means, brightly. The ways of God's statutes are full of pleasantness. He never asks us to give up anything without offering something better. He never has anything but our happiness and welfare as his desire. So, when our parents or teachers point out life's noblest paths, when duty calls us to some hard task, when Christ bids us to follow him, remember:

Do right and be blest,
Hold tight to the best,
Keep bright through the test,

and the crown shall be yours.—J. W. G. Ward.

## JANUARY 19. I Wonder Why!

TEXT: "And I looked . . . and I wondered." Isa. 63:5.

It is a good thing, young friends, to be able to wonder about things. When we look at things with surprise and admiration and awe we say, "Isn't that wonderful!" At other times we are puzzled and say, "I wonder why!" I am sure that you have said that very often. For example: you want to go on a picnic and it rains. Then you say, "I wonder why it always rains when we want to do something!" You have an accident, with a lot of pain and trouble. You wonder why that had to happen to you.

Yes, there are a good many things

that we do not understand. We cannot see why some boys and girls have to go through life without a father or mother or both. It isn't easy to understand why some things have to hurt us so much. A boy who had a good deal of trouble with earache asked his daddy once why he had to have so much pain with it. His father explained that pain was like the ringing of the doorbell when the house was on fire, so that the people would wake up and attend to it and save themselves. So pain, he said, made us attend to something that was wrong. "Yes," said the boy, "but why keep on ringing the bell after they are up? That's what my ear does."

Another boy said to his father, "I wonder why God made mosquitoes!" We wonder why it is so easy to do bad things and so hard to do good things.

We learn about God very early in life. About as soon as you were able to talk your mothers taught you to say your prayers. Then in the beginners' department of the Sunday School you were taught about God as your heavenly Father who made the world and knows and loves and cares for all his children. Then in just a few more years you began to say about a lot of things, "I wonder why!"

What we mean is that we are terribly puzzled. So we say, "I wonder why!"

Now I want to ask you to remember one thing. You are not the only one who is puzzled. You may be puzzled about God. But God may also be puzzled about you. Even God may say, "I wonder why!"

Here is a boy with a good father and mother who do everything they can for him, give him food and clothing and home and time to play and have a good time. The boy does not seem to be very grateful for it, and when father or mother ask him to do something about the home he gets sulky and cross about it. Don't you suppose God says, "I wonder why he acts that way!"

Here is a girl whose mother is just as kind to her as can be. And the little girl says, "Mother, you are just the best mother in the world." But sometimes that girl can talk just terribly mean to her mother. God is puzzled about that, I feel sure, and it may be that he says, "I wonder why!"

Well, there are a lot of things about God and this world which puzzle us and make us say, "I wonder why!" I cannot explain them. Nobody can, because God knows so much more than we do. But when you shake your head because you are puzzled about God, do not forget that God has to wonder about you every day.—Peter H. Pleune.

## JANUARY 26. About the Night

TEXT: "The darkness he called night." Genesis 1:5.

I have heard, and am sorry to think it, that there are boys and girls, and some older people too, who are afraid of the darkness of the night. Some are in fear when they go along a country lane in the dark, and some don't like to be alone even in a room of their own house without a light! They must fancy that God goes to sleep in the night and cannot take care of them as he does in the daytime. There are even people so wicked as to talk to children of bogies or ghosts who may come to do them hurt in the darkness. I hope you never tell such tales to your little brother or sister, because to tell a lie which frightens someone is the worst kind of lying.

You know that God never slumbers nor sleeps. He makes us sure of that by the things which he does in the night. He has made many flowers to bloom in the darkness, including the evening primrose, the great water lily, and the convolvulus. Then there are more butterflies on the wing in the darkness than there are in the daylight. It is true, the scientific men don't call them butterflies, but you and I may very properly call them butterflies of the night. Many caterpillars feed by night, and some of the most richly colored beetles are asleep all day and busy in the darkness. One of the sweetest songsters among the birds sings by night. And one reason why flowers open in the dark and butterflies sip their nectar in the night is, I believe, that you should be sure that God is not slumbering or sleeping, but keeps watch over us all by night as well as by day.

Have you ever thought that night is just the shadow of the world, which stretches out on the side of the earth opposite to the sun? Sometimes the shadow sweeps across the moon, and we say that there is an eclipse of the moon. There are people who are frightened when they see the moon eclipsed. They are terrified by a shadow—the shadow of the world on which they live!

How strange it would be to live in a world which had no shadow! And there are such worlds. They are lighted by two suns, and the inhabitants may see one sun rising while the other is setting.

One wonders whether the people who live in such a world know as much as we do of the vastness of the dominion of God. For it is to night that we owe our knowledge of the greatness of the universe. If we had never seen the stars, how little we should know of the power and glory of God! It is when we are being swept around through the shadow of the earth that we perceive that God has thousands and tens of thousands of other suns than ours, and millions and millions of other worlds which he is keeping and guiding through the immensity of space as a shepherd leads his flock. Think of that when you read or repeat the 23rd Psalm. The Lord who is your Shepherd is the Shepherd of myriads of worlds, and he thinks of the little flowers which open in the dark, and of the butterflies which flutter over them drinking honey in the stillness of the night. Why should you be afraid of darkness, or of anything, since the mighty God watches over you through day and night, through life and death, forever.—J. A. H.

## FEBRUARY 2. Walking with God

TEXT: "And Enoch walked with God." Gen. 5:22.

This is a short account to give of a very long life, but it is a very satisfactory account. What we are told is that "Enoch walked with God." And the question we have to try to answer is this: What sort of a walk is a walk with God? And in answering this question there are four thing about this walk of which we might think.

I. In the first place, if we walk with God we shall find that we have a safe walk. There are many places in which people walk that are very dangerous; but if we are walking with God, as Enoch was, he will guard us from danger, and make the path in which we are walking safe.

II. But in the second place, walking with God is a useful walk. Suppose that you and I were taking a walk through the wards of a hospital. It is full of people who are suffering from accidents and diseases of different kinds. And suppose, that like our blessed Lord, we had the power, as we went from one bed to another, to heal the sick and suffering people in that hospital. Then we might well say that our walk through that hospital was a useful one. Of course we have no such power as this to cure the diseases from which the bodies of men are suffering. Yet this may afford us a good illustration of what we can do for the souls that are suffering around us when we become Christians and walk with God.

III. Walking with God is a pleasant walk. When we are taking a walk there are several things that will help to make up the pleasure to be found in that walk. If we have a guide to show us the road; if we have a pleasant companion to talk with as we go on our way; if we have plenty of refreshments—nice things to eat and drink; if there are bright and cheerful prospects around and before us; and especially if we are sure of a nice comfortable home to rest in when our walk is ended, these will help to make it pleasant. But when we walk with God, as Enoch did, we have all these things, and more too. And these are sure to make a pleasant walk.

IV. Walking with God is a profitable walk. We see a good deal of walking done without much profit. But sometimes we hear of people who are able to make their walking pay. Jesus says that if we give a cup of cold water to one of his disciples, or if we suffer for him, or do any work for him, we "shall receive a manifold more in this present time, and in the world to come life everlasting." If such rewards are given to those who walk with him, then we may well say that that is profitable walking.—R. N.

**FEBRUARY 9. Where Our Flag Deserves to Wave**

In an Ohio town each morning the pupils of the central grammar school gathered about the flagpole for the simple flag-raising exercises.

One day the principal surprised the pupils by saying: "We shall have no flag-raising today. Yesterday afternoon, on their way home, some of the boys of this school tipped over a vegetable cart belonging to an Italian, and then as his carrots and potatoes rolled in the street, ran off laughing. Some of the girls also laughed at the incident. This Italian is Antonio Appolonio, and he lives at 8 Cedar Street. I happen to know that Mr. Appolonio has taken out his first naturalization papers. That means that he is thinking of becoming an American citizen. I wonder if he will be as anxious to do so if he believes this is the kind of people Americans are. We call ours an American school, but the American flag stands for a square deal to everybody. I would like the boys here to be thinking what ought to be done before we have a right to fly the flag over our schoolhouse."

That evening ten humble-looking boys knocked at 8 Cedar Street, presented the astonished Appolonio with ten dollars, and said they were sorry for their rudeness. They all shook hands with him, and the last boy to leave slipped a small American flag into his hands.—From *Be Square,* Forbush (Charles Scribner's Sons, publishers).

**FEBRUARY 16. A Good Indian**

The story is told of an Indian boy who had set his heart upon buying his mother a beautiful blanket for her birthday. For weeks, however, he had caught no animal whose skin was valuable enough to buy so fine a gift. Early one morning, Moe came again to one of his traps. Across the snow he saw the tracks of a large fox, but leading from the trap were the footprints of the storekeeper whom all the Indians distrusted and disliked. The trap was now quite empty. Only a little while before it had held the valuable fox.

Moe vowed that he would never forget this injury. He told himself over and over that "a good Indian never forgets." Late in the afternoon as he left the mission school he saw all the women of the village gathered upon the shore. A storm had come up. The fishing nets, set far out where the bay joined the sea, would certainly be cut adrift. There had not been time to call the men from their work in the forest. However, the women on the shore were not thinking about the nets. They were looking at the figure of the storekeeper. Fearing to lose even a little profit, should his nets be destroyed, he had started out in the storm to bring them in. Now he clung to the side of his overturned boat while his wife wrung her hands upon the shore. The men were at their work. There was no one to help.

The lad thought first that it served the storekeeper quite right. Now he would not have to get even with him. But through his mind kept ringing words he had heard again and again in the mission school, words which he had always thought might be all right for white people, but not for Indians. "If thine enemy hunger, feed him; if he thirst, give him drink." Suddenly he knew that these words were for Indians, too.

Before the frightened women knew what he was about, Moe had shoved a boat out into the foaming water and was pulling toward the drowning man. He finally reached him and somehow got him into the boat. Before the boat reached the shore, however, it was overturned by the giant waves. Moe held on and at the same time helped the storekeeper. After a terrible buffeting they were washed up on the shore, unconscious, nearly drowned, but yet alive. When finally the Indian lad opened his eyes, he saw the storekeeper beside him, and there was an amazed and questioning look in the man's eyes. He whispered, "You saved my life! Why?"

Proudly Moe answered: "A good

Indian forgives. He returns good for evil."—Dorthy LaCroix Hill.

## FEBRUARY 23. Judgment

Boys and girls, I read the other day a story which teaches one of the most important lessons of life. It is a lesson that older persons find more difficult to learn than young people. If we learn it early in life, it is all the better. Jesus taught the lesson in Matt. 7:1—"Judge not, that ye be not judged." Here is the story.

A busy little fellow stood watching a neighbor woman plant seeds in a flowerbed. Soon after the job was completed she returned to find a deep furrow in the soft soil where she had placed the seed. In a nice rage she went to see the little culprit's mother to whom she accused him of tearing up her flowerbed "on purpose," adding that he was a "bad, mean boy" and she was going to call the police. An angry person who talks of police is terrifying to a four-year-old, but Peter was fortunate in that his mother was fair, neither was she hasty in her judgment. Going into session with the child, she asked, "What did you think you were doing, son, when you dug up Mrs. Brown's seeds?"

Peter lived on the desert and only a few days before he had been his father's helper as an irrigating ditch was being dug around their own newly made rosebed. "I didn't dig up her seeds, Mummy, I just fixed a water ditch for her plants when they grow up," was the naïve reply. Without bothering first to get his own explanation of the affair, many a mother would have punished Peter because she failed to interpret his actions correctly, and because she failed to understand what prompted him to do the apparently destructive thing.

Someone long ago gave us the rule: "Judge the deed by the friend and not the friend by the deed."—Author Unknown.

## MARCH 2. About Good Temper

What are we here in the world for? Why were we born? Lots of people have the mistaken idea that they are here in the world to make themselves very happy and everybody else very good. But the truth is exactly the opposite. We have *one* to make good, many to make happy. Now a good-tempered boy or girl makes everyone glad who comes near. But if a boy is selfish and crabbed, or a girl is peevish and screws up her face in that strange fashion that some girls have, then everybody is made uncomfortable.

Quarreling is one way to be unhappy and to make other people unhappy too. Did you ever hear the story of the two squirrels who tried to quarrel? The story is told that there were two squirrels who lived together so happily that they never had a cross word. But one day one of them said, "Let us get up a quarrel, for a change. Two-legged people quarrel, so why shouldn't we?" "All right," said the other, "but how?" They tried all sorts of ways, but it was no good; they could not quarrel. One or the other was always giving in, and the quarrel never came off. But at last the one that had made the suggestion brought two acorns, and said, "Now we are going to quarrel. You are to say that those acorns are yours, and I'll say that they are mine; then we shall have a quarrel and fight like the two-legged folks do. Now all ready. I'll begin. These acorns are mine." And the other said, "Very well, you are quite welcome to them." And the first replied, "You simpleton, don't you know that it takes two to make a quarrel?"

If we only understood one another better we should never quarrel at all. It seems a great pity to hear young folks, boys or girls, snapping and finding fault and quarreling. I think the religion of young people is much centered in being kind and loving and helpful. At the same time I don't think that such things are very far away from the center of the religion of grown people too.—Adapted from B. J. Snell.

## MARCH 9. They Haven't Learned

"He Hasn't Learned" is the caption above the picture of a three-year-old Boston terrier with his face so full of porcupine quills that it is difficult to see the dog. He is waiting for a veterinarian to remove the quills. Since Rex suffered the same experience a year ago, one wonders just how good this three-year-old dog's memory is.

Then there was Mops, an older dog whose sins could not be laid to a poor memory. Though a model of virtue in his city home, Mops was not strong enough to resist the temptations of farm life. He chased a thickly bequilled porcupine and suffered the penalty. The removeal of even one quill was too much for Mops' master, so he took the tortured animal for a seven-mile ride and paid a veterinarian ten dollars to have the job completed.

For a few days it seemed as if Mops had learned, but the wounds had hardly healed when he chased another porcupine. When the fight was over Mops didn't go to his master for help; instead, he ran yelping to the family car and sat waiting to be taken to town to the doctor. Mops' memory was not at fault; he was simply a creature of weak morals. After the third expensive trip to town, Mops was safely locked indoors just before the evening hour when porcupines walk abroad.

Foolish dog, we say. As foolish as human beings. Instead of avoiding experiences that have brought us nothing but trouble, we return to the same old places, commit the same old sins and faults, and make the same old pleas for help.

Animals, including the human variety, can be so foolish! How about it, boys and girls?

## MARCH 16. It Paid to Listen

There was a time here in America, boys and girls, when ice and what goes with it, ice cream and cold drinks, were not so common as they are now. There was no refrigerator that made ice in the home. In some homes there was a large box with two parts, in one a cake of ice was kept, and the milk and vegetables in the other.

Where did they get ice in summer? In the villages and small towns there was generally a crude sort of building near a pond. This building was called an ice house. In winter the ice in the pond was cut into large cakes and pulled into the ice house and buried in sawdust. The sawdust kept it from melting too rapidly and some of it lasted into the summer.

I read that one summer a man was working in an ice house and happened to drop his valuable watch in the sawdust. He and his fellow workers searched for two hours and could not find it. Lunch time arrived and with great disappointment they left the building. On their return an hour or so later, imagine their surprise to find a small boy standing there with the watch in his hand.

"How did you find it?" they inquired.

The boy replied, "I just lay down in the sawdust and heard it ticking."

That reminds me of the text in the Bible, "Be still and know that I am God."—H.

## MARCH 23. The Greatest of These (A Fable)

A Persian ruler once had a wonderful pearl, white and pure and of great price, and this pearl he wished to give to the one of his three sons who would show the greatest nobility.

One day he called them to him and said, "During all this past year, what is the greatest deed you have done?"

The oldest son spoke promptly: "When I took my last journey, a merchant gave me some valuable jewels to deliver to safekeeping. He kept no account of them. I could easily have kept one, or even two, and the merchant would not have missed them. But I gave up the chance of becoming rich, and delivered every one of the jewels to safety."

"You did well, my son, you were honest," said the ruler; "but could you have done differently without having great shame?"

The second son told his story modestly. He said, "I was watching a child play by the lake. Soon he fell in, and I at once plunged in after him and so saved his life."

"You did well, my son, you were brave," said the ruler; "but you could not have left the child to drown."

The third son hesitated. Finally he spoke. "I was coming over the mountain one day, and I saw a man who hates me, and has done me great harm. He was asleep and had rolled near the edge of a great precipice. One push would have sent him over Just passing him by would have left him to move in his sleep and fall to his death. But I waked him gently, and told him of his danger, and he abused me for it."

"My son," declared the ruler, "the pearl is yours. You did right, without the hope of reward, to one who had done you wrong."—*Sunshine Magazine.*

**MARCH 30. The Children's Share in Palm Sunday (Palm Sunday)**

At the time of an election of a President of this country I received a letter from a very interesting little girl of ten years. One of the candidates visited the little city where she lived. What interested me most in her letter was to see how so young a girl was so deeply interested in the election. She told how as school children they insisted on being let out of school that they might greet the great man and hear him speak. They all went, and you can tell how they felt, for the letter added, "How glad we all were that he won!"

That reveals how interested children are in all that is going on. And, plainly, it is not something new in the world and in the nature of childern. They had this same alertness and interest two thousand years ago. Today is the anniversary of Palm Sunday. Two thousand years ago the Bible account tells us that as Jesus arrived at the Jerusalem Temple the children were there and joined in shouting, "Hosanna to the Son of David!"

When children are interested they are very deeply interested. That was an enthusiastic crowd of children who welcomed Jesus that day—on the first Palm Sunday.

What does Palm Sunday mean? It means that Jesus was making an offer of himself to be the Messiah, the spiritual King of the Jews, and the universal King. The children welcomed him then. Children can welcome and love him still. He once said, "Suffer the little children to come unto me, and forbid them not; for of such is the kingdom of God." And he once said to older people, "Unless you become as little children you cannot enter the kingdom of God." That meant that we who are older must become teachable and trustful, humble and affectionate as are little children.

Some people seem to think that children are too young to love Christ. How young is a child when too young to love its mother or father? No child who is old enough to love them but is old enough to love the Saviour, to learn to love him, to be taught to love him. Not any of you are too young to be Christians. You are just right! Children's love is especially warm and genuine and trustful.

That is the happy thought and glad fact that this Palm Sunday celebration can bring to you boys and girls, and also to all us older people. "Forbid them not." "Of such is the kingdom."—G. H.

**APRIL 6. Gordon's Easter**

Gordon wriggled a little in his pew beside his father. It was Easter Sunday, and the church was beautiful with flowers and stately with palms.

Gordon liked music, and the big pipe organ pealed softly through the church and seemed to send its solemn music deep into his heart and soul. This was exactly the way Easter should be, he thought: fragrance and color of flowers, deep thrill of organ music, glow of light through stained-glass windows. It made a fellow feel as if he could never be anything but straight and clean and true, whatever he was doing: going to school or playing ball or running a race. It was too bad that feeling didn't last. He'd often noticed that almost as soon as he passed through the door, the everyday feeling rose to the top, and he felt wrongly and sometimes did wrongly, too. Although it had happened weeks ago, the memory of one wrong act still sent the blood rushing to his face.

He hadn't been fair. He had let dad believe that Jack Lennon broke the expensive tube of the radio, when he, Gordon, had done it himself. And then one night dad had come home and said that Jack had asked for a Saturday job carrying handbills. "I refused though I know he needs the money. I don't think I needed to tell him why," dad said gravely. "A boy who destroys property and then sneaks out without confessing it—well, I don't want him working for me."

The music went on and on; sometimes it was singing voices; sometimes it was the organ. The lights streamed in through the colored windows. There was an especially lovely window in the front of the church; it was like a picture painted with precious jewels. In the center stood the figure of Jesus.

Gordon had often looked at that picture, but today he saw it as he never had before. The face was beautiful. A smile seemed to tremble on the lips, and yet there was sadness in the eyes. How gentle and strong they were, those eyes. Gordon breathed deep; it seemed as if they were gazing at him.

The minister was reading from the Bible—"And when the Sabbath was past, Mary Magdalene, and Mary, the mother of James, bought spices, that they might come and anoint him. And very early on the first day of the week, they come to the tomb when the sun was risen. And they were saying among themselves, Who shall roll us away the stone from the door of the tomb? And looking up, they see that the stone is rolled back: for it was exceeding great."

The minister paused and looked up from the Bible, saying; "Remember, young people, boys and girls, there is never anything so big that it can keep you from Jesus if you really want to be his friend."

Then there was more music, and presently came the time when five boys and girls stood in the front of the church to take the vows of church membership. The grave, kind eyes of the pictured Jesus looked steadily down into Gordon's, as if the pictured Jesus were asking, "Why doesn't he come, too?"

And Gordon's heart had to whisper back, "A boy can't come when he hasn't played fair."

And then he remembered the words, almost as if the pictured Christ were speaking them to him: "There is never anything that can keep you from Jesus if you really want to be his friend."

Why, those words were meant for him!

Gordon took his Sunday School paper, wrote on the margin of it, and handed it to his father. "Dad, Jack didn't break that radio tube. I broke it." The minister was saying again, "Will you come?" And Gordon walked down the aisle.—Florence Crannell Means.

### APRIL 13. "Give Him a Cheer, Boys!"

There is a story told of a fireman who was rescuing a child trapped in the top floor of a burning building. The ladder was not quite long enough to reach the window, and although the fireman tried again and again to reach the child, it seemed as though he would never do it. The crowd below waited, breathless and anxious. Suddenly someone shouted "Give him a cheer, boys!" and immediately there was a great shout of encouragement. The firemen made one more desperate effort, reached the child, and brought him down safely.

Whenever we see anyone doing a difficult task, it always helps if we can give him a word of encouragement. How ready Jesus was to give a word of encouragement and praise to all sorts and conditions of people. We think of his praise for the widow who cast her last two coins into the temple treasury; for the Syrophoenician mother who came to him on behalf of her daughter; for the Samaritan leper who came back to give thanks; and for the Roman centurion who came to him on behalf of his servant. In all these characters Jesus found something to commend. He could see the latent qualities of faith and love and gratitude which others overlooked. May God grant that when we come face to face with Christ there may be something in us that calls forth his praise, and may we hear his voice saying, "Well done, good and faithful servant."—J. J. Wilmshurst.

### APRIL 20. Acoustics

I was once minister of a church that had poor acoustics in the sanctuary. When I spoke to the boys and the girls in the front pews those who sat in the center could not hear me very well. A church ought to have good acoustics. That is, people in any part of the building should be able to hear everything that is spoken from the pulpit or the chancel.

But I have been wondering whether you have good acoustics inside yourself; whether I have good acoustics inside me. The Bible says that our lives are like temples, like churches. Is there good hearing inside our temples?

So I have a question to ask this morning. Here it is: Can you hear a silence?

You may think that a queer question, Can you hear a silence? It isn't so queer. When my own son was a small boy we moved from New York City to a small town in Iowa. New York City was very noisy. The street cars, the automobiles, the crowds of people made it so. In our new home sometimes when we were at the table eating a meal I would say "Listen!" Then we would listen carefully, and we couldn't hear a thing. It was dead silence. We had lots of fun listening to silence.

There is a Bible story about a man by the name of Elijah who was listening for the voice of God. One day he heard the crash and crack of a great wind blowing in the mountains; great trees were blown down, and the rocks rolled down the mountainside. Elijah said, "God must be speaking in the great wind." But he could not hear God speaking in the wind.

Then there was a great earthquake with its deep brass rumble and Elijah said, "God will speak in the earthquake." But he could not hear the voice of God in the earthquake.

After the earthquake there was a fire. A fire generally follows an earthquake. Elijah listened to the fire as it swept across the mountains; but God did not speak in the fire.

After the fire there was a stillness, silence. It was a silence like that to be found on the top of a high mountain; or a silence like that of a little hidden valley; or a silence like that of a deep hidden canyon. In the gentle stillness Elijah heard the voice of God.

I hope that your acoustics are good so that when there is a deep, deep silence inside your temple you may hear the silence and in it the voice of God.

Boys and girls. I do hope that you will listen to silences. Think about this: some people never became great and good, they never rise above the ordinary level of life, because they never listen to silence. They miss the voice of God.—H.

### APRIL 27. Acoustics Again

Last Sunday I talked to you boys and girls about acoustics. We mentioned the acoustics of this building, our temple, and the problems of hearing and of sound.

Then we talked about the temple of our hearts, and wondered whether we could hear a silence. I hope that during last week some of you were listening to silences. Let us do so now. Quiet! Perfectly quiet! Now, everybody listen to the silence. . . .

I am sure that all of us know the story that I am going to tell.

It is about a boy who was sleeping in the ancient temple. It was pretty dark, I think, with just one or two little oil lamps burning. As he lay upon his cot, probably half asleep and half awake, the little boy heard the silence and in the silence a voice, "Samuel!" It was his name. He answered, "Here I am!" Then he ran to the priest in another part of the temple and said, "Here I am, you called me."

But Eli, the priest, said, "I didn't call you. Lie down again."

And all was silent once more. Then the voice, "Samuel!"

The listening boy answered, "Here am I." And again he ran to the priest and as before the priest said that he had not called.

Samuel lay down again. I feel quite sure that he was not asleep. He was alert and wide-eyed and listening. The voice was unmistakable. "Samuel! Samuel!" When Samuel went to the priest again, the old man was wiser than before. He realized that it was God speaking to the boy in the silence.

Then the boy went back to his cot, and when God spoke again Samuel answered, "Speak, Lord, your servant hears."

God did speak. That was the beginning of great things for that boy. He became God's man. He became God's servant. How God used his life is a wonderful story which you boys and girls can read in the Bible books which bear the name of Samuel.—H.

## MAY 4. The Deaf Musician

This is the third Sunday, boys and girls, that I am talking to you about acoustics; especially about hearing in the midst of silence. Remember that last Sunday we heard about Samuel who answered God's call in the temple, when the temple in which he slept was all silent in the nighttime.

This morning, first of all, I wish you would turn to a hymn in the hymnbook. It begins:

> Joyful, joyful we adore Thee,
> God of glory, Lord of love.

We'll ask our organist to play it through. Notice that it is a very joyful hymn.

Now look at the name at the top on the left side—Henry van Dyke. He is one of America's great poets. He wrote the words of the hymn.

On the right side you will find the name of Ludwig van Beethoven. He wrote the joyous music of the hymn.

Now here is an interesting fact that you may already know. Beethoven was a deaf man, not a little hard of hearing, but totally deaf. That means that he lived in a silence. But in that silence he could hear music, and he could write that music down, and we can now sing this lovely hymn to music which he wrote.—H.

## MAY 11. "I Forgot!"

Ben had a habit of forgetting to do things. He started to leave for school one morning and his mother exclaimed, "Why, Ben! Your shirt is not buttoned, and you haven't even combed your hair!"

"Oh," he said, putting his books down, "I guess I forgot to do it."

When he was ready to leave again, Mother called, "Please stop by Mrs. Allen's on your way home. She has a dress pattern for me."

"All right," Ben answered, and was gone out the front door.

After he returned from school in the afternoon, Mother asked, "Did you get the pattern from Mrs. Allen?"

"Oh, I'm sorry" Ben answered. "I came right by her house and forgot to stop. I'll go back now."

"Never mind," Mother sighed. "I'll get the pattern some other time."

After supper Ben settled down to his homework. Mother and Daddy were reading. Suddenly there was a scratching and whining at the back door.

Daddy looked up from his newspaper. "Ben, did you feed your puppy tonight?"

Ben got up quickly. "No, I forgot!" He rushed out to the kitchen to get food for his pet.

The next morning when Mother called, "Breakfast is ready! Ben hurried to the table. Mother and Daddy were already seated. But Ben's place was not set.

"Isn't there a place for me?" he asked in surprise.

"Oh!" Mother exclaimed, getting up to go into the kitchen. "I forgot to set your place!"

After school that afternoon, Ben came whistling into the house; but he stopped short when he saw what Mother looked like. Her dress was not ironed, her stockings had ugly, long runs in them, and her hair was hanging down in her eyes.

"Mother!" he cried in amazement. "What in the world happened to you?"

"Me?" Mother asked, looking surprised. "Oh, I guess I forgot to fix myself up today." She disappeared into the bedroom and soon came back looking neat as usual.

Ben was tired for supper. He finished his homework quickly and started to bed. But he found his blanket folded neatly beside his pillow, right in the center of his bed! And no linen at all! He called out, "Mother, my bed is not made!"

Mother instantly appeared at the bedroom door with two sheets and a pillowcase. "Oh, I did the washing today," she said, "and I forgot to put fresh linen on your bed."

As she started making Ben's bed, he went around to the other side to help her. He looked across the bed with questioning eyes. "You did not really forget, did you, Mother?"

"What do you think?" Mother asked wisely, her eyes twinkling.

"I think you just pretended to forget things today, to teach me a lesson," he said.

Mother smiled and said nothing.

"Well, I don't like the way you did today," Ben said, tucking in a sheet. "So I guess I'd better try to remember things from now on."—Ellen E Morrison.

## MAY 18. The Order of Service

Well, boys and girls, suppose that we mix things up tomorrow. I'll tell you how we'll do it. Let's have the sun rise at ten o'clock in the morning! Let's surprise the people and have it rise in the West instead of the East. Then we'll have the moon rise in the East and meet the sun overhead—a full moon and a bright sun—it will be the brightest day in the history of the world. It's fun to think about such things and let your imagination expand; but it can't be done. Why not?

Because the sun and the moon and the stars and the world don't caper like a goat.

But what has a goat got to do with it? Well, someone noticed that you can't tell how a goat is going to jump. He jumps all sorts of ways when he feels fine. Now the Latin word for he-goat is *caper*, and so when a goat jumps about we say that he capers. From this we get an English word "caprice." It really means going every which way.

Let the sun rise at ten o'clock tomorrow, and the next day at four o'clock, and the next day after that at six o'clock, one could not tell when the sun was going to rise. We might well say under such conditions that the sun capers; it would rise by caprice.

Instead of that the sun rises every day so that man can discover the exact second of each rising, and the moon and the stars do the same. The seasons come and go in regularity. Life is that way; the big dog never grows into a puppy, but the puppy grows into a big dog. Apples never grow on orange trees, nor do roses grow on ivy. You see, the world has *order* in it. Everything has its own place and its own right time.

A certain wise man once said, "Order is heaven's first law."

So it comes about that we human folk learn this lesson from God. We learn to do thinks in order. There is a time for everything.

We have an *Order of Service*. This morning, first we had music on the organ, then the choir sang, then we all sang the doxology. After that there was a short prayer, followed by the Lord's Prayer. So in the church service we try to do things decently and in order. We believe that God loves order, because he himself has caused the universe to show order.

It is a great thing to learn the lesson of order. The order in life is babyhood, boyhood and girlhood, maturity, old age. At each place in life certain things ought to happen. I think it is in order for you to play a lot out-of-doors. It is in order that you learn a lot at school. It is in order that you become kind and learn to do useful things. It is in order that you learn to follow Christ and give your lives to him.

Most of the great Christians of the world learned to follow Christ when they were boys and girls.

Don't get out of order. Learn to follow Christ now. To wait until later might be like having the sun rise for you at ten o'clock or late in the afternoon.—H.

## MAY 25. Forget Not All His Benefits

TEXT: "Forget not all his benefits." Ps. 103:2.

A statesman of ancient Greece was once talking with a friend when his friend said, "O that some one would teach me to remember!" The statesman answered, "Nay, rather teach me to forget." That was long centuries ago, but I think that today there is not one of us but still would gladly learn that art of forgetting some things. What we would gladly forget we often best remember. What we would gladly remember we too often forget.

Now I am sure of this, if there be one thing we might be expected to remember it is God's loving-kindness. To the angels in heaven it must seem incredible that any here today should have forgotten the benefits of God. David made no mistake. He knew the temptation to forget, and you and I still know it too. Let us think a little on our forgetfulness of the benefits of God. "Forget not all his benefits."

I. And first, why are we all so likely to forget them? It is because we are so accustomed to them. Someone has said that if all the stars in heaven were to cease shining for a hundred years and then were suddenly to flash out again, there would not be an eye in all the earth but would be raised heavenward, and there would not be a heart but would break forth in hymns of praise to God. But the stars are shining every night. And you and I are accustomed to them. So with God's benefits. Did they come rarely, singly, unexpectedly, how we should prize them! But they have been over us like the heavens, round us like the air, under us like the earth ever since we were born. And we are so accustomed to them that our hearts are not responsive.

II. Now let us consider some simple hints for mastering this forgetfulness. How can we have better memories for all God's benefits?

1. First, let us strive to see God's hand in all that befalls us. Let us blot out from our dictionaries all such words as fate, misfortune, luck. Remember we are children of a King, not children of chance. Let us honor God by seeing in everything some movement of our heavenly Father's hand.

2. Again, let us go over our blessings in detail. Begin and try to count them. And for the first time we will learn how deeply and how hopelessly we are in our Father's debt. We must get to it benefit by benefit if we want to know what we owe God. David knew that. David did that. He cried to his soul, "Forget not all his benefits." Then he began to number them. Who forgiveth all thine iniquities—one. Who healeth all thy diseases—two. Who redeemeth that life from destruction—three. Who crowneth thee with loving-kindness and with tender mercies—four. And so on through a whole psalm. I wonder if you could sing a psalm like that?

3. If God has given us health and strength, sight and hearing, parents and homes, and a thousand things besides, and we have forgotten them all and never thanked him for them, how ungrateful we are! And yet we hope to meet him in the future!

4. If you would not forget God's benefits, see that you live in close companionship with his Son our Saviour. A gift is always a gift. But when a gift comes from one we love it has a double value in our eyes. It is the giver that makes the gift precious.

So with God's loving-kindness. Strive to take all as out of his hands. "Forget not all his benefits."—G. H. M.

## JUNE 1. Straight Rowing

Many of our boys and girls will be going to camp this summer. Some will be going to the lakes and for them especially I have a story that may help them with their rowing.

"Let me row back to camp," requested a little girl while on the lake one day. Hoping to help her avoid the beginner's usual zigzag course, the counselor passed on to her what had been taught him the first time he took the oars.

"Head your boat toward the place you want to reach," he explained, "then pick out some object lying in a direct line over the stern of the boat. By steering that way you'll save yourself lots of useless rowing."

In a short time the girl was headed very much off her course. The counselor explained once more, and corrected her direction, but in a few minutes she was pointing even farther amis. He reproved her mildly.

"But," she protested, "that's exactly what I'm doing."

"What object are you steering by?" he asked, sensing a misunderstanding.

"Why, that red boat going across the lake!"

That sounds amusing, but I know a lot of boys and girls, and a lot of their elders, who do just that foolish thing—they steer by the shifting fancy or fad or fashion of what someone else is doing. To steer a boat one needs to set one's eyes on a permanent object; to steer a life one has to direct one's course by some guiding principle that has stood the test of the ages. Wise men do this and I am sure you boys and girls want to be wise. It is such guiding principles that we learn in Sunday School and church. —Adapted from J. S. Royer.

## JUNE 8. Wishing for Wings

TEXT: "Oh that I had wings like a dove! for then I would fly away, and be at rest." Ps. 55:6.

King David was one of the wisest of men; yet he is not ashamed to tell us that one day he could not help wishing for what he knew was impossible. He wished for wings. The reason was that he was so grieved with the wickedness of a great many of the people among whom he lived that he longed to get away to some quiet valley, among lonely mountains and forests where he could be alone with God. So he said, "Oh that I had wings like a dove! for then would I fly away, and be at rest."

Other people beside King David have wished for wings. A little boy was sitting in school one bright summer morning. Looking up from his book, he could see through the open window many birds hopping among the trees, and the swallows skimming over the grass. And he could not help saying to himself, "Oh that I had wings! for then I would fly out of school, and do nothing but play with the birds in the sunshine." He did not know that the birds were not at play, but hard at work, catching flies and grubs to feed their young ones. Perhaps you knew that boy! Or was it a girl you knew who wished for wings? Well, let me give a word of advice about this.

Don't spend your time in wishing for wings, or anything else that is impossible. Not that there is anything wrong in a wish, unless what we wish for is wrong. Wishes will come flying into our minds as little birds sometimes hop in an open window. But do not pet and feed and fondle them. Let them fly away again. There is nothing wrong in King David's saying, "Oh that I had wings!" but it would have been very wrong and very foolish if he had wasted his time in longing for wings and murmuring and grumbling because he could not have them. Wishing is profitless work even for possible things. No one ever reached the top of a mountain, or even the top of a ladder, by wishing he were up there. No! you must climb step by step.

God gave Kind David something much better than wings. Often God denies our wishes that he may give us something better than we ask or think. A pair of dove's wings would be useless unless you had a dove's body; or eagle's, unless you had an eagle's body. "Oh, but that's just what I should like—to be a bird, just for a little time." Is it? Then, perhaps, you would wish for legs like a gazelle, or fins like a whale. One can't have everything. And yet I remember that St. Paul says to real Christians, "All things are yours, . . . and ye are Christ's."

The Lord Jesus needed no wings to ascend to heaven. And we need no wings to get near enough to him to talk to him. When you pray to him he listens, and hears every word as though he stood close to you. Ask him to help you use your hands and feet in his service. Love to him will be better than the winged shoes you read of in the old Greek fables. It will make your feet swift and your hands nimble for every duty and every kindness. It will give wings to your thoughts, so that they will fly up to him, and then come back fresher and more earnest to your work. Then, when the time comes, he will give you what is far better than wings: he will come and receive you unto himself, that where he is, there you may be also. —E. B. Conder.

## JUNE 15. The Dew Drier

Robert didn't like to wear his shoes and stockings. "I get so tired of putting them on every morning and taking them off every night," he complained one morning to his mother. "I wish I were the little black boy in the picture on Uncle Jake's desk!"

Uncle Jake heard Robert's complaint, "Do you mean the picture of Kaveke, the dew drier, Robert?" asked his uncle.

Robert was surprised at his uncle's voice. "Why, yes," he answered. "He doesn't have to bother with his shoes and stockings. He goes barefooted, and has nothing to do but play. I'd like to be Ka— what do you call him, Uncle?"

"But Kaveke has work to do, and a very important, dangerous work." Then Uncle Jake, who had been a missionary in Africa, told Robert about the little African boy in the picture on his desk.

"Kaveke is what they call a 'dew drier.' You see, the grass in parts of Africa grows very tall—sometimes fifteen feet tall. Sometimes the trails are almost hidden by the grass. And the dew is sometimes so heavy that drops from one grass blade will almost form a shower, and the first one to go along the trail paths in the morning is drenched. A dew drier is sent ahead to shake off the worst of the dew. Usually it is a boy."

"That would be fun!" exclaimed Robert. "It would be like a shower in the bathroom! I think I'd like to be a dew drier."

"Just wait. Suppose there is a line of porters starting out with their packs at dawn. The poor little dew drier, often not much older than you are, is rudely awakened—not at all the way Mother calls you. Then, often before he gets any breakfast, he is sent out into the tall grass ahead of the men to shake off the dew. Each step he takes drenches him. At times he is almost choked with the water. It's cold water, too, and the grass is so matted that it is all he can do to work his way through the tough stems. And if he does not go fast enough, the men push him along as he shivers in the cold showers."

"That doesn't sound so good," said Robert, for he did not like cold showers.

"I haven't told you the worst," continued Uncle. "The dew drier never knows when a hungry leopard or hyena may dart out into the path looking for his breakfast. When that happens, the little dew drier is no more. Kaveke had a very narrow escape."

"Oh, I'm sorry for Kaveke," said Robert, seriously. "Uncle Jake, can't we bring Kaveke over here? There are no wild animals here."

"We tried to get Kaveke into our school, but his father, who is at the head of the pack carriers for his village, said he needed Kaveke to work as a dew drier, and so wouldn't let him come. Maybe someday, when Kaveke gets older, and there are other boys to take his place as dew drier, he will come to school."

Robert was quiet for a long time. He went and looked at Kaveke's picture again. Then he slipped his hand into Uncle's, and said, "Uncle Jake, I don't think shoes and stockings are so hard to wear, after all."—From *Sunshine Magazine* which kindly permits extracts.

## SEPTEMBER 14. Catfish

It was very clever of these New England fishermen to hit on the plan of putting a catfish in among the codfish. At one time—perhaps they still do it—some fishermen used to have special tanks aboard their ships in which they kept live fish caught far out in the ocean. They wanted the fish to come on to the market as fresh as possible, for then the fish would fetch a good price. The difficulty was, however, that the cod, although was perfectly fresh and plump, were not in the best condition. You see, they had nothing to do during the long journey to port except lie about lazily. And that's not good for codfish any more than it is for us. It was then that the fishermen thought of this idea. Catfish and codfish, they well knew, are not very fond of each other. Place the catfish in with the cod and it would keep them "on their toes"; to avoid the enemy they would have to dodge this way and that, swimming, turning, diving. The arrangement worked perfectly. The codfish, instead of being fat and flabby, now came into the shops in prime condition.

Beethoven was little more than a lad when great musicians showered on him their praises and good wishes. During a visit to Vienna he met Mozart, who declared that one day he would "make a noise in the world." He was only twenty-two when Haydn heard him playing, and listened entranced for two hours. But what a difficult character Beethoven was in those days! He was proud, overbearing, full of fads, and his manners were dreadful. He also had a thoroughly bad temper. He might find a note a little out of tune and down his fist would come crashing on the keys. But quietly drawing near was something that was to change all that. His doctors informed him that his dullness of hearing would never leave him. And it didn't; it got worse and worse until he became almost stone deaf. It was a blow that stunned him. A sadder thing could hardly happen to one whose life was so bound up with beautiful music. But it made a new man of him. Instead of dragging him down, it acted as a spur to drive him on to greater things. The man that was deaf produced so many glorious symphonies!

Walter Scott was not two years old when he lost the use of his right leg. All his life he was lame. But Walter took this, as he took many other things, in the right spirit. At school he refused to allow it to spoil his fun and games. Later on in life it was the same. A good thing for us, too, and for all who are fond of a good story. He would tramp for miles the countryside he loved so well. That, of course, was the way he came into touch with the people who live again in his books. His health often troubled him, but he carried on bravely with his writing. There were other difficulties he had to meet, still he would let nothing daunt him. The worst trial of all was yet to come. A business into which he had put much money failed, and he was left with a debt of £130,000. Although he was responsible for only part of that debt he felt he ought to pay it all off. He would do it with his pen and he nearly succeeded. It took toll of health and strength, but what a victory he won!

We have trials and temptations that we may overcome them. We meet difficult things and disappointments in God's plan for us, but if our life is to be beautiful, healthy, useful, we must meet them and beat them. And this we are able to do "through Christ, which strengtheneth" us.—J. Macleod.

### SEPTEMBER 21. The Sun and the Earthen Lamp

"'Who is there to take up my duties?' asked the setting sun. The world remained dark and silent. Then said the earthen lamp, 'I will do what I can, my master.'" Thus wrote the Bengali poet, Rabindranath Tagore.

I have stood on the New York City side of the Hudson River when the sun was setting behind the Jersey hills. Its call came across the water, "Who is there to take up my duties?" Then I heard a small electric bulb answer, "I will do what I can, my master," and send a gleam across the water to the sun. And when another bulb called out the same reply a little baby saw it shining and clapped its hands for joy. And another bulb called out to the sun fast disappearing, "I will do what I can, my master," and long, long, until the hours of early morning, it gave light for a boy who studied from books the deep things of life. The bulb was not aware that it had a share in the making of a great man. So one by one, hundreds of them, thousands, millions, the bulbs kept calling out to the setting sun, "I will do what I can, my master," and the city became light, almost as light as day. I walked the streets of the city everywhere, except where there were no bright electric bulbs, for there was darkness.

I have no power to describe what this world or any portion of it would be without Christ in it. They write of darkest Africa but I have never been in the darkness there. I have never set my foot where there was not some of the

Christ light shining in the lives of men. Wherever there is love, wherever there is any joy, wherever there is peace, or kindness, or goodness, there the light of God is shining somewhat. With his light gone there would be hatred, and bitterness, and enmity, and violence, and evil.

But the visible presence of Christ is gone—as in the night the sun has sunk into the west so Christ is not here. And yet the sun is here. I look up at the moon and I know the sun's rays are streaming to it and illuminating it that it may brighten the night for us. I know that every bit of light is sunlight, the sun is here, and so the Christ is also here. The Christ calls out to the world, "Who is there to take up my duties?" The world remains dark and silent. Then says some man, "I will do what I can, my Master," and brightens a corner for the Christ. Some mother hears the Christ call and answers, "I will do what I can, my Master," and as she leans over the crib she sheds the light of Christ upon her babe. A noble man makes the same reply and he sheds the light of Christ upon some youth struggling to be great, and he creates the career of that youth. Men, women, boys and girls call out, "I will do what I can, my Master," and so upon the darkness of his world there shines the light of hundreds, thousands, millions, all shining for Him—and that is why the world is not in absolute darkness.—H.

## SEPTEMBER 28. Christ's Ship

Why is a church like a ship? That sounds like a riddle, doesn't it? And you may think that I am joking with you, for, of course, we know that a church isn't at all like a ship. To compare a church and a ship won't offer many similarities.

Yet in a way a church and a ship are very much alike. Long ago our forefathers thought so, too. They gave a name to that part of the church which is between the side aisles and which extends from the front porch to the front of the auditorium. The word they used is "nave."

The word "nave" means ship. But why should they call the place where the congregation sits a nave? Because for them the church was indeed like a ship in that a well-built ship is able to weather any storm and to move according to a sure course from one port to another. And, furthermore, at the helm of a ship is an experienced captain who will guide the ship safely.

So our forefathers thought of the church as a spiritual ship which stays afloat through all kinds of troubles and difficulties and moves the hearts of men from the port of our need of God to the port of God's love. And they knew also that at the head of the church is a great and good captain, Christ himself, and he knows the way we should go and he guides his church through storm and calm.

I think that it is very exciting to imagine that the church is like a great ship and it is very wonderful to know that at the helm of our church is our spiritual captain, Jesus Christ.—Charles L. Wallis.

## OCTOBER 5. Christianity that Shows

Nancy was named to serve on a high school committee which included four boys. At their first meeting the teacher in charge was late arriving and one of the boys began to tell an off-color story. Nancy quickly rose and walked to the farthest window, to be out of hearing.

A tall boy named Jim also left the group and noisily sharpened his pencil until the teacher appeared.

Both young people were Christians and their Christianity was showing.

This is World-wide Communion Day and our attention is directed to the church in many lands. Our thoughts go back to the early days when the missionaries went out to carry the gospel in distant places. Very often what they said did not bring much response, but by what they did their Christianity was showing, and this eventually had great effect.

I am reminded of two great missionaries of whom this is especially true. They come to mind because one month from today, Nov. 5, is the 200th anniversary of the death of Hans Egede. It is of him and his wife that I am going to tell you. (See Theme No. 5, Section VI, in this *Manual*.)

Ĕ-gĕ-dĕ is a strange name. I wonder whether you can guess where such a name came from. Hans Egede was born on an island off the coast of northern Norway. He went to school in Denmark. Finally he and his wife Gertrude went to Greenland as missionaries.

There disappointment followed disappointment as they worked among the Greenlanders. The language was very strange and most difficult to learn. The natives refused to accept their messages and often mocked and insulted them. The cold of the country through long winters seemed almost unendurable.

Then a pestilence broke out. The home of the missionaries was filled with the sick and dying. Pastor and Mrs. Egede went out to the villages without fear of catching the pestilence. Two or three thousand of the Greenlanders died. Afterward Mrs. Egede died. After fifteen years of disappointment and misfortune Hans Egede thought that he had failed.

But what was the fact? All through those years the Christianity of Hans Egede and his wife was showing. The natives wouldn't listen, but they were forced to see. They saw the Christianity that they spurned in the courage and patience and kindness of the two missionaries. Again, I say, their Christianity was showing. The Egedes showed Christianity to the Greenlanders. They showed Christianity to the people of Denmark. They gave to the whole Christian world an example of splendid worth.

Is your Christianity showing?—H.

## OCTOBER 12. A Wonderful New Idea

This is the story of two friends, Simone and Arturio, who lived in the little village of Tornia in Italy, not far from Palermo. They were humble, but contented goat shepherds.

One day Simone heard about a wonderful new idea which the wise men of the world were trying to introduce. These wise men had discovered that God wanted all men to live on the same level, and that all good people ought to do something about it.

Simone was very much impressed by it all. This was a project for him and his good friend, Arturio, whom he immediately won over. Sitting on the hillside, the two friends surveyed the orange groves in the valley. Pointing with his finger, Simone called the attention of Arturio to a particularly well-kept orange grove.

"You see," he said, "that is the grove of Gabriele Pocci. He has thirty orange trees, while his neighbors only have a dozen. Let's do something about it!" And Arturio enthusiastically agreed to co-operate with his friend.

On the very next day Simone was lustily swinging his ax in the grove of Gabriele Pocci till all but a dozen trees had been chopped down. Then he went in search for his turncoat friend, Arturio. He found him in one of the neighbor's gardens.

"Arturio," he said, "I thought we had agreed to create equality among these villagers."

"But that's just what I'm doing, Simone. See, I have planted eighteen new trees in the garden of these poor people."—Paul W. Brauer.

## OCTOBER 19. Proclaiming Peace

Many churches have towers or steeples in which are housed churchbells. These bells are rung on Sunday mornings when it is time for Sunday School and church. The bell is a very important part of the church for it represents the duty of the church to proclaim the gospel. Most bells are large and heavy. Perhaps at times you have pulled the bell rope and you know that it takes quite a tug to sound the notes of the bell.

Usually we say that the place where the bell is hung is the belfry. Originally a belfry had no association at all with a church. The belfry was a tall wooden tower and was mounted on wheels. Centuries ago this tower was moved about by soldiers who from the top of the tower could scale the walls of an enemy city or from that height could bombard an enemy with deadly arrows.

That was years and years ago. After a while the belfry became useless, mostly because enemy cities were no longer surrounded by walls. So the belfry was used for other purposes. It was sometimes set in the middle of the village square. Watchmen at the top of the belfry could warn the citizens of dangers. Because the church had been built near the center of the community, it was natural that the belfry should be placed next to the church.

When this was done, the watchmen in the tower also announced the times for church services. Later a bell was put in the tower and this bell served the same purpose. In time the tower became a part of the church building itself. But no longer did the tower serve primarily for military purposes but rather to proclaim God's peace.

Today when the church bell rings we don't board up our homes and prepare to fight an enemy. No, when we hear the familiar sound of the bell we open our homes and we go to church to pray that God may give peace and good will to all mankind.—Charles L. Wallis.

### OCTOBER 26. Noah's Partner

The legends which abound in the Midrash are of many varieties. Some recount the exploits of Biblical heroes, others revolve around the great sages of Talmudic times, and not a few are simply adaptations from the common folklore of Western civilization. Still others partake of the nature of fables with clearly-drawn moral lessons. Sometimes such fables stand alone without reference to a Biblical text. More often, as in the present example, they are told by way of commentary on a Scriptural verse.

Text: "And Noah began to be an husbandman, and he planted a vineyard." Gen. 9:20.

Just as Noah began to set the roots of the grapevine into the soil, Satan sauntered up and queried, "What are you planting, friend Noah?"

"A vineyard," replied the erstwhile sailor.

"What's it good for?"

"Why," said the new husbandman proudly, "its fruits are sweet when they are dried as well as when they are newly-plucked, and besides, they make a beverage which gladdens the heart."

"Would you like me to help you plant the vineyard?" asked Satan guilessly.

"Delighted," replied Noah.

Whereupon Satan seized a lamb and slaughtered it upon the grapevine before Noah's amazed eyes. Immediately thereafter he dispatched a lion in similar fashion, next a monkey, and finally a pig. Taking the blood of all his hapless victims, Satan proceeded to water the vineyard.

And thus it ofttimes is when a man quaffs one goblet of wine he becomes a lamb, meek and lowly of spirit. With the second draught he fancies himself mighty as a lion, and goes about boasting of his prowess. If he persists in his drinking he is transformed into a monkey, grimacing and capering and acting shamelessly without knowing what he does. When he is completely drunken, he becomes a pig—wallowing in the mire and filth.

And all these things befell even Noah who was a righteous man.—*Midrash Tanhuma,* 13.

### NOVEMBER 2. The Most Important Thing on a Ship

Some of you may have crossed the ocean on one of the great transatlantic liners. The last time I crossed I began to investigate the interior of the big vessel to find out for you, boys and girls, what was the most important thing on a ship.

Naturally enough I went to the captain, for he is the head of the ship, and he is supposed to know everything about ships, and he does, too. I said to him:

"Captain, what is the most important thing on board your ship? I want to find out for my boys and girls, and I want to be sure I'm right."

He replied: "I hardly know, there are so many things that are important. But what is most important is not very easy to say in such a complex thing as this vast vessel."

I asked the captain then if he was considered the most important. He said: "No, I am not. There was a captain on this ship before me, and there will be one after me."

Then I made all sorts of guesses, and asked if it was the compass.

He said: "No, unless the stars go out, we can navigate the ship by them."

I was growing impatient, and again I asked: "What is the most important thing, then, anyway? I want to know."

This time he said: "Ask the chief engineer."

So I went to the chief engineer. On the way I thought to myself: "I know the most important thing. It is the engine."

Quite hopeful and pleased at the happy thought, I approached the chief engineer away down in the engine room. After greeting him I ventured to say: "Sir, I am trying to find out what is the most important thing on your ship. I know it's not the captain, nor the compass. I think it is the engine."

He said I was wrong. "You see," he explained, "if the engine goes out of commission and becomes disabled we can hoist a sail and make the shore that way."

"Then I must begin my inquiry all over again," I said. "If it's not any of these, will you please show me?"

"Follow me," he commanded, and I did. He took me down to a dark place, away down a lot of long steel ladders. When we reached what I thought must surely be the bottom of the ship, we stopped. It was pitch dark. Switching on an electric light I found myself in front of a great black thing. It was a huge iron tank. Pointing to it, the engineer said:

"The most imporant thing on board the ship is contained in that tank."

I looked in, and I was never more surprised in my life. I wonder if you guess what it was. O-I-L, oil, just oil.

"Without the oil, the coal, the water, the engines, the engineers, the compass, all would be of no use," the chief engineer told me. "Without the oil the engines could not run, and the rudder would not work to steer the ship to shore. The voyage would not be a success, the ship could not be maintained. She would be open to all kinds of dangers."

This is true of life.

Oil is a smooth, a gentle thing, and gentleness is one of the most important things in life. What is the highest type of man? A gentleman. It is the gentleness of God that makes us great.

Once a group of people traveled around the world together. They were closely associated for six months. You might think that there would be little frictions and misunderstandings and even quarrels develop among them during that time. But these did not happen. After the trip was over the group decided that their harmony and enjoyment was due to a single member of the group. She was always pouring oil on troubled waters, as we say. Whenever she saw a misunderstanding developing she was always there with her gentle spirit setting matters right. The group called her "The Oil Can."—Adapted from George Adam.

## NOVEMBER 9. Two Kings

Once Alexander the Great visited a king in an outlying corner of the world. The king acted as a magistrate and invited his guest to sit beside him. Two men came before the court. One said: "I have bought a house from this man, and while repairing it, a treasure was found. I offered to return it to him, but he refuses to accept it."

The other said: "I knew nothing of the treasure, and it does not belong to me. Since I sold him the house and lot, the treasure is his property."

The king said: "Have you a son?" and to the other: "Have you a daughter?"

"Yes," was the answer from each.

"Then," continued the king, "let them marry and keep the treasure as their dowry."

The king thereupon turned to Alexander and said: "Did I not judge wisely?"

Alexander smiled and replied: "I would have cut off the heads of both of them and taken the treasure for myself."

The king shook his head. "Does the sun shine in your land?"

"Yes," was Alexander's answer.

"Does the rain fall in your land?"

Again the answer was "Yes."

"And are there cattle and sheep in your country?"

"Yes," said Alexander.

"Then most assuredly," said the king, "it is only for the sake of the animals, and not for yours, that the sun shines and the rain falls."—*Midrash Tanhuma.*

**NOVEMBER 16. Thank You!**

Gratitude is a very lovely and quite rare virtue.

That it is lovely is brought out by the manner in which the peoples of the earth say "Thank you." I have collected a few.

There is the French word *merci.* That sounds like our English word "mercy." And the word "mercy" in our Bible is often translated "loving-kindness." You have done me a loving-kindness! *Merci!*

*Danke schön*—we can catch the word *danke* and "thank" as sister words. The Germans add the word for beautiful, *schön*—Thanks beautiful. It was a beautiful thing for you to do—Thanks beautiful.

The Japanese say *Arigato gozaimus.* Pronounce these words just as though they were English, with no accent on any syllable. The very sound is melodious—*arigato. Arigato gozaimasu* means "it is precious." I hold in my hand the gift you have given me; I say "It is precious."

The Chinese in one of their dialects say *Do shě,* or *Shě shě.* This means "Many thanks." The Orientals have a way of doubling a word to express the plural, and so the Chinese are apt to say "Thanks-thanks."

In Italian and Spanish the word for "thanks" is like our English word "grace." It was a gracious thing for you to do. It comes from the Latin word *gratus* which means "pleasing." Thank you, you did a pleasing thing, *Grazie! Gracias!*

This reminds us that we have two words in English which carry this same idea, "gratitude" and "thanksgiving." "Gratitude" comes from the Latin through the Norman-French. "Thanksgiving" is Anglo-Saxon. It is really *think-giving.* "Thank" is the second grade of "think." I gave the matter second thought—I thank you.

Thank you is the expression of a lovely virtue.

Gratitude is a rare virtue. This was brought to my attention when my son was about fourteen years of age. It was at that time that everybody was reading *The Making of an American* by Edward Bok. I was deeply impressed by the book, and I said to Winchester, my son, "I have never told you before that you *must* read anything, but you *must* read the first chapter of *The Making of an American.*" He was quite willing. I knew that if he read the first chapter he would read the book through, which is what I wanted to have happen. There is in the book a chapter which tells of Edward Bok's experience as a boy collecting autographs. One day Winchester looked up and said, "Dad, I'm going to collect autographs and the first one I'm going to get is Edward Bok's." He sent his letter and back came the autograph on a slip of paper decorated for just that purpose.

Then Winchester sent a letter to Mr. Bok thanking him for the autograph. And this letter received a reply. In Mr. Bok's letter he said that he had sent thousands of autographs in response to requests and that this was the first time that anyone had sent him a letter of thanks.

Thanksgiving is a very rare virtue and a very lovely one—H.

**NOVEMBER 23. A Story for Thanksgiving**

I suppose you know there are stories so old they seem like new when told again. I have such a story this morning, told to me by an old gentleman past ninety years of age, who said that he heard it when he was a small boy. It is a Thanksgiving story.

It tells of two angels who were sent down from heaven to gather flowers from the earth. It was not roses or lilies or violets that they were to seek, but blossoms from the lives of boys and girls and men and women.

One of the angels was the Angel of Thanksgiving. He carried a large basket for he expected to bring back to heaven a great many flowers of thanksgiving.

The other angel was named the Angel of Petition. A petition, as you know, is a wish expressed to God, a desire for something good or fine or beautiful. This angel carried a small basket, because, he thought, the children of earth are so filled with gratitude for the blessings they have that they will give little thought to what things they may want.

But when the angels returned, what do you think? The Angel of Petition brought his basket full and upon his shoulders was an overflowing sack. The Angel of Thanksgiving had only a few blossoms to lay at the feet of God.

I wonder what would happen if the Angels came to gather blossoms this week. Perhaps they will. Who knows? —H.

**NOVEMBER 30. A Boy's Finest Memory**

This is the First Sunday of Advent, the beginning of the Christmas season. The story that I am going to tell comes from a Christmas card and was written by Cecil B. DeMille. You may have heard it, but I feel sure that it is worth hearing again. Here it is just as Mr. DeMille wrote it:

During this festive Christmas season, churches all over the country will overflow with worshipers. It wasn't always that way . . .

When I was a boy of ten, our community church, in order to stimulate interest among parishioners, decided to hold services every morning at 8 A.M. for a week. Since we couldn't afford a resident minister, one was acquired from the outside. I do not remember his name. But I shall never forget his strong, kindly face and his prominent red beard.

My father, who was very active in the church, sent me off one cold and rainy morning. I walked alone to the small, wooden sanctuary through a murky gloom. Upon arriving, I could see that no one was present but the red-bearded minister and me.

I was the congregation.

Embarrassed I took a seat, wondering anxiously what he would do. The hour for the service arrived. Surely he would tell me politely to run along home.

With calm and solemn dignity the minister walked into the pulpit. Then he looked down on me and smiled—a smile of great warmth and sincerity. In the congregation sat a solitary child, but he commenced the service as if the church were crowded to the walls.

A ritual opened the services, followed by a reading lesson to which I gave the responses. Then the minister preached a short sermon. He talked earnestly to me—and to God. When it came time for the offering, he placed the collection plate on the altar railing. I walked up and dropped my nickel into the plate.

Then he did a beautiful thing. He came down to the altar to receive my offering. As he did this, he placed his hand on my head. I can still feel the thrill and sensation of his gentle touch. It won my belief and strengthened my faith. The spirit of truth was in the church with us that morning.

None of us can tell at what moment we step into a boy's life and by a demonstration of love and faith turn him in God's direction.—*Guideposts,* Carmel, N.Y.

**DECEMBER 7. His Name—Jesus**

All of you know that this is Christmas month and that Christmas Day is not far away. You know, too, that Christmas Day is the birthday of Jesus whom the world has learned to love and worship.

Today in this service I am going to give a name to a little child and I know that you are glad to be here while I do so. Then I thought that you might like to know something about the name that was given to the little child born so long ago on the first Christmas.

His name was Jesus. We do not give that name to boys and girls now, except in Spanish-speaking countries. I suppose that we like to keep it sacred, for him alone. Long ago it was a very common name—a name like John or William or Harry. Joshua and Jesus were really the same name, just as today we use Richard or Dick for the same person.

Another thing about the name is its meaning. Jesus means *Saviour*. That is a lovely meaning. Jesus came to the world to be its Saviour. When he became a man he told stories about saving people. Then, too, he told a story about a shepherd saving a sheep that was lost. So Jesus saves us—he saves us from evil and makes us good; he saves us from uselessness and make us useful; he saves us from living selfishly and helps us to live lives of service.

Now a father and a mother are going to bring their little child to be named. I wonder what the name of the little boy shall be. Listen carefully for it. Remember that the little Babe who was born long ago is now the living Christ and the friend of all little children.—H.

### DECEMBER 14. Mary-Jo's Christmas Gift

"Well, it's about time that you children tell us what you want for a Christmas gift," said Mrs. Babcock one evening toward Christmas when all were gathered at the dinner table.

"I know what I want," cried Jimmy, waiting for just such an opportunity to tell.

"Anybody could guess," said Uncle George, "a basketball."

"That's it," said Jimmy, and added, "What do you want, Mary-Jo?"

"A new Bible with a concordance," answered Mary-Jo.

"What's a con—? What's that word, Mary-Jo?" asked Jimmy.

"A concordance. Don't you know what a concordance is? I'll show you after dinner."

After dinner Jimmy and Mary-Jo drew up their chairs close together and Mary-Jo began, "You see my old Bible is about worn out and it doesn't have a concordance. I borrowed Mrs. Sweetser's Bible, with a concordance, to show what I want. Now, Jimmy, you give me a word and I'll tell you whether you can find it in the Bible and what the Bible says about it."

Jimmy was a little puzzled, but looking out the window where the snow was falling, he said, "Snow."

Mary-Jo turned the pages of the concordance with Jimmy watching carefully. Finally she said, "Second Samuel 23:20," and read, "And Benaiah, the son of Jehoiada, the son of a valiant man, of Kabzeel, who had done many acts, he slew two lionlike men of Moab: he went down also and slew a lion in the midst of a pit in time of snow."

"Say, Sis, that's some story. I didn't know there were things like that in the Bible. He had no gun in those days. I wonder if he had a knife. I'll bet he killed that lion hand to hand."

"Here's another, Jimmy, 'He giveth snow like wool.' God gives snow like wool."

Jimmy looked out the window and remarked, "I think it's even whiter than wool."

Then Mary-Jo read, "Isaiah 1:18—'Come now, and let us reason together, saith the Lord: though your sins be as scarlet, they shall be as white as snow; though they be red like crimson, they shall be as wool.' When you do something mean or have a bad thought," added Mary-Jo, "God makes you clean again, if you are sorry and ask his forgiveness."

"I understand," said Jimmy. "That concordance is a wonderful thing."

Just then Mrs. Babcock came into the room and Jimmy said, "Mom, I want a Bible with a concordance for Christmas."

When Christmas morning came both Mary-Jo and Jimmy had beautifully bound Bibles, each with a concordance, from their father and mother. Uncle George gave Jimmy a basketball and Mary-Jo a gold bracelet that she wanted. —H.

**DECEMBER 21. Christmas Morning at the Babcocks**

Christmas morning was the time for opening gifts in the Babcock household—Christmas morning after breakfast. You can imagine that Jimmy and Mary-Jo could scarcely wait to have the meal over so that they could explore under the Christmas tree.

But this Christmas morning the breakfast table itself had its own wondreful attractions. When the family gathered, there in the center of the table was a crisp new one hundred dollar bill. And laid out neatly at each of the five plates was another bill just like the one in the center.

Uncle George was the first to exclaim, "What's all this? A hundred dollar bill!"

"I've got one, too!" yelled Jimmy. "That's a fortune! And Mom and Dad and Mary-Jo! Gee! Five hundred dollars!"

"There's one in the middle of the table, too," said Uncle George.

"Where did it come from?" asked Jimmy, as he searched his father's face for an answer, but he knew immediately that this father did not know. A glance at his mother told him that she didn't know. It must be Mary-Jo.

"Come on, Sis, where did you get six hundred dollars?"

"First fruits," was Mary-Jo's answer.

"First fruits, what do you mean? another one of your . . ." but Jimmy withheld his usual criticism.

Finally Uncle George persuaded Mary-Jo to tell.

"Well," said Mary-Jo, "do you remember last spring when I asked you all whether I might have the first basket of strawberries from our plants, and the first lug of peaches from our tree, and the first bunches of grapes from our vines."

"Yes, I remember," said Uncle George.

"I wanted them because in our Sunday School lesson there was a verse that I wanted to try out in a practical way. I've learned it to memory: 'Thou shalt take of the first of all the fruit of the earth, which thou shalt bring of thy land that the Lord thy God giveth thee, and shalt put it in a basket, and shalt go unto the place which the Lord thy God shall choose to place his name there.'

"Where did you take the fruit?" asked her mother.

"To old Mrs. Boone, down the street. God surely must have his name with that good old lady, I thought."

"But she died about two months ago," remarked Mr. Babcock.

"Yes, and she left a will. After everything was cleared up there was just six hundred dollars left and she willed that to me. The lawyer called me in yesterday and gave me the money."

"But that money's all yours," said Jimmy.

"No," replied Mary-Jo, "the fruits were not mine; they belonged to all of us. You gave them just as much as I did. These five hundred dollars belong to all of us."

"What about that hundred dollar bill in the center of the table?" asked Jimmy.

"You may put it in the offering plate at the Christmas service this morning," returned Mary-Jo.—H.

**DECEMBER 28. A Chapel at Home**

John and his brothers were playing in their yard when their mother called.

"Jack," she said, "do you know what day it is?"

"Yes, Mother." John answered. "It is my day. I'll be right in." And immediately he tossed the ball to his brother Charles and started toward the house. As he did so his mother came out to meet him, and he took her arm as they entered the house.

You see, Mrs. Wesley had a somewhat unusual custom of setting aside an hour a week for reading and talking with each of her nineteen children. John's hour was always just after tea things were cleared away on Thursday afternoons.

John and his mother went into a little room that was called, by the Wesley children, "Our Little Sanctuary." The afternoon sun made lovely patterns on the floor as it shone through a small stain-glassed window. On the wall opposite the window hung a picture of Jesus. Below it stood a small table which bore two tall candles and an open Bible. In a corner of the little room, beside another table on which a number of good books were arranged, was a comfortable armchair. And beside it was a hassock.

John took his place on the hassock and his mother used the chair. They both bowed for a few minutes of silent prayer. Next, they sang a favorite hymn together and then Mrs. Wesley read from the Bible. For a few minutes they talked about what they had read, and repeated from memory some of the beautiful verses that John had learned by heart. Mrs. Wesley helped John to find several other great passages and he selected a new one to memorize. More conversation followed—about religion, about school, about home problems. Finally John and his mother knelt before the little altar, composed of the table with the candles and Bible, and prayed aloud. It was a pleasant hour for both Mrs. Wesley and her son.

Years later, when John was a student at Oxford University, he thought often of the "Little Sanctuary" at home. He missed it so much. Then an idea came to him. Why not invite some of his friends to share such an hour with him? So the "Holy Club" was formed of students who planned to be methodical in their religious devotions, as Mrs. Wesley was in the training of her children. Other students made fun of them and called them "Methodists." But they did not mind. And strange as it seems, the name lasted and the "Holy Club" grew until today the whole Methodist Church looks back with honor upon John's "Holy Club" and upon the "Little Sanctuary" in the Wesley home. —Author Unknown.

# SECTION IX. *Hymnology*

For anniversaries of hymn writers and composers of music see No. 6 under Section I of this volume.

Selected hymns are given under each Morning Service in Section VII.

The new hymns given below are printed with the permission of The Hymn Society of America.

## A NEW HYMN ON THE HOME

O God, Who to a Loyal Home
St. Leonard C.M.D.

Words: Harry Emerson Fosdick, 1956.

Tune: Henry Hiles, 1867

O God, who to a loyal home
  Didst trust Thy Son divine,
Where faithful love and patient work
  Make daily life benign;
With contrite shame Thy grace we claim,
  And lift to Thee our prayer:
Redeem our oft unworthy homes
  Till all is Christ-like there.

Deliver us from sins which harm
  Our homes, and mar their peace,
May selfless and devoted love
  Make strife and discord cease.
With anxious zeal, for mankind's weal
  And world-wide peace we pray.
But all in vain, if wayward homes
  Cause childhood's steps to stray.

Thou art our Father, and from Thee
  All faithful fam'lies spring;
To homes where love and honor dwell
  Thou dost Thy blessing bring.
O God of love, send from above
  Thy succor, swift and strong,
That from such homes stout souls may come
  To triumph over wrong.

We pray that childhood's latent pow'rs
  May grow to bless mankind;
That we may guide aright young lives,
  For unguessed good designed.
O Father God, whose Son has trod
  Such lowly paths as we,
Help us to build on earth true homes,
  Till we come home to Thee. Amen.

## NEW HYMNS FOR YOUTH BY YOUTH

O God of Truth, The Power of Nations Free

Toulon 10.10.10.10

Words: Daniel B. Merrick, Jr., 1955

Tune: The Geneva Psalter, 1551

O God of truth, the power of nations free;
Source of all wisdom, strength and liberty;
Giver of faith, on whom our hopes depend;

Hear us as hymns of praise to thee ascend.

Armed by thy might, our fathers set us free;
Bind us to them in faith and loyalty;
Set high our aims that justice may prevail;
Fill us with love, and hope that cannot fail.

Fix high our purpose in this fateful hour;
Save from the shame that blights the gift of power;
Forgive our foolish pride, we humbly pray,
Yet grant us courage equal to our day.

Thus let us falter not at duty's call,
Which bids us seek a brotherhood for all,
Building through all the coming years with thee
A Commonwealth united, strong and free. Amen.

### Come Forth, O Christian Youth

Diademata S.M.D.

Words: Mary Ellen Jackson, 1955
Tune: George J. Elvey, 1868

Come forth, O Christian youth,
A task before us lies;
The world awaits the strength and zeal
Which youthful heart supplies.
We seek to win mankind
To choose Christ's nobler way,
And usher in true brotherhood
For ev'ry man today.

Stand firm, O Christian youth,
With trust in God alone,
That we may live our Christian faith
And make Christ truly known.
Be ours to show all men
The path His feet have trod,
To make all life a sacrament
And holy unto God.

Grow strong, O Christian youth,
Be loyal, brave and true,
And strive with courage for the right
In what we say and do.
Thus may our words and deeds
Be worthy in God's sight,
And manifest to all mankind
His way of truth and light.

Give all, O Christian youth,
And nought from Christ withhold;
His Kingdom claims us for its own;
His Spirit keeps us bold!
As pilgrims in the world
Yet followers of the Way,
God make us faithful citizens
Till his eternal day. Amen.

## MUSIC SUITABLE FOR CHURCH WEDDINGS

These selections have been compiled by Eugene L. Nordgren, Minister of Music at The House of Hope Presbyterian Church, St. Paul, Minn.

*Before the Ceremony:*

| | |
|---|---|
| Prelude in G Major | J. S. Bach |
| Prelude in D Major | " |
| Air for the G String | " |
| Blessed Jesus at Thy Word | " |
| Blessed Jesus, We Are Here | " |
| Cathedral Prelude and Fugue | " |
| Deck Thyself, My Soul with Gladness | " |
| God, My Shepherd, Walks Beside Me | " |
| How Brightly Shines the Morning Star | " |

| | |
|---|---|
| I Stand at Heaven's Portals | J. S. Bach |
| A Mighty Fortress Is Our God | " |
| In Thee Is Gladness | " |
| If Thou Art Near (*Bist Du Bei Mir*) | " |
| * Jesu, Joy of Man's Desiring | " |
| Little G Minor Fugue | " |
| Lord Jesus, Be Present Now | " |
| Now Let Every Tongue Adore Thee | " |
| Our Father Who Art in Heaven | " |
| St. Anne's Fugue | " |
| Sinfonia from Wedding Cantata No. 196 | " |
| Romance Sans Paroles | Bonnet |
| My Inmost Heart Rejoices | Brahms |
| Rigaudon (Gray) | Campra |
| Suite in F (first three movements) | Corelli |
| Preludio (9th Violin Sonata) | " |
| Prelude on Brother James' Air | Darke |
| * Sonata in G (soft movement) Breitkopf | Elgar |
| Andante (from "Grande Piece Symphonique") | Cesar Franck |
| Cantabile | " |
| Concerto No. 13 in F (Larghetto, Allegro) | Handel |
| Thanks Be to Thee | Handel |
| * Water Music (J. Fischer) | " |
| The Faithful Shepherd (H. W. Gray) | " |
| Overture to the "Occasional Oratorio" (Gray) | " |
| Adagio from the "Occasional Oratorio" (Gray) | " |
| Aria in F Major (Concerto Grosso No. 12) | " |
| Andante (Concerto in F) | " |
| Wedding Music | Concordia Press |
| Praeludium (H. W. Gray) | Jarnefelt |
| Chant de Mai | Jongen |
| Prayer | " |
| Benediction (Marks) | Karg-Elert |
| Improvisation in E | " |
| Fanfare | Lemmens |
| The Heavens Declare the Glory | Marcello |
| Slow Movements of the Sonatas | Mendelssohn |
| The King of Love | Milford |
| The Guardian Angel (Ditson) | Pierne |
| Trumpet Tune and Peal (Schott & Co.) | Purcell |
| Trumpet Voluntary (Gray) | " |
| Largo (12th Sonata) | " |
| Benedictus (Peters) | Max Reger |
| Rondo (Concerto for the Flute) (Gray) | Rinck |
| Benedictus | Alex Rowley |
| The Lord Is My Shepherd | Schubert |
| Carillon (Gray) | Leo Sowerby |
| Andante (Gray) | Stamitz |
| Carillon (24 pieces in free style) | Vierne |
| Seven Sketches on Verses from the Psalms (The Lord Is My Shepherd: He Leadeth Me Beside Still Waters) | Whitlock |
| * Andante Catabile (Fourth Symphony) | Widor |
| Prelude on Rhosymedre (The King of Love) | R. Vaughan Williams |

*Entrance and Exit Music Other than the Traditional Wedding Marches*

| | |
|---|---|
| God My Shepherd Walks Beside Me | Bach |
| Recessional (Toccata on "O Perfect Love") | Clokey |
| March from the Occasional Overture | Handel |
| Processional | Handel-Buszin |
| Now Thank We All Our God | Karg-Elert |
| Nuptial Processional | Kreckel |
| Psalm XIX and XX | Marcello |
| Carillon Sortie | Mulet |
| Largo | Purcell |
| Trumpet Tune | " |
| Trumpet Voluntary | " |
| Grand Choir Dialogue | Gigout |
| Solemn Melody | Davies Walford |

* Played at the wedding of Princess Elizabeth, November, 1947.

*Vocal Solos*

| | |
|---|---|
| The Lord Is My Shepherd (from the Anthem) | Schubert |
| Jesu, Joy of Man's Desiring | Bach |
| O Perfect Love | Barnby |
| God, My Shepherd, Walks Beside Me | Bach |
| Beloved, Let Us Love One Another | Sowerby |
| The Twenty-third Psalm | Malotte |
| The God of Love My Shepherd Is | Thiman (Novello) |
| O Lord Most Holy | Cesar Franck |
| Set Me As a Seal | Clokey (J. Fischer) |
| The Lord's Prayer | Malotte |
| Love One Another (from the anthem "Blessed Be the God") | S. S. Wesley |
| O Bless the House | Markworth (Concordia) |
| O Perfect Love | Willan (Gray) |
| O Perfect Love | Sowerby (Gray) |
| O Perfect Love | Burleigh (Presser) |
| O Christ Who Once Hast Deigned | Lloyd (Concordia) |
| Be Thou but Near (Sacred Words) | Bach |
| Entreat Me Not To Leave Thee (Song of Ruth) | Gounod (G. Schirmer) |
| Sanctus | Gounod |
| A Wedding Prayer | Diggle (G. Schirmer) |
| Holy Spirit We Come to Thee | Virginia Weatherbee Powell (Manuscript) |
| Though I Speak with the Tongue (Fourth Serious Song) | Brahms |
| Wedding Song | Schutz (Chantry Press) |
| Eternal Father | Huntington Woodman |
| Wedding Blessings | Bunjes |
| Love Never Faileth | Ward-Stephen (Chappell) |

*Hymns*

| | |
|---|---|
| Love Divine, All Love Excelling | (Sing to Hyfrydol) |
| Praise My Soul The King of Heaven | |
| Joyful, Joyful We Adore Thee | |
| The King of Love My Shepherd Is | |

Fairest Lord Jesus
O Love Divine and Golden
O Perfect Love
Now Thank We All Our God

*Anthems*

Set Me As a Seal — William Watton (Oxford Maxern Anthems) A 86